# Beginning Java Web Services

Henry Bequet

Meeraj Moidoo Kunnumpurath

Sean Rhody

Andre Tost

*Wrox Press Ltd.* ®

# Beginning Java Web Services

First Printed in September 2002

Published by Wrox Press Ltd,
Arden House, 1102 Warwick Road, Acocks Green,
Birmingham, B27 6BH, UK
Printed in the United States
ISBN 1-86100-753-1

# Trademark Acknowledgments

Wrox has endeavored to provide trademark information about all the companies and products mentioned in this book by the appropriate use of capitals. However, Wrox cannot guarantee the accuracy of this information.

# Credits

**Authors**
Henry Bequet
Meeraj Moidoo Kunnumpurath
Sean Rhody
Andre Tost

**Managing Editor**
Joanna Mason

**Commissioning Editor**
Craig A. Berry

**Technical Editors**
Dipali Chittar
Kalpana Garde
David Mercer
Arunkumar Nair

**Project Managers**
Cilmara Lion
Beth Sacks
Abbas Rangwala

**Author Agent**
Nicola Phillips

**Cover**
Natalie O'Donnell

**Technical Reviewers**
Jeelani Basha
Richard Bonneau
Scott Bonneau
Ersin Eser
Anne Horton
Romin Irani
Margarita Isaveya
Dan Jepp
Don Reamy
Sandeep Saluja
Dave Whitney

**Production Coordinator**
Abbie Forletta

**Production Assistant**
Neil Lote

**Illustrations**
Santosh Haware
Manjiri Karande

**Index**
Martin Brooks
Andrew Criddle

**Proof Reader**
Chris Smith

# About the Authors

## Henry Bequet

Henry Bequet is an Architect with Iteration Software (http://www.iteration.com), a Silicon Valley company focused on real-time business intelligence. Henry is a SUN-certified Java 2 programmer who specializes in developing scalable distributed web applications using XML, SOAP, Java, C++, and C#.

Henry was born in rainy Belgium but he now lives in sunny Boulder, Colorado with his wife and two children where he enjoys software development, skiing, and roller-skating.

*A book like this one would not be possible without the work and support of many people. I would like to apologize in advance for any omission in this list of the wonderful people who helped me along the way.*

*Special thanks go to Ken Gardner, Chairman and CEO of Iteration Software, for his unconditional support and trust.*

*I also want to acknowledge the team at Wrox press that supported me in this endeavor: Craig Berry and Cilmara Lion. Many thanks to the reviewers of the book: Jeelani Basha, Richard Bonneau, Scott Bonneau, Ersin Eser, Anne Horton, Romin Irani, Margarita Isaveya, Dan Jepp, Don Reamy, Sandeep Saluja, and Dave Whitney.*

*Finally, special thanks go to my family, Anne-Françoise, Julie, and Christophe who make the journey worthwhile.*

*To all, my warmest thanks and deepest appreciation.*

Henry contributed Chapters 3, 4, 5, and 7 to this book.

## Meeraj Moidoo Kunnumpurath

Meeraj works with EDS as a Senior Information Specialist.

*"Mariam...*
*Do you know Allah's Prophet (SA) use to call Fathima (RA), my dear little daughter...*
*My dear little daughter,*
*you are my dreams when I sleep*
*you are my tears when I cry*
*you are my smile when I am happy*
*you are the one, who taught me what unconditional love is.*

*I am grateful to Allah that he has given me you."*

Meeraj contributed Chapters 2, 9, and 11 to this book.

## Sean Rhody

Sean Rhody is a Partner with Computer Sciences Corporation where he serves as a Program Architect for CSC Consulting Group. Sean is actively involved in the design, development and delivery of distributed systems in a number of industries.

Sean is also the Editor-in-Chief of Web Services Developers Journal (http://www.wsj2.com) and was the Founding Editor of Java Developers Journal.

Sean lives in Flemington, NJ and can be reached at s-rhody@rcn.com.

Sean contributed Chapters 1 and 10 to this book.

## Andre Tost

Andre Tost works as a Solution Architect for IBM's WebSphere Software Group in Rochester, Minnesota. In his current assignment, he helps IBM's strategic software partners to integrate with IBM middleware products. Before that, he had various development and architecture roles in IBM's SanFrancisco and WebSphere Business Components development organizations. He started programming in early 1996 in the SanFrancisco project had has been developing in this language ever since. For the past year or so, he has been closely following the evolution of web services technologies and spends a large portion of his time consulting and teaching programming workshops about it.

Andre was born and raised in Northern Germany and moved his family to (cold!) Minnesota in 1998. Being a football fan (meaning the real football that Americans call soccer), he likes to play and watch the game. Fortunately, Rochester has quite an active soccer scene with plenty of playing opportunities. Besides spending his time on programming and soccer, he likes to be with his wife and his two boys (they're two and five years old and think that being a programmer at IBM must be the biggest fun one have possibly have – oh well...).

Andre contributed Chapters 6 and 8 to this book.

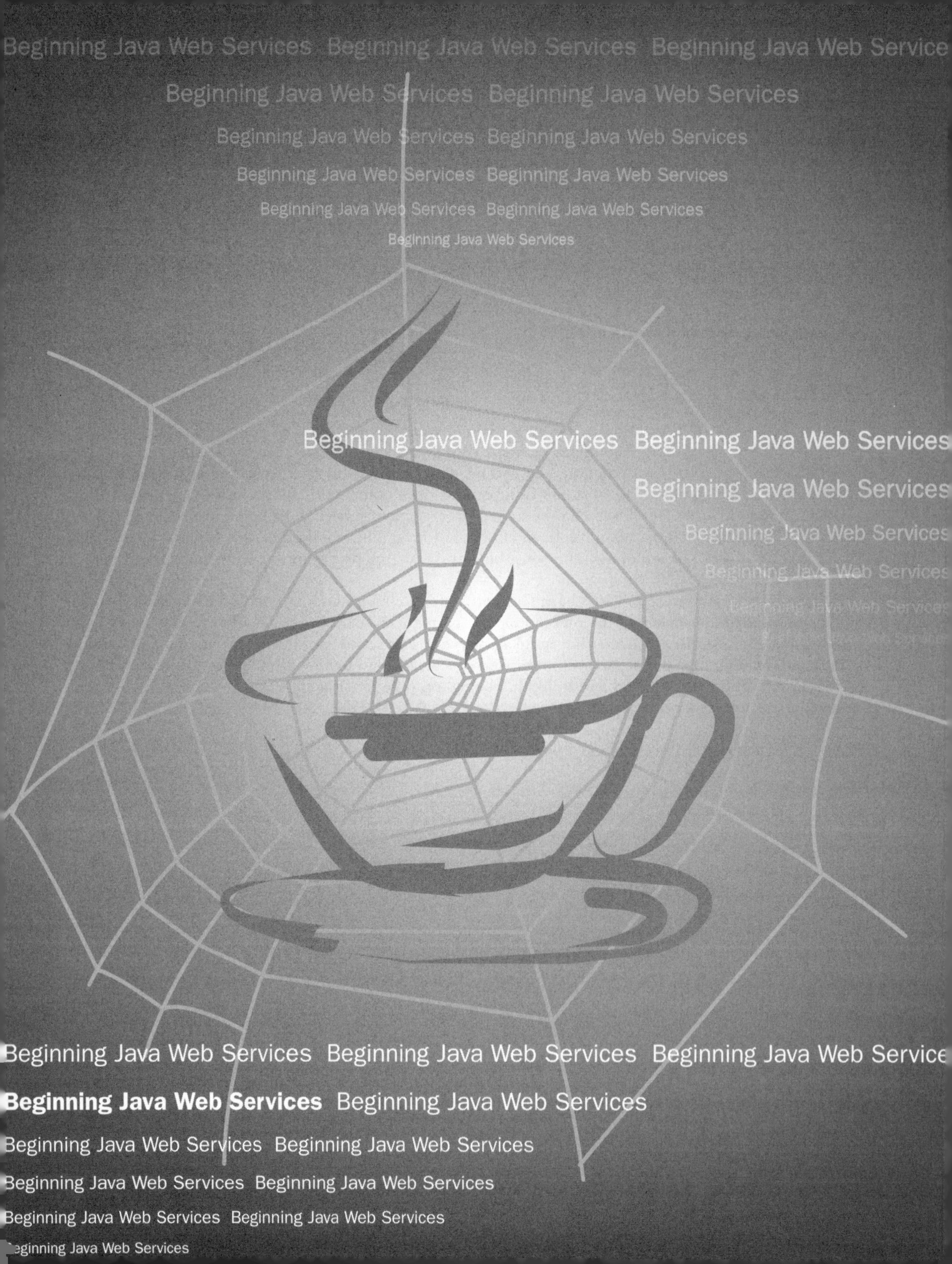

# Table of Contents

# Table of Contents

# Table of Contents

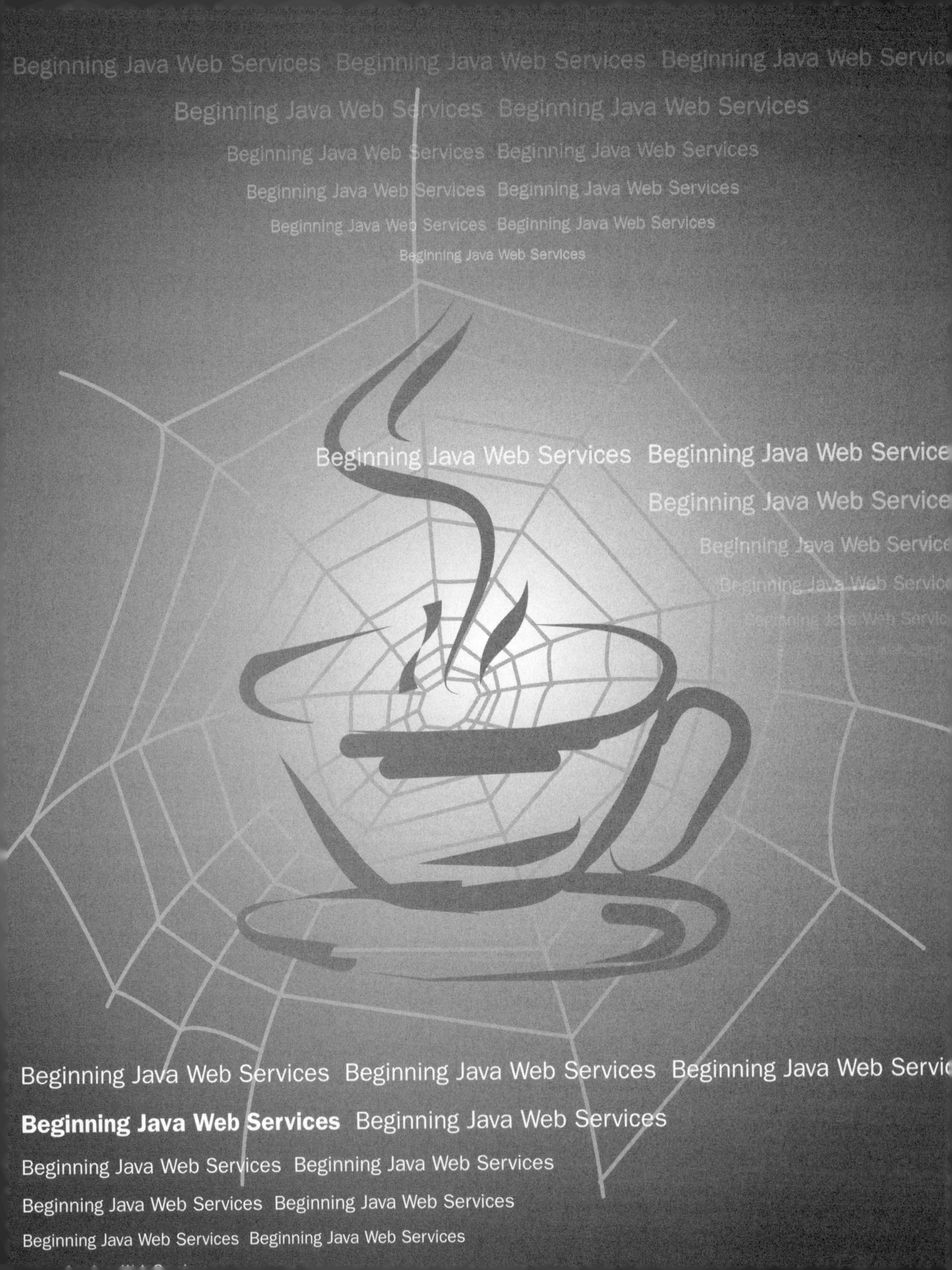

Beginning Java Web Services  Beginning Java Web Services  Beginning Java Web Service

Beginning Java Web Services  Beginning Java Web Services

Beginning Java Web Services  Beginning Java Web Services

Beginning Java Web Services  Beginning Java Web Services

Beginning Java Web Services  Beginning Java Web Services

Beginning Java Web Services

Beginning Java Web Services  Beginning Java Web Service

Beginning Java Web Service

Beginning Java Web Service

Beginning Java Web Service

Beginning Java Web Servic

Beginning Java Web Services  Beginning Java Web Services  Beginning Java Web Servic

**Beginning Java Web Services**  Beginning Java Web Services

Beginning Java Web Services  Beginning Java Web Services

Beginning Java Web Services  Beginning Java Web Services

Beginning Java Web Services  Beginning Java Web Services

# Introduction

Today Java developers are successfully adopting web services as the latest technology in application development. There are many benefits for web services as compared to the previous technologies. The key benefit of web services is that they allow applications to interoperate through the Web regardless of the language, platform, and operating system.

This book is an introduction to web services with Java and introduces the relevant specifications and APIs that will be utilized. It looks at the different ways in which we can build web services using the Java platform and at the tools, technologies, and protocols that we will need to work with. In this book we will introduce technologies such as XML, SOAP, UDDI, and WSDL and explain how to use them.

## What's Covered in this Book?

This book teaches web services by explaining how they work. It focuses on using Java for building web services.

In Chapter 1 we will introduce web services and outline the various components of a web services system. We will give an introduction to how Java is used as the development language and platform for web services.

In Chapter 2 we will look at how XML makes it possible to exchange data in a programming language-independent way. Here we will cover topics such as XML Namespaces, XML Schema, and XML Protocols.

Chapter 3 will introduce Axis and explain its installation and configuration. We will go over server-side and client-side development using the Axis API. Also we will give a brief introduction to debugging web services using TCPMon.

In Chapter 4 we will explain the fundamental differences between RPC-SOAP and Document-SOAP. We will expand the example that we introduced in Chapter 3 with some document processing.

In Chapter 5 we will use the WSDL document to generate a (static) client-side proxy. We will add custom data types to our sample web service to show how the complexity translates into WSDL.

In Chapter 6 we will look at the invocation models for web services, both static and dynamic. We will take a look at some non-SOAP web services such as the Web Services Invocation Framework (WSIF).

We will describe the concept of web services publishing in Chapter 7. We will look at short examples in UDDI and WSIL and also briefly describe JAXR.

In Chapter 8 we will see what exactly asynchronous web services are. We will discuss two of the APIs, namely: the Java API for XML-based Messaging or JAXM, and the Java Message Service (JMS) API.

In Chapter 9 we will cover the various security issues relevant to web services and the security solutions that address these issues.

In Chapter 10 we will focus on some tools available commercially that can make the design, development, and deployment of web services a simple, straightforward task.

In the case study in Chapter 11 we will illustrate the use of web services to integrate disparate applications within an enterprise. The domain selected in the case study is an online shopping system that will be integrated to various other systems within the enterprise using web services.

## Who Is this Book For?

This book is for Java developers who need to get started with developing web services for their Java-based applications. No knowledge of web services or XML is required; however, familiarity with web-based Java programming would be advantageous. The book provides complete setup, configuration, and deployment instructions for all the web service development tools required (see below).

## What You Need to Use this Book

To run the samples in this book you need to have:

- ❑ Java 2 Platform, Standard Edition SDK v1.3, or better (http://java.sun.com/j2se/)
- ❑ Apache Axis, beta 3, or better (http://xml.apache.org/axis/index.html)
- ❑ Apache Tomcat 4, or better (http://jakarta.apache.org/tomcat/index.html)
- ❑ Xerces2 Java Parser 2, or better (http://xml.apache.org/xerces2-j/index.html)
- ❑ IBM's Web Services Toolkit version (WSTK) 3.2, or better (http://www.alphaworks.ibm.com/tech/webservicestoolkit/)
- ❑ IBM's WebSphere SDK for Web Services (WSDK) (http://www-106.ibm.com/developerworks/webservices/wsdk/)
- ❑ Java XML Pack, Summer '02 Update Release, or better (http://java.sun.com/xml/downloads/javaxmlpack.html)
- ❑ JSSE 1.0.3 (http://java.sun.com/products/jsse/index-103.html)
- ❑ BEA WebLogic Workshop (http://www.bea.com/products/weblogic/platform/index.shtml)
- ❑ IBM's Websphere Studio Application Developer 4.03 or better (http://www-3.ibm.com/software/ad/studioappdev/)

The complete source code for the samples is available for download from our web site at http://www.wrox.com/.

# Conventions

To help you get the most from the text and keep track of what's happening, we've used a number of conventions throughout the book.

## Try It Out – An Example

*Try It Out* is our way of presenting practical examples. Whenever something important is being discussed, you will find this section. This will help you understand the problem better. *Try It Out* is followed by:

### How It Works

This section gives you a step-by-step explanation to the example discussed in the *Try It Out* section. It will tell you exactly what is going on.

> **These boxes hold important, not-to-be-forgotten information, which is directly relevant to the surrounding text.**

*While the background style is used for asides to the current discussion.*

As for styles in the text:

- ❑  When we introduce them, we **highlight** important words
- ❑  We show keyboard strokes like this: *Ctrl-K*
- ❑  We show filenames and code within the text like so: `persistance.properties`
- ❑  Text on user interfaces and URLs are shown like this: Menu

We present code in two different ways:

```
In our code examples, the code foreground style shows new, important, pertinent
code.
While code background shows code that's less important in the present context, or
has been seen before.
```

On the occasions when we'll be running a command from the DOS command line, it will be shown as:

```
java ServiceTest
```

# Customer Support

We always value hearing from our readers, and we want to know what you think about this book: what you liked, what you didn't like, and what you think we can do better next time. You can send us your comments, either by returning the reply card in the back of the book, or by e-mail to feedback@wrox.com. Please be sure to mention the book title in your message.

# How to Download the Sample Code for the Book

When you visit the Wrox site http://www.wrox.com/ simply locate the title through our Search facility or by using one of the title lists. Click on Download in the Code column, or on Download Code on the book's detail page.

The files that are available for download from our site have been archived using WinZip. When you have saved the attachments to a folder on your hard-drive, you need to extract the files using a de-compression program such as WinZip. When you extract the files, the code is usually extracted into chapter folders. When you start the extraction process, ensure your software (WinZip) is set to use folder names.

# Errata

We've made every effort to make sure that there are no errors in the text or in the code. However, no one is perfect and mistakes do occur. If you find an error in one of our books, like a spelling mistake or faulty piece of code, we would be very grateful for your feedback. By sending in errata you may save another reader hours of frustration, and of course, you will be helping us provide even higher quality information. Simply e-mail the information to support@wrox.com; your information will be checked and if correct, posted to the errata page for that title, or used in subsequent editions of the book.

To find errata on the web site, go to http://www.wrox.com/, and simply locate the title through our Advanced Search or title list. Click on the Book Errata link, which is below the cover graphic on the book's detail page.

# E-Mail Support

If you wish to directly query a problem in the book with an expert who knows the book in detail then e-mail support@wrox.com, with the title of the book and the last four numbers of the ISBN in the subject field of the e-mail. A typical e-mail should include the following things:

❑ The **title of the book**, **last four digits of the ISBN (7531)**, and **page number** of the problem in the Subject field.

❑ Your **name**, **contact information**, and the **problem** in the body of the message.

We *won't* send you junk mail. We need the details to save your time and ours. When you send an e-mail message, it will go through the following chain of support:

❑ Customer Support – Your message is delivered to our customer support staff who are the first people to read it. They have files on most frequently asked questions and will answer anything general about the book or the web site immediately.

❑ Editorial – Deeper queries are forwarded to the technical editor responsible for that book. They have experience with the programming language or particular product, and are able to answer detailed technical questions on the subject.

❑ The Authors – Finally, in the unlikely event that the editor cannot answer your problem, they will forward the request to the author. We do try to protect the authors from any distractions to their writing; however, we are quite happy to forward specific requests to them. All Wrox authors help with the support on their books. They will e-mail the customer and the editor with their response, and again all readers should benefit.

The Wrox Support process can only offer support to issues directly pertinent to the content of our published title. Support for questions that fall outside the scope of normal book support is provided via the community lists of our http://p2p.wrox.com/ forum.

# p2p.wrox.com

For author and peer discussion join the P2P mailing lists. Our unique system provides **programmer to programmer**™ contact on mailing lists, forums, and newsgroups, all in addition to our one-to-one e-mail support system. If you post a query to P2P, you can be confident that it is being examined by the many Wrox authors and other industry experts who are present on our mailing lists. At p2p.wrox.com you will find a number of different lists to help you, not only while you read this book, but also as you develop your applications.

To subscribe to a mailing list just follow these steps:

**1.** Go to http://p2p.wrox.com/

**2.** Choose the appropriate category from the left menu bar

**3.** Click on the mailing list you wish to join

**4.** Follow the instructions to subscribe and fill in your e-mail address and password

**5.** Reply to the confirmation e-mail you receive

**6.** Use the subscription manager to join more lists and set your e-mail preferences

## *Why this System Offers the Best Support*

You can choose to join the mailing lists or you can receive them as a weekly digest. If you don't have the time, or facility, to receive the mailing list, then you can search our archives. Junk and spam mails are deleted, and your own e-mail address is protected by the unique Lyris system. Queries about joining or leaving lists, and any other general queries about lists, should be sent to listsupport@wrox.com.

# Introducing Java Web Services

Ideally, it would be easy to define what web services are and what technologies and components make up a web service. Unfortunately, most of the industry has some trouble with a common definition of web services.

According to the Gartner Group:

> *"Web services are software components that interact with one another dynamically via standard Internet technologies, making it possible to build bridges between IT systems that otherwise would require extensive development efforts."*

Forrester Research says that web services are:

> *"Software designed to be used by other software via Internet protocols and formats."*

There are probably as many definitions as there are companies promoting web services. But as we begin our discussion on web services, and how to interact with them using Java, we should probably try to define them ourselves. We will do that first by describing them, listing some of their characteristics, and then by showing the standards that make up web services. We will look at how web services relate to Java as an implementation language, a hosting platform, and as a consumer of web services. In short, this book is an introduction to understanding, building, and using web services in the context of Java programming.

In this chapter we will look at:

- ❑  What web services are
- ❑  A brief discussion on XML
- ❑  The business reasons for web services
- ❑  The technical reasons for web services
- ❑  Java and web services

# Web Services Basics

Let's begin by describing what web services are and what they do. Web services:

❑ Are independent of language, development tool, and platform

❑ Are based on industry-accepted open standards

❑ Are loosely coupled, service-based applications that present an API for communication using established protocols to facilitate connectivity and reduce complexity

❑ Allow automated and direct machine-to-machine communication regardless of the systems involved

❑ Allow the discovery of published web services utilizing a common mechanism for searching for and publishing services

As we mentioned, another way to define web services is to list the standards by which people would judge whether a particular application is a web service. This is more difficult than it appears, because there is no one standard specification for a web service. Nevertheless, the standard definition includes the following:

❑ **Extensible Markup Language** or **XML** for data representation in an independent fashion. XML is used not only for the data definition, but also in all of the descriptions within other protocols (for example, the SOAP envelope, which will be addressed in Chapter 2).

❑ **HyperText Transfer Protocol** or **HTTP** for transportation across the Internet or within Intranets. This provides the mechanism for both data transport and for request/response types of communication.

❑ **Simple Object Access Protocol** or **SOAP**, which provides a mechanism for request/response definition and allows conversations in a Remote Procedure Call (RPC) format.

❑ **Universal Description, Discovery and Integration** or **UDDI**, which provides a means of locating services via a common registry of providers and services.

❑ **Web Services Description Language** or **WSDL**, which provides the detailed information necessary to invoke a particular service. WSDL and UDDI are somewhat complementary, but also overlap in certain areas.

Some people will argue that other protocols, such as messaging, business process management, security or overall management of the application that provides the service also belong to the definition, but to date there has not been complete agreement over inclusion of these items in the industry accepted definition of web services.

## Service-Oriented Architecture (SOA)

A concept that we will encounter frequently during our discussions is that of software as a service, or a **Service-Oriented Architecture (SOA)**. The concept of designing software as a service, independent of a user interface has been a part of the software engineering landscape for well over a decade. Early attempts at distributed computing such as the Distributed Computing Environment (DCE) and the Common Object Request Broker Architecture (CORBA) led to the realization that the business logic of an application is not necessarily coupled with the presentation logic. It could be completely decoupled and offered as a service with a defined Application Programming Interface (API).

The Internet, with HTML as a presentation layer, lacked all but the most basic programming constructs, helping to drive the adoption of SOA as a more common design philosophy. Mobile or wireless devices such as cell phones and PDAs with micro-browsers or other presentation schemes highlighted the need to separate the presentation from the business logic.

The separation of the logic into a service provides a number of benefits. The user interface is no longer required to run on the same physical tier as the business logic, and both can be scaled independently. Several platforms exist that provide strong support for services, such as Java and .NET. Both provide transaction management, persistence and some state management, removing many of the complexities of service design (for example, writing thread-safe, multi-threaded code).

The introduction of Java, with the concept of "write once, read anywhere", accelerated the adoption of service-oriented architectures, first with Enterprise JavaBeans (EJB) and then with the release of the entire Enterprise platform (J2EE), which provided particular paradigms for implementing user interfaces (specifically JavaServer Pages and servlets) as well as increased support for the development of services.

It was quickly realized that for services to be truly neutral and platform independent, a neutral representation of the data exchanged between the client and the service was needed. The Extensible Markup Language (XML) proved to be the needed component.

In an all-Java environment, these would likely be enough, but most corporate environments are not homogeneous. Not every program can utilize RMI to communicate with the server, and the interface exposed by the J2EE server for services leaves out some of the features that we need (like discovery).

A web service is the next logical abstraction of the services architecture. It makes the discovery, description, and invocation of services (for example, written in Java) simple and transparent to clients running on any machine, language, and platform. So, an Active Server Page or an application written in Delphi and running on a Windows PC can easily access services written in Java and running on Unix or a mainframe.

The diagram below represents the typical service contact of Service-Oriented Architecture:

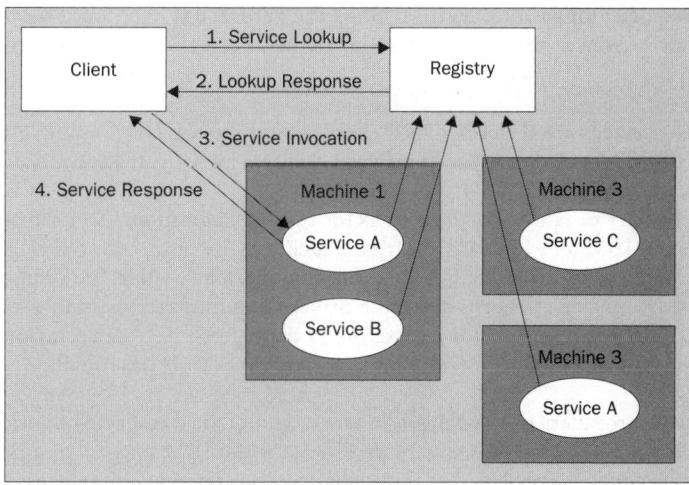

A client contacts a public registry to locate a particular service. It then contacts that service to obtain the service signature to understand the data that is required for the operation, and the data that is returned. Note that data is a very loose term – the return will be in XML in web services, but what is represented in that XML may be a document, an array, or a list of data.

Once the client understands the service signature, it can invoke the service and receive a response. This may be done in a single invocation, or the client and the service may communicate multiple times in a conversation to complete a business transaction.

There are a number of observations that need to be made regarding this diagram:

❑ First of all, it should be noted that a machine (usually identified by an IP address) could host more than one service.

❑ It should also be noted that a service could be provided by more than one source (for example, Machine 1 and Machine 3 both host Service A).

❑ A client would interrogate the registry to obtain the correct service location (a URL in most cases), and then invoke the service.

For web services this is an idealized representation. A UDDI registry would handle the service lookup and response, but the identification of a specific service would typically be by human intervention rather than by automatic recognition.

> One of the biggest debates in the web services community is to what degree UDDI will actually be used, and whether it will be used on a global basis, or within industries. Most insiders predict that UDDI will not be a global registry on the same scale as the Domain Naming Service (DNS), which helps locate particular machines (for example, www.wrox.com is a DNS lookup that ties to a particular server).

Once a service has been identified, the client would need to examine the description – in the form of an XML-based WSDL document – of the service to understand the particulars of the invocation. In most cases, this would require human intervention. Once the WSDL has been understood, an invocation can take place. This may be one or more conversations between the client and the service to accomplish a business task.

In many cases, web services are described as a client, searching a UDDI registry, finding a service, and using it automatically. This won't happen for a variety of reasons – some technical and some social.

First of all, UDDI doesn't provide any provisions for service guarantees. So for example, if you wish to purchase a hard drive, IBM and Joe's Hard Drive Shack may be at the same level. There's no way to know that IBM provides a 99% satisfaction level (if in fact it does), while Joe's Hard Drive Shack won't even provide an RMA service to return defective drives. You may still want to deal with Joe (maybe his prices are insane), but there's no way for a machine to distinguish between a major multi-national corporation and the fellow down the street who sells parts out of his basement.

Additionally, locating providers of hard drives doesn't mean that the service interface (described via WSDL) is the same. Joe may want your credit card only, while IBM may be in a position to accept a purchase order. So to invoke a service, human intervention is once again a necessity.

*This is a hypothetical situation and in no way implies that IBM provides a web service that sells hard drives via purchase orders. Or that Joe's Hard Drive Shack, if it exists, only takes credit cards.*

There is an effort underway to create a web services MetaData specification, which might answer some of these questions. Industry standardization of service interfaces could also alleviate some of these issues as well, but for the moment they exist.

The second observation is that a complete business transaction may involve more than one invocation of a service function. In cases such as these, the atomicity of the entire conversation is critical. This means that if a business transaction, such as ordering a hard drive requires multiple invocations, then there needs to be some mechanism for ensuring that the whole transaction completes or is rolled back.

*Work is underway on what is known as the "Business Transaction Protocol" to address this need, but for now be warned – it's definitely possible to create only a portion of a business transaction. This should be no surprise to experienced coders – the same situation has existed in databases and other transactional systems for years. Web services currently lack a standard protocol for addressing this need.*

# What are Web Services?

Let's start with an example that might help us to understand the characteristics of web services.

> **Having agreed upon the technologies involved in web services (HTTP, XML, SOAP, WSDL, and UDDI), we can infer that a web service is a software component that provides a consistent, transparent API for invocation of services by using message-oriented transport mechanisms, which can be dynamically located and bound, and by utilizing XML for data representation and transformation.**

As such, any client that can bind itself to the particular service, regardless of client platform, language or hardware, can invoke a web service.

Consider a simple application designed to let us monitor the checkbook. This is a standalone, single-user application with a simple purpose to keep track of debits and credits for our checking account. Suppose we have several accounts in different banks. Each month we receive a statement generated by each bank's computer listing the transactions. Then we enter them into the program and make sure we haven't missed anything or that the bank hasn't made a mistake.

Now we connect our computer to the Internet. The banks can send us statements via e-mail, but we still have to enter them into the program manually because the program was not designed to be aware of other applications. Therefore, the developer adds a data import facility in the next version of the program. Let's assume it's fairly basic and requires a fixed format, one that not all of the banks follow. Some banks may put the transaction type first, some may put the date, and some may put the amount first. The next release of the software won't be for another year. So, even though this is useful to an extent, we will have to do other things if we don't want to type the data in.

We may use a spreadsheet to manipulate the data from the bank and translate it into the format required by the checkbook program. This reduces the time to enter the data, but why can't the checkbook program talk directly to the bank whenever we want, or automatically get the information without us having to do anything at all (other than review it so we don't bounce a check)?

The answer is that our program and all the software involved in the communication, such as the bank's mainframe accounting system, need to communicate with one another. Since it's not just the checkbook program but other vendors' programs too that are involved, we need to move towards standards and approaches that facilitate application interoperability. Web services provide us with a platform in which these issues can be handled.

Of course there are alternatives such as Electronic Data Interchange (EDI), private leased lines for communication, which essentially render the system a giant, client-server application, and object technologies, such as Common Object Request Broker Architecture (CORBA), and Enterprise JavaBeans (EJB). These technologies have salient points but exhibit some drawbacks when compared to web services.

EDI requires too much overhead and requires intense effort to implement. Business reasons usually preclude allowing outside companies access to internal applications in the manner of a client-server program, and the more the number of companies interacting, the more likely it is that they will use different systems, requiring multiple terminals and not allowing transparency of data. CORBA and EJB provide fairly robust communication mechanisms, but the APIs are either complex (CORBA), or proprietary (EJB). Web services allow us to make the service available to anyone we want, regardless of computer, as long as Internet access (or intranet if we are only within a company) is available.

To solve our dilemma, we need to develop several things. First of all, to address the common problem of data opaqueness, we need a way to represent our data in a format that our applications can understand. We need to describe elements of arbitrary complexity in data in such a way that an application can clearly distinguish the elements. It must be self-describing, so that any application that receives the data will be able to use what it needs without being written expressly for that data format. There are a number of choices available for solving this data problem.

We could try to establish an industry standard for the data interchange. Industries have attempted this with EDI before, but unfortunately EDI is fairly limited in its capacity. We could develop a programming interface, but that reflects the underlying language or platform of the system, which is not optimal. Or we could use XML to encode the data, which is the approach that web services takes. This has the advantage of establishing a neutral format for the data, regardless of the systems involved. With the banking example, we can see how XML can help us.

Suppose Bank A sends its data like this:

```
12/2/2002,DEBIT,123.45, SHOPRITE AUTOMATIC TRANSACTION
12/4/2002,CHECK,1200.00,1270
12/27/2002,CREDIT,4999.00, PAYROLL DIRECT DEPOSIT
```

We can see that the format is date, transaction type, amount, and description. The data is comma separated, the amount is in dollars, and the dates use the American format – month, day, and year. In this case, we can see that the record length is variable, as are the field lengths.

Bank B may use a different format. Suppose it sends its data like this:

```
CR2002-11-230000000123.45          Payroll Deposit
DT2002-12-010000000050.00          Shoprite Auto Trans
CK2002-12-020000012345.00          Check# 2001
```

We can see that Bank B formats the data as transaction type, date, amount, and description. The record length and field lengths are fixed, with the amount being padded with zeros, the description right justified, the transaction type using abbreviations (a code of some sort), and the date is in year, month, and day.

We as humans can see it. Computer applications may not be able to do the same. We need something that will let us describe the data, so the application can be sure of what it means. This is where XML comes in.

# XML – Extensible Markup Language

This book is not intended to provide extensive coverage of XML. For a detailed look at XML, see *Professional XML 2nd Edition* from Wrox Press (ISBN 1-86100-505-9). Nevertheless, a brief description of the basics of XML will be helpful. Chapter 2 will cover more advanced topics such as XML Namespaces.

As we have seen, XML stands for Extensible Markup Language. Like HTML, and its predecessor, SGML, XML uses tags to define elements of a document.

XML was envisioned to be a self-describing language that would allow both humans and computers to read or use the data described by an XML document with equal facility. XML provides a facility for creating tags, embedding additional information within the tags, and providing a validation mechanism, which allows a computer program to validate that the document is well formed and complete (unlike HTML, which can be malformed). Extensive information on XML is available at http://www.w3.org/XML.

To begin with, XML is case sensitive (unlike HTML), and requires either an opening and closing tag, or a tag that both opens and closes an element. An element name must begin with a letter, an underscore, or a colon, though in practice the colon should not be used. The name must not begin with the string "XML" in any combination of upper or lowercase.

An XML document consists of an optional prolog, which typically describes the version of XML, a body, which contains the information, and an optional epilog, which contains comments or processing instructions.

Within the body, there are **elements**. These elements may contain other elements – they are the basic building blocks of XML. Elements are delimited by **tags**, which consist of an element type name enclosed between angle brackets (< >). Each element must have a start tag and an end tag. Optionally an empty element (one with no data, just instructions) can be included using the format: `<element name />`. So for example, a tag might be:

```
<account_number>1571</account_number>
```

or:

```
<level name="1"/>
```

Elements can be nested within other elements at an arbitrary depth. The second tag example shown above also illustrates the concept of **attributes** within a tag – the tag is `level`, but the attribute is `name`.

Another important aspect of XML is the comment, which in XML is indicated like this:

```
<!-- …Some Comment Text … -->
```

Occasionally data elements may contain characters that would otherwise be recognized as part of the markup language (–, <, >). To make sure that these characters are not misinterpreted, XML includes a tag known as `CDATA`. The tag looks like:

```
<! [CDATA […]]>
```

This means that anything within the inner brackets `[…]` is not interpreted by the XML system as XML, but rather as a data element. This allows us to include a variety of information in a tag that would otherwise be interpreted as XML and displayed or processed incorrectly.

## Document Type Definitions

Earlier we discussed the ability to validate an XML document as a significant advantage of XML. In order to validate an XML document, a validation program must be able to reference the document's **Document Type Defintion (DTD)**. It defines the document's vocabulary. It also allows a **parser** (a software program that can interpret XML to a certain extent) to validate the document's conformity to the definition. For more information on DTD visit http://www-106.ibm.com/developerworks/library/buildappl/.

DTDs are fairly esoteric. They contain a number of elements that help describe a document, but these elements do not necessarily lend themselves to easy inspection, as they define a specific grammar and taxonomy for elements of a document. A document needs a DTD to be validated, and multiple documents can have a common DTD.

## XML Example

Here's an example XML document, taken from the book *Professional XML 2nd Edition* from Wrox Press (ISBN 1-86100-505-9):

```
<holiday>
    <journey>
        <from>London Gatwick</from>
        <to>Orlando, Florida</to>
        <date>2000-02-15 11:40 </date>
        <flight>BA1234 </flight>
    </journey>
    <journey>
        <from> Orlando, Florida </from>
        <to> London Gatwick </to>
        <date>2000-03-01 18:20 </date>
        <flight>BA1235</flight>
    </journey>
```

```
    <visit>
        <hotel>Orlando Hyatt Regency </hotel>
        <arrival>2000-02-15</arrival>
        <departure>2000-03-01</departure>
    </visit>
</holiday>
```

We can see that a holiday consists of multiple journeys, plus multiple visits (in this case, only one). Each `journey` element has nested elements that describe the end points of the journey, plus the date and the flight.

Each `visit` describes the lodging, plus the date of arrival and departure. There could, of course, be multiple visits.

This document describes a high-level holiday, the journeys required to accomplish it, and the visits needed to complete the holiday. It omits the prolog and epilog. Still it is a good example of the kind of encoding that an XML document provides.

In our data, let's see how we can define a transaction. We will need to know the start and end of the transaction data, the type of transaction, the amount of the transaction, the date of the transaction, and a description. Bank A data could look like this in XML:

```
<statement>
  <transaction type="debit">
     <date>
         <month>12</month>
         <day>2</day>
         <year>2002</year>
     </date>
     <amount>123.45</amount>
     <description>SHOPRITE AUTOMATIC TRANSACTION</description>
  </transaction>
  <transaction type="check" number="1270">
     <date>
         <month>12</month>
         <day>4</day>
         <year>2002</year>
     </date>
     <amount>1200.00</amount>
     <description>1270</description>
  </transaction>
  <transaction type="credit">
     <date>
         <month>12</month>
         <day>27</day>
         <year>2002</year>
     </date>
     <amount>4999.00</amount>
     <description>PAYROLL DIRECT DEPOSIT</description>
  </transaction>
</statement>
```

The `statement` element is important as the top level can have only one set of data. This element encapsulates as many transactions as are needed.

Bank B data would look like this:

```
<statement>
  <transaction type="credit">
      <date>
          <year>2002</year>
          <month>11</month>
          <day>23</day>
      </date>
      <amount>123.45</amount>
      <description>Payroll Deposit</description>
  </transaction>
  <transaction type="debit">
      <date>
          <year>2002</year>
          <month>12</month>
          <day>1</day>
      </date>
      <amount>50.00</amount>
      <description>Shoprite Auto Trans</description>
  </transaction>
  <transaction type="check" number="2001">
      <date>
          <year>2002</year>
          <month>12</month>
          <day>2</day>
      </date>
      <amount>12345.00</amount>
      <description>Check 2001</description>
  </transaction>
</statement>
```

This is a complete XML document, though not fully informative. We are missing the prolog and the epilog sections. Additionally, there is no DTD that tells us what the data format is.

Let us suppose that Bank A orders the elements of a date as month, day, year while Bank B orders them as year, month, day. Since the tag completely specifies the type of information, an application can read the data correctly regardless of the order. Since XML is text based, it can be transmitted over HTTP and can also traverse firewalls and proxy servers easily.

Now we have solved one problem – that of representing the data – but we still have several other problems left to tackle. We need a way to discover how the bank offers this information, and ways to describe the service and to ask for the information once we have located the service and understood how to invoke it. UDDI, WSDL, and SOAP are candidates for this type of operation. It's important to note that subsets of these standards are also appropriate candidates.

An all-SOAP solution is certainly a possibility, although it presupposes the ability to locate and define the API for a service. But that presupposition is often the case, and thus a number of web services protocols may be unnecessary at the lowest level. They exist, however, because the lowest level is not the only level on which interaction takes place. Other topics such as business transactions must take precedence over pure interaction based protocols.

**Universal Description, Discovery and Integration (UDDI)** is the means by which services can be published. It is a standard developed and promulgated by a consortium of software vendors and other interested business parties. Information on UDDI can be found at http://www.uddi.org.

Why do we need to locate a service? It is for the same reason we need a phone book. While we may remember the phone numbers of a few friends, when we need access to someone we don't know, we go to the phone book and look them up. We use the white pages or a telephone directory, when we want to look someone up by name and the yellow pages when we want to look them up by category of business.

This is a good area to compare to J2EE's method of finding services. In order to locate a J2EE service, we need to know its complete JNDI name. While JNDI is useful, it does not provide the category hierarchy of UDDI. It is also completely bound to Java, and does not allow clients of other languages to access its functionality.

UDDI allows service providers to establish a provider identity, known as the business entity and register the services it is willing to provide. Business services provide binding information that allows for identification of the type of information to be sent to access the services and a tModel, which gives directions to the calling application as to where to access the service. UDDI uses XML to describe services. UDDI and tModel will be explained in greater detail in Chapter 7.

There are multiple ways of identifying services. As an example, Bank A and Bank B would both register with UDDI as business entities and would describe the services they provide, in this case statement provision.

Now that we know how to locate a service, we need a description of the service so we know how to use it. For this we will use **Web Services Description Language (WSDL)**, which is an XML grammar for describing network services as collections of communication endpoints capable of exchanging messages. WSDL represents a contract between the service requestor and the service. The abstract definition of endpoints and messages is separated from their concrete network deployment or data format bindings. This is also an XML document – in this case one – for describing web services.

We need WSDL to understand the semantics of a particular service. It allows us to define the data types used by the service, the message to be used, and even the binding to a particular invocation mechanism (usually SOAP). Although Bank A and Bank B share a common statement format, they may have different WSDL descriptions. Bank A may require the account number and password, while Bank B may require the account number and social security number of the owner.

Next, we need **Simple Object Access Protocol (SOAP)**. This allows us to actually invoke a service – pass a document containing information needed by the service from our application to the service and receive a reply. Bank A and Bank B have different computer systems. SOAP allows us to contact the appropriate computer, transmit our message, and get our reply. It's important to note that SOAP is also based on XML and that each SOAP message is an XML document.

Now that we know a little about what web services are, let us take a brief look at why we need them.

# Business Reasons for Web Services

There are both business and technical reasons for web services. Our discussion will begin with some of the business reasons for web services and try to briefly outline what business needs are driving the creation of standards and why. While not every business will have all of these needs, most will have at least some of them.

Probably the most common problem in software development is the need to extend the life of a system or program that was written some time ago. The Year 2000 (Y2K) crisis illustrated this problem effectively, driving home the fact that software often outlives even the most optimistic lifespan estimates of its authors. Y2K was caused by a set of shortcuts used by developers to gain speed, efficiency, or space in code written as early as forty years ago. When the time came to correct these shortcuts, people discovered all sorts of additional surprises.

One of the biggest challenges was that the code wasn't documented and the authors had long since retired. Another was that there were incompatibilities between versions of the languages used like the difference between modern English and the archaic style used by Shakespeare. There were differences in the size of variables from version to version, causing difficulties for anyone who made assumptions about variable lengths.

The lessons Y2K taught us are still valid and in many cases developers are creating smaller, more localized versions of the Y2K crisis in companies across the globe. If we look closely, we'll see a number of common problems. These include:

❑ **Hardware Dependence**
Assumptions about word size, byte ordering, and variable length can cause difficulties. For example, if we assumed that an integer was two bytes and had an array of integers that held ten integers, we could assume that the array was twenty bytes long. In some languages, we could access the individual bytes and perform operations on them. Now if we try interfacing this with a system on a different platform, one that defines an integer as four bytes, all of our operations would be wrong.

❑ **Language Dependence**
Systems are usually written in single programming language. However, that is beginning to change as languages have varying concepts of design, such as procedural or object-oriented.

❑ **Data Opaqueness**
The lack of a common, transparent format for data and its representation leads to all kinds of problems. Differences in the format of data representation drive up the cost of any integration project.

❑ **Paradigm Inadequacies**
The most common programming paradigm is to build a system based on the requirement to perform a business task. Usually this system has user interface, business logic, and some data. Until recently, the concept of building a system did not include the idea that other systems may want to access the business logic or data of the system.

As an analogy, consider building a house and after it has been built deciding that you want a patio deck with French doors. Unfortunately, the wall you want to put the door in has wiring, plumbing, and heating on it, because you never considered the possibility that you might want a door there. In the world of computer software, programs such as screen scrapers were the first attempt to access mainframe, terminal-based software by using personal computers. Although this approach lessened the problems faced by companies as they tried to make their systems work together, it didn't totally remove them.

The basic problem is to make applications on one computer talk to applications on another computer, or a set of other computers. Thanks to advances in computer technology, computers of any make can communicate by sending electronic signals to each other. What to do with these signals is the concern of operating systems and applications.

## Enterprise-to-Enterprise Connectivity

Even after the demise of the dotcom era, the Internet does have a significant influence on the way most corporations do business.

Fundamentally, the adoption of the Internet was about breaking down communication barriers. Some of these barriers were technical while others were simply posturing for business purposes. The worldwide reach of the Internet has allowed customers, partners, and employees to challenge the traditional means of doing business.

Communication needed between enterprises is supplied very elegantly by web services. Large corporations, companies with many divisions and lines of services have a wide network of relationships with other business concerns, as well as with their customers. In any enterprise, electronic communication is a prerequisite.

Corporations utilize a variety of means to communicate with one another. File transfer is common, as is the use of Electronic Data Interchange (EDI) messages.

EDI transactions generally work from implementation guidelines that specify fixed message formats. Traditional EDI refers to the use of rigid transaction sets with business rules embedded in them. This model simply does not work in today's rapidly changing business environment. EDI works fine, as long as you keep within your supply chain and have stable content. But business today does not always have that kind of predictability, and EDI transactions has been found difficult to map from one industry to another, and even between different segments of the same industry.

What is the state of EDI today? Industry statistics indicate that the use of EDI in B2B exchanges is far out in front of other web protocols. An IDC study calculated the total value of goods and services exchanged in business-to-business electronic commerce in 2001 at $2.3 trillion, with EDI transactions valued at $1.8 trillion or about 78 percent of that total, and Internet-based e-commerce providing the remaining $0.5 trillion.

E-mail is also used to exchange information. Unfortunately, none of these mechanisms are appropriate for the needs of the business. File transfer is not standardized, EDI is standardized but not easily adaptable, and e-mail is not sufficient in itself to accomplish the task, which is to exchange information.

The Internet era made corporations aware of their need to communicate. At the same time, it also made them aware of the challenges they faced in doing so due to their existing infrastructure. It was no coincidence that the startups were first to market in many cases, building a presence in the face of larger corporations and moving at a dizzying pace since they had no legacy infrastructure. They were able to build their Internet-based businesses quickly because they didn't have to figure out how to integrate their six separate purchasing systems to deliver product.

The challenge faced by IT staff throughout the industry is to do more with less. Old systems must be perpetuated, not replaced. Yet, every new system added to the mix requires interfaces to every other system. As seen in the diagram below, adding one new system requires multiple new interfaces to be created: (n-1) where n is the total number of systems after the addition:

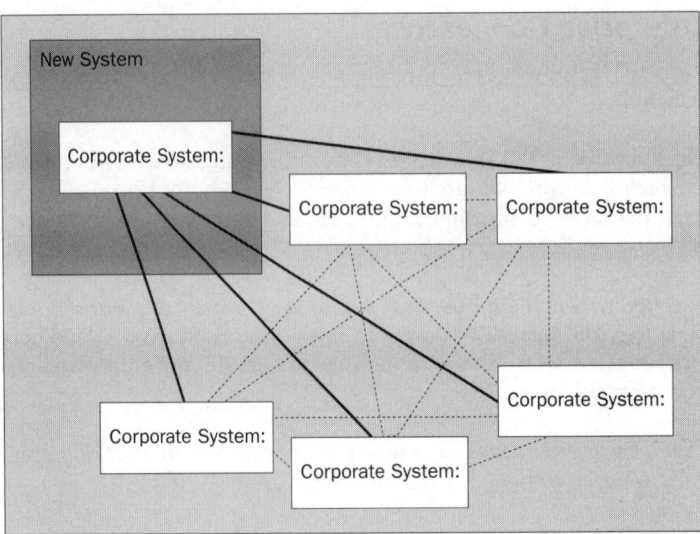

### Enterprise Application Integration

Enterprise Application Integration (EAI) is an attempt to solve part of that problem. EAI introduces a hub or bus concept. Interfaces are written to the hub, with each system requiring only a single interface rather than multiple interfaces:

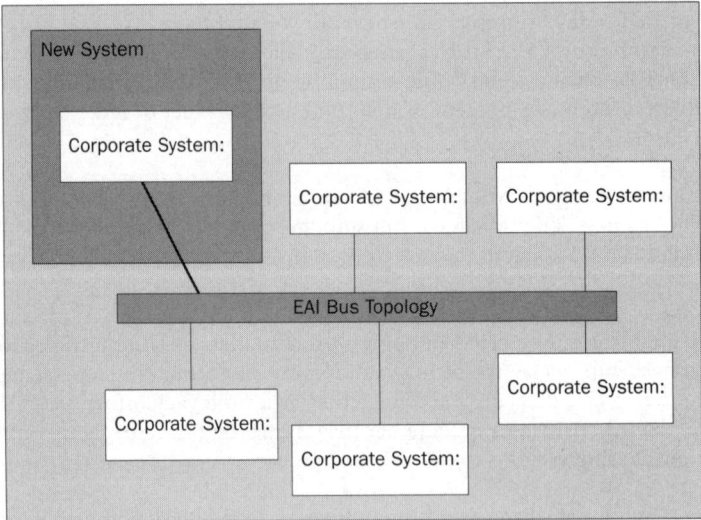

From a business perspective, EAI is about doing more with less. For example, EAI enables multiple billing systems to function as a single billing conglomerate. From an external perspective, this amalgamation allows users to think of billing as a single system, even though it may be a conglomerate of multiple applications. It allows a business to create a standard interface for its systems so as to reduce the complexity of making them interoperate. From an internal perspective, EAI is a definite aid.

However, it breaks down at the borders of the corporation, as it is proprietary and not truly Internet based. The proprietary nature of EAI solutions means that at the enterprise level, a single, simple interface does not exist between corporations. Companies using different EAI products once again had to write multiple interfaces and since not all corporations use EAI, other interfaces needed to be developed as well:

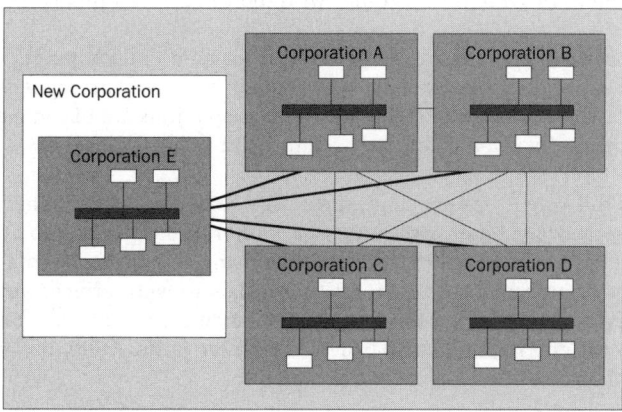

Web services solve that problem. The UDDI registry allows a company to advertise its services to any and all. WSDL allows it to describe the interfaces by which it delivers these advertised services. SOAP allows for the transmission of messages adhering to the interfaces between cooperating partners. Since the technology is based on open standards, implementations on a wide variety of platforms exist, removing the need for proprietary interfaces. It is worth noting that all the major EAI vendors either already support web services, or will support them in the near future.

A number of simplifications are at work here. We have not touched the topic of security at all. Neither have we discussed what business services should be exposed through UDDI. Also we have not looked at situations where more than two corporations need to interact in the same business transaction. Nevertheless, we have begun to solve the basic business problem – allowing corporate systems to interact with one another. We will look at the answers to some of those questions (such as security) in later chapters. However, it is worth looking at application integration from a business perspective as well.

## Application Integration

We also have the problem of application integration. Major corporations have a number of systems, often because of mergers and acquisitions or multiple lines of business having differing needs. One of the consequences of this type of environment is difficulty in obtaining timely and accurate information about the state of a corporation. Another consequence is that duplicate systems and data exist.

Often, the question of "System of Record" becomes an issue. "System of Record" is the concept that the repository should be the only receptacle for the data, the system of record against which copies are compared. An example is the concept of a customer record. If a company employs a billing system, an accounting system, an inventory system, a tracking system, and a manufacturing system, all of these may have some concept of a customer. Depending upon which transaction, or what state, the question of which system is the master, the true data, becomes a key question. At times it can be impossible to designate the key system. Money is lost when records don't match and shipments are sent to the wrong address, or not billed, or shipped twice.

Another issue is the use of multiple systems for fulfillment of a business process. A corporation might take orders via its web site. To do so, it needs to have a web application. It needs to access inventory and track work in progress. It may use a third party provider to do credit card transactions, while having an accounting application to track the funds. It might do its own shipping, or might use a different shipping firm each time. It might have to provide interim status of an order. All these systems need to be coordinated to provide the customer with their order in a timely, seamless fashion.

When we consider that these systems are likely to reside on different computers with different operating systems, and that the applications are likely to be written in different languages, we can start to gain an appreciation for the task of the corporate IT staff. Package solutions are of some aid, as they typically provide some mechanisms for interaction, but it's important to have some means of uniting these systems.

While EAI has filled this role to some extent, the ability to use the same technology within the enterprise that we use between enterprises once again offers a unique way to achieve simplification and reduce costs through the use of standards. Rather than using a proprietary solution within the enterprise and writing interfaces or intermediate programs to translate to web services, building the application bridge using web services ensures that services within the enterprise can be at any time migrated to services provided by the enterprise to it's partners. This type of flexibility is crucial to success in an environment where the rules of business change swiftly.

# Technical Reasons for Web Services

In reality, the technical reasons are often at the heart of the business reason as the inability to do things technically often escalates into a business problem. There are many reasons for selecting web services; mentioned here are a few of the more prevalent ones.

## Service-Oriented Architecture

Code within an application contains a mixture of presentation logic, business logic, and storage code, running on a single machine. Client-server technology moved the storage code to a centralized database server, but left the remaining architecture unchanged. In this model, adding a web interface, or adapting for a cell phone, or integrating into a messaging system requires massive changes to the application structure, even though the business logic could remain unchanged. The diagram below illustrates typical application architecture before the concept of **Service-Oriented Architecture (SOA)**:

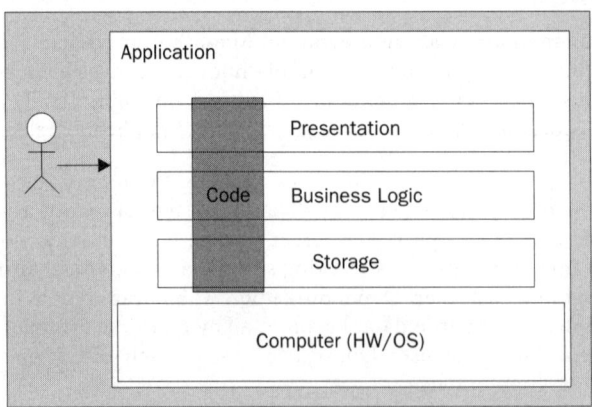

Basically, SOA implies the design of an application as a set of services. Demand for this design approach and technologies to support it have increased with the rise of the Internet. HTML made a poor application programming language, but was fairly adequate for providing a presentation layer. SOA divides the design of an application into services. A client can make use of a service to accomplish a task. This became a useful concept when people needed to add a web interface, an internal interface, interact with the financial system, and let users look at things on their cell phones. The service concept let developers design code that could be accessed in a number of ways (these ways or layers could, in fact, also be considered services in their own right).

In the figure below, the presentation of the interface to the user is separated from the business logic, which in turn is separated from the storage logic. Each partition can run on separate hardware platforms and perform discrete tasks. Adding a new system that makes use of the business logic requires no change in the code or the application structure:

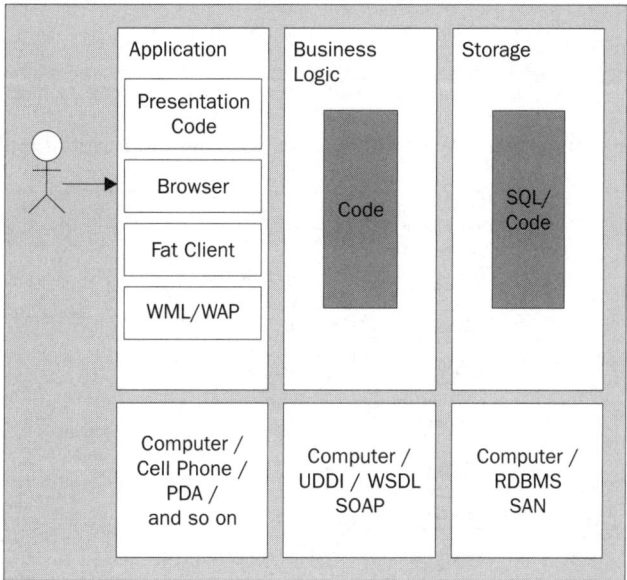

Web services fits perfectly into the concept of SOA – it is built around the principles of service-oriented architecture. It also provides abstraction of the interface from the implementation language and platform independence.

Let us look at our checkbook application again, but from a different view. We started by assuming that it was a single-user desktop application. Now let's suppose that we want to share it among other users (maybe we've started a small business and want to try to use it in multi-user mode to track orders). As it was written for a single user, with no concept of services, we would have a lot of difficulty modifying it to work for multiple users:

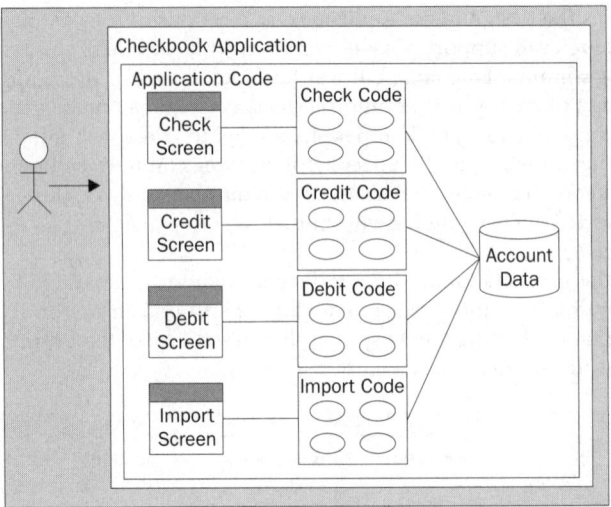

Now, if the checkbook application were written as an SOA design, it would look something like this:

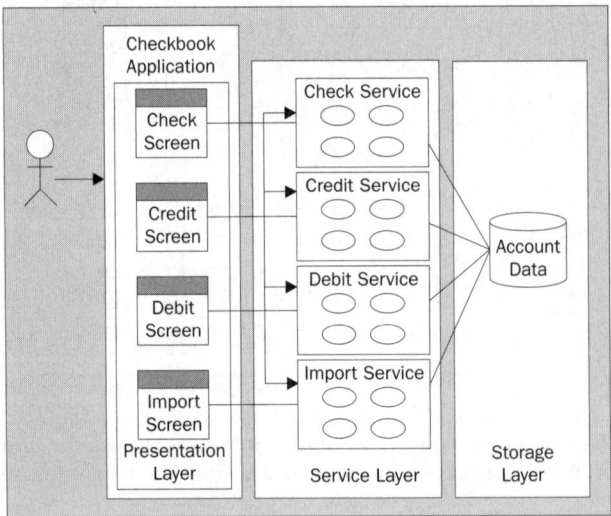

Now we can treat the application as the presentation code, or any other code that makes use of the service. We might have other applications such as direct banking, that do not need a user interface at all, but make use of the services. Also, notice that we can define the Import Service simply by utilizing the other services – there is no need to duplicate the code of those services. This illustrates that the service layer may call into itself and that there may be a chain of services that fulfill a particular business need.

With this type of design we can create other clients and distribute them as needed – as HTML pages, applications, wireless apps, and so on. The SOA design provides tremendous flexibility.

## *Platform Independence*

A related technical issue is that of **platform independence**. In an enterprise, it is rare to have one single platform, hardware or software. More commonly, there is a mix of hardware and software from multiple vendors. One goal of platform independence is that programs may run anywhere, but a related and more important objective is to acquire ability to ignore the platform a particular service or application runs on. In reality, true portability of applications isn't nearly as important as this ability. Most applications, especially custom applications, will run on a particular platform. It is important that the platform does not become a limitation to the accessibility of the application by other platforms.

Web services provide platform independence. The main protocols of web services are ubiquitous – XML is platform neutral and HTTP, which provides the most common transport mechanism, is available on almost every platform. By designing applications to be web-services enabled, we can achieve the power of platform independence and allow clients to access our business services in whatever manner necessary, from any platform needed.

## *Consolidation and Abstraction*

One of the issues in IT support is the cost of maintenance. As the number of systems and applications grows, these costs can skyrocket. A common approach to solving this problem is **consolidation** of systems. The idea is that multiple systems perform some of the same tasks. Thus by removing some of the systems we can have the same functionality with fewer moving parts and reduce costs by reducing hardware, licensing, or personnel. Mergers and acquisitions often result in this type of environment with different systems performing the same tasks. For example, one company may use Peoplesoft, the other SAP. When the companies are merged, both systems may need to be retained for some time.

One of the approaches to consolidation is **abstraction**. Abstraction is a classic pattern in computer software, providing an API layer between the software being abstracted and the software that uses the services. By abstraction, changes in the implementation behind the API are not necessarily exposed to the client, making it easier to do design modifications.

In the case of duplicate systems, creating an abstraction allows for migration of functionality from one system to another at an ordered pace. Once the abstraction is in place, clients call an interface that provides the services. Where the service is executed is not meaningful – as long as the service is provided the client is satisfied. This way, IT staff can begin the task of reducing duplication. Once the API is in use, portions of one system can be migrated to the other and eventually one of the duplicate systems can be retired. No user needs to know when this happens, because the services do not change.

Obviously, web services fits quite nicely into this arena as well. UDDI and WSDL provide the building blocks for creating an API to abstract the systems in question and the routing information in WDSL allows services to be redirected as needed to allow parts of a system to be turned off without disruption of service.

# Java and the Web Services Stack

Until this point, we have discussed Java only in passing. The first part of the chapter was intended to provide a feel for the concepts of web services, which are not confined to any single language or platform.

At this point, a couple of valid questions might be: Why Java at all? What need is there for Java as a platform, or as a programming language? The answer is that, as with all services and applications the actual implementations still need to be written in a programming language and run on a platform. In this book we will be using the Java platform, with Java as the development language, along with HTML (via JSP) and XML. For the sake of this discussion we will be referencing the Java SDK version 1.4. Let's look at the diagram below:

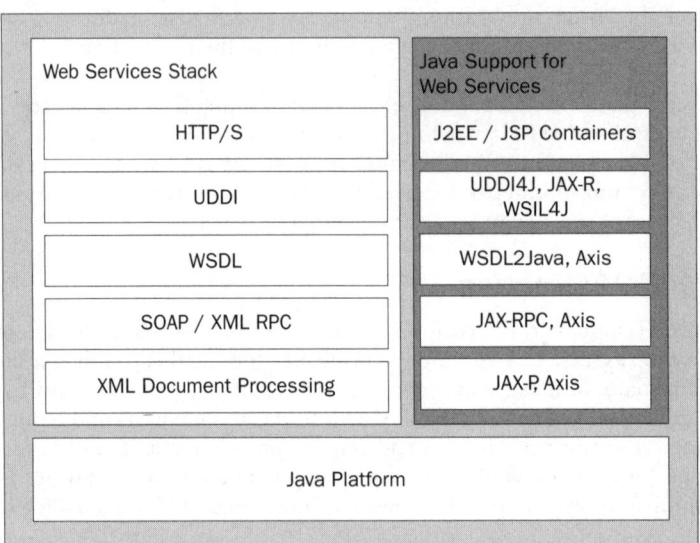

The diagram above illustrates the web services stack and some of the key Java features that support it. At the bottom of the stack is the Java Development Kit (JDK) that contains the Java Runtime Environment (JRE) and represents the basic Java platform, the virtual machine. There are many ways that Java APIs can support web services; this diagram shows the web services stack and its relationship to Java APIs that affect each layer, rather than how web services are implemented using Java technologies. What this means is that this book is about using Java technology with web services, rather than building things like a UDDI registry in Java. The following sections explain the previous diagram in detail.

# Standard Transport Mechanism

The standard protocol for web services is the **Hypertext Transfer Protocol (HTTP)** and its encrypted variant, **HTTP/S**. The HTTP protocol is a simple request/response paradigm and is synchronous. This means that any call to a service waits until the service responds. Sometimes this is referred to as blocking on a call. If the service crashes or takes an inordinate amount of time to respond, the call may time out and the caller would then consider the invocation as a failure. As with an ordinary web page, a web service is invoked using a **Universal Resource Locator (URL)** that allows the service to be contacted. HTTP allows for invocation of URLs and ensures that the request and response are routed correctly.

The HTTP/S protocol provides an encrypted channel between the HTTP server (the web server or whatever software is providing HTTP support) and the client (your browser, application, and so on). Typically, this is done when using a username and password to authenticate the user of the service. Chapter 9 will examine security issues in greater detail.

Third-party providers offer elements that enable Java to support HTTPS. J2EE (Java 2 Platform, Enterprise Edition) servers provide an environment that includes HTTP/S as part of their implementation of the Java servlet container. Standalone JSP containers also provide the necessary functionality.

### Asynchronicity and Other Protocols

HTTP and HTTP/S are not the only mechanisms possible for communication and the request/response model is not sufficient for everyone's needs. Some computing tasks may take a significant amount of time – they may be calculation intensive, or may need human input via some workflow mechanism. For example, first time shoppers may have to receive human approval if their initial order is over a specified dollar figure. So not all web service requests can necessarily be completed in a synchronous fashion; we also need asynchronicity.

**Asynchronicity** is the ability for a client to communicate with a service in a fashion outside the publish/subscribe, request/response mechanism. It is important because many business transactions require multiple conversations to record a business transaction. Not all of these conversations can be accounted for in synchronous invocations.

Java provides several different mechanisms for asynchronous communication. In the J2EE specification, the Java Messaging Service (JMS) provides facilities for a number of paradigms, including point-to-point and multicast messaging. The Java API for XML Messaging (JAX-M) provides an asynchronous service for web services and implements a pure Java version of the SOAP protocol. These technologies will be covered in detail in Chapter 8.

# Discovery via UDDI

UDDI allows for the registration of an entity as a service provider as well as the ability to register the services the company is willing to provide. Although a global UDDI registry is often discussed, many developers predict the rise of industry-specific, private or semi-private registries rather than one global UDDI registry similar to the DNS service for networking.

Java provides the Java API for XML Registries (JAXR) to allow developers to access a UDDI registry, query its contents, and make entries. Querying the UDDI registry can be done via URL access as well; it is not limited to API access.

The use of JAXR to access the UDDI registry will be seen in detail in Chapter 7, where we will also discuss several utilities (UDDI4J and WSIL4J) that allow for quick conversions between UDDI XML and Java objects/classes. We will also discuss the Axis tool as an implementation of XML RPC and related APIs. It is an implementation of the SOAP submission to W3C by the Apache organization (http://xml.apache.org/axis).

# Description via WSDL

WSDL is the language used for specifying detailed information about a service, which allows an application to understand how to invoke the service and what parameters are required. An actual WSDL document is complex and includes elements such as imports, types, schemas, messages, ports, bindings, and services. The details of WSDL will be covered in Chapter 5.

Java supports WSDL via several tools. The Java2WSDL tool, which is part of the IBM web services Toolkit allows for the generation of WSDL from a Java class, while the WSDL2Java tool, also a part of the toolkit, allows developers to generate Java class stubs from a WSDL document.

An example of a WSDL document taken from the `StockQuote` example in Chapter 5 is shown below. We can see that a number of messages are defined, particularly one for a `getQuoteRequest` and one for a `getQuoteResponse`, which allows us to request a stock quote and receive a reply. Note that the messages start with `<wsdl:message ...>`. You can also see the definition of the operation, named `GetQuote`, and its relationship to the two messages. It's envisioned that UML modeling tools will be able to generate WSDL documents such as that shown below. The WSDL document is as follows:

```xml
<?xml version="1.0" encoding="UTF-8" ?>
<wsdl:definitions targetNamespace="http://stockquote.iws.wrox.com"
  xmlns="http://schemas.xmlsoap.org/wsdl/"
  xmlns:SOAP-ENC="http://schemas.xmlsoap.org/soap/encoding/"
  xmlns:impl="http://stockquote.iws.wrox.com-impl"
  xmlns:intf="http://stockquote.iws.wrox.com"
  xmlns:wsdl="http://schemas.xmlsoap.org/wsdl/"
  xmlns:wsdlsoap="http://schemas.xmlsoap.org/wsdl/soap/"
  xmlns:xsd="http://www.w3.org/2001/XMLSchema">

<wsdl:message name="Exception" />
<wsdl:message name="getQuoteRequest">
  <wsdl:part name="in0" type="SOAP-ENC:string" />
</wsdl:message>

<wsdl:message name="getQuoteResponse">
  <wsdl:part name="return" type="SOAP-ENC:string" />
</wsdl:message>

<wsdl:portType name="StockQuote">
  <wsdl:operation name="getQuote" parameterOrder="in0">
    <wsdl:input message="intf:getQuoteRequest" />
    <wsdl:output message="intf:getQuoteResponse" />
    <wsdl:fault message="intf:Exception" name="Exception" />
  </wsdl:operation>
</wsdl:portType>
<wsdl:binding name="StockQuoteSoapBinding" type="intf:StockQuote">
  <wsdlsoap:binding style="rpc"
    transport="http://schemas.xmlsoap.org/soap/http" />
  <wsdl:operation name="getQuote">
    <wsdlsoap:operation soapAction="" />
    <wsdl:input>
      <wsdlsoap:body
        encodingStyle="http://schemas.xmlsoap.org/soap/encoding/"
        namespace="http://stockquote.iws.wrox.com" use="encoded" />
    </wsdl:input>
    <wsdl:output>
      <wsdlsoap:body
        encodingStyle="http://schemas.xmlsoap.org/soap/encoding/"
        namespace="http://stockquote.iws.wrox.com" use="encoded" />
    </wsdl:output>
```

```
      </wsdl:operation>
    </wsdl:binding>

    <wsdl:service name="StockQuoteService">
      <wsdl:port binding="intf:StockQuoteSoapBinding" name="StockQuote">
        <wsdlsoap:address
          location="http://localhost/axis/services/StockQuote"/>
      </wsdl:port>
    </wsdl:service>
  </wsdl:definitions>
```

# Invocation via SOAP

Simple Object Access Protocol or SOAP is one of the many binding protocols available to WSDL, but it is the standard and most commonly used one for web services. SOAP allows a web service to be invoked by a client application irrespective of the language, in which the client and providing application are implemented. Java provides the Java API for XML RPC (JAX-RPC) to allow developers to execute Remote Procedure Calls (RPC). JAX-RPC implements a pure Java version of the SOAP protocol. The use of JAX-RPC and SOAP via the use of the Axis toolkit is illustrated in Chapter 3. The following diagram shows the representation of a SOAP message:

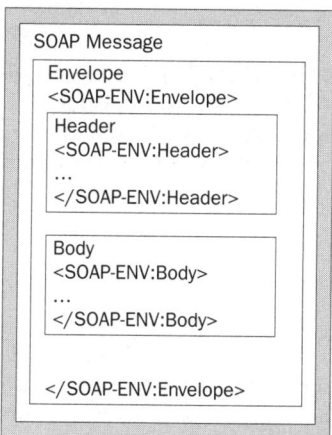

This diagram shows the anatomy of a SOAP message. It includes the envelope, header, and body. SOAP may use HTTP to accomplish communication between a client and a service, which must provide a SOAP processor to decode the message. Common web servers such as IIS and Apache provide such processors.

The envelope marks the beginning and end of a SOAP message. The header is optional, and can be used to describe attributes of the message. The body is required and contains the actual message, which may be one or more blocks of information.

As a preview of things to come, here is a snippet of a SOAP message that we will look at in detail in Chapter 4. You can see the start of the envelope, with the tag <SOAP-ENV:Envelope …>. It defines the schema and the namespaces to be used. Then within the envelope, we see the body, which begins with the <SOAP-ENV:Body> tag. Within the body is a response from the HelloWorld service to a call on the SayHello method:

```
<?xml version="1.0" encoding="UTF-8"?>
<SOAP-ENV:Envelope
   xmlns:SOAP-ENV="http://schemas.xmlsoap.org/soap/envelope/"
   xmlns:xsd="http://www.w3.org/2001/XMLSchema"
   xmlns:xsi="http://www.w3.org/2001/XMLSchema-instance">
   <SOAP-ENV:Body>
     <ns1:sayHelloResponse
        SOAP-ENV:encodingStyle="http://schemas.xmlsoap.org/soap/encoding/"
        xmlns:ns1="urn:helloworld">
        <sayHelloReturn xsi:type="xsd:string">Hello Reader!</sayHelloReturn>
     </ns1:sayHelloResponse>
   </SOAP-ENV:Body>
</SOAP-ENV:Envelope>
```

# Data/Document Processing Using XML

Java provides the Java API for XML Processing (JAXP) to facilitate the processing of an XML document. It includes mechanisms for parsing and manipulating XML documents such as the DOM and SAX representations of an XML document, as well as an implementation of XSLT. Chapter 4 will expand on the examples from Chapter 3 and will demonstrate document processing using JAXP and the Axis toolkit.

While we are discussing Java and XML we need to discuss two topics – DOM and SAX. DOM stands for Document Object Model and is one way for Java developers to access and influence XML documents. SAX stands for the Simple API for XML, and also provides an API for XML access via Java. To a certain extent, the choice of DOM or SAX is left to the programmer, but it is also part of the design specification for a particular service.

# Summary

In this chapter we discussed some of the reasons that led to the development of web services. We looked at the shortcomings in a number of programming models related to distributed applications and examined how web services provided an excellent way to support both internal and external abstraction of systems. We discussed XML, SOAP, UDDI, and WSDL as they relate to the creation and publishing of web services.

We also discussed the infrastructure of web services, and covered how XML, SOAP, and RPC reflect its reality.

From a Java perspective we also included a variety of documents. We examined how web services relate to Java and what Java APIs are available. These included JAX-M, JAX-R, JAX-P, and JAX-RPC. We briefly outlined these relationships and mentioned the chapters in which they will be covered in detail. Let us now proceed with the rest of this book for a detailed description of web services.

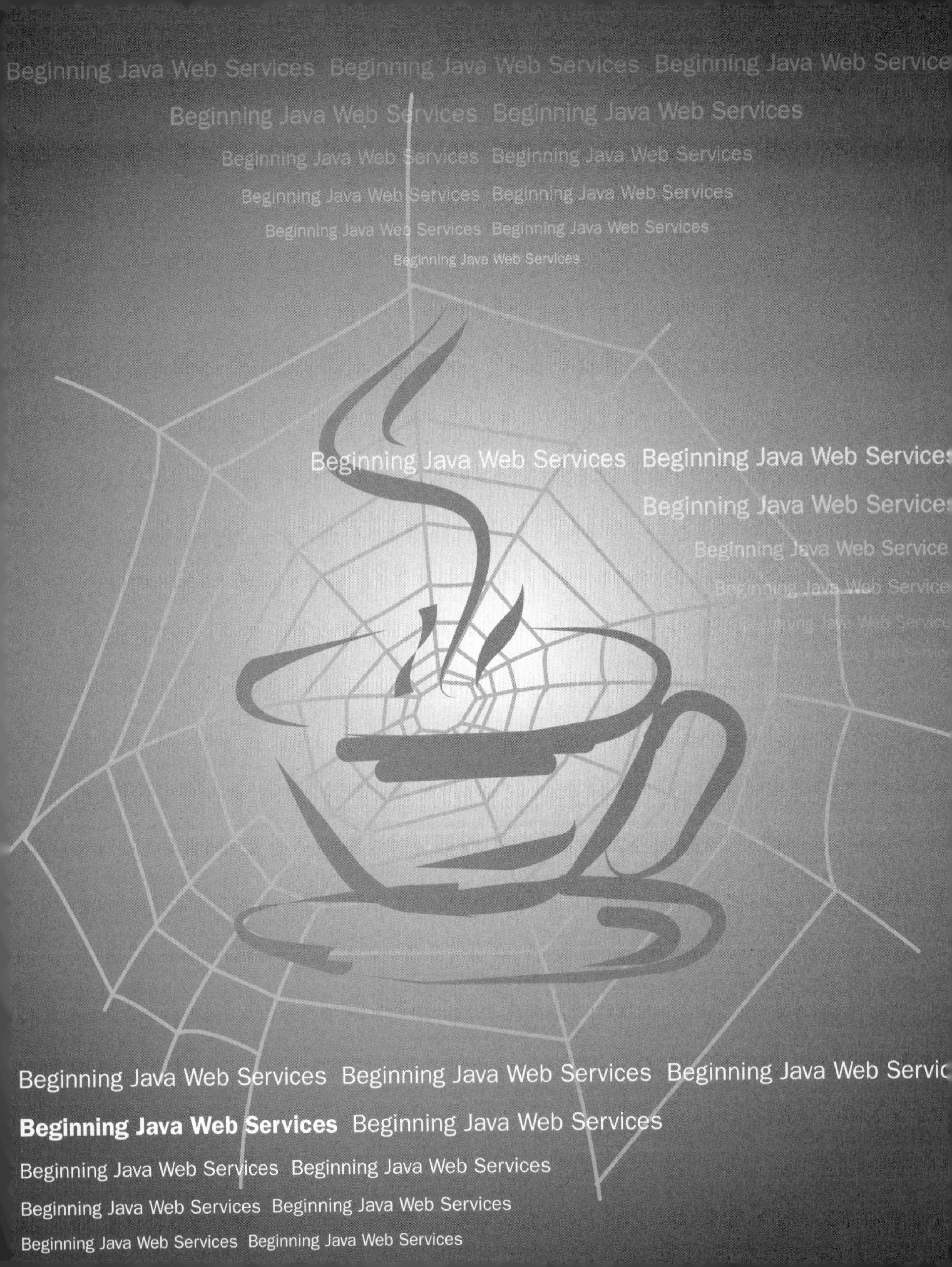
Beginning Java Web Services Beginning Java Web Services
Beginning Java Web Services Beginning Java Web Services
Beginning Java Web Services Beginning Java Web Services
Beginning Java Web Services Beginning Java Web Services
Beginning Java Web Services Beginning Java Web Services
Beginning Java Web Services
Beginning Java Web Services
Beginning Java Web Services Beginning Java Web Services
Beginning Java Web Services Beginning Java Web Services
Beginning Java Web Services Beginning Java Web Services
Beginning Java Web Services Beginning Java Web Services
Beginning Java Web Services Beginning Java Web Services

# Parsing Data Using XML

In the last chapter we had a whirlwind tour of web services. From this chapter onwards we will cover the individual technologies involved in implementing web services in further detail. We will focus on how XML is used in web services and the various aspects of XML that are relevant to web services. The topics that are covered in this chapter are as follows:

- ❏ **XML Namespaces**
  We will look at XML Namespaces that are used quite extensively in both **Web Service Description Language (WSDL)** documents that describe web services, and **Simple Object Access Protocol (SOAP)** envelopes that represent web service requests and responses.

- ❏ **XML Schema**
  We will look at XML Schema, which addresses many shortcomings that are associated with **Document Type Definitions (DTD)**, traditionally used for constraining the contents of XML documents.

- ❏ **Processing XML documents**
  We will look at the various options available for producing and consuming XML documents. Here we will cover the **Document Object Model (DOM)** and the **Simple API for XML (SAX)**. We will also cover the **Java API for XML Processing (JAXP)** for writing XML applications that are not tightly coupled to XML parser vendors.

- ❏ **XML Protocols**
  We will look at the various protocols available for using XML to represent remote procedure requests and responses. Since SOAP is the dominant protocol used in web services, we will cover that in more detail. We will also cover the simpler but less efficient XML-RPC protocol.

> **Please note that this chapter doesn't cover the basics of XML. It assumes basic knowledge of XML. For a more comprehensive coverage of XML please refer to** *Professional Java XML* **published by Wrox Press (ISBN 1-86100-285-8).**

# The Evolution of XML

In the past few years XML has evolved as the de facto standard for document markup with human readable tags. Since its advent, XML has found its way into a variety of applications such as:

- ❏ Configuration Information
- ❏ Publishing
- ❏ Electronic Data Interchange
- ❏ Voice Mail Systems
- ❏ Vector Graphics
- ❏ Remote Method Invocation
- ❏ Object Serialization

XML can be used to customize tags that are relevant to the domain we work on. As a result of this extensibility XML has been adopted by diverse industries for representing the data relevant to their domain.

What makes XML an integral element of enterprise computing is that XML documents are simple text documents with a platform-neutral way of representing data. An XML document produced by an application running on Microsoft Windows can easily be consumed by an application running on Sun Solaris.

XML is a descendant of the **Standard Generalized Markup Language (SGML)**, which is a very powerful but complicated markup language. XML simplifies most of SGML's complexity and provides a powerful way of creating document markup. The XML 1.0 specification was made a Recommendation by the W3C in early 1998. Since then, it has evolved into one of the most powerful technologies in enterprise computing. Over the past few years many other complementary technologies have also evolved that extend the power of XML. These technologies include:

- ❏ **XSL Transformations**
  Used for transforming XML documents from one form to another

- ❏ **XSL Formatting Objects**
  Used for describing layout of viewable XML documents

- ❏ **XPath**
  Used for selecting nodes arbitrarily from XML documents

- ❏ **XLink**
  Used for linking XML documents in a manner similar to HTML hyperlinks

- ❏ **XML Base**
  Used in conjunction with XLink for defining a base URI for XML documents (this is similar to the functionality provided by the HTML base tag)

- ❏ **XML Schema**
  Used for defining rules for a valid XML document

❑ **XPointer**
Used as an extension of XPath for pointing to arbitrary structures within an XML document

❑ **XML Query**
Used for extracting data from XML documents

❑ **SOAP**
Used for exchanging structured and typed information between applications in a decentralized, distributed environment using XML

❑ **XML Encryption**
Used for encrypting specific portions of an XML document

❑ **XML Key Management**
Used for describing the protocols for distributing and registering public keys

❑ **XML Signature**
Used for digitally signing specific portions of an XML document

In the next few sections we will be covering those XML-related technologies that are relevant to web services. We can obtain all the XML-related specifications from http://www.w3c.org/XML/.

# Processing XML Documents

In this section we will cover the various technologies for processing XML documents. Processing XML documents mainly involves:

❑ Creating XML documents from scratch

❑ Parsing XML data available from external sources to ensure the well formedness and validity of the XML content

The various examples that we will cover in this chapter will be built around a stock quote XML example that will be used throughout the book. The structure of the XML document is shown below:

```
<?xml version="1.0"?>

<stock_quotes>

  <!-- EDS -->
  <stock_quote>
    <symbol>EDS</symbol>
    <when><date>2002-6-21</date><time>13:33</time></when>
    <price type="ask" value="32.32"/>
    <price type="open" value="32.8"/>
    <price type="dayhigh" value="33.1"/>
    <price type="daylow" value="32.16"/>
    <change>+0.239</change><volume>67552600</volume>
  </stock_quote>

  <!-- Sun-->
  <stock_quote>
```

```
      <symbol>SUNW</symbol>
      <when><date>2002-6-21</date><time>13:33</time></when>
      <price type="ask" value="5.93"/>
      <price type="open" value="5.67"/>
      <price type="dayhigh" value="6.01"/>
      <price type="daylow" value="5.56"/>
      <change>+0.239</change>
      <volume>67552600</volume>
   </stock_quote>

   <!-- IBM-->
   <stock_quote>
      <symbol>IBM</symbol>
      <when><date>2002-6-21</date><time>13:33</time></when>
      <price type="ask" value="69.01"/>
      <price type="open" value="69.51"/>
      <price type="dayhigh" value="71.39"/>
      <price type="daylow" value="71.39"/>
      <change>+0.239</change>
      <volume>67552600</volume>
   </stock_quote>

   <!-- Microsoft -->
   <stock_quote>
      <symbol>MSFT</symbol>
      <when><date>2002-6-21</date><time>13:33</time></when>
      <price type="ask" value="51.25"/>
      <price type="open" value="51.31"/>
      <price type="dayhigh" value="52.79"/>
      <price type="daylow" value="50.64"/>
      <change>+0.239</change>
      <volume>67552600</volume>
   </stock_quote>

   <!-- DOW Jones -->
   <stock_quote>
      <symbol>^DJI</symbol>
      <when><date>2002-6-21</date><time>13:33</time></when>
      <price type="ask" value="8448.19"/>
      <price type="open" value="8540.47"/>
      <price type="dayhigh" value="8621.95"/>
      <price type="daylow" value="8448.19"/>
      <change>+0.239</change>
      <volume>67552600</volume>
   </stock_quote>

   <!-- NASDAQ -->
   <stock_quote>
      <symbol>^IXIC</symbol>
      <when><date>2002-6-21</date><time>13:33</time></when>
      <price type="ask" value="1360.62"/>
      <price type="open" value="1390.41"/>
      <price type="dayhigh" value="1395.29"/>
      <price type="daylow" value="1360.22"/>
      <change>+0.239</change>
      <volume>67552600</volume>
   </stock_quote>
```

```
    <!--Standard & Poor -->
    <stock_quote>
      <symbol>^GSPC</symbol>
      <when><date>2002-6-21</date><time>13:33</time></when>
      <price type="ask" value="884.58"/>
      <price type="open" value="905.36"/>
      <price type="dayhigh" value="907.84"/>
      <price type="daylow" value="884.46"/>
      <change>+0.239</change>
      <volume>67552600</volume>
    </stock_quote>

  </stock_quotes>
```

The XML document above defines the quotes for some well-known stocks and market indices. Note that in a real-world scenario, this document would come from a web site such as Reuters, Yahoo Finance, or Financial Times that provides online stock quotes.

Each quote shows the ticker symbol of the stock that is quoted, the date on which the quote was received, the ask price, open price, highest and lowest prices for the day, change in price since open, and the volume of the stocks. We will have a look at how the stock quote XML can be created from scratch, how an external file that contains the stock quote XML can be parsed to check for validity and well formedness, and how an in-memory XML structure representing the stock_quote can be queried to find various information regarding the stock quotes.

The two prevalent APIs available for processing XML documents are:

❑ **DOM**
   DOM is a W3C recommendation for processing XML documents. The DOM API loads the whole XML document into memory as a tree structure and allows the manipulation of the structure of the document by adding, removing, and amending the nodes.

❑ **SAX**
   SAX is an event-driven approach for processing XML documents. The SAX API parses XML documents dynamically instead of loading the whole document into memory.

Both DOM and SAX define an API in terms of interfaces and exceptions. To use them in our applications, we need to have classes that implement these interfaces. Fortunately, there are high quality XML parsers available, which implement both SAX and DOM APIs. In this chapter, we will be using the Xerces parser. It can be obtained from http://xml.apache.org/xerces2-j/index.html.

# Document Object Model

DOM is a W3C recommendation that provides an API for treating XML documents as a tree of objects. It loads an entire XML document into memory and allows us to manipulate the structure of the XML document by adding, removing, and amending the elements and/or attributes.

## Evolution of DOM

The initial DOM specification was put forward to provide portability to HTML documents. This allowed various elements of an HTML document to be treated as part of an object tree.

The list below illustrates the various levels of DOM that evolved over the past few years:

❑ **DOM Level 1**
This became a W3C recommendation in mid 1998. It defined the basic interfaces that represent the various components of an XML document like the document itself, elements, attributes, PIs, and CDATA sections.

❑ **DOM Level 2**
This became a recommendation in late 2000 and most importantly added support for XML namespaces. Level 2 also modularized DOM into:

❑ **Core**
This builds on Level 2, defining interfaces for manipulating the structure of XML documents

❑ **Views**
Covers presentation of a document in different types of views

❑ **Events**
Allows events and event listeners to be associated with XML nodes

❑ **Style**
Deals mainly with style sheets

❑ **Traversal and Range**
Deals with traversal of XML documents and the definition of ranges between arbitrary points in an XML document

❑ **DOM Level 3**
This is currently a working draft and builds on Level 2. Main additions include loading and storing of XML documents from and to external sources.

In this section we will be covering the DOM Level 2 core API. However, the Xerces implementation provides full support to all the Level 2 modules, and also provides experimental support to the Level 3 features.

## *DOM Level 2 Core Architecture*

The diagram below depicts the main interfaces in the DOM Level 2 core API:

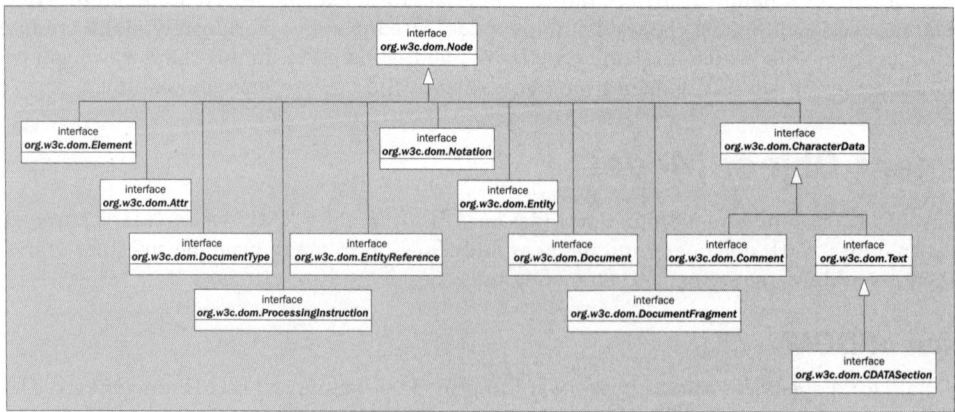

In DOM, every component that makes up an XML document is treated as a **node**. Each of these nodes is represented as an interface that defines methods specific to that node. The different types of nodes include:

- ❑   `org.w3c.dom.Element`
- ❑   `org.w3c.dom.Attr`
- ❑   `org.w3c.dom.DocumentType`
- ❑   `org.w3c.dom.ProcessingInstruction`
- ❑   `org.w3c.dom.Notation`
- ❑   `org.w3c.dom.Entity`
- ❑   `org.w3c.dom.Document`
- ❑   `org.w3c.dom.DocumentFragment`
- ❑   `org.w3c.dom.Comment`
- ❑   `org.w3c.dom.Text`
- ❑   `org.w3c.dom.CDATASection`

The behavior common to all the node types is defined in the `org.wc.dom.Node` interface.

### Node Interface

The `Node` interface defines methods that represent the common behavior of all types of nodes. The methods defined on this interface are mainly used for:

- ❑   Getting information regarding the node's parent node, child nodes, and sibling nodes
- ❑   Getting information about the node itself, such as the local name, attributes, and namespace URI
- ❑   Adding and removing of nodes and attributes

### Document Interface

The `Document` interface extends the `Node` interface and represents the XML document itself. The most important aspect of this interface is that it acts as a factory for creating other types of nodes such as elements, attributes, texts, comments, CDATA sections, and so on. Nodes created by a document can be attached only to the owning document. However, this interface provides methods for importing nodes owned by other documents as well. Let us now look at an example.

### Try It Out – Creating the Stock Quote Document

Now we will discuss a small example that uses the DOM API to build the stock quote XML document from scratch and then save it to a file called `stock_quote.xml`.

**1.** We will read the stock quotes data from a database table. The SQL scripts shown overleaf will create the required table and add the sample data:

```
CREATE TABLE Quotes (
    symbol VARCHAR(30),
    ask_price FLOAT,
    open_price FLOAT,
    dayhigh_price FLOAT,
    daylow_price FLOAT,
    change_price FLOAT,
    volume FLOAT
);

INSERT INTO Quotes VALUES
    ('EDS', 32.32, 32.80, 33.10, 32.16, -1.63, 5470100);
INSERT INTO Quotes VALUES
    ('SUNW', 5.93, 5.67, 6.01, 5.56, +0.239, 67552600);
INSERT INTO Quotes VALUES
    ('IBM', 69.01, 69.51, 71.39, 71.39, -1.99, 10428600);
INSERT INTO Quotes VALUES
    ('MSFT', 51.25, 51.31, 52.79, 50.64, -0.55, 48166900);
INSERT INTO Quotes VALUES
    ('^DJI', 8448.19, 8540.47, 8621.95, 8448.19, -94.29, -1);
INSERT INTO Quotes VALUES
    ('^IXIC', 1360.62, 1390.41, 1395.29, 1360.22, -36.63, -1);
INSERT INTO Quotes VALUES
    ('^GSPC', 884.58, 905.36, 907.84, 884.46, -21.46, -1);
```

2. We will then run the SQL scripts shown above in our database management system to create the Quotes table. We have used MySQL in this case.

*To learn more about MySQL please refer to* Beginning Databases with MySQL *from Wrox Press (ISBN 1-86100-692-6).*

3. Download Xerces from http://xml.apache.org/dist/xerces-j/ and install it on your machine. (This should simply be a case of unzipping the files to a directory such as C:\Xerces2.)

4. Store the class shown below in a file called StockCoreDOMGenerator.java. (You can obtain the source code from http:\\www.wrox.com).

```java
package com.wrox.jws.stockcore;

import org.w3c.dom.Document;
import org.w3c.dom.Element;
import org.w3c.dom.Attr;

import org.apache.xerces.dom.DocumentImpl;

import java.io.PrintWriter;
import java.io.FileWriter;

import java.sql.*;
import java.util.GregorianCalendar;

public class StockCoreDOMGenerator {
```

This is the document that holds the stock quotes data:

```
private Document doc;
```

This string array holds the various types of prices associated with the stock:

```
private static String TYPES[] = {"ask", "open", "dayhigh", "daylow"};
```

This variable holds the name of the file to which the stock data is written:

```
private static final String STOCK_FILE = "stock_quote.xml";
```

This interface contains the names of the elements and attributes used to build the stock quotes data:

```
private static interface Markup {

  public static final String STOCK_QUOTES = "stock_quotes";
  public static final String STOCK_QUOTE = "stock_quote";

  public static final String SYMBOL = "symbol";

  public static final String WHEN = "when";
  public static final String DATE = "date";
  public static final String TIME = "time";

  public static final String PRICE = "price";
  public static final String TYPE = "type";
  public static final String VALUE = "value";

  public static final String CHANGE = "change";
  public static final String VOLUME = "volume";

}
```

The interface shown below contains the various properties required for connecting to the database. The driver and the JDBC URL we have used here are specific to MySQL database. If you are using a different DBMS, you will have to change this to match your DBMS:

```
private static interface Database {

  public static final String URL =
                  "jdbc:mysql:/localhost:3306/Quotes";
  public static final String USER = "sa";
  public static final String PASSWD = "";
  public static final String SQL = "SELECT * FROM Quotes";
  public static final String DRIVER = "org.gjt.mm.mysql.Driver";

}
```

The constructor creates the document and the root element:

```
public StockCoreDOMGenerator() {
  doc = new DocumentImpl();

  Element root = doc.createElement(Markup.STOCK_QUOTES);
  doc.appendChild(root);
}
```

This method adds the specified stock data to the XML document:

```
private void addStock(String symbol, String quote[], String change,
    String volume) {

  GregorianCalendar cal = new GregorianCalendar();
  String date = cal.get(cal.YEAR) + "-" + cal.get(cal.MONTH) +
    "-" + cal.get(cal.DATE)   ;
  String time = cal.get(cal.HOUR_OF_DAY) + ":" + cal.get(cal.MINUTE);

  Element root = doc.getDocumentElement();

  Element stockQuoteEl = doc.createElement(Markup.STOCK_QUOTE);
  root.appendChild(stockQuoteEl);

  Element symbolEl = doc.createElement(Markup.SYMBOL);
  symbolEl.appendChild(doc.createTextNode(symbol));
  stockQuoteEl.appendChild(symbolEl);

  Element whenEl = doc.createElement(Markup.WHEN);
  Element dateEl = doc.createElement(Markup.DATE);
  dateEl.appendChild(doc.createTextNode(date));
  whenEl.appendChild(dateEl);
  Element timeEl = doc.createElement(Markup.TIME);
  timeEl.appendChild(doc.createTextNode(time));
  whenEl.appendChild(timeEl);
  stockQuoteEl.appendChild(whenEl);

  for(int i = 0; i < 4; i++) {
    Element priceEl = doc.createElement(Markup.PRICE);
    priceEl.setAttribute(Markup.TYPE, TYPES[i]);
    priceEl.setAttribute(Markup.VALUE, quote[i]);
    stockQuoteEl.appendChild(priceEl);
  }

  Element changeEl = doc.createElement(Markup.CHANGE);
  changeEl.appendChild(doc.createTextNode("+0.239"));
  stockQuoteEl.appendChild(changeEl);
  Element volumeEl = doc.createElement(Markup.VOLUME);
  volumeEl.appendChild(doc.createTextNode("67552600"));
  stockQuoteEl.appendChild(volumeEl);

}
```

This method serializes and saves the XML document to an external file:

```
private void saveDocument() throws Exception {
  PrintWriter writer = new PrintWriter(new FileWriter(STOCK_FILE));
  writer.println(((DocumentImpl)doc).saveXML(doc));
  writer.close();
}
```

The `main()` method adds a set of stock quote data to the XML by reading the data from the database and saves it to an external file:

```
public static void main(String args[]) throws Exception  {
  StockCoreDOMGenerator generator = new StockCoreDOMGenerator();

  Class.forName(Database.DRIVER);
  Properties props = new Properties();
  props.put("user", Database.USER );
  props.put("password", Database.PASSWD );

  Connection con = DriverManager.getConnection(Database.URL, props);
  Statement stmt = con.createStatement();
  ResultSet res = stmt.executeQuery(Database.SQL);

  try {
    while(res.next()) {
      generator.addStock(res.getString(1), new String[]{res.getString(2),
        res.getString(3),res.getString(4),res.getString(5)},
        res.getString(6),res.getString(7));
    }
  } finally {
    if(res != null) res.close();
    if(stmt != null) stmt.close();
    if(con != null) con.close();
  }

  generator.saveDocument();

  System.out.println("Stock quotes saved successfully");

  }
}
```

**5.** Set the classpath to include the `xercesImpl.jar` and `xmlParserAPI.jar` files available with Xerces distribution:

```
set classpath=%classpath%;C:\Xerces2\xercesImpl.jar;
            C:\Xerces2\xmlParserAPIs.jar;
```

*Here, C:\Xerces2 is our Xerces installation directory.*

**6.** Now compile the file `StockCoreDOMGenerator.java` (assuming we are in the `\Chp02\src` directory) by giving the following command:

```
javac -d ..\classes com\wrox\jws\stockcore\StockCoreDOMGenerator.java
```

**7.** Run the class. Please make sure that the database driver is available in the classpath when running the application. You will need to switch to the `\Chp02\classes` directory now in order for this to run:

```
java -classpath %classpath%;%mysql_home%\mm.mysql-2.0.4-bin.jar
    com.wrox.jws.stockcore.StockCoreDOMGenerator
```

This will produce the following output in the command window:

**Stock quotes saved successfully**

### How It Works

Now we will have a look at some of the key aspects of the class `StockCoreDOMGenerator`. Here we create an instance of the XML document by using the Xerces-specific implementation of the DOM `Document` interface:

```
doc = new DocumentImpl();
```

The document object is used to create the root element and it is attached to the document:

```
Element root = doc.createElement(Markup.STOCK_QUOTES);
doc.appendChild(root);
```

This method adds a quote to the stock quotes data. The method takes the symbol, various prices, and the net volume:

```
private void addStock(String symbol, String quote[], String change,
    String volume) {

GregorianCalendar cal = new GregorianCalendar();
String date = cal.get(cal.YEAR) + "-" + cal.get(cal.MONTH) +
    "-" + cal.get(cal.DATE)   ;
String time = cal.get(cal.HOUR_OF_DAY) + ":" + cal.get(cal.MINUTE);
```

First the root element is retrieved from the document object:

```
Element root = doc.getDocumentElement();
```

Create the `stockQuoteEl` element and append it to the root element:

```
Element stockQuoteEl = doc.createElement(Markup.STOCK_QUOTE);
root.appendChild(stockQuoteEl);
```

Create the `symbolEl` element and append it to the `stockQuoteEl` element:

```
Element symbolEl = doc.createElement(Markup.SYMBOL);
symbolEl.appendChild(doc.createTextNode(symbol));
stockQuoteEl.appendChild(symbolEl);
```

Create the `whenEl` element:

```
Element whenEl = doc.createElement(Markup.WHEN);
```

Create the `dateEl` element and append it to the `whenEl` element:

```
Element dateEl = doc.createElement(Markup.DATE);
dateEl.appendChild(doc.createTextNode(date));
whenEl.appendChild(dateEl);
```

Create the `timeEl` element and append it to the `whenEl` element:

```
Element timeEl = doc.createElement(Markup.TIME);
timeEl.appendChild(doc.createTextNode(time));
whenEl.appendChild(timeEl);
```

Append the `whenEl` element to the `stockQuoteEl` element:

```
stockQuoteEl.appendChild(whenEl);
```

Append the various `priceEl` elements to the `stockQuoteEl` element:

```
for(int i = 0; i < 4; i++) {
   Element priceEl = doc.createElement(Markup.PRICE);
```

Add the `TYPE` and `VALUE` attributes to the `priceEl` element:

```
   priceEl.setAttribute(Markup.TYPE, TYPES[i]);
   priceEl.setAttribute(Markup.VALUE, quote[i]);
   stockQuoteEl.appendChild(priceEl);
}
```

Create the `changeEl` element and append it to the `stockQuoteEl` element:

```
Element changeEl = doc.createElement(Markup.CHANGE);
changeEl.appendChild(doc.createTextNode("+0.239"));
stockQuoteEl.appendChild(changeEl);
```

Create the `volumeEl` element and append it to the `stockQuoteEl` element:

```
Element volumeEl = doc.createElement(Markup.VOLUME);
volumeEl.appendChild(doc.createTextNode("67552600"));
stockQuoteEl.appendChild(volumeEl);
```

The following method uses the DOM Level 3 functionality provided by the Xerces implementation to serialize the document to an external file:

```
private void saveDocument() throws Exception  {
```

Open a print writer to the file to which the XML data is written:

```
PrintWriter writer = new PrintWriter(new FileWriter(STOCK_FILE));
```

Use the Xerces-specific document implementation to serialize and save the XML data to an external file:

```
writer.println(((DocumentImpl)doc).saveXML(doc));
writer.close();
```

Now we will have a look at the `main()` method. First, we construct an instance of the class:

```
StockCoreDOMGenerator generator = new StockCoreDOMGenerator();
```

Load the database driver and get a connection to the database:

```
Class.forName(Database.DRIVER);
Connection con = DriverManager.getConnection(Database.URL, props);
```

Create a SQL statement and execute the query:

```
Statement stmt = con.createStatement();
ResultSet res = stmt.executeQuery(Database.SQL);
```

Iterate through the resultset and call the method for adding stocks by passing the information read from the database:

```
while(res.next()) {
  generator.addStock(res.getString(1), new String[]{res.getString(2),
    res.getString(3),res.getString(4),res.getString(5)},
    res.getString(6),res.getString(7));
}
```

Then we close the database resources:

```
if(res != null) res.close();
if(stmt != null) stmt.close();
if(con != null) con.close();
```

Finally we store the XML document to an external file:

```
generator.saveDocument();

System.out.println("Stock quotes saved successfully");
```

In this example we created the stock quote XML from scratch using the DOM interfaces. In the following example we will use the Xerces DOM parser to parse the contents of the text file we generated in the last example to an in-memory DOM structure.

## Try It Out – Parsing Stock Quote Data

Here, the parser will verify the contents of the text file for the well formedness constraints for XML documents. The text file we will parse will contain the stock quote for more than one symbol.

**1.** Store the contents of the class below to a file called `StockCore.java`:

```
package com.wrox.jws.stockcore;

import org.w3c.dom.Document;
import org.w3c.dom.Element;
import org.w3c.dom.Attr;
import org.w3c.dom.NodeList;

import org.apache.xerces.parsers.DOMParser;
import org.xml.sax.InputSource;

public class StockCore {
```

The string variable that contains the name of the file containing the stock quote XML data:

```
private static final String STOCK_FILE = "stock_quote.xml";

private Document doc;
public Document getDocument() { return doc; }
```

The constructor parses the XML document:

```
public StockCore() throws Exception {
  InputSource in = new InputSource(
    getClass().getClassLoader().getResourceAsStream(STOCK_FILE));

  DOMParser domParser = new DOMParser();
  domParser.parse(in);
  doc = domParser.getDocument();

}
```

The `main()` method simply calls the constructor to parse the XML document:

```
public static void main(String args[]) throws Exception {
  StockCore stockCore = new StockCore();
  System.out.println("Stock quotes loaded.");
}
}
```

**2.** Compile the file `StockCore.java` (again making sure the Xerces JAR files are in the classpath):

```
javac -d ..\classes com\wrox\jws\stockcore\StockCore.java
```

**3.** The `StockCoreDOMGenerator` class should have saved the file `stock_quote.xml` in the `\chp02\classes` directory. If not copy it there yourself.

**4.** Switch to the `\chp02\classes` directory and run the class:

```
java com.wrox.jws.stockcore.StockCore
```

This will produce the following output:

Stock quotes loaded

### How It Works

Let's look at some of the key aspects of the `StockCore` class:

We first create an input source pointing to the file containing the stock quote data:

```
InputSource in =
    new InputSource(getClass().getResourceAsStream(STOCK_FILE));
```

Then we create the Xerces DOM parser:

```
DOMParser domParser = new DOMParser();
```

Finally we parse the document itself and store the reference to the parsed document:

```
domParser.parse(in);
doc = domParser.getDocument();
```

## Try It Out – Examining the Contents of a DOM Structure

In this example, we will expand the `StockCore` class to add functionality for inspecting the contents of the stock quotes DOM structure. Here, the application will take the ticker symbol as a command-line argument and print the ask price if the symbol is available in the stock quotes data.

**1.** Add the following method to our current `StockCore.java` file. This is the new method that is added to get the ask price for a specified symbol:

```
public String getQuote(String symbol) {
    Element root = doc.getDocumentElement();
    NodeList stockList = root.getElementsByTagName("stock_quote");

    for(int i = 0; i < stockList.getLength(); i++) {
```

```
        Element stockQuoteEl = (Element)stockList.item(i);
        Element symbolEl =
          (Element)stockQuoteEl.getElementsByTagName("symbol").item(0);
        if(!symbolEl.getFirstChild().getNodeValue().equals(symbol))
          continue;

        NodeList priceList = stockQuoteEl.getElementsByTagName("price");

        for(int j = 0; j < priceList.getLength(); j++) {
          Element priceEl = (Element)priceList.item(0);
          if(priceEl.getAttribute("type").equals("ask"))
            return priceEl.getAttribute("value");
        }
      }
      return"";

    }
```

**2.** We also need to modify the `main()` method so that it first parses the XML by calling the constructor and then calls the method to get the ask price for the symbol passed in as the commandline argument:

```
    public static void main(String args[]) throws Exception {
      if(args.length != 1) {
        System.out.println("Usage: java dom.StockCore <symbol>");
        System.exit(0);
      }

      StockCore stockCore = new StockCore();
      System.out.println("The ask price for " + args[0] + " is " +
        stockCore.getQuote(args[0]));
    }
```

**3.** Recompile the file `StockCore.java` (with the Xerces JARs in the classpath):

```
javac -d ..\classes com\wrox\jws\stockcore\StockCore.java
```

**4.** Run the class:

```
java com.wrox.jws.stockcore.StockCore EDS
```

This should produce the following output:

The ask price of EDS is 32.32.

### How It Works

Now let us take a look at some of the key aspects of this new version of the class `StockCore` and see how it works.

The first step of our `getQuote()` method is to get the `root` element of the document:

```
Element root = doc.getDocumentElement();
```

The method `getElementsByTagName()` returns all the elements in the document with the specified tag name. `NodeList` is a DOM interface that represents a list of nodes. Use this method to get all the `stock_quote` elements in the document:

```
NodeList stockList = root.getElementsByTagName("stock_quote");

for(int i = 0; i < stockList.getLength(); i++) {
  Element stockQuoteEl = (Element)stockList.item(i);
```

Then we get the `symbol`, which is the child element of the `stock_quote` element:

```
Element symbolEl =
  (Element)stockQuoteEl.getElementsByTagName("symbol").item(0);
```

The `getFirstChild()` method returns the first child of the current node. The `getNodeValue()` method returns the value of the node. The value of the node depends on the type of the node. In this case the first child of the `symbol` element is the text node and this will return the content of the `symbol` element. If this content doesn't match the passed `symbol`, process the next `stock_quote` element:

```
if(!symbolEl.getFirstChild().getNodeValue().equals(symbol))
  continue;
```

Get the list of prices for the matched symbol:

```
NodeList priceList =
  stockQuoteEl.getElementsByTagName("price");

for(int j = 0; j < priceList.getLength(); j++) {
  Element priceEl = (Element)priceList.item(0);
```

The `getAttribute()` method returns the value of the named attribute. In this case we return the value of the attribute called `value` of the `price` element, if the value of the `type` attribute is "ask":

```
if(priceEl.getAttribute("type").equals("ask"))
  return priceEl.getAttribute("value");
```

# SAX

DOM is a powerful API for loading an XML document into memory, and inspecting and manipulating its contents. However, this is not very efficient for processing large documents or in cases where we are not interested in the contents of the whole document or where we just want to verify the validity of the document. This is where SAX comes into the picture. SAX is the acronym for **Simple API for XML** parsing.

Members of the `xml-dev` mailing list defined the SAX 1.0 API in mid 1998. The current release of SAX version 2.0 provides advanced features including support for namespaces, which is significantly different from version (1.0) and this section will be concentrating on the 2.0 API.

SAX provides an event-driven approach for parsing XML documents. SAX parsers parse XML documents sequentially and emit events indicating start and end of the document, elements, text content etc. Applications interested in processing these events can register implementations of callback interfaces provided by the SAX API with the parser.

## SAX Architecture

In SAX, the parser can be configured with a variety of callback handlers. When the parser scans an external stream that contains XML markup, it will report the various events involved to these callback handlers. These events include the following:

- ❑ Beginning of the document
- ❑ End of the document
- ❑ Namespace mapping
- ❑ Errors in well-formedness
- ❑ Validation errors
- ❑ Text data
- ❑ Start of an element
- ❑ End of an element

The SAX API provides interfaces that define the contract for these callback handlers. When we write XML applications that use SAX, we can write implementations for these interfaces and register them with a SAX parser. The diagram below depicts the important classes and interfaces in the SAX API:

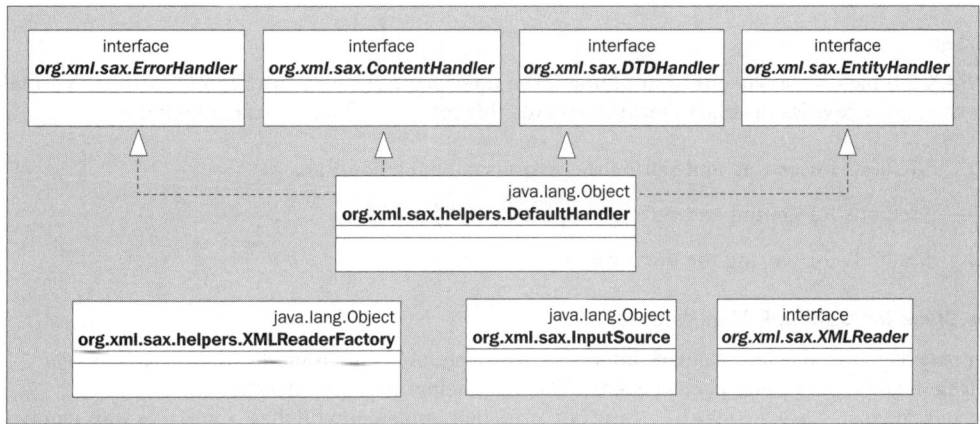

### SAX Event Handlers

In this section, we will see the various event handlers available in the SAX 2.0 API, which can be used for receiving relevant events associated with parsing XML documents:

❏ org.xml.sax.ContentHandler
This interface is implemented by classes that need to be notified about events associated with the contents of the document. The events handled by this interface include:

❏ Start and end of the document

❏ Start and end of prefix mappings

❏ Start and end of elements

❏ Occurrence of character data, processing instructions, and ignorable whitespace

❏ org.xml.sax.DTDHandler
This interface is implemented by classes that need to be notified about events associated with the contents of the DTD. The events handled by this interface include notation and unparsed entity declarations.

❏ org.xml.sax.EntityResolver
Entity resolver can be used for resolving entities like external DTDs and so on.

❏ org.xml.sax.ErrorHandler
This interface is implemented by classes that need to be notified about errors that occur during parsing the XML document. The events handled by this interface include errors, fatal errors, and warnings encountered during parsing the document.

### Input Source

The SAX parser uses the class org.xml.sax.InputSource that can wrap a variety of input streams like:

❏ Byte stream

❏ Character stream

❏ A source identified by a public ID

### SAX Parser

The SAX 2.0 parser class needs to implement the interface org.xml.sax.XMLReader. Normally, the parser vendor provides the class that implements this interface. This interface includes:

❏ Methods for getting and setting the various callback handlers

❏ Methods for getting and setting properties and features

❏ Methods for parsing the documents

### Adapter Class for Callback Handlers

Earlier we had looked at four callback interfaces, which should be registered with the parser to get notification about the various parsing events. The SAX helper API provides the org.xml.sax.helpers.DefaultHandler class that implements all these interfaces with empty implementations. Hence, the only thing we need to do is to extend this class and override the required methods.

If we are interested only in the start and end of the document, we may write an implementation as shown below:

```
import org.xml.sax.helpers.DefaultHandler;

public class MyDocumentHandler extends DefaultHandler
{
  public void startDocument() { System.out.println("Document started"); }

  public void endDocument() { System.out.println("Document ended"); }
}
```

## Try It Out – Parsing the Stock Quotes XML Using SAX

In this section we will write a version of StockCore class that will parse the stock_quote.xml file using the SAX API. Please note that the SAX parser will not create the document for us. Hence we will create the DOM document from the SAX events emitted by the parser during parsing.

**1.** Store the contents of the following class to a file called StockCoreHandler.java. This class is the handler, which we will register with our SAX parser to receive notifications about key events:

```
package com.wrox.jws.stockcore.sax;

import org.xml.sax.helpers.DefaultHandler;
import org.xml.sax.Attributes;
import org.xml.sax.SAXParseException;
import org.xml.sax.SAXException;

import org.w3c.dom.Document;
import org.w3c.dom.Element;
import org.apache.xerces.dom.DocumentImpl;

import java.util.Stack;

public class StockCoreHandler extends DefaultHandler {
  private Stack elements;
```

This is the reference to the document that is created from the parser events:

```
  private Document doc;
  public Document getDocument() { return doc; }
```

This method is called when the parser encounters character data:

```
  public void characters(char[] ch, int start, int length) {
    Element current = (Element)elements.peek();
    current.appendChild(doc.createTextNode(new String(ch, start, length)));
  }
```

This method is called when the parser encounters the end of the document:

```
public void endDocument()   {
  doc.appendChild((Element)elements.pop());
}
```

This method is called when the parser encounters the end of an element:

```
public void endElement(String namespaceURI, String localName,
    String qName) {
  if(elements.size() != 1) elements.pop();
}
```

This method is called when the parser encounters the start of the document:

```
public void startDocument() {
  elements = new Stack();
  doc = new DocumentImpl();
}
```

This method is called when the parser encounters the start of an element:

```
public void startElement(String namespaceURI, String localName,
    String qName, Attributes atts) {
  Element child = doc.createElement(qName);

  for(int i = 0; i < atts.getLength(); i++) {
    child.setAttribute(atts.getQName(i), atts.getValue(i));
  }

  if(elements.empty()) {
    elements.push(child);
  } else {
    Element parent = (Element)elements.peek();
    parent.appendChild(child);
    elements.push(child);
  }

}
```

The three methods shown below are called in the case of parsing errors:

```
public void error(SAXParseException ex) throws SAXException {
  throw ex;
}

public void fatalError(SAXParseException ex) throws SAXException {
  throw ex;
}

public void warning(SAXParseException ex) throws SAXException {
  throw ex;
}

}
```

2. Store the class shown below into a file called `StockCore.java`. Most of it is similar to the DOM version, the major difference being the use of SAX parser instead of the DOM parser. Hence only the bits that are different from the DOM version are shown below:

```
package com.wrox.jws.stockcore.sax;
```

Import the SAX parser:

```
import org.apache.xerces.parsers.SAXParser;
```

```
public class StockCore {
   ...
```

The constructor now uses the SAX parser to parse the document:

```
   public StockCore() throws Exception {
     InputSource in = new InputSource(
       getClass().getClassLoader().getResourceAsStream(STOCK_FILE));

     SAXParser saxParser = new SAXParser();
     StockCoreHandler handler = new StockCoreHandler();
     saxParser.setContentHandler(handler);
     saxParser.setErrorHandler(handler);

     saxParser.parse(in);
     doc = handler.getDocument();
   }
   ...
}
```

3. Compile the files `StockCoreHandler.java` and `StockCore.java` (we are in the `\Chp02\src` directory):

**javac -d ..\classes com\wrox\jws\stockcore\sax\*.java**

4. Switch to the `\Chp02\classes` directory and run the class:

**java com.wrox.jws.stockcore.sax.StockCore EDS**

This will produce the same output as the DOM example:

The ask price of EDS is 32.32.

### How It Works

In this example we use a SAX parser. Since the SAX parser doesn't generate the document for us, we create a callback handler called `StockCoreHandler` by extending the `org.xml.sax.helper.DefaultHandler` class and override the required callback methods to create the document from the information provided by the callback method arguments. We will use the same handler instance as our content and error handlers.

First we will have a look at the key aspects of the class `StockCoreHandler`. The `Stack` stores the elements when they are parsed by the SAX parser:

```
private Stack elements;
```

The `Document` object stores the parsed stock quotes data:

```
private Document doc;
public Document getDocument() { return doc; }
```

The parser calls this method when it encounters the start of the `Document`. Here we initialize the `Document` and the `Stack` that stores the `elements` that are parsed:

```
public void startDocument() {
  elements = new Stack();
  doc = new DocumentImpl();
}
```

The parser calls this method when it encounters the start of an element. It passes the namespace URI, local name, qualified name, and attributes associated with the element. Please note that namespaces, qualified name, local names, etc. will be covered in detail a little later. At this moment, just note that qName will give us the name of the element that is currently being parsed:

```
public void startElement(String namespaceURI, String localName,
    String qName, Attributes atts) {
```

Create the `Element` and set the attributes. The `Attributes` class represents the aggregation of all attributes present in the element:

```
Element child = doc.createElement(qName);
for(int i = 0; i < atts.getLength(); i++) {
  child.setAttribute(atts.getQName(i), atts.getValue(i));
}
```

If the `Stack` is empty, the parser is parsing the `Document` element. Hence push the `Document` element to the `Stack`:

```
if(elements.empty()) {
  elements.push(child);
```

If the `Stack` is non-empty, we are at an intermediate element. Hence retrieve the last element from the stack and append the current element as a child to the last element:

```
} else {
  Element parent = (Element)elements.peek();
  parent.appendChild(child);
  elements.push(child);
}
```

The parser calls this method when it encounters character data. Here we use it to add the text content for the elements:

```
public void characters(char[] ch, int start, int length) {
  Element current = (Element)elements.peek();
  current.appendChild(doc.createTextNode(new String(ch, start, length)));
}
```

This method is called when the parser encounters the end of an element. We use this method to remove the last element that was added to the stack, unless there is only one element left in the stack. In that case it is the Document element:

```
public void endElement(String namespaceURI, String localName,
    String qName) {
  if(elements.size() != 1) elements.pop();
}
```

This method is called at the end of the document and we use it to retrieve the Document element from the stack and add it to the document:

```
public void endDocument() {
  doc.appendChild((Element)elements.pop());
}
```

The three methods shown below come from the ErrorHandler interface and are used to notify errors during parsing. These methods take an exception that represents the parsing error as their argument. We simply throw this exception back to abort parsing:

```
public void error(SAXParseException ex) throws SAXException {
  throw ex;
}

public void fatalError(SAXParseException ex) throws SAXException {
  throw ex;
}

public void warning(SAXParseException ex) throws SAXException {
  throw ex;
}
```

Now we will have a look at the changes made to the StockCore class, to use the SAX parser. The main changes are in the constructor and are shown below:

```
public StockCore() throws Exception  {
  InputSource in = new InputSource(
    getClass().getClassLoader().getResourceAsStream(STOCK_FILE));
```

Instantiate the SAX parser:

```
SAXParser saxParser = new SAXParser();
```

Create the callback handler used for content and error handling:

```
StockCoreHandler handler = new StockCoreHandler();
saxParser.setContentHandler(handler);
saxParser.setErrorHandler(handler);
```

Parse the document and retrieve the document from the handler:

```
saxParser.parse(in);
doc = handler.getDocument();
```

Please note that we will also have to import the SAXParser class instead of the DOMParser class.

### Factory-Based Approach for Creating Parsers

As already mentioned, the XMLReader is generally implemented by parser vendors. If we start hard-coding the class names of the vendor implementations in our applications, our applications will become tightly coupled to the vendor implementations. To avoid this, the SAX helper package provides a factory-based approach for creating parsers using org.xml.parser.helper.XMLReaderFactory.

This class provides two methods for writing vendor-neutral parser code. The first method is:

```
static XMLReader createXMLReader(String className) throws SAXException.
```

This method takes the name of the class that implements the interface XMLReader and returns an instance. Please note that the specified class should be available in the classpath.

The second method is:

```
static XMLReader createXMLReader() throws SAXException.
```

This method performs the following logic to return an XMLReader instance:

❑ The system property org.xml.sax.driver is checked for the class name
❑ The file META-INF/services/org.xml.sax.driver is checked in the available JAR files at run time
❑ Parser vendors may provide a default implementation

## Features and Properties

Even though the SAX helper API provides a vendor-neutral way of creating parsers using a factory approach, the vendors may need to provide specific features and properties in their parser implementations.

This can be done in a vendor-neutral way by specifying them using the setFeature() and setProperty() method specified in the XMLReader interface. Both these methods will throw a SAXNotRecognizedException if the specified feature/property is not recognized and SAXNotSupportedException if it is recognized and not supported. The features are set using Boolean values true or false, whereas properties are set as Java objects.

The table below summarizes some of the general features supported by the Xerces parser:

| Feature | Description | Default |
|---|---|---|
| http://xml.org/sax/features/namespaces | Performs Namespace processing | True |
| http://xml.org/sax/features/validation | Validates the document | False |
| http://apache.org/xml/features/validation/dynamic | Validates only if grammar is specified | False |
| http://apache.org/xml/features/validation/schema | Turns on schema validation | False |
| http://apache.org/xml/features/validation/schema--full-checking | Enables full schema grammar constraint checking | False |
| http://apache.org/xml/features/validation/schema/normalized-value | Exposes normalized values for elements and attributes | True |
| http://xml.org/sax/features/external-general-entities | Includes external general entities | True |
| http://xml.org/sax/features/external-parameter-entities | Includes external parameter entities | True |
| http://apache.org/xml/features/validation/warn-on-duplicate-attdef | Warns on duplicate attribute declaration | True |

The table below summarizes some of the properties supported by the Xerces parser:

| Property | Description | Type |
|---|---|---|
| http://apache.org/xml/properties/schema/external-schemaLocation | Defines a list of schema locations for schemas with target namespace | String |
| http://apache.org/xml/properties/schema/external-noNamespace SchemaLocation | Defines a list of schema locations for schemas without target namespace | String |

We will have a look at using features and properties in a parsing example in a later section on XML schemas for validating XML documents.

# The Java API for XML Processing

In the examples we have seen so far, we have been using Xerces-specific classes. One drawback of using this approach in XML-based applications, is that at a later stage if we decide to change our parser vendor, we will have to change all the hard-coded class names in our application. JAXP offers a vendor-neutral approach for writing SAX and DOM applications. It provides a factory-based approach for creating DOM and SAX parsers and wrappers around vendor-specific DOM and SAX parsers encapsulating DOM and SAX parsers respectively. It also provides support for XSL transformations.

JAXP is part of both J2EE 1.3 and J2SE 1.4 and includes the following packages:

- ❑ `java.xml.parsers`
  Contains classes that provide a factory-based approach for DOM- and SAX-based XML processing

- ❑ `java.xml.transform`
  Contains generic transformation API

- ❑ `java.xml.transform.dom`
  Contains DOM-specific transformation APIs

- ❑ `java.xml.transform.sax`
  Contains SAX-specific transformation APIs

- ❑ `java.xml.tranform.stream`
  Contains stream- and URI-specific transformation API

## JAXP Factory Classes for XML Processing

The diagram below depicts the classes provided by JAXP for writing vendor-neutral XML applications:

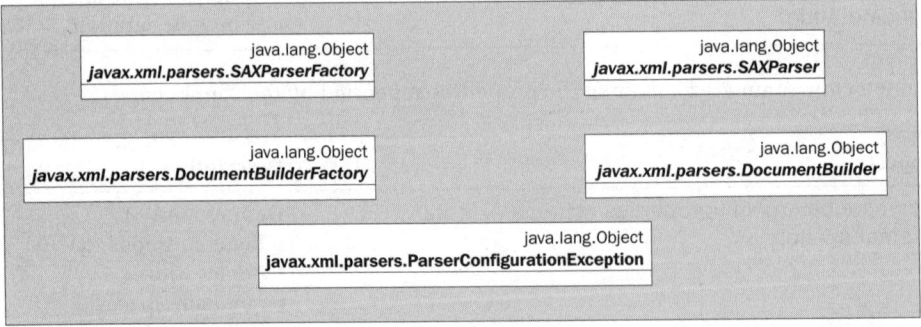

The `SAXParserFactory` class provides factory methods for creating `SAXParser` instances. The `SAXParser` class acts as a thin wrapper around the SAX `XMLReader` interface. The parser implementation to be used at run time is defined using the system property `javax.xml.parsers.SAXParserFactory` to specify the factory to be used.

This can also be specified in the `jaxp.properties` file in the `\lib` directory of the JRE installation or it may also use the JAR services API to look in the file `META-INF/services/javax.xml.parsers.SAXParserFactory`. If none of these things are specified the parser vendor may choose to use a default parser factory.

The DocumentBuilderFactory class provides factory methods for creating DocumentBuilder instances. The DocumentBuilder class provides methods for parsing XML documents into DOM trees, creating new XML documents, and so on. The parser implementation to be used at run time is defined using the system property javax.xml.parsers.DocumentBuilderFactory to specify the factory to use.

This can also be specified in the jaxp.properties , or it may also use the JAR services API to look in the file META-INF/services/javax.xml.parsers.DocumentBuilderFactory. If none of these things specified the parser vendor may choose to use a default parser factory.

## Try It Out – Using JAXP with DOM StockCore

In this section, we will look at removing the Xerces-specific code from the DOM version of the StockCore class.

**1.** Take the StockCore.java file that we developed for the DOM parser example and copy it into a new directory for the JAXP examples. Make the following changes:

```
package com.wrox.jws.stockcore.jaxp;

import org.w3c.dom.Document;
import org.w3c.dom.Element;
import org.w3c.dom.Attr;
import org.w3c.dom.NodeList;

import javax.xml.parsers.DocumentBuilder;
import javax.xml.parsers.DocumentBuilderFactory;

import org.xml.sax.InputSource;

public class StockCore {
```

The constructor now uses the JAXP classes instead of the Xerces DOM parser:

```
public StockCore() throws Exception  {
  InputSource in = new InputSource(
    getClass().getClassLoader().getResourceAsStream(STOCK_FILE));

  DocumentBuilder domParser =
    DocumentBuilderFactory.newInstance().newDocumentBuilder();
  doc = domParser.parse(in);

}
```

**2.** Compile the new StockCore.java file:

```
javac -d ..\classes com\wrox\jws\stockcore\jaxp\StockCore.java
```

**3.** Switch directories and run the class:

```
java com.wrox.jws.stockcore.jaxp.StockCore EDS
```

This will produce the following output yet again:

The ask price of EDS is 32.32.

# XML Namespaces

As we have seen in the last chapter, web services use XML to define data representing the requests sent by the clients to the web services and the responses the clients receive from web services. These XML documents are defined as SOAP envelopes, and information about these web services is published using the standard WSDL documents. These documents are also XML documents that define information like parameter types, return types, protocol, and transport bindings about the web services.

The SOAP documents that represent web services and the WSDL documents that describe web services, contain markup coming from a variety of sources. For example, a WSDL document contains markup related to description of web services, the encoding scheme used, and XML Schema for defining the types of the information that are exchanged using web services.

When a single document contains markup originating from more than one source, a potential problem called 'name collision' arises. A single document can contain markup vocabulary from more than one source, especially if we are using XML Schema to constrain the contents of the document. XML Schema is covered in detail in the next section.

Name collision occurs when two elements with same names but totally different meanings are present in the same XML document. This problem is not as severe for attributes since the scope of an attribute is always the enclosing element and an element can never have duplicate attributes. This problem of name conflicts is solved by the simple yet elegant solution of XML namespaces. In this section we will look at how XML solves the age-old problem of name conflicts using namespaces.

We shall illustrate this problem with the help of an example. In the XML document representing our stock quotes, each `stock_quote` element has four `price` elements. However, each `price` element has a different meaning, as they represent `ask`, `open`, `dayhigh`, and `daylow` prices. These four elements have the same names and the only way we can distinguish one from the other is by looking at the value of the `type` attribute.

## Implementing Namespaces

Namespaces solve the problem of name ambiguity of elements and attributes by assigning **prefixes** to names. These prefixes are qualified to unique URIs. Namespaces allow us to take advantage of elements defined in other namespaces, and leverage that knowledge in our own XML documents. The ambiguity problem in the case of identical names is resolved by declaring that a particular element's (or attribute's) context is taken from a definition established in a separate namespace. We leverage that namespace by using the prefix format that qualifies the specified element.

The reason for using a combination of URIs and prefixes is that URIs are often very long and may contain characters that are not allowed in XML markup. Hence these URIs are mapped to shorter prefixes that are used to qualify the element and attribute names.

The following example shows how we can use XML namespaces to distinguish the price elements from one another, instead of using the `type` attribute:

```
<stock_quotes
  xmlns:ask="http://www.acme.com/Ask"
  xmlns:open="http://www.acme.com/Open"
  xmlns:dayHigh="http://www.acme.com/DayHigh"
  xmlns:dayLow="http://www.acme.com/DayLow">

  <!-- EDS -->
  <stock_quote>
    <symbol>EDS</symbol>
    <when>
     <date>7/18/2002</date>
     <time>3:12pm</time>
    </when>
    <ask:price value="32.32" />
    <open:price value="32.80" />
    <dayHigh:price value="33.10" />
    <dayLow:price value="32.16" />
    <change>-1.63</change>
    <volume>5470100</volume>
  </stock_quote>

  ...
<stock_quotes>
```

In the example shown above each `price` element is attached to a prefix qualified by a unique URI. By doing this we have removed the need of using the `type` attribute to distinguish the business meaning of the `price` element.

Here the prefixes `ask`, `open`, `dayHigh`, and `dayLow` attached to the elements representing the same are qualified by the `http://www.acme.com/Ask`, `http://www.acme.com/Open`, `http://www.acme.com/DayHigh`, and `http://www.acme.com/DayLow` namespaces respectively. Namespaces are defined using the following syntax:

```
xmlns:<Namespace Prefix>="<Namespace URI>"
```

Each namespace prefix defined in an XML document should be bound to exactly one URI. In the example above, for the element `<open:price>`, open is called the namespace prefix and `price` is called the local part. The complete name including the colon is called the **QName** or **qualified name**.

Assigning a namespace prefix to a URI is called **namespace binding**. This is done using the `xmlns` attribute. The scope of a namespace binding is the element within which the namespace binding is defined and all its child elements. Hence the prefixes in the above example can be used to qualify the `stock_quotes` element and all its child elements. We can declare the namespace binding in any element we like as shown below:

```
<stock_quotes
  xmlns:ask="http://www.acme.com/Ask"
  xmlns:open="http://www.acme.com/Open"
  xmlns:dayHigh="http://www.acme.com/DayHigh"
  xmlns:dayLow="http://www.acme.com/DayLow">
```

```
<!-- EDS -->
<stock_quote>
  <symbol>EDS</symbol>
  <dt:when xmlns:dt="http://www.acme.com/Dt">
    <dt:date>7/18/2002</dt:date>
    <dt:time>3:12pm</dt:time>
  </dt:when>
  <ask:price value="32.32" />
  <open:price value="32.80" />
  <dayHigh:price value="33.10" />
  <dayLow:price value="32.16" />
  <change>-1.63</change>
  <volume>5470100</volume>
</stock_quote>

...
<stock_quotes>
```

Here the namespace prefix dt is declared in the scope of the when element and can be used to qualify only that specific instance of when element and its children – date and time elements. Please note that in the above example, none of the elements and attributes apart from the price elements is qualified by a namespace and hence they don't belong to any namespace. In XML applications of considerable size and complexity, it is recommended that the namespace bindings be defined in the root element to avoid confusion.

## Default Namespaces

In an XML application where the majority of the markup comes from one source, prefixing all the markup elements can be tedious. To simplify this, we can define a default namespace for an element and its child elements. This is done by defining a namespace binding without the prefix for that element and not specifying any prefix for that element, and its children. However, default namespaces apply only for elements. Attributes without a prefix are not considered to be a part of any namespace.

The example below shows that all the elements in the stock quote XML belong to the default namespace http://www.acme.com/Stock apart from the price elements that are explicitly declared to belong to different namespaces:

```
<stock_quotes
  xmlns:ask="http://www.acme.com/Ask"
  xmlns:open="http://www.acme.com/Open"
  xmlns:dayHigh="http://www.acme.com/DayHigh"
  xmlns:dayLow="http://www.acme.com/DayLow"
  xmlns="http://www.acme.com/Stock">

  <!-- EDS -->
  <stock_quote>
    <symbol>EDS</symbol>
    <when>
      <date>7/18/2002</date>
      <time>3:12pm</time>
```

```
    </when>
    <ask:price value="32.32" />
    <open:price value="32.80" />
    <dayHigh:price value="33.10" />
    <dayLow:price value="32.16" />
    <change>-1.63</change>
    <volume>5470100</volume>
  </stock_quote>

...
<stock_quotes>
```

Now let's modify our `StockCore` example to use namespaces support.

## Try It Out – Using Namespaces to Get the Ask Price

In the versions of the `StockCore` class that we have so far covered in this chapter, we have been getting all the price elements for the specified symbol and checking whether the value of the `type` attribute is `ask` before returning the value of the value attribute. In this section we will modify that code to use namespaces support provided by the DOM API instead.

**1.** First we need to create the namespace-qualified version of our `stock_quote.xml` file. We've already seen the changes we're going to be making in the above section on namespaces. For simplicity, we'll just modify the `stock_quote.xml` file and save it as `stock_quote_ns.xml`:

```
<stock_quotes
   xmlns:ask="http://www.acme.com/Ask"

   <!-- EDS -->
   <stock_quote>
     <symbol>EDS</symbol>
     <when>
      <date>7/18/2002</date>
      <time>3:12pm</time>
     </when>
     <ask:price value="32.32" />
     <price value="32.80" />
     <price value="33.10" />
     <price value="32.16" />
     <change>-1.63</change>
     <volume>5470100</volume>
   </stock_quote>
```

Change all the other ask price elements as appropriate.

**2.** Store the contents of the class shown below in a file called `StockCore.java`:

```
package com.wrox.jws.stockcore.ns;

import org.w3c.dom.Document;
import org.w3c.dom.Element;
import org.w3c.dom.Attr;
```

```
import org.w3c.dom.NodeList;

import javax.xml.parsers.DocumentBuilder;
import javax.xml.parsers.DocumentBuilderFactory;

import org.xml.sax.InputSource;

public class StockCore {

  private static final String STOCK_FILE = "stock_quote_ns.xml";

  private Document doc;
  public Document getDocument() { return doc; }
```

The constructor now makes the JAXP document-builder class namespace aware:

```
public StockCore() throws Exception  {

  InputSource in = new InputSource(
    getClass().getClassLoader().getResourceAsStream(STOCK_FILE));
  DocumentBuilderFactory factory = DocumentBuilderFactory.newInstance();
  factory.setNamespaceAware(true);

  DocumentBuilder domParser = factory.newDocumentBuilder();
  doc = domParser.parse(in);

}
```

This method now uses the namespace support offered by the DOM API to get the value of the ask price:

```
public String getQuote(String symbol) {

  Element root = doc.getDocumentElement();
  NodeList stockList = root.getElementsByTagName("stock_quote");

  for(int i = 0; i < stockList.getLength(); i++) {
    Element stockQuoteEl = (Element)stockList.item(i);
    Element symbolEl =
      (Element)stockQuoteEl.getElementsByTagName("symbol").item(0);

    if(!symbolEl.getFirstChild().getNodeValue().equals(symbol)) {
      continue;
    }

    Element priceEl = (Element)stockQuoteEl.getElementsByTagNameNS(
      "http://www.acme.com/Ask", "price").item(0);

    return priceEl.getAttribute("value");
  }

  return "";
  }
}
```

**3.** Compile the file:

```
javac -d ..\classes com\wrox\jws\stockcore\ns\StockCore
```

**4.** Make sure we have `stock_quote_ns.xml` in the `\Chp02\classes` directory and run the class:

```
java com.wrox.jws.stockcore.ns.StockCore EDS
```

This will produce the familiar output:

The ask price of EDS is 32.32.

### How It Works

By default the JAXP `DocumentBuilderFactory` creates DOM parsers that are not namespace aware. However, if we call `setNameSpaceAware` method on `DocumentBuilderFactory` with a Boolean value of `true`, it will create `DocumentBuilder` instances that are namespace aware:

```
factory.setNamespaceAware(true);
```

Here instead of listing through all the price elements, we select only those price elements belonging to the namespace `http://www.acme.com/Ask` using the method `getElementsByTagNameNS()`. This method takes the namespace URI and the local name of the element as arguments:

```
Element priceEl = (Element)stockQuoteEl.getElementsByTagNameNS(
    "http://www.acme.com/Ask", "price").item(0);
```

Now we will have a detailed look at XML Schema.

# XML Schema

The contents of an XML document may be optionally constrained by a set of rules, defined either internally or externally, to the document. Traditionally, these rules were defined using DTD.

Shortcomings of DTD include:

❑ DTDs have very limited support for types

❑ DTDs have very limited support for namespaces

❑ DTDs use a non-XML syntax

❑ DTDs don't provide any mechanism for defining types and type extensions

This led to a far more powerful mechanism for constraining XML documents – XML Schema. XML Schema are now a W3C recommendation.

XML Schema is an XML application that can be used for defining the content model for XML applications. From a web services perspective, XML Schema is used extensively in WSDL documents for defining the types used in the web services. In this section, we will give a brief overview of XML Schema. Please note that a comprehensive coverage of XML Schema is beyond the scope of this chapter.

# XML Schema in Practice

We will cover the various aspects of XML Schema by developing a schema to constrain our stock quotes XML document.

If we look at the content model of the elements in the XML document that we discussed earlier, we will find the following types of elements:

❑ **Elements that contain child elements and/or attributes**
The example below shows an element that contain child elements:
`<when><date>2002-6-21</date><time>13:33</time></when>`
The example below shows an element that contains attributes:
`<price type="daylow" value="32.16"/>`

❑ **Elements that contain only text contents**
The snippet below shows an element that contains only text content:
`<time>13:33</time>`

XML Schema can be used to represent constraints on the content model of elements in an XML document. Elements that contain child elements and/or attributes are defined in a Schema document using complex types. Elements that don't contain child elements and attributes are defined using simple types.

Before we delve into the details of defining an XML Schema, we will take a look at a schema document for our stock quotes XML. An XML document that complies with the rules defined in a schema document is referred to as an **instance document** of that schema:

```
<xsd:schema xmlns:xsd="http://www.w3.org/2001/XMLSchema">

  <xsd:annotation>
    <xsd:documentation xml:lang="en">
      Schema for stock quotes.
    </xsd:documentation>
  </xsd:annotation>


  <xsd:element name="stock_quotes" type="StockQuotes"/>

  <xsd:complexType name="StockQuotes">
    <xsd:sequence>
      <xsd:element name="stock_quote" minOccurs="0" maxOccurs="unbounded">
        <xsd:complexType>
          <xsd:sequence>
            <xsd:element name="symbol" type="Symbol"/>
            <xsd:element name="when" type="When"/>
            <xsd:element name="price" type="Price" minOccurs="4"
              maxOccurs="4"/>
```

```
            <xsd:element name="change" type="xsd:double"/>
            <xsd:element name="volume" type="xsd:double"/>
          </xsd:sequence>
        </xsd:complexType>
      </xsd:element>
    </xsd:sequence>
  </xsd:complexType>

  <xsd:complexType name="When">
    <xsd:sequence>
      <xsd:element name="date" type="xsd:string"/>
      <xsd:element name="time" type="xsd:string"/>
    </xsd:sequence>
  </xsd:complexType>

  <xsd:complexType name="Price">
    <xsd:attribute name="type" type="xsd:string"/>
    <xsd:attribute name="value"     type="xsd:decimal"/>
  </xsd:complexType>

  <xsd:simpleType name="Symbol">
    <xsd:restriction base="xsd:string">
      <xsd:enumeration value="EDS"/>
      <xsd:enumeration value="SUNW"/>
      <xsd:enumeration value="IBM"/>
      <xsd:enumeration value="MSFT"/>
      <xsd:enumeration value="^DJI"/>
      <xsd:enumeration value="^IXIC"/>
      <xsd:enumeration value="^GSPC"/>
    </xsd:restriction>
  </xsd:simpleType>

</xsd:schema>
```

The schema shown above defines elements, attributes, and types. Elements and attributes defined in the schema are associated with a type. Elements can be one of the following types:

❑ A user-defined complex type like When

❑ A built-in simple type like xsd:string

❑ A user-defined simple type derived from a built-in simple type like Symbol

Attributes can either be built-in or user-defined simple types.

The markup elements peculiar to an XML Schema such as element, attribute, sequence, simpleType, complexType, restriction, enumeration, and so on belong to the namespace http://www.w3.org/2001/XMLSchema and are, by convention, qualified by the prefix xsd. In the section on namespaces we have seen that an XML document can contain markup vocabulary from more than one source. XML Schema documents are a classic example for this scenario.

Let's look at the different types in more detail.

# Simple Types

XML Schema defines a variety of simple types that can be used for attributes or elements containing only text content. These types include:

- ❏ `string`: Character strings in XML
- ❏ `integer`: Integer values
- ❏ `positiveInteger`: Positive integer values
- ❏ `negativeInteger`: Negative integer values
- ❏ `short`: Short integer values
- ❏ `decimal`: Arbitrary-precision decimal numbers
- ❏ `float`: IEEE single-precision 32-bit floating point
- ❏ `double`: IEEE double-precision 64-bit floating point
- ❏ `boolean`: Data type to support binary logic; either true or false
- ❏ `date`: A calendar date like 1973-06-31
- ❏ `time`: An instance of time that recurs every day
- ❏ `ID`: Represents an XML ID attribute type
- ❏ `IDREF`: Represents an XML IDREF attribute type
- ❏ `ENTITY`: Represents an XML entity attribute types

Please refer to the XML Schema data types for a complete list of built-in simple types.

## *User-Defined Simple Types*

In addition to the built-in simple types, we can define our own simple types that are derived from the built-in simple types. XML Schema provides a variety of mechanisms for restricting the values of built-in simple types for user-defined simple types. Please refer to the XML Schema specifications for a complete list of these mechanisms at http://www.w3.org/XML/Schema.

When a new simple type is defined, the base type is defined using the `restriction` element. Various elements are used within the `restriction` element for defining the restriction rules.

The example below defines a data type called `Symbol` that is derived from `xsd:string` for defining stock symbols restricted by a set of values:

```
<xsd:simpleType name="Symbol">
  <xsd:restriction base="xsd:string">
    <xsd:enumeration value="EDS"/>
    <xsd:enumeration value="SUNW"/>
    <xsd:enumeration value="IBM"/>
    <xsd:enumeration value="MSFT"/>
    <xsd:enumeration value="^DJI"/>
    <xsd:enumeration value="^IXIC"/>
    <xsd:enumeration value="^GSPC"/>
  </xsd:restriction>
</xsd:simpleType>
```

The example above uses the enumeration facet to define that the content of the symbol element should be one among the pre-defined set of values.

# Complex Types

Complex types are used to define content model for elements that contain child elements and/or attributes. The content model of an element defines the structure of its child nodes and the attributes it can and can't have. Complex types are defined using the XML Schema markup complexType as shown below:

```
<xsd:complexType name="when">
  <xsd:sequence>
    <xsd:element name="date" type="xsd:string"/>
    <xsd:element name="address" type="xsd:string"/>
  </xsd:sequence>
</xsd:complexType>
```

Complex type definitions generally contain element and attribute declarations that make up the content model for that type. Elements are declared using the element element, and attributes using the element attribute. The content model of complex types can be both – either complex types or simple types. The schema above defines that the When element should have exactly one date element with text content and one time element that also contains only text content, strictly in that order.

## Constraining Element Occurrence

The number of times an element may appear in a complex type is defined using the attributes minOccurs and maxOccurs in the type definition as shown below:

```
<xsd:complexType name="StockQuotes">
  <xsd:sequence>
    <xsd:element name="stock_quote" minOccurs="0" maxOccurs="unbounded">
      <xsd:complexType>
        <xsd:sequence>
          <xsd:element name="symbol" type="Symbol"/>
          <xsd:element name="when" type="When"/>
          <xsd:element name="price" type="Price" minOccurs="4"
            maxOccurs="4"/>
          <xsd:element name="change" type="xsd:double"/>
          <xsd:element name="volume" type="xsd:double"/>
        </xsd:sequence>
      </xsd:complexType>
    </xsd:element>
  </xsd:sequence>
</xsd:complexType>
```

The listing above states that the complex type StockQuotes may contain zero or more stock_quote elements and the stock_quote element should contain exactly four price elements.

The values for this minOccurs and maxOccurs may be a positive integer or the string unbounded. If neither the attributes is specified, the element should appear exactly once in the content model for the type. If both, minOccurs and maxOccurs are specified, the value of minOccurs should be less than or equal to that of maxOccurs.

If only `minOccurs` is specified, its value should be either 0 or 1 and similarly, if only `maxOccurs` is specified, its value should be greater than or equal to 1. However the value of `minOccurs` can be greater than one if it is specified with `maxOccurs`, but should not be greater than the value of the `maxOccurs` attribute.

The table below depicts the various possible combinations for the `minOccurs` and `maxOccurs` attributes:

| minOccurs | maxOccurs | Result |
| --- | --- | --- |
| 1 | 1 | Element must appear exactly once |
| 2 | unbounded | Element must appear at least two times |
| 0 | 1 | Element appear once |
| 0 | 2 | Element may be absent, or present once or twice |
| 4 | 4 | Element must appear exactly four times |
| 0 | 0 | Element must not appear |

## Constraining Attribute Occurrence

Attributes may appear either once or not at all. Attributes are declared with the `use` attribute to indicate whether they are `required`, `optional`, or `prohibited`. The `default` attribute can be used in attribute declaration to give a default value to the attribute when it is absent.

The example below states that the type of the attribute `type` is `string` and it is a required attribute. If the attribute is not present the schema processor will give the default value `ask`:

```
<xsd:attribute name="type" type="xsd:string" use="required" default="ask"/>
```

We can use the `fixed` attribute in an attribute declaration to state that the value of the attribute should be fixed. The example below states that the `type` attribute should be present and its value should always be `ask`:

```
<xsd:attribute name="type" type="xsd:string" use="required" fixed="ask"/>
```

The snippet below states that the type attribute shouldn't be present at all:

```
<xsd:attribute name="type" type="xsd:string" use="prohibited"/>
```

# Anonymous Data Types

XML Schema also allows types to be defined without associating a name with them. This is useful when an element can appear in only one context. The listing below shows the stock quotes type, but it doesn't define the type for the `stock_quote` type explicitly:

```
<xsd:complexType name="StockQuotes">
```

The stock quotes type defines zero or more `stock_quote` element without explicitly specifying its type:

```
<xsd:sequence>
  <xsd:element name="stock_quote" minOccurs="0" maxOccurs="unbounded">
    <xsd:complexType>
      <xsd:sequence>
```

The `stock_quote` element should contain exactly one `symbol`, one `when`, four `price`, one `change`, and one `volume` elements, exactly in that order:

```
        <xsd:element name="symbol" type="Symbol"/>
        <xsd:element name="when" type="When"/>
        <xsd:element name="price" type="Price" minOccurs="4"
          maxOccurs="4"/>
        <xsd:element name="change" type="xsd:double"/>
        <xsd:element name="volume" type="xsd:double"/>
      </xsd:sequence>
    </xsd:complexType>
  </xsd:element>
  </xsd:sequence>
</xsd:complexType>
```

# XML Schema and Namespaces

In the root element of an XML Schema document we may use the `targetNamespace` attribute to define the **target namespace**, a namespace that applies to all the types defined in the schema. In our example this includes `Symbol`, `When`, `StockQuotes`, etc.

A schema document can have only one target namespace. Target namespaces are important in validating an XML document against a schema. The listing below shows our original schema document with target namespace defined in it:

```
<xsd:schema
  xmlns:xsd="http://www.w3.org/2001/XMLSchema"
  targetNamespace="http://www.acme.com"
  xmlns:stock="http://www.acme.com">

  <xsd:annotation>
    <xsd:documentation xml:lang="en">
      Schema for stock quotes.
    </xsd:documentation>
  </xsd:annotation>

  <xsd:element name="stock_quotes" type="stock:StockQuotes"/>

  <xsd:complexType name="StockQuotes">
    <xsd:sequence>
      <xsd:element name="stock_quote" minOccurs="0" maxOccurs="unbounded">
        <xsd:complexType>
```

```
            <xsd:sequence>
              <xsd:element name="symbol" type="stock:Symbol"/>
              <xsd:element name="when" type="stock:When"/>
              <xsd:element name="price" type="stock:Price" minOccurs="4"
                maxOccurs="4"/>
              <xsd:element name="change" type="xsd:double"/>
              <xsd:element name="volume" type="xsd:double"/>
            </xsd:sequence>
          </xsd:complexType>
        </xsd:element>
      </xsd:sequence>
    </xsd:complexType>

    <xsd:complexType name="When">
      <xsd:sequence>
        <xsd:element name="date" type="xsd:string"/>
        <xsd:element name="time" type="xsd:string"/>
      </xsd:sequence>
    </xsd:complexType>

    <xsd:complexType name="Price">
      <xsd:attribute name="type" type="xsd:string"/>
      <xsd:attribute name="value"     type="xsd:decimal"/>
    </xsd:complexType>

    <xsd:simpleType name="Symbol">
      <xsd:restriction base="xsd:string">
        <xsd:enumeration value="EDS"/>
        <xsd:enumeration value="SUNW"/>
        <xsd:enumeration value="IBM"/>
        <xsd:enumeration value="MSFT"/>
        <xsd:enumeration value="^DJI"/>
        <xsd:enumeration value="^IXIC"/>
        <xsd:enumeration value="^GSPC"/>
      </xsd:restriction>
    </xsd:simpleType>

  </xsd:schema>
```

Note that now all the new types defined in the schema document are qualified with the target namespace. Now, we will see how to validate an XML document with a schema by using the target namespace:

```
<stock: stock_quotes xmlns:stock="http://www.acme.com">

  <stock_quote>
    <symbol>EDS</symbol>
    <when><date>2002-6-21</date><time>13:33</time></when>
    <price type="ask" value="32.32"/>
    <price type="open" value="32.8"/>
    <price type="dayhigh" value="33.1"/>
    <price type="daylow" value="32.16"/>
    <change>+0.239</change><volume>67552600</volume>
  </stock_quote>
  ...

</stock:stock_quotes>
```

In the instance document above, the namespace declaration for the root element matches the target namespace of the schema document. If an instance document needs to be valid according to a schema, the target namespace of the schema should be the same as the namespace for the elements in the instance document. The content of this document is validated against the schema as we shall seen soon.

# Qualified and Unqualified Locals

In the instance document shown above, only the root element is qualified by the target namespace. If we want all the elements and attributes to be qualified by the namespace during validation, we can use the `elementFormDefault` and `attributeFormDefault` attributes in the schema definition:

```
<xsd:schema
   xmlns:xsd="http://www.w3.org/2001/XMLSchema"
   targetNamespace="http://www.employee.com"
   xmlns:emp="http://www.employee.com"
   elementFormDefault="qualified"
   attributeFormDefault="qualified">
```

In this case all the elements and attributes should be explicitly qualified by the target namespace:

```
<stock:stock_quotes xmlns:stock="http://www.acme.com">

  <stock:stock_quote>
    <stock:symbol>EDS</stock:symbol>
    <stock:when>
      <stock:date>2002-6-21</stock:date>
      <stock:time>13:33</stock:time>
    </stock:when>
    <stock:price stock:type="ask" stock:value="32.32"/>
    <stock:price stock:type="open" stock:value="32.8"/>
    <stock:price stock:type="dayhigh" stock:value="33.1"/>
    <stock:price stock:type="daylow" stock:value="32.16"/>
    <stock:change>+0.239</stock:change>
    <stock:volume>67552600</stock:volume>
  </ stock:stock_quote>
  ...

</stock:stock_quotes>
```

Note that the default value for `elementFormDefault` and `attributeFormDefault` is `unqualified`. The `form` attribute can be used for overriding the global values defined for individual local elements and attribute declarations using the `elementFormDefault` and `attributeFormDefault`:

```
<attribute name="type" type="xsd:string" form="qualified"/>
```

# Schema Definition in Instance Documents

Instance documents can provide applications with the location of the schema document to be used for validation using the `schemaLocation` attribute:

```
<emp:employees
   xmlns:emp="http://www.employee.com"
```

The namespace `http://www.w3c.org/2001/XMLSchema-instance` contains the `schemaLocation` attribute used to specify hints about the schema that should be used to validate the document:

```
xmlns:xsi="http://www.w3.org/2001/XMLSchema-instance"
xsi:schemaLocation="http://www.employee.com
http://www.employee.com/Employee.xsd">
```

This attribute contains pairs of values. The first member of the pair is the target namespace and the second member is the physical location of the schema. When the schema documents don't have a target namespace their locations are defined using the attribute `noNamespaceSchemaLocation` as shown below:

```
<stock_quotes
   xmlns:xsi="http://www.w3.org/2001/XMLSchema-instance"
   xsi:noNamespaceSchemaLocation="stock_quote.xsd">
```

# Advanced Concepts

The XML features that are not covered in the chapter include:

❑ Including schema documents in other schema documents

❑ Importing types from one schema document to another

❑ Deriving complex types from other complex types

❑ Defining groups of elements and attributes that can be reused by different complex types

❑ List types

❑ Identity constraints similar to DTD IDs and IDREFs

❑ Substitution groups for designating certain element declarations as substitutes for others

*Please refer to* Professional XML Schema *from Wrox Press (ISBN-1-86100-547-4) for a comprehensive coverage of XML Schema.*

## Try It Out – Validating the Stock Quotes XML

In this section we will validate our stock quotes XML document with the schema we have developed in this section.

**1.** First, we need to specify the schema location in the document element of our XML document as shown below, and save it as `stock_quote_schema.xml`:

```
<stock_quotes
  xmlns:xsi='http://www.w3.org/2001/XMLSchema-instance'
  xsi:noNamespaceSchemaLocation='stock_quote.xsd'>
```

**2.** Store the contents of the schema document from the section above in a file called stock_quote.xsd.

**3.** We will use a JAXP SAX implementation of the StockCore class this time. The listing below shows the relevant modifications made to the StockCore class:

```
package com.wrox.jws.stockcore.schema;

import org.w3c.dom.Document;
import org.w3c.dom.Element;
import org.w3c.dom.Attr;
import org.w3c.dom.NodeList;

import javax.xml.parsers.SAXParser;
import javax.xml.parsers.SAXParserFactory;
import org.xml.sax.XMLReader;

import org.xml.sax.InputSource;
import org.apache.xerces.dom.DocumentImpl;

public class StockCore {
```

This interface defines the various schema constants used for validating the stock quotes document:

```
private static interface FeatureId {

  public static final String NAMESPACES =
    "http://xml.org/sax/features/namespaces";
  public static final String VALIDATION =
    "http://xml.org/sax/features/validation";
  public static final String SCHEMA_VALIDATION =
    "http://apache.org/xml/features/validation/schema";
  public static final String SCHEMA_FULL_CHECKING =
    "http://apache.org/xml/features/validation/schema-full-checking";

}

private static final String STOCK_FILE = "stock_quote_schema.xml";

private Document doc;
public Document getDocument() { return doc; }
```

The constructor now validates the stock quotes XML using the schema:

```
public StockCore() throws Exception  {

  InputSource in = new InputSource(
    getClass().getClassLoader().getResourceAsStream(STOCK_FILE));

  SAXParser saxParser = SAXParserFactory.newInstance().newSAXParser();
  XMLReader reader = saxParser.getXMLReader();

  reader.setFeature(FeatureId.NAMESPACES, true);
  reader.setFeature(FeatureId.VALIDATION, true);
  reader.setFeature(FeatureId.SCHEMA_VALIDATION, true);
  reader.setFeature(FeatureId.SCHEMA_FULL_CHECKING, true);

  StockCoreHandler handler = new StockCoreHandler();
  reader.setContentHandler(handler);
  reader.setErrorHandler(handler);

  reader.parse(in);
  doc = handler.getDocument();
}
```

**4.** We will also need a JAXP version of the `StockCoreHandler` class. This is very similar to the class we saw earlier when we first looked at SAX parsing:

```
package com.wrox.jws.stockcore.schema;

import org.xml.sax.helpers.DefaultHandler;
import org.xml.sax.Attributes;
import org.xml.sax.SAXParseException;
import org.xml.sax.SAXException;

import org.w3c.dom.Document;
import org.w3c.dom.Element;

import javax.xml.parsers.DocumentBuilder;
import javax.xml.parsers.DocumentBuilderFactory;

import java.util.Stack;

public class StockCoreHandler extends DefaultHandler
```

The only other change is that the `startDocument()` method now uses the JAXP calls to create the XML document instead of using the Xerces-specific document implementation:

```
public void startDocument() {
  try {
    elements = new Stack();
    DocumentBuilder builder =
      DocumentBuilderFactory.newInstance().newDocumentBuilder();
    doc = builder.newDocument();
  } catch(Exception ex){
    ex.printStackTrace();
  }
}
```

**5.** Now compile the files `StockCoreHandler.java` and `StockCore.java`:

```
javac -d ..\classea com\wrox\jws\stockcore\schema\*.java
```

**6.** Make sure the files `stock_quote.xsd` and `stock_quote_schema.xml` are in the execution directory and run the class:

```
java com.wrox.jws.stockcore.schema.StockCore EDS
```

This will produce the all too familiar output:

The ask price of EDS is 32.32.

### How It Works

The `FeatureID` interface defines the SAX features to enable schema-based validation:

```
private static interface FeatureId  {
```

This feature makes the parser namespace aware:

```
public static final String NAMESPACES =
    "http://xml.org/sax/features/namespaces";
```

This turns validation on:

```
public static final String VALIDATION =
    "http://xml.org/sax/features/validation";
```

This turns schema validation on:

```
public static final String SCHEMA_VALIDATION =
    "http://apache.org/xml/features/validation/schema";
```

This turns full compliance with schema features on:

```
public static final String SCHEMA_FULL_CHECKING =
    "http://apache.org/xml/features/validation/schema-full-checking";
```

Now we will have a look at the changes we need in the constructor to enable schema validation. Please note that we can also make the parser namespace aware by calling the `setNamespaceAware()` method on `SAXParserFactory` by passing the Boolean value `true`. Similarly to set validation on we can call the `setValidating()` method passing the Boolean value `true`:

```
reader.setFeature(FeatureId.NAMESPACES, true);
reader.setFeature(FeatureId.VALIDATION, true);
reader.setFeature(FeatureId.SCHEMA_VALIDATION, true);
reader.setFeature(FeatureId.SCHEMA_FULL_CHECKING, true);

StockCoreHandler handler = new StockCoreHandler();
reader.setContentHandler(handler);
reader.setErrorHandler(handler);

reader.parse(in);
doc = handler.getDocument();
```

Now let us take a look at XML protocols.

# XML Protocols

All protocols used for inter-process and inter-machine communication like HTTP, FTP, Telnet, TCP/IP, JRMP, and IIOP are based on the seven-layered **Open Systems Interconnect (OSI)** model determined by the **International Organization for Standardization (ISO)**. The seven-layered model is depicted in the diagram shown below:

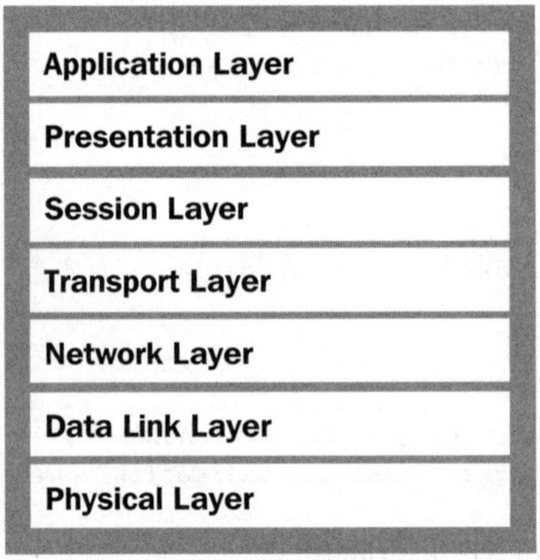

| Application Layer |
| Presentation Layer |
| Session Layer |
| Transport Layer |
| Network Layer |
| Data Link Layer |
| Physical Layer |

In the diagram above, the *Physical* layer takes care of how the bits are transmitted and the *Data Link* layer handles synchronization, blocking, and error and flow control. The network card driver provides the Physical and Data Link layers. The *Network* layer isolates the top layers from the Data Link layer and provides an abstraction of how a connection is made. Examples of network layer protocol are IP and X.25.

The *Transport* layer takes care of how the data is reliably transferred between two endpoints, and the *Session* layer provides an application-level abstraction of the connection. Protocols that handle these two layers include TCP and UDP. The *Presentation* layer decouples the applications from dependence on specific structured information and the *Application* layer interacts with the services. Examples of application-layer protocols are HTTP, FTP, Telnet, and so on.

The main goal of the layered architecture is to loosely couple the different aspects of data communication. When data is sent by the application layer it goes through the subsequent layers and each layer adds header information to the data frame. Similarly, when the physical layer receives data, each layer in the model strips off specific header information before it reaches the services. As the OSI model and the TCP/IP protocol stack were designed long before the advent of XML, in the TCP/IP implementation the application layer is a combination of both application and presentation layers.

Even though people were excited with the advent of XML as a standard for representing structured data, it still didn't become a de facto standard for data interchange and RPC calls between applications. This is because XML doesn't specify any semantics for representing remote procedures and it doesn't specify a standard way of representing the data that is interchanged between applications.

# XML-RPC

XML-RPC is a specification for representing remote procedure calls and results using XML in a simple yet powerful way. We can find the specification and information on the tools that implement the specification at http://www.xmlrpc.com. Note that XML-RPC is not an international standard, but it is increasingly becoming a de facto standard for performing remote procedure calls through an HTTP tunnel.

The most important thing about using XML for representing remote procedure calls is that it can sit on top of HTTP and pass through firewalls. This allows RPC calls to be made though firewalls, where most of the binary protocols like JRMP and IIOP won't work.

The basic way XML-RPC works is depicted in the diagram shown below:

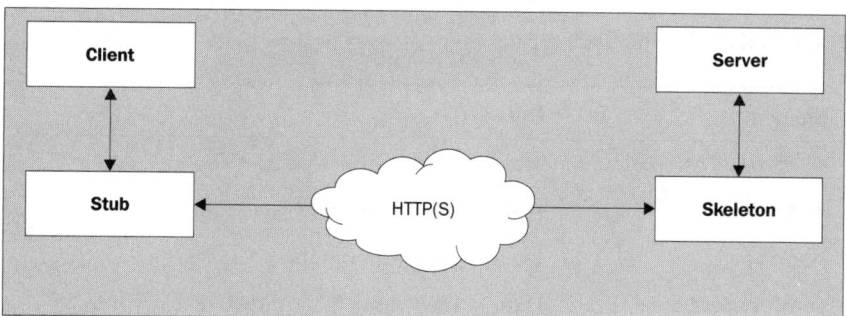

1. The client calls the remote procedure

2. The client stub marshals the call on to HTTP as a message

3. The server skeleton receives and marshals the message

4. The method call is executed on the server skeleton and the result is sent back to the client

The XML-RPC calls are sent to the server as HTTP post requests. There are currently implementations available in Java, C/C++, COM, Perl, Python, Tcl, PHP, Lisp, BASIC, JavaScript, and ASP.

## *XML-RPC Request*

The root element of the XML document that represents an XML-RPC request is represented by
methodCall. The root element must have a mandatory child methodName that represents the name
of the remote method and optional children representing the method parameters. The parameters are
encapsulated in a params element that may contain zero or more param elements. An example is
shown below:

```
<methodCall>
  <methodName>
    getSquareRoot
  </methodName>
  <params>
    <param>
      <value>
        <i4>64</i4>
      </value>
    </param>
  </params>
</methodCall>
```

The remote procedure getSquareRoot() is called with passing a parameter of type i4. The
parameters and results passed back and forth during the remote procedure calls are encapsulated in
value elements containing child elements representing the type of the value being passed with the
element content as the value itself. The actual mapping of the XML-RPC types to the types within the
implementation platform is specific to the implementation.

XML-RPC defines the following data types:

| Element | Data type |
|---|---|
| <i4> or <int> | 4 byte integer |
| <string> | A string of characters |
| <double> | Double-precision numbers |
| <dateTime.iso8601> | Date in the format YYYYMMDDTHH:mm:SS |

### *Complex Types*

XML-RPC also provides complex types for serializing application-specific data types. The complex data
types provided by XML-RPC are:

❑  Structures

❑  Arrays

Structures are represented by the element struct with embedded member elements to represent
the members of the structure. The example below shows how a Java class may be represented by
using structures:

```
public class Stock
{
  private String isin;
  private String sedol;
  private String shortCode;
  private double closingValue;
}
```

The struct elements may have other struct elements as nested members. The struct representation of the above class in XML-RPC may be represented as:

```
<struct>

  <member>
    <name>
      isin
    </name>
    <value>
      <string>
        GB12345
      </string>
    </value>
  </member>

  <member>
    <name>
      sedol
    </name>
    <value>
      <string>
        00897645
      </string>
    </value>
  </member>

  <member>
    <name>
      name
    </name>
    <value>
      <string>
        Chelsea Village
      </string>
    </value>
  </member>

  <member>
    <name>
      closingValue
    </name>
    <value>
      <double>
        1223.67
      </double>
    </value>
  </member>
</struct>
```

How a specific instance of the class is serialized to its `struct` representation is specific to the implementation.

Arrays are represented in XML-RPC using `array` elements with a nested data element. The `data` element encapsulates all the array members as value elements. The example below represents an integer array:

```
<array>
  <data>
     <value><i4>1</i4></value>
     <value><i4>2</i4></value>
     <value><i4>3</i4></value>
  </data>
</array>
```

## XML-RPC Response

XML-RPC responses are represented by XML documents with the root element as `methodResponse`. The content of the root element is governed by the result of the method call. For remote requests that don't cause any lower-level communication errors, the HTTP response status header should always be `200`. If the method call is successful, the response element will contain a list of values represented using the `value` elements that represents the result of the method call. An example is shown below:

```
<methodResponse>
   <value><i4>567</i4></value>
   <value><string>Test</string></value>
</methodResponse>
```

If the call fails due to business logic violation or an incorrect way of calling the method, the root element should contain a `fault` element. An example of the `fault` element is shown below:

```
<fault>
  <value>
    <struct>

      <member>
        <name>faultCode</name>
        <value>
          <i4>4</i4>
        </value>
      </member>

      <member>
        <name>faultString</name>
        <value>
          <string >Too many parameters</string>
        </value>
      </member>

    </struct>
  </value>
</fault>
```

Note that the `fault` element is represented as a structure with an integer element `faultCode`, representing an implementation-specific fault code and a string element `faultString`, representing the fault description.

## XML-RPC Implementations

Many implementations providing the framework for writing client and server code use XML-RPC. One popular Java implementation is available at http://xml.apache.org/xmlrpc/. This framework provides both a client-side and server-side API. The server-side API supports remote procedures bound to both standalone servers and J2EE web containers.

# SOAP

SOAP is a text-based protocol that uses XML for exchanging typed information in a decentralized environment. Please note that an exhaustive coverage of SOAP is beyond the scope of this chapter and book. In this section, we will take a whirlwind tour of SOAP envelopes, so that we can use them in our sample application.

## Basic Concepts

The party that sends the SOAP message is called a SOAP sender and the one who receives it is called a SOAP receiver. The path a SOAP message takes from the initial sender to the ultimate receiver is called a message path. A message path will contain an initial sender, an ultimate receiver, and zero or more SOAP intermediaries. Not all the information in the envelope may be intended to the ultimate receiver. The entities that process messages according to the rules defined by SOAP are called SOAP nodes.

The atomic unit of information exchanged between SOAP nodes is called a SOAP message. A SOAP message is an XML document with the root element SOAP envelope. The SOAP envelope may have a SOAP header and has a mandatory SOAP body. The header and body may have multiple units of information encapsulated within them qualified by namespace URIs, called header blocks and body blocks respectively. A SOAP fault is a special body block that contains the fault information generated by a SOAP Node.

The diagram below shows the basic structure of a SOAP message:

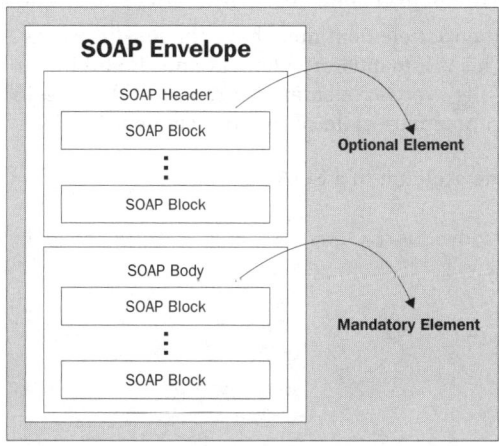

## *Message Exchange Model*

As we have already seen, SOAP nodes can be any one of the initial sender, ultimate receiver, or the intermediary. The roles performed by each node in the message path are defined by the SOAP actor name, specified as a URI. A SOAP node with an anonymous actor role is assumed as the ultimate receiver of the message. Each node in the message path is supposed to assume the roles of a special actor identified by the URI `http://www.w3.org/2001/06/soap-envelope/actor/next`. The SOAP specification doesn't define a way to link SOAP actor names to message routing.

The root elements of the SOAP header blocks may have an optional `actor` attribute qualified by the SOAP namespace to target them to specific SOAP nodes in the message path. Blocks without an explicit actor attribute are targeted for the ultimate receiver in the message path. The header block may also have an attribute called `mustUnderstand` belonging to the SOAP namespace, when set to 1, it mandates that the intended actor should process that block. If it can't process the block then it should raise a SOAP fault and stop doing any further processing.

## *Message Processing Rules*

If header blocks are targeted towards specific SOAP nodes by using the `actor` attribute and have the `mustUnderstand` attribute set to 1, are not understood by the targeted nodes then such nodes should generate a SOAP fault and stop further processing. For intermediary SOAP nodes, the messages may need to be passed to the next node in the message path. These messages should retain all the header and body blocks except the header blocks targeted to the node that processed the messages.

## *SOAP Envelope*

A SOAP envelope is an XML document that is exchanged between communicating peers. An envelope comprises the following:

❑ The document element of the SOAP envelope should have the local name `Envelope` and the namespace URI `http://www.w3.org/2001/06/soap-envelope`.

❑ This element may have an optional child element with local name as `Header` and the same namespace URI. Please note that, if this element is present it should be the first immediate child of the root element, and may be used for adding information to the envelope without prior agreement with the peers that are invloved in the interchange.

❑ The next child of the root element must have the local name as `Body` and the same namespace URI. This is a mandatory element and should be the second immediate child of the root element if the `Header` element is present. If the `Header` element is absent this should be the first immediate child of the root element.

The snippet below shows the skeleton of a SOAP message:

```
<env:Envelope xmlns:env="http://www.w3.org/2001/06/soap-envelope">
  <env:Header>
  ...
  </env:Header>
  <env:Body>
   ...
  </env:Body>
</env:Envelope>
```

The Header and the Body elements may contain elements from different namespaces, for example, our application-specific data that we intend to exchange.

### SOAP Header

SOAP header is the first immediate child element of the envelope. All immediate children of the header are called header blocks. Header blocks are used for extending the messages in a decentralized way by adding functionalities like authentication, transaction management, and so on.

All header elements must be namespace qualified. The header blocks may have the actor and mustUnderstand attributes to identify and mandate the SOAP node that processes the message. An example of a header attribute with mustUnderstand attribute set to 1 is shown below. The block is intended for the final receiver because the actor attribute is missing:

```
<env:Header>
  <authentication xmlns="http://myDomain/app" env:mustUnderstand="1">
    <user>Meeraj</user>
    <password>******</password>
  </authentication>
</env:Header>
```

In the above example the prefix, env, belongs to the SOAP envelope namespace.

## SOAP Body

SOAP body is used for encapsulating the mandatory information intended for the ultimate receiver of the message. A SOAP body element should be the first immediate child of the envelope if the header is absent and the second immediate child if the header is present. The SOAP body element may have multiple immediate children called body blocks, which are treated as separated entities. SOAP body content is used for marshaling RPC calls, exchanging messaging information, and so on. The example shows SOAP envelope with both header and body elements defined:

```
<env:envelope xmlns:env="http://www.w3.org/2001/06/soap-envelope">
  <env:Header>
    <auth:authentication xmlns:auth="http://myDomain/auth">
      <auth:user>Meeraj</auth:user>
      <auth:password>******</auth:password>
    </auth:authentication>
  </env:header>
  <env:body>
    <stock:getStockQuoteResponse
      xmlns:stock="http://www.acme.com/service">
      <stock_quote>
        <symbol>EDS</symbol>
        ...............
      </stock_quote>
    </stock:getStockQuoteResponse >
  </env:body>
</env:envelope>
```

### SOAP Fault

SOAP fault, if present, should be the first body block in the envelope and should appear only once in the envelope. The fault block is used for conveying error and status information in processing the messages. The fault block will have the following child elements:

- ❏ `faultcode`
  This will carry a code for the fault. The SOAP specification defines a small set of standard SOAP fault codes.

- ❏ `faultstring`
  This gives a more detail description of the message.

- ❏ `faultactor`
  This defines the SOAP node that caused the fault.

- ❏ `detail`
  This can be used for providing details of the fault like stack traces and so on.

The things that we have not covered in this section about SOAP are SOAP encoding, transport protocol binding, and RPC conventions. However, now we have enough grounding in SOAP to write simple web services, which accept and send SOAP envelopes.

The listing below shows an example SOAP fault:

```
<SOAP-ENV:Envelope
  xmlns:SOAP-ENV="http://schemas.xmlsoap.org/soap/envelope/">
<SOAP-ENV:Body>
  <SOAP-ENV:Fault>
    <faultcode>SOAP-ENV:Server</faultcode>
    <faultstring>Server Error</faultstring>
```

We can use the detail element to pass application specific error messages. Some of the Java implementations use this to pass stack traces:

```
      <detail>
        <e:myfaultdetails xmlns:e="Some-URI">
          <message>
            My application didn't work
          </message>
          <errorcode>
            1001
          </errorcode>
        </e:myfaultdetails>
      </detail>
    </SOAP-ENV:Fault>
  </SOAP-ENV:Body>
</SOAP-ENV:Envelope>
```

# Summary

We stated this chapter by covering the evolution of XML over the past few years. Then we looked at the processing of XML documents – both generation and parsing. We studied DOM and SAX; they are the two prevalent APIs for processing XML documents. We looked at generating an XML document from the data stored in a database. Then we went on to discuss using XML namespaces for avoiding name collisions.

XML Schemas were discussed to illustrate how to constrain the contents of an XML document. We then covered the various XML protocols available for exchanging structured and typed information between applications; here we covered both XML-RPC and SOAP.

Throughout the chapter we have been using the stock quotes data to illustrate how to create, parse, and validate XML documents in our various examples. This XML example will also be used in the subsequent chapters to illustrate the various aspects of web services.

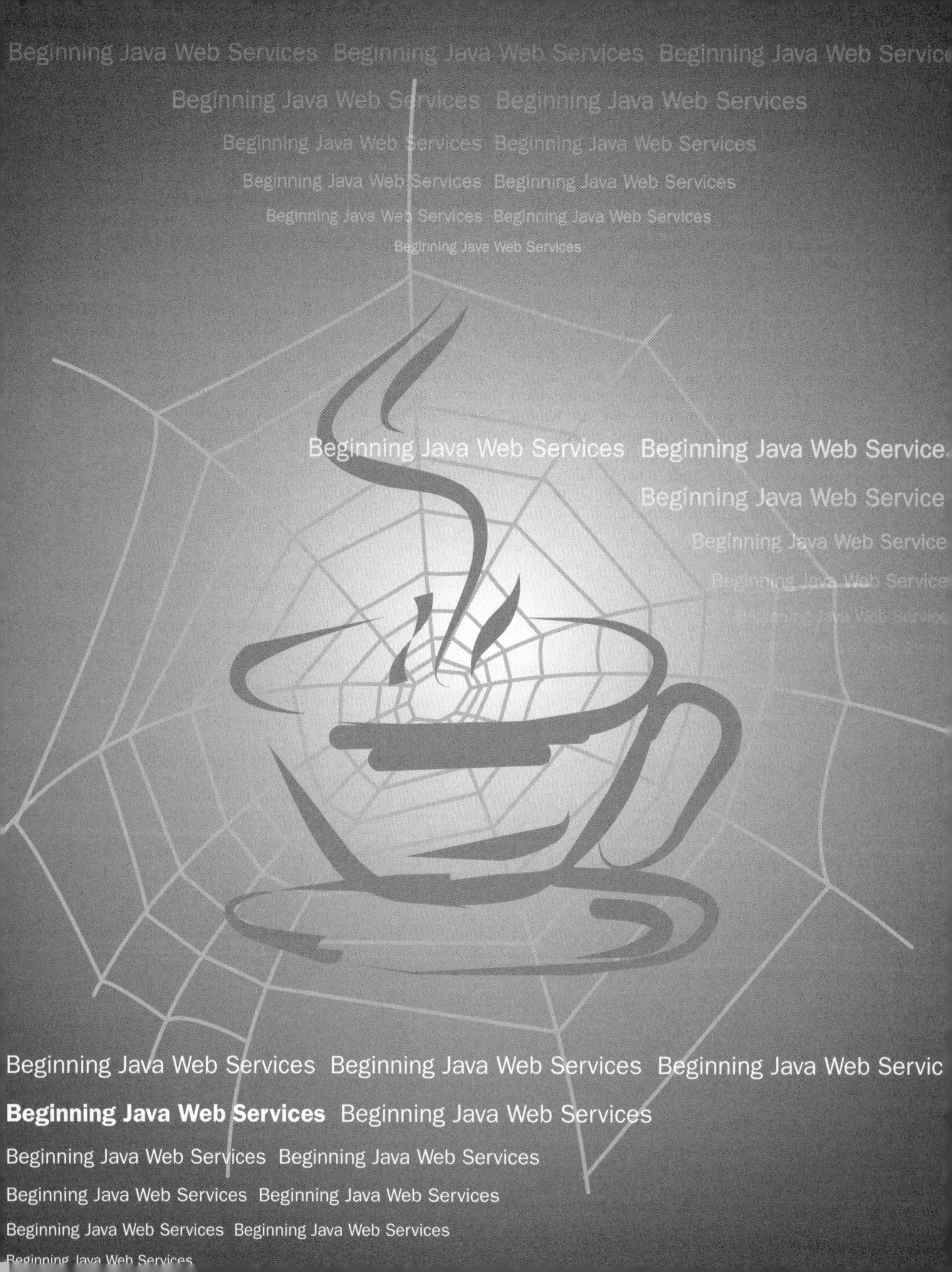
Beginning Java Web Services Beginning Java Web Services Beginning Java Web Services
Beginning Java Web Services Beginning Java Web Services
Beginning Java Web Services Beginning Java Web Services
Beginning Java Web Services Beginning Java Web Services
Beginning Java Web Services Beginning Java Web Services
Beginning Java Web Services
Beginning Java Web Services Beginning Java Web Services
Beginning Java Web Service
Beginning Java Web Service
Beginning Java Web Services Beginning Java Web Services Beginning Java Web Servic
Beginning Java Web Services Beginning Java Web Services
Beginning Java Web Services Beginning Java Web Services
Beginning Java Web Services Beginning Java Web Services
Beginning Java Web Services Beginning Java Web Services
Beginning Java Web Services

# Creating Web Services with Java

Chapters 1 and 2 explained the historical and technical background of web services. We discussed the evolution of distributed and interoperable protocols along with technologies that are used in web services such as XML, XML Schema, and SOAP. It is now time to get practical and create our first SOAP-based web service.

Specifically, in this chapter, we will:

- ❏ Introduce Axis, which is a **SOAP engine** (or framework).

- ❏ Discuss Tomcat, which is a **servlet engine**. Using this selected framework we will be writing a simple web service called `HelloWorld`.

- ❏ Look at a web service that uses a JAR file and a **deployment descriptor**. We will see that this additional level of complexity comes with added flexibility.

- ❏ Discuss **serialization and de-serialization** – we will focus on the process of mapping Java data types to and from XML documents.

Of course, our first task is to select a SOAP engine.

## The SOAP Engine

We saw earlier that a major goal of web services is to provide a language-neutral and vendor-neutral platform for distributed applications. In this chapter, we will go from theory to practice by having a close look at a SOAP engine. First of all, let's try to answer the question, which is probably on your minds: what is a SOAP engine? A (Java) SOAP engine is a set of Java classes that facilitate the server-side and client-side development of SOAP applications. Practically speaking, the SOAP engine contains core classes to perform the following operations:

- ❏ Serialize method calls into SOAP packets

- ❏ Deserialize SOAP packets into Java calls

- ❏ Wrap XML documents into SOAP packets

- ❏ Unwrap XML documents from SOAP packets

- ❏ Submit SOAP requests and handle the responses

- ❏ Accept SOAP requests and return the responses

The list of operations is open ended. There is no bounded definition of what a SOAP application is and therefore there is no boundary to what one can expect from the SOAP engine. For instance, if our application supports **asynchronous** operations, should the SOAP engine support the asynchronous traffic or should it put that burden on another component? We will revisit the issues surrounding asynchronous processing in Chapter 8.

> *A list of the popular tools for SOAP development (Java and others) can be found at* http://www.soaprpc.com/software/.

When it comes to selecting a SOAP engine, the Java developer has many options to choose from. At the time of writing, the most popular choices are:

- ❏ **Apache SOAP 2.2** (http://xml.apache.org/soap/index.html)
  The Apache SOAP engine is probably the most mature tool available to Java developers. However, it does not support more recent technologies such as the Web Services Definition Language (WSDL), which we cover in this book.

- ❏ **Apache SOAP 3.0** (http://xml.apache.org/axis/index.html)
  This Apache SOAP engine is also known as **Axis**. It is not really the next version of Apache SOAP, since it is a complete rewrite. According to the documentation, Axis stands for **Apache eXtensible Interaction System**.

- ❏ The **Web Services Developer Pack** (http://java.sun.com/webservices/)
  This package from Sun Microsystems is in fact a bundle of several technologies. For instance, we can use the **Java API for XML-Based Remote Procedure Call (JAX-RPC)**, the **Java API for XML Processing (JAXP)** for document-style SOAP, and so on.

- ❏ The IBM **Web Services Toolkit (WSTK)**
  (http://www.alphaworks.ibm.com/tech/webservicestoolkit)
  This download from IBM is similar to the Web Services Developer Pack in the sense that it also is a bundle of several technologies. It uses Axis as a SOAP engine and WebSphere as a web server. We discuss the WSTK in more detail in Chapter 7.

- ❏ The IBM **WebSphere SDK for Web Services (WSDK)**
  (http://www-106.ibm.com/developerworks/webservices/wsdk/)
  This is a more 'official' web services pack from IBM (compared to the beta code of the WSTK above). It also comes with Axis, as well as lots more components such as Xerces, a private UDDI registry, a test databases, WebSphere web server, etc. We will be using the WSDK in Chapter 10.

# Axis

We have decided to use Axis as the SOAP engine in this book, for the following reasons:

❑   Axis is a vendor-neutral offering.

❑   Axis has been adopted by several vendors. We mentioned IBM with WSTK, but other vendors such as Macromedia use the Axis implementation as part of their J2EE server (JRun).

❑   Axis provides an implementation of JAX–RPC. The goal is to provide an implementation that is compliant with JAX-RPC 1.0. At the time of writing, the current version of Axis is Beta 3.

❑   Axis provides an extensible implementation that allows for tremendous flexibility in customization.

> *Please note that, in the course of this book, not all the products we use are vendor neutral. For example, in Chapter 7, when we introduce the tools necessary for the publication and discovery of web services, we will rely on IBM's Web Services Developer Toolkit.*

Before we can start working with Axis, we need to make sure that we have two other software components. They are the Java Development Kit (1.3), and a JAXP-1.1-compliant XML parser such as Xerces or Crimson. (We will be using Xerces).

> *The Java API for XML Processing (JAXP) supports the parsing of XML documents. More details about JAXP can be found in Chapter 2.*

We will assume that you have the JDK already installed and that the environment variable `java_home` points to its installation directory, since will be making use of this variable in our examples.

## Try It Out – Download and Install Axis

The following instructions are for a computer running Windows 2000, but it is easy to adapt them for other platforms.

**1.**   To download Axis, point your browser to the URL http://xml.apache.org/axis.

**2.**   From the links given, select the **Releases** link presented under the **Download** section on the left hand side of the screen. At the time of writing, Axis is still in Beta so we downloaded `xml-axis-beta3.zip`.

> **Check the code download from** http://www.wrox.com **for any changes to these instructions on the release of later versions of Axis.**

**3.**   After the file is downloaded we decompress the files to C:\ and rename the directory `C:\xml-axis-beta3` as `C:\xml-axis`. This will help us to keep the path names in our classpath to a reasonable length. At the end of this process, the Axis directory on our machine will look like this:

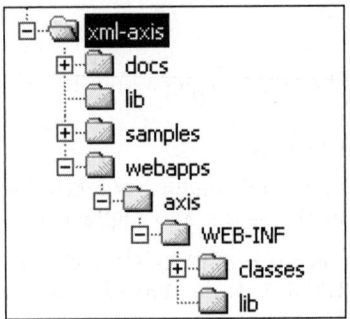

4. To simplify our life during development, we will use two environment variables (also known as shell variables):

❑ `axisDirectory`:
The Axis installation directory (in our case: `C:\xml-axis`)

❑ `jwsDirectory`:
The root directory where we will be putting the examples of this book (in our case `C:\Beginning_JWS_Examples`)

5. To run Axis we need only two files out of the Xerces package that we should have downloaded in the previous chapter:

❑ `xercesImpl.jar`:
A Java Archive File (JAR) file containing all the parser class files, which implement the standard APIs supported by the parser

❑ `xmlParserAPIs.jar`:
A Java Archive File (JAR) file containing the definitions of the standard APIs implemented by the parser

We will copy these two files into our `%jwsDirectory%\lib` directory, but feel free to put them anywhere else on your machine. The important part is to include these two JAR files in our classpath, while running Axis.

We are now ready to try out the Axis SOAP engine with a simple web service. In the next section we will discuss one such simple web service called `HelloWorld`, and run it ourselves.

# Writing a Web Service

Before getting into the details of creating a web service using Axis, let's have a look at the end product. The simplest possible service is a web service that returns fixed data such as an integer or a string. To convince ourselves that our web service responds to our input, we will write one that takes a string as input and returns a modified version of the input string. Specifically, if we send the string `Reader` to the service, it will respond with the string "Hello Reader!" The following figure depicts what we are trying to achieve:

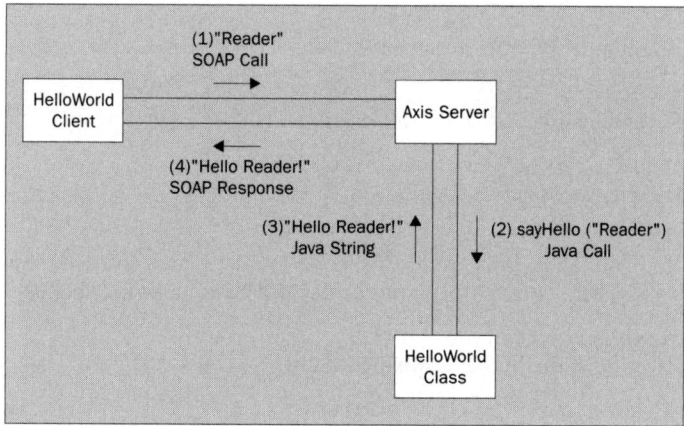

As shown in the above diagram, the sequence of events is as follows:

**1.** The `HelloWorld` client submits a SOAP request to the SOAP engine, Axis.

**2.** The Axis server receives the request and forwards it as a Java call to the `HelloWorld` class. Notice that we said, "class", not "service". In other words, we do not have to have to do anything special to morph our class into a web service under this scenario: we only write a simple Java class and the SOAP engine does the rest. We will discuss the specifics shortly.

**3.** The `sayHello()` method of our class simply returns a Java string back to Axis.

**4.** Axis serializes this Java string into a SOAP response, which in turns gets processed by the client.

Before we can actually try out the `HelloWorld` client, we must briefly discuss the HTTP server.

# SimpleAxisServer

To service remote calls over HTTP, we need a web server (it is also known as a HTTP Server). This server will be responsible for handling the HTTP requests (GET and POST). The web server listens to a socket port, typically 80 in production and 8080 in development. When a request arrives at this port from the client, the web server forwards the request to the appropriate software component for processing. In the case of a SOAP request, the proper software component will be the SOAP engine (in this case, Axis).

When it comes to choosing a web server, there are several options available to us. We will start with the easiest, the web server that comes with Axis (`SimpleAxisServer`): `org.apache.axis.transport.Web.SimpleAxisServer`.

In order to try out our `HelloWorld` example, we need to start up our server, but before starting the `SimpleAxisServer`, we need to make sure that the following JAR files are in the classpath (as mentioned, `%axisDirectory%` is the installation root for Axis, `%jwsDirectory%` is the installation root of our examples, and `%java_home%` is the JDK directory):

- ❑ `%axisDirectory%\lib\axis.jar`
  This JAR contains the Axis implementation.

- ❑ `%axisDirectory%\lib\jaxrpc.jar`
  This JAR contains the JAX-RPC declarations.

- ❑ `%axisDirectory%\lib\commons-logging.jar`
  This JAR contains Apache's logging capability.

- ❑ `%axisDirectory%\lib\tt-bytecode.jar`
  This JAR contains the TechTrader bytecode toolkit, which is set of classes used to modify Java bytecodes (see http://sourceforge.net/projects/tt-bytecode/ for details).

- ❑ `%axisDirectory%\lib\saaj.jar`
  This JAR contains the SOAP implementation.

- ❑ `%axisDirectory%\lib\log4j-core`
  This JAR contains the Log4J classes for additional logging.

- ❑ `%jwsDirectory%\lib\xercesImpl.jar` and
  `%jwsDirectory%\lib\xmlParserAPIs.jar`
  These JAR files contain the XML parser.

- ❑ `%java_home%\lib\tools.jar`
  This JAR is required to compile the JWS file.

*You may find it easiest to create a batch file such as the one included with the code download to set the classpath before you begin to compile or execute any of the example classes.*

Once you have this set up correctly, we can begin with our example.

## Try It Out – Hello World

Here are the steps to try out the `HelloWorld` service:

**1.** From within the `\Chp03\HelloWorld` directory, start the `SimpleAxisServer` by typing in the following command:

```
java org.apache.axis.transport.http.SimpleAxisServer
```

If all has gone well, you will see a message confirming that the server is starting on port 8080, like this:

*By default, the `SimpleAxisServer` listens to port 8080, but you can change the port by passing the port number (for example 8081) as a command-line argument.*

Once started, the `SimpleAxisServer` does not give the control back to the command prompt so we will have to open another one for running the client. At this point, we have a web server ready to process SOAP requests.

**2.** Now we need to install the `HelloWorld` web service. The code of the `HelloWorld` web service is listed below:

```java
public class HelloWorld {
  /**
   * Returns "Hello <sender>!".
   */
  public String sayHello(String sender) {
    return "Hello " + sender + "!";
  }
}
```

Installing a web service is usually referred to as **deployment**. For deploying the `HelloWorld` web service, we don't have to compile it as Axis will automatically do this for us. We just have to copy the `HelloWorld.java` (you can download the source code for this file from our web site **http://www.wrox.com**) file to the root directory of the `SimpleAxisServer` and rename it as `HelloWorld.jws` (**JWS** stands for **Java Web Service**):

> The **SimpleAxisServer** looks for JWS file in the directory where it was started up, and not in the Axis installation directory. So, from our screenshot opposite, you can see that we should copy the **HelloWorld.jws** file to **%jwsDirectory%\Chp03\HelloWorld\HelloWorld.jws**

This simple operation completes the deployment of the `HelloWorld` web service.

**3.** The last step that we need to complete before seeing `HelloWorld` in action is to build the client, `HelloWorldClient.java`.

As we can see from the following snippet, the code for the client is slightly more complex than the `HelloWorld` web service, but we will review it in detail shortly:

```java
// The Axis package is used to generate and handle the SOAP call
import org.apache.axis.client.Call;
import org.apache.axis.client.Service;
import org.apache.axis.encoding.XMLType;

// The rpc package is used to create the RPC call
import javax.xml.namespace.QName;
import javax.xml.rpc.NamespaceConstants;

// The java.net package gives us a URL class
import java.net.URL;

public class HelloWorldClient {
```

```
/**
 * Test main.
 */
public static void main(String args[]) {
  System.out.println("HelloWorld.main: Entering...");

  try {
    String   url    = "http://localhost:8080/HelloWorld.jws";
    String   sender = "Reader";
    Service  service = new Service();
    Call     call   = (Call) service.createCall();

    call.setTargetEndpointAddress(new URL(url));
    call.setSOAPActionURI("sayHello");
    call.setEncodingStyle(NamespaceConstants.NSURI_SOAP_ENCODING);
    call.setOperationName(new QName("urn:helloworld", "sayHello"));
    //call.setReturnType(XMLType.XSD_STRING);

    String hello = (String)call.invoke(new Object[] { sender } );

    System.out.println("The Web Service returned: " + hello);
    System.out.println ("HelloWorld.main: All done!");

  } catch (Exception exception) {
    System.err.println("Caught an exception: " + exception);
  }
}
}
```

Compiling this code can easily be achieved by the following command. We have assumed that this is saved in the `%jwsDirectory%\Chp03\HelloWorld` directory (as you will see from the code download):

**`javac HelloWorldClient.java`**

> **Remember you need to have set your classpath to include the Axis and Xerces JAR files, as described earlier.**

**4.** The command to run the `HelloWorldClient` is:

**`java HelloWorldClient`**

```
C:\WINNT\System32\cmd.exe                                    _ □ X

C:\Beg_JWS_Examples\Chp03\HelloWorld>java HelloWorldClient
HelloWorld.main: Entering...
The Web Service returned: Hello Reader!
HelloWorld.main: All done!

C:\Beg_JWS_Examples\Chp03\HelloWorld>_
```

Congratulations! You have deployed and tested your first web service.

If everything works as described, read on. However, in case you experienced any problems the next section deals with some common problems you might encounter.

## Troubleshooting

It is frustrating to try out something for the first time and have it fail repeatedly. Here are a few common exceptions that may get thrown up while trying out the `HelloWorld` example:

❑   Caught an exception: java.io.FileNotFoundException: HelloWorld.jws (The system cannot find the file specified)"

This error occurs when Axis is unable to find the JWS file. It is a very common problem the first time you work with a JWS file. To fix the problem, stop the `SimpleAxisServer` and double-check that the `HelloWorld.jws` file is present **in the directory where you started the `SimpleAxisServer`**. After verifying that the file is present, restart the `SimpleAxisServer`.

❑   Caught an exception: java.lang.RuntimeException: Compiler not found in your classpath. Make sure you added 'tools.jar'

This error occurs when Axis is unable to locate the `tools.jar` file. The reason is that without `tools.jar`, Axis cannot compile the JWS file. Please ensure that the `tools.jar` file is in your classpath.

❑   Caught an exception:

There can be several reasons for this error. In this case the window where the Axis server is running will probably contain a stack trace, from which we can usually find out the cause. As with Java development, the problem is likely to be a missing JAR file in the classpath. Make sure that the classpath (server and client) contains all the files that we listed above. Note that when we get an error like this one, the Axis server might crash. If this happens remember to restart it.

### How It Works

The code of the `HelloWorld` web service is very simple. This web service is made up of just one Java method, `sayHello()`. Its implementation is rather trivial and does not contain any Axis-specific code.

Most of the work is actually in the client, so let's have a closer look at that code. The imported `org.apache.axis` package contains Axis's implementation of the JAX-RPC package. The imported `javax.xml` package contains the declarations (without the implementation) of the classes and interfaces defined by JAX-RPC. The client code is contained in `HelloWorld.main()`:

```
public static void main(String args[]) {
    System.out.println("HelloWorldClient.main: Entering...");

    try {
        String  url     = "http://localhost:8080/HelloWorld.jws";
        String  sender  = "Reader";
        Service service = new Service();
        Call    call    = (Call) service.createCall();
```

The URL of our web service is `localhost:8080`, port 8080 on the local machine. The `Service` class models a remote web service and the `Call` class models a remote procedure call to a (remote) web service.

Once we have a `Call` object, we must give it enough information to generate the SOAP packet, that is:

- ❏ The remote URL
- ❏ The SOAP action (`sayHello`)
- ❏ The encoding (`SOAP`)
- ❏ The remote method to call (`sayHello()`)
- ❏ The type of the object returned by the remote procedure (`String`)

The SOAP action is optional, but some servers use it as a hint of the method being called. Setting the return type is also discretionary when talking to Axis because it puts type information in the SOAP response. This is not necessarily the case with other SOAP engines, so to be safe you might want to specify the return type explicitly. We will examine the SOAP request and response shortly.

The code that performs all this is listed here:

```
call.setTargetEndpointAddress(new URL(url));
call.setSOAPActionURI("sayHello");
call.setEncodingStyle(SOAPConstants.URI_NS_SOAP_ENCODING);
call.setOperationName(new QName("urn:helloworld", "sayHello"));
//call.setReturnType(XMLType.XSD_STRING);
```

The actual call to the remote procedure is done through `call.invoke()` (notice the cast to a `String`):

```
String hello = (String)call.invoke(new Object[] { sender } );
```

The remainder of the code prints the string returned by the web service. It also contains the exception-handling code.

As we have said before, the bulk of the `HelloWorld` implementation is in the client. When we introduce WSDL in Chapter 5, we will see that it is possible to automatically generate a proxy for handling the details of setting up the `Service` and the `Call` objects.

Let's now have a look at the SOAP packets transmitted between the client and the server.

## Try It Out – SOAP Debugging

Axis comes with a very useful class `tcpmon` (TCP monitor). It is a Swing-based utility used for setting up a TCP tunnel between our client (`HelloWorldClient`) and the server (the `HelloWorld` web service).

**1.** The first step is to start the `tcpmon` utility (Remember to set the same classpath as in the `HelloWorld` client):

**java org.apache.axis.utils.tcpmon**

This command should display a Window as shown below into which we can enter the values shown here (the text fields are empty by default):

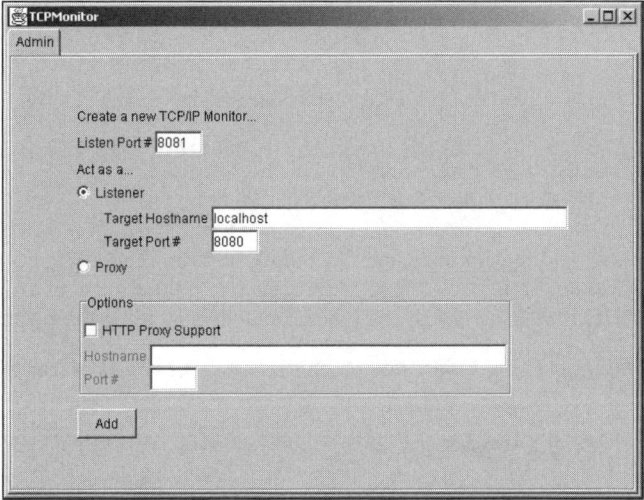

> **Do not use the same port values for the Listen Port and the Target Port or else we will get into an infinite loop.**

**2.** Once we've entered the values as shown above screenshot, click on the Add button. This will create a new tab in the window labeled Port 8081.

**3.** Click on the Port 8081 tab, to show its contents. The display should now look like the following:

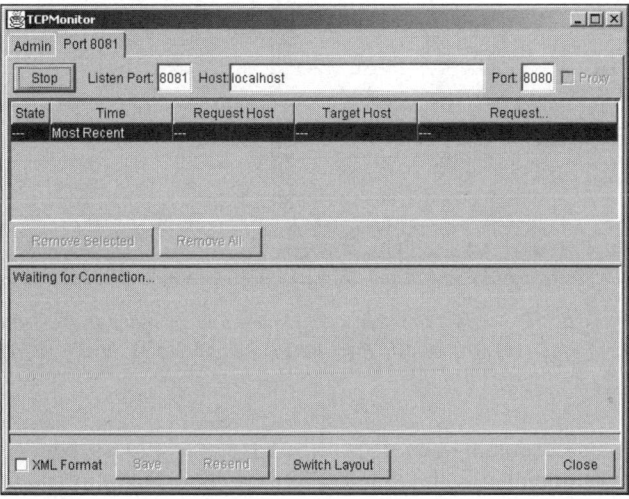

**4.** Since we have set up the `tcpmon` utility to listen to port 8081, we need to modify our client to submit its requests to port 8081. This is relatively simple; we just have to change one line in our code for `HelloWorld`. For this we will open the file `HelloWorldClient.java` in a text editor and change the value as shown below:

```
public static void main(String args[]) {
    System.out.println("HelloWorldClient.main: Entering...");
    try {
        String  url     = "http://localhost:8081/HelloWorld.jws";
        String  sender  = "Reader";
        Service service = new Service();
```

**5.** The JWS file should remain unchanged. Compile and run the modified `HelloWorldClient`. After the execution of `HelloWorldClient.main()`, the display of `tcpmon` should look like this (we can switch between a vertical and a horizontal display using the **Switch Layout** button):

*When running this example make sure that the `SimpleAxisServer` is listening to port 8080, its default value.*

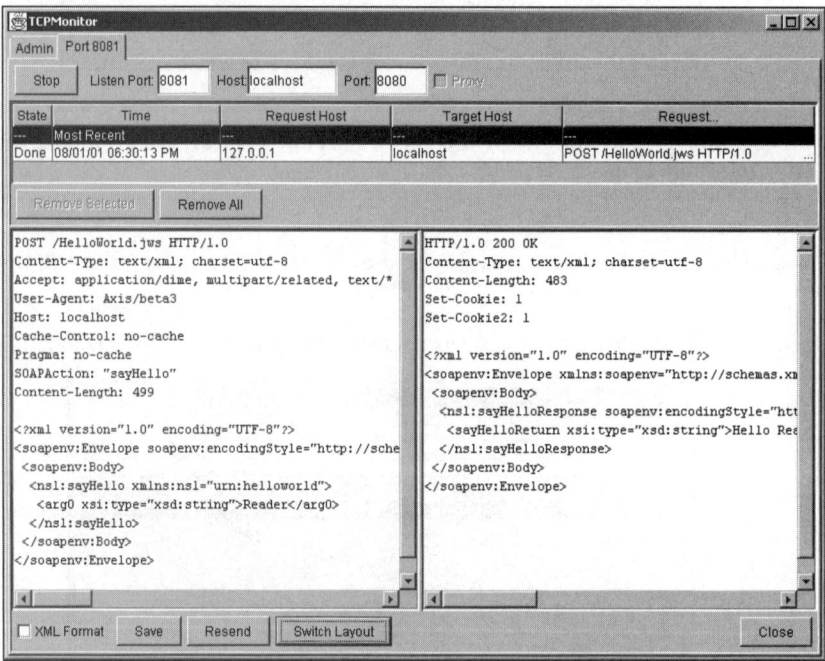

*Note that it is theoretically possible to modify the request and resend it to the server. If you want to do so, keep in mind that you must modify the Content Length HTTP header to reflect the change.*

### How It Works

Let's start with the request submitted by `HelloWorld.main()`. The request starts with an HTTP header that contains information such as the HTTP verb (POST), the version of the protocol, the length and type of the content, and the optional `SOAPAction` header that we discussed previously:

```
POST /axis/HelloWorld.jws HTTP/1.0
Content-Length: 505
Host: localhost
Content-Type: text/xml; charset=utf-8
SOAPAction: "sayHello"
```

Note that the HTTP header is terminated by an empty line and followed by the content of the document. The SOAP request is an RPC call to the `sayHello()` method of the web service qualified with the `urn:helloworld` namespace:

```
<?xml version="1.0" encoding="UTF-8"?>
<SOAP-ENV:Envelope SOAP-
ENV:encodingStyle="http://schemas.xmlsoap.org/soap/encoding/" xmlns:SOAP-
ENV="http://schemas.xmlsoap.org/soap/envelope/"
xmlns:xsd="http://www.w3.org/2001/XMLSchema"
xmlns:xsi="http://www.w3.org/2001/XMLSchema-instance" xmlns:SOAP-
ENC="http://schemas.xmlsoap.org/soap/encoding/">
  <SOAP-ENV:Body>
    <ns1:sayHello xmlns:ns1="urn:helloworld">
      <arg0 xsi:type="xsd:string">Reader</arg0>
    </ns1:sayHello>
  </SOAP-ENV:Body>
</SOAP-ENV:Envelope>
```

The response is a SOAP response to the RPC and it is a return value. Once again the HTTP header is terminated by an empty line and followed by the SOAP envelope:

```
HTTP/1.0 200 OK
Content-Type: text/xml; charset=utf-8
Content-Length: 489
Set-Cookie: 1
Set-Cookie2: 1

<?xml version="1.0" encoding="UTF-8"?>
<SOAP-ENV:Envelope xmlns:SOAP-ENV="http://schemas.xmlsoap.org/soap/envelope/"
xmlns:xsd="http://www.w3.org/2001/XMLSchema"
xmlns:xsi="http://www.w3.org/2001/XMLSchema-instance">
 <SOAP-ENV:Body>
    <ns1:sayHelloResponse SOAP
      ENV:encodingStyle="http://schemas.xmlsoap.org/soap/encoding/".
     xmlns:ns1="urn:helloworld">
      <sayHelloReturn xsi:type="xsd:string">Hello Reader!</sayHelloReturn>
    </ns1:sayHelloResponse>
  </SOAP-ENV:Body>
</SOAP-ENV:Envelope>
```

As we can see from this example, when it comes to debugging SOAP applications, the `tcpmon` utility can be a priceless asset. Now let's spend some time in discussing the working of the TCP Monitor.

The following diagram shows how the message flow is modified for `HelloWorld`:

When we set the listening port to 8081, we instructed `tcpmon` to listen to TCP/IP (and therefore HTTP) connections on port 8081. We also modified the client to connect to 8081 rather than 8080. When the request comes in to port 8081 (label (1) in the figure above), `tcpmon` does two things. Firstly, it displays the request in its GUI (label 2) and secondly, it forwards the same request to the target host (label 3).

In our case, the target host is port 8080 where the `SimpleAxisServer` is waiting for the request. From the point of view of the server (in our case the `SimpleAxisServer`), nothing has changed (labels 4 and 5). When the response is ready, it does not come back to our client, instead it first comes back to `tcpmon` (label 6). When `tcpmon` receives the response it updates it GUI (label 7) and simultaneously forwards the response to the client (label 8), the `HelloWorld.main()` that submitted the request to port 8081.

Note that the use of `tcpmon` is not restricted to SOAP traffic alone; we can use it for our HTML or JSP development.

Let's now shift our attention to a production-grade servlet engine, Tomcat.

# Using Tomcat as the HTTP Server

We had mentioned in passing that the `SimpleAxisServer` was not production-worthy. It has several shortcomings, such as:

❑ **It is not robust**
As we said earlier, the server will crash and consequently stop serving all HTTP requests. This is simply not acceptable in a production environment.

❑ **It is not secure**
It provides no security mechanism whatsoever. A robust security mechanism is one of the prerequisites for a production-grade server.

❑ **It is not scalable**
The `SimpleAxisServer` can only serve one request at a time because it is single threaded. As a result, it cannot handle high workloads in a production environment.

So, is it fair to say that the `SimpleAxisServer` is useless? Absolutely not! Its main advantages are its simplicity and lightweight nature. These advantages are very handy during web service development. As `SimpleAxisServer` is single threaded, we can be sure that the server is performing no other work while we are working on our code. This is a major asset when it comes to debugging or profiling. Also, being lightweight, the `SimpleAxisServer` will start quickly. So make sure that you do not forget the appropriate uses of the `SimpleAxisServer` once you have learned how to set up Axis with a servlet engine.

In this book we will be using Tomcat 4, which is the most current version at the time of writing (4.0.4 to be precise). Tomcat is an attractive solution as it is an open source (vendor-neutral) servlet engine. It is also the servlet reference implementation selected by Sun. Other servlet engine implementations provided by WebSphere or WebLogic application servers are also available. We will be talking about application servers in Chapter 10.

Tomcat addresses the main concerns raised about the `SimpleAxisServer`:

❑ **Robustness**
   The crash of a servlet will not bring down the server.

❑ **Security**
   It implements the J2EE security specifications. See http://java.sun.com/j2ee for a short introduction to J2EE.

❑ **Scalability**
   It is a multi-threaded server that can, under some circumstances, be replicated across several machines.

We have touched on the fact that these desired features came at the expense of simplicity. The first manifestation of this added complexity is the download and installation of Tomcat. But don't worry; with the instructions provided in the coming pages, setting up Tomcat with Axis will be a breeze.

## Try It Out – Installing Tomcat

Let's go through the steps of installing Tomcat.

**1.** The recent release of Tomcat (Tomcat 4.0.4) can be obtained from
http://jakarta.apache.org/builds/jakarta-tomcat-4.0/release/v4.0.4/bin/:

*It's quite possible that there will be a later build by the time you're reading this; however, the instructions should be identical; only the version number will be different.*

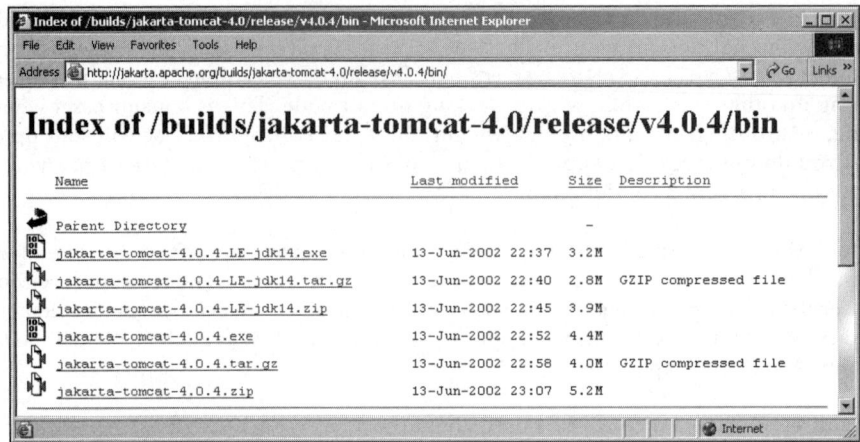

For Windows platform, the easiest method is to download and run the `jakarta-tomcat-4.0.4.exe` file.

**2.** Run the executable. After we've agreed to the license, the `jakarta-tomcat-4.0.4` displays the following dialog box:

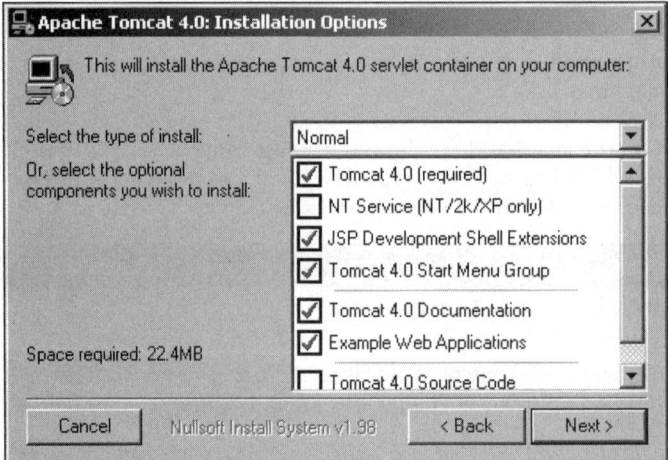

**3.** Select the optional components that you might need. Note that in this book we will not use the source code or the NT service.

**4.** The next screen prompts for the installation directory. We will use `C:\Tomcat4.0` but any other directory will do just fine:

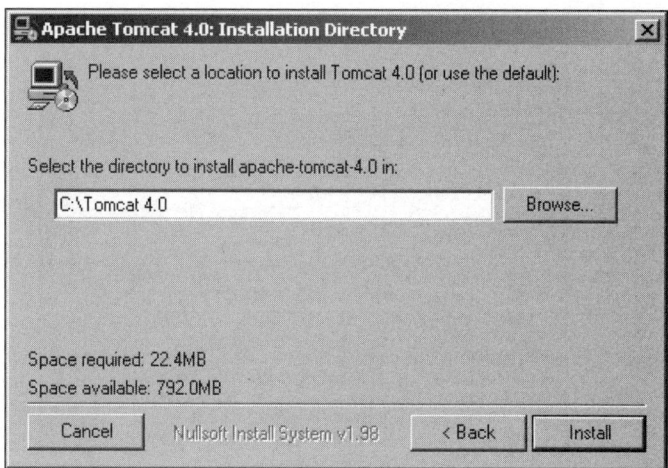

**5.** At the end of the installation, our Tomcat installation directory should look like this:

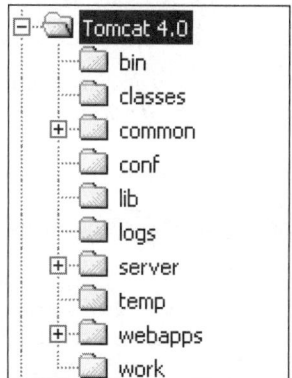

**6.** We will define a `catalina_home` environment variable to represent the Tomcat installation directory (in our case `C:\Tomcat4`). In Windows 2000 this can be done through the **Environmental Variables** tab in the **System** control panel applet:

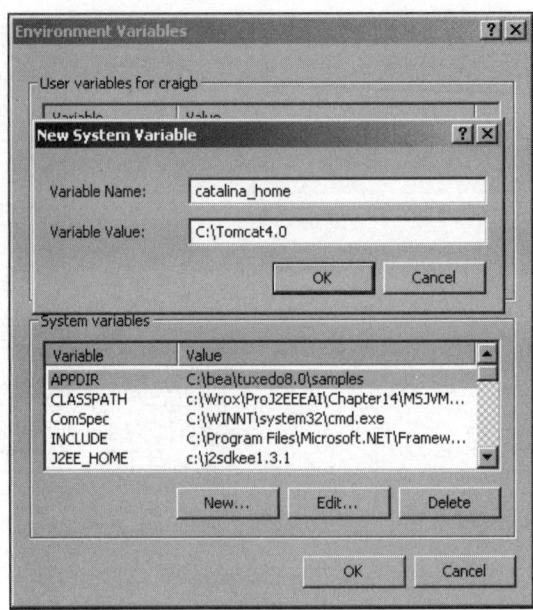

*Catalina was the code name for the Tomcat 4.0 development. It is still used in several places, including the .sh and .bat files that come with the installation.*

**7.** To test the installation, simply run `%catalina_home%\bin\startup`:

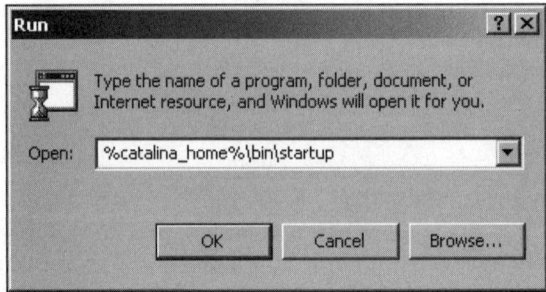

This launches the Tomcat server in a new window that looks like the following:

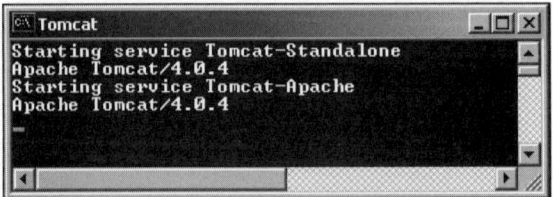

*If you would rather run Tomcat from within the same window (perhaps to see any exceptions thrown) then the command is `%catalina_home%\bin\catalina run`.*

**8.** At this point, our Tomcat server is listening to port 8080 for HTTP requests (providing you have stopped our SimpleAxisServer listening on 8080). By navigating to the URL http://localhost:8080, we can view its home page:

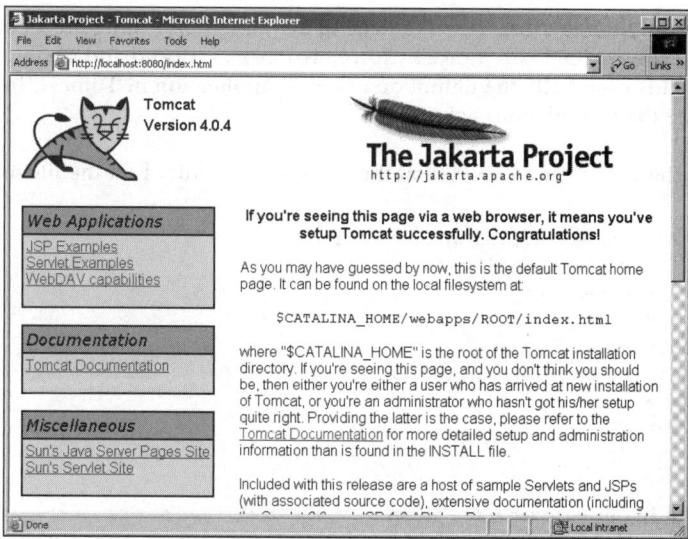

Now that we have Tomcat running correctly, we can focus our attention back to SOAP development and modify our Tomcat installation to run with Axis.

## Try It Out – Modify Tomcat to Work with Axis

We need to modify Tomcat's default installation to make it suitable for running Axis inside Tomcat. We must:

❑   Alter the classpath to include the Axis JAR files we mentioned previously

❑   Install the Axis servlet

**1.** There are several ways to modify the classpath used by Tomcat. A straightforward way is to edit the `%catalina_home%\bin\setclasspath.bat` file using a text editor, like so:

```
rem Set standard CLASSPATH
rem Note that there are no quotes as we do not want to introduce random
rem quotes into the CLASSPATH
set CLASSPATH=%JAVA_HOME%\lib\tools.jar
set CLASSPATH=%classpath%;%axisDirectory%\lib\axis.jar
set CLASSPATH=%classpath%;%axisDirectory%\lib\commons-logging.jar
set CLASSPATH=%classpath%;%axisDirectory%\lib\jaxrpc.jar
set CLASSPATH=%classpath%;%axisDirectory%\lib\log4j-core.jar
set CLASSPATH=%classpath%;%axisDirectory%\lib\tt-bytecode.jar
set CLASSPATH=%classpath%;%axisDirectory%\lib\saaj.jar

set CLASSPATH=%classpath%;%jwsDirectory%\lib\xercesImpl.jar
set CLASSPATH=%classpath%;%jwsDirectory%\lib\xmlParserAPIs.jar

rem Set standard command for invoking Java.
```

**109**

**2.** The easiest way to install the Axis servlet in Tomcat is to copy the `%axisDirectory%\webapps\axis` directory into the `%catalina_home%\webapps\ROOT` directory.

Another solution that has the advantage of avoiding duplicating the `webapps\axis` directory is to edit the `%catalina_home%\conf\server.xml` and add a **context** to Tomcat for Axis. A context is essentially the definition of a web application in Tomcat. In our case, we will be following the second approach.

Here is the modification needed in the `server.xml` file. Edit the file using any text editor:

```
          <name>mail.smtp.host</name>
          <value>localhost</value>
        </parameter>
      </ResourceParams>
    </Context>
    <Context docBase="c:\xml-axis\webapps\axis" path="/axis"/>
  </Host>
 </Engine>
</Service>
```

Note that in our case we have given `c:\xml-axis\webapps\axis` as the docBase, since this is the path for our `%axisDirectory%\webapps\axis` directory (recall we installed Axis in the directory `C:\xml-axis`).

**3.** Stop Tomcat with the following command:

**`%catalina_home%\bin\shutdown`**

**4.** After Tomcat has stopped, restart it by typing this command in order to load the Axis web application:

**`%catalina_home%\bin\startup`**

> If you get classpath errors now when you try to start Tomcat, then copy the `axis.jar` file into Tomcat's `\common\lib` directory and then remove the relevant `set classpath` line in the batch file.

**5.** Once Tomcat restarts, we should be able to navigate to the Axis home page; the URL is http://localhost:8080/axis/index.html. If the modifications were carried out correctly, our browser will display the Axis home page:

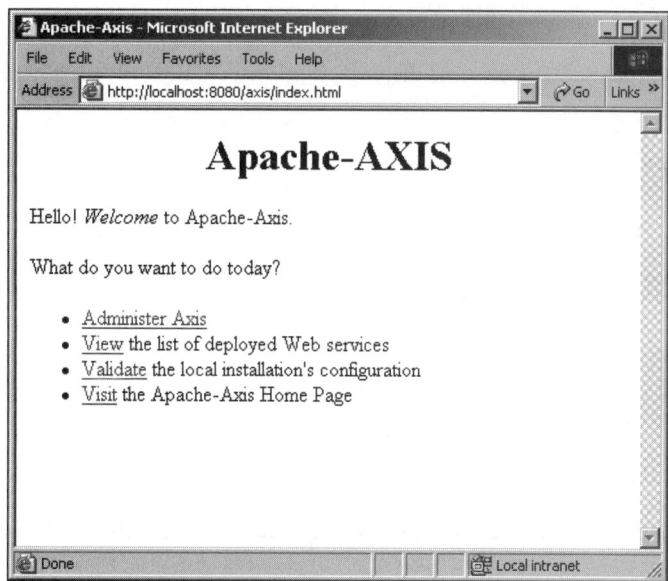

The **Administer Axis** link provides a way to start and stop Axis. When the Axis server is stopped, any request returns a SOAP fault. The **View** link provides a list of the registered web services (more on this later).

*Note that when it comes to the installation and configuration of Tomcat, we have barely scratched the surface. Among other things, we have not described how to set up Tomcat with a production web server like Apache or IIS, but the instructions that we have reviewed in this section are enough to start our development efforts. For detailed documentation on how to set up Tomcat in a production environment, you can visit the http://jakarta.apache.org/tomcat/index.html.*

We are now ready to deploy the `HelloWorld` service inside Tomcat.

## Try It Out – HelloWord (Reprise)

The method of using a Java Web Service (JWS) file still works with Axis running as a servlet hosted by Tomcat. We will, however, need to make a small change in the `HelloWorldClient.java` file.

**1.** First we need to modify the `HelloWorldClient.java` file. Since Axis is now running as the Axis web application inside Tomcat, the `HelloWorld` service changes to http://localhost:8080/axis/HelloWorld.jws (the earlier URL was http://localhost:8080/HelloWorld.jws). So open the `HelloWorldClient.java` file in a text editor and make the following change to it:

```
public static void main(String args[]) {
  System.out.println("HelloWorldClient.main: Entering...");
  try {
    String   url    = "http://localhost:8080/axis/HelloWorld.jws";
    String   sender = "Reader";
    Service  service = new Service();
    Call     call    = (Call) service.createCall();
...
```

The `HelloWorld.jws` file remains unchanged.

**2.** Assuming that `HelloWorld` is the current directory, the following command will recompile the client:

```
javac HelloWorldClient.java
```

**3.** Copy the `HelloWorld.jws` file to the `%axisDirectory%\webapps\axis` directory.

**4.** The command to run the client is identical to the `SimpleAxisServer` example:

```
java HelloWorldClient
```

We should get exactly the same exciting result as before.

Before trying out this example make sure that Tomcat is running and that the `SimpleAxisServer` is stopped. Note that the exceptions thrown by the (Tomcat) server are logged in the file `localhost.log.date`, where `date` represents the date on which the log file was created. This file is in the `%catalina_home%\logs\` directory.

### How It Works

The main difference between the `SimpleAxisServer` and running Axis inside Tomcat is that Tomcat handles the HTTP requests and passes them as servlet requests to Axis. For more information on the servlet methodology, please refer to http://java.sun.com/products/servlet. This situation is depicted in the high-level diagram below:

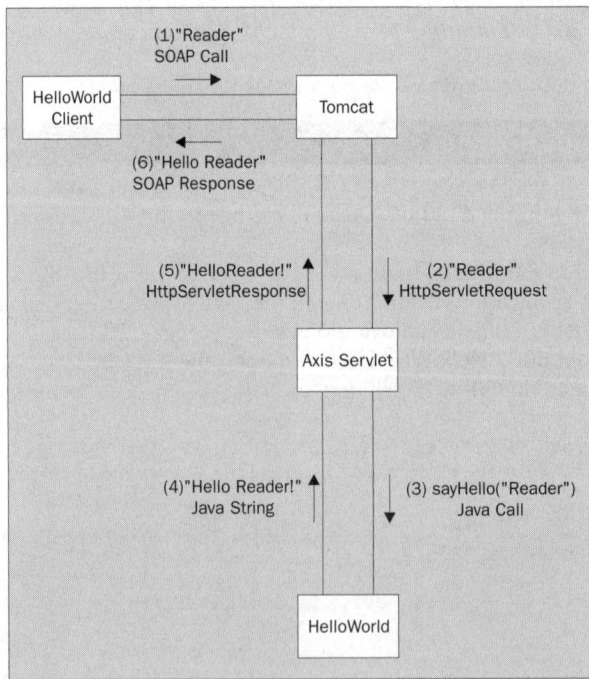

As we can see above, the request from the client goes to Tomcat on port 8080. Tomcat then creates an instance of the `AxisServlet` class, and calls it with the SOAP call repackaged in a servlet-specific data structure: `HttpServletRequest`. The `AxisServlet` parses the requests and transforms it into a Java call for our web service: `HelloWorld`. On the return side, the `AxisServlet` generates a SOAP response from the Java return value and puts it inside another servlet-specific data structure, an `HttpServletResponse`. Finally, Tomcat uses that data to create the HTTP response sent back to the client.

Using JWS files might not be the best deployment strategy for a production web site. Some of the arguments against using JWS are:

❑ The source code of our web service is available to everybody

❑ The entire source must be in the JWS files, or the JAR files must be manually copied to the `lib` directory

❑ The amount of configuration required is limited (see below for more details)

However, like the `SimpleAxisServer`, the use of JWS files is quick and easy.

There is an alternative to JWS-based web services. Instead of using a JWS file we can use **compiled Java classes** and **deployment descriptors**. This form of deployment is also called **manual or custom deployment**.

# Manual Deployment – StockQuote

To explain the process of manual deployment better, we need to take a more complex example than `HelloWorld`. We will work with a stock quote service that provides web service-based stock quotes over the Internet. To show a realistic scenario that involves the use of class libraries, we will divide the web service into two classes:

❑ The `StockCore` class, which deals with the details of getting the stock quote. This was developed in Chapter 2.

❑ The `StockQuote` class, which exposes the functionality as a web service.

The `StockQuote` class contains one method that defines the interface of the web service and one `main()` method that acts as the client to the web service. The following diagram shows the organization of the application:

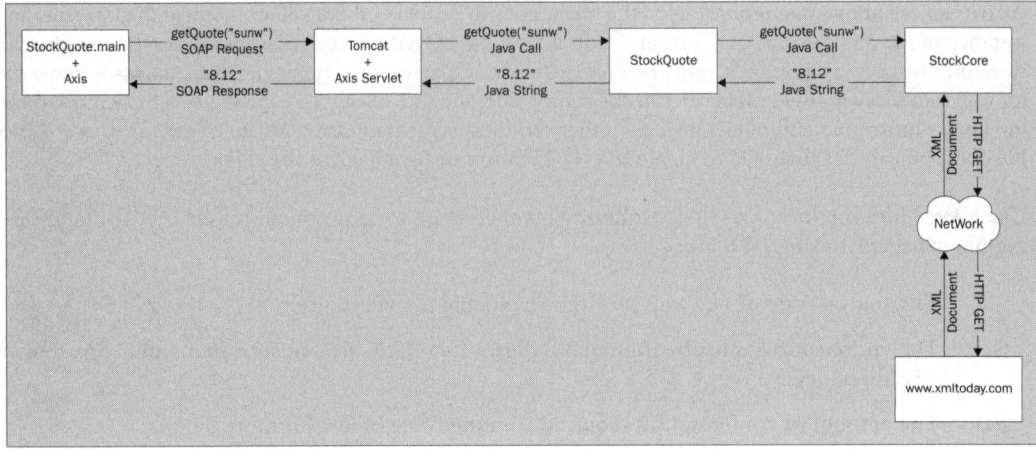

The figure above shows that a request to StockQuote is made of the following steps:

**1.** The client code builds a SOAP request with the help of the Axis runtime similarly to how we did with the HelloWord.main().

**2.** The Axis runtime sends the SOAP request over HTTP to Tomcat, which then invokes the Axis servlet. The Axis servlet then **de-serializes** the SOAP request, in other words, the Axis servlet builds a Java call for the StockQuote class (StockQuote.getQuote("SUNW")). We will revisit the issue of **serialization** (Java to XML) and **de-serialization** (XML to Java) at the end of this chapter.

**3.** The StockQuote.getQuote() method gets the actual value of the stock using the StockCore class that we build in Chapter 2.

**4.** Upon the return of the method, Axis serializes the stock quote into a SOAP response.

**5.** On the client side, Axis **de-serializes** the SOAP response into a Java string that can easily be used by the client code.

We will now compile, deploy, and test the StockQuote web service. But first, we'll need to use the functionality we developed in the StockCore example in the last chapter as a JAR file. We'll begin our next example by turning StockCore.class into stockcore.jar in order to use it as a library for the rest of the example.

## Try It Out – StockQuote

In order to build our stock quote service, the first steps will involve making our stockquote.jar file available to the stockquote service. To manually build the stockcore.jar file, follow these simple steps:

**1.** From the \Chp02\StockCore\classes\ directory run the following command (assuming you have a compiled version of StockCore.class in the com\wrox\jws\stockcore directory:

```
jar -cf stockcore.jar com\wrox\jws\stockcore\StockCore.class
```

**2.** Place `stockcore.jar` in the `%axisDirectory%\webapps\axis\WEB-INF\lib\` path so that we have it in our classpath.

**3.** Here is the code for `StockQuote.java` (to be placed in the `\Chp03\StockQuote\src` directory):

```java
package com.wrox.jws.stockquote;

import org.apache.axis.client.Call;
import org.apache.axis.client.Service;
import org.apache.axis.encoding.XMLType;
import org.apache.axis.utils.Options;

import javax.xml.rpc.ParameterMode;
import javax.xml.namespace.QName;

import com.wrox.jws.stockcore.StockCore;

public class StockQuote {

  public String getQuote(String ticker) throws Exception {
    StockCore stockcore = new StockCore();
    return stockcore.getQuote(ticker);
  }
```

The `StockQuote.main()` method is used as a client for testing:

```java
public static void main(String [] args) {
  final String methodName = "StockQuote.main";

  try {
    if(args.length != 1) {
      System.err.println("StockQuote Client");
      System.err.println(
        "Usage: java com.wrox.jws.stockquote.StockQuote" +
        " <ticker-symbol>");
      System.err.println(
        "Example: java com.wrox.jws.stockquote.StockQuote sunw");
      System.exit(1);
    }

    // Replace the following URL with what is suitable for
    // your environment
    String endpointURL = "http://localhost:8080/axis/servlet/AxisServlet";
    Service service    = new Service();
    Call    call       = (Call)service.createCall();

    call.setTargetEndpointAddress(new java.net.URL(endpointURL));
    call.setOperationName(new QName("StockQuote", "getQuote"));
    call.addParameter("ticker", XMLType.XSD_STRING, ParameterMode.IN);
    call.setReturnType(org.apache.axis.encoding.XMLType.XSD_STRING);
```

```
        String ret = (String)call.invoke(new Object[] { args[0] });

        System.out.println("The value of " + args[0] + " is: " + ret);

    } catch (Exception exception) {
        System.err.println(methodName + ": " + exception.toString());
        exception.printStackTrace();
    }
  }
}
```

**4.** To compile `StockQuote` class, type in the following commands (we need the `StockCore` class in our classpath so we reference the copy we stored in Axis):

```
javac -classpath %classpath%;%axisDirectory%\webapps\axis\
        WEB-INF\lib\stockcore.jar
    -d ..\classes StockQuote.java
```

**5.** Once the class file is compiled, we need to copy it into the `\classes` directory of the Axis web application. Depending which methodology you elected to use to modify Tomcat to run with Axis (see *Try It Out – Modify Tomcat to Work with Axis* earlier in this chapter), you will either copy the compiled file to the `\webapps` directory inside Axis or to the `\axis` directory inside Tomcat. We mapped the Axis application to our Axis installation directory so, here is what our `\axis` directory should look like:

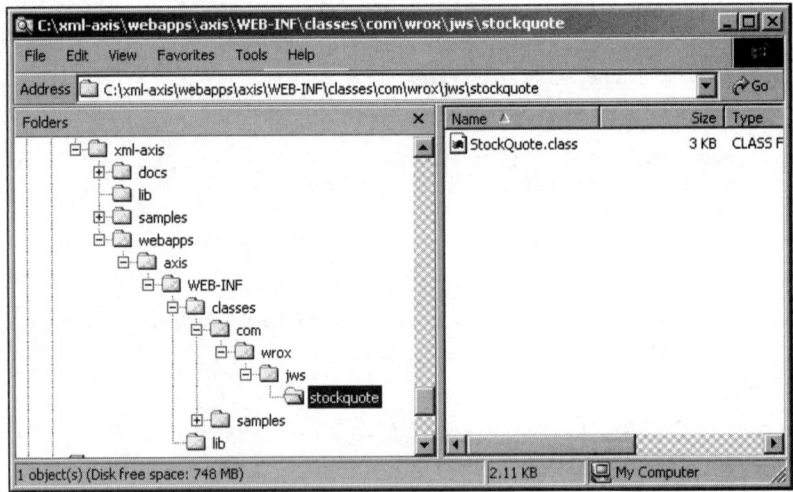

**6.** Now we need to tell Axis that `StockQuote` is a valid web service. This is done with the help of a **deployment descriptor** and the **Axis `AdminClient`** (make sure that Tomcat is running before launching these commands).

Save this deployment descriptor into a file called `StockQuote.wsdd`:

```
<deployment xmlns="http://xml.apache.org/axis/wsdd/"
  xmlns:java="http://xml.apache.org/axis/wsdd/providers/java">
<service name="StockQuote" provider="java:RPC">
  <parameter name="className" value="com.wrox.jws.stockquote.StockQuote"/>
  <parameter name="allowedMethods" value="getQuote"/>
</service>
</deployment>
```

**7.** The following command sends the deployment descriptor to Axis for processing (assuming that \src is still our current directory):

**java org.apache.axis.client.AdminClient ..\StockQuote.wsdd**

Here is how it looks on our client machine:

```
C:\WINNT\System32\cmd.exe                                          _ □ ×

C:\Beg_JWS_Examples\Chp03\StockQuote\src>java org.apache.axis.client.AdminClient
 ..\StockQuote.wsdd
- Processing file ..\StockQuote.wsdd
- <Admin>Done processing</Admin>

C:\Beg_JWS_Examples\Chp03\StockQuote\src>
```

*Bear in mind that Tomcat should not be running when we are building the example. It might give some errors as the* stockcore.jar *and* StockQuote.class *files are likely to be locked by Tomcat. However, when trying out the example, make sure that Tomcat is running.*

**8.** We will examine the deployment descriptor in detail shortly. For now, we will check whether the StockQuote service has been successfully deployed. For this we will visit the URL http://localhost:8080/axis/servlet/AxisServlet:

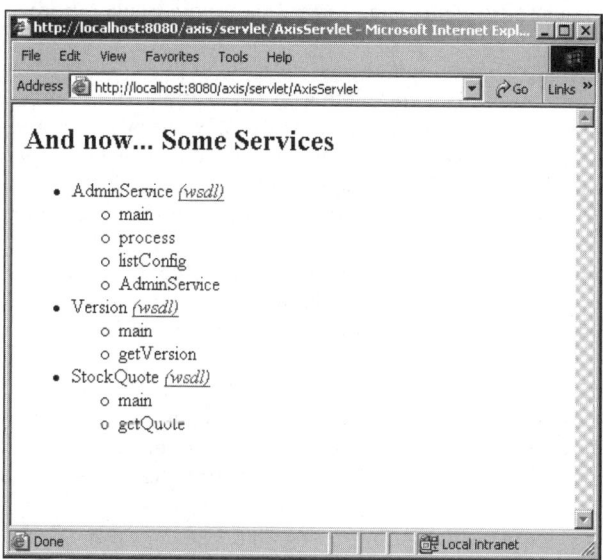

You can see that there is now a web service called StockQuote with two methods: main and getQuote that correspond to our class.

**9.** Copy the `stock_quote.xml` file to the `%axisDirectory%\webapps\axis\WEB-INF\classes` directory; otherwise we'll get an exception when `StockCore` can't load the source XML document.

**10.** Now we can test our `StockQuote` class. As you will recall we built a test harness into the `StockQuote` class itself in the `main()` method. Therefore, we can run it either on the class we copied to Axis (from the `%axisDirectory%\webapps\axis\WEB-INF\classes` directory) or our original compiled class (from the `\Chp03\StockQuote\classes` directory):

```
java com.wrox.jws.stockquote.StockQuote IBM
```

All being well, this should return the following result:

```
C:\WINNT\System32\cmd.exe                                            _ □ ×

C:\Beg_JWS_Examples\Chp03\StockQuote\classes>java com.wrox.jws.stockquote.StockQ
uote IBM
The value of IBM is: 69.01

C:\Beg_JWS_Examples\Chp03\StockQuote\classes>_
```

### How It Works

Before jumping into the code for StockQuote, it is worth spending a few moments to review what we achieved and compare it to the JWS-based implementation.

Our first step was to compile the `StockQuote.java` file. This step solved the first problem we mentioned with JWS; our source code is no longer accessible to everybody.

The second step was to copy the compiled class along with its dependency (`stockcore.jar`). In fact, nothing prevents us from installing a complete web application with libraries and resource files. This brings up an important point: our application does not have to be contained inside the Axis web application. We are free to define our own web application completely separated from Axis. The security implications of this simple fact are significant since this allows our application to run completely isolated from other web services deployed on the same machine.

The third and last step before running the client was the actual deployment. The `AdminClient` can easily deploy or un-deploy a web service. All this sounds a little too easy, but there is a catch. What is there to prevent a malicious client from un-deploying all our web services from a server?

The Axis designers are aware of this potential security breach, so by default **remote administration** is not allowed on Axis. In other words, we are only permitted to deploy and un-deploy web services from the local machine. However it is possible to allow remote administration by modifying the `\axis\WEB-INF\server-config.wsdd` file and setting the `enableRemoteAdmin` attribute to `true` instead of `false`:

```
...
<handler name="MsgDispatcher"
 type="java:org.apache.axis.providers.java.MsgProvider"/>
 <service name="AdminService" provider="java:MSG">
  <parameter name="allowedMethods" value="AdminService"/>
  <parameter name="enableRemoteAdmin" value="true"/>
  <parameter name="className" value="org.apache.axis.utils.Admin"/>
  <namespace>http://xml.apache.org/axis/wsdd/</namespace>
 </service>
 <service name="Version" provider="java:RPC">
...
```

If you plan on using remote administration in your deployed web services, be sure to secure access to the web site.

Let's now focus our attention to the StockQuote.java file (the full source code can be downloaded from our web site). The imports of the org.apache.axis and javax.xml packages are identical to what we saw in HelloWorld. Once again they are only required for the client portion of this sample (contained in the main() method). The import of com.wrox.jws.stockcore.StockCore gives us access to the StockCore class.

Most of the server-side work is done in the getQuote() method:

```
public class StockQuote {

    public String getQuote(String ticker) throws Exception {
        StockCore stockcore = new StockCore();
        return stockcore.getQuote(ticker);
    }
```

As we can see from the above code snippet, the method getQuote() takes a string as input (the ticker symbol of the stock we are interested in) and returns the current stock value as a string.

The class also contains a main() method to test the service; this is very similar to the HelloWorld.main() method, which we reviewed previously. A notable difference is in the invocation of the StockQuote service, which is shown below:

```
...
call.setReturnType(org.apache.axis.encoding.XMLType.XSD_STRING);

String ret = (String)call.invoke(new Object[] { args[0] });

System.out.println("The (delayed) value of " + args[0]
  + " is: " + ret);
...
```

Armed with the implementation of our web service, we can now focus on the deployment descriptor: StockQuote.wsdd. The outermost element, <deployment/>, tells us that the XML document is an Axis deployment descriptor. The deployment descriptor is Axis specific since the namespace is "http://xml.apache.org/axis/wsdd/". The Java namespace is used for Java providers, or in other words, web services implemented as a Java class.

For each web service that we deploy, we will have one `<service/>` element in the deployment descriptor. In our example, we deploy the `StockQuote` service as a Java class and we use the Remote Procedure Call (RPC) methodology. The meanings of the `classname` and `allowedMethods` attributes are self-explanatory. Instead of listing methods (separated by commas or spaces), we can specify `"*"` to allow all the methods to be invoked.

It is worth mentioning that Axis instantiates the class that we specify using the default constructor, hence the requirement that the default constructor (for example, `StockQuote()`) must be defined and public. Without further instructions in the deployment descriptor Axis instantiates a new object with every request. Since creating an object with every request can be wasteful at times, Axis supports three modes of object creation, also referred as **scoping**:

❑ **Request**
   This is the default: a new object is created with every request to the server

❑ **Session**
   The object will exist for the duration of the session

❑ **Application**
   One object will be created for the entire application

To specify different scoping, simply set the `scoping` attribute to the desired value in the `<service/>` element:

```
  ...
    <parameter name="allowedMethods" value="getQuote"/>
    <parameter name="scope" value="session"/>
  </service>
</deployment>
```

When deciding on the scope of a web service it is important to keep two things in mind:

❑ **Threading**
   When using the request scope, our web service object will be created and used in the same thread. It is not necessarily the case with the session and application scopes; the `SimpleAxisServer` is single-threaded, but Tomcat and other production-grade servers are multi-threaded.

❑ **Security**
   When using the application scope, all clients will use the same object and any residual state from one request might affect another request. In addition to the added complexity of developing thread-safe web services, this is clearly a security risk, which we must consider during our design and balance it against the benefits of sharing object instances across client requests.

This concludes our description of Tomcat as a container for Axis. Before concluding this chapter, we need to discuss an important topic: **serialization**.

# Market Example

*The code for the* `Market` *class can be found in the* `\Chp03\Market` *directory.*

We will use the `Market` class to show how data types are serialized and deserialized by the Axis framework. The `Market` class is a modified version of the `StockQuote` class. It returns more information through the `MarketData` class. The `MarketData` class contains the following instance data:

- The ticker symbol
- The ticker symbol value as a string
- The ticker symbol value as a double
- The values of the three major US stock indices (DOW, NASDAQ, and S&P 500)

Before looking at the `Market` class in action, we need to discuss some background information on the mappings between Java and XML.

# Java/XML Mappings

We have seen that `HelloWorld.main()` uses Axis to serialize Java data types into XML data types and that the Axis server deserializes the XML data types into Java data types. That serialization/deserialization process for a request is briefly summarized in the following diagram:

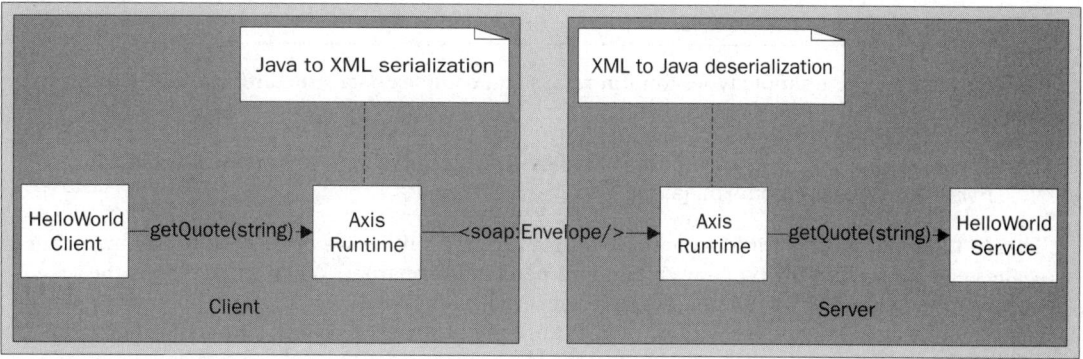

The only data type exchanged between the client and the server in the case of `HelloWorld` is a string. On the calling side, the string argument of `HelloWorld.getQuote()` is serialized as follows:

```
<arg0 xsi:type="xsd:string">Reader</arg0>
```

Note that the return string value is serialized in the same way.

The following table describes how Axis implements the XML to Java mapping for simple data types:

| Simple Type | Java Type |
|---|---|
| xsd:string | java.lang.String |
| xsd:integer | java.math.BigInteger |
| xsd:int | int |
| xsd:long | long |
| xsd:short | short |
| xsd:decimal | java.math.BigDecimal |
| xsd:float | float |
| xsd:double | double |
| xsd:Boolean | boolean |
| xsd:byte | byte |
| xsd:dateTime | java.util.Calendar |
| xsd:base64Binary | byte[] |
| xsd:hexBinary | byte[] |

We can combine these simple types to form arrays and complex data structures (we will see an example shortly).

> *The specific mapping rules are defined in the JAX-RPC specification, which can be downloaded from* http://java.sun.com/xml/jaxrpc/.

Thanks to the serialization infrastructure built in Axis, most times we don't need to pay much attention to these mappings. Simple types are a hundred percent transparent. When we deployed the StockQuote example we did not specify what serialization needed to be used. The same goes for arrays; for instance, if our web service returns an array of strings Axis will automatically handle the serialization and deserialization without further instructions from the web service developer or consumer. The mapping for complex types is almost handled automatically. We must specify how to handle the serialization but the default mechanism provided by Axis will take care of the details for us. The serialization information is part of the deployment descriptor.

Let's see how this works in practice with the Market class.

## Try It Out – The Market and MarketData Classes

The market example contains two classes: the Market class is the web service, and the MarketData class gets the data returned by Market.getQuote(). Our first step is to compile these two classes.

**1.** The MarketData class contains a stock quote with the market indices. Save this code in a file called MarketData.java in the \Chp03\Market\src directory):

```
package com.wrox.jws.stockquote;

import com.wrox.jws.stockcore.StockCore;
```

```java
public final class MarketData {

  public transient String DOW   = "^DJI";
  public transient String NASDAQ = "^IXIC";
  public transient String SP500  = "^GSPC";

  String ticker;          // The ticker symbol.
  String stringValue;     // The value of the stock as a string
  double doubleValue;     // The value of the stock as a double
  double indices[];       // The DOW, the NASDAQ, and the S&P 500 values

  /**
   * Empty Market constructor. For the bean serializer.
   */
  public MarketData() {}

  /**
   * Market constructor. Simply pass in the ticker symbol and the
   * constructor will do the rest.
   *
   * @param ticker The ticker symbols to get a quote for (e.g. sunw)
   * @throws exception If anything goes wrong
   */
  public MarketData(String ticker) throws Exception {
    this.ticker = ticker;

    StockCore stockcore = new StockCore();

    stringValue = stockcore.getQuote(ticker);
    doubleValue = Double.parseDouble(stringValue);
    indices     = new double [3];
    indices[0]  = Double.parseDouble(stockcore.getQuote(DOW));
    indices[1]  = Double.parseDouble(stockcore.getQuote(NASDAQ));
    indices[2]  = Double.parseDouble(stockcore.getQuote(SP500));
  }

  /**
   * Public get and set methods. Used by the bean serializer
   */
  public double[] getIndices() {
    return indices;
  }
  public void setIndices(double indices[]) {
    this.indices = indices;
  }
  public String getTicker() {
    return ticker;
  }
  public void setTicker(String ticker) {
    this.ticker = ticker;
  }
  public double getDoubleValue() {
    return doubleValue;
  }
  public void setDoubleValue(double doubleValue) {
    this.doubleValue = doubleValue;
  }
}
```

**2.** The `Market` class contains the web service and a test client in the `Market.main()`. Save this code in a file called `Market.java` in a `\Chp03\Market\src` directory):

```java
package com.wrox.jws.stockquote;

import org.apache.axis.client.Call;
import org.apache.axis.client.Service;
import org.apache.axis.encoding.XMLType;
import org.apache.axis.utils.Options;
import org.apache.axis.encoding.ser.BeanSerializerFactory;
import org.apache.axis.encoding.ser.BeanDeserializerFactory;

import javax.xml.rpc.ParameterMode;
import javax.xml.namespace.QName;

public class Market {

  /**
   * Returns a delayed quote for the ticker symbol passed in. This one line
   * method is the only method of the service thanks to the simplicity of
   * Axis and the use of our StockCore class that we developed in Chapter 2.
   *
   * @param ticker The ticker symbol of the the stock
   */
  public MarketData getQuote(String ticker) throws Exception {
    return new MarketData(ticker);
  }
}
```

The `main()` method is used as a client of the `StockQuote` SOAP service. This method is used for testing purposes and as such is not part of the `StockQuote` web service. In a production mode, it is usually preferable to isolate test methods like this one in a separate test class that is not included in the web service distribution:

```java
  /**
   * @param args The ticker symbols to get a quote for (e.g. sunw)
   */
  public static void main(String [] args) {
    final String methodName = "Market.main";

    try {
      if(args.length != 1) {
        System.err.println("Market Client");
        System.err.println(
          "Usage: java com.wrox.jws.stockquote.Market <ticker-symbol>");
        System.err.println(
          "Example: java com.wrox.jws.stockquote.Market sunw");
        System.exit(1);
      }

      // Replace the following URL with what is suitable for your
      // environment
```

```
                String endpointURL =
                   "http://localhost:8080/axis/servlet/AxisServlet";
                Service service    = new Service();
                Call    call       = (Call)service.createCall();

                // Setup input arguments
                call.setTargetEndpointAddress(new java.net.URL(endpointURL));
                call.setOperationName(new QName("Market", "getQuote"));
                call.addParameter("ticker", XMLType.XSD_STRING, ParameterMode.IN);

                // register the MarketData class
                QName qName = new QName("http://stockquote.jws.wrox.com",
                   "MarketData");
                call.registerTypeMapping(MarketData.class, qName,
                   BeanSerializerFactory.class, BeanDeserializerFactory.class);

                call.setReturnType(new QName("marketData"));

                MarketData data = (MarketData)call.invoke(new Object[] { args[0] });

                System.out.println("The (delayed) value of " + args[0]
                   + " is: " + data.doubleValue + " (NASDAQ is "
                   + data.indices[1] + ")");

            } catch (Exception exception) {
                System.err.println(methodName + ": " + exception.toString());
                exception.printStackTrace();
            }
        }
    }
}
```

**3.** Compiling `Market` and `MarketData` is similar to the `StockQuote` example. Assuming that the current directory is `src`, the following instructions will compile and run the example on the Windows platform. Be sure to include all the JAR files that we used earlier (including `StockQuote.jar`) in the classpath:

```
javac -d ..\classes com\wrox\jws\stockquote\MarketData.java
javac -d ..\classes com\wrox\jws\stockquote\Market.java
```

**4.** Once we have compiled these two classes, we will need to copy them into the Axis web application directory (we used Tomcat 4, but you could also use the `SimpleAxisServer`).

**5.** To deploy the Market web service manually we need the following `MarketDeploy.wsdd` file:

```
<deployment xmlns="http://xml.apache.org/axis/wsdd/"
            xmlns:java="http://xml.apache.org/axis/wsdd/providers/java">
  <service name="Market" provider="java:RPC">
   <parameter name="className" value="com.wrox.jws.stockquote.Market"/>
   <parameter name="allowedMethods" value="getQuote"/>
  </service>
  <beanMapping qname="ns:MarketData"
   xmlns:ns="http://stockquote.jws.wrox.com"
   languageSpecificType="java:com.wrox.jws.stockquote.MarketData"/>
</deployment>
```

**6.** Make sure that Tomcat (or the `SimpleAxisServer`) is running and listening on port 8080, and run the `AdminClient` to deploy the `Market` service as shown below (assuming that `src` is still your current directory):

```
java org.apache.axis.client.AdminClient ..\MarketDeploy.wsdd
```

Here is how it should look:

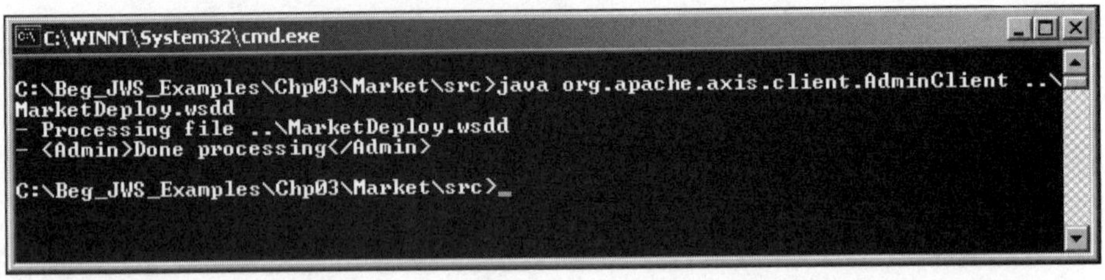

```
C:\WINNT\System32\cmd.exe                                          _□×

C:\Beg_JWS_Examples\Chp03\Market\src>java org.apache.axis.client.AdminClient ..\
MarketDeploy.wsdd
- Processing file ..\MarketDeploy.wsdd
- <Admin>Done processing</Admin>

C:\Beg_JWS_Examples\Chp03\Market\src>_
```

**7.** Our last step is to run the `Market` client with the following command (from either the `Chp03\Market\classes` directory or the `%axisDirectory%\webapps\axis\WEB-INF\classes` directory):

```
java com.wrox.jws.stockquote.Market SUNW
```

**8.** The output should be similar to the following screenshot:

```
C:\WINNT\System32\cmd.exe                                          _□×

C:\Beg_JWS_Examples\Chp03\Market\classes>java com.wrox.jws.stockquote.Market SUN
W
The value of SUNW is: 5.93 (NASDAQ is 1360.62)

C:\Beg_JWS_Examples\Chp03\Market\classes>_
```

### How It Works

Let's have a closer look at the response as it contains the serialization of the `MarketData` class:

```
(HTTP Header omitted from this listing)
<?xml version="1.0" encoding="UTF-8"?>
  <SOAP-ENV:Envelope
    xmlns:SOAP-ENV="http://schemas.xmlsoap.org/soap/envelope/"
    xmlns:xsd="http://www.w3.org/2001/XMLSchema"
    xmlns:xsi="http://www.w3.org/2001/XMLSchema-instance">
    <SOAP-ENV:Body>
      <ns1:getQuoteResponse
        SOAP-ENV:encodingStyle=
          "http://schemas.xmlsoap.org/soap/encoding/"
      xmlns:ns1="Market">
      <getQuoteReturn href="#id0"/>
```

The first part of the listing shows the SOAP header for an RPC return value; it is similar to what we saw in `StockQuote`. The return value is actually a reference to another element in the file, the `href="#id0"` attribute indicates that the element to look for is identified with the `id="id0"` attribute (see below):

```
    </ns1:getQuoteResponse>
    <multiRef id="id0"
      SOAP-ENC:root="0"
      encodingStyle="http://schemas.xmlsoap.org/soap/encoding/"
      xsi:type="ns3:MarketData"
      xmlns:SOAP-ENC="http://schemas.xmlsoap.org/soap/encoding/"
      xmlns:ns2=
        "http://schemas.xmlsoap.org/soap/envelope/:encodingStyle"
      xmlns:ns3="http://stockquote.jws.wrox.com">
```

The `<multiRef/>` element is a placeholder for data that might be referenced multiple times. In this case, however, it is only referenced once in `<getQuoteReturn/>`.

Inside the `<multiRef/>` element, we will find the actual data of the `MarketData` object. The first instance data to get serialized is the array of index values (DOW, NASDAQ, S&P500). Notice that the type of each element is double and that the array encoding is defined as SOAP encoding (`"http://schemas.xmlsoap.org/soap/encoding/"`). Also, the name of the element is the name of our instance data (indices):

```
    <indices xsi:type="SOAP-ENC:Array"
      SOAP-ENC:arrayType="xsd:double[3]">
      <item>9925.25</item>
      <item>1615.73</item>
      <item>1067.14</item>
    </indices>
```

The remaining instance data items are the ticker symbol (string), its value as a double, and the three constants for US market indices. If we want to avoid the serialization of these constants by Axis, we need to remove them from the class definition (marking them as `transient` does not work as of Axis Beta 2):

```
    <ticker xsi:type="xsd:string">sunw</ticker>
    <doubleValue xsi:type="xsd:double">6.89</doubleValue>
    <DOW xsi:type="xsd:string">^DJI</DOW>
    <NASDAQ xsi:type="xsd:string">^IXIC</NASDAQ>
    <SP500 xsi:type="xsd:string">^GSPC</SP500>
  </multiRef>
 </SOAP-ENV:Body>
</SOAP-ENV:Envelope>
```

Let's now review the code of `Market`, `MarketData`, and their deployment descriptor.

We will start with the `Market` class. A quick glance at the code below shows us that the `getQuote()` method is modified to return an instance of `MarketData` rather than a string as we did in `StockQuote`:

```
public MarketData getQuote(String ticker) throws Exception {
  return new MarketData(ticker);
}
```

The input argument is still the same: the ticker symbol of the stock we are interested in. As we mentioned previously, the `MarketData` class contains the ticker symbol, its value, and the values of the major US stock indices:

```
public final class MarketData {

   public String DOW    = "^DJI";
   public String NASDAQ = "^IXIC";
   public String SP500  = "^GSPC";

   String ticker;          // The ticker symbol.
   String stringValue;     // The value of the stock as a string
   double doubleValue;     // The value of the stock as a double
   double indices[];       // The DOW, the NASDAQ, and the S&P 500 values

   ...
   public MarketData(String ticker) throws Exception {
      this.ticker = ticker;

      StockCore stockcore = new StockCore();

      stringValue = stockcore.getQuote(ticker);
      doubleValue = Double.parseDouble(stringValue);
      indices     = new double [3];
      indices[0]  = Double.parseDouble(stockcore.getQuote(DOW));
      indices[1]  = Double.parseDouble(stockcore.getQuote(NASDAQ));
      indices[2]  = Double.parseDouble(stockcore.getQuote(SP500));
   }
```

The development of the `MarketData` class is straightforward thanks to the `StockCore` class that we built earlier. The remainder of the `MarketData` code contains the set and get methods, which follow the JavaBean pattern.

Prior to running the client, we deployed the `Market` web service with the following descriptor. This deployment descriptor is similar to `StockQuote.wsdd`. The key difference is the serialization information contained in the `<beanMapping/>` element:

```
<deployment xmlns="http://xml.apache.org/axis/wsdd/"
  xmlns:java="http://xml.apache.org/axis/wsdd/providers/java">
  <service name="Market" provider="java:RPC">
    <parameter name="className"
      value="com.wrox.jws.stockquote.Market"/>
    <parameter name="allowedMethods" value="getQuote"/>
  </service>
  <beanMapping qname="ns:MarketData"
    xmlns:ns="http://stockquote.jws.wrox.com"
    languageSpecificType=
  "java:com.wrox.jws.stockquote.MarketData"/>
</deployment>
```

The `<beanMapping/>` element contains the necessary information for the **bean serializer** to perform the Java to XML serialization and XML to Java deserialization. It is a helper class provided by Axis to serialize and deserialize instances of classes that follow the JavaBean pattern. For the purpose of this discussion, a JavaBean is a Java class with a public default constructor and (public) set/get methods to set and get the values of instance data. Note that the JavaBean specification also requires the implementation of the `Serializable` interface, but we will not use that interface in this discussion.

That wraps up our final example, but before we finish off the chapter, let's quickly discuss the `<beanMapping/>` element in more detail.

## beanMapping Element

`<beanMapping/>` specifies the following information:

❑ **A QNAME (and its namespace)**
An XML namespace-qualified name (QName) that identifies the element to be serialized and deserialized. In the `Market` web service example the element is
`http://stockquote.jws.wrox.com:MarketData`.

❑ **A language-specific (for example Java or C#) type**
The data type that will be used to represent the element in a specific language, in our case Java.

When the bean serializer needs to generate XML from a Java data structure (serialize), it goes through the following steps:

❑ **Create an XML element for the data structure**
This element is either a place holder (`<multiRef/>`) or bears the same name as the Java data structure (for example `<indices/>`).

❑ **Serialize each data element that supports a get method**
For instance `stringValue`, `doubleValue` in the case of `MarketData`.

When the bean serializer needs to generate a Java data structure from an XML document (deserialize), it goes through the following steps:

❑ **Create a Java class for the XML element**
This is done using the public default constructor.

❑ **Deserialize each data element that supports a set method**
The bean serializer reads the data from the XML document and calls the set method corresponding to the data. For instance, from our previous example, when encountering the `<doubleValue/>` element, it calls the `MarketData.setDoubleValue` to set the value of `MarketData.doubleValue`.

As long as the data being exchanged in SOAP packets can be represented by JavaBeans, they can be serialized and deserialized using the bean serializer. This is the case with most types of data, but sometimes, a bean will not do the job. For instance, if the object that needs to be serialized contains runtime-only data structures like references that would be too expensive to exchange with every call then we might have to write our own serializer. A potential use of **custom serializers** is the optimization of the data being transferred, for instance, we could write a custom serializer for strings that compresses the data when it reaches a certain size.

Before considering the use of a custom serializer, take note of the fact that they have the potential of limiting interoperability. For more detail about custom serializers, please refer to the user's guide that comes with Axis (`%axisDirectory%\docs\users-guide.html`).

# Summary

We have covered a lot of topics in this chapter. After installing Axis, we created a very simple web service called `HelloWorld`. The `HelloWorld` service defines one method, `getQuote()`, which takes a string as its input argument and modifies the input before returning it to the client. We also saw that thanks to the Axis framework and the Java Web Service (JWS) concept, the creation of a web service based on a Java class was a trivial exercise. After deploying and testing the `HelloWorld` service, we used `tcpmon` to look at the SOAP packets as they traveled between the client and the server.

We then downloaded and configured Tomcat to run with Axis as a production-ready replacement for the `SimpleAxisServer`, and tested Tomcat and Axis using `HelloWorld`. We then developed the `StockQuote` web service using a packaged library, namely `StockCore`. This more realistic web service allowed us to introduce Axis deployment descriptors and the flexibility that they provide.

We concluded the chapter with the `Market` example, which returns a structure and an array that can be serialized and de-serialized by the bean serializer provided by Axis.

This chapter has given us enough information to create and deploy our own web services. In the next chapter, we will discuss techniques for describing the features of web services in a platform- and language-independent manner.

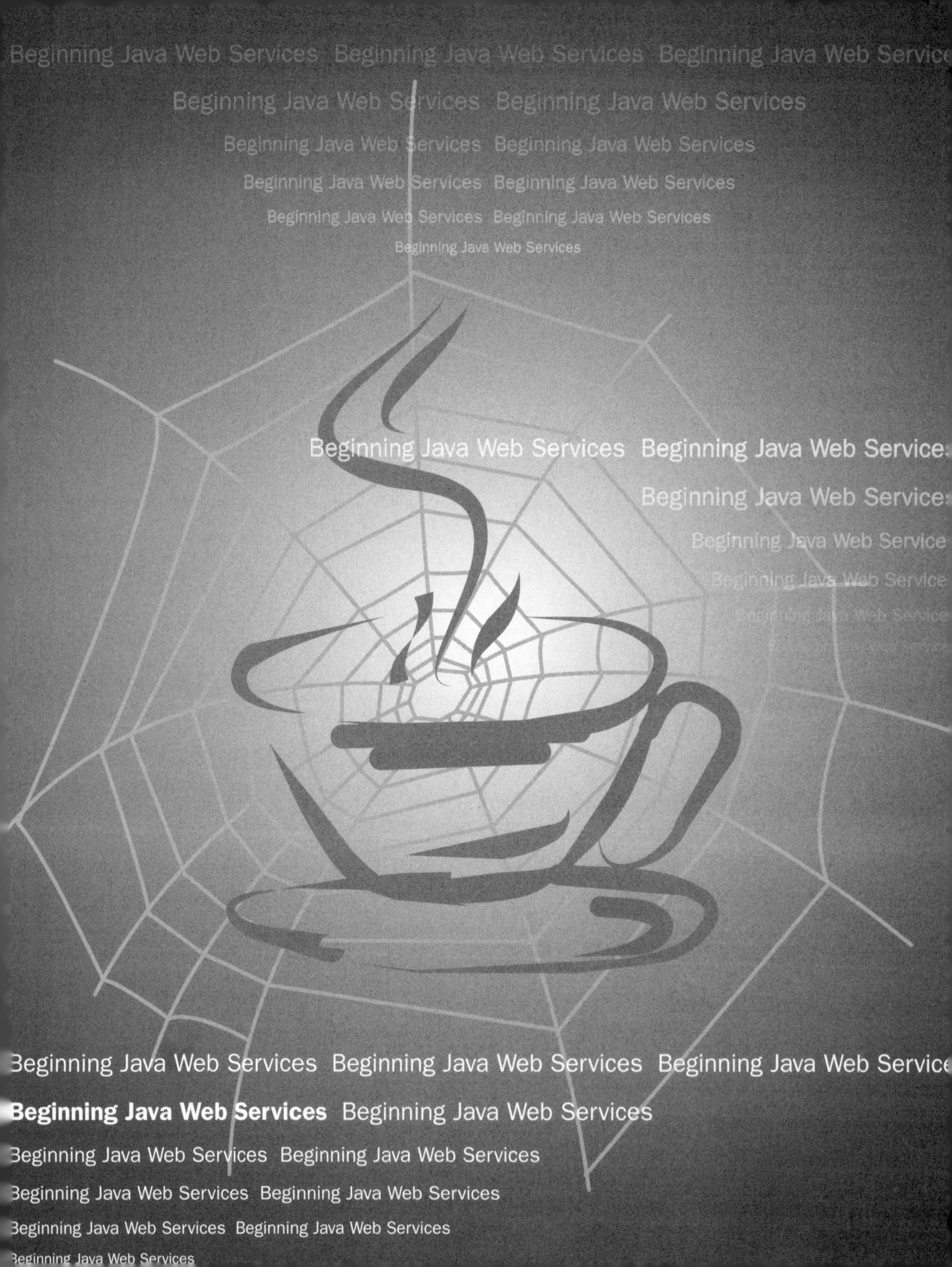
Beginning Java Web Services

# Transferring Data with Web Services

In the previous chapter, we created our own web service using the Remote Procedure Call (RPC) model. More specifically, we designed a Java class named StockQuote with a single method, getQuote(), that we called it over a network using the SOAP protocol. The fact that the data exchanged between the client and server was in the form of an XML document was incidental; in fact we could have used another protocol such as JRMP.

In this chapter, we will take another point of view – we will regard the XML documents that transit between the caller and the web service as essential. This type of SOAP development is called **document-style** SOAP programming.

In this chapter we shall discuss:

- ❏ An overview of document-style SOAP development
- ❏ The Document Object Model (DOM) and the Simple API for XML (SAX) to compare the pros and cons of both models
- ❏ A modified version of StockQuote – Portfolio, which will allow us to illustrate the concepts of document-style SOAP development

Let us begin by comparing RPC and document-style SOAP development.

## RPC versus Document-Style

As shown by the diagrams overleaf, from an external perspective, RPC-style and document-style SOAP development are similar.

❑ **RPC-style SOAP development**
In this, the client makes a remote method call to a web service instantiated on the server. At a macro level, the client submits a SOAP request and gets a SOAP response:

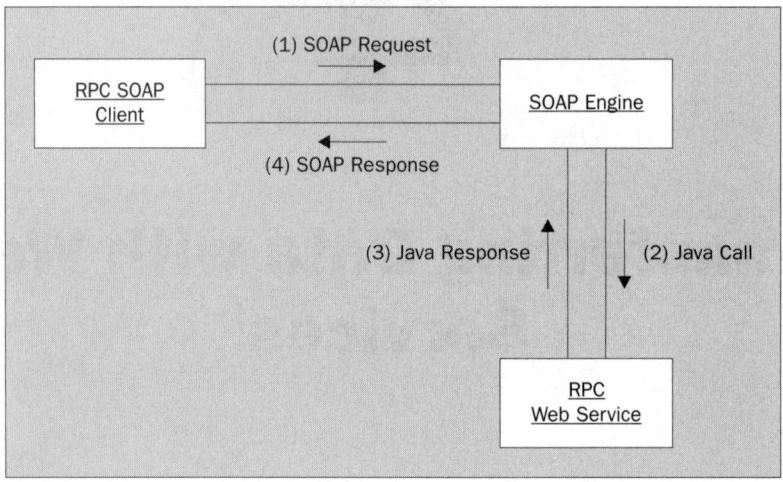

❑ **Document-style SOAP development**
In this, the client submits an XML document to a web service instantiated on the server. Here also, at a macro level, the client submits a SOAP request and gets a SOAP response:

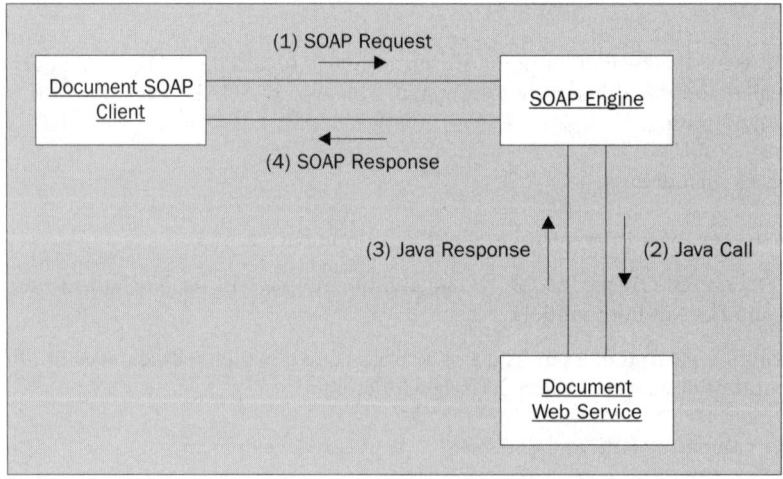

However, when we look at them from an internal perspective, things are different.

❑ **RPC-style SOAP development:**

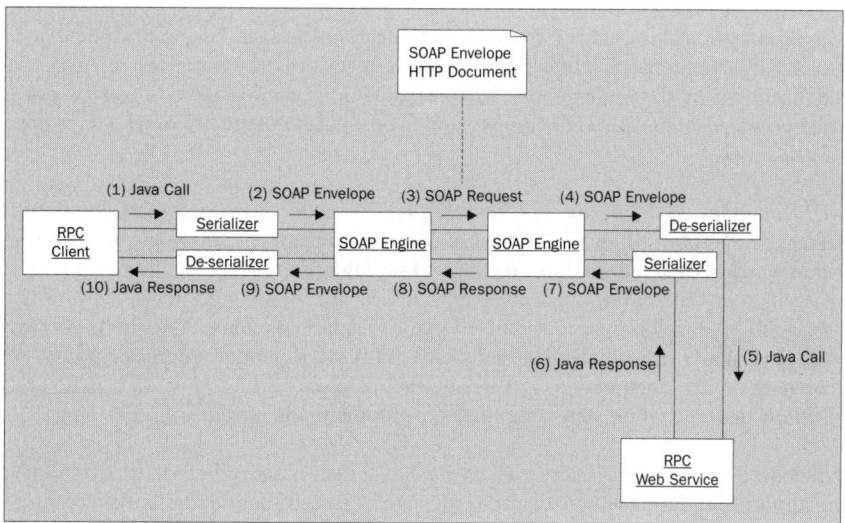

❑ **Document-style SOAP development:**

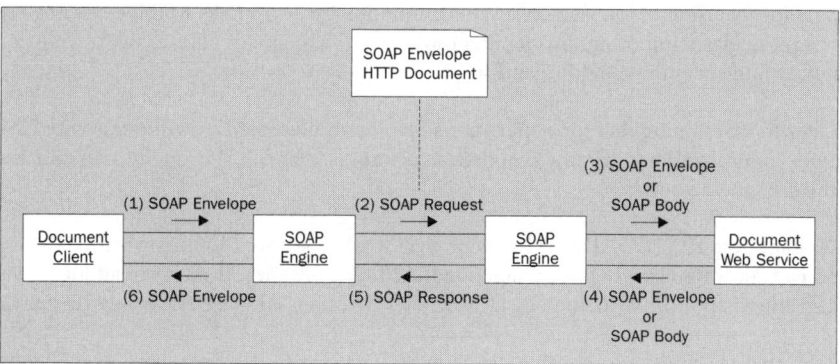

The main differences between these two are:

❑ **Serialization and Deserialization**
In document-style SOAP development, the client does not need to serialize a Java call and its arguments into an XML document. Conversely, the server does not need to deserialize the XML document into a Java call and data types.

❑ **Semantic**
In RPC-style SOAP development, the client and the server are forced to adhere to a well-defined programming model – the client calls a method with possible arguments, and the server returns one value as a response. In document-style, an XML document is exchanged and the meaning of each element is left to the interpretation of the participants. In addition, the client and the web service can bundle multiple documents in the request and the response.

**135**

By looking at the last two diagrams, we can also infer that the reliance on the SOAP engine is minimized when using the document-style model. This simplification of the SOAP infrastructure is mostly due to the absence of a serialization engine.

As there is no serialization/deserialization process, applications designed using document-style ought to be faster than their RPC counterparts. However, that is not necessarily the case; one can argue that in document-style, the serialization is up to the developer, since at some point we will have to convert our Java data into XML and vice-versa. Also, the XML documents involved can be potentially much larger than the simple request-response types.

Now that we have reviewed the distinctions between RPC and document-style development, it is appropriate to ask ourselves the question, when should we use them? Unfortunately, there are no easy rules that we can apply to decide which style to adopt; but there are a few guidelines.

Document-style SOAP development is at home when we want to exchange data between two or more parties. This is particularly true when we already have an XML document representing the data as we can simply exchange the XML document as-is, without having to convert it to Java data structures. The removal of the serialization/deserialization steps simplifies development and speeds up processing.

Another application that lends itself very well to the use of document-style SOAP development is a data transforming application. For instance, consider the case of a customer database that contains names and addresses, but no demographic information like income, family size, neighborhood type, and so on. In order to improve our knowledge of the customers, we can submit their records to a demographic data enhancement service, which will return the customer data along with the desired demographics. We can then process the enhanced data for inclusion in our database. This methodology also works well for keeping records up-to-date, which is particularly important for demographic data that changes constantly (people get married, have children, move up the economic ladder, and so on).

Finally, it is worth mentioning that for applications that manipulate XML documents with XSLT, having an XML document is preferable to having Java data structures since an XSLT engine can automatically transform the document.

On the other hand, the RPC SOAP development style works very well if the problem can easily be modeled with method calls or if we already have a functional API. For instance, if we were adding a web service access layer to a distributed application written in DCOM or RMI, then RPC SOAP would be our first choice.

Later on in the chapter, when we examine the code of our `Portfolio` example, we will look at creating and parsing an XML document. But before bringing the discussion to a practical level, we must discuss the support provided by Axis for document-style SOAP development.

The easiest way to get more familiar with document-style SOAP development is to try it out with an example.

# The StockQuote Deployment

In Chapter 3, we deployed the `StockQuote` web service using the `AdminClient` provided by Axis where we simply submitted an XML document to Axis for processing:

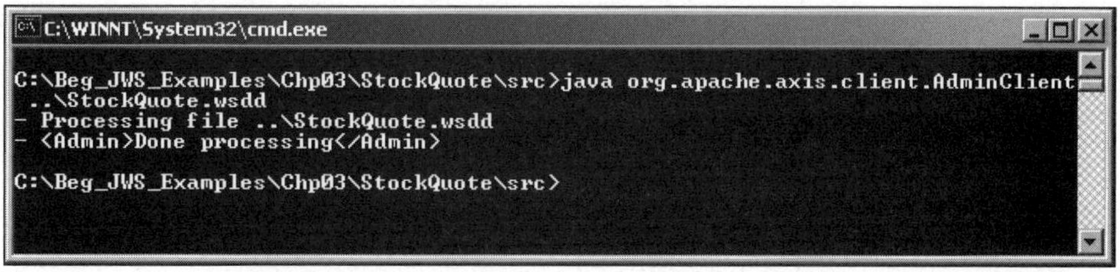

```
C:\WINNT\System32\cmd.exe                                               _ □ ×

C:\Beg_JWS_Examples\Chp03\StockQuote\src>java org.apache.axis.client.AdminClient
..\StockQuote.wsdd
- Processing file ..\StockQuote.wsdd
- <Admin>Done processing</Admin>

C:\Beg_JWS_Examples\Chp03\StockQuote\src>
```

In other words, we are already familiar with document-style processing since we used it in the submission of a deployment descriptor. Note that only the deployment/un-deployment of the StockQuote web service is considered document-style SOAP programming; the StockQuote service uses the RPC model.

This simple example shows us that document-style SOAP development is more natural than we might think. If we were to re-design the deployment descriptors with an RPC API, we would have to define an interface that supports the dynamic nature of deployment descriptors. This interface would then involve arrays, variable number of arguments, and possibly method overloading, thus making it more complicated than its document-style counterpart.

If we have an XML background, we will be more likely to favor the simple XML schema over an informal description of Java methods (such as Javadoc) with several special cases. This last point touches on another characteristic of document-style SOAP development – XML documents are typically more expressive and therefore more succinct than their RPC counterparts. We will illustrate these points when we review the Portfolio example.

To take a closer look at what is happening here, we will have to talk in more detail about how deployment descriptors are handled in Axis.

In the SOAP request for the deployment of StockQuote, the portion shown below is passed to the service:

```
POST /axis/services/AdminService HTTP/1.0
Content-Length: 587
Host: localhost
Content-Type: text/xml; charset=utf-8
SOAPAction: "AdminService"

<?xml version="1.0" encoding="UTF-8"?>
<SOAP-ENV:Envelope
xmlns:SOAP-ENV="http://schemas.xmlsoap.org/soap/envelope/"
xmlns:xsd="http://www.w3.org/2001/XMLSchema"
xmlns:xsi="http://www.w3.org/2001/XMLSchema-instance">
  <SOAP-ENV:Body>
    <deployment
      xmlns="http://xml.apache.org/axis/wsdd/"
      xmlns:java="http://xml.apache.org/axis/wsdd/providers/java">
      <service name="StockQuote" provider="java:RPC">
        <parameter name="className"
          value="com.wrox.jws.stockquote.StockQuote"/>
        <parameter name="allowedMethods" value="getQuote"/>
      </service>
    </deployment>
  </SOAP-ENV:Body>
</SOAP-ENV:Envelope>
```

The actual document that is typically processed by a web service is the document fragment residing inside the `<deployment>` element (more on that in a moment):

```
<deployment
  xmlns="http://xml.apache.org/axis/wsdd/"
  xmlns:java="http://xml.apache.org/axis/wsdd/providers/java">
  <service name="StockQuote" provider="java:RPC">
    <parameter name="className"
      value="com.wrox.jws.stockquote.StockQuote"/>
    <parameter name="allowedMethods" value="getQuote"/>
  </service>
</deployment>
```

If we look closely at the HTTP header of the previous SOAP request, we will see that the target web service is `AdminService()`, which is an Axis built-in web service that handles the deployment and un-deployment of web services.

Since our goal is to discuss document-style support in Axis, we don't need to know about all the intricacies of the `AdminService()` implementation. For our discussions, we are only concerned about the method that handles the incoming requests (deployment and un-deployment descriptors). As indicated by the `SOAPAction` in the HTTP header, this method bears the same name as its class (this is not always the case):

```
public Element[] AdminService(Vector xml) throws Exception
```

The signature of the `AdminService()` method contains one argument, `java.util.Vector`, and returns one array of `org.w3c.dom.Element` objects. This might look surprising at first, as we might have expected to see something along the lines of:

```
public Document AdminService (Document document) throws Exception
```

As a matter of fact, this second signature was a perfect fit; it was the signature of document-style web services in early versions of Axis. However, this signature had two shortcomings:

❏ **Only one document is passed in**
If we go back to the SOAP specification, we will see that it is perfectly legal to pass more than one XML document as part of a SOAP packet. With the second `AdminService()` signature, only one document is passed to the web service.

❏ **Only one document is returned**
Same problem as mentioned previously, but with the return value. If we pass more than one document as input, we might expect to return more than one document.

The remainder of `AdminService()` contains few surprises (the `MessageContext` is used by Axis to keep track of the state of a message):

```
MessageContext msgContext = MessageContext.getCurrentContext();
log.debug(JavaUtils.getMessage("enter00", "Admin:AdminService"));
Document doc = process( msgContext, (Element) xml.get(0) );
```

The process() method handles the deployment descriptor. We can see above that the first element of the vector is passed to the process() method. In other words, if we were to send multiple deployment descriptors as part of the SOAP message, only the first one would be treated. The return value of the process is an org.w3c.dom.Document that we convert to an org.w3c.dom.Element, since it is the return type expected by Axis:

```
Element[] result = new Element[1];
result[0] = doc.getDocumentElement();
log.debug(JavaUtils.getMessage("exit00", "Admin:AdminService") );
return result;
}
```

*The class that contains the call to the* AdminService() *method is* org.apache.axis.providers.java.MsgProvider. MsgProvider *is the built-in provider for document-style web services in Axis.* RPCProvider *is the same package that we used in the previous chapter. It is the built-in provider for RPC-style web services.*

Before looking at a more complete example, let's mention that Axis also supports a special form of document-style web services, called **full message service**. With full message service, not only the content of the SOAP body, but also the entire SOAP envelope is passed to the callback method. This description sheds some light on the difference between the client and the server that we saw in the earlier diagram – the client submits a SOAP envelope, full message services are handed a SOAP envelope, and other services deal with the SOAP body.

In the next section we will demonstrate and review the main example of this chapter, Portfolio.

# Portfolio

To illustrate document-style SOAP development, we will develop a Portfolio example. This application is a refinement of the StockQuote example, which we wrote in the previous chapter. The Portfolio example supports three basic features:

❑   The user of the service can add stocks to their portfolio

❑   The user of the service can remove stocks from their portfolio

❑   The user of the service can get the status of their portfolio

The following figure illustrates the flow of data in the Portfolio application. Predictably, it follows the structure that we described earlier for document-style development. The Portfolio example is not a full message service; it only deals with the body that is inside its root element <portfolio/>:

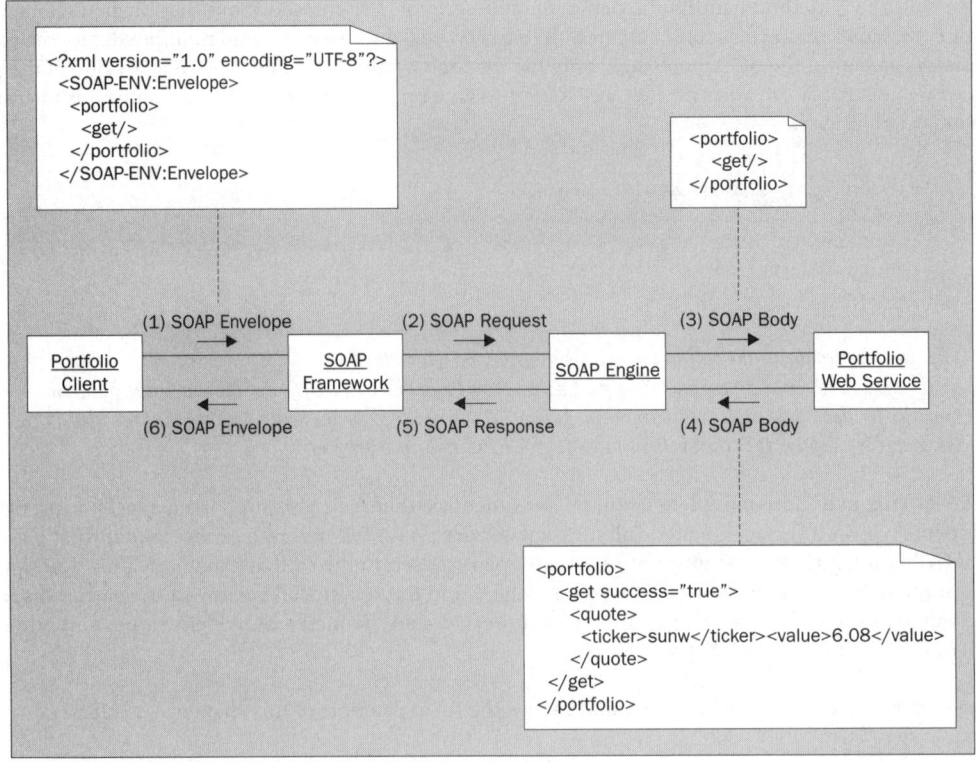

Since it is an example, in the interest of keeping the discussion focused on document-style SOAP development, we have introduced a few limitations in it. The main restrictions are:

❑ The application does not provide a GUI; it only provides a command line interface to modify and retrieve the portfolio. The portfolio is displayed in raw XML.

❑ The portfolio is not persistent; in other words, if the serverside of the SOAP engine (for example, the SimpleAxisServer or Catalina) is restarted, we will lose our portfolio.

❑ The application supports only one portfolio.

Note that, these restrictions have little to do with SOAP development and will not interfere with our main objective of describing the issues faced by a SOAP developer in working with the document-style paradigm.

## Try It Out – Portfolio Example

Trying out the Portfolio sample is similar to what we did for StockQuote: we need to compile, deploy, and test the web service.

**1.** Here is the entire implementation of Portfolio:

```java
package com.wrox.jws.stockquote;

import java.util.Vector;
import java.util.Set;
import java.util.HashSet;
import java.util.Collections;
import java.util.Iterator;

import java.net.URL;

import javax.xml.parsers.DocumentBuilderFactory;
import javax.xml.parsers.DocumentBuilder;

import org.apache.axis.client.Call;
import org.apache.axis.client.Service;
import org.apache.axis.message.SOAPEnvelope;
import org.apache.axis.message.SOAPBodyElement;
import org.apache.axis.utils.XMLUtils;

import org.w3c.dom.Document;
import org.w3c.dom.Element;
import org.w3c.dom.Node;
import org.w3c.dom.NodeList;

import com.wrox.jws.stockcore.StockCore;

public class Portfolio {
    // The valid commands from the user. These are also the valid XML elements
    final static String addCommand    = "add";
    final static String removeCommand = "remove";
    final static String getCommand    = "get";

    // Attribute to be added to commands to give a status; might be true/false
    final static String successAttribute = "success";

    final static String nameSpaceURI = "Portfolio"; // portfolio ns URI
    final static String portfolioTag = "portfolio"; // Root of the document
    final static String tickerTag = "ticker"; // A ticker inside add or remove
    final static String quoteTag = "quote";    // A quote (response to a get)
    final static String valueTag = "value";    // A value (inside a quote)

    // Our (simplistic) portfolio
    static Set portfolioSet = Collections.synchronizedSet(new HashSet());

    /**
     * Creates a <quote/> element with the values passed in. The result should
     * look like the following XML:
     *     <quote>
     *        <ticker>ticker</ticker>
     *        <value>value</value>
     *     </quote>
     *
     * This method is used internally to build the document fragment returned
```

```
 * by the <get/> command.
 *
 * @param document the document that will contain the element
 * @param tickerName the ticker symbol for the stock (e.g. sunw)
 * @param tickerValue the value of the stock (e.g. 100.00)
 * @return the newly created <quote/> element
 */
private static Element createQuote(Document document,
    String tickerName, String tickerValue) {

  // Create the elements and text nodes
  Element quote      = document.createElement(quoteTag);
  Element ticker     = document.createElement(tickerTag);
  Element value      = document.createElement(valueTag);
  Node    nameText   = document.createTextNode(tickerName);
  Node    valueText  = document.createTextNode(tickerValue);

  // Create the hierarchy
  ticker.appendChild(nameText);
  value.appendChild(valueText);
  quote.appendChild(ticker);
  quote.appendChild(value);

  return quote;
}

/**
 * Process a set of commands. The valid commands are:
 *   <get/>
 *   <add><ticker>ticker1</ticker>...<ticker>tickern</ticker></add>
 *   <remove><ticker>ticker1</ticker>...<ticker>tickern</ticker></remove>
 *
 * The output document depends on the input commands. For add and remove,
 * we simply echo the command with the attribute success="true". For the
 * get command, we list the portfolio using the following format:
 *   <get success="true">
 *     <quote>
 *       <ticker>ticker1</ticker>
 *       <value>value1</value>
 *     </quote>
 *     ...
 *     <quote>
 *       <ticker>tickern</ticker>
 *       <value>valuen</value>
 *     </quote>
 *   </get>
 *
 * @param command the command in the form of an xml document
 * @return the resulting XML document
 */
public static Element[] portfolio(Vector xmlDocument) throws Exception {

  Document requestMessage =
```

```
        ((Element)xmlDocument.get(0)).getOwnerDocument();
    Document responseMessage = (Document)requestMessage.cloneNode(true);

    Element[] result = new Element[1];
    result[0] = portfolio(requestMessage.getDocumentElement(),
      responseMessage.getDocumentElement());

    return result;
}

/**
 * Called by the public version of portfolio. Useful for testing as
 * inproc.
 *
 * @param requestElement the <portfolio/> element of the request
 * @param requestElement the <portfolio/> element of the response
 * @return the modified requestElement
 */
private static Element portfolio(Element requestElement,
    Element responseElement) throws Exception {

  // We traverse the document and process each command as we go
  NodeList nodes = responseElement.getChildNodes();
  for(int nodeIndex = 0; nodeIndex < nodes.getLength(); nodeIndex++) {
    Node currentNode = nodes.item(nodeIndex);

    if(currentNode instanceof Element) { // Ignore anything else
      Element commandElement = (Element)currentNode;
      String  commandName    = commandElement.getTagName();
      boolean success        = true;

      if(commandName.equals(addCommand) ||
         commandName.equals(removeCommand)) {
        // We get the list of ticker symbols to add/remove
        NodeList tickerNodes = commandElement.getChildNodes();
        for(int tickerIndex = 0; tickerIndex < tickerNodes.getLength();
            tickerIndex++) {
          Node currentTickerNode = tickerNodes.item(tickerIndex);
          if(currentTickerNode instanceof Element) {
            Element tickerTag  = (Element)currentTickerNode;
            String  tickerName = tickerTag.getFirstChild().getNodeValue();

            // Add/Remove the ticker to/from the list. We do not return an
            // error for non-exisitent ticker symbols.
            if(commandName.equals(addCommand)) {
              portfolioSet.add(tickerName);
            } else { // remove
              portfolioSet.remove(tickerName);
            }
          }
        }
      } else if(commandName.equals(getCommand)) {
        Iterator tickers = portfolioSet.iterator();
```

```
            StockCore stockcore = new StockCore();
            // We loop on the ticker symbols passed in and add the value
            while(tickers.hasNext()) {
              String  tickerName  = (String)tickers.next();
              String  tickerValue = stockcore.getQuote(tickerName);
              Element quote       =
                        createQuote(responseElement.getOwnerDocument(),
                                    tickerName, tickerValue);

              // Be sure to add the quote element as a child of the command
              commandElement.appendChild(quote);
            }
          } else {
            // Unknown command, we mark it as failure
            success = false;
          }

          commandElement.setAttribute(successAttribute,
            new Boolean(success).toString());
        }
      }

  return responseElement;
}

/**
 * Display usage information and leave.
 *
 * @arg error Error message
 */
private static void usage(String error) {
  System.err.println("Portfolio Client: " + error);
  System.err.println(
    "  Usage        : java com.wrox.jws.stockquote.Portfolio "
    + "<command> [<ticker-symbols>]");
  System.err.println(
    "  Valid Commands: add, remove, get; get takes no ticker symbols.");
  System.err.println(
    "  Examples: java com.wrox.jws.stockquote.Portfolio get");
  System.err.println(
    "            : java com.wrox.jws.stockquote.Portfolio add sunw msft ");
  System.exit(1);
}

/**
 * The main is a client test for the Portfolio service. It modifies the
 * portfolio with the stocks passed in as arguments using the add an
 * remove commands in the XML document submitted to server. It also gets
 * the status of the portfolio with the get command, which takes no
 * argument.
 *
 * @param args The command and the ticker symbols (e.g. sunw msft ibm)
```

```java
    */
    public static void main(String [] args) {
      final String methodName = "Portfolio.main";

      try {
        // Validate the arguments
        if(args.length < 1) {
          usage("Please specify one command: add, remove, or get.");
        } else if(args[0].equals(addCommand) ||
                  args[0].equals(removeCommand)) {
          if(args.length == 1) {
            usage(
              "You need to specify at least one ticker for add and remove.");
          }
        } else if(args[0].equals(getCommand)) {
          if(args.length > 1) {
            usage("You may not specify any ticker for get.");
          }
        } else {
          usage("Unknown command: " + args[0] + ".");
        }

        // We create an XML document for the request.
        // We start by creating a parser
        DocumentBuilderFactory documentBuilderFactory = null;
        DocumentBuilder        parser                 = null;

        // We need a namespace-aware parser
        documentBuilderFactory = DocumentBuilderFactory.newInstance();
        documentBuilderFactory.setNamespaceAware(true);
        parser = documentBuilderFactory.newDocumentBuilder();

        // We create the document for the request (the XML document that will
        // be embedded inside the SOAP body).
        Document document = parser.newDocument();
        Element  element  = document.getDocumentElement();

        // The <portfolio/> element is the root of our document;
        Element requestElement = document.createElementNS(nameSpaceURI,
                                        portfolioTag);
        Element command        = document.createElement(args[0]);

        requestElement.appendChild(command);

        // We add the list of ticker symbols
        for(int index = 1; index < args.length; index++) {
          Element ticker = document.createElement(tickerTag);

          ticker.appendChild(document.createTextNode(args[index]));
          command.appendChild(ticker);
        }

        // Unless the command is a get, we add the get command
```

```
        if(!args[0].equals(getCommand)) {
            requestElement.appendChild(document.createElement(getCommand));
        }

        Element result = null;
        boolean local = false;  // set to true for local test (inproc)

        if(local) {
            // Local test, no SOAP
            result = portfolio(requestElement,
                (Element)requestElement.cloneNode(true));
        } else {
            // We create a SOAP request to submit the XML document to the
            // server. You might need to replace the following URL with what is
            // suitable for your environment
            String  endpointURL =
                    "http://localhost:8080/axis/servlet/AxisServlet";
            Service service      = new Service();
            Call    call         = (Call)service.createCall();

            // Create a SOAP envelope to wrap the newly formed document
            SOAPEnvelope    requestEnvelope = new SOAPEnvelope();
            SOAPBodyElement requestBody     =
                            new SOAPBodyElement(requestElement);
            requestEnvelope.addBodyElement(requestBody);

            // Set the endpoint URL (address we are talking to) and method name
            call.setTargetEndpointAddress(new URL(endpointURL));
            call.setSOAPActionURI(portfolioTag); // method name = tag name

            // Submit the document to the remote server
            SOAPEnvelope responseEnvelope = call.invoke(requestEnvelope);

            // Get the <portfolio/> element from the response
            SOAPBodyElement responseBody =
                (SOAPBodyElement)responseEnvelope.getBodyElements().get(0);
            result = responseBody.getAsDOM();
        }

        // Display the output
        System.out.println("Document from server: ");
        XMLUtils.PrettyElementToStream(result, System.out);
    } catch (Exception exception) {
        System.err.println(methodName + ": " + exception.toString());
        exception.printStackTrace();
    }
  }
}
```

2. Compiling `Portfolio.java` is also similar (you can refer to Chapter 3 for a discussion about the classpath). Assuming that `src` is the current directory, the following command will compile `Portfolio.java`:

```
javac -d ..\classes Portfolio.java
```

**3.** The `Portfolio.class` file needs to find its way into the `classes` directory of our Axis installation as shown in the following screenshot:

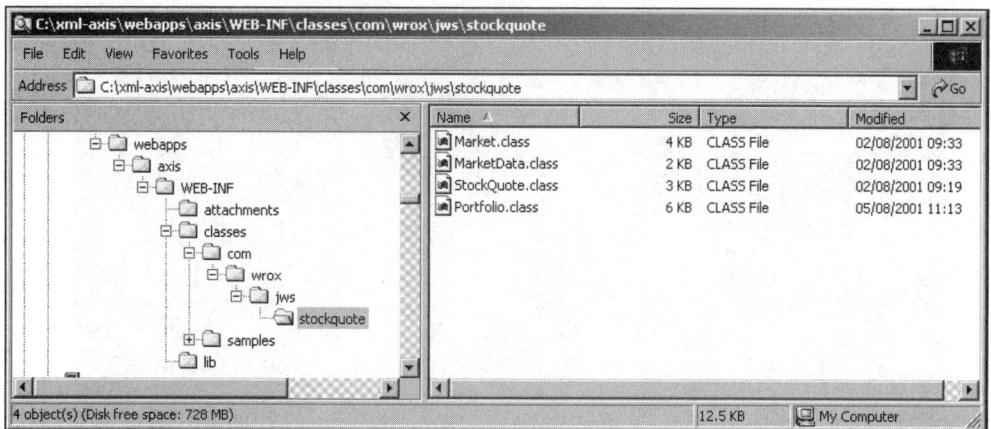

Also, make sure the `stockcore.jar` is in the `lib` directory.

**4.** Now, we need to deploy the `Portfolio` web service:

```
java org.apache.axis.client.AdminClient ..\Portfolio.wsdd
```

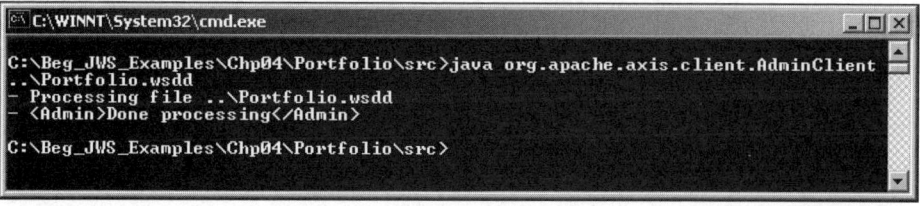

The `Portfolio.main()`, our test client, takes the following commands as arguments:

❑ `add`
This command adds a stock to the portfolio. It takes one argument: the symbol of the stock to add.

❑ `remove`
This command removes a stock from the portfolio. It takes one argument: the symbol of the stock to remove.

❑ `get`
This command returns the portfolio with the stock values. It takes no parameter.

**5.** Here is the command for adding `SUNW`, `MSFT`, and `IBM` to the portfolio:

```
java com.wrox.jws.stockquote.Portfolio add SUNW MSFT IBM
```

**6.** The following screenshot shows the results of the execution on a Windows machine:

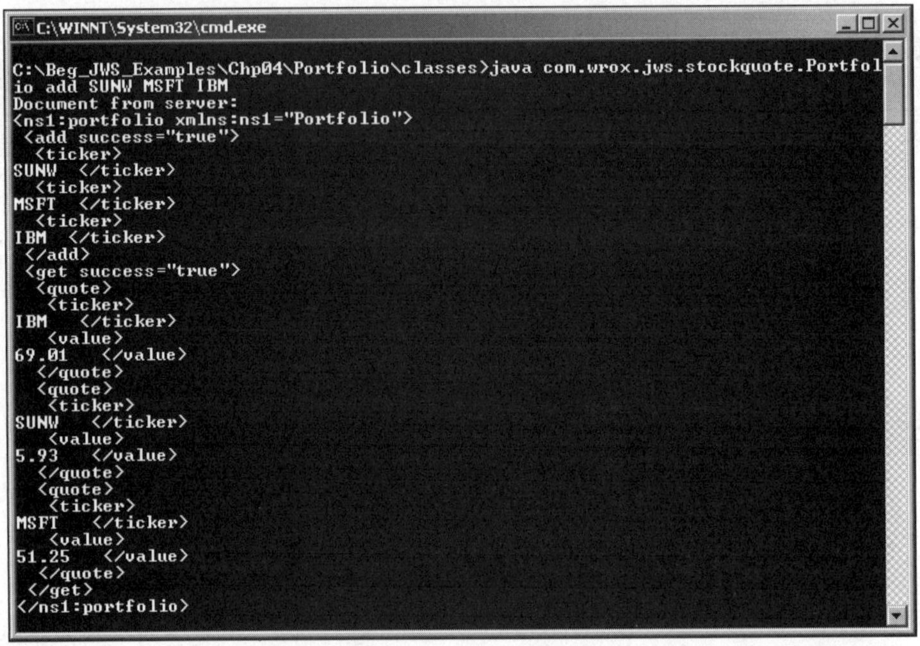

### How It Works

`Portfolio.main()` sends the following SOAP request to the server:

```
POST /axis/servlet/AxisServlet HTTP/1.0
Content-Length: 330
Host: localhost
Content-Type: text/xml; charset=utf-8
SOAPAction: "portfolio"

<?xml version="1.0" encoding="UTF-8"?>
<SOAP-ENV:Envelope xmlns:SOAP-ENV="http://schemas.xmlsoap.org/soap/envelope/"
xmlns:xsd="http://www.w3.org/2001/XMLSchema"
xmlns:xsi="http://www.w3.org/2001/XMLSchema-instance">

<SOAP-ENV:Body>
  <ns1:portfolio xmlns:ns1="Portfolio">
    <add>
      <ticker>SUNW</ticker><ticker>MSFT</ticker><ticker>IBM</ticker>
    </add>
    <get/>
  </ns1:portfolio>
</SOAP-ENV:Body>
</SOAP-ENV:Envelope>
```

As you can see, the request is a simple XML document, which is based on the specified command-line parameters. The `<get/>` element is always added by the client when the `add` or `remove` commands are given as input. This allows the user to see the effect of the command without having to resubmit an additional XML document to the server.

The response from the server contains the response document wrapped in a SOAP envelope and an HTTP response (the document has been slightly modified for presentation):

```
HTTP/1.1 200 OK
Content-Type: text/xml; charset=utf-8
Content-Length: 517
Date: Thu, 13 Jun 2002 13:45:40 GMT
Server: Apache Tomcat/4.0.3 (HTTP/1.1 Connector)

<?xml version="1.0" encoding="UTF-8"?>
<SOAP-ENV:Envelope xmlns:SOAP-ENV="http://schemas.xmlsoap.org/soap/envelope/"
xmlns:xsd="http://www.w3.org/2001/XMLSchema"
xmlns:xsi="http://www.w3.org/2001/XMLSchema-instance">
  <SOAP-ENV:Body>
    <ns1:portfolio xmlns:ns1="Portfolio">
      <add success="true">
        <ticker>SUNW</ticker><ticker>MSFT</ticker><ticker>IBM</ticker>
      </add>
      <get success="true">
        <quote><ticker>SUNW</ticker><value>5.93</value></quote>
        <quote><ticker>MSFT</ticker><value>51.25</value></quote>
        <quote><ticker>IBM</ticker><value>69.01</value></quote>
      </get>
    </ns1:portfolio>
  </SOAP-ENV:Body>
</SOAP-ENV:Envelope>
```

As you can see, the response document is similar to the request document. If we look at the `<add/>` and `<get/>` elements, we can see that the `Portfolio` web service added the attribute `success="true"` to inform the requester that the transaction was a success. The inner data of the `<add/>` element is identical to the request, but the `<get/>` element contains the value of the stocks we are interested in.

> *Note that in the interest of brevity, the* `Portfolio` *web service could have removed the inner data of the* `<add/>` *element. Another fact worth noting about the documents that are exchanged between the client and the server is the absence of type information; this is because of the implicit contract between the participants. The type information is optional.*

The existence of a more formal contract than a simple RPC paradigm is what usually allows document-style SOAP to be more expressive and therefore reduces the amount of information that has to be exchanged for the dialog to be successful.

Note that after running the previous command, we will get the same output from the `get` command since the stocks have been stored in the portfolio (the value of stocks might change):

```
java com.wrox.jws.stockquote.Portfolio get
```

```
C:\WINNT\System32\cmd.exe                                    _ □ ×
C:\Beg_JWS_Examples\Chp04\Portfolio\classes>java com.wrox.jws.stockquote.Portfol
io get
Document from server:
<ns1:portfolio xmlns:ns1="Portfolio">
 <get success="true">
  <quote>
   <ticker>
IBM   </ticker>
   <value>
69.01   </value>
  </quote>
  <quote>
   <ticker>
SUNW   </ticker>
   <value>
5.93   </value>
  </quote>
  <quote>
   <ticker>
MSFT   </ticker>
   <value>
51.25   </value>
  </quote>
 </get>
</ns1:portfolio>
```

The XML document for the get command contains only one element inside <portfolio/> (the SOAP
envelope and body are not shown):

```
...
<ns1:portfolio xmlns:ns1="Portfolio"><get/></ns1:portfolio>
...
```

Let's now review the Portfolio code.

We use DOM and JAXP to parse the request and build the response (please refer to Chapter 2 for an
introduction to JAXP and DOM):

```
import javax.xml.parsers.DocumentBuilderFactory;
import javax.xml.parsers.DocumentBuilder;
```

We will rely on the Axis API on the client side and on the server side. We will get into the specifics shortly.
The actual stock quote values will be provided by StockCore.

As you can see in the implementation, the Portfolio class contains several constants that will come in
handy when we build and parse the XML documents. Their meaning should be self-explanatory.

The next line of code contains the declaration of the back-end data store for our portfolio. As we said
previously, no mention is made of persistence. Note that since it is our only (non final) data structure that will
survive from call to call, it is worth synchronizing it. This saves us from having to manually protect the
statements that modify the back-end store. Also we are using a set since in our sample it does not make much
sense to ask for the same stock quote more than once:

```
// Our (simplistic) portfolio
static Set portfolioSet = Collections.synchronizedSet(new HashSet());
```

The next method requires a short preamble. We have seen that in response to a `get` command, `Portfolio` returns a list of `<quote/>` elements, one for each stock in the portfolio. The `createQuote()` method creates a `<quote/>` element for a specific document. We have to pass the target document as an input argument since it is not legal to create an element with one document and insert it in another. The `createQuote()` method returns a reference to the newly created `<quote/>` element, which is now ready for insertion inside a `<get/>` element:

```
private static Element createQuote(Document document,
String tickerName, String tickerValue) {

// Create the elements and text nodes
Element quote    = document.createElement(quoteTag);
Element ticker   = document.createElement(tickerTag);
Element value    = document.createElement(valueTag);
Node nameText  = document.createTextNode(tickerName);
Node valueText = document.createTextNode(tickerValue);

// Create the hierarchy
ticker.appendChild(nameText);
value.appendChild(valueText);
quote.appendChild(ticker);
quote.appendChild(value);

return quote;
```

The next method, which is simply called `portfolio()`, is at the core of the interface between Axis and a document-style web service. You will notice that its structure is similar to what we saw in the `Admin` web service. Here are the steps performed by `portfolio()`:

**1.** Extract the XML document passed by the user from the first element of the vector. Once again, only one document is processed per request.

**2.** Create the response document. In this case, we simply clone the request since the schema of the request is (very) similar to the schema of the response.

**3.** Call an overloaded version of the `portfolio` method, which returns an `Element`.

**4.** Wrap the `Element` inside an array and return it to Axis for inclusion inside a SOAP envelope.

The code structure is as follows:

```
public static Element[] portfolio(Vector xmlDocument)throws Exception {

  Document requestMessage  =
    ((Element)xmlDocument.get(0)).getOwnerDocument();
  Document responseMessage = (Document)requestMessage.cloneNode(true);

  Element[] result = new Element[1];
  result[0] = portfolio(requestMessage.getDocumentElement(),
  responseMessage.getDocumentElement());

  return result;
}
```

The next method is a private version of `portfolio()` that takes two arguments – the element of the request document and the element of the response document. Its return value is superfluous since it returns the (hopefully modified) request element:

```
private static Element portfolio(Element requestElement,
    Element responseElement) throws Exception {
```

The algorithm implemented by `portfolio` is straightforward:

❑ Traverse the child elements of `<portfolio/>` in the response document, which at the beginning, is identical to the request document.

❑ Process commands as they are encountered and add the necessary child elements (`<quote/>`) and create a `success` (Boolean) attribute.

The following loop traverses each command:

```
// We traverse the document and process each command as we go
NodeList nodes = responseElement.getChildNodes();
for(int nodeIndex = 0; nodeIndex < nodes.getLength(); nodeIndex++) {
  Node currentNode = nodes.item(nodeIndex);
```

For each command, we test if it is an `Element`. In other words, we ignore any text inside `<portfolio/>` and outside the children elements.

```
if(currentNode instanceof Element) {  // Ignore anything else

  Element commandElement = (Element)currentNode;
  String commandName = commandElement.getTagName();
  boolean success = true;
```

The `add` and `remove` commands are handled in the same block of code, as their processing is similar. For this, we need to extract the ticker symbol from the `<ticker/>` element and modify the portfolio data structure with a `Set.add()` and `Set.remove()` respectively:

```
if(commandName.equals(addCommand) ||
    commandName.equals(removeCommand)) {
  // We get the list of ticker symbols to add/remove
  NodeList tickerNodes = commandElement.getChildNodes();
  for(int tickerIndex = 0; tickerIndex < tickerNodes.getLength();
      tickerIndex++) {
    Node currentTickerNode = tickerNodes.item(tickerIndex);
    if(currentTickerNode instanceof Element) {
      Element tickerTag  = (Element)currentTickerNode;
      String  tickerName = tickerTag.getFirstChild().getNodeValue();

      // Add/Remove the ticker to/from the list. We do not return an
      // error for non-exisitent ticker symbols.
      if(commandName.equals(addCommand)) {
        portfolioSet.add(tickerName);
      } else { // remove
        portfolioSet.remove(tickerName);
      }
    }
  }
}
```

To process the `get` command, we simply loop over the ticker symbols defined in the portfolio, get the quote using `StockCore`, and add a `<quote/>` element with the help of the `createQuote()` method that we reviewed earlier:

```
    } else {
      if(commandName.equals(getCommand)) {
          Iterator tickers = portfolioSet.iterator();

          // We loop on the ticker symbols passed in and add the
          //value
          while(tickers.hasNext()) {
            String  tickerName  = (String)tickers.next();
            String  tickerValue = StockCore.getQuote(tickerName);
            Element quote =
            createQuote(responseElement.getOwnerDocument(),
            tickerName, tickerValue);

            // Be sure to add the quote element as child of the
            // command
            commandElement.appendChild(quote);
          }
      } else { // Unknown command, we mark it as failure
        success = false;
      }
```

Any other command is unknown so we mark it with `success="false"`. The statement below sets the success attribute to the value held by the variable `success` (`true` or `false`):

```
      commandElement.setAttribute(successAttribute,
        new Boolean(success).toString());
    }
  }

  return responseElement;
}
```

This completes the definition of the `Portfolio` web service. The remainder of the quote contains the implementation of the test client.

The `usage()` method that displays help about the command-line arguments is self-explanatory:

```
private static void usage(String error) {
  System.err.println("Portfolio Client: " + error);
  System.err.println(
    " Usage          : java com.wrox.jws.stockquote.Portfolio "
    + "<command> [<ticker-symbols>]");
  ...
```

The main task of the client is to build the XML document that constitutes the request. We will, once again, use DOM and its Xerces implementation to achieve this objective.

The beginning part of the `main()` method simply collects the arguments from the user and exits with an error message, in case it does not like what was passed to it.

Things start getting more appealing when we begin to build the document. As we can see below, we need to have a namespace-aware parser (this is not the default). This requirement comes from our `<portfolio/>` that is qualified with the `Portfolio` namespace (the full request was listed earlier) – `<ns1:portfolio xmlns:ns1="Portfolio">`.

```
// We create an XML document for the request. We start by creating
// a parser
DocumentBuilderFactory documentBuilderFactory = null;
DocumentBuilder        parser                 = null;

// We need a namespace-aware parser
documentBuilderFactory = DocumentBuilderFactory.newInstance();
documentBuilderFactory.setNamespaceAware(true);
parser = documentBuilderFactory.newDocumentBuilder();
```

Armed with a parser, we can now build a document. Things are not as easy as they were in the server case, as we do not have a document that we can morph into the request. Note that it would be a valid alternative design to start with two literal documents for add and remove and modify them to add the ticker symbols passed as arguments. In that implementation, we would read the documents into a DOM and transform them using the `org.w3c.dom` API as we did for the web service.

After creating a document, we get a hold of its element and use it to append the command element (`<add/>` or `<remove/>`) that we create using the document:

```
// We create the document for the request (the XML document that
// will be embedded inside the SOAP body).
Document document = parser.newDocument();
Element  element  = document.getDocumentElement();

// The <portfolio/> element is the root of our document;
Element requestElement =
   document.createElementNS(nameSpaceURI, portfolioTag);
Element command        = document.createElement(args[0]);
requestElement.appendChild(command);
```

Our next task is to create the list of `ticker` symbols for the command. This code should look familiar since it is similar to what we did on the server side, when we created the list of tickers based on the portfolio data structure:

```
// We add the list of ticker symbols
for(int index = 1; index < args.length; index++) {
  Element ticker = document.createElement(tickerTag);
  ticker.appendChild(document.createTextNode(args[index]));
  command.appendChild(ticker);
}

// Unless the command is a get, we add the get command
if(!args[0].equals(getCommand)) {
  requestElement.appendChild(document.createElement(getCommand));
}
```

As we mentioned earlier and as seen in the statement above, we also add a `<get/>` element (command), unless the user gave us a `get` command to begin with.

If we look below, we will see that we have a `boolean` variable to differentiate between a local test and a remote test. This is useful to save time during development and easy to achieve thanks to our private version of portfolio:

```
Element result = null;
boolean local = false;  // set to true for local test (inproc)

if(local) {
  // Local test, no SOAP
  result = portfolio(requestElement,
  (Element)requestElement.cloneNode(true));
} else {
```

The case that requires our attention is the remote case. This code is not very different from the `StockQuote` client that we developed in Chapter 3. The main difference is that we add the request element, `<portfolio/>`, to the SOAP body via the Axis `SOAPBodyElement`:

```
// We create a SOAP request to submit the XML document to the
// server. You might need to replace the following URL with
// what is suitable for our environment
String  endpointURL =
  "http://localhost:8080/axis/servlet/AxisServlet";
Service service = new Service();
Call call = (Call)service.createCall();

// Create a SOAP envelope to wrap the newly formed document
SOAPEnvelope    requestEnvelope = new SOAPEnvelope();
SOAPBodyElement requestBody     =
  new SOAPBodyElement(requestElement);
requestEnvelope.addBodyElement(requestBody);

// Set the endpoint URL (address we are talking to) and
// method name
call.setTargetEndpointAddress(new URL(endpointURL));
call.setSOAPActionURI(portfolioTag); // method name = tag name
```

In the document-style version of a SOAP call, we pass the envelope to the `Call` object and we get an envelope back as a result, or an exception when things go awry:

```
// Submit the document to the remote server
SOAPEnvelope responseEnvelope = call.invoke(requestEnvelope);
```

We extract the `<portfolio/>` element from the response. Once again, it would be legal to have a response with more than one root element. We then assign the DOM of the response to the result variable. The remainder of the code displays the DOM and handles any exception thrown our way:

```
// Get the <portfolio/> element from the response
SOAPBodyElement responseBody =
  (SOAPBodyElement)responseEnvelope.getBodyElements().get(0);
result = responseBody.getAsDOM();
...
```

The deployment descriptor for `Portfolio`, `Portfolio.wsdd` looks a lot like `StockQuote.wsdd` that we introduced in the previous chapter:

```
<deployment xmlns="http://xml.apache.org/axis/wsdd/"
    xmlns:java="http://xml.apache.org/axis/wsdd/providers/java">
<service name="Portfolio" provider="java:MSG">
  <parameter name="className"
    value="com.wrox.jws.stockquote.Portfolio"/>
  <parameter name="allowedMethods" value="portfolio"/>
</service>
</deployment>
```

> *To deploy a document-style web service as a full message web service, add the*
> `FullMessageService` *parameter to our deployment descriptor*
> `<parameter name="FullMessageService" value="true" />`.

Aside from the class name and the allowed method, the provider is different – `provider="java:MSG"`. In the case of RPC, the provider was `provider="java:RPC"`. The `java:MSG` attribute value tells Axis to instantiate an `org.apache.axis.providers.java.MsgProvider` object. The main task of the `MsgProvider.processMessage()` method, the only method defined in `MsgProvider`, is to instantiate our class, extract the document from the SOAP envelope, and pass it to our method. In the case of a full message service, the SOAP envelope is passed as-is.

This concludes our review of the `Portfolio` class. Before closing this chapter on document-style SOAP development, it is worth spending a few lines discussing our XML parsing strategy.

# SAX versus DOM

In the `Portfolio` example, both on the client and server side, we manipulated the XML document using DOM, which provided us with an easy-to-use interface. However, this facility comes with one noteworthy disadvantage – the entire document must be loaded in memory. If the document is very large, this requirement might significantly hamper the performance of our application.

The preferred way to handle large documents is to use the Simple API for XML (SAX) that we covered in Chapter 2. The methodology used by SAX is radically different from that of DOM – we register a callback class that implements the `org.xml.sax.DocumentHandler` interface, and, for document-related events, methods of this interface get called by the parser (for example, the beginning or the end of an element).

A similar methodology could be implemented as part of Axis, where we would get a callback function with a stream as input argument and a stream as output argument. Alas, at the time of this writing, such support does not exist in Axis. If our application needs to handle large XML documents, our best bet is to write a servlet that uses SAX to parse the requests and document fragments.

# Summary

Document-style SOAP development differs from RPC-style in a significant way. In the RPC model, the client is bound to the procedure call paradigm, whereas in the document-style model, the client is bound to what can be expressed through an XML document. This freedom requires a contract that defines the semantics of the requests and responses.

Practically, the implementation of a document-style web service requires the implementation of a callback method that uses the DOM for its input arguments and return value. We first looked at the structure of the `Admin` web service to see how a document-style web service interfaces with Axis. We then wrote a modified version of the `StockQuote` example, `Portfolio`, which used the document-style model as an interface to a simplistic portfolio management application. We also made extensive use of the DOM to create and manipulate the request and the response.

We concluded the chapter by briefly discussing the drawbacks of using the DOM and mentioned a SAX-based servlet as an alternative.

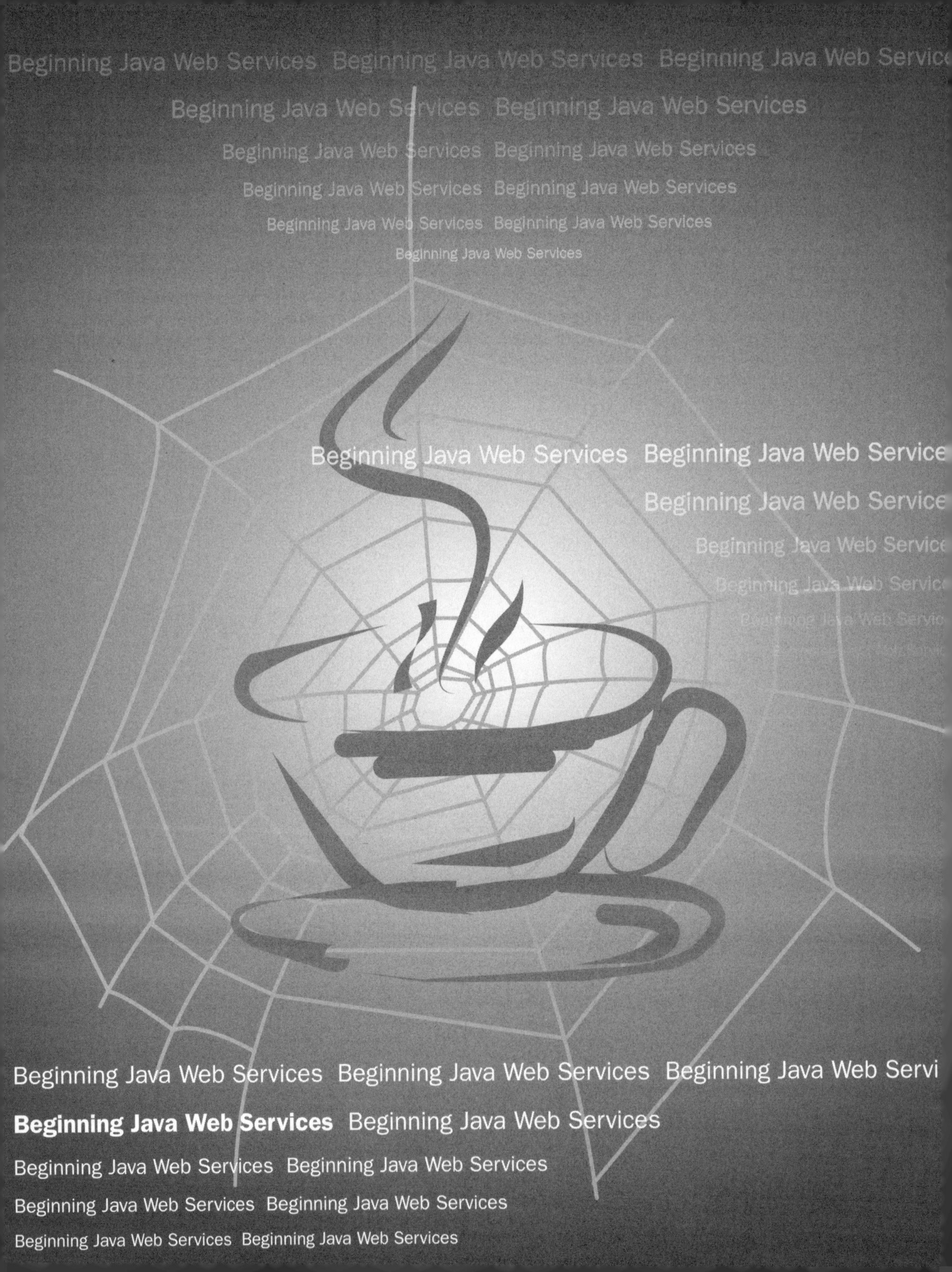
Beginning Java Web Services Beginning Java Web Services Beginning Java Web Service
Beginning Java Web Services Beginning Java Web Services
Beginning Java Web Services Beginning Java Web Services
Beginning Java Web Services Beginning Java Web Services
Beginning Java Web Services Beginning Java Web Services
Beginning Java Web Services
Beginning Java Web Services Beginning Java Web Service
Beginning Java Web Service
Beginning Java Web Service
Beginning Java Web Servic
Beginning Java Web Services Beginning Java Web Services Beginning Java Web Servi
Beginning Java Web Services Beginning Java Web Services
Beginning Java Web Services Beginning Java Web Services
Beginning Java Web Services Beginning Java Web Services
Beginning Java Web Services Beginning Java Web Services

# Describing Web Services

One of the major goals of web services is to provide a framework for electronic commerce (e-commerce) or electronic business (e-business). This framework is made up of official standards such as HTTP, HTML, and XML. In this context, 'official' implies international organizations such as the **World Wide Web Consortium** (W3C) with enough clout to entice developers to use them. The framework is also made of standards that have been proposed to organizations such as the W3C. SOAP, which we have spent some time describing in the first part of this book, is one such standard.

As we saw in the earlier chapters, SOAP has been designed to encode **Remote Procedure Calls** (RPC) or XML documents for their transit over a network. **Interoperability** or encoding data to be processed by remote computers is not the goal, but mandatory for successful e-commerce. The description and publication capabilities of a web service are as important as the actual processing of the data and its encoding.

To ensure a wide acceptance, the description of web services must conform to some standard. Without some agreement among buyers and sellers of web services, it would be close to impossible for a consumer to compare the services of two or more providers. The criteria that immediately come to mind, are name, description, and price.

Apart from this, the protocols used for calling a web service are equally important. Does the service support SOAP or is it simply accessible via HTTP GET? Does the service only support HTTP or does it support SMTP as well? These questions are fundamental when it comes to choosing one web service over another. It would do us no good to select a web service based on a better price if that service did not support the only protocol we are familiar with.

Usually, software vendors provide some textual description of what their products are capable of achieving. This human-readable description of a product is poorly suited for automated processing. A more formal description is needed for computer programs to make sense of it. It is also important to remember that we do not want to forgo the benefits of a human-readable description. The **Web Services Description Language** (WSDL) is an attempt at addressing this dual need.

In a nutshell, WSDL defines an XML dialect to describe the capabilities of a web service.

The use of XML is a reasonable balance between a machine-readable and a human-readable document.

We hinted earlier that a description is necessary but not sufficient. As a web service developer, we would be hard pressed to sell our components if we had no place to advertise them. The UDDI specification proposes an answer to this. We will discuss UDDI and other publishing technologies available to web services in Chapter 7.

In this chapter:

❑ We will start with a high-level view of the specification of a web service. Here, we will describe the WSDL top-level elements.

❑ We will then go from theory to practice by looking at a WSDL document that describes our simple StockQuote web service.

❑ We will then look into a complex version of this web service, which uses more complex data structures such as arrays and custom data types.

❑ We will also review a brief example that shows how client-side development is eased with the use of WSDL.

Let's begin with an overview of WSDL.

# WSDL Overview

*The specification for WSDL can be found at http://www.w3.org/TR/wsdl.*

As we mentioned previously, WSDL provides a description of a web service in terms of **endpoints** and the **messages** traveling to and from the endpoints. A more intuitive way of looking at a WSDL document is to state that it answers four questions about a web service:

❑ **What do you do?**
This question is answered both in machine-readable and human-readable forms. The human-readable answers can be found in the <name/> and <documentation/> elements. The answer in machine-readable terms comes from the <message/> and the <portType/> elements.

❑ **What language do you speak?**
What data types do you use? This question is answered using the <types/> elements.

❑ **How do I talk to you?**
How does a client talk to the service? HTTP? SMTP? This question is answered using the <binding/> elements.

❑ **Where do I find you?**
Where can I find this web service? What is its URL? The answer is in the <service/> elements.

The following figure shows a high-level picture of the WSDL specification:

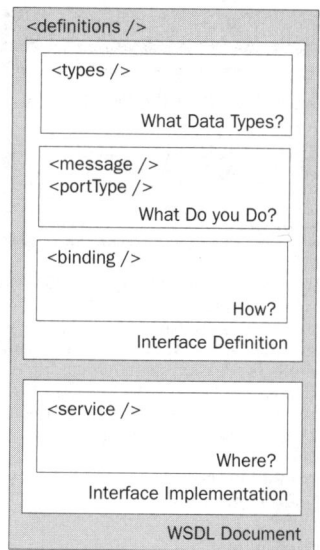

Instead of describing each WSDL element in abstract terms, we will look at the WSDL that describes the StockQuote web service developed in Chapter 3 (the instructions for building, deploying, and testing StockQuote can be found in Chapter 3 along with the code).

# A WSDL Document for StockQuote

Instead of writing a WSDL document from scratch, we will use the tools provided by Axis to generate the WSDL document from our Java class as shown below:

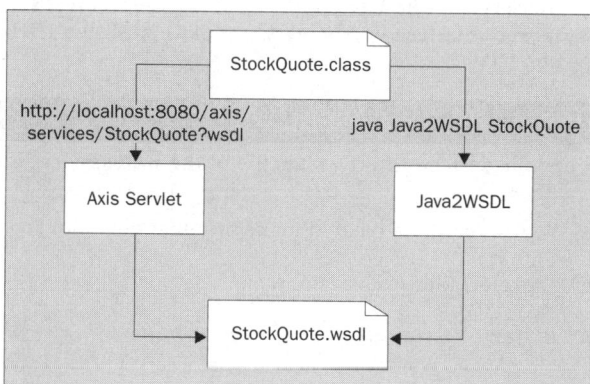

As we can see from the diagram, there are two ways to generate a WSDL document from an existing web service. We will be looking at both methods as they each have their pros and cons. Let's start with the Axis servlet.

## Try It Out – Generate WSDL Using the Axis Servlet

The easiest way to generate a WSDL document for a web service deployed with Axis is to navigate to the http://<server-name>/services/<service-name>?wsdl URL as shown in the screenshot:

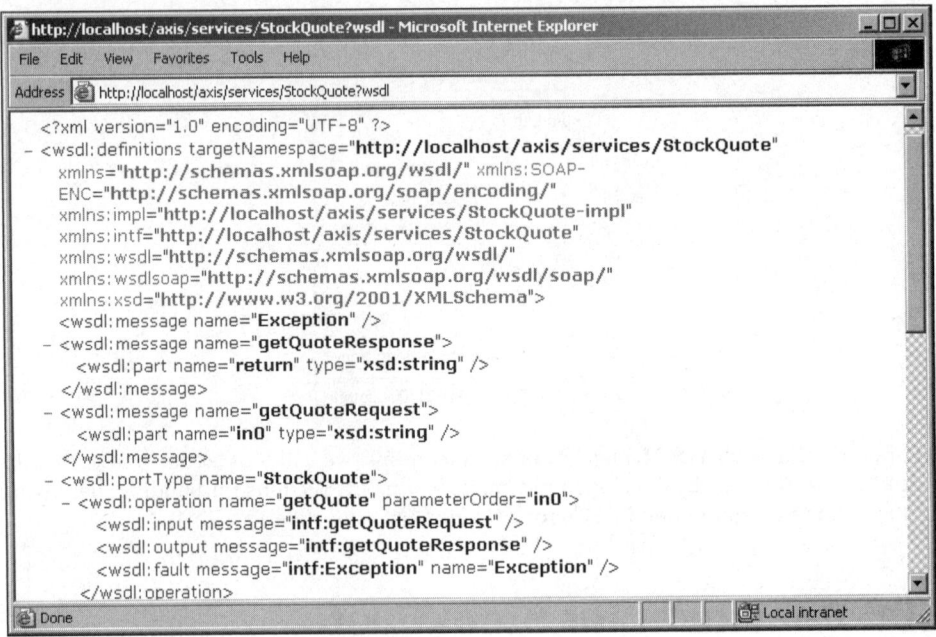

### How It Works

When the Axis servlet detects the `?wsdl` trailer on a valid web service URL, it generates the WSDL based on the class file of the service. The URL trailer is not case sensitive, so `?WsDl` works just as well. This built-in support in the web interface will be very useful to publish a URL for the description of a web service in a registry like UDDI.

## Try It Out – Generate WSDL with Java2WSDL

In this second method, one needs access to the class file of the web service to use the `Java2Wsdl` tool.

**1.** Prior to running `Java2Wsdl`, we need to make sure that the following files are in our classpath:

The Xerces (XML parser) files:
```
xercesImpl.jar
xmlParserAPIs.jar
```

The JAR files distributed with Axis (see Chapter 3 for more details):
```
axis.jar
commons-logging.jar
tt-bytecode.jar
jaxrpc.jar
```

The WSDL for Java package contains the WSDL to Java and Java to WSDL classes that we use in this chapter. It comes with Axis and can be found in the `lib` directory with the other JAR files distributed with Axis:
`wsdl4j.jar`

The `.class` file (not the `.java` file) of the `StockQuote` example that we developed in Chapter 3:
`StockQuote`

**2.** Here is the `Java2WSDL` command for creating the `StockQuote.wsdl` file:

```
java org.apache.axis.wsdl.Java2WSDL com.wrox.jws.stockquote.StockQuote
-l http://localhost:8080/axis/services/StockQuote
```

**3.** Now we can check whether the `StockQuote.wsdl` file has been created:

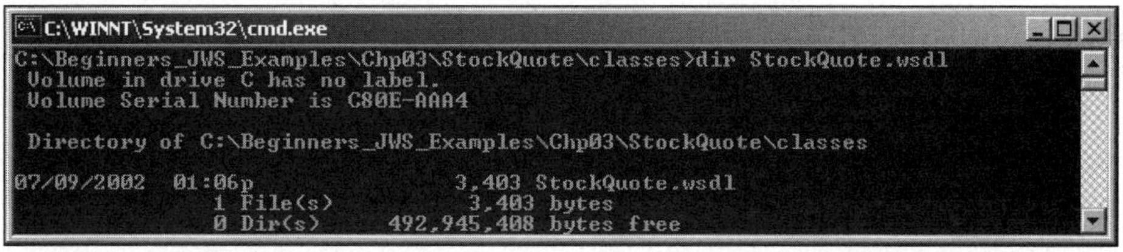

```
C:\WINNT\System32\cmd.exe                                           _ □ ×
C:\Beginners_JWS_Examples\Chp03\StockQuote\classes>dir StockQuote.wsdl
Volume in drive C has no label.
Volume Serial Number is C80E-AAA4

Directory of C:\Beginners_JWS_Examples\Chp03\StockQuote\classes

07/09/2002  01:06p               3,403 StockQuote.wsdl
               1 File(s)         3,403 bytes
               0 Dir(s)    492,945,408 bytes free
```

Be sure to indicate the actual location (`-l http://...`) of the service since it is not available in the class file. The `Java2Wsdl` supports more options, which we can see by running the class without any command-line arguments.

Regardless of the methodology that we use to generate the WSDL document, the result will be the same as shown below. It would be a good idea to take a few moments to go through that document and compare it to the high-level block diagram shown earlier in this chapter. Do not focus on the details for now; have a look at the elements and their high-level meanings as stated in the block diagram:

```
<?xml version="1.0" encoding="UTF-8"?>

<wsdl:definitions
  targetNamespace="http://localhost/axis/services/StockQuote"
  xmlns="http://schemas.xmlsoap.org/wsdl/"
  xmlns:SOAP-ENC="http://schemas.xmlsoap.org/soap/encoding/"
  xmlns:impl="http://localhost/axis/services/StockQuote-impl"
  xmlns:intf="http://localhost/axis/services/StockQuote"
  xmlns:wsdl="http://schemas.xmlsoap.org/wsdl/"
  xmlns:wsdlsoap="http://schemas.xmlsoap.org/wsdl/soap/"
  xmlns:xsd="http://www.w3.org/2001/XMLSchema">
<wsdl:message name="Exception"/>

<wsdl:message name="getQuoteRequest">
  <wsdl:part name="in0" type="xsd:string"/>
</wsdl:message>
```

```
        <wsdl:message name="getQuoteResponse">
          <wsdl:part name="return" type="xsd:string"/>
        </wsdl:message>

        <wsdl:portType name="StockQuote">
          <wsdl:operation name="getQuote" parameterOrder="in0">
            <wsdl:input message="intf:getQuoteRequest"/>
            <wsdl:output message="intf:getQuoteResponse"/>
            <wsdl:fault message="intf:Exception" name="Exception"/>
          </wsdl:operation>
        </wsdl:portType>

        <wsdl:binding name="StockQuoteSoapBinding" type="intf:StockQuote">
          <wsdlsoap:binding style="rpc"
            transport="http://schemas.xmlsoap.org/soap/http"/>
          <wsdl:operation name="getQuote">
            <wsdlsoap:operation soapAction=""/>
            <wsdl:input>
              <wsdlsoap:body
                encodingStyle="http://schemas.xmlsoap.org/soap/encoding/"
                namespace="http://localhost/axis/services/StockQuote"
                use="encoded"/>
            </wsdl:input>

            <wsdl:output>
              <wsdlsoap:body
                encodingStyle="http://schemas.xmlsoap.org/soap/encoding/"
                namespace="http://localhost/axis/services/StockQuote"
                use="encoded"/>
            </wsdl:output>
          </wsdl:operation>
        </wsdl:binding>

        <wsdl:service name="StockQuoteService">
          <wsdl:port binding="intf:StockQuoteSoapBinding" name="StockQuote">
            <wsdlsoap:address
              location="http://localhost/axis/services/StockQuote"/>
          </wsdl:port>
        </wsdl:service>
      </wsdl:definitions>
```

We shall now explain the different elements in this WSDL document section by section.

# The definitions Element

The root of every WSDL document is the `<definitions/>` element. In other words, a WSDL document is simply a list of definitions. As we can see from the document, the `<definitions/>` element defines several namespaces and each namespace corresponds to:

```
targetNamespace="http://localhost/axis/services/StockQuote"
```

The `targetNamespace` is the namespace of our web service. When we look at the `<types/>` element, we will see that it allows the **XML Schema** contained in a WSDL document to refer to itself. As is always the case with namespaces, a document does not necessarily exist at the specified URL.

*XML Namespaces and Schema were introduced in Chapter 2.*

The default namespace of our document is `http://schemas.xmlsoap.org/wsdl/`:

```
xmlns="http://schemas.xmlsoap.org/wsdl/"
```

It is the namespace used to reference WSDL elements, like `<definitions/>` or `<portType/>`. Note that in our example, the default namespace is redefined with the prefix `wsdl`. In other words, `<portType/>` is equivalent to `<wsdl:portType/>` in this document. The namespace used to describe SOAP encoding is `http://schemas.xmlsoap.org/soap/encoding`:

```
xmlns:SOAP-ENC="http://schemas.xmlsoap.org/soap/encoding/"
```

For example, if we wanted to specify that an array should be encoded using SOAP encoding, we would qualify the encoding with (`SOAP-ENC:Array`). We will see an example of array encoding later in the chapter.

The next attributes define the implementation and definition namespaces for `StockQuote`:

```
xmlns:impl="http://localhost/axis/services/StockQuote-impl"
xmlns:intf="http://localhost/axis/services/StockQuote"
```

Conceptually, a web service can be separated into two WSDL files:

❑ Document for the definition of the interface of the web service (elements `<types/>`, `<message/>`, `<portType/>`, and `<bindings/>`)

❑ Document for the implementation of the web service (element `<service/>`)

For simplicity, we will use only one file here, and consequently we will only work with the `http://localhost/axis/services/StockQuote` namespace, prefixed with `intf`:

```
xmlns:wsdlsoap="http://schemas.xmlsoap.org/wsdl/soap/"
xmlns:xsd="http://www.w3.org/2001/XMLSchema">
```

The remaining two namespaces are for SOAP elements (`<body/>`) and XML Schema definition elements (`<xsd:string/>`).

Note that the `<definitions/>` element can also define the name of the service via the `name` attribute:

```
...
<wsdl:definitions
  name="StockQuote"
  targetNamespace="http://localhost/axis/services/StockQuote"
  xmlns="http://schemas.xmlsoap.org/wsdl/"
...
```

However, the `Java2WSDL` class does not generate that attribute.

Let's conclude this review of the `<definitions/>` root element by mentioning that WSDL also supports a `<document/>` element for the definition of a human-readable description of the web service. For instance, the following modification of our WSDL document is valid:

```
<?xml version="1.0" encoding="UTF-8"?>

<wsdl:definitions
...
   xmlns:xsd="http://www.w3.org/2001/XMLSchema">
   <wsdl:document>
     The StockQuote service provides near real-time stock quote
     at a very   affordable price.
   </wsdl:document>
...
```

# The message Element

The `<message/>` element gives information about the data that travels from one endpoint to another. More specifically, the `<message/>` element depicts a **one-way message** (more on this later). To describe an RPC method call, one needs an **input message** and an **output message**. This becomes obvious if we look at the WSDL generated by Axis:

```
...
   <wsdl:message name="getQuoteRequest">
     <wsdl:part name="in0" type="xsd:string"/>
   </wsdl:message>

   <wsdl:message name="getQuoteResponse">
     <wsdl:part name="return" type="xsd:string"/>
   </wsdl:message>
...
```

The `getQuote()` method is described in terms of a request (the method call) and a response (the return value). Messages are grouped into operations that can be compared to Java methods, and these operations are grouped into port types that can be compared to Java classes.

The name of the `<message/>` element simply provides a unique identifier (within the document) for the one-way message. Each argument of the call is described with the `<part/>` element. Like all WSDL elements, it can be qualified by a unique name. To have `Java2WSDL` generate part names with meaningful names rather than the `in0`, `in1` that we have in our document, we can use a class file compiled with debug information (that is by using `javac -g` rather than `javac`). For instance, `in0` would be replaced by `ticker`:

```
...
   <wsdl:message name="getQuoteRequest">
     <wsdl:part name="ticker" type="xsd:string"/>
   </wsdl:message>
...
```

The most important attribute here is the `type` attribute; it specifies an XML Schema data type. More precisely, the value of the `type` attribute must be a namespace-qualified XML Schema element, also known as **QName**. In this particular case, we use the `xsd` (XML Schema Definition) prefix, which refers to `http://www.w3.org/2001/XMLSchema`, the XSD namespace. We can also use our own data type definitions.

> *Beware of tools that are still using older XML schema namespaces like `http://www.w3.org/1999/XMLSchema`, because they might be the source of interoperability problems. Typically the solution is to manually edit the WSDL file and replace the older namespace with the 2001 version.*

The `getQuote()` method defines only one argument. Consequently, the `<message/>` element in our WSDL document contains only one `<part/>` element. If the method signature contains multiple elements, we can simply specify multiple `<part/>` elements. For instance, consider the following variation of `getQuote()`:

```
public void getQuotes(String ticker1, String ticker2);
```

It would be described by the following WSDL `<message/>` element:

```
<wsdl:message name="getQuoteRequest">
  <wsdl:part name="ticker1" type="xsd:string"/>
  <wsdl:part name="ticker2" type="xsd:string"/>
</wsdl:message>
```

Let's see how messages can be grouped to form **port types** and **operations**.

# The portType Element

The `<portType/>` element describes and defines the operations (or methods) supported by the web service. Operations can have `input` messages, `output` messages, and `fault` messages. In our example, we have an RPC call that has one `input` message, one `output` message, and one `fault` message:

```
...
<wsdl:portType name="StockQuote">
  <wsdl:operation name="getQuote" parameterOrder="in0">
    <wsdl:input message="intf:getQuoteRequest"/>
    <wsdl:output message="intf:getQuoteResponse"/>
    <wsdl:fault message="intf:Exception" name="Exception"/>
  </wsdl:operation>
</wsdl:portType>
...
```

Note that the `input`, `output`, and `fault` messages must specify a message that is defined elsewhere in the WSDL document (for example `getQuoteRequest()`). As mentioned before, the `<portType/>` element can roughly be compared to the concept of a Java class. It would be more correct to compare a port type to an interface since a port type only defines operations (methods), and not instance data.

> *The order of definitions is not relevant in a WSDL document. For instance, we can define an operation that refers to a message defined later in the document.*

WSDL supports four modes of operations:

- **One-way**

  A message is sent to an endpoint of the service. For instance, a client sends a message to a web service via SMTP or calls a method with a `void` return type over HTTP. In this case, only an input message appears in the operation:

- **Request-Response**

  This mode of operation is the most common. In this case, an `input`, an `output`, and an optional `fault` element appear in the operation. A non-void method call like `getQuote()` is an example of a request-response operation:

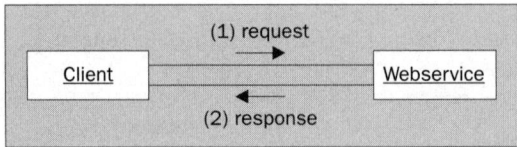

- **Solicit-Response**

  In this transmission mode, the endpoint is the client of another endpoint. The format of the operation is similar to the request-response mode, but the output is listed before the input. A possible use of this mode is an advertisement to which different clients can send different responses:

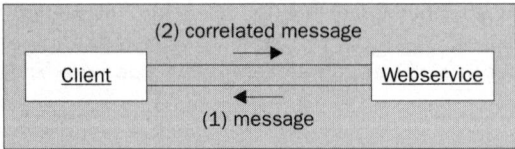

- **Notification**

  This mode is another version of the one-way transmission primitive where the endpoint sends the message rather than receives it. In this case, the operation only contains an output message. This is similar to event notification in GUI development:

So far we have only answered one of the four questions that we identified earlier – What do we do? We know what a web service does, the messages that can be exchanged between the clients and the endpoints, to form operations that can be further aggregated into port types.

At this point, we still do not know how the operations are going to travel across the wire. How will RPC calls be encoded? Will they use SOAP? Will they be simple HTTP GETs? Answering the 'how' of a web service is the essence of the `<binding/>` element that we introduce in the next section.

# The binding Element

The `<binding/>` element brings the discussion to a more practical level. It describes how the operations defined in a port type are transmitted over the network. Since it applies to a port type, a `<binding/>` element must specify a port type defined somewhere else in the document. In our example, the binding refers to the only port type that we have defined – `StockQuote`:

```
<wsdl:binding name="StockQuoteSoapBinding" type="intf:StockQuote">
```

The value of the `name` attribute specifies a unique identifier for this binding. The next element, `<wsdlsoap:binding/>` belongs to the `http://schemas.xmlsoap.org/wsdl/soap` namespace, and is part of the WSDL specification. Elements in that namespace define a **SOAP extension** to WSDL, which allows one to define the details of SOAP elements like the body and the envelope right in the WSDL file.

The `<wsdlsoap:binding/>` element indicates that the binding describes how the `StockQuote` port type will be accessed via SOAP:

```
<wsdlsoap:binding style="rpc"
  transport="http://schemas.xmlsoap.org/soap/http"/>
```

The value of the style attribute indicates that the SOAP message will follow the Remote Procedure Call (RPC) format – a request followed by a response or a fault if things go badly. More specifically, a call to `getQuote()` will be encoded with a SOAP envelope and a SOAP body as in the following example:

```
<?xml version="1.0" encoding="UTF-8"?>

<SOAP-ENV:Envelope
  SOAP-ENV:encodingStyle="http://schemas.xmlsoap.org/soap/encoding/"
  xmlns:SOAP-ENV="http://schemas.xmlsoap.org/soap/envelope/"
  xmlns:xsd="http://www.w3.org/2001/XMLSchema"
  xmlns:xsi="http://www.w3.org/2001/XMLSchema-instance"
  xmlns:SOAP-ENC="http://schemas.xmlsoap.org/soap/encoding/">

  <SOAP-ENV:Body>
    <ns1:getQuote xmlns:ns1="StockQuote">
      <ticker xsi:type="xsd:string">sunw</ticker>
    </ns1:getQuote>
  </SOAP-ENV:Body>

  </SOAP-ENV:Envelope>
```

In our WSDL document, the `transport` attribute indicates the SOAP transport that will be used. In this case, we use HTTP. Another valid value for indicating the use of the SMTP transport that we mentioned earlier would be `http://schemas.xmlsoap.org/soap/SMTP`.

In the WSDL document snippet below, we further qualify how a call to the `getQuote()` method gets translated into a valid SOAP document:

```
<wsdl:operation name="getQuote">
  <wsdlsoap:operation soapAction=""/>
```

The `Java2WSDL` does not specify a `soapAction` attribute for the SOAP action header, but it is usually a good idea to do so since some servers use this header as a hint to allow or deny a request.

The next element is the `<input/>` element that defines the format of the SOAP body. The `<body/>` element is part of the SOAP extensions for WSDL that we mentioned earlier. It is used to describe the input and output messages of our SOAP calls. In the case of our example, the encoding style is standard SOAP:

```
<wsdl:input>
  <wsdlsoap:body
    encodingStyle="http://schemas.xmlsoap.org/soap/encoding/"
    namespace="http://localhost/axis/services/StockQuote"
    use="encoded"/>
</wsdl:input>
```

Another possible value for the `use` attribute is literal, as in `use="literal"`. In this case, the argument is an XML document fragment. This type of encoding saves space because the XML special characters like '<' or '>' do not have to be escaped with '&lt;' or '&gt;'. However, this saving comes at the expense of coding – the client and server must manually serialize and de-serialize the data. For this reason, literal XML works best when exchanging data structures that are already represented as XML documents in the code.

As seen below, the description of the output packet is identical to the input, except for the `<wsdl:output/>` element:

```
<wsdl:output>
  <wsdlsoap:body
    encodingStyle="http://schemas.xmlsoap.org/soap/encoding/"
    namespace="http://localhost/axis/services/StockQuote"
    use="encoded"/>
  </wsdl:output>
</wsdl:operation>
</wsdl:binding>
```

Now, we have the answer to the *what* and the *how* of a web service. We still need to define the implementation of the web service. In Java terms, we have the Javadoc for our web service, but we still need a class file or a JAR file. In web service terms, we need to answer the 'where' question that we posed earlier, by giving a URL to the server hosting the service. This question is answered in the next section.

# The service Element

The `<service/>` element specifies where to find the web service. In our example, the web service can be found on `localhost`:

```
<wsdl:service name="StockQuoteService">
  <wsdl:port binding="intf:StockQuoteSoapBinding" name="StockQuote">
    <wsdlsoap:address
      location="http://localhost/axis/services/StockQuote"/>
  </wsdl:port>
</wsdl:service>
```

As for the other WSDL elements that we have seen so far, the `name` attribute uniquely identifies the service in the WSDL document.

The `<service/>` element is a collection of `<port/>` elements. If we continue the analogy to the Java language, we could say that the port types are classes and the ports are objects. A `port` must refer to an existing binding (defined somewhere else in the document). In this example, it refers to the `StockQuoteSoapBinding`, which itself refers to the `StockQuote` port type.

Once we have specified the binding for our service, we need to specify protocol-specific data for the actual location of the web service. In our case, we use the SOAP extensions for WSDL to specify the location of the service: `http://localhost/axis/services/StockQuote`.

We will see shortly how a WSDL document can be used to automatically generate client-side proxies to ease the burden of SOAP development. First, we will have a look at two more WSDL elements: `<import/>` and `<types/>`. Let's start with the `<import/>` element that allows us to organize our WSDL documents better.

# The import Element

Very often, the `<service/>` element will be segregated into its own WSDL document for practical reasons. Among other things, it allows clients to bind to one well-defined interface and switch implementations at will. To satisfy that requirement, the `Java2WSDL` Axis tool that we used earlier can be invoked to create two files: one for the **interface definition** and one for the **interface implementation** as shown in the following diagram:

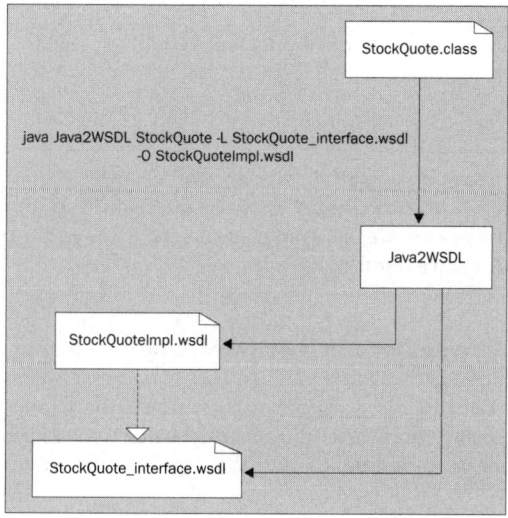

## Try It Out – Generate a WSDL Interface Definition Document

The following command creates two files, `StockQuote_interface.wsdl` and `StockQuoteImpl.wsdl` (make sure that the JAR files and `StockQuote.class` are in our classpath prior to running the command):

```
java org.apache.axis.wsdl.Java2WSDL com.wrox.jws.stockquote.StockQuote
-l http://localhost:8080/axis/services/StockQuote -O StockQuoteImpl.wsdl
-L StockQuote_interface.wsdl
```

### How It Works

The `StockQuote_interface.wsdl` document is the `StockQuote.wsdl` document reviewed earlier, minus the `<service/>` element. The `StockQuoteImpl.wsdl` document (listed below) is made of the `<definitions/>` and `<service/>` elements that we are now familiar with, plus the `<import/>` element:

```
<?xml version="1.0" encoding="UTF-8"?>

<wsdl:definitions
  targetNamespace="http://stockquote.iws.wrox.com-impl"
  xmlns="http://schemas.xmlsoap.org/wsdl/"
  xmlns:SOAP-ENC="http://schemas.xmlsoap.org/soap/encoding/"
  xmlns:impl="http://stockquote.iws.wrox.com-impl"
  xmlns:intf="http://stockquote.iws.wrox.com"
  xmlns:wsdl="http://schemas.xmlsoap.org/wsdl/"
  xmlns:wsdlsoap="http://schemas.xmlsoap.org/wsdl/soap/"
  xmlns:xsd="http://www.w3.org/2001/XMLSchema">

  <wsdl:import
    location="StockQuote_interface.wsdl"
    namespace="http://stockquote.iws.wrox.com"/>
  <wsdl:service name="StockQuoteService">
    <wsdl:port binding="intf:StockQuoteSoapBinding" name="StockQuote">
      <wsdlsoap:address
        location="http://localhost/axis/services/StockQuote"/>
    </wsdl:port>
  </wsdl:service>
</wsdl:definitions>
```

> Be sure to specify the '`-L StockQuote_interface.wsdl`' option. Otherwise **Java2WSDL** will simply generate an import statement without a location, which is going to be useless unless we hand-modify it.

The `<import/>` element allows us to include one WSDL document into another. In this particular case, we import `StockQuote_interface.wsdl`. The `<import/>` element also specifies the namespace `http://stockquote.iws.wrox.com`, which is the namespace of our interface definition. Note that the interface file is useful on its own since it gives us a definition of the web service. This definition could be shared among developers that would each provide their own implementation of the web service.

We will now wrap up our review of WSDL with the `<types/>` elements that allows us to extend the data types provided by XML schemas. We will use the `Market` service that we developed back in Chapter 3 as an example of a web service that uses custom types.

# The types Element

We can use `Java2WSDL` to generate the WSDL document for the `Market` example (make sure that the Axis JAR files we mentioned previously and `Market.class` are in the classpath prior to running that command):

```
java org.apache.axis.wsdl.Java2WSDL com.wrox.jws.stockquote.Market
-1 http://localhost/axis/services/Market
```

Please note that, we can also use the Axis servlet to generate the WSDL file, for this simply navigate to http://localhost/axis/services/Market?wsdl.

The generated WSDL document, `Market.wsdl` looks like:

```
<?xml version="1.0" encoding="UTF-8"?>
<wsdl:definitions targetNamespace="http://stockquote.iws.wrox.com"
  xmlns="http://schemas.xmlsoap.org/wsdl/"
  xmlns:SOAP-ENC="http://schemas.xmlsoap.org/soap/encoding/"
  xmlns:impl="http://stockquote.iws.wrox.com-impl"
  xmlns:intf="http://stockquote.iws.wrox.com"
  xmlns:wsdl="http://schemas.xmlsoap.org/wsdl/"
  xmlns:wsdlsoap="http://schemas.xmlsoap.org/wsdl/soap/"
  xmlns:xsd="http://www.w3.org/2001/XMLSchema">
```

The `<definitions/>` element is identical to the WSDL file we generated for `StockQuote`. However, the `<types/>` element that we see below is new. It contains the XML Schema for the `MarketData` class. Note that there is no schema for the `Market` class since we only use its methods and we never return or pass it as data. When required, Java2WSDL automatically adds the schema:

```
<types>
  <schema
    targetNamespace="http://stockquote.iws.wrox.com"
    xmlns="http://www.w3.org/2001/XMLSchema">
    <complexType name="MarketData">
      <sequence>
        <element name="DOW" nillable="true" type="xsd:string"/>
        <element name="NASDAQ" nillable="true" type="xsd:string"/>
        <element name="SP500" nillable="true" type="xsd:string"/>
```

The `MarketData` class starts with three strings. This might seem wasteful, but the `nillable="true"` attribute allows these strings to be omitted.

Keep in mind that most automated tools, including the bean serializer, which we discussed in Chapter 3, will include these values. When we generate a Java client based on the WSDL file, we will also see that these strings' values are fairly useless unless we manually modify the code and initialize the strings to meaningful values ("^DJI", "^IXIC"). Note that the `static` instance also suffers from the same ailment.

The rest of the sequence element contains the elements generated from the `MarketData` instance data, that is the ticker symbol, the double value, and the array of doubles for the market indices:

```
<element name="ticker" nillable="true" type="xsd:string"/>
<element name="doubleValue" type="xsd:double"/>
<element name="indices" nillable="true"
    type="intf:ArrayOf_xsd_double"/>
  </sequence>
</complexType>
```

The indices are defined as an array of doubles encoded according to the SOAP encoding rules:

```
<complexType name="ArrayOf_xsd_double">
  <complexContent>
    <restriction base="SOAP-ENC:Array">
      <attribute ref="SOAP-ENC:arrayType"
        wsdl:arrayType="xsd:double[]"/>
    </restriction>
  </complexContent>
</complexType>
<element name="MarketData" nillable="true" type="intf:MarketData"/>
  </schema>
</types>
```

Apart from the addition of the types and minor changes like the one shown below for the return value of `getQuote()`, the remainder of `Market.wsdl` is identical to `StockQuote.wsdl`:

```
...
  <wsdl:message name="getQuoteResponse">
    <wsdl:part name="return" type="intf:MarketData"/>
  </wsdl:message>
...
```

This presentation of the `<types/>` element concludes our overview of WSDL. In the next section we will use WSDL documents to develop web service clients.

# WSDL-Based Clients

Using the WSDL documents we have generated, we will be able to automatically create client classes that provide an interface to the web service.

## Java Clients

In this section, we will create a Java **stub class** and the Java classes necessary to support it. The following diagram shows the relationship between the client and the server when using a stub:

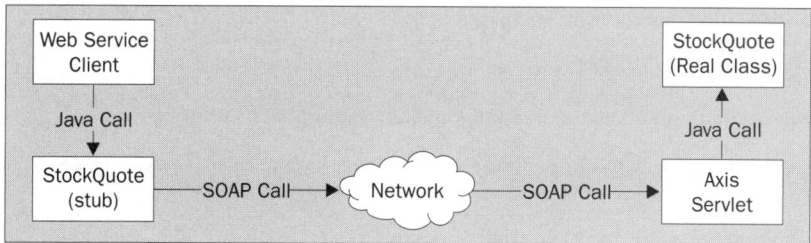

When calling the getQuote() method, our application calls the stub class, which takes care of **serializing** (from Java to XML) our inputs and sending them over the network via a SOAP call. When the call completes, the stub class also takes care of **deserializing** (from XML to Java) the return value. From the point of view of our application, everything looks as if we are making a local Java call.

Well, almost, because the stub will throw a java.rmi.RemoteException when something goes wrong. Keep in mind that we could be calling a service written in C++, C#, or Perl and running on an operating system that may be different from the one hosting our client application. This level of integration across platforms and programming languages is a major component in the success of web services.

It's apparent from this discussion that the WSDL file is the glue that binds web services and their clients together. Without the WSDL file, .NET and Java would not have a common language.

## The StockQuoteClient

The StockQuoteClient is a WSDL-based client that uses the StockQuote example that we developed in Chapter 3.

### Try It Out – StockQuoteClient

The first step is to generate the stub and its supporting classes. For this example, that step is optional as these classes are provided with the code.

*If we want to regenerate the stub and its supporting class, we should make sure that Exception.java and all its references are deleted. This topic is discussed in the* How It Works *section below.*

**1.** To generate the stub class that is used by StockQuoteClient, Axis provides the WSDL2Java class:

```
java org.apache.axis.wsdl.WSDL2Java StockQuote.wsdl
```

*At the time of this writing, the version of WSDL2Java that comes with Axis (Beta 3) contains some minor problems. We will make special note of these problems as we go through the example. Hopefully, those caveats will have been addressed by the time you read these lines.*

**2.** Build the stub and the client. The client code is contained in the StockQuoteClient class:

```
package com.wrox.jws.stockquote;

public class StockQuoteClient {
  /**
   * The main is used as a client of the StockQuote SOAP service.
   *
   * @param args The ticker symbols to get a quote for (e.g. sunw)
   */

  public static void main(String [] args) {
    final String methodName = "StockQuoteClient.main";

    try {
      if(args.length != 1) {
        System.err.println("StockQuote Client");
        System.err.println("  Usage:
          java com.wrox.jws.stockquote.StockQuoteClient <ticker-symbol>");
        System.err.println("  Example:
          java com.wrox.jws.stockquote.StockQuoteClient sunw");
        System.exit(1);
      }

      // We create a service (StockQuoteService is the interface)
      StockQuoteService stockQuoteService = new StockQuoteServiceLocator();

      // We get a stub that implements the Service Description
      //Interface (SDI)
      StockQuote stockQuote = stockQuoteService.getStockQuote();

      // We call getQuote
      String quote = stockQuote.getQuote(args[0]);

      System.out.println("The (delayed) value of " + args[0]
        + " is: " + quote);
    } catch (Exception exception) {
      System.err.println(methodName + ": " + exception.toString());
      exception.printStackTrace();
    }
  }
}
```

**3.** Building the example is similar to what we did in Chapter 3 for StockQuote and Market. Keep in mind that we need to compile the client, the stub, and the supporting classes. Also, make sure that our classpath matches the earlier one (src is the current directory):

```
javac -d ..\classes StockQuote.java
javac -d ..\classes StockQuoteService.java
javac -d ..\classes StockQuoteServiceLocator.java
javac -d ..\classes StockQuoteSoapBindingStub.java
javac -d ..\classes StockQuoteClient.java
```

**4.** To run the StockQuoteClient, simply use the following command (make sure that our class path contains the files that we compiled in the previous step):

```
java com.wrox.jws.stockquote.StockQuoteClient IBM
```

**5.** The output is:

The value of IBM is: 69.01

**6.** Unsurprisingly, the net result of the command is identical to the client that we developed in Chapter 3. The differences reside in the methodology, which involves the creation of a stub class as we describe in the next section.

### How It Works

The first command that we executed in the previous section was `WSDL2Java`. The execution of that command creates the following files:

- ❑ `Exception.java`
  We have seen earlier, in the `StockQuote.wsdl` file, that the `Exception` class is thrown when a fault is received. Since the `WSDL2Java` class does not know (solely from the WSDL file) that the exception is really a `java.lang.Exception`, it generates a `com.wrox.jws.stockquote.Exception`. One way to avoid this caveat is to rely only on `java.rmi.RemoteException`, since it is thrown by every service method. In other words, we can simply ignore the generated `Exception` class.

- ❑ `StockQuote.java`
  The `StockQuote` interface corresponds to the `StockQuote portType` in the WSDL file. It extends `java.rmi.Remote`. This interface is called the **Service Definition Interface** (SDI).

- ❑ `StockQuoteSoapBindingStub.java`
  This class is the stub class that we mentioned earlier. It implements the SDI (`StockQuote` in our case).

- ❑ `StockQuoteService.java`
  The `StockQuoteService` interface is derived from the `<service/>` element in WSDL. It defines three methods – one method to get the URL of the web service, one method per port to get a stub, and one to get a stub class for an arbitrary URL. This interface is implemented by the **service locator**.

- ❑ `StockQuoteServiceLocator.java`
  This class implements the `StockQuoteService` interface. It is a class factory for the stub (see below for details).

Thus, we can refine the previous diagram to include the supporting classes of the stub (numbers in circles indicate the order of execution):

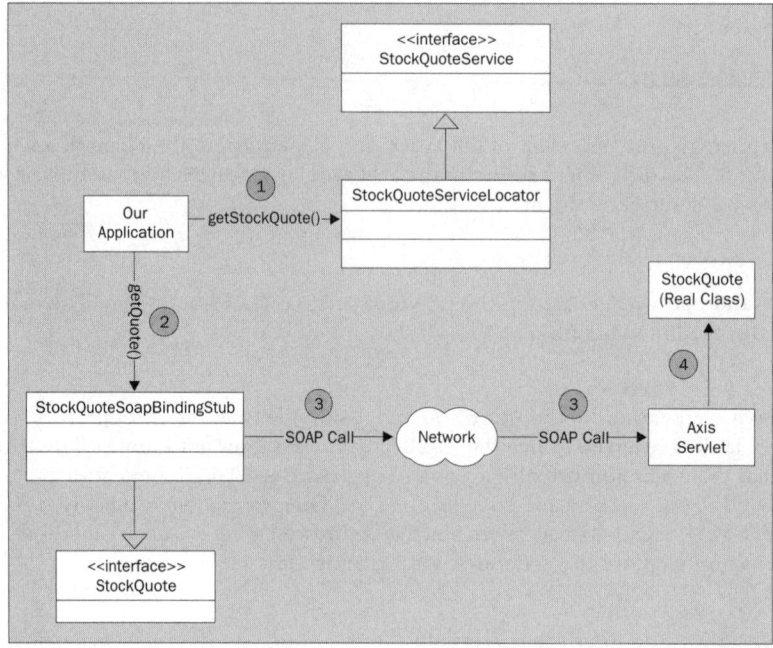

The following table summarizes the rules of class/interface creation when using WSDL2Java:

| WSDL Element | Java Class or Interface |
| --- | --- |
| For each element in `<types/>` | A Java class |
| `<portType/>` | A Java interface |
| `<binding/>` | A stub class |
| `<service/>` | A service interface |
| | A service implementation (the locator) |
| `<fault/>` | A Java class |

Note that WSDL2Java follows the rules of JAX-RPC that we mentioned in Chapter 3.

Now we have a basic understanding of the WSDL2Java tool. Let's see how we can use the classes generated from WSDL when developing StockQuoteClient.

If we look at the listing above, we will notice that since all generated classes are in the com.wrox.jws.stockquote package along with this client, we don't need to import anything.

After dealing with the only possible argument, a stock ticker, we reach the essence of the client code. First, we get a reference to the StockQuoteService interface by creating an instance of the StockQuoteServiceLocator class:

```
    // We create a service (StockQuoteService is the interface)
    StockQuoteService stockQuoteService = new StockQuoteServiceLocator();
```

Next, we get a reference to the `StockQuote` interface (the one that implements `getQuote()`) through the `getStockQuote()` method:

```
    // Get a stub that implements the Service Description Interface (SDI)
    StockQuote stockQuote = stockQuoteService.getStockQuote();
```

Third, and last, we call the `getQuote` method as we would call any other local interface:

```
    // We call getQuote
    String quote = stockQuote.getQuote(args[0]);

    System.out.println("The (delayed) value of " + args[0]
      + " is: " + quote);
```

To compare the simplicity of this approach to the relative complexity of an Axis client, we can go back to the `main()` method of `StockQuote` or `Market` that we developed in Chapter 3.

## The MarketClient

The `StockQuoteClient` class was a fairly trivial example since it only used strings as input and output. To see for ourselves what happens when we use complex data types, we will use `WSDL2Java` to generate a stub for the `Market` web service.

### Try It Out – MarketClient

1. If we want to generate the stub and its supporting classes (they are included with the code of this chapter), the following command will do the trick (use the same classpath as before):

```
java org.apache.axis.wsdl.WSDL2Java Market.wsdl
```

2. Now we build the stub and client. The `MarketClient` class is listed below. As you can see, it is very similar to the `StockQuoteClient`:

```
package com.wrox.jws.stockquote;

public class MarketClient {
  /**
   * The main is used as a client of the Market SOAP service.
   *
   * @param args The ticker symbols to get a quote for (e.g. sunw)
   */
  public static void main(String [] args) {
    final String methodName = "MarketClient.main";

    try {
      if(args.length != 1) {
```

```
            System.err.println("Market Client");
            System.err.println("  Usage:
              java com.wrox.jws.stockquote.MarketClient <ticker-symbol>");
            System.err.println("  Example:
              java com.wrox.jws.stockquote.MarketClient sunw");
            System.exit(1);
        }

        // We create a service (StockQuoteService is the interface)
        MarketService marketService = new MarketServiceLocator();

        // We get a stub that implements the Service Description
        // Interface (SDI)
        Market market = marketService.getMarket();

        // We call getQuote
        MarketData marketData = market.getQuote(args[0]);

        System.out.println("The (delayed) value of " + args[0]
          + " is: " + marketData.getDoubleValue() + ", and the NASDAQ is: "
          + marketData.getIndices()[1]);
    } catch (Exception exception) {
        System.err.println(methodName + ": " + exception.toString());
    }
  }
}
```

**3.** Building the code is analogous to what we did for StockQuoteClient (use the same class path and the current directory is src):

```
javac -d ..\classes Market.java
javac -d ..\classes MarketService.java
javac -d ..\classes MarketServiceLocator.java
javac -d ..\classes MarketSoapBindingStub.java
javac -d ..\classes MarketData.java
javac -d ..\classes MarketClient.java
```

**4.** Now, to test the stub and the client, we run the command:

```
java com.wrox.jws.stockquote.MarketClient SUNW
```

**5.** Here is the output of an execution of MarketClient for SUNW:

The value of SUNW is: 5.93, and the NASDAQ is: 1360.62

Here also, we have the same output as what we saw in Chapter 3.

### How It Works

The notable difference between the StockQuoteClient and the MarketClient is the MarketData class. The appearance of the MarketData class conforms to the rules that we mentioned earlier – one Java class is generated per entry in the <types/> element.

Functionally, the client-side `MarketData` class is equivalent to the server-side version. The main differences are the initialization of final values, the removal of a constructor, and the addition of the `equals()` method. However, there are a few caveats that are worth pointing out, so let's quickly review the code for the `MarketData` class generated by `WSDL2Java`:

```
package com.wrox.jws.stockquote;

public class MarketData implements java.io.Serializable {
    private java.lang.String DOW    = "^DJI";
    private java.lang.String NASDAQ = "^IXIC";
    private java.lang.String SP500  = "^GSPC";
    private java.lang.String ticker;   // attribute
    private double doubleValue;   // attribute
    private double[] indices;   // attribute

    public MarketData() {
```

We modified the DOW, NASDAQ, and SP500 variables with the initializations shown above. By default, these three strings are initialized to `null`. As we can see below, without these changes the `getDow()` method would be useless:

```
public java.lang.String getDOW() {
    return DOW;
}
```

The `getNASDAQ()` and `getSP500()` methods follow the same pattern.

The next method is `getIndices()`, which returns the values of the three major US stock indexes:

```
public double[] getIndices() {
    return indices;
}
```

To be able to use the `getIndices()`, one needs to know that `index=0` corresponds to DOW, `index=1` to NASDAQ, and `index=2` to SP500. This could be indicated in the documentation of the web service. The remainder of this listing contains no surprises.

The other classes generated from the `Market.wsdl` file are analogous to the ones generated for `StockQuote`.

Using the stub for `Market` contains no new ideas as one can see in the code below. The `MarketClient.java` file, which comes with the code for this chapter, contains the entire code:

```
// We create a service (StockQuoteService is the interface)
MarketService marketService = new MarketServiceLocator();

// Get a stub that implements the Service Description Interface (SDI)
Market market = marketService.getMarket();
```

```
            // We call getQuote
            MarketData marketData = market.getQuote(args[0]);

            System.out.println("The (delayed) value of " + args[0]
              + " is: " + marketData.getDoubleValue() + ", and the NASDAQ is: "
              + marketData.getIndices()[1]);
```

During testing, if we happen to get an error like 'could not find deserializer for type http://localhost/axis/services/StockQuote:MarketData', be sure to double-check our deployment descriptor for the Market service for the QName and its name space. The client and server must use the same names (QName and namespace) for the deserializer to be registered properly.

# Summary

In this chapter, we have covered the important topic of web service description. It is an important topic for two reasons. First, we want people to be able to read descriptions of the services that we provide. Without that knowledge, nobody would be able to use the software that we develop. Second, we want tools like WSDL2Java to automatically read a description of our web services and provide their users with a quick interface to our web services.

A technology that has the potential of transforming that dream into reality is the Web Service Description Language (WSDL), an XML dialect. We reviewed the elements that make up a WSDL document and saw that WSDL answers three fundamental questions about web service by describing them in terms of endpoints and the messages that transit between these endpoints.

The four questions about web services that are addressed by WSDL are:

❑ **What?**
The machine-readable answer to that question is in the `<message/>` and `<portType/>` elements. The human-readable answer is in the `<name/>` and `<document/>` elements.

❑ **Which?**
This tells us about the language used and is found in the `<types/>` element.

❑ **How?**
The answer can be found in the `<binding/>` elements.

❑ **Where?**
The answer is specified in the `<service/>` elements.

We concluded the chapter by generating stub classes for StockQuote and Market using their respective WSDL documents.

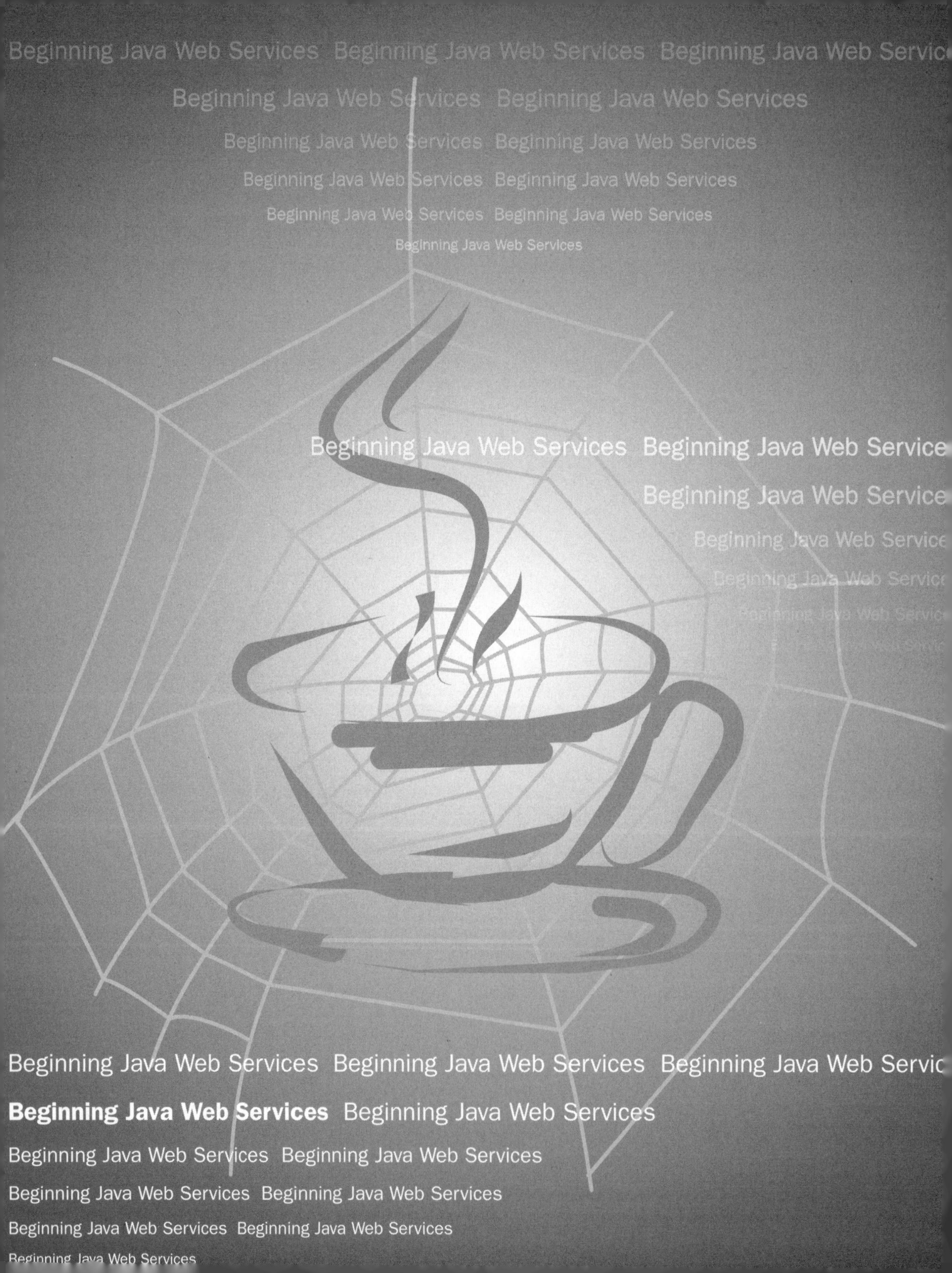
Beginning Java Web Services Beginning Java Web Services
Beginning Java Web Services Beginning Java Web Services
Beginning Java Web Services Beginning Java Web Services
Beginning Java Web Services Beginning Java Web Services
Beginning Java Web Services
Beginning Java Web Services Beginning Java Web Services
Beginning Java Web Services Beginning Java Web Services
Beginning Java Web Services Beginning Java Web Services
Beginning Java Web Services Beginning Java Web Services
Beginning Java Web Services

# Invoking Web Services

By now it is apparent that web services are all about connecting applications over a network, allowing them to communicate. These applications do not necessarily know about each other in any depth; they don't have to be written in the same programming language, or even run on the same platform or operating system. The standards and specifications that we have read about in the previous chapters, and will read about in the following chapters, are all based on the fact that they should allow application-to-application communication regardless of platform, programming language, or even the network protocol that is used.

This implies that when talking about web services, we have to distinguish between the **requester**, or client, and the **provider**, or server, of a web service. The only contract between the two is the description of the web service, namely the WSDL document that contains the abstract definition of the offered interface and the protocol information that a client needs to bind to that service.

So far we have looked at some of the basic principles of web services, namely how XML makes it possible to exchange data in a programming language-neutral way, and how to describe functions in an abstract fashion using WSDL.

In this chapter, we shall see:

- ❑ Web services invocation models – static and dynamic
- ❑ Java API for XML-based RPC, or JAX-RPC
- ❑ Non-SOAP web services

An example of the last point above is the **Web Services Invocation Framework (WSIF)**, which was initially developed by IBM and has been being donated to Apache as an open source project. We will take a look at some examples that show how to develop client code that takes a WSDL definition at run time and creates the appropriate invocation constructs based on that definition.

# Web Services Invocation Models

WSDL not only delivers information about the functional interface that is offered by a web service, it also describes details of the protocol that can be used to access that service. Most web services that are built today use the SOAP protocol as their communication protocol. A client that invokes a service will build an XML message, which has the `<Envelope>` element as its root element and carries a message that complies with the SOAP specification. For example, the Apache SOAP implementation uses the namespace of the envelope's `<Body>` element as an identifier for the service that is invoked. This kind of information is needed by a client that wants to access the service, but is not really part of the service interface – it is protocol information, or, according to the WSDL specification, binding information.

We spend a great deal of time in this book discussing SOAP and its various implementations, most notably the Apache Axis package. However, if you think that web services can only be implemented and consumed using SOAP, you are mistaken. While SOAP is presently the dominant protocol used in the marketplace for web services, we expect that this will change over time to include many other protocols as well.

Web services may not exclusively be built to support SOAP as the communication protocol, which means that we want to build client code that is based on the service's interface definition, not on its run time environment. In other words, if a service happens to exist in the same address space that the client is running in, there is no reason to marshal and unmarshal all the data and send it out over an HTTP connection, if a local Java or RMI/IIOP call would do the job just fine.

In other cases, however, we may know that SOAP is the only way we will ever use to access a service. For example, the .NET platform currently only supports SOAP over HTTP as its communication protocol (unless you happen to be in a pure .NET environment; but we as Java programmers are not, are we?). Thus, if we want to take advantage of a service that has been implemented on either the Internet or on an intranet using .NET, SOAP may be the only choice. In these cases, a static client invocation model may be the right choice. Let's now look at the two invocation models in detail.

## Static Invocation Model

This model is the more common one. We have to learn about an existing web service, probably by accessing its WSDL description, potentially by finding it in a UDDI registry and generating code that somehow wraps the invocation of the service in a Java class. This is because, after all, we don't want everyone who uses this new service to write tons of code creating XML artifacts that encode the invocation of that service. This would mean converting all Java objects into XML structures of some sort.

Moreover, in the common case that this service is available via SOAP over HTTP, we would have to write code that generates the right type of HTTP request. We can make our lives easier by generating Java code, which converts a web service definition into a Java interface and a client side implementation of this interface that clients can use as if the service was available as a local Java class. To make this clear, let us reuse the `StockQuote` example from Chapter 3.

Here is the WSDL document again that describes the service:

```
<?xml version="1.0" encoding="UTF-8"?>
<wsdl:definitions
  targetNamespace="http://localhost:8080/axis/services/StockQuote"
  xmlns="http://schemas.xmlsoap.org/wsdl/"
  xmlns:SOAP-ENC="http://schemas.xmlsoap.org/soap/encoding/"
  xmlns:impl="http://localhost:8080/axis/services/StockQuote-impl"
  xmlns:intf="http://localhost:8080/axis/services/StockQuote"
  xmlns:wsdl="http://schemas.xmlsoap.org/wsdl/"
  xmlns:wsdlsoap="http://schemas.xmlsoap.org/wsdl/soap/"
  xmlns:xsd="http://www.w3.org/2001/XMLSchema">
  <wsdl:message name="Exception"/>

  <wsdl:message name="getQuoteRequest">
    <wsdl:part name="in0" type="xsd:string"/>
  </wsdl:message>

  <wsdl:message name="getQuoteResponse">
    <wsdl:part name="return" type="xsd:string"/>
  </wsdl:message>

  <wsdl:portType name="StockQuote">
    <wsdl:operation name="getQuote" parameterOrder="in0">
      <wsdl:input message="intf:getQuoteRequest"/>
      <wsdl:output message="intf:getQuoteResponse"/>
      <wsdl:fault message="intf:Exception" name="Exception"/>
    </wsdl:operation>
  </wsdl:portType>

</wsdl:definitions>
```

This WSDL definition does not contain any information about the actual protocol that could be used to invoke this service. However, it describes the interface of this service in an abstract, or, a programming language-neutral way. We'll get to the protocol part in a little while.

To build a Java client with the static invocation model, which uses this web service, we have to create a representation of the service that is Java-based, and not XML-based. In other words, we have to generate a Java interface that matches the operations and messages defined in the WSDL document. Until recently, every provider of Java-based web services solutions chose their own way of doing this, providing proprietary tools within their environment. Luckily, this has now changed with the creation of a standard Java API that describes this, namely the **Java API for XML-based RPC**, or **JAX-RPC**.

For example, the StockQuote service that we showed above can be represented in Java by the following interface:

```
package com.wrox.jws.StockQuote;

public interface StockQuote extends java.rmi.Remote {

  public java.lang.String getQuote(java.lang.String in0) throws
    java.rmi.RemoteException, com.wrox.jws.StockQuote.Exception;
}
```

Looking at this example, we can easily see that the `<portType>` defined in the WSDL extract above, named `StockQuote`, was turned into a Java interface called `StockQuote`. Similarly, the operation in that port type, `<operation name="getQuote">`, was turned into a method called `getQuote()` on the Java interface.

So, the first step in the process is to generate a Java interface that represents the port type in the WSDL document.

We learned in the previous chapter that WSDL not only contains the definition of the offered web service interface, it also contains information about how to access that service. This information is called the protocol binding, and is represented by the `<binding>` element in the WSDL document. Most commonly, this protocol binding defines the additional information needed to access a web service via SOAP over HTTP.

For example, we could enhance the WSDL document for our `StockQuote` service with the following protocol binding:

```
<definitions ...>
  ...
  <wsdl:binding name="StockQuoteSoapBinding" type="intf:StockQuote">
  <wsdlsoap:binding style="rpc"
    transport="http://schemas.xmlsoap.org/soap/http"/>
    <wsdl:operation name="getQuote">
      <wsdlsoap:operation soapAction=""/>
      <wsdl:input>
        <wsdlsoap:body
          encodingStyle="http://schemas.xmlsoap.org/soap/encoding/"
          namespace="http://localhost:8080/axis/services/StockQuote"
          use="encoded"/>
      </wsdl:input>
      <wsdl:output>
        <wsdlsoap:body
          encodingStyle="http://schemas.xmlsoap.org/soap/encoding/"
          namespace="http://localhost:8080/axis/services/StockQuote"
          use="encoded"/>
      </wsdl:output>
    </wsdl:operation>
  </wsdl:binding>

  <wsdl:service name="StockQuoteService">
    <wsdl:port binding="intf:StockQuoteSoapBinding" name="StockQuote">
      <wsdlsoap:address
        location="http://localhost:8080/axis/services/StockQuote"/>
    </wsdl:port>
  </wsdl:service>

</definitions>
```

The `<binding>` element describes everything we need to know to build a SOAP request message that the web service can understand, and it also defines what kind of return data we can expect from that service. We can generate code that knows how to build such a request and map it to the Java interface that we have generated in the first step. This allows client application developers to use this code to interact with the web service.

What exactly this code looks like depends on the SOAP package that we use. As mentioned above, the JAX-RPC standard only defines an API, namely how to map WSDL port types into a Java interface; it does not define how to implement the invocation of the actual request.

If we use the Apache Axis package, however, the `getQuote` operation from our WSDL is turned into the following implementation:

```java
public class StockQuoteSoapBindingStub extends org.apache.axis.client.Stub
  implements com.wrox.jws.stockquote.StockQuote {
...
  public java.lang.String getQuote(java.lang.String in0)
      throws java.rmi.RemoteException, com.wrox.jws.stockquote.Exception
  {
    if (super.cachedEndpoint == null) {
      throw new org.apache.axis.NoEndPointException();
    }
    org.apache.axis.client.Call call = createCall();
    javax.xml.rpc.namespace.QName p0QName =
      new javax.xml.rpc.namespace.QName("", "in0");
    call.addParameter(p0QName,
      new javax.xml.rpc.namespace.QName("http://www.w3.org/2001/XMLSchema",
        "string"),
      java.lang.String.class,
      javax.xml.rpc.ParameterMode.IN);

    call.setReturnType(
      new javax.xml.rpc.namespace.QName("http://www.w3.org/2001/XMLSchema",
        "string"));
    call.setUseSOAPAction(true);
    call.setSOAPActionURI("");
    call.setOperationStyle("rpc");

    call.setOperationName(new javax.xml.rpc.namespace.QName(
      "http://localhost:8080/axis/services/StockQuote", "getQuote"));

    Object resp = call.invoke(new Object[] {in0});

    if (resp instanceof java.rmi.RemoteException) {
      throw (java.rmi.RemoteException)resp;
    } else {
      try {
        return (java.lang.String) resp;
      } catch (java.lang.Exception e) {
      return (java.lang.String) org.apache.axis.utils.JavaUtils.
        convert(resp, java.lang.String.class);
      }
    }
  }
}
```

Given this rather lengthy chunk of code, it is pretty obvious that we wouldn't want to write it ourselves (and it is only an extract of a class that is in reality even longer). Luckily, there are tools available as part of the Apache Axis package that generate this code for us. However, this snippet shows that the generated code implements the Java interface we saw earlier, representing the abstract interface of the service. This allows clients to use the SOAPBindingStub class as a local proxy, hiding the SOAP interaction from the client developer and offering a standard Java interface.

The second step in the static invocation model is the generation of a stub that implements the interface generated in first step, and contains the implementation of the protocol binding defined in the WSDL document.

The following diagram shows the structure of a static web services client:

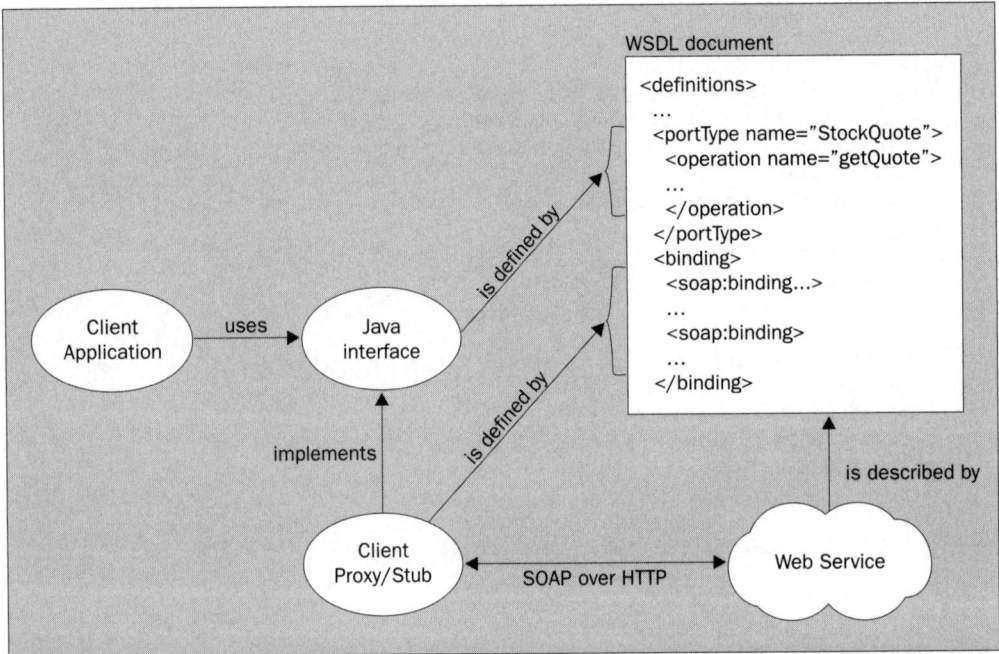

This diagram shows that the WSDL document represents the contract between the web service and its client. The client need not know how the web service was implemented, which programming language was used, and on which platform it exists. Different parts of the WSDL document are used to create a Java interface and a Java class (which implements that interface) that hide the details of the service from the client. The model is called the static model because code that represents the service is generated at development time.

If the WSDL document changes, the code must be regenerated and the client code must be recompiled to take those changes into account. For example, if a new operation is offered in a newer version of the service, a new Java interface and stub must be generated, so that the client can take advantage of it. In this case, however, existing operations can still be used as before.

There is no automatic way to find out if a WSDL document has changed, or, in other words, whether a compiled Java stub still matches the interface described in the document. If a service provider updates the service, the client may or may not still work, depending on the changes. If an incompatible change was made, the client will receive a runtime error.

In general, it is fair to say that versioning of web services is currently not supported by any standard. Web services request messages do not carry a version number or anything like that. This means that any change to a web service will typically lead to disruption of the users of that service, so care should be taken to avoid this situation whenever possible.

This is not the case in the dynamic invocation model, which we will look at next.

# Dynamic Invocation Model

One of the promises of web services technology in general is to increase the level of automation in application-to-application communication. This means that applications can establish a communication path without knowing any details about each other (beyond the WSDL document describing their web services interfaces), or that changes to an existing system, or service, can be utilized without requiring manual changes to the user of that system.

Universal Discovery, Description, and Integration (UDDI) registries, as we shall see in Chapter 7, contain information about businesses and the services they offer, many of which may be web services represented by various WSDL documents. It should be possible for applications to use these registries to dynamically discover and use services with little, if any, manual intervention. Given this as a goal, we need a way for a client to use a service without the generation of code for interfaces and stub classes as described by the static invocation model.

Clients must be able to make decisions about which service to invoke and over which protocol, based on the definitions in the WSDL document for that service. If this document changes, the client must be able to adapt to that change without having to re-implement the client code.

In this case, the overall programming model that we use for web services remains the same as before: the service is represented by its WSDL interface definition and its protocol bindings. We use Java code to wrap the invocation of the service on the client, so that the client developer need not know or care about how to build requests for different protocols. This means that the client developer only needs to care about the functional interface of a service, and not about how it is invoked.

## Protocol Independence

We have mentioned several times now that the description of a web service in a WSDL document is a key piece of information for developing clients, which consume that service. A WSDL document contains two layers of information, and we can handle both of them statically or dynamically. These layers are:

- ❏ The interface definition (represented by the `<portType>` element)
- ❏ The protocol bindings (represented by the `<bindings>` and `<service>` elements)

We now want to develop Java code that uses this service in a dynamic way, by using the WSDL definitions at runtime to create proper requests – in a format that the server can understand, as outlined in the WSDL definition.

Let us assume that a web service is available over a certain protocol, for example, SOAP over HTTP. In that case, the `<port>` element, which is contained in the `<service>` element, carries information about where the service is located, so that a client can send a request to that service. Our client should not have any hard-coded dependency on the target URL, but rather it should read this address from the WSDL document at run time. Then, if the address ever changes, perhaps because the service is moved to a new server, the client code does not have to change.

Another example of information that can change and should therefore not be hardwired into the client code is information about how exactly to build the request and response messages. For example, the service provider might choose to change a service to use the 'literal XML' encoding scheme rather than the default SOAP encoding scheme (discussed later in this chapter). Again, in the dynamic programming model, the client code can adjust to those changes because the encoding scheme is interpreted at run time and the right encoding is applied when building a request and receiving the response.

Also, a WSDL document could contain information allowing us to invoke a service over several protocols at the same time. Most web services today utilize SOAP over HTTP. In the future, however, the invocation of a web service could be done over RMI/IIOP (which is the protocol used for Enterprise JavaBeans invocations), or over a messaging layer using the Java Messaging Service (JMS), just to name two examples.

This is useful if we want to build a system that uses a common programming model for its components – namely accessing those components via WSDL-defined interfaces, regardless of whether they are local or remote.

## Interface Independence

The interface description in WSDL, more specifically the `<portType>` element, contains information about the structure of the messages that a web service sends and receives. In other words, it defines the input parameters of the service as well as the return type. To achieve interface independence in the client code, this code must interpret this information at run time to build the right request and properly interpret the returned response.

For example there could be a situation where an existing web service may change its interface over time. A newer version of a web service could require additional parameters to be passed along, and we want to develop client code that can automatically adjust to those changes and pass along those additional parameters to the service when required. Again, these kinds of scenarios will be less common and will only occur in highly dynamic environments. Most usages of the dynamic invocation model will be based on protocol independence and not on interface invariance.

Now that we have described the two invocation programming models, we can go a level deeper and look at a standard Java API that supports both models, namely JAX-RPC.

# JAX-RPC

If we were to describe the main purpose of JAX-RPC in one sentence, we could say that this API defines the rules for turning WSDL port-type information into Java and vice versa. These rules apply on both the client and the server side. Consider the case where we have existing Java code that we want to offer to clients over a web services layer. One of the things we have to do is describe the interface of our Java code in WSDL, and JAX-RPC tells us how to do that. Similarly, if we have the WSDL description of a given web service and want to invoke that web service in our client Java application, we can use an implementation of the JAX-RPC API to turn this WSDL description into a Java interface.

Since this chapter is all about how to consume web services, the second scenario is what we will focus on here. However, many of the things we will discuss apply to both the client and the server.

As mentioned, JAX-RPC supports both the invocation models described earlier. We will look at the classes that are used for both of them in detail. For the code examples, we will use the Apache Axis beta 3 package, which implements the JAX-RPC interface. You can find detailed information about how to obtain Axis and how to install it in Chapter 3.

## Java to WSDL Mapping

As we mentioned above, JAX-RPC defines how to map Java code into WSDL definitions. The specification can be found at http://java.sun.com/xml/downloads/jaxrpc.html#jaxrpcspec. The rules for this are pretty straightforward, so let us simply go through each of them here:

- ❑ **Basic Java types are mapped to basic XML Schema types.**
  This rule means that if we are dealing with the common data types like `String`, `Integer`, `Boolean`, and so on, we can map them directly to data types that are defined for XML Schemas.

- ❑ **Primitive types use Holder classes.**
  A primitive type is something that Java defines that does not inherit from `java.lang.Object`, such as `int` or `short`. For these to be handled properly, a so-called `Holder` class is used that carries the value of the primitive type within a real object.

- ❑ **JavaBean classes are mapped to an XML Schema structure.**
  If a class contains a value object, in other words, is an object of a class that holds data and is serializable, it gets converted into an XML Schema describing the structure of the data. For example, a Java class that looks like this:

  ```
  public class Person {
    public String firstName;
    public String lastName;
    public int age;
  }
  ```

  maps to this XML Schema definition:

  ```
  <complexType name="person">
    <all>
      <element name="firstName" nillable="true" type="string">
      <element name="lastName" nillable="true" type="string">
      <element name="age" nillable="true" type="int">
    </all>
  </complexType>
  ```

❑ **Java artifacts are mapped to the appropriate WSDL artifacts.**
This is described in the following table:

| Java | WSDL |
|------|------|
| Package | WSDL document |
| Interface | `portType` |
| Method | `operation` |
| Exception | `fault` |

❑ **The Java interface must extend `java.rmi.Remote` and each method must throw a `java.rmi.RemoteException`.**
This is in line with how remote invocations over RMI are done in Java. Each method that can be called over RMI (for example, methods exposed by an Enterprise JavaBean) must throw `java.rmi.RemoteException`. A web service is typically invoked over a network, hence the rule about adding the exception.

There are more rules and more details to this, but we have covered the most important parts. Normally, we would use a tool to generate the appropriate WSDL file for our Java code, and this tool will have all of the details implemented.

# WSDL to Java Mapping

The previous section described the mapping of existing Java code into WSDL. Here we are looking at the opposite scenario where WSDL information is turned into Java code. This set of rules is used on both the server and the client side. On the server, it defines what the concrete implementation of the described service in Java will look like. This can be used to create skeletons in Java for a given, possibly standardized, WSDL document.

In this chapter the client-side case is more relevant for us. An existing web service is represented by its WSDL document. This can now be used to generate clients, which follow the static programming model. It is also used by dynamic clients, which build the appropriate request and response structures at run time.

Let us look at the rules that are defined for this mapping:

❑ **Basic XML Schema types are mapped to basic Java types.**
This is basically the same rule as for the opposite case described above.

❑ **XML structures and complex types are mapped to a JavaBean.**
If the WSDL document uses message parts that are complex types, or XML structures, then these are mapped to plain JavaBeans that contain the elements of the structure as their attributes. An example for this is the simple `Person` class we listed above. Just in this case, the process is done in the opposite direction, starting with the WSDL document and creating Java code from that.

❏ **Enumerations are turned into public static final attributes.**
   Defining the attributes is the most common way of simulating enumerations in Java. For example, assume the following enumeration in XML (the Java package names for these classes are generated from the namespace of the WSDL document, but how exactly the mapping is done depends on the implementation):

```
<simpleType name="MonthType">
  <restriction base="xsd:string">
    <enumeration value="January"/>
    <enumeration value="February"/>
    ...
  </restriction>
</simpleType>
```

This maps to the following Java class:

```
public class MonthType implements java.io.Serializable {

  private java.lang.String _value_;
  private static java.util.HashMap _table_ = new java.util.HashMap();

  // Constructor
  protected MonthType(java.lang.String value) {
    _value_ = value;
    _table_.put(_value_,this);
  };

  public static final java.lang.String _January = "January";
  public static final java.lang.String _February = "February";
  public static final java.lang.String _March = "March";
  ...
  public static final MonthType January = new MonthType(_January);
  public static final MonthType February = new MonthType(_February);
  public static final MonthType March = new MonthType(_March);
  ...
  public java.lang.String getValue() { ...}

  public static MonthType fromValue(java.lang.String value)
    throws java.lang.IllegalStateException { ... }
  public static MonthType fromString(String value)
    throws java.lang.IllegalStateException { ... }
  public boolean equals(Object obj) { ... }
  public int hashCode() { ... }
  public String toString() { ... }
}
```

❏ **WSDL artifacts are mapped to the appropriate Java artifacts.**
   The same mappings between Java artifacts and WSDL artifacts apply as in the opposite case described previously. In other words, a document maps to a package, a port type maps to a class and each operation maps to a method in that class.

# Service Mapping

The mapping of the `<service>` element in WSDL is not quite as straightforward as those for the other elements that we have looked at so far, so we will take a little more time to have a look at it. As we shall see in Chapter 7, the `<service>` element defines where a web service can be found through its contained `<port>` elements.

JAX-RPC defines an interface called `javax.xml.rpc.Service`. A concrete class implementing the interface must exist at run time. The `Service` interface contains methods that a client can use to invoke the actual web service.

There are two different styles that clients can use in order to invoke a web service using the `Service` interface. One is the use of a proxy object, which is returned by one of the `getPort()` methods of the `Service` interface. This proxy object exposes the methods of the web service locally, by turning the WSDL port type into Java.

Previously we had generated an interface called `StockQuote` from the WSDL document. This interface had one method on it, namely `getQuote()`. Using the `getPort()` method returns a run-time object that implements the `StockQuote` interface and will route all invocations of the `getQuote()` method to the actual web service. The proxy is created at run time and no code is generated.

The other choice we have is the use of a `javax.xml.rpc.Call` object. A `Call` object represents one invocation of a web service. It allows us to set parameters and other invocation variables, and then execute the request. We will go through both invocation styles in more detail below.

First, let's have a look at the methods that are defined in the `Service` class. Here is the entire interface. You will find this interface in every JAX-RPC-compliant implementation:

```java
package javax.xml.rpc;

import javax.xml.rpc.encoding.TypeMappingRegistry;
import javax.xml.rpc.handler.HandlerRegistry;
import javax.xml.rpc.namespace.QName;

public interface Service {

  public java.rmi.Remote getPort(QName portName, Class proxyInterface)
    throws ServiceException;

  public java.rmi.Remote getPort(Class serviceDefInterface)
    throws ServiceException;

  public Call createCall(QName portName) throws ServiceException;

  public Call createCall(QName portName, String operationName)
    throws ServiceException;

  public Call createCall(QName portName, QName operationName)
    throws ServiceException;
```

```
   public Call createCall() throws ServiceException;

   public Call[] getCalls() throws ServiceException;

   public HandlerRegistry getHandlerRegistry();

   public java.net.URL getWSDLDocumentLocation();

   public QName getServiceName();

   public java.util.Iterator getPorts();

   public TypeMappingRegistry getTypeMappingRegistry();
}
```

## The getPort() Method

We will just pick the most important methods here and look at them in detail, so let's get started with the getPort() method:

```
public java.rmi.Remote getPort(QName portName, Class proxyInterface)
   throws ServiceException;
```

A port is the actual location of a web service. How we describe this location depends on the protocol that is used to access the service. For example, if the service is accessible via SOAP over HTTP, then the location is a URL, to which you can send the request message.

Each <service> element can have multiple <port> elements in it, and each one can be retrieved from the Service class using the getPort() method. We specify the port we are looking for by passing its QName. This is the fully qualified name of the <port> element in the WSDL document. We will have a look at this in more detail before explaining the getPort() method.

Here is the complete WSDL document again that we use for this example. This document will serve as the basis for most examples that will follow below. We can find the namespace of this WSDL document in the <definitions> element:

```
<?xml version="1.0" encoding="UTF-8"?>
<wsdl:definitions
   targetNamespace="http://localhost:8080/axis/services/StockQuote"
   xmlns="http://schemas.xmlsoap.org/wsdl/"
   xmlns:SOAP-ENC="http://schemas.xmlsoap.org/soap/encoding/"
   xmlns:impl="http://localhost:8080/axis/services/StockQuote-impl"
   xmlns:intf="http://localhost:8080/axis/services/StockQuote"
   xmlns:wsdl="http://schemas.xmlsoap.org/wsdl/"
   xmlns:wsdlsoap="http://schemas.xmlsoap.org/wsdl/soap/"
   xmlns:xsd="http://www.w3.org/2001/XMLSchema">
   <wsdl:message name="Exception"/>
```

```
<wsdl:message name="getQuoteRequest">
  <wsdl:part name="in0" type="xsd:string"/>
</wsdl:message>

<wsdl:message name="getQuoteResponse">
  <wsdl:part name="return" type="xsd:string"/>
</wsdl:message>

<wsdl:portType name="StockQuote">
  <wsdl:operation name="getQuote" parameterOrder="in0">
    <wsdl:input message="intf:getQuoteRequest"/>
    <wsdl:output message="intf:getQuoteResponse"/>
    <wsdl:fault message="intf:Exception" name="Exception"/>
  </wsdl:operation>
</wsdl:portType>

<wsdl:binding name="StockQuoteSoapBinding" type="intf:StockQuote">
  <wsdlsoap:binding style="rpc"
                    transport="http://schemas.xmlsoap.org/soap/http"/>
  <wsdl:operation name="getQuote">
  <wsdlsoap:operation soapAction=""/>
  <wsdl:input>
    <wsdlsoap:body
     encodingStyle="http://schemas.xmlsoap.org/soap/encoding/"
     namespace="http://localhost:8080/axis/services/StockQuote"
     use="encoded"/>
  </wsdl:input>
  <wsdl:output>
    <wsdlsoap:body
     encodingStyle="http://schemas.xmlsoap.org/soap/encoding/"
     namespace="http://localhost:8080/axis/services/StockQuote"
     use="encoded"/>
  </wsdl:output>
  </wsdl:operation>
</wsdl:binding>

<wsdl:service name="StockQuoteService">
```

We will take the `<port>` element here as our example to illustrate the concept of fully qualified names in XML. The `<port>` element is defined like this:

```
<wsdl:port binding="intf:StockQuoteSoapBinding" name="StockQuote">
  <wsdlsoap:address
   location="http://localhost:8080/axis/services/StockQuote"/>
</wsdl:port>
</wsdl:service>
</wsdl:definitions>
```

So, the local name `StockQuote` and the namespace `http://localhost:8080/axis/services/Stockquote` can be used to build a `QName` instance like this:

```
QName portQN = new QName("http://localhost:8080/axis/services/StockQuote",
   "StockQuote");
```

Many of the APIs in JAX-RPC require fully qualified names for elements, so you will notice this kind of code throughout all the samples.

## Try It Out – Using the getPort() Method

Now that we know how to build a `QName` instance, we can build a client application that invokes our stock quote service.

**1.** Save the above WSDL document in a file called `StockQuote.wsdl`, saved in a `\Chp06\ServiceTest` directory.

**2.** We now want to generate the `StockQuote` service interfaces and classes, similar to those we saw earlier in the chapter. To do this we need to run the WSDL2Java tool. First let's make sure we have the `wsdl4j.jar` file that ships with Axis in our classpath:

**set classpath=%classpath%;%axisDirectory%\lib\wsdl4j.jar**

Now run the following command to generate the necessary classes (assuming we're in the `\Chp06\ServiceTest` directory):

**java org.apache.axis.wsdl.WSDL2Java StockQuote.wsdl**

This will create five `.java` files in a new `\localhost` subdirectory:

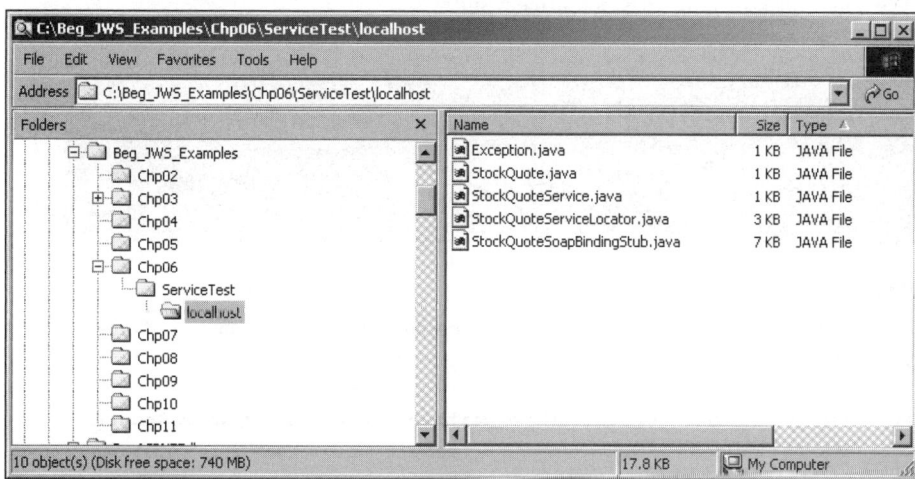

**3.** Now compile these generated classes:

**javac localhost\*.java**

**4.** Write the following example code in `ServiceTest.java` in the
`\Chp06\ServiceTest` directory:

```
import javax.xml.rpc.*;
import javax.xml.namespace.*;

import localhost.*;

public class ServiceTest {

  public static void main(String args[]) throws java.lang.Exception {
    QName portQN = new
      QName("http://localhost:8080/axis/services/StockQuote",
      "StockQuote");
    QName serviceQN = new
      QName("http://localhost:8080/axis/services/StockQuote",
      "StockQuoteService");
    Service service = ServiceFactory.newInstance().createService(
      new java.net.URL("file:stockquote.wsdl"), serviceQN);

    StockQuote port = (StockQuote)service.getPort(portQN, StockQuote.class);
    System.out.println("IBM stock price is : " + port.getQuote("IBM"));
  }
}
```

**5.** Finally execute our `ServiceTest` class:

**`java ServiceTest`**

We'll get our now familiar stock price result:

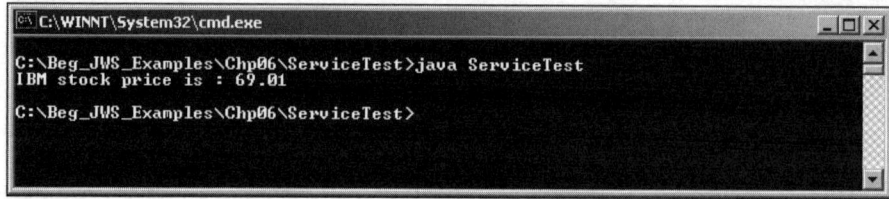

### How It Works

Getting back to the `getPort()` method, we can see that the returned object is of type
`java.rmi.Remote`:

```
public java.rmi.Remote getPort(QName portName, Class proxyInterface)
    throws ServiceException;
```

Here is where the service definition interface comes into play. In the `StockQuote` example that we
used earlier, this service definition interface is the `StockQuote` interface. A client can now downcast
the returned object from the `getPort()` method to an instance of `StockQuote`. Moreover, the class
of the returned interface is passed to the method in the second parameter. Here is how a client would
use this method:

```
...
QName portQN = new
   QName("http://localhost:8080/axis/services/StockQuote",
   "StockQuote");
QName serviceQN = new
   QName("http://localhost:8080/axis/services/StockQuote",
   "StockQuoteService");

Service service = ServiceFactory.newInstance().createService(
   new java.net.URL("file:stockquote.wsdl", serviceQN);
StockQuote port = (StockQuote)service.getPort(portQN, StockQuote.class);
System.out.println("The current stock price is " + port.getQuote("IBM"));
...
```

In this example, the `Service` object is instantiated using the `ServiceFactory` class, passing the URL of the WSDL document to it, plus the fully qualified name of the service within that document. There are other ways of creating a `Service` object, and we will revisit this later in an example. Then, the `getPort()` method is used to return a proxy that can be used by the client to invoke the service.

This client code reads the WSDL document for the web service at run time and can therefore react to changes made in that document. However, it takes advantage of the generated `StockQuote` class. Thus, we see a mix of the static and the dynamic invocation models here. Note that the location of the service, its URL, is not hard-coded in the client but it is read from the WSDL file at run time. This is done by using the `getPort()` method. The method will read the endpoint definition, or location, from the WSDL document.

## Other Variations

Let us look at some other variations. The following method is a variation of the method described above:

```
public java.rmi.Remote getPort(Class serviceDefInterface)
    throws ServiceException;
```

It does not require a port name to be passed and is used typically when there is only one port defined in the WSDL document.

The `getPorts()` method returns a collection of all ports defined in a WSDL document:

```
public java.util.Iterator getPorts();
```

In fact, it returns an `Iterator` allowing us to retrieve the fully qualified names of the ports as instances of the `QName` class. These names can then be used to retrieve individual proxy objects for each port using one of the `getPort()` methods described above.

## The createCall() Method

Moving on, we create a `Call` object from a given port name as shown in the code snippet below. A `Call` object can be used to make an invocation of a service, if no generated service definition interface (`StockQuote` in our example) is available. You will note that the programming style we use in this case is very different from the example above, where the returned dynamic proxy was used. If you are familiar with the use of reflection in the Java language, you may find that this is a similar style:

```
public Call createCall(QName portName) throws ServiceException;
```

The `Call` interface defines methods for setting parameters for a request. For example, coming back to the `StockQuote` example, we can set one parameter on the request for the ticker symbol of the requested stock. We can also set things like the name of the operation, the endpoint address, the encoding style, and other attributes on a `Call` object. Let us see this method now in practice.

## Try It Out – Using the createCall() Method

**1.** Save the following code example in the `CallTest.java` file:

```java
import javax.xml.rpc.*;
import javax.xml.namespace.*;

public class CallTest {

  public static void main(String args[]) throws java.lang.Exception  {

    Service service = ServiceFactory.newInstance().createService(null);
    Call call = service.createCall();
    call.setTargetEndpointAddress(
      "http://localhost:8080/axis/services/StockQuote");
    call.setOperationName(new QName(
      "http://localhost:8080/axis/services/StockQuote", "getQuote"));

    QName stringQN = new QName("http://www.w3.org/2001/XMLSchema",
      "string");

    call.addParameter("in0", stringQN, ParameterMode.IN);
    call.setReturnType(stringQN);

    String res = (String) call.invoke(new Object[] {"IBM"});

    System.out.println("IBM : " + res);
  }
}
```

**2.** Run the following commands for compiling and executing the code:

```
javac CallTest.java
java CallTest
```

The output will be as follows:

### How It Works

Using this approach, we have much finer control over how an individual request is built – and how the response is handled. First, we have to build a `Service` object and retrieve a `Call` object from it:

```
    ...
        Service service = ServiceFactory.newInstance().createService(null);
        Call call = service.createCall();
    ...
```

Now we can set attributes on the `Call` object. Note that these attributes can be retrieved from the WSDL document.

For example, let us look at the `in0` parameter, which we will add to the `Call` object next. This parameter maps to the content of the request message defined in WSDL:

```
    <wsdl:message name="getQuoteRequest">
      <wsdl:part name="in0" type="xsd:string"/>
    </wsdl:message>
```

Here is the definition of the operation and request message again, for our reference:

```
    <wsdl:message name="getQuoteResponse">
      <wsdl:part name="return" type="xsd:float"/>
    </wsdl:message>

    <wsdl:portType name="StockQuote">
      <wsdl:operation name="getQuote" parameterOrder="in0">
        <wsdl:input message="intf:getQuoteRequest"/>
        <wsdl:output message="intf:getQuoteResponse"/>
        <wsdl:fault message="intf:Exception" name="Exception"/>
      </wsdl:operation>
    </wsdl:portType>
```

The `<wsdl:input>` element refers to a message named `intf:getQuoteRequest`. This message is defined above, with one part in it, named `in0`. The name of this part is used as the parameter name when adding the parameter to the `Call` object:

```
        QName stringQN = new QName("http://www.w3.org/2001/XMLSchema",
          "string");
        call.addParameter("in0", stringQN, ParameterMode.IN);
```

The JAX-RPC specification dictates that those names have to match. Moreover, if we had more than one part listed in the `<wsdl:message>` element, then each one would be mapped to a parameter on the `Call` object, and their sequence as defined in the `<wsdl:message>` element must be preserved.

Finally, we indicate what response type we expect and invoke the service:

```
        call.setReturnType(stringQN);
        String res = (String) call.invoke(new Object[] {"IBM"});
        System.out.println("IBM : " + res);
```

Note that we as client developers are responsible for making sure that the attributes we set on the `Call` object are correct according to the WSDL definition. If we set one of these values incorrectly (for example, by using the wrong order of parameters), a run-time error may occur later when we call the service. This sequence can also be defined explicitly by using the `parameterOrder` attribute on the `<operation>` element.

Earlier, we described the case where a proxy object is created at run time, which can then be used to invoke a service. The right request message is built based on the definitions in the WSDL document. Here, we have more fine-grained control over how the message is built – and also how the response is handled, but we have to write more code manually, and we have to make sure that this code properly maps the WSDL definition.

Let us look at some other variations. Above, we have looked at one method that we can use to obtain a `Call` object. The `Service` interface defines a number of methods that allow us to create and retrieve `Call` objects, which can then be used similarly to the example above. These methods differ in how we define which operation we would like to be represented by the `Call` object. There is also a method to obtain an array of `Call` objects, one object per operation defined in the WSDL document, namely the `getCalls()` method.

# Type Mapping

One method on the `Service` interface that we have not talked about yet is the `getTypeMappingRegistry` method. Here is its signature:

```
public TypeMappingRegistry getTypeMappingRegistry();
```

This is a good time to talk in more detail about type mapping. The goal is pretty simple: web services technology is based on the exchange of XML messages. We want to build applications in Java, so we need to find a way to convert XML constructs into Java objects. That is where the type mapping registry comes in handy. This registry contains an entry for each data type that a web service deals with, namely its XML type definition, Java type definition, and how to convert one into the other. This last part is defined by a couple of interfaces called `Serializer` and `Deserializer`. A `Serializer` turns a Java object into an XML string, and a `Deserializer` does the opposite.

Most implementations of JAX-RPC will come with a set of predefined serializers and deserializers, which can convert the most common data types. So, if we use basic types like `String`, `Integer`, or `Boolean` on our web services interface, we won't have to do anything. The mapping between XML Schema types and Java types for those is well defined.

On top of the `Serializer` and `Deserializer` classes for the basic types, the Apache Axis package contains a `BeanSerializer` class and a `BeanDeserializer` class. These two classes can handle the conversion of a JavaBean into an XML document and vice versa.

Effectively, this means that we should not have to worry about type mapping too much, at least not in the beginning stage. It may become more of an issue if complex data types are exchanged via a web service link. Still, in most cases, we will use tooling to create the right serializer and deserializer code.

# JAX-RPC and SOAP

The JAX-RPC API was defined in a way that lets us use it independently of the protocol that is used to invoke a web service. However, most if not all web services today use SOAP as the invocation protocol. So there is a special section in the specification that explains how to use JAX-RPC with respect to SOAP only.

Interaction with a web service over SOAP can happen in one of two ways, or styles. One style is called `rpc` style and the other one is called `document` style (for more information on this refer to Chapter 4). In short, `rpc` style means that the invocation of a web service is viewed as a function invocation, where parameters are passed into the function and a result value is received back. The `document` style means that we are sending an XML document to a web service, and may or may not get another XML document back as a response. We will try below to explain common rules of thumb to define which one to use, and you will find other references to this throughout the book.

On top of the invocation style, there are two main ways of encoding data into a SOAP message: one is to use the default SOAP encoding as defined in the SOAP specification, the other one is called **literal XML**. With literal encoding (or rather, no encoding at all) you don't encode any of the data, but add a chunk of XML to the SOAP body.

In almost all cases, only two combinations of these are used: web services either support RPC-style invocation with default SOAP encoding, or they support document style with literal XML encoding. The JAX-RPC specification requires that any implementation of the API supports the two combinations mentioned above – the other possible combinations are optional. In fact, the specification requires that the client-side API does not differ between the two cases, so that we can use web services for both styles in the same way. There is an exception to that rule in a case where there is no easy mapping of a type defined in WSDL to a Java type. We will get to that in a second.

So when do we choose one way over the other? In many cases, the choice will be determined by the implementation of the web service.

Let's assume we have an application that can process XML documents as part of its external interface. It may store XML documents in a database, or process them in some other way. Now we want to add a web-services layer to that application, to make it accessible via SOAP, just to name one option. In that case, document style with literal XML encoding will probably be the easier choice, because we can define the XML constructs that our application already deals with and define them as messages in our WSDL definition for the new service. All of the parsing and interpreting of these XML messages is already done within our application, so there is no need to add another layer to it where this is done again.

On the other hand, we may have an application that has a pure Java-based external interface. Clients using this application pass Java objects to it and get Java objects returned. In those cases, if we add a web services wrapper around the application, we will want to support RPC style with default SOAP encoding as this gives us a more object-based view on a web service, where we send parameters to the service and get a return value. This is the reason that the style attribute in the WSDL bindings for SOAP deserves its name. The question is whether our service lets clients make a remote procedure call, or whether we exchange documents with our clients. Obviously, there is gray area in between those, and some tools don't even give a choice to begin with and simply force the developer into one style over the other.

The JAX-RPC specification states that interfaces do not change between the two styles. In other words, you cannot tell from the generated interfaces which style has been defined in the WSDL document for a web service. The differences between the styles are handled strictly in the underlying runtime. The specification defines how a given WSDL type definition is turned into a remote service interface in Java. In the case of basic data types, or simple structures, this is a straightforward thing, and the specification defines how to map those types into Java.

A problem, however, exists if some of the defined message parts cannot be mapped to Java. One example for this is if an XML Schema defines attributes to be part of an XML document. Attributes cannot be mapped to Java types. So what do we do? In these cases, the interface will contain an object that simply wraps the XML construct. We will have a look at an example for this in a second, but first let us see where this 'XML object wrapper' comes from.

There is a standard Java API, called **JAXM**, or **Java API for XML Messaging**, which describes how to send and receive XML-based messages in Java. One aspect of this specification deals with the notion of sending and receiving SOAP messages. The JAX-RPC API takes advantage of some classes that have been defined for JAXM and describe XML documents containing SOAP messages. One of these classes is called `javax.xml.soap.SOAPElement`. It provides basic methods for building and/or parsing an XML element.

JAX-RPC takes advantage of the `SOAPElement` class by saying that whenever a type cannot be mapped into Java according to the JAX-RPC rules it shows up as a `SOAPElement` in the interface. It is then up to the requester to build the right object, and up to the service provider to parse it, because no automatic way is defined to turn it into a regular object. In most cases, this will occur when the web service uses document style and literal XML encoding.

## Try It Out – Complex Type Mapping

Let's enhance and modify the WSDL document for the stock quote web service that we have been using before, to see how this works.

**1.** Modify the WSDL document:

```xml
<?xml version="1.0" encoding="UTF-8"?>
<wsdl:definitions
   targetNamespace="http://localhost/axis/services/StockQuote"
   xmlns="http://schemas.xmlsoap.org/wsdl/"
   xmlns:SOAP-ENC="http://schemas.xmlsoap.org/soap/encoding/"
   xmlns:impl="http://localhost/axis/services/StockQuote-impl"
   xmlns:intf="http://localhost/axis/services/StockQuote"
   xmlns:wsdl="http://schemas.xmlsoap.org/wsdl/"
   xmlns:wsdlsoap="http://schemas.xmlsoap.org/wsdl/soap/"
   xmlns:xsd="http://www.w3.org/2001/XMLSchema"
   xmlns:types="http://localhost/StockQuote">
<types>
  <xsd:schema elementFormDefault="qualified"
     targetNamespace="http://localhost/StockQuote">
    <xsd:element name="GetQuote">
      <xsd:complexType>
        <xsd:sequence>
          <xsd:element minOccurs="0"
            maxOccurs="1"
```

```
                  name="StockSymbol"
                  type="xsd:string" />
               <xsd:element minOccurs="0"
                  maxOccurs="1"
                  name="AdditionalInfo"
                  type="xsd:anyType" />
            </xsd:sequence>
            <attribute name="theAttribute"
               type="xsd:string"
               use="optional"/>
          </xsd:complexType>
        </xsd:element>
      </xsd:schema>
   </types>

   <wsdl:message name="Exception"/>

   <wsdl:message name="getQuoteRequest">
     <wsdl:part name="in0" element="types:GetQuote"/>
   </wsdl:message>

   <wsdl:message name="getQuoteResponse">
     <wsdl:part name="return" type="xsd:string"/>
   </wsdl:message>

   <wsdl:portType name="StockQuote">
     <wsdl:operation name="getQuote" parameterOrder="in0">
       <wsdl:input message="intf:getQuoteRequest"/>
       <wsdl:output message="intf:getQuoteResponse"/>
       <wsdl:fault message="intf:Exception" name="Exception"/>
     </wsdl:operation>
   </wsdl:portType>

   <wsdl:binding name="StockQuoteSoapBinding" type="intf:StockQuote">
     <wsdlsoap:binding style="document"
       transport="http://schemas.xmlsoap.org/soap/http"/>
     <wsdl:operation name="getQuote">
       <wsdlsoap:operation soapAction=""/>
       <wsdl:input>
         <wsdlsoap:body use="literal"
           namespace="http://localhost/axis/services/StockQuote"/>
       </wsdl:input>
       <wsdl:output>
         <wsdlsoap:body
           namespace="http://localhost/axis/services/StockQuote"
           use="literal"/>
       </wsdl:output>
     </wsdl:operation>
   </wsdl:binding>

   <wsdl:service name="StockQuoteService">
     <wsdl:port binding="intf:StockQuoteSoapBinding" name="StockQuote">

       <wsdlsoap:address
         location="http://localhost:8080/axis/services/StockQuote"/>
     </wsdl:port>
   </wsdl:service>
</wsdl:definitions>
```

**2.** Invoke the `WSDL2Java` tool in Axis:

```
java org.apache.axis.wsdl.WSDL2Java stockquote_complextype_document.wsdl
```

This creates a number of Java classes, just as before. One of them is called `StockQuoteSoapBinding.java`:

```
package localhost;

public interface StockQuoteSoapBinding extends java.rmi.Remote {

  public java.lang.String getQuote(localhost.GetQuote in0) throws
    java.rmi.RemoteException, localhost.Exception;
}
```

The `WSDL2Java` tool also creates a class named `GetQuote` for us – we will explain it below:

```
package localhost;

public class GetQuote implements java.io.Serializable {
  private java.lang.String stockSymbol;
  private java.lang.Object additionalInfo;
  private java.lang.String theAttribute;  // attribute

  public GetQuote() {}

  public java.lang.String getStockSymbol() {
    return stockSymbol;
  }

 ... // additional getters and setters left out here
  // Type metadata
  private static org.apache.axis.description.TypeDesc typeDesc =
    new org.apache.axis.description.TypeDesc(GetQuote.class);

  static {
    org.apache.axis.description.FieldDesc field = new
      org.apache.axis.description.AttributeDesc();
    field.setFieldName("theAttribute");
    typeDesc.addFieldDesc(field);
    field = new org.apache.axis.description.ElementDesc();
    field.setFieldName("stockSymbol");
    field.setXmlName(new
      javax.xml.rpc.namespace.QName("http://localhost/StockQuote",
      "StockSymbol"));
    typeDesc.addFieldDesc(field);
    field = new org.apache.axis.description.ElementDesc();
    field.setFieldName("additionalInfo");
    field.setXmlName(new
      javax.xml.rpc.namespace.QName("http://localhost/StockQuote",
```

```
     "AdditionalInfo"));
   typeDesc.addFieldDesc(field);
};


/**
 * Return type metadata object
 */
public static org.apache.axis.description.TypeDesc getTypeDesc() {
   return typeDesc;
}


/**
 * Get Custom Serializer
 */
public static org.apache.axis.encoding.Serializer getSerializer(
   String mechType, Class _javaType, javax.xml.rpc.namespace.QName _xmlType)
{
   return
   new  org.apache.axis.encoding.ser.BeanSerializer(_javaType,
     _xmlType,typeDesc);
};


/**
 * Get Custom Deserializer
 */
public static org.apache.axis.encoding.Deserializer getDeserializer(
   String mechType, Class _javaType,
   javax.xml.rpc.namespace.QName _xmlType) {
   return
     new  org.apache.axis.encoding.ser.BeanDeserializer(
     _javaType, _xmlType,typeDesc);
};
}
```

### How It Works

Let's walk through what is going on here. First, we changed the getQuoteRequest message in the WSDL definition to contain a complex type instead of a string:

```
<wsdl:message name="getQuoteRequest">
  <wsdl:part name="in0" element="types:GetQuote"/>
</wsdl:message>
```

This complex type, called GetQuote, is described in an XML Schema, embedded in the <types> element. Note that the complex type contains two elements and one attribute. One element, called StockSymbol, is a string. The other one, called AdditionalInfo, is an anyType. You will notice later that our JAX-RPC implementation, the Apache Axis package, maps this type to a Java object. The optional attribute is called theAttribute and is a string:

```
<xsd:schema elementFormDefault="qualified"
  targetNamespace="http://localhost/StockQuote">
  <xsd:element name="GetQuote">
    <xsd:complexType>
      <xsd:sequence>
        <xsd:element minOccurs="0"
          maxOccurs="1"
          name="StockSymbol"
          type="xsd:string" />
        <xsd:element minOccurs="0"
          maxOccurs="1"
          name="AdditionalInfo"
          type="xsd:anyType" />
      </xsd:sequence>
      <attribute name="theAttribute"
        type="xsd:string"
        use="optional"/>
    </xsd:complexType>
  </xsd:element>
</xsd:schema>
```

Besides adding a complex type, we have changed the SOAP operation style from rpc to document, and the encoding from the SOAP default encoding to literal:

```
<wsdl:binding name="StockQuoteSoapBinding" type="intf:StockQuote">
  <wsdlsoap:binding style="document"
    transport="http://schemas.xmlsoap.org/soap/http"/>
  <wsdl:operation name="getQuote">
    <wsdlsoap:operation soapAction=""/>
    <wsdl:input>
      <wsdlsoap:body
        use="literal"
        namespace="http://localhost/axis/services/StockQuote"/>
    </wsdl:input>
    <wsdl:output>
      <wsdlsoap:body
        namespace="http://localhost/axis/services/StockQuote"
        use="literal"/>
    </wsdl:output>
  </wsdl:operation>
</wsdl:binding>
```

The StockQuoteSoapBinding interface looks similar to the service interface that we have seen before. The only difference is that the getQuote() method now does not take a string as its only parameter, it takes an object of type localhost.GetQuote instead:

```
...
public java.lang.String getQuote(localhost.GetQuote in0) throws
    java.rmi.RemoteException, localhost.Exception;
...
```

This parameter maps to the `GetQuote` type definition in the WSDL document. The `WSDL2Java` tool generated the `GetQuote` class for us to represent this data type. There are a few interesting things to note about this class. First of all, it contains properties that map to the elements of the `GetQuote` type. There is also the attribute, `theAttribute`, mapped to a property of this class. The JAX-RPC specification defines support for attributes as optional, so other implementations may not be able to handle it, or may even deal with it in a different way (for example, by using the `SOAPElement` class out of JAXM).

```
public class GetQuote implements java.io.Serializable {
    private java.lang.String stockSymbol;
    private java.lang.Object additionalInfo;
    private java.lang.String theAttribute;  // attribute
...
}
```

The `GetQuote` class also has a property called `typeDesc`, which contains metadata about the structure of the mapped XML document. Here you can see that the attribute is handled differently from the elements:

```
// Type metadata
private static org.apache.axis.description.TypeDesc typeDesc =
    new org.apache.axis.description.TypeDesc(GetQuote.class);

static {
    org.apache.axis.description.FieldDesc field = new
        org.apache.axis.description.AttributeDesc();
    field.setFieldName("theAttribute");
    typeDesc.addFieldDesc(field);
    field = new org.apache.axis.description.ElementDesc();
    field.setFieldName("stockSymbol");
    field.setXmlName(new
        javax.xml.rpc.namespace.QName("http://localhost/StockQuote",
        "StockSymbol"));
    typeDesc.addFieldDesc(field);
    field = new org.apache.axis.description.ElementDesc();
    field.setFieldName("additionalInfo");
    field.setXmlName(new
        javax.xml.rpc.namespace.QName("http://localhost/StockQuote",
        "AdditionalInfo"));
    typeDesc.addFieldDesc(field);
};
```

This type description object is also used by two other methods, namely the `getSerializer` and the `getDeserializer` methods. The `Serializer` and `Deserializer` classes are in charge of turning the appropriate XML pieces in the SOAP message into Java and vice versa:

```
public static org.apache.axis.encoding.Serializer getSerializer(
    String mechType, Class _javaType,
    javax.xml.rpc.namespace.QName _xmlType) {
    return
    new org.apache.axis.encoding.ser.BeanSerializer(
        _javaType, _xmlType, typeDesc);
```

```
  };

  /**
   * Get Custom Deserializer
   */
  public static org.apache.axis.encoding.Deserializer getDeserializer(
    String mechType, Class _javaType,
    javax.xml.rpc.namespace.QName _xmlType) {
    return
      new  org.apache.axis.encoding.ser.BeanDeserializer(
      _javaType, _xmlType,typeDesc);
  };
```

Let's now look at the same WSDL document but with a few modifications added to it.

## Try It Out – Complex Type Mapping with SOAP Encoding

We can now take the same WSDL document as a basis and see what happens when we change the invocation style to rpc and the encoding style to literal.

**1.** Modify the code example accordingly:

```
<?xml version="1.0" encoding="UTF-8"?>
<wsdl:definitions
  targetNamespace="http://localhost/axis/services/StockQuote"
  xmlns="http://schemas.xmlsoap.org/wsdl/"
  xmlns:SOAP-ENC="http://schemas.xmlsoap.org/soap/encoding/"
  xmlns:impl="http://localhost/axis/services/StockQuote-impl"
  xmlns:intf="http://localhost/axis/services/StockQuote"
  xmlns:wsdl="http://schemas.xmlsoap.org/wsdl/"
  xmlns:wsdlsoap="http://schemas.xmlsoap.org/wsdl/soap/"
  xmlns:xsd="http://www.w3.org/2001/XMLSchema"
  xmlns:types="http://localhost/StockQuote">
  <types>
    <xsd:schema elementFormDefault="qualified"
      targetNamespace="http://localhost/StockQuote">
      <xsd:element name="GetQuote">
        <xsd:complexType>
          <xsd:sequence>
            <xsd:element minOccurs="0"
              maxOccurs="1"
              name="StockSymbol"
              type="xsd:string" />
            <xsd:element minOccurs="0"
              maxOccurs="1"
              name="AdditionalInfo"
              type="xsd:anyType" />
          </xsd:sequence>
          <attribute name="theAttribute"
            type="xsd:string"
            use="optional"/>
```

```
          </xsd:complexType>
        </xsd:element>
      </xsd:schema>

    </types>
    <wsdl:message name="Exception"/>

    <wsdl:message name="getQuoteRequest">
      <wsdl:part name="in0" element="types:GetQuote"/>
    </wsdl:message>

    <wsdl:message name="getQuoteResponse">
      <wsdl:part name="return" type="xsd:string"/>
    </wsdl:message>

    <wsdl:portType name="StockQuote">
      <wsdl:operation name="getQuote" parameterOrder="in0">
        <wsdl:input message="intf:getQuoteRequest"/>
        <wsdl:output message="intf:getQuoteResponse"/>
        <wsdl:fault message="intf:Exception" name="Exception"/>
      </wsdl:operation>
    </wsdl:portType>

    <wsdl:binding name="StockQuoteSoapBinding" type="intf:StockQuote">
      <wsdlsoap:binding style="rpc"
        transport="http://schemas.xmlsoap.org/soap/http"/>
      <wsdl:operation name="getQuote">
        <wsdlsoap:operation soapAction=""/>
        <wsdl:input>
          <wsdlsoap:body
            use="encoded"
            encodingStyle="http://schemas.xmlsoap.org/soap/encoding/"
            namespace="http://localhost/axis/services/StockQuote"/>
        </wsdl:input>
        <wsdl:output>
          <wsdlsoap:body
            namespace="http://localhost/axis/services/StockQuote"
            encodingStyle="http://schemas.xmlsoap.org/soap/encoding/"
            use="encoded"/>
        </wsdl:output>
      </wsdl:operation>
    </wsdl:binding>

    <wsdl:service name="StockQuoteService">
      <wsdl:port binding="intf:StockQuoteSoapBinding" name="StockQuote">
        <wsdlsoap:address
          location="http://localhost:8080/axis/services/StockQuote"/>
      </wsdl:port>
    </wsdl:service>
  </wsdl:definitions>
```

**2.** Use the `WSDL2Java` tool in Axis again to generate the client code for this new service definition:

```
java org.apache.axis.wsdl.WSDL2Java stockquote_complextype_rpc.wsdl
```

### How It Works

The only difference between this WSDL document and the one in the previous example is the invocation style and encoding. Both of these values are defined in the `<wsdlsoap:binding>` element:

```
<wsdlsoap:binding style="rpc"
  transport="http://schemas.xmlsoap.org/soap/http"/>
    <wsdl:operation name="getQuote">
      <wsdlsoap:operation soapAction=""/>
      <wsdl:input>
        <wsdlsoap:body
          encodingStyle="http://schemas.xmlsoap.org/soap/encoding/"
          use="encoded"
          namespace="http://localhost/axis/services/StockQuote"/>
      </wsdl:input>
      <wsdl:output>
        <wsdlsoap:body
          namespace="http://localhost/axis/services/StockQuote"
          encodingStyle="http://schemas.xmlsoap.org/soap/encoding/"
          use="encoded"/>
      </wsdl:output>
    </wsdl:operation>
  </wsdl:binding>
```

Most of the generated code is exactly the same. Clients using this code will not be different. In other words, the interface hides the details of these things from the client developer.

# Non-SOAP Web Services

Most web services today are invoked using SOAP over HTTP. This makes sense, since web services technology started out as something that would allow applications to communicate with each other over the Internet in a standard way.

What we see today, however, is a trend towards building service-oriented architecture. While the concept has been around for some time, we now have a widely used mechanism to implement it, namely, web services. This expands the concept of application-to-application communication beyond the Internet and SOAP over HTTP. Applications are connected internally, in an intranet, or even on the same computer. For an application developer, the type of protocol used to invoke a service should be transparent. The run time system should pick the best protocol depending on how and where a service is deployed.

For example, assume that a JavaBean provides some business logic. To make this business logic available as a web service, we typically add or generate a servlet that can receive SOAP over HTTP requests, for example, by using the Apache Axis package. This servlet will then map request messages for the web service into Java calls to the JavaBean. But what if the requester of the service happens to be running in the same process, like the JavaBean with the business logic? Obviously, we can spare the overhead of creating an XML message and sending it over HTTP. We might as well make a local Java call.

# Non-SOAP Protocol Bindings in WSDL

To allow this kind of optimization, we need to find a way for a service to describe how it can be accessed over different protocols. The WSDL `<binding>` element is the perfect place for this. In fact, it is meant for exactly this purpose. The WSDL specification defines protocol bindings for SOAP and HTTP, but it also states that new bindings can be defined.

So, in our example above, we could define bindings that allow a local Java call instead of going over SOAP. Note, however, that no mechanism exists today to pick the best protocol to be used at run time. The type of binding to be used is still a decision made while developing the client code. Future web services implementations may offer such functionality.

## Using Java Bindings in WSDL

Here is an example of what the Java bindings for our `StockQuote` example could look like:

```xml
<?xml version="1.0" encoding="UTF-8"?>
<wsdl:definitions
   targetNamespace="http://localhost/axis/services/StockQuote"
   xmlns="http://schemas.xmlsoap.org/wsdl/"
   xmlns:SOAP-ENC="http://schemas.xmlsoap.org/soap/encoding/"
   xmlns:impl="http://localhost/axis/services/StockQuote-impl"
   xmlns:intf="http://localhost/axis/services/StockQuote"
   xmlns:wsdl="http://schemas.xmlsoap.org/wsdl/"
   xmlns:wsdlsoap="http://schemas.xmlsoap.org/wsdl/soap/"
   xmlns:java="http://schemas.xmlsoap.org/wsdl/java/"
   xmlns:xsd="http://www.w3.org/2001/XMLSchema">
   ...
   <wsdl:binding name="StockQuoteJavaBinding" type="intf:StockQuote">
     <java:binding/>
   </wsdl:binding>

   <wsdl:service name="StockQuoteService">
     <wsdl:port binding="intf:StockQuoteJavaBinding" name="StockQuote">
       <java:address class="com.wrox.jws.StockQuote"/>
     </wsdl:port>
   </wsdl:service>
</wsdl:definitions>
```

The WSDL listing above contains the regular definitions for the messages and operations of the service. What is interesting here, and why this example is different from all the others that we have looked at so far, is the `<binding>` and `<port>` elements.

Let us look at the `<binding>` element first:

```xml
<wsdl:binding name="StockQuoteJavaBinding" type="intf:StockQuote">
   <java:binding/>
</wsdl:binding>
```

As usual, the `<wsdl:binding>` element contains a child element that indicates the specific protocol that is supported. In this case, it is the `<java:binding>` element. Here, this element is empty, because there is no protocol-specific information needed.

The `<port>` element contains the location of the service implementation; in this case it is just a Java class:

```
<wsdl:port binding="intf:StockQuoteJavaBinding" name="StockQuote">
  <java:address class="com.wrox.jws.StockQuote"/>
</wsdl:port>
```

At runtime, we can interpret this binding by simply invoking a method on the Java class as defined in the `<java:address>` element.

*Note that WSDL documents can contain multiple binding and port elements, so that we can define several ways of accessing a web service. Clients can then choose the method that is best for them.*

### Other Examples

Another example for a useful WSDL protocol binding is the **Java 2 Connector Architecture (JCA)**. This architecture, which is part of the J2EE standard, defines how certain back-end non-J2EE environments called **Enterprise Information Systems (EIS)** can be connected to a J2EE application server in a transactional and secure way. Explaining the connector architecture goes well beyond the scope of this book, but what we can note here is that it is the recommended way in Java to connect to existing legacy applications and databases. This allows for integration of existing environments into new J2EE-based solutions. The J2EE application server can include the legacy backend into its transactional control and connections to backends can be pooled and shared among clients.

We mentioned earlier that web services technology plays a big role in Enterprise Application Integration. A JCA connector provides the 'plumbing' to make this possible. We can invoke requests to an EIS via the connector, which will then pass it on to the backend. Thus, if we can define a WSDL binding for JCA as the protocol, we can view the backend that we want to integrate as a web service and leave the hard work of getting the invocation done to the connector.

Here is what the stock quote bindings for a sample JCA connector, going over CICS in this case, would look like:

```
<?xml version="1.0" encoding="UTF-8"?>
<wsdl:definitions
  targetNamespace="http://localhost/axis/services/StockQuote"
  xmlns="http://schemas.xmlsoap.org/wsdl/"
  xmlns:SOAP-ENC="http://schemas.xmlsoap.org/soap/encoding/"
  xmlns:impl="http://localhost/axis/services/StockQuote-impl"
  xmlns:intf="http://localhost/axis/services/StockQuote"
  xmlns:wsdl="http://schemas.xmlsoap.org/wsdl/"
  xmlns:wsdlsoap="http://schemas.xmlsoap.org/wsdl/soap/"
  xmlns:cics="http://schemas.xmlsoap.org/wsdl/cics/"
  xmlns:xsd="http://www.w3.org/2001/XMLSchema">
  <wsdl:message name="Exception"/>

  <wsdl:message name="getQuoteRequest">
    <wsdl:part name="in0" type="xsd:string"/>
  </wsdl:message>
```

```
     <wsdl:message name="getQuoteResponse">
       <wsdl:part name="return" type="xsd:string"/>
     </wsdl:message>

     <wsdl:portType name="StockQuote">
       <wsdl:operation name="getQuote" parameterOrder="in0">
         <wsdl:input message="intf:getQuoteRequest"/>
         <wsdl:output message="intf:getQuoteResponse"/>
         <wsdl:fault message="intf:Exception" name="Exception"/>
       </wsdl:operation>
     </wsdl:portType>

     <wsdl:binding name="StockQuoteJCABinding" type="intf:StockQuote">
       <format:typemapping style="COBOL" encoding="COBOL">
         <format:typemap typename="Symbol"
           formattype="StockSymbol.ccp:SYMBOL"/>
       </format:typemapping>
       <operation name='getQuote'>
         <cics:operation functionName="GETQUOTE" />
       <input>
         ...
       </input>
       <output>
         ...
       </output>
     </wsdl:binding>

     <wsdl:service name="StockQuoteService">
       <wsdl:port binding="intf:StockQuoteJCABinding" name="StockQuote">
         <cics:address connectionURL="..." serverName="CICS_A" />
       </wsdl:port>
     </wsdl:service>
   </wsdl:definitions>
```

Note that these bindings are not standardized. We won't go into any detail here about how to build and use a JCA connector, or how exactly the bindings above are built and used. This was just to show the idea of non-SOAP binding protocols and how they could be mapped to a WSDL document. Obviously, if these bindings were part of a standard, that would improve portability between implementations by different vendors, making it desirable that such standardization takes place in the near future.

In order to use web services that have been defined this way, we need a Java client implementation that can interpret these protocol bindings at run time and generate the right kind of invocation.

# The Web Services Invocation Framework (WSIF)

So far in this chapter, we have looked at static and dynamic ways to invoke web services. In many cases, this involved the generation of code, based on the WSDL definition for a service. Thus, the client code introduced so far never showed a truly dynamic invocation model. In JAX-RPC, we either generated a service interface and used a proxy via the `javax.xml.rpc.Service.getPort` method or we created a `Call` object and set all of the parameters of the invocation manually.

In this section, we want to focus on an alternative approach to web service invocation, which is more dynamic and, most of all, completely independent from any protocol. Thus, the same client code can support not only invocations via SOAP over HTTP, but also invocations that are simple local Java calls or calls over a JCA connector, just to name two examples.

The WSIF provides an API and runtime that does exactly what we are looking for – invocation of web services independent from the supported protocol. Originally developed by IBM, it is in the process of being turned into an open source project at the Apache foundation. At the time of this writing, there are nightly builds of WSIF at Apache, but no external driver has been released yet. As part of this transition of WSIF into an open source project, the package names will have changed from being based on `com.ibm.wsif` to `org.apache.wsif`. We will stick with the `com.ibm.wsif` package names here, but you should have no problem converting the code to work with latest release from Apache once there are external releases of it.

WSIF depends on a package called WSDL4J, which is an open source Java API for reading and creating WSDL documents (WSDL4J is also the base for a proposed standard Java API to process WSDL. The proposal is captured under JSR 110: http://jcp.org/jsr/detail/110.jsp). In other words, it provides us with an interface that lets us interpret an existing WSDL document, or build a brand new one. It contains Java wrapper classes for all of the elements defined in WSDL. For example, there is a class called `javax.wsdl.Operation`, and also one called `javax.wsdl.PortType`. At the top of the WSDL4J API class hierarchy is a class called `javax.wsdl.Definition`, which captures most of the WSDL document.

Invoking a web service through WSIF is based on the WSDL document that describes that service. No code is generated upfront; all handling is done at run time.

## Try It Out – Invoking a Web Service with WSIF

Let us step through an example that shows how to invoke a web service with WSIF. We will invoke the stock quote web service that we have used before. Assume here that a file named `stockquote.wsdl` exists.

**1.** We first need to get hold of the WSIF package. At the time of writing this was easier said than done because it was still in transition from IBM to Apache. Eventually you should be able to download it from the Apache site, but at the time of writing we downloaded it from Alphaworks (http://alphaworks.ibm.com/tech/wsif).

**2.** Save the following example code in `WSIFSample.java`:

```java
import javax.wsdl.*;
import org.xml.sax.*;
import java.io.*;
import com.ibm.wsdl.xml.*;
import com.ibm.wsif.*;

public class WSIFSample {

    public static void main(String[] args) throws Exception {
```

```
    Definition def = WSDLReader.readWSDL(null,
      new InputSource("http://localhost:8080/axis/stockquote.wsdl"));
    WSIFDynamicPortFactory dpf = new WSIFDynamicPortFactory(def);
    WSIFPort port = dpf.getPort();
    WSIFMessage input = port.createInputMessage();
    WSIFMessage output = port.createOutputMessage();
    WSIFMessage fault = port.createFaultMessage();

    WSIFPart inputPart =
      new WSIFJavaPart(java.lang.String.class, "IBM");
    input.setPart("in0", inputPart);
    port.executeRequestResponseOperation("getQuote",
      input, output, fault);
    WSIFPart outputPart = output.getPart("return");
    System.out.println("\tResult : " + outputPart);
  }
}
```

**3.** Run the following commands to compile and execute it:

```
javac WSIFSample.java
java WSIFSample
```

*The IBM version of WSIF also requires an Apache SOAP installation but presumably when the project is fully moved to Apache this will be replaced by Axis.*

```
C:\WINNT\System32\cmd.exe                                                _ □ ×

C:\Beg_JWS_Examples\Chp06\WSIF>javac WSIFSample.java

C:\Beg_JWS_Examples\Chp06\WSIF>java WSIFSample
        Result : com.ibm.wsif.WSIFJavaPart@5e5a50

C:\Beg_JWS_Examples\Chp06\WSIF>_
```

## How It Works

Notice that this approach focuses a lot on the definitions made in the WSDL document. That is everything we need to do. We will now walk through a code sample that shows how these steps look in Java code.

Step 1 was to read in the WSDL document and store it in a `javax.wsdl.Definition` object (note that the package declarations are omitted to make the code more readable):

```
Definition def = WSDLReader.readWSDL(null,
  new InputSource("http://localhost:8000/axis/stockquote.wsdl"));
```

Next, the dynamic port factory is created. All type mapping between the XML types declared in the WSDL and the Java classes that are used in the client is defined on this factory:

```
WSIFDynamicPortFactory dpf = new WSIFDynamicPortFactory(def);
```

Note that to make a dynamic call, Java classes must already exist for the types that are declared in the `<types>` element of the WSDL document (or in the schema that is included via an `<import>` element). In our case, this is not needed since all the types the stock quote web service handles are basic data types. In case of a WSDL definition that defines complex types on its interface, a mapping is needed, and the port factory is the place to add such mappings.

> **The next release of WSIF is scheduled to take advantage of yet another technology that will define a way to handle this dynamically. This dynamic handling is done through the notion of generic Java objects that map an XML tree. You can find out more about this technology at http://www.alphaworks.ibm.com/tech/jrom.**

Now we can retrieve the `com.ibm.wsif.WSIFPort` object and wrap the messages and parts:

```
WSIFPort port = dpf.getPort();

WSIFMessage input = port.createInputMessage();
WSIFMessage output = port.createOutputMessage();
WSIFMessage fault = port.createFaultMessage();

WSIFPart inputPart = new WSIFJavaPart(java.lang.String.class, "IBM");
input.setPart("in0", inputPart);
```

If we wanted to write a completely generic client, that is, a client that can read and interpret any WSDL document, we would have to add code here that reads the part definitions and fills in appropriate values. For example, in our stock quote case, the input message contains one part of type string. We can map this into the code above. To make this dynamic, we would have to read the part definition from the WSDL document. Then we would detect, for this case, that the input message contains one part that is of type `String`. Given this information, we could build the `com.ibm.wsif.WSIFPart` object. Note, however, that this can turn into rather lengthy code, especially in cases where we have to deal with complex data types.

We are now ready to invoke the service with `executeRequestResponseOperation()` on the `com.ibm.wsif.WSIFPort` object:

```
port.executeRequestResponseOperation("getQuote", input, output, fault);
```

This is the only place where the `<operation>` is referenced by its name. The result of the call can now be retrieved from the output message:

```
WSIFPart outputPart = output.getPart("return");
```

An important thing that this code shows is that the service is invoked independently from the actual protocol that is used. In other words, this code will work for a SOAP binding as well as for an HTTP binding of the service, and no additional client package is required. The WSIF uses something called a **dynamic provider** for this. Based on the specification in the WSDL document, a provider that implements the right protocol is used. For example, if `<soap:binding>` is specified, a class called `WSIFDynamicProvider_ApacheSOAP` is used to make the call. However, this never shows up in the client code. This means that we could write our own extension to WSIF to support our own protocol bindings, by supplying a specific dynamic provider.

This example shows how we can deal with a web service on a WSDL level, without requiring any knowledge about the protocol it supports and how the service was implemented. The use of an abstract API like WSDL4J together with additional support for dynamic invocation as provided by the WSIF makes this possible.

# Summary

In this chapter, we have seen that there are different ways in which a client can invoke web services. In the static model, tools are used to generate client-side classes from the WSDL definition of a service. These classes can then be used by client developers who, consequently, don't have to worry about the network protocol that is used to invoke a service, or how to build responses for it, and interpret responses from it.

In the dynamic model, client-side objects are generated at run time, from the WSDL definition of the service. This still allows client code to be developed without any knowledge about the actual invocation mechanism. In other words, client programmers don't have to know the details of SOAP to use a service. There are variations to the dynamic model, one of which promotes client classes that are completely independent from any kind of predefined code.

Both static and dynamic invocations of web services can be done using the classes and interfaces defined in the JAX-RPC API. This API will standardize the access to web services for the J2EE world. For example, it specifies how to obtain a reference to a proxy object that can handle interaction with a WSDL-based web service. These proxies can be generated or created at run time by the JAX-RPC environment.

Finally, we learned how web services technology is not restricted to SOAP. Invocations to existing services can be made over a variety of protocols, for example, via RMI/IIOP or JMS. The supported protocol can be described in the <binding> element in WSDL. A run-time environment that takes advantage of these new bindings is the WSIF. It allows dynamic clients to be built strictly based on a service WSDL document. These clients can then build valid requests for that web service based on the supported access protocols.

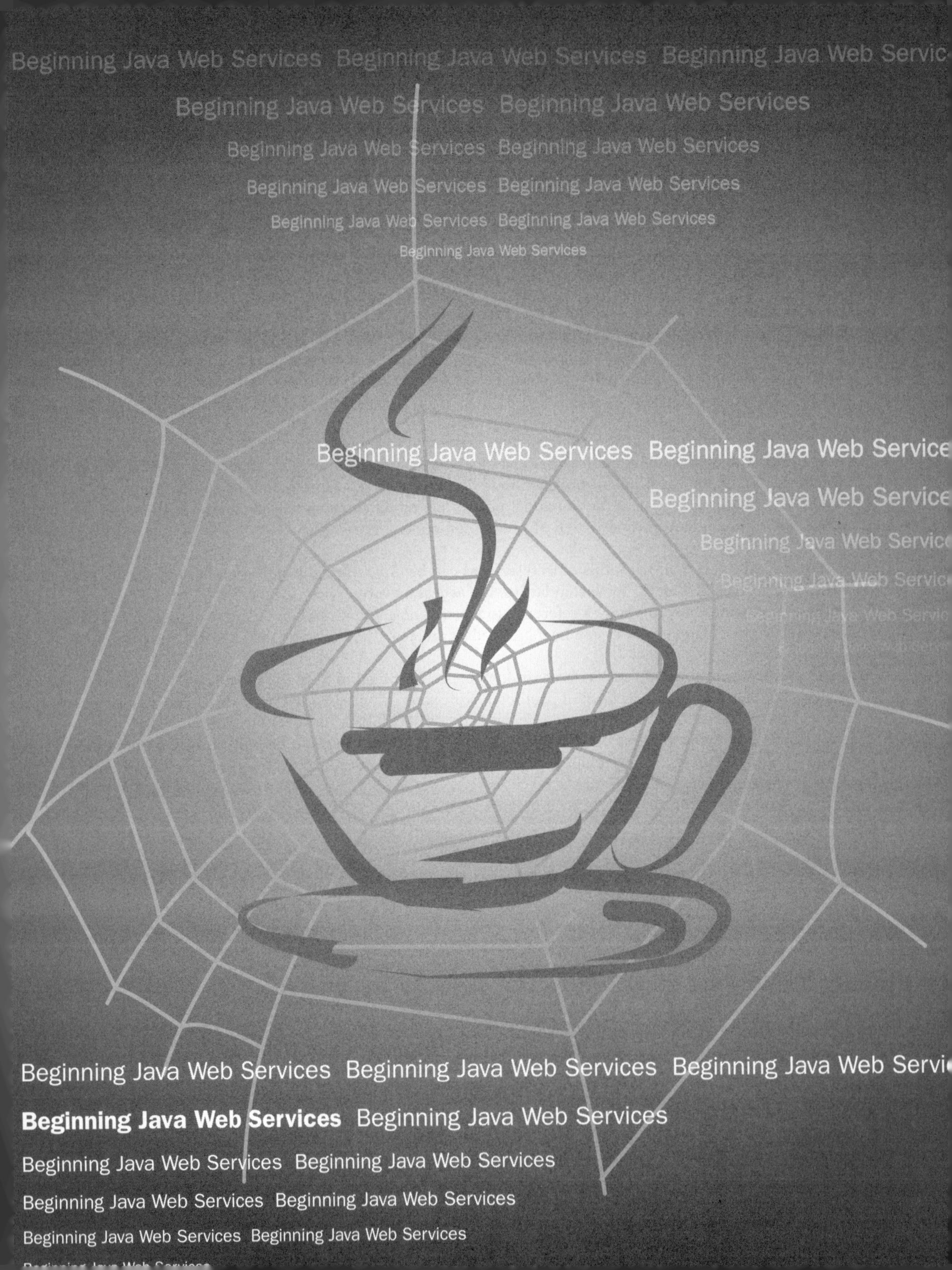

Beginning Java Web Services Beginning Java Web Services Beginning Java Web Servic
Beginning Java Web Services Beginning Java Web Services
Beginning Java Web Services Beginning Java Web Services
Beginning Java Web Services Beginning Java Web Services
Beginning Java Web Services Beginning Java Web Services
Beginning Java Web Services
Beginning Java Web Services Beginning Java Web Service
Beginning Java Web Service
Beginning Java Web Servic
Beginning Java Web Services Beginning Java Web Services Beginning Java Web Servi
**Beginning Java Web Services** Beginning Java Web Services
Beginning Java Web Services Beginning Java Web Services
Beginning Java Web Services Beginning Java Web Services
Beginning Java Web Services Beginning Java Web Services

# Publishing and Discovering Web Services

In Chapter 5, we reviewed the Web Service Description Language (WSDL), which provided us with a standard way to describe web services in human and machine terms. As we mentioned in that chapter, having a description of the functionality and interface for our software is only half the battle when it comes to selling. We must have some well-known forum where software developers can **publish** their WSDL files, and where potential web service users can **discover** what is available. This situation is similar to what we face while running a bricks-and-mortar business – the business owner advertises in media such as the newspaper, the radio, or the Yellow Pages.

The Yellow Pages, or more generally the phonebook, is the model we are interested in when it comes to publishing web services. A key argument in favor of modeling the advertisement of web services after the phonebook is the fact that it provides more structure than other media. We will expand on this structure and its generalization to web services.

In this chapter we will see:

- ❑ Issues concerning web service publishing
- ❑ An overview of UDDI
- ❑ UDDI data structures
- ❑ Programming UDDI
- ❑ Some other publishing technologies: WS-Inspection and JAXR

We will see how the **Universal Description, Discovery, and Integration (UDDI)** industry standard extends the phonebook metaphor to provide a framework for the publication of web services. Armed with a good understanding of the concepts in UDDI, we will go from theory to practice:

- ❑ We will publish our `StockQuote` web service to publicly available UDDI registries
- ❑ We will also examine how a potential customer could find `StockQuote`

Let's start our journey in web service publishing by formalizing the problem that we are facing. A better definition of our problem will help us understand why UDDI is such a good solution.

*In this chapter, we will use the terms registering and publishing interchangeably.*

# Web Service Publishing and Advertising

At first glance, the problem is simple – John, a software developer, has written a web service and the WSDL document that describes it. The question is – How can John reach Mary, another software developer and potential user of John's web service?

*Note that for the purpose of our discussion, a web service user is a software developer. We won't assume that someone has put a GUI on top of a web service to make it available to non-programmers.*

If we assume that there is some public forum or global registry where John could advertise his web service, then the situation would reflect that depicted in the following diagram:

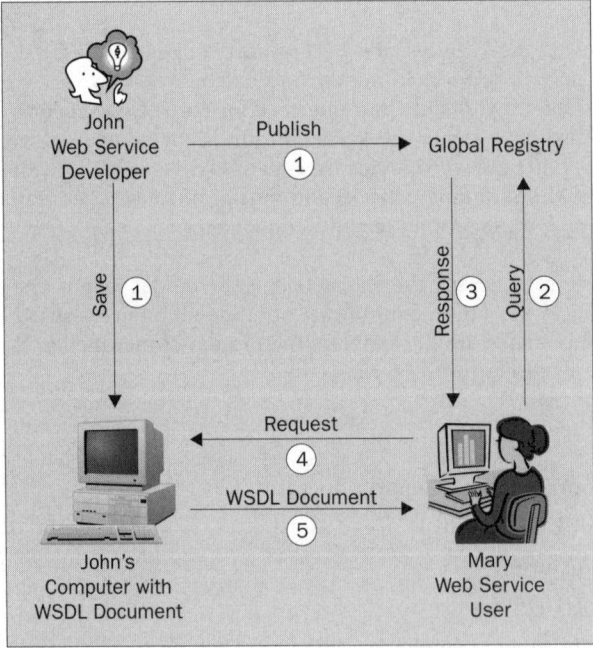

The steps are straightforward:

1.  John publishes the web service to a global registry. At the same time, he saves the WSDL document describing his web service on his publicly available server.

2.  Mary queries the global registry.

**3.** She gets a response from the global registry. When the response is positive, it contains at least one URL to a WSDL document. In this case, the URL points to John's machine.

**4.** Mary requests the WSDL document.

**5.** Mary receives the WSDL document.

We will refine the description of these steps shortly. Note that the diagram shown previously stops at the download of the WSDL file, which we will consider as the end of the discovery process for the remainder of our discussion.

We can see from the diagram that the global registry does not contain all the information. For instance the WSDL file, which we could compare to a brochure from a business, stays on John's computer. This is akin to a phonebook where we can get basic information on the purpose of the business, its phone number, and its address, but more detailed information such as a prospectus has to be retrieved from the business itself.

> *The concept of a **directory** has been used in the software industry for quite some time now. For instance, the X.500 and the well-known **Lightweight Directory Access Protocol (LDAP)** are standards for the sharing of information without being repositories of all the information.*

Let's spend a few more minutes discussing certain other issues regarding the global registry, which can be inferred from the previous diagram.

# Universal

A phonebook must be usable by most people in the target audience. For instance, a phonebook in French published in Tuscaloosa, a city in Alabama, would have little chances of making any impact. To minimize the risk of irrelevancy, the global registry shown in the earlier diagram must be universal.

The fact that anybody who can read the local language can use a phonebook to find the name of a business, should translate into something like anybody with access to a computer can use the registry to find the name of a web service. In other words, any solution that will allow John to publish his web service must be accessible on most systems. For instance, a solution only available on an AppleTalk network using the Extended Binary-Coded Decimal Interchange Code (EBCDIC) would hardly qualify.

So if a universal web services registry should not use EBCDIC, what should it use? It should rely on standards that are accepted by a majority of companies (for example Microsoft, IBM, Sun, BEA) and implemented on a majority of platforms (for example Linux, Windows, Solaris, AIX). Standards such as HTTP, Unicode, XML, and SOAP would meet these two criteria.

# Description

So far, we have agreed that our web service phonebook must be available on most platforms, but we still have not put any content in the phonebook. Simply stated, the registry must provide some form of description of web services. Ideally that description should meet the two requirements that we stipulated for WSDL in Chapter 5 – human readability and machine readability.

# Discovery

When we open the phonebook, we can either look up businesses by name (White Pages) or by category (Yellow Pages), so the web service phonebook must also have some classification. As we mentioned in the previous paragraph, the taxonomy should be friendly to both humans and machines.

> *Note that this issue of discovering components is not new to the software industry. Among other possibilities, the Common Object Request Broker Architecture (CORBA) supports a locator capability.*

# Integration

This last requirement is similar to the ubiquity of the registry that we mentioned previously, but is more concerned with the use of the web service. Once Mary has found that John's web service is a perfect match for her problem, it would be quite a disappointment to find out that she cannot use the software because it is limited to a platform or a programming language that she does not have access to. So our web service should be easy to integrate into existing applications, or at least be functional on many platforms.

# UDDI Overview

UDDI and other technologies address the requirements that we presented in the previous section. We will be spending most of our time on UDDI, but we will also discuss some of the possible alternatives.

As web services are quite popular at the time of writing, there is a tendency to assume that everything about them is quite revolutionary. This is not necessarily so, especially when it comes to UDDI. We have already mentioned existing technologies like XML and HTTP that solve, at least partially, the problems tackled by UDDI. More precisely, we will see shortly that UDDI consists mainly of existing technologies and standards.

Let's start our discussion of UDDI with some historical perspective.

# History of UDDI

UDDI grew out of the collaboration of three major industry players – IBM, Microsoft, and Ariba. IBM and Ariba have been active for a few years in the back-end services that make Business-to-Business (B2B) applications possible. IBM and Microsoft were among the companies that collaborated on the SOAP specification. Ariba and Microsoft have collaborated in the XML space for BizTalk and commerce XML (cXML). A notable absentee from the list is Sun Microsystems that embraced UDDI a couple of weeks after its announcement. Sun Microsystems is now a member of the UDDI community.

The UDDI organization runs a web site at http://www.uddi.org that serves both as a documentation site and as a registry of services available over the web. The community of companies that support UDDI is growing steadily and at the time of this writing, counts over 300 members.

During the summer of 2001, Ariba dropped out of the triumvirate, and now IBM and Microsoft run the site. However, the support of UDDI is not fading as other companies like HP, SAP, and more recently non-software companies such as NTT (Nipon Telephone & Telegraph) have joined the fray to operate their own UDDI registry.

The UDDI registry on http://www.uddi.org went live on May 2, 2001.

# Core Technologies

To satisfy the goal of ubiquity that we discussed in the requirements phase, the architects of UDDI decided to rely as much as possible on existing open and interoperable standards. The major technologies that UDDI relies on are:

- ❏ TCP/IP, HTTP, and HTTPS
- ❏ XML, XML Schemas, and WSDL
- ❏ SOAP

Some of us might argue that packaging open protocols under one umbrella is no technology, but in the mind of the UDDI partners, allowing providers and consumers of web services to keep their existing solutions was a key requirement, because the partners themselves have radically different solutions to common problems.

# Methodology

Before diving into the methodology proposed by UDDI, let's talk about its applicability. UDDI is not exclusively reserved for web services. As we will see shortly, the methodology, the model, and the taxonomies (discussed next) proposed by UDDI apply quite nicely to products other than web services.

Let's modify the earlier diagram that showed the interactions between John and Mary to explain the approach proposed by UDDI:

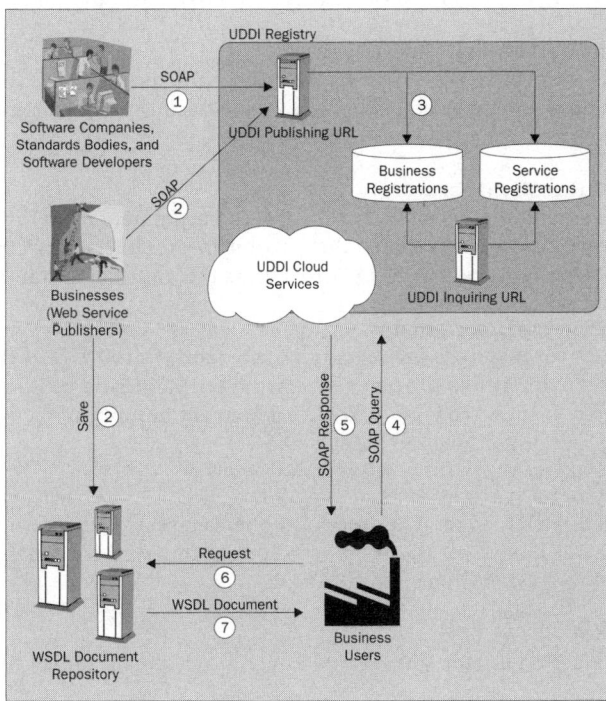

Fundamentally, nothing has changed between the earlier diagram of John and Mary and the one above. Again, the methodology described here is heavily geared towards web services described in WSDL, but other scenarios are also possible.

UDDI registries are linked to one another to form a global view of the available web services. This global view formed by the public UDDI registries is called the **UDDI cloud**.

The process presented in the above diagram consists of seven steps:

1.  **Publish Web Service Types**
    In this first step, we separate the roles that were actually played by John in the earlier figure. The separation is based on splitting a web service into a web service type and a web service occurrence, in the same way that we would split an object between a class and the instance of a class.
    The type of service should span more than one company to promote reuse. Specifically, when two web services share the same WSDL interface definition, a consumer can easily switch from one to the other. This is a practical example of the benefits gained from the split of a WSDL document into two documents.

2.  **Publish Web Service**
    It is the responsibility of businesses and software developers to publish web services according to the specifications published in Step 1. In the case of `StockQuote`, we will assume the roles of web service type publisher and web service publisher at the same time.
    It is important to point out that the publishing of web service types and their implementations is done using SOAP. In case we are worried about security, we will be glad to know that the integrity of the data in transit is protected via the UDDI account and the use of HTTPS.

3.  **Register Business and Service Identifiers**
    This is another refinement of our earlier diagram – the business and the services are registered separately. A many-to-one relationship allows one business to register all the web services that it supports under the same business entity.

4.  **Query a UDDI Registry (Discovery)**
    Based on the fact that the businesses are registered separately from the services that they provide, this querying process can be done by businesses or by services. Once again, the API to query the UDDI registry uses SOAP packets as the underlying transport mechanism.

5.  **Retrieve Web Service Description**
    The information coming from the registry is only partial since UDDI is based on the directory model. Typically, things like the name, a short description, and business contacts can be retrieved directly from UDDI, but a WSDL document describing the web service interface and endpoints will be retrieved in Steps 6 and 7.

6.  **WSDL Query**
    The URL of the WSDL document describing the web service is returned in Step 5. Commonly, this will be the URL of the web service followed by `?WSDL` as in http://myserver/Services/StockQuote?WSDL.

7.  **WSDL Retrieval**
    The WSDL requested in Step 6 is returned over a transport protocol like HTTP

We will see shortly that Steps 1 to 3 constitute the publishing process which is modeled by the **publishing API** and that Steps 4 to 7 make up the querying process, modeled by the **inquiry API**.

Now that we have a better understanding of the high-level process, we can spend some time in discussing the details. We have already reviewed WSDL in detail, so we need to concentrate on the model used to store and query web services. Notice that the UDDI designers kept the phonebook metaphor in mind when defining their model.

# The UDDI Data Model

In this section, we will have a look at how the data is archived in a UDDI registry. First, we will have a high-level overview and discuss the organization of the database. Then we will look at the model with finer granularity and review the data types. We will use this knowledge when writing code against a UDDI registry.

## Organization

To store business and service registrations, a UDDI registry uses an organization similar to a phonebook and contains three distinct types of page, as follows:

- ❑ **White Pages**
  As in an everyday phonebook, the White Pages are indexed by the names of the businesses. They contain information like the business name, contact, and phone numbers. In addition, they contain data that we usually do not find in a phonebook, such as credit ratings.

- ❑ **Yellow Pages**
  These sort businesses by category. In other words, the Yellow Pages represent taxonomy. In the phonebook, the definition of the taxonomies is typically up to the phone company or the publisher, but this solution would not satisfy the requirement of universal support.
  Rather than inventing new taxonomies from scratch, the UDDI architects decided to support well-established classifications like the North American Industry Classification System (NAICS), which provides common industry definitions for Canada, Mexico, and the United States (http://www.census.gov/epcd/www/naics.html). There is also support for an UN-sponsored taxonomy (see http://www.uddi.org for details).

- ❑ **Green Pages**
  These contain the business and the technical descriptions of web services. When using WSDL, the technical information is contained within the WSDL document. We will see how this works in practice shortly.

Now that we have a grasp on the organization of the UDDI registry, let's zoom in and review the data structures.

## Data Structures

The following UDDI data structures are used during the publication and discovery of web services:

- ❑ `businessEntity`
  This contains general information about the service provider, and a collection of services (the `businessServices` element).

❏ businessService
The businessService record is the essence of the Green Pages since it contains the business and technical descriptions of a web service. It is a container for a set of related web services. Examples of related web services are all the services for shipping or all the services for customer relationships management. The technical description of a web service is stored in a bindingTemplate container.

❏ bindingTemplate
This is a container for a set of tModels (type of service), the actual technical description of the service. More precisely, a bindingTemplate is a container for tModelInstanceInfo records, which refer to the tModel.

❏ tModel
This is metadata about the service; it is a *model* for a *type* of service. We will be looking at tModel in detail.

These data structures are represented in the following diagram:

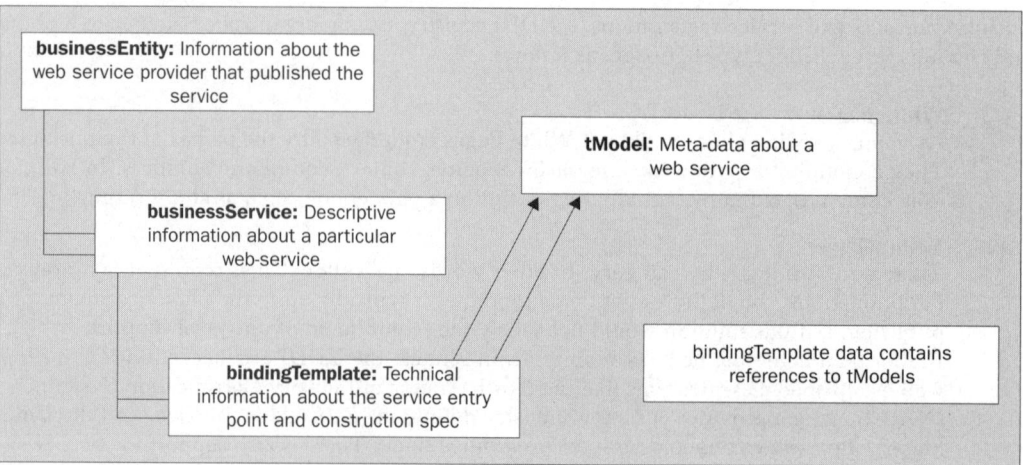

### tModel

The tModel records contain three kinds of fields:

❏ The name of the service

❏ The description of the service

❏ A set of URL pointers to the actual specifications of the web service

The specification for a tModel defines three attributes and five elements as we can see in the following XML schema snippet (the full UDDI schema can be found at http://www.uddi.org/schema/uddi_1.xsd):

```
<element name="tModel">
  <type content="elementOnly">
    <group order="seq">
      <element ref="name" />
      <element ref="description" minOccurs="0" maxOccurs="*" />
      <element ref="overviewDoc" minOccurs="0" maxOccurs="1" />
      <element ref="identifierBag" minOccurs="0" maxOccurs="1" />
      <element ref="categoryBag" minOccurs="0" maxOccurs="1" />
    </group>
    <attribute name="tModelKey" minOccurs="1" type="string" />
    <attribute name="operator" type="string" />
    <attribute name="authorizedName" type="string" />
  </type>
</element>
```

The attributes of a tModel are:

❑  tModelKey
   The unique key assigned to the tModel. It is the only required attribute.

❑  Operator
   The name of the UDDI registry site operator. For example, IBM UDDI Test Registry.

❑  AuthorizedName
   The name of the person who registered the tModel. For example, Ron LeBossy.

The elements of a tModel are:

❑  name
   A unique, human-readable identifier for the tModel record. The name is a required element.

❑  description
   A locale-aware description of the tModel record. The description is locale-aware because it
   carries a locale identifier, for example en.

❑  overviewDoc
   A container for remote descriptions and information. For instance, the overview URL contains
   a URL to a document that describes the web service. A recommended language to specify the
   description of a web service in a tModel is WSDL that we introduced in the previous chapter.

❑  identifierBag
   An optional list of name-value pairs that can be used during search.

❑  categoryBag
   A container for one or more name-value pairs called key references. These allow for a flexible
   taxonomy of tModels. If WSDL is used to describe the service, then the tModel should be
   classified using the uddi-org:types taxonomy with the type wsdlSpec. We will use this
   model when registering the StockQuote service.

When using WSDL to describe a web service, the UDDI organization recommends a mapping between UDDI and WSDL data. This mapping is shown in the following diagram:

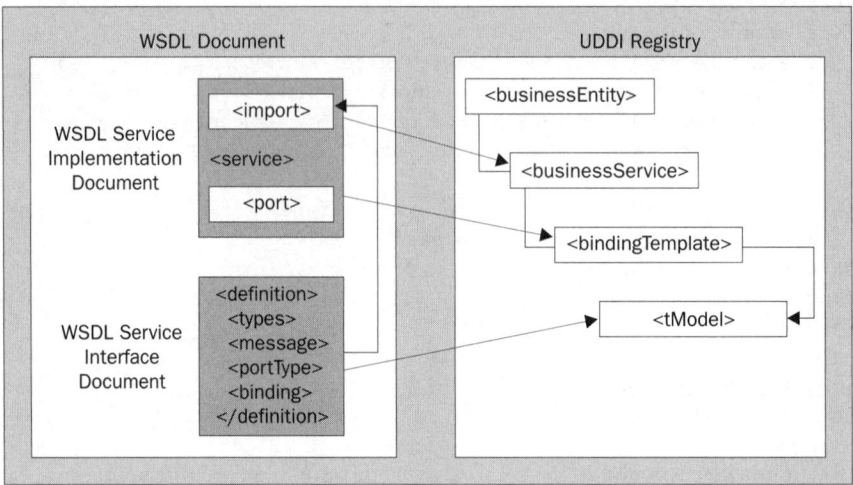

As we have just described, the tModel defines the type of web service, so it should come as no surprise that it is mapped to the definition of the web service – <wsdl:types/>, <wsdl:message/>, <wsdl:portType/>, and <wsdl:binding/>.

The <wsdl:port/>, which defines the URL of the web service finds its UDDI incarnation in the <uddi:bindingTemplate/> element. Finally, the WSDL implementation document corresponds to the <uddi:businessService/> element and its binding templates.

There are a couple of data structures that we have not discussed in detail because they are seldom used. For example, the operationalInfo structure includes data about the publishing of an entity, such as the creation time. The publisherAssertion structure provides a way to couple business entities stored in the registry.

This completes our UDDI overview. In the next section, we will go from theory to practice by looking at how John and Mary use UDDI as a facilitator of e-business.

# Programming UDDI

We have seen in the UDDI overview that it provides four main capabilities. We can:

1. Register businesses
2. Register web service types
3. Register web services
4. Query for web services

We will start this section by publishing a business in the `RegisterBusiness` example and then we will publish a service along with its type in the `RegisterService` example. For the sake of brevity, we will combine the query of the UDDI registry with the registration.

*Note that the UDDI operators (IBM, Microsoft, HP) provide a GUI to both register and find web services according to the taxonomies that we have discussed in the UDDI overview. Before starting the next section, it might be a good idea to navigate to one of them and experiment with the concepts that we have discussed so far.*

IBM maintains a test registry and a production registry:

❑ We can find the test UDDI registry at:
https://www-3.ibm.com/services/uddi/testregistry/protect/registry.html.

❑ The production UDDI registry can be found at:
https://www-3.ibm.com/services/uddi/protect/registry.html.

We do not need a user name to query the registry, but we need to obtain a valid login in order to register our own business and services. To obtain a user name and password, simply follow the **First Time** link as shown in the screenshot below. The process of getting an account is straightforward – enter a user name and password along with the contact information. Remember to keep the user name-password combination handy since we will be requiring it to run the `RegisterService` example:

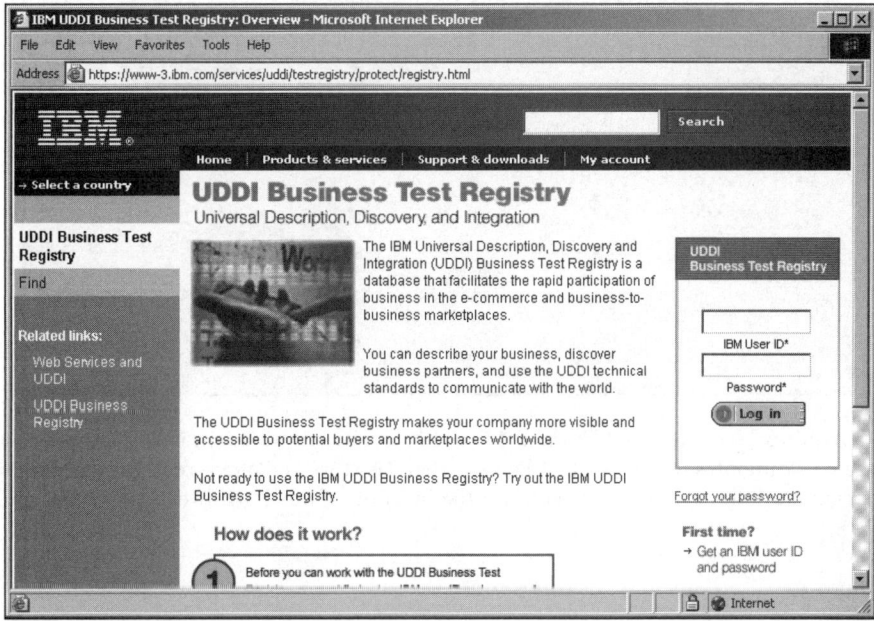

This URL is to register new business and services (notice the HTTPS). To simply query the registry, follow the **Find** link above; this will take us to a URL that does not use HTTPS.

UDDI requests are in fact SOAP packets. So to program against a UDDI registry, one could put together SOAP packets using, for instance, the Axis client API, and call UDDI methods. There is an easier path – use the UDDI for Java API (UDDI4J API) from IBM that comes with the Web Service Toolkit (WSTK). The main benefit of the UDDI4J package is that it provides a hierarchical model of the UDDI registry, which is (mostly) isolated from the intricacies of the UDDI SOAP API.

Our next step will be to install the WSTK on our computer.

# Web Services Toolkit (WSTK)

Download the latest version of WSTK from http://www.alphaworks.ibm.com/tech/webservicestoolkit.

Once the installation file is downloaded to our machine, we can start the actual installation by double-clicking on it. Now, the first screen will appear. As we can see from the following screenshot, the current version at the time of this writing is 3.2:

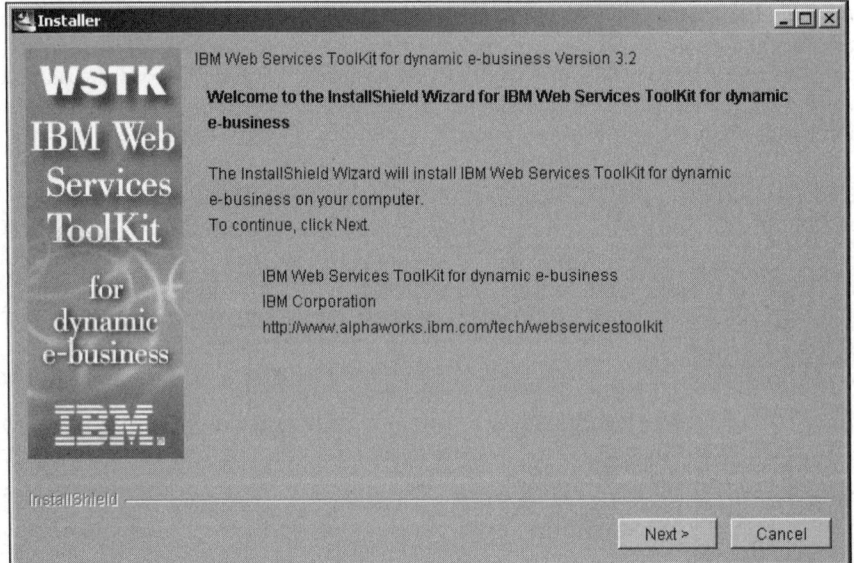

WSTK 3.2 requires Java (Standard Edition) 1.3 or higher. The installation is not without a few detours, so let's take a few minutes to review it. When we click Next we see one screen for the unavoidable license agreement, followed by one to confirm the location of our JDK directory (in our case it's C:\jdk1.4):

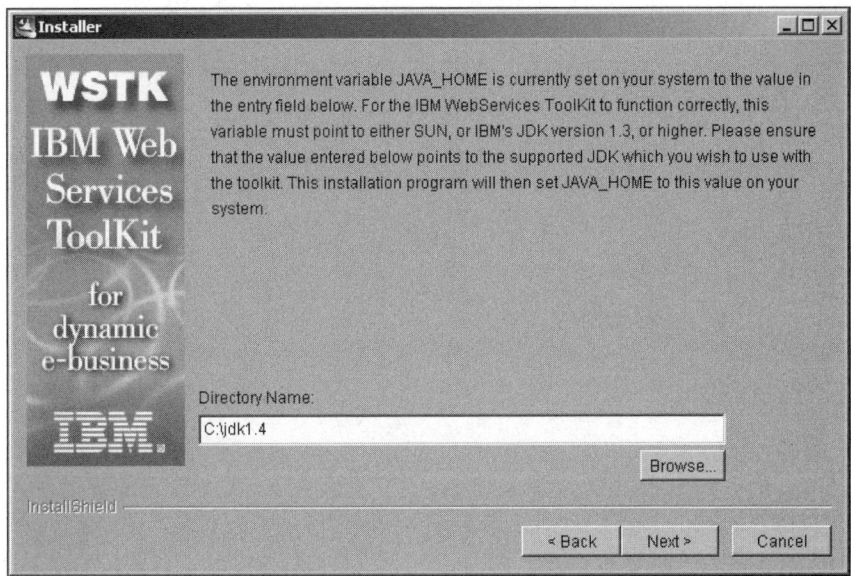

The next screen asks us for the WSTK installation directory. In our case, we will be installing it in the C:\Wstk directory:

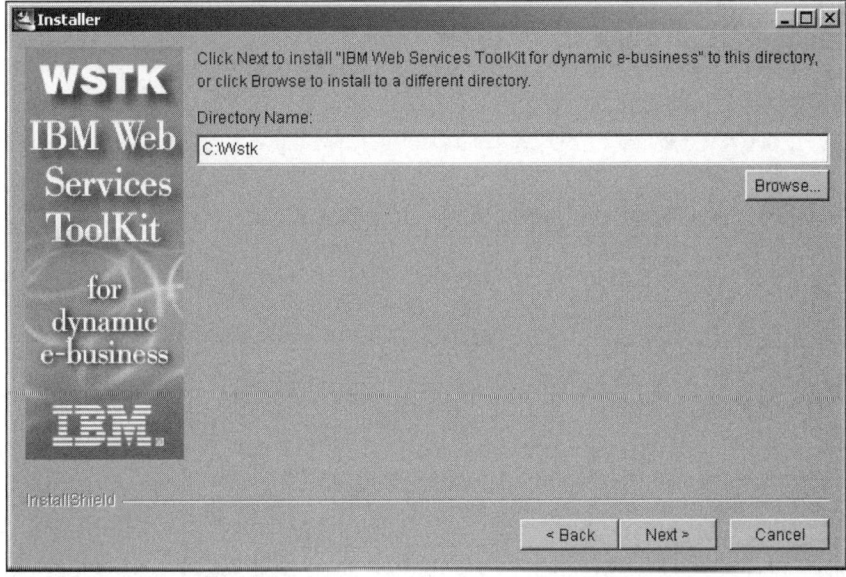

During the installation, an environment variable called wstk_home is also created; it contains the value of the WSTK installation directory.

Then it asks us whether we want to perform a Typical Installation or a Custom Installation. We will select the Typical Installation:

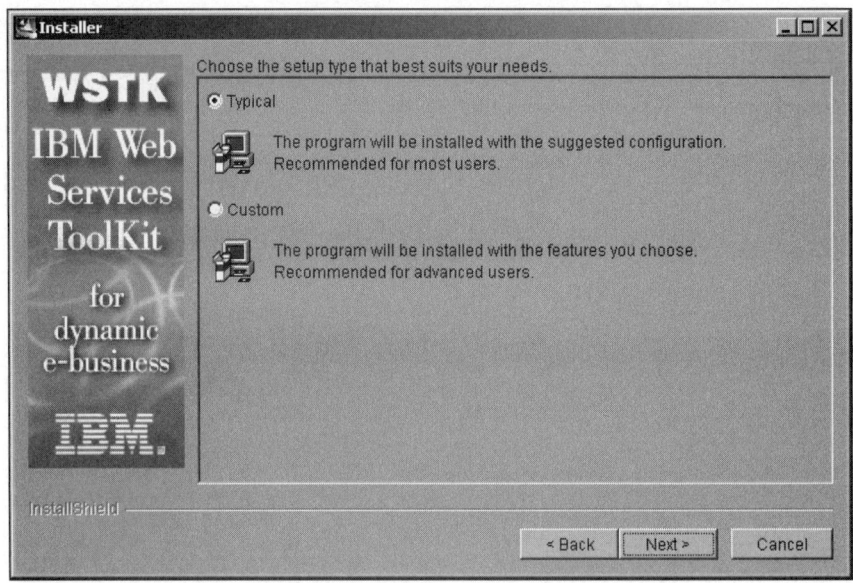

Things get slightly more demanding at the end of the installation process when the setup asks us to configure several components as shown in the following screenshot:

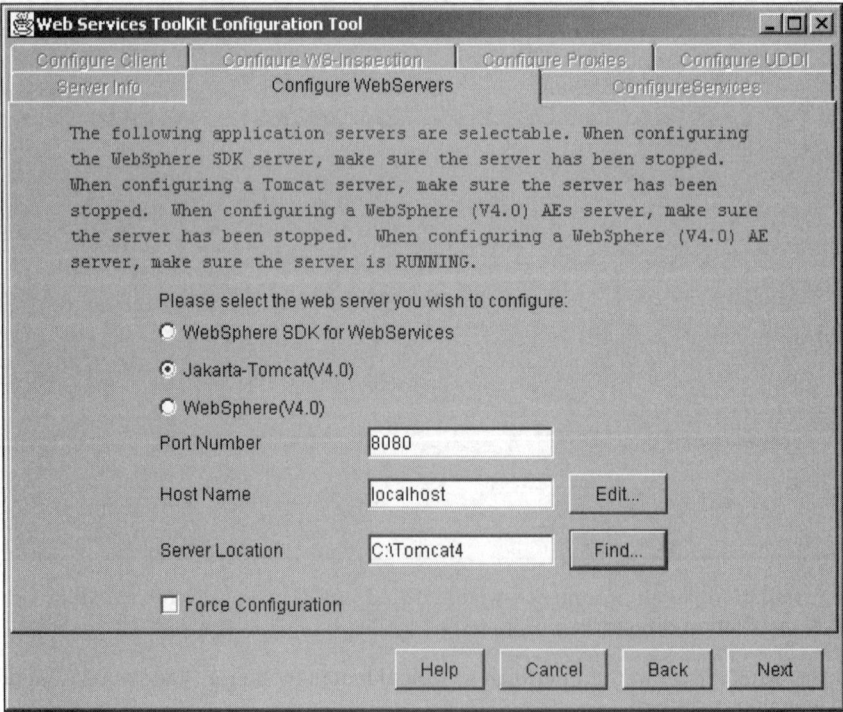

If we change our mind later about one of our choices regarding the configuration of WSTK, we can invoke the configuration tool by typing `%wstk_home%\bin\wstkconfig` (wstk_home is the directory where WSTK is installed).

The following components need to be configured (use **Next** and **Back** buttons to navigate between the different tabs):

❑ **Server Info**
  This tab provides information about the servers that we can use with WSTK. We can use WebSphere SDK, Jakarta Tomcat, or WebSphere (v 4.0).

❑ **Configure Web Servers**
  This option allows us to configure the web server for working with WSTK. We will be using Tomcat. Please refer to Chapter 3 for specifics on the Tomcat installation. For configuring Tomcat, we will use the parameters shown in the previous screenshot.

❑ **Configure Services**
  WSTK comes with several web services; however, we will not be using them in this book. So we can safely select the web services that we would like to try and unselect the others. However, beware that any web service that we select will be added to our `WebApps` directory, thereby making the process of loading our servlet engine (much) slower.

❑ **Configure WS-Inspection**
  Accept the defaults. We will have a short discussion on WS-Inspection at the end of this chapter.

❑ **Configure Proxies**
  If we are working through a proxy, we will have to configure WSTK for our proxy.

❑ **Configure UDDI**
  We need to enter the user name and password for the UDDI registry (IBM, Microsoft). We will assume that we have an account on the IBM Test Registry for the remainder of this chapter. Adapting our discussions to another registry like Microsoft's is straightforward.

❑ **Configure Client**
  We need to enter the host name and port numbers that will be used by clients. Since we are using Tomcat on the local machine, we need to enter `localhost` for the host name and `8080` for the port number.

*The IBM and Microsoft UDDI registries are linked since they are part of the UDDI cloud that we mentioned earlier. So after a few hours, a business created in one shows up in the other. However, beware of interoperability issues. A business created in one UDDI registry cannot be edited in another. For instance, we cannot create a business in the IBM registry and add services to it using the Microsoft registry. We will get an `E_operatorMismatch` error with a description stating that the business is invalid.*

Now that we have an account with a UDDI provider and the software packages to facilitate the use of UDDI, we can move on to our first example in which we will publish the web service that we developed in Chapter 3.

# Publishing the jws Business

We know that the goal of publishing a web service is providing a service for someone or something. It is therefore not surprising to find out that the first step in registering a web service is actually to register a **business**. A new business can be registered via the GUI provided by most operators or it can be registered programmatically. We illustrate the latter in the `RegisterBusiness` example.

## Try It Out – Publishing a Web Service

The `RegisterBusiness` class adds a business entity called `jws` to the IBM UDDI test registry.

**1.** Write the following into the `RegisterBusiness.java`:

```
package com.wrox.jws.stockquote;

import org.uddi4j.UDDIException;
import org.uddi4j.client.UDDIProxy;
import org.uddi4j.response.DispositionReport;
import org.uddi4j.datatype.business.BusinessEntity;
import org.uddi4j.datatype.Name;
import org.uddi4j.response.AuthToken;
import org.uddi4j.response.BusinessDetail;
import org.uddi4j.response.BusinessList;
import org.uddi4j.response.BusinessInfo;
import org.uddi4j.util.FindQualifier;
import org.uddi4j.util.FindQualifiers;
import java.util.Vector;

public class RegisterBusiness {
```

The `RegisterBusiness` class contains only one method, `main()`, in which we register a business and then query for its existence:

```
public static void main (String args[]) {
    String methodName = "com.wrox.jws.stockquote.Register";
    System.out.println(methodName + ": Starting...");

    // Enable https
    System.setProperty("java.protocol.handler.pkgs",
        "com.ibm.net.ssl.internal.www.protocol");
    java.security.Security.addProvider(new com.ibm.jsse.JSSEProvider());
    // Construct a UDDIProxy object
    UDDIProxy proxy = new UDDIProxy();

    try {
        String bizName = "jws";
        String username = "hbequet";
        String password = "wroxpress";
        String inquiryURL =
            "http://www-3.ibm.com/services/uddi/testregistry/inquiryapi";
        String publishURL =
            "https://www-3.ibm.com/services/uddi/testregistry" +
            "/protect/publishapi";
```

```
    // Select the desired UDDI server node
    proxy.setInquiryURL(inquiryURL);
    proxy.setPublishURL(publishURL);

    // Set the transport to use Axis (default is Apache SOAP)
    System.setProperty("org.uddi4j.TransportClassName",
      "org.uddi4j.transport.ApacheAxisTransport");

    System.out.println("  Getting authorization tokens...");

    // Get an authorization token from the UDDI registry
    AuthToken token = proxy.get_authToken(username, password);
    // The minimal business entity contains a business name.
    Vector bizEntities = new Vector(1);
    BusinessEntity bizEntity  = new BusinessEntity("", bizName);
    bizEntities.addElement(bizEntity);

    System.out.println("  Saving business...");

    // Save the business. We get an instance of BusinessDetail in return
    BusinessDetail bizDetail = proxy.save_business
      (token.getAuthInfoString(), bizEntities);

    System.out.println("  Business saved!");

    String bizKey = ((BusinessEntity)(bizDetail.getBusinessEntityVector().
      elementAt(0))).getBusinessKey();

    System.out.println("  Business key: " + bizKey);
    System.out.println("  Verifying results...");
```

The next section of code queries UDDI for the business that we just registered. Typically, this step is not performed in a production application:

```
    // To check that everything went fine, we find the business that we
    // just added using its name (the only thing we have saved).
    Vector names = new Vector(1);
    names.add(new Name(bizName));

    BusinessList bizList = proxy.find_business(names, null, null, null,
      null, null, 0);
    Vector bizInfoVector =
      bizList.getBusinessInfos().getBusinessInfoVector();
    System.out.println("  We found the following businesses:");

    for(int index = 0; index < bizInfoVector.size(); index++) {
      BusinessInfo bizInfo =
        (BusinessInfo)bizInfoVector.elementAt(index);
      System.out.print("    - " + bizInfo.getNameString());

      if(bizInfo.getBusinessKey().equals(bizKey)) {
        System.out.print(" (the one we just added)");
      }
      System.out.println();
    }
```

The remainder of the code contains our exception handling:

```
        } catch(UDDIException uddiException) {
          DispositionReport report = uddiException.getDispositionReport();

          if(report != null) {
            System.err.println(methodName + ": Caught UDDIException!");
            System.err.println("    UDDIException faultCode:"
              + uddiException.getFaultCode()
              + "\n      Operator:" + report.getOperator()
              + "\n      Generic:" + report.getGeneric()
              + "\n      Errno:"   + report.getErrno()
              + "\n      ErrCode:" + report.getErrCode()
              + "\n      InfoText:" + report.getErrInfoText());
          }
        } catch (Exception exception) {
          System.err.println(methodName + ": Caught Exception!");
          exception.printStackTrace();
        }
        System.out.println(methodName + ": All done!");
      }
  }
```

Let's now build and test the `RegisterBusiness` class.

Building `RegisterBusiness` requires `uddi4j.jar`, `xmlParserAPIs.jar`, and `ibmjsse.jar` in our classpath. The `ibmjsse.jar` file contains the support for HTTPS. JSSE stands for Java Secure Socket Extension.

> *Note that if we are using the JDK 1.4 or have another JSSE JAR file in our classpath, we can omit* `ibmjsse.jar` *from the classpath.*

To compile the file `RegisterBusiness.java` file on Windows 2000, change to the `Register\src` directory and type the following commands (or their equivalent, in case of the Linux platform):

```
set classpath=%wstk_home%\uddi4j\lib\uddi4j.jar;%wstk_home%\lib\ibmjsse.jar;
        %jwsDirectory%\lib\xmlParserAPIs.jar;

javac -d ..\classes com\wrox\jws\stockquote\RegisterBusiness.java
```

These commands will produce a `RegisterBusiness.class` file in the `register\classes\com\wrox\jws\stockquote` directory.

Before running the `RegisterBusiness` class, let's have a look at the IBM UDDI Test Registry. If we log on successfully, the page should look like the following, with no businesses and no services listed:

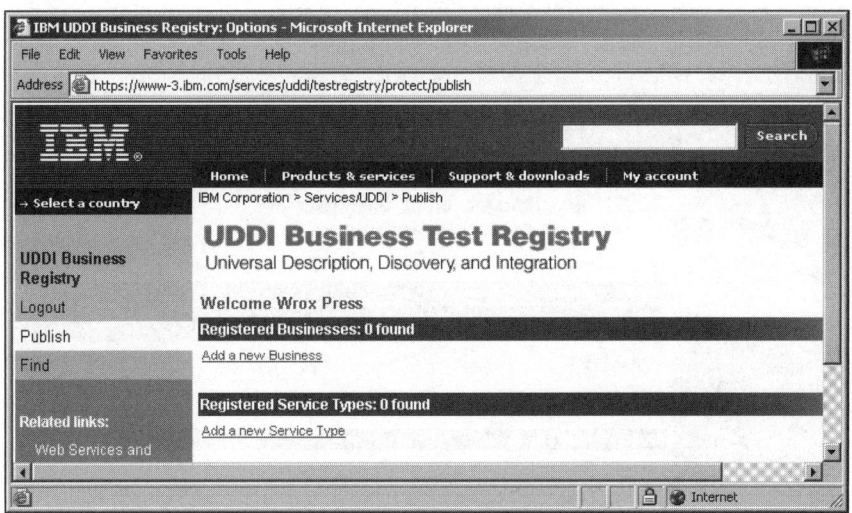

Now if we run the example with the following command (make sure that `RegisterBusiness.class`, `ibmjsse.jar` and `uddi4j.jar` are in our classpath and that we are in the `Register\classes` directory):

```
java com.wrox.jws.stockquote.RegisterBusiness
```

we will get the following result:

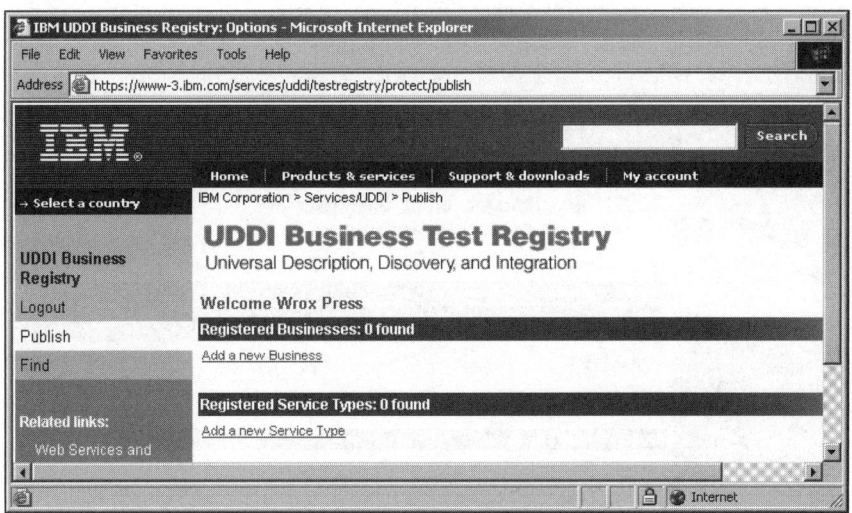

The refreshed browser page should show that the `jws` business has been registered successfully:

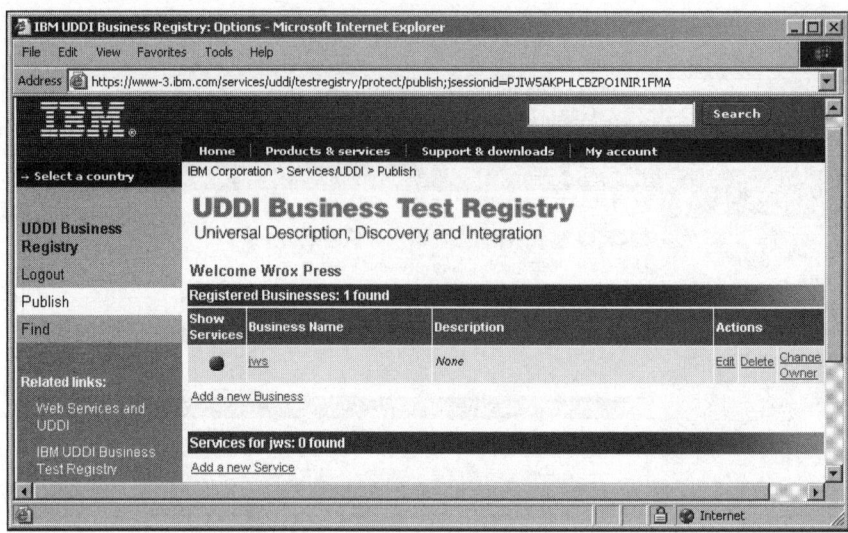

The business still has not registered any services, but we will address that shortcoming in the next section.

> *Note that the business key is a **Universal Unique Identifier** (UUID) – 2BA70F90-993A-11D6-9880-000629DC0A53. A UUID is a 128-byte number generated with an algorithm that guarantees its uniqueness. Typical implementations rely on the address of the computer and the time of the day.*

Bear in mind that if we try to run the RegisterBusiness class a second time against the IBM test registry, we will get an error since we can only register one business:

```
C:\WINNT\System32\cmd.exe                                         _ |□| x
C:\Beginners_JWS_Examples\Chp07\Register\classes>java com.wrox.jws.stockquote.Re
gisterBusiness
com.wrox.iws.stockquote.Register: Starting...
    Getting authorization tokens...
    Saving business...
com.wrox.iws.stockquote.Register: Caught UDDIException!
    UDDIException faultCode:Client
        Operator:www.ibm.com/services/uddi
        Generic:2.0
        Errno:10160
        ErrCode:E_accountLimitExceeded
        InfoText:E_accountLimitExceeded (10160) Save request exceeded the quantity
limits for the given structure type. businessEntity
com.wrox.iws.stockquote.Register: All done!

C:\Beginners_JWS_Examples\Chp07\Register\classes>
```

Let's now have a closer look at the implementation of the RegisterBusiness class.

### How It Works

The RegisterBusiness class adds a business entity called jws to the IBM UDDI test registry. As we can see in the following listing, we make extensive use of the UDDI4J (org.uddi4j) package that comes with WSTK. The uddi4j.jar file can be found in the uudi4j\lib directory under the WSTK installation directory:

```
package com.wrox.jws.stockquote;

import org.uddi4j.UDDIException;
// Other imports omitted from this listing
```

We will discuss each class that we import from the UDDI4J package as we encounter them in the code:

```
public class RegisterBusiness {

  public static void main (String args[]) {
    String methodName = "com.wrox.jws.stockquote.Register";
```

We use the `methodName` variable to prefix our messages with the fully qualified `main()` method .

```
    // Enable https
    System.setProperty("java.protocol.handler.pkgs",
      "com.ibm.net.ssl.internal.www.protocol");
    java.security.Security.addProvider(new com.ibm.jsse.JSSEProvider());
```

We have seen earlier in this chapter that publishing to a UDDI directory entails the use of HTTPS for security reasons. If we don't enable HTTPS, the call to `setPublishURL()` below will fail with an "unknown protocol" error.

The next step is to create a UDDI proxy that will take care of generating the SOAP calls to UDDI and parsing the SOAP results from UDDI. Note that this proxy is different from the WSDL-generated proxy that we discussed in Chapter 5 since it is a generic proxy not tied to a specific web service:

```
    // Construct a UDDIProxy object
    UDDIProxy proxy = new UDDIProxy();

    try {
      String bizName    = "jws";
      String username   = "hbequet";
      String password   = "wroxpress";
      String inquiryURL =
        "http://www-3.ibm.com/services/uddi/testregistry/inquiryapi";
      String publishURL =
        "https://www-3.ibm.com/services/uddi/testregistry/" +
        "protect/publishapi";
```

To run the example, we will need to update the user name and password to what we specified when we created the user account with the provider, as we discussed earlier. The `inquiryURL` is the URL used to query UDDI and the `publishURL` is the URL used to publish businesses and web services in UDDI.

Feel free to replace the IBM UDDI test registry URL by another provider. For instance, the following URLs are for the Microsoft UDDI registry (remove the "test." at the beginning of the URL to get to the production site):

- ❏ http://test.uddi.microsoft.com/inquire
- ❏ https://test.uddi.microsoft.com/publish

Once again, the publishing URL is protected through HTTPS. The next two lines of code simply tell the proxy which URL to use:

```
// Select the desired UDDI server node
proxy.setInquiryURL(inquiryURL);
proxy.setPublishURL(publishURL);
```

Now, we need to tell the UDDI4J package what SOAP client package to use when sending requests to the UDDI provider. Since we have been using Axis in most of this book, we will use it here as well:

```
// Set the transport to use Axis (default is Apache SOAP)
System.setProperty("org.uddi4j.TransportClassName",
    "org.uddi4j.transport.ApacheAxisTransport");
```

The next statement requires a little bit of background information. The security model used by UDDI is based on user name and password arguments passed in every call. However, this implies that for every call, the server will have to perform credential validation. To lessen the burden on the server, the UDDI protocol contains the following compromise – the caller must obtain a security token from the server and pass that security token with every request to UDDI. To add an extra level of safety, the security token is only valid for a limited period of time. We will discuss other security models in detail later in the book, but for now, let's get a security token from the UDDI operator:

```
// Get an authorization token from the UDDI registry
AuthToken token = proxy.get_authToken(username, password);
```

In the following section of code, we create a `BusinessEntity` structure and submit it to the UDDI operator for registration. The `BusinessEntity` is a container for information about the business; in other words, it stores the White and Yellow Pages data.

Note that we have to use a vector since the API is geared toward the registration of several businesses with one call to minimize network traffic. A more detailed discussion of the data types defined by UDDI can be found at http://www.uddi.org/pubs/DataStructure-V2.00-Open-20010608.pdf:

```
// The minimal business entity contains a business name.
Vector bizEntities = new Vector(1);
BusinessEntity bizEntity = new BusinessEntity("", bizName);
bizEntities.addElement(bizEntity);

// Save the business. We get an instance of BusinessDetail in return
BusinessDetail bizDetail = proxy.save_business(
    token.getAuthInfoString(), bizEntities);
```

As we mentioned earlier, the security token must be passed with each call that requires authentication. It is worth pointing out that more detailed information about the business such as the address, the phone number, and contact information can be added to the `BusinessEntity` structure.

The return value of `save_business()` is a `BusinessDetail` structure that contains most of the information saved in the registry. We use it in the next section of code to display the business key, a unique identifier assigned by the UDDI operator. Once again, notice the use of the vector that makes the API a little tedious:

```
String bizKey = ((BusinessEntity)(bizDetail.getBusinessEntityVector()
    elementAt(0))).getBusinessKey();
```

If we have got this far, then our business has been successfully registered. If something goes wrong, we are likely to get an `UDDIException` or an `IOException`. We handle all exceptions at the end of this method. The rest of the code goes back to the UDDI registry and verifies that our business actually got registered. In practice this is not necessary, but it is a good time for a short introduction to UDDI queries.

The code to query a UDDI registry is similar to the publishing code, except for two main differences – the inquiry URL differs from the publishing URL, and the inquiry URL does not require the use of HTTPS. As we can see below, to query UDDI, we simply pass the business name. We will discuss more complicated queries based on taxonomies shortly. Once again, notice the use of vectors:

```
// To check that everything went fine, we find the business that we
// just added using its name (the only thing we have saved).
Vector names = new Vector(1);
names.add(new Name(bizName));

BusinessList bizList = proxy.find_business(names, null, null, null,
    null, null, 0);
```

The last argument of the `find_business()` method specifies the maximum number of rows returned in the result (0 means no maximum). The other arguments specify more criteria like the URL or the taxonomy of the business. The return value of `find_business()` is a vector of `BusinessInfo` structures that we use to print the business name and key:

```
Vector bizInfoVector =
  bizList.getBusinessInfos().getBusinessInfoVector();
System.out.println("  We found the following businesses:");
for(int index = 0; index < bizInfoVector.size(); index++) {
  BusinessInfo bizInfo =
    (BusinessInfo)bizInfoVector.elementAt(index);
  System.out.print("    - " + bizInfo.getNameString());

  if(bizInfo.getBusinessKey().equals(bizKey)) {
    System.out.print(" (the one we just added)");
  }
  System.out.println();
}
```

The last task on our list is to take care of errors. The UDDIException class gives us detailed information about what went wrong. As we might expect from an API that uses SOAP, UDDI returns errors in the form of SOAP packets. The error message contains a <uddi:dispositionReport/> element that is a container for a <uddi:result/> element, which holds the error code and the error info. The DispositionReport class models the error message as we can see in the exception handling block below:

```
    } catch(UDDIException uddiException) {
      DispositionReport report = uddiException.getDispositionReport();

      if(report != null) {
        System.err.println(methodName + ": Caught UDDIException!");
        System.err.println("    UDDIException faultCode:"
          + uddiException.getFaultCode()
          + "\n     Operator:" + report.getOperator()
          + "\n     Generic:"  + report.getGeneric()
          + "\n     Errno:"    + report.getErrno()
          + "\n     ErrCode:"  + report.getErrCode()
          + "\n     InfoText:" + report.getErrInfoText());
      }
    } catch(Exception exception) {
      System.err.println(methodName + ": Caught Exception!");
      exception.printStackTrace();
    }

    System.out.println(methodName + ": All done!");
  }
}
```

Let's now move to the next level and register the StockQuote service.

# Publishing StockQuote

We will assume that we have created a business on the IBM Test Registry by running the RegisterBusiness example using our own UDDI account (that is with the user name and password that we obtained from the UDDI operator as previously).

## Try It Out – Registering a Web Service

1. As we can see, the code of RegisterService has quite a few similarities to the RegisterBusiness class:

```
package com.wrox.jws.stockquote;

import org.uddi4j.UDDIException;
import org.uddi4j.client.UDDIProxy;
import org.uddi4j.response.DispositionReport;
import org.uddi4j.datatype.service.BusinessService;
import org.uddi4j.datatype.Name;
import org.uddi4j.datatype.binding.AccessPoint;
import org.uddi4j.datatype.binding.BindingTemplates;
import org.uddi4j.datatype.binding.BindingTemplate;
import org.uddi4j.datatype.binding.TModelInstanceDetails;
import org.uddi4j.datatype.binding.TModelInstanceInfo;
import org.uddi4j.response.AuthToken;
import org.uddi4j.response.ServiceDetail;
import org.uddi4j.response.ServiceList;
import org.uddi4j.response.ServiceInfos;
import org.uddi4j.response.ServiceInfo;
import org.uddi4j.response.BusinessList;
import org.uddi4j.response.BusinessInfo;
import org.uddi4j.util.CategoryBag;
import org.uddi4j.util.KeyedReference;
import java.util.Vector;

public class RegisterService {

  private static final String businessKey =
    "2BA70F90-993A-11D6-9880-000629DC0A53";
  private static final String bizName = "jws";

  // The following values are for the category of
  // WSDL-described web services
  private static final String keyName = "uddi-org:types";
  private static final String keyValue = "wsdlSpec";
  private static final String tModelKey =
    "uuid:C1ACF26D-9672-4404-9D70-39B756E62AB4";

  // Beginning of the main() method omitted from this listing

      // Get an authorization token from the UDDI registry
      AuthToken token = proxy.get_authToken(username, password);

      // We create the StockQuote service
      String serviceName = "StockQuote";
      BindingTemplates bindingTemplates = new BindingTemplates();
      BindingTemplate bindingTemplate = new BindingTemplate();
      Vector bndVector = new Vector();
      Vector tVector = new Vector();

      // We need a tModel reference to a web service described with WSDL
      TModelInstanceDetails tModelInstanceDetails =
        new TModelInstanceDetails();
      TModelInstanceInfo tModelInstanceInfo = new TModelInstanceInfo();
```

```
tModelInstanceInfo.setTModelKey(tModelKey);
tVector.addElement(tModelInstanceInfo);
tModelInstanceDetails.setTModelInstanceInfoVector(tVector);

// The access point is through http
AccessPoint accessPoint = new AccessPoint(
  "localhost/axis/servlet/AxisServlet", "http");

bindingTemplate.setTModelInstanceDetails(tModelInstanceDetails);
bindingTemplate.setAccessPoint(accessPoint);
bindingTemplate.setBindingKey("");
bindingTemplate.setDefaultDescriptionString("Unsecure Stock quotes.");
bndVector.addElement(bindingTemplate);
bindingTemplates.setBindingTemplateVector(bndVector);

BusinessService service = new BusinessService("");
Vector sVector = new Vector(); // services
Vector sdVector = new Vector(); // service details

// We add the binding templates to the business service
service.setBindingTemplates(bindingTemplates);

// We set the default service name (in English)
service.setDefaultNameString("StockQuote", "en");

// Create a category bag with the WSDL tModel
CategoryBag categoryBag = new CategoryBag();
KeyedReference keyedReference = new KeyedReference(keyName,
  keyValue, tModelKey);
categoryBag.add(keyedReference);

// Save the service and its description in the UDDI registry
service.setDefaultDescriptionString("Stock quotes over the web");
service.setBusinessKey(businessKey);
service.setCategoryBag(categoryBag);
sVector.addElement(service);

ServiceDetail serviceDetail = proxy.save_service(
  token.getAuthInfoString(), sVector);

// We print the service key of the service we just added
sdVector = serviceDetail.getBusinessServiceVector();
System.out.println("      Name        : "
  + ((BusinessService)sdVector.elementAt(0)).getDefaultName());
System.out.println("      Service key : "
  + ((BusinessService)sdVector.elementAt(0)).getServiceKey());

System.out.println("   ----- Done Adding -----");
// Find jws
System.out.println("   Searching for jws and its services...");
Vector names = new Vector(1);
names.add(new Name(bizName));
```

```
    BusinessList bizList = proxy.find_business(names, null, null, null,
       null, null, 0);
    Vector bizInfoVector =
       bizList.getBusinessInfos().getBusinessInfoVector();

    System.out.println("  Found " + bizInfoVector.size()
       + " entry(ies):");

    // List the businesses
    for(int ndx = 0; ndx < bizInfoVector.size(); ndx++) {
      BusinessInfo businessInfo =
         (BusinessInfo)bizInfoVector.elementAt(ndx);
      System.out.println("    entry[" + ndx + "]: "
         + businessInfo.getNameString() + " ("
         + businessInfo.getDefaultDescriptionString()
         + "), \n      business key is: "
         + businessInfo.getBusinessKey());

      // For each business, we list the services
      ServiceInfos serviceInfos = businessInfo.getServiceInfos();
      Vector       siv         = serviceInfos.getServiceInfoVector();

      System.out.println("    There is(are) "
         + siv.size() + " service(s) registered for "
         + businessInfo.getNameString());

      for(int svcNdx = 0; svcNdx < siv.size(); svcNdx++) {
        ServiceInfo serviceInfo = (ServiceInfo)siv.elementAt(svcNdx);
        System.out.println("        "
           + serviceInfo.getNameString() + ", service key is: "
           + serviceInfo.getServiceKey());
      }
    }
  } catch(UDDIException uddiException)  {
    DispositionReport report = uddiException.getDispositionReport();
```

```
// Remainder of code is similar to RegisterBusiness
```

**2.** Let's now build and test the RegisterService class. Building and testing the RegisterService example is similar to what we did for RegisterBusiness (using the same classpath and assuming that our current directory is src):

```
javac -d ..\classes RegisterService.java
```

```
java com.wrox.jws.stockquote.RegisterService
```

After running this command, we will see:

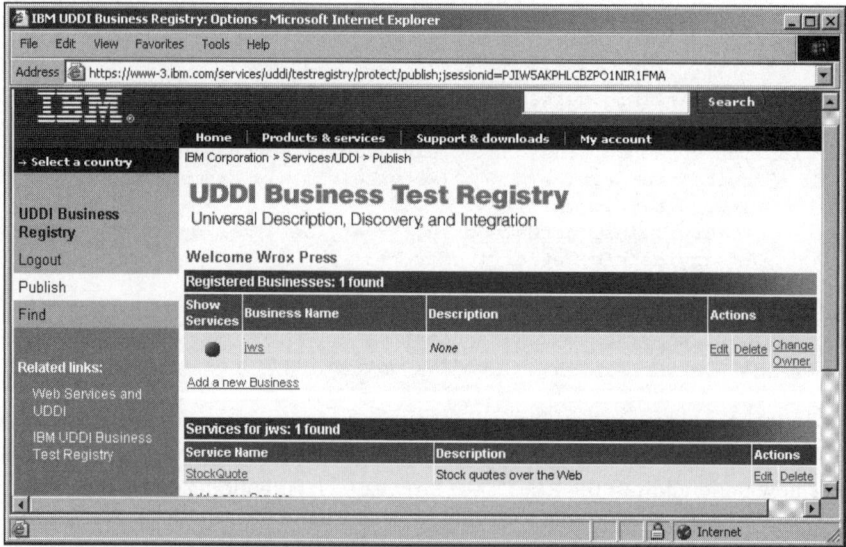

**3.** We can double check that our service got added to the UDDI registry by visiting the web page as shown in the following screenshot:

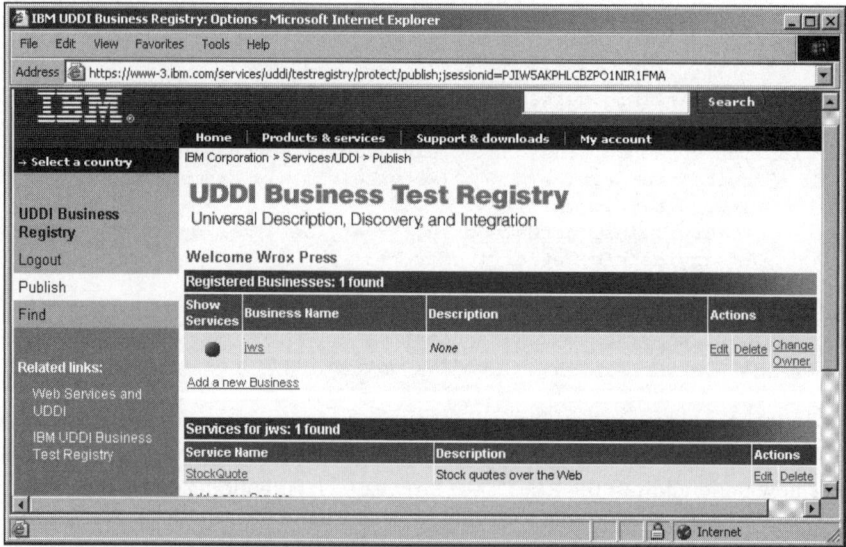

**4.** If we drill down into the details of the StockQuote service (this can be done by clicking on the StockQuote service link), we will see the additional information that we have provided (access point, WSDL-described web service, and so on):

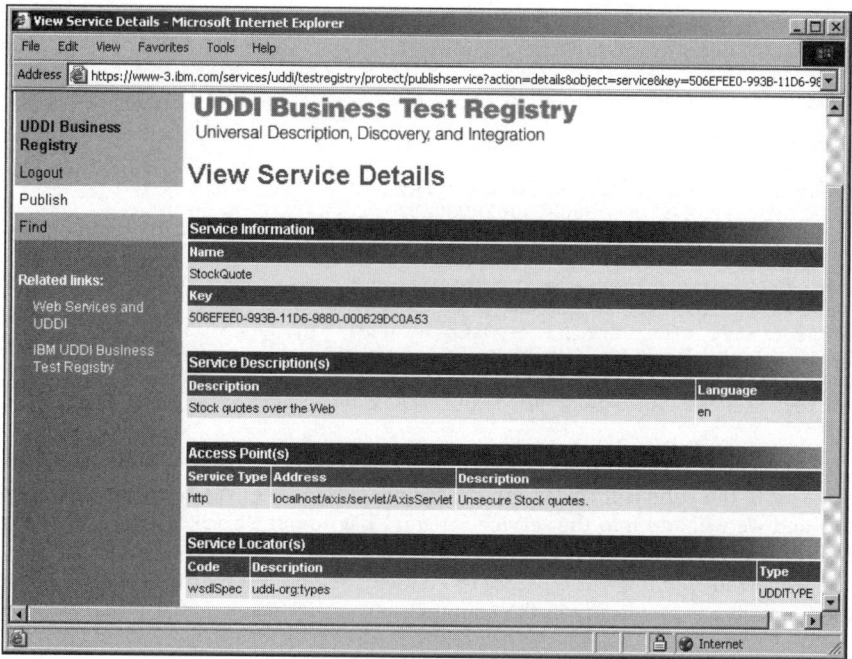

Let's now examine the code of the RegisterService class.

### How It Works

The RegisterService example registers the StockQuote web service, but can easily be modified to register any web service. Similar to RegisterBusiness, we also query the UDDI registry for the service that we publish. We have mentioned previously that in UDDI, one organizes web services as part of a business, so we must obtain a business key for our business prior to registering one or more web services.

One possibility would be to cut and paste the code around the find_business() call that we reviewed in the previous example and take the business key out of the business info structure. For the sake of simplicity, we will hardcode the business key that we obtained from the previous registration – 368D90C0-A5D6-11D6-A687-000629DC0A7B.

When you are ready to run this example on your machine, be sure to replace the value above with the actual business key obtained while registering the business (the RegisterBusiness example above echoes the business key when it runs).

Let's now look the code of RegisterService in detail:

```
package com.wrox.jws.stockquote;

import org.uddi4j.UDDIException;
// Other import omitted from this listing
import java.util.Vector;
```

We will describe the new classes that we import from the UDDI4J package as we encounter them in the code. Again, we need to use a vector for most data types since the API is designed to minimize network roundtrips:

```
public class RegisterService {

    private static final String businessKey =
        "2BA70F90-993A-11D6-9880-000629DC0A53";
    private static final String bizName = "jws";

    // The following values are for the category of
    // WSDL-described web services
    private static final String keyName = "uddi-org:types";
    private static final String keyValue = "wsdlSpec";
    private static final String tModelKey =
        "uuid:C1ACF26D-9672-4404-9D70-39B756E62AB4";
```

The business has been registered previously under the name jws with the business key listed above. The tModelKey in the code is for a WSDL-described web service. We will register the service using this tModel and we will add it to the service category bag to put StockQuote in the taxonomy of web services described by WSDL. The key name and value constitute the keyed reference that we described earlier when we introduced the categoryBag element. We have already explained the relationship between these data types previously in the chapter.

The beginning of the main() method is mostly borrowed from the RegisterBusiness example (enabling HTTPS, setting up the transport, and so on). Things start to get different when we initialize the data structures for a service:

```
    // Beginning of the main() method omitted from this listing
    // Get an authorization token from the UDDI registry
    AuthToken token = proxy.get_authToken(username, password);

    // We create the StockQuote service
    String serviceName = "StockQuote";
    BindingTemplates bindingTemplates = new BindingTemplates();
    BindingTemplate bindingTemplate = new BindingTemplate();
    Vector bndVector = new Vector();
    Vector tVector = new Vector();

    // We need a tModel reference to a web service described with WSDL
    TModelInstanceDetails tModelInstanceDetails =
        new TModelInstanceDetails();
    TModelInstanceInfo tModelInstanceInfo = new TModelInstanceInfo();
    tModelInstanceInfo.setTModelKey(tModelKey);
    tVector.addElement(tModelInstanceInfo);
    tModelInstanceDetails.setTModelInstanceInfoVector(tVector);
```

As we can see in the code, we use the WSDL tModel to define the type of the service. It is an acceptable solution since we expect the users of StockQuote to rely solely on WSDL to discover the service. An alternative is to define our own business service type (that is, our own tModel) and use it to register the web service. For specifics on how to create your own tModel, please refer to the UDDI4J documentation.

In the next section of code, we define an access point and we initialize the binding template that will hold the data structures for the registration of `StockQuote`. The access point is simply the URL that customers can use to access our service. In this case, we simply register an HTTP access point that we qualify with the unsecure label since the data will travel unencrypted. We use the default port 80, but we can specify an alternative port such as 8081, `localhost:8081/axis/servlet/AxisServlet`:

```
// The access point is through http
AccessPoint accessPoint = new AccessPoint(
    "localhost/axis/servlet/AxisServlet", "http");

bindingTemplate.setTModelInstanceDetails(tModelInstanceDetails);
bindingTemplate.setAccessPoint(accessPoint);
bindingTemplate.setBindingKey("");
bindingTemplate.setDefaultDescriptionString("Unsecure Stock quotes.");
bndVector.addElement(bindingTemplate);
bindingTemplates.setBindingTemplateVector(bndVector);
```

We now have enough information to create a business service structure. However, we still need to add a `categoryBag` to this service to include it in the taxonomy of WSDL-described web services.

The argument of the `BusinessService` constructor is the operator-assigned key for the business service. By passing an empty key, we tell the UDDI operator that we want a new service to be created. We can modify an existing service by passing a valid business service key:

```
BusinessService service = new BusinessService("");
Vector sVector = new Vector(); // services
Vector sdVector = new Vector(); // service details

// We add the binding templates to the business service
service.setBindingTemplates(bindingTemplates);

// We set the default service name (in English)
service.setDefaultNameString("StockQuote", "en");

// Create a category bag with the WSDL tModel
CategoryBag categoryBag = new CategoryBag();
KeyedReference keyedReference = new KeyedReference(keyName,
    keyValue, tModelKey);
categoryBag.add(keyedReference);

// Save the service and its description in the UDDI registry
service.setDefaultDescriptionString("Stock quotes over the web");
service.setBusinessKey(businessKey);
service.setCategoryBag(categoryBag);
sVector.addElement(service);
```

If we look at the previous lines of code, we will see that we create a keyed reference to identify the `categoryBag` for the taxonomy. We then add that category bag to the service. Notice the initialization of the mandatory business key. The default description is optional.

Our service is now complete and ready for registration. Similar to `RegisterBusiness`, we use the `UDDIProxy` class to save the service. The returned value is a service detail class that contains the key generated by the UDDI operator among other values, as we can see in the following print statements:

```
ServiceDetail serviceDetail = proxy.save_service(
   token.getAuthInfoString(), sVector);

// We print the service key of the service we just added
sdVector = serviceDetail.getBusinessServiceVector();
System.out.println("     Name        : "
   + ((BusinessService)sdVector.elementAt(0)).getDefaultName());
System.out.println("     Service key : "
   + ((BusinessService)sdVector.elementAt(0)).getServiceKey());
```

If we were not verifying the UDDI registration then this example would be complete.

Querying the UDDI registry for services is similar to `RegisterBusiness`; we run the query through the `proxy` object. In the following code snippet we query all the services associated to our business, but we can also directly query for a service via the `UDDIProxy.find_service()` method:

```
// Find jws
System.out.println("   Searching for jws and its services...");
Vector names = new Vector(1);
names.add(new Name(bizName));

BusinessList bizList = proxy.find_business(names, null, null, null,
   null, null, 0);
```

The `UDDIProxy.find_service()` method provides more sophisticated query capabilities than a simple name-based lookup. For instance, we can run a query that is based on taxonomies (category bags). In addition to WSDL-described services, we can query for standard taxonomies like the Universal Standard Products and Services Classification (UNSPSC), which is a hierarchical classification of products and services. For more information, we can go to the UNSPSC home page http://eccma.org/unspsc/.

For more specifics on UDDI query, check the UDDI4J documentation. But for now, let's go back to our example. As we just saw in the code, the list of businesses that match our criteria is assigned to `bizList`. We then use `bizList` to get a vector of `BusinessInfo` objects:

```
Vector bizInfoVector =
   bizList.getBusinessInfos().getBusinessInfoVector();
System.out.println("   Found " + bizInfoVector.size()
   + " entry(ies):");
```

Finally, we loop through the results to display the businesses and services that were returned by UDDI:

```
// List the businesses
for(int ndx = 0; ndx < bizInfoVector.size(); ndx++) {

   BusinessInfo businessInfo =
      (BusinessInfo)bizInfoVector.elementAt(ndx);
   System.out.println("     entry[" + ndx + "]: "
```

```
     + businessInfo.getNameString() + " ("
     + businessInfo.getDefaultDescriptionString()
     + "), \n          business key is: "
     + businessInfo.getBusinessKey());

     // For each business, we list the services
     ServiceInfos serviceInfos = businessInfo.getServiceInfos();
     Vector siv = serviceInfos.getServiceInfoVector();

     System.out.println("      There is(are) "
       + siv.size() + " service(s) registered for "
       + businessInfo.getNameString());

     for(int svcNdx = 0; svcNdx < siv.size(); svcNdx++) {
       ServiceInfo serviceInfo = (ServiceInfo)siv.elementAt(svcNdx);
       System.out.println("          "
         + serviceInfo.getNameString() + ", service key is: "
         + serviceInfo.getServiceKey());
     }
   }
 } catch(UDDIException uddiException) {
```

The remainder of the code is identical to `RegisterBusiness` so we won't explain it again.

We have only scratched the surface of what can be done with UDDI and the UDDI4J package, but the examples that we reviewed provide us with a solid base for further learning.

Now that we have some practical experience with UDDI, it is time to take a step back and see what the technology can accomplish for us. If we recall the advertising problem that we described at the beginning of this chapter and compare it to what we have discussed about UDDI, we will see that, by and large, UDDI solved the issues that we identified, namely the following:

❑   **Universal**
    The UDDI cloud is accessible through HTTP and SOAP, which are available on most platforms in use today, and are open interoperable specifications.

❑   **Description**
    The UDDI registry provides both local (tModels) and remote descriptions (WSDL documents) of web services.

❑   **Discovery**
    The UDDI cloud provides a query mechanism by name and by taxonomies.

❑   **Integration**
    The web services registered in UDDI use standard protocols like HTTP and SOAP.

So, is it true to say that everything is rosy in web service land? Not quite. As we will discuss in the following section, UDDI will have to overcome some flaws if it is to become the first choice when it comes to publishing and advertising web services.

# Other Publishing Technologies

According to a study conducted by SalCentral and WebServicesArchitect, close to 50% of the data stored in the production UDDI cloud is inaccurate. This is not surprising if we consider the fact that UDDI registration is not moderated; in other words anybody can put anything in the UDDI cloud. The details of the SalCentral/WebServicesArchitect research can be found at http://www.salcentral.com/uddi/default.asp.

To be convinced that a moderator is important, let's ask ourselves the following question – how accurate would the phone book be, if it were up to all the businesses and individuals to enter and keep their data up-to-date? Another analogy worth mentioning is the HTML publishing surge that we saw a few years ago – a lot of people wanted to publish their pages over the web, but very few wanted to maintain the accuracy of the data that they published. Even inside an enterprise, too often we see out-of-date departmental web sites.

Another shortcoming of UDDI is the lack of restricted communities; there is no equivalent in the UDDI cloud to our intranets and extranets.

In this section, we will take a short look at two potential solutions to these shortcomings. We will first look at setting up a private UDDI registry and then we will look at a specification that complements UDDI by supporting local publication of web services – the **Web Service Inspection Language (WSIL)**.

Let's start with a discussion on setting up a private UDDI registry.

## Private UDDI Registries

Setting up a private UDDI registry answers the weaknesses that we mentioned earlier:

❑ A private UDDI registry can easily be moderated and therefore limit the inaccuracies that inevitably creep into the database.

❑ A private UDDI registry, by definition, can be restricted to an intranet or an extranet.

However, these features come at a price – as its name implies, a private UDDI registry is not part of the cloud and can therefore not be used to gain new customers. It is only a valid medium to publish web services to our partners and co-workers. Another way to look at a private UDDI registry is to think of it as a corporate phonebook.

First, it is destined to be used by a specific, well-targeted audience and as such can contain proprietary information. Second, because the users usually know what they are looking for, a sophisticated taxonomy is not always required; only the largest companies have a phonebook with Yellow Pages.

One could argue that using UDDI is not required when the information is only going to be published to an intranet or an extranet. There is at least one good reason why the extra complexity and expense of a private UDDI registry over a homegrown solution (for example, a SQL or an LDAP database) are warranted. The reason is that UDDI is a standardized protocol, so if we use UDDI both internally and externally, we will be able to leverage our development for our private registry when we do go to the UDDI cloud.

When it comes to setting up a private UDDI registry, there are several solutions to choose from. One that is relatively easy to setup is the lightweight UDDI server that comes with the WebSphere Software Development Kit for Web Services (WSDK).

## Try It Out – Setting up a Private UDDI Registry

Our first step in setting up a private registry is to download the WSDK.

**1.** We can download WSDK from http://www-106.ibm.com/developerworks/webservices/wsdk/ (follow the Download link on the right):

The download and setup process of WSDK will be reviewed in details in Chapter 10. For now, we are simply interested in getting a private UDDI registry up and running, so we will focus on that portion of WSDK.

After answering the obligatory registration questions, we will be prompted to download an .exe file for the Windows platform or a .tar file for Linux platform. At the time of this writing, the .exe for Windows is ibm-wsdk-131-w32.exe:

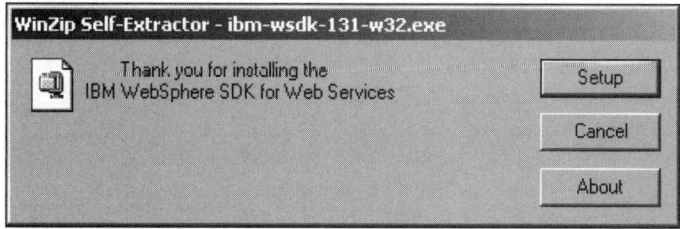

Click on Setup, enter the installation directory, (we will be installing it to C:\WSDK). We will assume that the installation directory is the wsdk_home shell variable for the purpose of this discussion. Note that we will need to restart our machine after the setup is finished.

2. To enable the WebSphere UDDI implementation, we must run the WSDK configuration utility by typing the following command (or its equivalent for our installation):

```
%wsdk_home%\bin\wsdkconfig.bat
```

3. When the GUI comes up, select the default (Lightweight application server) as shown on the following screenshot:

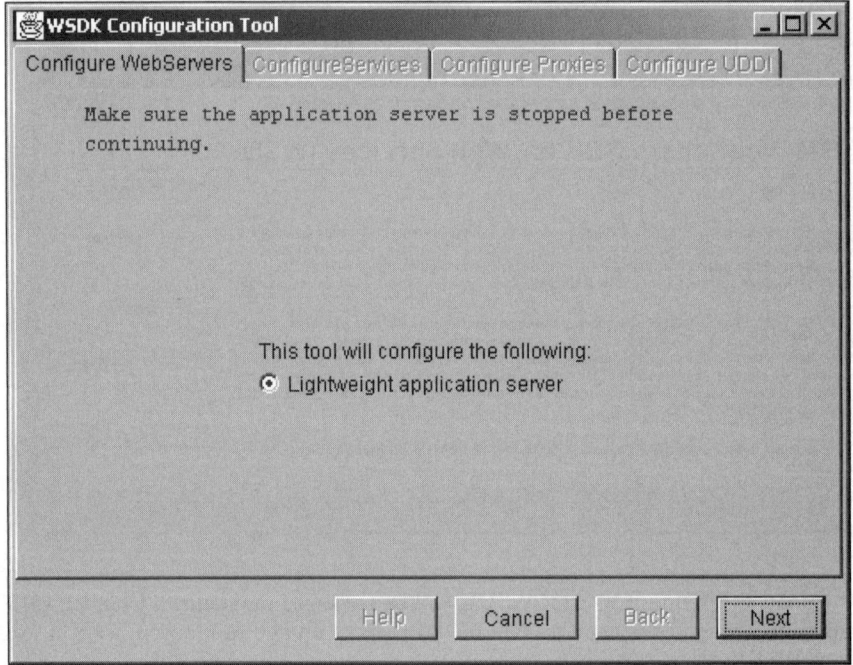

Then click on the Next button until we get to the UDDI configuration tab:

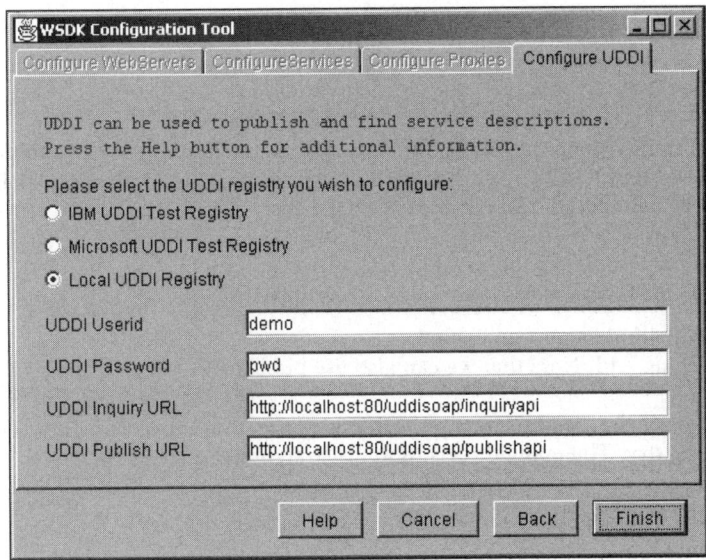

Once again, the defaults should suit us well. Click on Finish to set up the lightweight UDDI server (the process might take a few minutes).

**4.** To start the UDDI server, simply type the following command (or its equivalent for our installation) in a command (shell) window:

```
%wsdk_home%\WebSphere\bin\startServer
```

There is also a `stopServer` command to stop the UDDI server.

**5.** Once the server is running, navigate our browser to the following URL http://localhost/uddigui. Note that we are using the default port: 80. If everything goes as expected, we should see the following screen:

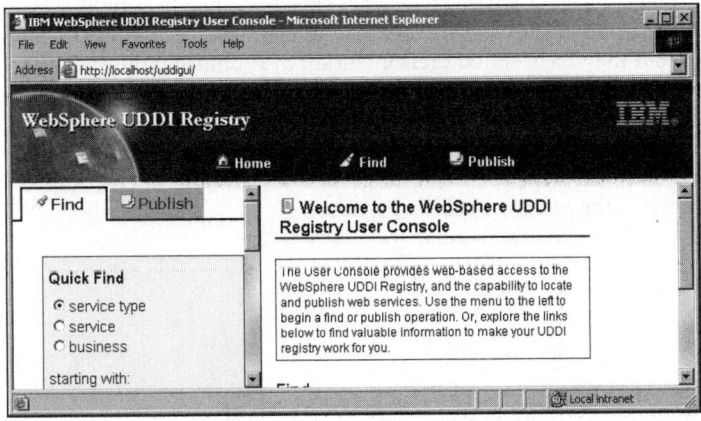

*The WSDK UDDI registry comes with a default login. The user name is* demo, *and the password is* pwd.

### How It Works

This UDDI GUI is simpler than the IBM public site and is functional. We can run the `RegisterBusiness` and `RegisterService` examples against the following URLs (or their equivalent for our installation) to test our local UDDI registry:

❑ http://localhost/uddisoap/inquiryapi
The inquiry API. Note that we can also use inquiryAPI.

❑ http://localhost/uddisoap/publishapi
The publishing API. Note that we can also use publishAPI.

We will have to register the `jws` business prior to registering the `StockQuote` service, as we did for the public UDDI registry. The manual registration is straightforward:

**1.** Click on the Publish tab as shown in the previous screenshot

**2.** Enter the business name (`jws`)

**3.** Finally, click on the Publish now link

There is also an Advanced publish link that allows us to enter other information like an address, a contact, and so on.

We said earlier that a significant drawback of a private UDDI registry is that it does not participate in the UDDI cloud. There is a solution that bridges the public UDDI cloud and a private registry. This solution also comes with a price – a new XML dialect: the WSIL.

# WS-Inspection

The motivation behind the **WS-Inspection** specification is simple – allow web service users to query a web server rather than a central registry. The WS-Inspection specification is a proprietary specification jointly proposed by IBM and Microsoft. At the time of this writing, the specification is still in the hands of both companies, but they have stated their intention of submitting the specification to a standards body. The text of the specification can be found at http://www-106.ibm.com/developerworks/webservices/library/ws-wsilspec.html.

Going back to John and Mary, the following diagram illustrates the interactions between the web service publisher and user when they rely on WS-Inspection:

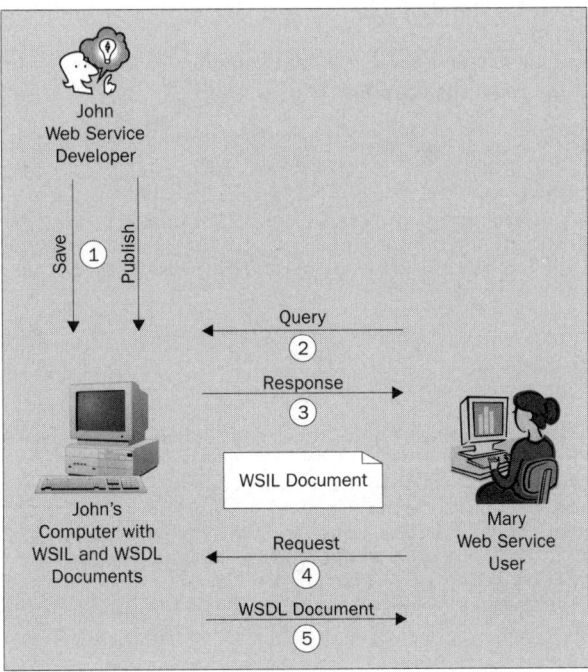

This diagram is slightly different from the first one we looked at in this chapter; here Mary queries John's web site for the WSIL document that contains the list of web services that John supports. This approach is actually complementary with UDDI, because nothing forbids John to publish in a WSIL document web services that are also available from the UDDI cloud as shown on the following figure:

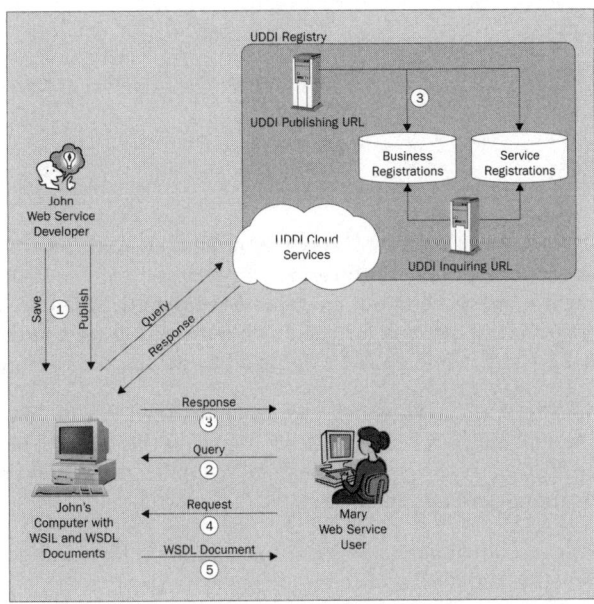

In this case, John's computer is simply a gateway to a UDDI registry (public or private).

Without any more delays, let's have a look at a WSIL document for the `StockQuote` and `Market` web services that we used in the previous chapter:

```xml
<?xml version="1.0" encoding="UTF-8"?>

<inspection
  xmlns="http://schemas.xmlsoap.org/ws/2001/10/inspection/"
  xmlns:wsilwsdl="http://schemas.xmlsoap.org/ws/2001/10/inspection/wsdl/"
  xmlns:wsiluddi="http://schemas.xmlsoap.org/ws/2001/10/inspection/uddi/"
  xmlns:uddi="urn:uddi-org:api">

  <service>
    <name xml:lang="en-US">
      StockQuoteService
    </name>
    <description referencedNamespace="http://schemas.xmlsoap.org/wsdl"
      location="http://localhost/axis/services/StockQuote?wsdl">
      <wsilwsdl:reference endpointPresent="true">
        <wsilwsdl:implementedBinding
          xmlns:interface="http://stockquote.jws.wrox.com">
            interface:StockQuoteSoapBinding
        </wsilwsdl:implementedBinding>
      </wsilwsdl:reference>
    </description>
  </service>

  <service>
    <name xml:lang="en-US">MarketService</name>
    <description referencedNamespace="http://schemas.xmlsoap.org/wsdl"
      location="http://localhost/axis/services/Market?wsdl">
      <wsilwsdl:reference endpointPresent="true">
        <wsilwsdl:implementedBinding
          xmlns:interface="http://stockquote.jws.wrox.com">
          interface:MarketSoapBinding
        </wsilwsdl:implementedBinding>
      </wsilwsdl:reference>
    </description>
  </service>

</inspection>
```

As we can see, the WSIL document is an XML document with an `<inspection>` root element. The namespace of the specification is `http://schemas.xmlsoap.org/ws/2001/10/inspection`, which we use as the default namespace in our example document. Inside the `<inspection>` element, there is a set of `<service>` elements, one for each web service that we want to publish. One can also have `<businessDescription/>` elements to publish businesses (we will see an example shortly).

In the example above, the definition of the web service is included in situ, but it is also possible to have a link to another WSIL document or a UDDI registry (more on this later). The `<name>` element is the name of the web service. The `<description>` element contains the actual description of the web service along with its location (for example, `StockQuote.wsdl`).

The `referencedNamespace` attribute is the namespace of the referenced document. Since in this case the web service is described using WSDL, its name space is `http://schemas.xmlsoap.org/wsdl`.

You will notice that the `<reference/>` element is not part of the default namespace; rather it is part of `http://schemas.xmlsoap.org/ws/2001/10/inspection/wsdl`, prefixed by `wsilwsdl` in this document. This methodology of supporting WSDL in WSIL through extensions is similar to what we saw with the support for SOAP inside WSDL documents.

This allows the specification to accommodate new description formalisms by simply adding a namespace rather than modifying the specification. In our example, the `<wsilwsdl:implementedBinding/>` element indicates which WSDL bindings are defined in the referenced WSDL document. The `<wsilwsdl:implementedBinding/>` element is optional.

You will also notice that our WSIL document declares the namespace for web services published in UDDI `http://schemas.xmlsoap.org/ws/2001/10/inspection/uddi` with the prefix `wsiluddi`. As a matter of fact, it is fairly easy to modify our WSIL document to reference a UDDI entry. Notice the use of the `<link>` element and the fact that we publish a business rather than a service.

```xml
<?xml version="1.0"?>

<inspection
  xmlns:wsiluddi="http://schemas.xmlsoap.org/ws/2001/10/inspection/uddi/"
  xmlns="http://schemas.xmlsoap.org/ws/2001/10/inspection/">
  <link referencedNamespace="urn:uddi-org:api">
    <wsiluddi:businessDescription
      location="http://www.ibm.com/uddi/inquiryapi">
      <wsiluddi:businessKey>
        368D90C0-A5D6-11D6-A687-000629DC0A7B
      </wsiluddi:businessKey>
      <wsiluddi:discoveryURL useType="businessEntity">
        http://www-3.ibm.com/services/uddi/testregistry/uddiget?
          businessKey=368D90C0-A5D6-11D6-A687-000629DC0A7B
      </wsiluddi:discoveryURL>
    </wsiluddi:businessDescription>
  </link>
</inspection>
```

The UDDI-specific elements are:

❑ `<wsiluddi:businessDescription/>` element
  This contains a URL to the description of the business

❑ `<wsiluddi:businessKey/>` element
  This contains the UDDI business key

❑ `<wsiluddi:discoveryURL/>` element
  This contains the discovery URL along with the necessary argument (a UDDI business key)

Let's wrap up our review of the WSIL document above by saying that the `endPointPresent="true"` attribute simply states that the WSDL contains a WSDL `<service/>` element. An interface definition WSDL document would not contain a `<service/>` element, and as such would have `endPointPresent="false"` attribute.

Publishing the web services available on a given web site using WSIL is not enough because potential users must have a standard URL to go to. The same problem existed with WSDL and was solved by adding the `?WSDL` trailer to the web service URL as we saw in Chapter 5 (for example, http://localhost/axis/StockQuote?WSDL).

Here the convention must be web site-wide since the purpose of WSIL is to publish all the web services available on a given web site. The well-known WSIL URL is inspection.wsil. For instance, if our web services are at http://www.wroxpress.com/axis, then our WS-Inspection document should be at http://www.wroxpress.com/axis/inspection.wsil.

There are at least three ways to make the inspection.wsil URL available for all to browse:

❑ Hardcode a WSIL document

❑ Generate a WSIL document with the DOM

❑ Use the WSIL4J package available with the WSTK

> *At the time of this writing, WSIL4J (WSTK 3.2) does not automatically recognize the web services published by Axis, but according to the documentation, that feature is planned for a future release.*

Solution 1 and 2 are straightforward and do not involve concepts specific to web services. Solution 3 is worth investigating since it has the potential of simplifying the creation and processing of WSIL documents.

The WSIL4J (%wstk_home%\wsil4j) package comes with two examples – one to read a local WSIL document and one to read a remote WSIL document. Alas, there is no example that creates a WSIL document, so we will go through one.

## Try It Out – Generate a WSIL Document

The Inspection example provides an implementation of the inspection.wsil URL that produces the WSIL document that we just reviewed. The Inspection class is a servlet. If you are not familiar with servlet development do not worry; we will be discussing all the steps necessary to get the Inspection class working.

**1.** The code of the Inspection class is listed below:

```
package com.wrox.jws.stockquote;

import org.apache.wsil.WSILDocumentFactory;
import org.apache.wsil.WSILDocument;
import org.apache.wsil.WSILException;
import org.apache.wsil.Service;
import org.apache.wsil.ServiceName;
import org.apache.wsil.Description;
import org.apache.wsil.QName;

import org.apache.wsil.extension.wsdl.Reference;
import org.apache.wsil.extension.wsdl.ImplementedBinding;

import org.apache.wsil.impl.ServiceNameImpl;
import org.apache.wsil.impl.DescriptionImpl;
import org.apache.wsil.impl.extension.wsdl.WSDLExtensionBuilder;
import org.apache.wsil.impl.extension.wsdl.ReferenceImpl;
import org.apache.wsil.impl.extension.wsdl.ImplementedBindingImpl;
import org.apache.wsil.xml.XMLWriter;

import java.io.IOException;
import java.io.InputStream;
```

```java
import java.io.InputStreamReader;
import java.net.URL;
import java.net.URLConnection;

import javax.servlet.ServletException;
import javax.servlet.http.HttpServlet;
import javax.servlet.http.HttpServletRequest;
import javax.servlet.http.HttpServletResponse;

public class Inspection extends HttpServlet {

  // Minimal doGet implementation.
  public void doGet(HttpServletRequest req, HttpServletResponse res)
    throws ServletException, IOException {

    WSILDocument document = createDocument();
    XMLWriter writer = new XMLWriter();

    try {
      writer.writeDocument(document, res.getWriter());
      res.setContentType("text/xml");
    } catch (WSILException wsilException) {
      throw new ServletException("Cannot generate WSIL dcoument: "
        + wsilException);
    }
  } // doGet

  // Comments omitted from this listing
  private void addService(WSILDocument document, String name,
    String location, String bindingUriNamespace, String bindingName) {

    Service stockQuoteService = document.createService();
    ServiceName stockQuoteServiceName = new ServiceNameImpl();
    Description stockQuoteDescription = new DescriptionImpl();

    // We add a <name/> element for the English language
    stockQuoteServiceName.setText(name);
    stockQuoteServiceName.setLang("en-US");
    stockQuoteService.addServiceName(stockQuoteServiceName);

    // We add a <description/> element (location + referenced namespace)
    stockQuoteDescription.setLocation(location);
    stockQuoteDescription.setReferencedNamespace(
      "http://schemas.xmlsoap.org/wsdl");

    // We add a reference element to a SOAP binding:
    Reference refBinding = new ReferenceImpl();
    ImplementedBinding stockQuoteBinding = new ImplementedBindingImpl();

    refBinding.setEndpointPresent(Boolean.TRUE);
    stockQuoteBinding.setBindingName(
      new QName(bindingUriNamespace, bindingName));
    refBinding.addImplementedBinding(stockQuoteBinding);

    stockQuoteDescription.setExtensionElement(refBinding);
    stockQuoteService.addDescription(stockQuoteDescription);
    document.getInspection().addService(stockQuoteService);
  }
```

```
  // Create a WSIL document with two services: StockQuote and Market
  private WSILDocument createDocument() throws WSILException {
    String methodName =
      "com.wrox.jws.stockquote.Inspection.createDocument";
    WSILDocument document = null;

    document = WSILDocumentFactory.newInstance().newDocument();
    addService(document, "StockQuoteService",
      "http://localhost/axis/services/StockQuote?wsdl",
      "http://stockquote.jws.wrox.com", "StockQuoteSoapBinding");

    addService(document, "MarketService",
      "http://localhost/axis/services/Market?wsdl",
      "http://stockquote.jws.wrox.com", "MarketSoapBinding");

    return document;
  }
```

The remainder of the code contains the `main()` method that is used as a test case.

**2.** Building the `Inspection` example requires that we include the following JAR files in our classpath:

❑ `%jwsDirectory%\lib\xmlParserAPIs.jar`
  The Xerces parser is required since WSIL is an XML document

❑ `%wstk_home%\uddi4j\lib\uddi4j.jar`
  `wstk_home` is where we installed the Web Service Toolkit

❑ `%wstk_home%\wsil4j\lib\wsil4j.jar`

❑ `%catalina_home%\common\lib\servlet.jar`
  `catalina_home` is where we installed Tomcat (Catalina)

**3.** Once you have built the class file (`Inspection.class`), make sure that you put it under `%axisDirectory%\webapps\axis\WEB-INF\classes`, where `axisDirectory` is your Axis installation directory. For instance, on Windows, type the following commands, assuming that the `src` directory is our current directory (it is best to stop Tomcat before building):

```
javac -d %axisDirectory%\webapps\axis\WEB-INF\classes
 com\wrox\jws\stockquote\Inspection.java
```

> The order of the `<servlet/>` and `<servlet-mapping/>` elements is constrained by the DTD. So make sure that all the servlet definitions come before the servlet mappings in `web.xml`. If `web.xml` does not follow the constraints of its DTD we will get a validation error when Tomcat comes up.

**4.** Before being able to test our example, we need to define it as a servlet. To include `inspection.wsil` as a servlet, make sure that you add the following lines to the `web.xml` of your Axis installation (`%axisDirectory%\webapps\axis\WEB-INF\web.xml`):

```
...
<servlet>
    <servlet-name>inspection</servlet-name>
    <servlet-class>com.wrox.jws.stockquote.Inspection</servlet-class>
</servlet>

<servlet-mapping>
    <servlet-name>inspection</servlet-name>
    <url-pattern>inspection.wsil</url-pattern>
</servlet-mapping>
...
```

**5.** Note that you might want to make a backup copy of the `web.xml` file before modifying it. Next, we will test the `Inspection` class. After starting Tomcat, you should be able to navigate to the `inspection.wsil` URL and see the following result:

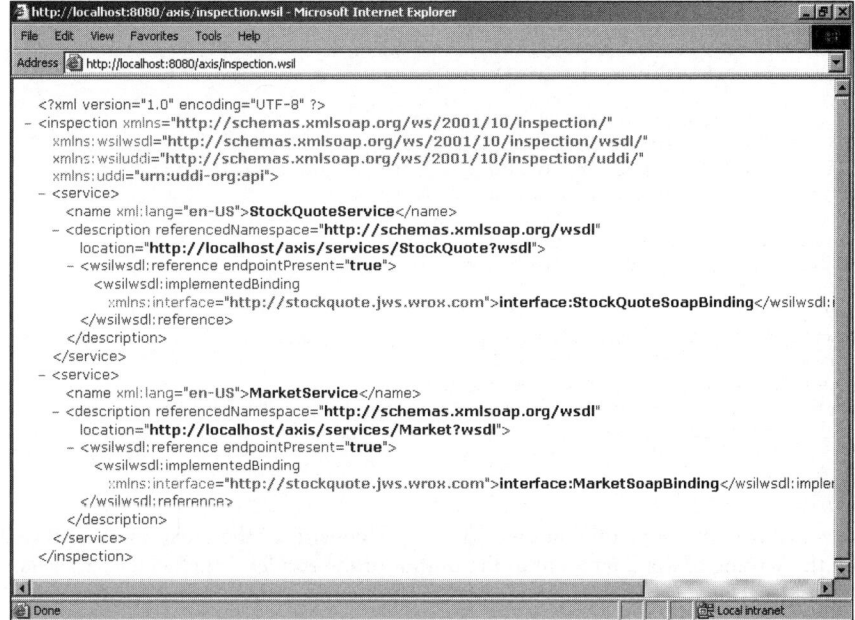

Before proceeding with a review of the code, it is necessary to point out a few facts.

The WSIL4J package models the structure of a WSIL document by exposing a hierarchy with a model that is similar to the DOM API. For instance, if we look at the `<service/>` element, it is modeled with a `org.apache.wsil.Service` object and always contained inside a `org.apache.wsil.Inspection` element, which itself is part of a `org.apache.wsil.WSILDocument`. One creates a service with a call `WSILDocument.createService()`.

### How It Works

Let's now have a closer look at the `Inspection` class:

```
package com.wrox.jws.stockquote;

import org.apache.wsil.WSILDocumentFactory;
// Other imports removed from this listing
```

We will review the `org.apache.wsil` classes as we encounter them in the code. The `java.io` and `java.net` packages are simply used for the test code that reads the WSIL document from the `inspection.wsil` URL:

```
import java.io.IOException;
import java.io.InputStream;
import java.io.InputStreamReader;
import java.net.URL;
import java.net.URLConnection;
```

The `javax.servlet` classes are used to implement a minimalist version of `doGet()`:

```
import javax.servlet.ServletException;
import javax.servlet.http.HttpServlet;
import javax.servlet.http.HttpServletRequest;
import javax.servlet.http.HttpServletResponse;

public class Inspection extends HttpServlet {
  // Minimal doGet implementation.
  public void doGet(HttpServletRequest req, HttpServletResponse res)
    throws ServletException, IOException  {

    WSILDocument document = createDocument();
    XMLWriter    writer   = new XMLWriter();

    try {
      writer.writeDocument(document, res.getWriter());
      res.setContentType("text/xml");
    } catch (WSILException wsilException) {
      throw new ServletException("Cannot generate WSIL dcoument: "
        + wsilException);
    }
  } // doGet
```

As you can see above, the implementation of `doGet()` consists of the creation of the WSIL document followed by the writing of the document to the output of the servlet. The `XMLWriter` class that comes with the WSIL4J package is handy to write any WSIL document to a `java.io.OutputStream` or to a `java.io.Writer`.

The next method in the `Inspection` servlet is the `addService()` method, which adds a service to the `<inspection/>` element of the document passed as argument. The goal of `addService()` is to produce a document fragment like the following in the case of `StockQuote`:

```
<service>
 <name xml:lang="en-US">StockQuoteService</name>
 <description

   referencedNamespace="http://schemas.xmlsoap.org/wsdl"
   location="http://localhost/axis/services/StockQuote?wsdl">

  <wsilwsdl:reference endpointPresent="true">
   <wsilwsdl:implementedBinding
   xmlns:interface="http://stockquote.jws.wrox.com">
   interface:StockQuoteSoapBinding
   </wsilwsdl:implementedBinding>
  </wsilwsdl:reference>
 </description>
</service>
```

Here is the code for `addService()`:

```
private void addService(WSILDocument document, String name,
   String location, String bindingUriNamespace, String bindingName) {

   Service stockQuoteService = document.createService();
   ServiceName stockQuoteServiceName = new ServiceNameImpl();
   Description stockQuoteDescription = new DescriptionImpl();
```

Notice that we need the document to create a service, but that the elements inside the service can be created standalone and must be added through `add*` methods, as we can see below for the service name:

```
   // We add a <name/> element for the English language
   stockQuoteServiceName.setText(name);
   stockQuoteServiceName.setLang("en-US");
   stockQuoteService.addServiceName(stockQuoteServiceName);
```

The `<description/>` is a little more complex since we want to include a binding for SOAP. First, we set the location and the namespace to WSDL:

```
   // We add a <description/> element (location + referenced namespace)
   stockQuoteDescription.setLocation(location);
   stockQuoteDescription.setReferencedNamespace(
     "http://schemas.xmlsoap.org/wsdl");
```

Next, we create the reference element and the binding:

```
   // We add a reference element to a SOAP binding:
   Reference refBinding = new ReferenceImpl();
   ImplementedBinding stockQuoteBinding = new ImplementedBindingImpl();

   refBinding.setEndpointPresent(Boolean.TRUE);
   stockQuoteBinding.setBindingName(
     new QName(bindingUriNamespace, bindingName));

   refBinding.addImplementedBinding(stockQuoteBinding);

   stockQuoteDescription.setExtensionElement(refBinding);
   stockQuoteService.addDescription(stockQuoteDescription);
```

**269**

As you can see, we add the `<description/>` element to the `<service/>` element. Finally, we must not forget to add the created service to the `<inspection/>` element:

```
        document.getInspection().addService(stockQuoteService);
    }
```

Thanks to the `addService()` method, adding a `<service/>` element for `StockQuote` and `Market` is relatively trivial:

```
    // Create a WSIL document with two services: StockQuote and Market
    private WSILDocument createDocument() throws WSILException {

      String methodName = "com.wrox.jws.stockquote.Inspection.createDocument";
      WSILDocument document = null;
      document = WSILDocumentFactory.newInstance().newDocument();

      addService(document, "StockQuoteService",
        "http://localhost/axis/services/StockQuote?wsdl",
        "http://stockquote.jws.wrox.com", "StockQuoteSoapBinding");

      addService(document, "MarketService",
        "http://localhost/axis/services/Market?wsdl",
        "http://stockquote.jws.wrox.com", "MarketSoapBinding");

      return document;
    }
```

This concludes our detailed review of the `Inspection` class.

The WSIL example that we reviewed is fairly simple, but it should give us enough information to get started with our own project. We can enhance this example by adding links to other WSIL documents, or by adding links to UDDI registries (public or private).

# Java for XML Registries

If there is a design that has been copied over and over, it is the two-tier design for database access first popularized by ODBC, and more recently by JDBC. The **Java API for XML Registries (JAXR)** is no exception, since it is a two-tier architecture to access data stored in XML. As you can see from the following figure, JAXR can be used in the case of John and Mary:

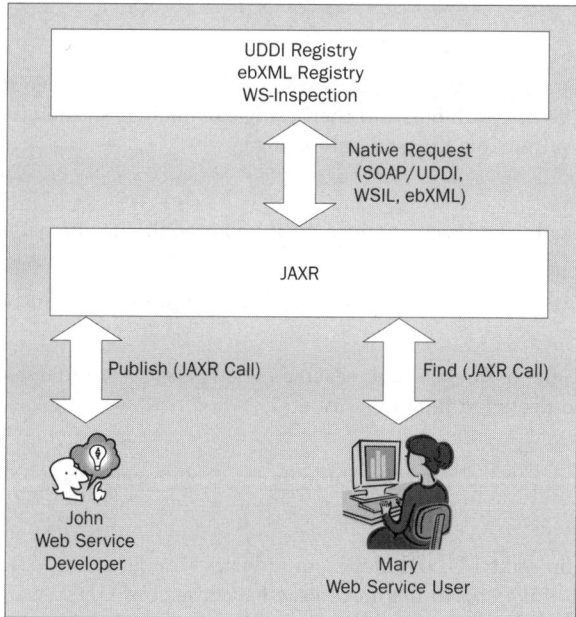

*Electronic business XML (ebXML) is a specification sponsored by the United Nations Centre for Trade Facilitation and Electronic Business (UN/CEFACT) and by the Organization for the Advancement of Structured Information Standards (OASIS).*

This architecture is also similar to the UDDI4J package that we used in this chapter to access a UDDI registry. However, there are at least two significant differences:

❑   **UDDI4J was designed specifically for UDDI registries**
JAXR, on the other hand, provides an abstraction that can be used to access most XML registries.

❑   **UDDI4J was written by IBM and donated to open source**
JAXR is the product of the Java Community Process (JCP). Whether or not the open process produced a better mousetrap is probably a matter of taste.

The JAXR specification can be downloaded from http://java.sun.com/xml/jaxr. At the time of this writing, the latest version of JAXR comes with the Java Web Service Developer Pack 1.0 (Java WSDP 1.0), which can be downloaded from http://java.sun.com/webservices/webservicespack.html.

Given the tendency of XML to generate new specifications, like dandelions on a spring lawn, a unifying technology like JAXR is likely to succeed in the long run. Once again, this is not unlike ODBC and JDBC that mostly isolate our database developments from the vendor-specific intricacies and peculiarities. Alas, at the time of this writing, only UDDI and ebXML registries are supported, so there is little JAXR can do to help us in the UDDI/WSIL world.

# Summary

This chapter gave us the opportunity to review web service publishing. We started our discussion with a more formal definition of the problem, and then using the analogy of the ubiquitous phonebook, we identified four main requirements for web publishing:

❏  **Universal**
    A directory of published web services must be accessible to the widest possible audience

❏  **Description**
    A web service registry must provide some description of the published web services

❏  **Discovery**
    It must be possible to query a web service registry using intuitive searches like names, geography, and provided functionality

❏  **Integration**
    A published web service must be usable on most platforms, using most programming languages

We focused our attention on the UDDI cloud, an industry standard, and described why it satisfies our requirements. We then moved on to the more practical subject of UDDI development using the UDDI4J package with two examples: `RegisterBusiness` and `RegisterService`.

We wrapped up the chapter with a review of other web service publishing technologies than the UDDI cloud. We saw that setting up a private UDDI registry allowed us to service an intranet or an extranet. We also introduced the WS-Inspection specification and its Web Service Inspection Language (WSIL) as a way to bridge the gap between a local and a global XML registry. We concluded the chapter with a short introduction to the Java API for XML Registries (JAXR), which supports a standardized API to XML registries like UDDI and ebXML, but does not yet support WSIL.

In the next chapter, we'll look at how we can we can use messaging to send and receive web services asynchronously.

# Asynchronous Web Services

Up to this point, we have learned the basics of web services – how to create and consume them using Java. The examples we discussed so far have mostly relied on SOAP communication between the requester and the provider of a web service. This meant that the requester of the service sent a request envelope and the provider returned a response envelope.

In this chapter, we will focus on scenarios where the request is not followed by an immediate response. Instead, a request is sent out and the caller is not blocked until the response arrives. The caller can pick up the response, if there is one, at a later time. We call web services implementing such scenarios **asynchronous web services**. After we have looked at it from a programming model perspective, we can apply what we learned there to different web service scenarios like **message-based web services**.

The implementations of this type of web services are different from those of synchronous, RPC–style web services. They are also accessed in a different manner. Overall, there are many possibilities regarding the use of message-based web services. In this chapter we shall be discussing two of them. Namely:

- ❑  The **Java API for XML-based Messaging** or **JAXM**, which allows us to build and process generic XML messages with special support for SOAP messages.

- ❑  The **Java Message Service (JMS)** API. This is another standard Java interface for messaging. We can send SOAP messages over this layer, or we can send invocations for web services over this interface in some other format.

As we can see, there are many options for implementing and accessing web services in an asynchronous manner. By the time we complete this chapter, we will be in a position to understand what these options are.

# Programming Models Revisited

We cannot stress it enough: web services are all about allowing applications to interact with each other. So far, we have been focusing on synchronous communication. An application (the requester) communicates with another application (the provider) by invoking a function that the provider exposes in the form of a web service. After invoking this exposed function, the requester process blocks itself, until a response from the invoked service comes back.

In some cases, this blocking of the process is not acceptable; to say the least, this is not a productive use of our computing resources. The invoked web service may take a long time to complete its function. Instead of waiting for the reply, this waiting time of the requester can be used to perform some other task. Moreover, the called web service might not return any data, or the requester might not need the returned data immediately. In these types of scenarios, it is sufficient for us to trigger the execution of a remote function, without having to wait for its completion.

For example, let's assume that a business firm has two distinct software packages – one of them is an Enterprise Resource Planning (ERP) system, which apart from doing other functions is also responsible for handling the new orders placed by a customer. The other software package runs on the manufacturing floor and controls the manufacturing process for these orders.

These systems are loosely coupled. In other words, on getting an order, the ERP system will trigger some processes in the manufacturing system, so that the ordered products are actually build. At the same time, the manufacturing system will possibly send updates about the status of an order back to the ERP system.

Now, these two interactions can be asynchronous, as they do not require immediate feedback from the invoked service. Besides, it also possible that the triggered processes (for example, the manufacturing of a product) might take hours or sometimes even days to complete. In such a case, the ERP system cannot be kept waiting till the manufacturing system completes its work. A diagram showing these two systems is as follows:

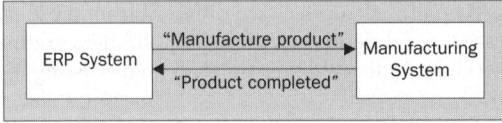

In these types of daily settings, asynchronous message-based systems have been deployed for a long time. The advent of web services doesn't change this fundamental approach. It merely puts formalization around the model of system interaction, thereby making it easier for us to implement these systems. The implementation gets easier as the communication between existing subsystems is based on open standards, which work across heterogeneous platforms and different programming languages.

## Message-based Web Services

The term **message-based web service** is somewhat redundant because a web service is always invoked through a request message by a requester. In the web services scenarios that we discussed in the previous chapters, we considered the request message to be an invocation of a function, which accepts parameters and returns a result. In this case, though, we talk about a generic message that contains a bunch of data, which a client passes to a server. The data that is sent by a requester to the provider is not meant to be interpreted as a collection of parameters to a function.

So, what does the programming model for these services look like? On a high level, the various systems that communicate in this environment are generally more event-driven than systems in other environments. A particular type of activity in one system (like the arrival of a customer order) leads to an event, which triggers other activities in another system (or systems). As a result, this can lead to environments where many processes can be taking place at the same time.

One crucial issue is how we map these characteristics in our web services. We have already seen that web services are described by using port types in WSDL. Each port type consists of one or more operations. There are four types of operations – request-response, one-way, solicit-response, and notification. What we have looked at so far were the request–response operations where the requester blocks after sending the request message until it gets the response message.

For message-based web services, which are using asynchronous communication to interact with their counterparts, one-way operations are more common. Note that WSDL does not mandate that request-response operations have to be handled synchronously. A requester could send a request message, continue to do other work, and receive the response to the request at a later time. However, in most cases this style of interaction would be implemented by using multiple one-way operations.

Keep in mind, though; that the WSDL specification does not mandate the use of synchronous or asynchronous communication; this is left to the underlying protocol to determine. WSDL maintains a strict separation between the interface of a service and the protocol that is used to invoke it. This means that we can have, for example, a request-response operation and still use an asynchronous protocol to handle the invocation of such an operation.

Speaking of protocols, is SOAP (the primary protocol for web services) a synchronous protocol or an asynchronous one? The answer is, that it is neither. The specification does not mandate the use of a certain network protocol to transmit a SOAP message, and at its very core, SOAP defines one-way messages.

This means that a SOAP request does not have to lead to a SOAP response. If we are using SOAP over HTTP, then we will make a synchronous request, because HTTP is a synchronous protocol. However, even in this case, the SOAP specification does not mandate that a SOAP response be returned. Thus, we could implement a compliant run time environment that supports asynchronous web service invocations, using SOAP over HTTP.

Besides, SOAP can also be used over other network protocols. For example, we could use SOAP over a messaging environment supporting the Java Message Service (JMS).

JMS defines an API that allows us to send and receive messages from a queue. Thus, this API supports asynchronous communication between programs 'out of the box', which makes it easier to implement asynchronous web services.We will look at this case in more detail later on.

JMS also defines a way for broadcasting messages to multiple receivers by a **publish-subscribe mechanism**. In this case, clients subscribe to a certain 'topic'. Whenever a message is published on that topic, it is automatically forwarded to all subscribers, which could be used in web services scenarios, too. So, given that SOAP can be used for asynchronous, message based web services, what other protocols are available? We have already mentioned JMS. In the previous chapter, we saw that in WSDL, we can describe the details of accessing a web service in the <binding> element. In this element, we can also define information that describes how to communicate with a web service over JMS. However, note that so far, this is not standardized.

### Message-Driven Bean (MDB)

In all cases where JMS is used as a transport layer for web services – be it transporting SOAP envelopes or data that was formatted in some other way, we need some process to receive the messages arriving for a service. The Java 2 Platform, Enterprise Edition (J2EE) specification defines a special kind of Enterprise JavaBean (EJB) for this purpose, it is known as **Message-Driven Bean** (**MDB**).

An MDB is configured to receive messages from a particular JMS queue or topic. Whenever a message arrives on a queue or topic that an MDB is configured for, the J2EE application server will automatically receive this message and forward it to this MDB.

We will look at this setup again in more detail later. For now, just keep in mind that from a programming model perspective, an MDB is the most common way to receive web services invocations for services using JMS as the transport layer. After receiving the invocations, the MDB will forward them to the actual web service:

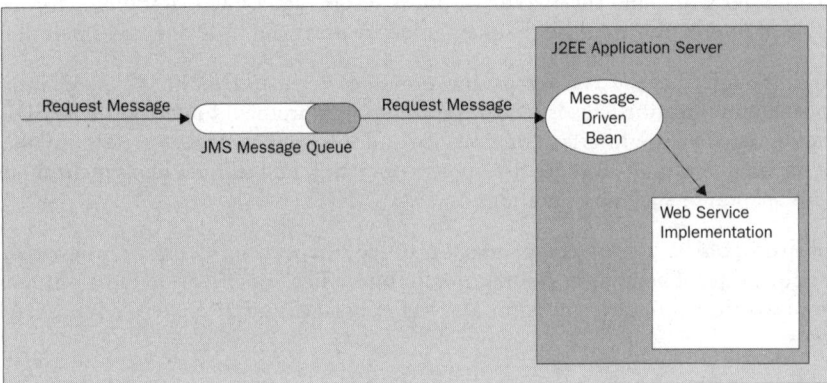

If there is a response (depending on whether the operation was defined as a request-response, or a one-way operation), it is sent back to the requester in the same way. That is, the MDB will pick up the returned data, format it into a SOAP message, and send it to an output message queue. This queue is likely to be different from the receiver queue, and from there the requesting client can pick up the response.

If we wanted to build a solution that does not require a full J2EE application server environment with its support for MDBs, we would have to develop some code that can receive messages from a JMS queue and forward them to a web service. The advantage that the MDB and the J2EE environment brings us is that the reception of the message and the invocation of the service run in a secure and transactional environment. Moreover, if we are using an MDB, we don't have to write any JMS code, the J2EE application server will take care of that for us.

Now that we have looked at things from a programming model perspective, let's look at their implementation in Java.

# The JAXM API

*The latest JAXM specification can be obtained from http://java.sun.com/xml/downloads/jaxm.html and the SAAJ specification from http://java.sun.com/xml/downloads/saaj.html.*

As we mentioned earlier, the Java API for XML-based Messaging, or JAXM, provides us with a set of interfaces for building and processing generic XML messages, with special support for SOAP messages. These interfaces focus more on a messaging approach to web services, as opposed to the more procedural approach of JAX-RPC (discussed in the previous chapter).

The most recent version of JAXM specification is version 1.1. The JAXM 1.0 specification was split up into two new specifications, namely JAXM 1.1 and SOAP with Attachments API for Java (SAAJ) 1.1.

JAXM depends on SAAJ, so generally we get both of them in one set; however, they are available in separate packages as well. The reason for creating a separate package is to allow other packages (most notably JAX-RPC) to take advantage of the SOAP classes in SAAJ, without creating a dependency on all of JAXM. This split into two specifications is also reflected in the Java packages – the JAXM specification defines classes in the `javax.xml.messaging` package, whereas the SAAJ specification uses the `javax.xml.soap` package.

> *Since both APIs are so closely related, for our discussions in this chapter we will only refer to JAXM, but please note that it will implicitly include SAAJ also.*

JAXM defines a messaging interface for both synchronous and asynchronous communication. This communication can follow both a request-response and a one-way protocol. For example, we could execute a request-response scenario in an asynchronous fashion. This means a client would send out a request to a service, then do some other work and come back later to pick up the response for the request.

> *Note that in this case, the client needs to implement a mechanism to correlate a response message or any acknowledgement to a particular request message. JAXM does not provide any built-in support for this.*

The messages that we send and receive in JAXM are SOAP messages. Even though it is possible, other message protocols are not defined at this time. The fact that SOAP messages are exchanged also implies that on one side of the equation, the sender or the receiver can have a non-JAXM implementation. A JAXM client can send a SOAP message to a web service that was implemented using a different interface, as long as both of them support the same SOAP format.

For example, we could take a WSDL definition of a web service and generate a JAXM client proxy class for it. However, if the web service is using 'RPC' style then using JAX-RPC may be the easier way.

# The Provider

JAXM also supports two styles of sending a SOAP message. It can use a so-called JAXM **provider**, or it can send messages directly. If no provider is used, the message can only be sent synchronously through HTTP, to a concrete URL.

A provider is a piece of code that picks up a message from a JAXM sender, and forwards it to the actual destination on the sender's behalf. Similarly, the provider receives a message on behalf of the JAXM receiver and forwards it to this receiver. This decouples the JAXM sender and receiver from the actual implementation of the message transport, since that is handled by the provider. However, note that to take advantage of a provider, a JAXM application needs to run in a J2EE container (for example, either run as part of a servlet application or as part of an EJB application). In this chapter we will be using Tomcat's web container.

The diagram below shows a typical scenario of sending a SOAP message over JAXM:

In this scenario, the client uses any SOAP-client implementation to build and send a SOAP message. This message goes over HTTP to a JAXM provider on the receiver side, which delivers the message to the service. This message could also be forwarded to another endpoint over another protocol such as SMTP.

As we have seen in the earlier chapters, SOAP does not define the content of any message. The specification only states that a SOAP message is contained within a root element called <Envelope>. This root element can have two children – namely <Header> and <Body>. The content of these elements is not defined. Higher-level standards can be used to define what this content looks like.

For example, the ebXML standard, which is an effort sponsored by OASIS and the United Nations, defines rules and data structures that can be used for electronic data interchange between companies. As part of this, it specifies message formats that are needed, in particular B2B scenarios. These formats are based on SOAP. JAXM provides the concept of a **Profile** to enable us to add definitions about these higher-level formats thereby helping us to build messages conforming to these formats. For example, there is an ebXML profile, which defines the additional fields available in the SOAP header. If a JAXM client uses a profile, both the sender and the receiver of the message have to agree on the same content.

# Synchronous Communication

As we mentioned above, JAXM supports both synchronous and asynchronous communication. There are two different programming models to deal with either one. For the synchronous model, JAXM does not require the use of a provider; rather each sender communicates directly with the receiver of a message. The javax.xml.soap.SOAPConnection class contains a call() method that allows sending a SOAP request message and waiting for the response document to be returned.

## Installing the Java XML Pack

The examples in this chapter will take advantage of the JAXM reference implementation in the **Java XML (JAX) Pack** (at the time of writing this was in its Summer 02 incarnation). We can download this package from http://java.sun.com/xml/downloads/javaxmlpack.html.

The package comes in a zip file, which we can extract into a new directory. For example, if we extract the contents of the zip file into our C: drive, we will find the package at C:\java_xml_pack-summer-02. It contains a number of subdirectories with implementations for the various XML APIs. The JAXM implementation will be in the C:\java_xml_pack-summer-02\jaxm-1.1 directory.

*Hereafter we'll refer to the installation directory of the JAX Pack by the variable %JAX_Pack%.*

For compiling and running the examples given in this chapter, we will need the following JAR files in our classpath:

- ❑ %JAX_Pack%\jaxm-1.1\lib\jaxm-api.jar

- ❑ %JAX_Pack%\jaxm-1.1\lib\saaj-api.jar

- ❑ %JAX_Pack%\jaxm-1.1\lib\commons-logging.jar

- ❑ %JAX_Pack%\jaxm-1.1\lib\dom4j.jar

- ❑ %JAX_Pack%\jaxm-1.1\lib\mail.jar

- ❑ %JAX_Pack%\jaxm-1.1\lib\activation.jar

- ❑ %JAX_Pack%\jaxm-1.1\jaxm\jaxm-runtime.jar

- ❑ %JAX_Pack%\jaxm-1.1\jaxm\saaj-ri.jar

- ❑ %JAX_Pack%\jaxp-1.2\jaxp-api.jar

- ❑ %JAX_Pack%\jaxp-1.2\sax.jar

- ❑ %JAX_Pack%\jaxp-1.2\xercesImpl.jar

- ❑ %JAX_Pack%\jaxp-1.2\xalan.jar

- ❑ %JAX_Pack%\jaxp-1.2\dom.jar

## Try It Out – Sending a Synchronous Request over JAXM

Let's now look at an example that shows us how to send a synchronous request using the javax.xml.soap.SOAPConnection class:

**1.** Save the following code as TestJAXMSync.java:

```
import javax.xml.messaging.*;
import javax.xml.soap.*;

import javax.xml.transform.*;
import javax.xml.transform.stream.*;

public class TestJAXMSync {

  public static void main(String args[]) throws Exception {

    // build a SOAP message
    MessageFactory mf = MessageFactory.newInstance();
    SOAPMessage message = mf.createMessage();
```

```
SOAPPart part = message.getSOAPPart();
SOAPEnvelope envelope = part.getEnvelope();
SOAPBody body = envelope.getBody();

// set up some namespace declarations in the envelope
envelope.addNamespaceDeclaration("xsd",
  "http://www.w3.org/2001/XMLSchema");
envelope.addNamespaceDeclaration("xsi",
  "http://www.w3.org/2001/XMLSchema-instance");
envelope.addNamespaceDeclaration("SOAP-ENC",
  "http://schemas.xmlsoap.org/soap/encoding/");

// build the element in the body: <getQuote>...</getQuote>
Name name1 = envelope.createName("getQuote");
SOAPBodyElement bodyElement = body.addBodyElement(name1);

// build the parameter element:
// <arg0 xsi:type="xsd:string">IBM</arg0>
SOAPFactory soapFactory = SOAPFactory.newInstance();
SOAPElement arg0 = soapFactory.createElement("arg0");
Name name3 = soapFactory.createName("type", "xsi",
  "http://www.w3.org/2001/XMLSchema-instance");
arg0.addAttribute(name3, "xsd:string");
arg0.addTextNode("IBM");

//add the parameter element to the getQuote element
bodyElement.addChildElement(arg0);

// use a connection factory to create a new connection
SOAPConnectionFactory factory =
  SOAPConnectionFactory.newInstance();
SOAPConnection conn = factory.createConnection();

// create an end point and make the call
URLEndpoint endpoint =
  new URLEndpoint("http://localhost:8080/axis/services/StockQuote");
SOAPMessage response = conn.call(message, endpoint);

// interpret response
System.out.println("Result:");
TransformerFactory tFact = TransformerFactory.newInstance();
Transformer transformer = tFact.newTransformer();
Source src = response.getSOAPPart().getContent();
StreamResult result=new StreamResult(System.out);
transformer.transform(src, result);
System.out.println();
  }
}
```

**2.** Compile the file, (make sure that the JAR files that we listed earlier are in the classpath):

`javac TestJAXMSync.java`

**3.** To run the program type:

`java TestJAXMSync`

We will get the following output:

```
C:\WINNT\System32\cmd.exe                                          _ □ ×
C:\Beg_JWS_Examples\Chp08>java TestJAXMSync
Result:
<?xml version="1.0" encoding="UTF-8"?>
<soapenv:Envelope xmlns:soapenv="http://schemas.xmlsoap.org/soap/envelope/" xmln
s:xsd="http://www.w3.org/2001/XMLSchema" xmlns:xsi="http://www.w3.org/2001/XMLSc
hema-instance">
 <soapenv:Body>
  <getQuoteResponse soapenv:encodingStyle="http://schemas.xmlsoap.org/soap/encod
ing/">
   <getQuoteReturn xsi:type="xsd:string">69.01</getQuoteReturn>
  </getQuoteResponse>
 </soapenv:Body>
</soapenv:Envelope>

C:\Beg_JWS_Examples\Chp08>_
```

### How It Works

Since this chapter is about asynchronous communication with a web service, we will not cover this example in great detail. There is a detailed explanation about SOAP message creation later in the chapter when we get to the asynchronous example. Here, let us just have look at the code that is specific to the synchronous case.

To send a synchronous request, we need to create a SOAPConnectionFactory. This factory object lets us create a SOAPConnection. Sending the request is done by using the call() method, passing in the actual SOAP message and an instance of URLEndpoint. The URLEndpoint object represents the address of the web service that we send the request to:

```
// use a connection factory to create a new connection
SOAPConnectionFactory factory =
  SOAPConnectionFactory.newInstance();
SOAPConnection conn = factory.createConnection();

// create an end point and make the call
URLEndpoint endpoint =
  new URLEndpoint("http://localhost:8080/axis/services/StockQuote ");
SOAPMessage response = conn.call(message, endpoint);
```

In this example, no provider is used and the call is synchronous. In other words, the calling process will block until the response is returned. As we mentioned before, the receiver of the message can be a JAXM application or any other application that can receive and process a SOAP message.

# Asynchronous Communication

In this section we will be covering asynchronous communication in greater detail. We will also discuss senders and receivers of asynchronous messages.

## Sending Asynchronous Messages

There are five steps involved in sending a message asynchronously. They are:

**1.** Obtain an instance of `javax.xml.messaging.ProviderConnectionFactory`.

**2.** Create a `javax.xml.messaging.ProviderConnection` object.

**3.** Create a `javax.xml.soap.MessageFactory` object.

**4.** Create a `javax.xml.soap.SOAPMessage` object and populate it.

**5.** Send the message to its target.

We will walk through each of these steps here by looking at an example class that sends an asynchronous request to a web service via JAXM.

### Try It Out – Building an Empty SOAP Message

Now let us look at an example which building a new SOAP message and print it out on the screen:

**1.** Save the code shown below in a file called as `TestJAXM1.java`:

```java
import javax.xml.messaging.*;
import javax.xml.soap.*;

public class TestJAXM1 {

  public static void main(String args[]) throws Exception {

    MessageFactory msgFactory = MessageFactory.newInstance();
    SOAPMessage message = msgFactory.createMessage();
    message.writeTo(System.out);
    System.out.println("\n");
  }
}
```

**2.** The command for compiling and running the example is:

```
javac TextJAXM1.java
java TextJAXM1
```

This will give us the following output:

### How It Works

This code is pretty straightforward. In order to create a new `SOAPMessage` object, we create a `MessageFactory` object, which returns a new and empty SOAP message:

```
MessageFactory msgFactory = MessageFactory.newInstance();
SOAPMessage message = msgFactory.createMessage();
```

Finally, we take advantage of the `writeTo()` method in the `SOAPMessage` class to print the content of the message on the screen:

```
message.writeTo(System.out);
```

## Providers and Profiles

Earlier we mentioned that a provider is needed for asynchronous communication. A JAXM application gets access to a provider by using a `javax.xml.messaging.ProviderConnectionFactory` object. The application will use this factory object to create new `javax.xml.messaging.ProviderConnection` objects, which are later used to send the actual message. We will get to that in a little while. Note that, by using the factory and the `javax.xml.messaging.ProviderConnection` instance, an application does not have any dependency on the provider, nor does it know which provider it is using.

So, how does the application get access to the correct `javax.xml.messaging.ProviderConnectionFactory` object? According to the JAXM specifications, it is expected that a JAXM application using asynchronous communication will exist in a J2EE container. Let us discuss briefly what this means.

J2EE provides two types of container – the EJB container and the web container. In both the cases, the code that runs in the container is under control of the J2EE application server. This means, among many other things, that the code has access to information stored in a name server using the **Java Naming and Directory Interface (JNDI)**. While we can store all kinds of things in a JNDI name server, typically we use it to store references for commonly used objects.

In the case of JAXM, we store the `javax.xml.messaging.ProviderConnectionFactory` object in the JNDI name server. Normally, the object is configured by the application server administrator and then created at run time whenever the application server is started. A reference to this object is then stored in the JNDI name server, from where the application can pick it up through a normal lookup.

Here is a code snippet that shows us how to use the JNDI name server to find a `javax.xml.messaging.ProviderConnectionFactory` instance:

```
Context context = new InitialContext();
ProviderConnectionFactory factory =
  context.lookup("myProviderConnectionFactory");
```

However, the use of JNDI in J2EE containers is beyond the scope of this book, and we won't go into any more detail about it here. Luckily an alternative approach exists; the `javax.xml.messaging.ProviderConnectionFactory` class provides a static method called `newInstance()`, which returns a `javax.xml.messaging.ProviderConnectionFactory` for the default provider. This default provider depends upon the environment in which the application is running and also on the JAXM implementation

Once we have created a connection object over which we can send a message, we have to create the message. To do so, we use a `javax.xml.soap.MessageFactory` object. There can be different types of message factory objects, supporting different types of SOAP messages. Previously, we said that JAXM uses profiles to support different types of standard SOAP message formats; here is where these profiles come into play.

A `MessageFactory` object knows how to create a message. Thus, for different profiles, there are different `MessageFactory` objects. While creating a `MessageFactory` object from a `javax.xml.messaging.ProviderConnection` object, we have to specify the profile for the new message. For example, to build a message that follows the ebXML definitions, we would create the `MessageFactory` like this:

```
MessageFactory msgFactory = connection.createMessageFactory("ebxml");
```

For our examples, we will use the profile that comes with the Java XML Pack, namely the `soaprp` profile. This profile acts as a simple example for what a profile can look like and allows for the exchange of basic SOAP messages.

## Try It Out – Installing the JAXM Provider in Tomcat

Before we are able to use a JAXM Provider we need to set up the JAXM Reference Implementation in the form of a web application. Therefore, we will configure it to work without Tomcat installation. The process is not unlike installing Axis.

**1.** We need to make sure the JAXM JAR files are loaded into Tomcat's classpath. So copy all the JAR files from the `%JAX_HOME%\jaxm-1.1\lib` and `%JAX_HOME%\jaxm-1.1\jaxm` directories into `%CATALINA_HOME%\common\lib`.

**2.** Next we also need some of the JAXP JARs, so copy `jaxp-api.jar` from the `%JAX_HOME%\jaxp-1.1` directory into `%CATALINA_HOME%\common\lib`.

**3.** Unfortunately the SOAP JAR that we installed with Axis conflicts with the JAXM installation so we need to remove the classpath reference to Axis' `saaj.jar` file in Tomcat's `setclasspath.bat` file (which we set in Chapter 3):

```
...
set CLASSPATH=%classpath%;%axisDirectory%\lib\log4j-1.2.4.jar
set CLASSPATH=%classpath%;%axisDirectory%\lib\tt-bytecode.jar
rem set CLASSPATH=%classpath%;%axisDirectory%\lib\saaj.jar
...
```

**4.** To install the provider itself, all we need to do is copy the `jaxm-provider.war` file (from the `%JAX_HOME%\jaxm-1.1\jaxm` directory) to the `%CATALINA_HOME%\webapps` directory:

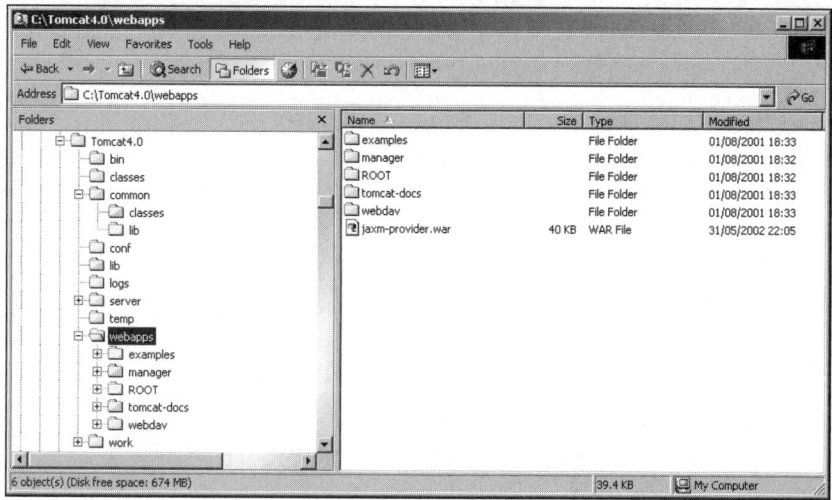

The next time we start Tomcat, it will automatically deploy this web application for us.

**5.** In order to test that our JAXM provider installation was successful, we'll also install one of the applications that comes with JAXM.

Copy the `jaxm-soaprp.war` file from the `%JAX_HOME%\jaxm-1.1\samples` directory to the `%CATALINA_HOME%\webapps` directory.

**6.** Start up Tomcat.

**7.** Browse to http://localhost:8080/jaxm-soaprp/ to test the JAXM installation:

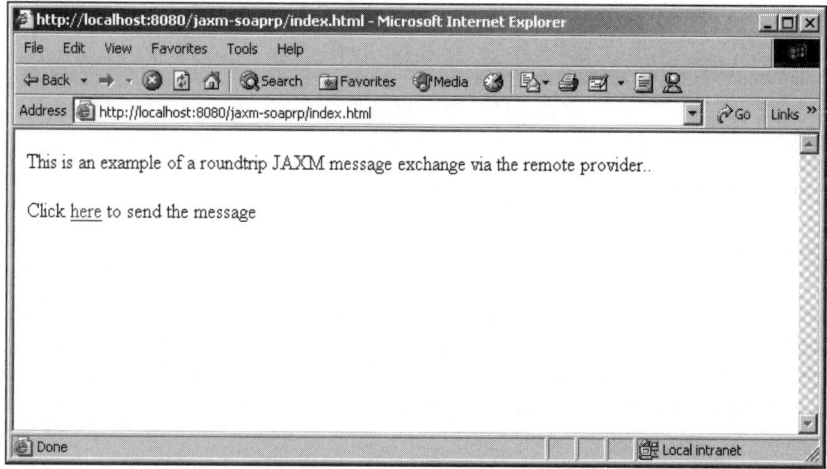

Now we're read to code.

## Try It Out – Building an Empty SOAP Message for a Profile

Let's build a SOAP message that can be used with a provider and which follows a certain profile.

**1.** Here is the complete listing of the example application, entitled `TestJAXM2.java`:

```java
import javax.xml.messaging.*;
import javax.xml.soap.*;

import com.sun.xml.messaging.jaxm.soaprp.*;

public class TestJAXM2 {

  public static void main(String args[]) throws Exception {

    ProviderConnectionFactory factory =
      ProviderConnectionFactory.newInstance();
    ProviderConnection connection = factory.createConnection();

    ProviderMetaData metaData = connection.getMetaData();
    String[] supportedProfiles = metaData.getSupportedProfiles ();
    String profile = null;

    for(int i = 0; i < supportedProfiles.length; i++) {
      if(supportedProfiles[i].equals("soaprp")) {
        profile = supportedProfiles[i];
        break;
      }
    }

    MessageFactory msgFactory = connection.createMessageFactory(profile);
    SOAPMessage message = msgFactory.createMessage();

    message.writeTo(System.out);
    System.out.println("\n");

  }
}
```

**2.** Compile the code:

`javac TestJAXM2.java`

**3.** The `javax.xml.messaging.ProviderConnection` implementation class uses a file called `client.xml` to find the right provider. The client will exchange some initialization message with the provider to learn about available profiles, and so on. Here is what the `client.xml` file for our example should look like:

```
<?xml version="1.0" encoding="ISO-8859-1"?>

<!DOCTYPE ClientConfig
  PUBLIC "-//Sun Microsystems, Inc.//DTD JAXM Client//EN"
  "http://java.sun.com/xml/dtds/jaxm_client_1_0.dtd">

<ClientConfig>
  <Endpoint>
    The JAXM client
  </Endpoint>

  <CallbackURL>
    http://localhost:8080/dummy
  </CallbackURL>

  <Provider>
    <URI>http://java.sun.com/xml/jaxm/provider</URI>
    <URL>http://localhost:8080/jaxm-provider/sender</URL>
  </Provider>

</ClientConfig>
```

This file must be available on the classpath of the client. If we have the current directory (".") in our classpath, we can simply create the file in the current directory.

**4.** Now we can run the class:

```
java TestJAXM2
```

It creates the following output:

## How It Works

There are a number of important steps that are executed here. Let us now look at each of these steps in detail.

As mentioned earlier, for our examples, we are using the Java XML Pack, Summer 02. The JAXM implementation in this package comes with a default `javax.xml.messaging.ProviderConnectionFactory` object that can be obtained through the `newInstance()` method, like this:

```
ProviderConnectionFactory factory = ProviderConnectionFactory.newInstance();
```

The factory object can now be used to create a `javax.xml.messaging.ProviderConnection` object. This is a straightforward operation:

```
ProviderConnection connection = factory.createProviderConnection():
```

A regular SOAP message does not contain any information about the receiver of the message. Thus, we have to add additional information here. The `javax.xml.messaging.ProviderConnection` implementation class uses the `client.xml` file to find the right provider:

```
<?xml version="1.0" encoding="ISO-8859-1"?>

<!DOCTYPE ClientConfig
  PUBLIC "-//Sun Microsystems, Inc.//DTD JAXM Client//EN"
  "http://java.sun.com/xml/dtds/jaxm_client_1_0.dtd">

<ClientConfig>
  <Endpoint>
    The JAXM client
  </Endpoint>

  <CallbackURL>
    http://localhost:8080/dummy
  </CallbackURL>

  <Provider>
    <URI>http://java.sun.com/xml/jaxm/provider</URI>
    <URL>http://localhost:8080/jaxm-provider/sender</URL>
  </Provider>

</ClientConfig>
```

The `<CallbackURL>` element describes the address to which the provider can send back messages destined for this client. In our case, however, the client is a command-line application that cannot receive any messages. We will be covering the acceptance of asynchronous JAXM messages later in the chapter. So, for now, we can simply put a dummy address here.

The `<Provider>` element describes the address of the provider. In our case, we installed the JAXM SOAPRP provider from the Java XML Pack into Tomcat 4 so the URL will be at http://localhost:8080/jaxm-provider/.

Part of using a profile is always to make sure that both sides agree on the structure of message. In fact, that is what profiles are all about – making sure that both parties can build and interpret the messages they exchange. The Java XML Pack comes with two predefined profiles – one for ebXML and one for SOAPRP. For example, one of them is the `com.sun.xml.messaging.jaxm.soaprp.SOAPRPMessageImpl` class, which adds endpoint definitions to the SOAP message to tell the provider where a message should go.

We can check the `javax.xml.messaging.ProviderConnection` object, to make sure it supports the profile we want to use (in this case, the `soaprp` profile), and then create a `MessageFactory` instance:

```
ProviderMetaData metaData = connection.getMetaData();
String[] supportedProfiles = metaData.getSupportedProfiles();
String profile = null;

for(int i =0 ; i < supportedProfiles.length; i++) {
  if(supportedProfiles[i].equals("soaprp")) {
    profile = supportedProfiles[i];
    break;
  }
}
```

Once we have obtained the `MessageFactory` object, we can use it to build the actual SOAP message and print it out on the screen:

```
MessageFactory msgFactory = connection.createMessageFactory(profile);
SOAPMessage message = msgFactory.createMessage();
message.writeTo(System.out);
```

## Populating SOAP Messages

The `javax.xml.soap.MessageFactory` object allows the creation of message objects, specifically, SOAP message objects. The `javax.xml.soap.SOAPMessage` class represents SOAP messages. Each `javax.xml.soap.SOAPMessage` object, regardless of the profile that it is created for, contains at least four other objects in it. They are:

❑ A `javax.xml.soap.SOAPPart` object
As its name indicates, the SAAJ specification supports SOAP attachments. If a SOAP message, with attachment, is sent, it contains multiple parts – the SOAP part and one or more other parts (the actual attachments). As SAAJ considers each `SOAPMessage` object as one that potentially has an attachment, it stores the actual SOAP message in the `SOAPPart` attribute.

❑ A `javax.xml.soap.SOAPEnvelope` object
In the `SOAPPart` object, we find a `SOAPEnvelope` object. This object represents the content of the actual `<Envelope>` element and all of its children.

❑ A `javax.xml.soap.SOAPHeader` object

❑ A `javax.xml.soap.SOAPBody` object
Obviously, once we have access to the envelope object, we can retrieve the values of the `<Header>` and `<Body>` elements from within that envelope.

Here is an example that shows how to parse an existing `javax.xml.soap.SOAPMessage` object and retrieve its content:

```
// receive the SOAP message from somewhere, we will cover this later
SOAPMessage message = …
SOAPPart part = message.getSOAPPart();
SOAPEnvelope envelope = part.getEnvelope();
SOAPHeader header = envelope.getHeader();
SOAPBody body = envelope.getBody();
```

Before we can start adding new content to the message, we have to briefly discuss another topic – **names**. Elements in an XML document have a name that is defined within a namespace. Which means that each name has two parts to it – the actual name, and the name of the namespace in which it is defined. When we add new elements to our SOAP message, we need to give them fully qualified names. Note that the names do not *have* to be fully qualified, but it is recommended that we always create new elements that way. JAXM provides the `javax.xml.soap.Name` interface to describe the name of an element.

The steps for adding a new element to a SOAP envelope are:

- ❑ Obtain the `javax.xml.soap.SOAPEnvelope` object
- ❑ Get the `javax.xml.soap.SOAPHeader` or `javax.xml.soap.SOAPBody` object from it, as appropriate
- ❑ Use the `javax.xml.soap.SOAPEnvelope.createName()` method to create a name for the new element
- ❑ Add a new element using either the `javax.xml.soap.SOAPHeader.addHeaderElement()` method or the `javax.xml.soap.SOAPBody.addBodyElement()` method
- ❑ Add content to the new element as needed

Let us build an example for this. Here, we will assume that we want to create a request message for the stock quote example that we have worked with in the earlier chapters.

*The stock quote service is a synchronous service, thus it is not a perfect example here. However, since we are familiar with its interface, we will reuse it here to make it easier to understand the code. More specifically, we will send an asynchronous message to our service and simply ignore the (synchronous) response.*

## Try It Out – Populating the SOAP Message

This example populates a SOAP message, which can then be sent to the stock quote web service we used before. The creation of that message is similar to what we have shown in the previous example above:

**1.** Save this code in a file called as `TestJAXM3.java`:

```java
import javax.xml.messaging.*;
import javax.xml.soap.*;

import com.sun.xml.messaging.jaxm.soaprp.*;

public class TestJAXM3 {

  public static void main(String args[]) throws Exception {

    ProviderConnectionFactory factory =
      ProviderConnectionFactory.newInstance();
    ProviderConnection connection = factory.createConnection();

    ProviderMetaData metaData = connection.getMetaData();
    String[] supportedProfiles = metaData.getSupportedProfiles();
    String profile = null;

    for(int i = 0; i < supportedProfiles.length; i++) {
```

```
        if(supportedProfiles[i].equals("soaprp")) {
          profile = supportedProfiles[i];
          break;
        }
      }

      MessageFactory msgFactory = connection.createMessageFactory(profile);
      SOAPMessage message = msgFactory.createMessage();

      SOAPPart part = message.getSOAPPart();
      SOAPEnvelope envelope = part.getEnvelope();
      SOAPBody body = envelope.getBody();

      // set up some namespace declarations in the envelope
      envelope.addNamespaceDeclaration("xsd",
        "http://www.w3.org/2001/XMLSchema");
      envelope.addNamespaceDeclaration("xsi",
        "http://www.w3.org/2001/XMLSchema-instance");
      envelope.addNamespaceDeclaration("SOAP-ENC",
        "http://schemas.xmlsoap.org/soap/encoding/");

      // build the element in the body: <getQuote>...</getQuote>
      Name name1 = envelope.createName("getQuote");
      SOAPBodyElement bodyElement = body.addBodyElement(name1);

      // build the parameter element: <arg0 xsi:type="xsd:string">IBM</arg0>
      SOAPFactory soapFactory = SOAPFactory.newInstance();
      SOAPElement arg0 = soapFactory.createElement("arg0");
      Name name3 = soapFactory.createName("type", "xsi",
        "http://www.w3.org/2001/XMLSchema-instance");
      arg0.addAttribute(name3, "xsd:string");
      arg0.addTextNode("IBM");

      //add the parameter element to the getQuote element
      bodyElement.addChildElement(arg0);

      message.writeTo(System.out);
    }
}
```

**2.** Compile and run the code:

```
javac TestJAXM3.java
java TestJAXM3
```

Here is the output from the example:

*How It Works*

In this example, we create a new `SOAPMessage` object as we have done before. This object will already have a `SOAPPart` and a `SOAPEnvelope` with empty body and header elements.

From the `SOAPMessage` object, we retrieve the `javax.xml.soap.SOAPPart` and `javax.xml.soap.SOAPEnvelope` objects. The `javax.xml.soap.SOAPEnvelope` allows us to obtain the `javax.xml.soap.SOAPBody` element, like so:

```
SOAPPart part = message.getSOAPPart();
SOAPEnvelope envelope = part.getEnvelope();
SOAPBody body = envelope.getBody();
```

Next, we define the namespace declarations for the envelope. These are standard definitions that we can always add to our envelope:

```
envelope.addNamespaceDeclaration("xsd",
  "http://www.w3.org/2001/XMLSchema");
envelope.addNamespaceDeclaration("xsi",
  "http://www.w3.org/2001/XMLSchema-instance");
envelope.addNamespaceDeclaration("SOAP-ENC",
  "http://schemas.xmlsoap.org/soap/encoding/");
```

The next two lines add the `<getQuote>` element to the body. This is a simple element with only a local (not fully qualified) name. The `addBodyElement()` method returns a reference to the new element, which will use later:

```
Name name1 = envelope.createName("getQuote");
SOAPBodyElement bodyElement = body.addBodyElement(name1);
```

To create a new element within the `<getQuote>` element, we need an instance of `javax.xml.soap.SOAPFactory`. This factory object provides methods to create new XML artifacts needed within a body or header:

```
SOAPFactory soapFactory = SOAPFactory.newInstance();
```

The `<arg0>` element is again built with a local name only:

```
SOAPElement arg0 = soapFactory.createElement("arg0");
```

This new element, `<arg0>` has one attribute and one text node inside of it. The attribute is fully namespace qualified, which means that we have to create another `javax.xml.soap.Name` object. Adding the attribute and the text node is straightforward:

```
Name name3 = soapFactory.createName("type", "xsi",
  "http://www.w3.org/2001/XMLSchema-instance");
arg0.addAttribute(name3, "xsd:string");
arg0.addTextNode("IBM");
```

**294**

What happens here is that the SOAP factory creates a `Name` object first, before adding the new attribute to the element. The `type` parameter represents the name of the parameter that is set to the web service. The `xsi` parameter serves as the prefix for all entries further down that are scoped to the same namespace. Finally, `http://www.w3.org/2001/XMLSchema-instance` is the URI (note that this is not necessarily a valid URL) that is used to uniquely identify elements that are part of the XML Schema data-types namespace.

## Sending the Message

Now we have a complete SOAP message that we can send to the target. In the asynchronous case the message is not directly sent to the target. Instead, it gets forwarded to the provider, which then delivers it to the final destination. How this is done depends on the selected profile.

### Try It Out – Sending the Message

Here is the complete source for the test application that sends the message.

**1.** Save the listing given below in a file called `TestJAXMAsync.java`:

```java
import javax.xml.messaging.*;
import javax.xml.soap.*;

import com.sun.xml.messaging.jaxm.soaprp.*;

public class TestJAXMAsync {

  public static void main(String args[]) throws Exception {

    ProviderConnectionFactory factory =
      ProviderConnectionFactory.newInstance();
    ProviderConnection connection = factory.createConnection();

    ProviderMetaData metaData = connection.getMetaData();
    String[] supportedProfiles = metaData.getSupportedProfiles();
    String profile = null;

    for(int i = 0; i < supportedProfiles.length; i++) {
      if(supportedProfiles[i].equals("soaprp")) {
        profile = supportedProfiles[i];
        break;
      }
    }
    MessageFactory msgFactory = connection.createMessageFactory(profile);
    SOAPRPMessageImpl message =
      (SOAPRPMessageImpl)msgFactory.createMessage();

    message.setFrom(
      new Endpoint("http://localhost:8080/someclient"));
    message.setTo(new Endpoint("http://localhost:8080/myservice"));

    SOAPPart part = message.getSOAPPart();
```

```
    SOAPEnvelope envelope = part.getEnvelope();
    SOAPBody body = envelope.getBody();

    // set up some namespace declarations in the envelope
    envelope.addNamespaceDeclaration("xsd",
      "http://www.w3.org/2001/XMLSchema");
    envelope.addNamespaceDeclaration("xsi",
      "http://www.w3.org/2001/XMLSchema-instance");
    envelope.addNamespaceDeclaration("SOAP-ENC",
      "http://schemas.xmlsoap.org/soap/encoding/");

    // build the element in the body: <getQuote>...</getQuote>
    Name name1 = envelope.createName("getQuote");
    SOAPBodyElement bodyElement = body.addBodyElement(name1);

    // build the parameter element: <arg0 xsi:type="xsd:string">IBM</arg0>
    SOAPFactory soapFactory = SOAPFactory.newInstance();
    SOAPElement arg0 = soapFactory.createElement("arg0");
    Name name3 = soapFactory.createName("type", "xsi",
      "http://www.w3.org/2001/XMLSchema-instance");
    arg0.addAttribute(name3, "xsd:string");
    arg0.addTextNode("IBM");

    //add the parameter element to the getQuote element
    bodyElement.addChildElement(arg0);

    message.writeTo(System.out);
    connection.send(message);
  }
}
```

**2.** The provider must be configured properly to understand and process messages that are sent to it. The provider is configured through a file called `provider.xml`. It contains entries that define the protocol used for communication (that is, HTTP), plus additional entries for each target that we will send a message to.

This file can be found at `%CATLINA_HOME%\webapps\jaxm-provider\WEB-INF`. We need to configure a new endpoint to match that which we defined in the class above (`"http://localhost:8080/myservice"`). To do this add a new `<Endpoint/>` element to the `provider.xml` file, like so:

```
<?xml version="1.0" encoding="ISO-8859-1"?>

<!DOCTYPE ProviderConfig
  PUBLIC "-//Sun Microsystems, Inc.//DTD JAXM Provider//EN"
  "http://java.sun.com/xml/dtds/jaxm_provider_1_0.dtd">

<ProviderConfig>
<!--profile definition for 'ebxml' left out here -->
  <Profile profileId="soaprp">
    <Transport>
```

```
    <Protocol>
      http
    </Protocol>

    <Endpoint>
      <URI>
        http://www.wombats.com/soaprp/sender
      </URI>
      <URL>
        http://127.0.0.1:8080/jaxm-provider/receiver/soaprp
      </URL>
    </Endpoint>

    <Endpoint>
      <URI>
        http://localhost:8080/myservice
      </URI>
      <URL>
        http://localhost:8080/axis/services/StockQuote
      </URL>
    </Endpoint>

  <ErrorHandling>
     <Retry>
        <MaxRetries>
         3
        </MaxRetries>
        <RetryInterval>
         2000
        </RetryInterval>
     </Retry>
  </ErrorHandling>
...
</ProviderConfig>
```

**3.** Stop and restart Tomcat.

**4.** Now compile and run the code:

```
javac TestJAXMAsync.java
java TestJAXMAsync
```

Here is what the output on the screen will look like:

In the Tomcat window you should see the message being processed:

```
Tomcat                                                                   _ □ X
Starting service Tomcat-Standalone
Apache Tomcat/4.0.4
Starting service Tomcat-Apache
Apache Tomcat/4.0.4
- Processing InitConnection
- Putting in toBeSent queue
- put in soaprp store
- Trying to send message to... http://localhost:8080/axis/services/StockQuote
- Message sent
-
```

### How It Works

Most of the code for this example is exactly as we have described before. What is new here is that we define the two endpoints for our communication with the stock quote service, namely the originator and the destination. As shown in the code extract below, the
com.sun.xml.messaging.jaxm.soaprp.SOAPRPMessageImpl class defines two attributes for this:

```
MessageFactory msgFactory = connection.createMessageFactory(profile);
SOAPRPMessageImpl message = (SOAPRPMessageImpl)msgFactory.createMessage();

message.setFrom(new Endpoint("http://localhost:8080/someclient"));
message.setTo(new Endpoint("http://localhost:8080/myservice"));
```

Note that, in this case we use a dummy originator address, because we cannot receive any response messages anyway. We had already defined this dummy receiver in the client.xml file when we configured the client. The code also shows that the target address, http://localhost:8080/myservice is defined in the provider.xml file to be at the concrete URL
http://localhost:8080/axis/services/StockQuote.

The provider.xml file configures a profile called soaprp for this provider. Within the profile definition, it specifies that an endpoint URI named http://localhost:8080/myservice is to be translated into a concrete URL, namely http://localhost:8080/axis/services/StockQuote. This allows for redirecting messages to different endpoint URLs without having to change any code.

Another interesting setting here is the <ErrorHandling> element:

```
<ErrorHandling>
   <Retry>
      <MaxRetries>
       3
      </MaxRetries>
      <RetryInterval>
       2000
      </RetryInterval>
   </Retry>
</ErrorHandling>
```

It specifies that the provider should try to send a message three times if necessary to the target. Note that the client will not be blocked for the duration of this; after all, we are making an asynchronous call.

The following diagram describes how a client finds a provider and sends a message to it:

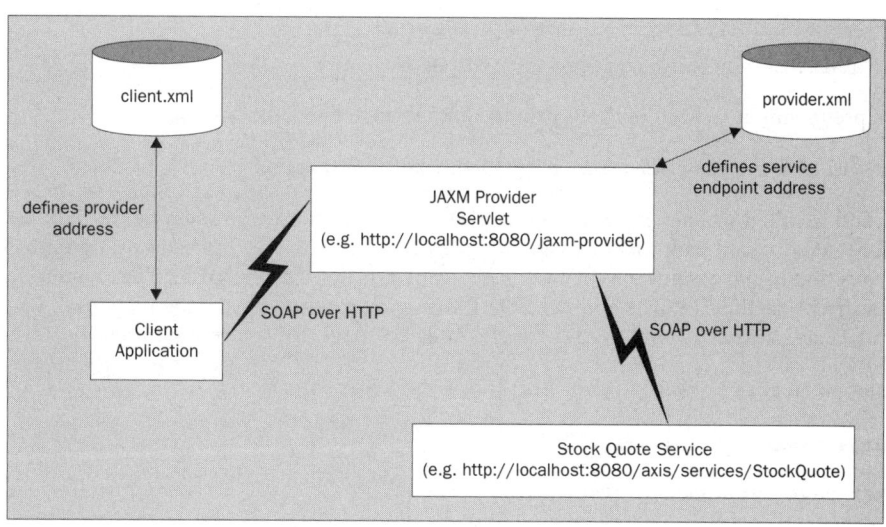

The provider then delivers the message to the destination based on the information found in the provider.xml file.

We are finally ready to send the message! The following line of code shows that we can use the send() method on the javax.xml.messaging.ProviderConnection object to do that:

```
connection.send(message);
```

*Note that, the SOAP <Header> element contains additional fields, which will tell the provider where to send the message.*

Now that we know how to send a message asynchronously using a provider, we can look at setting up an application to receive the message.

## Receiving Asynchronous Messages

The only protocol for asynchronous communication that is supported in the Java XML Pack, Summer 02, is HTTP. In other words, we can only send and receive messages over HTTP. The typical receiver of an HTTP request is a servlet. As a result, our receiver application will be wrapped in a servlet.

In a more realistic example, with a more sophisticated messaging provider, we would most likely use JMS as the communication vehicle for the message exchange. In the next section, we will be talking about the use of JMS in such a scenario. For now, let us just say that a service, which is based on JMS and running in a J2EE application server, would have an MDB as its access point.

In this case, however, we are using HTTP. Even though HTTP is a synchronous protocol, the use of the provider decouples the receiving and processing of a message from the sending of that message. We have seen in the previous section that the message is handed off to the provider without waiting for any response to come back. So how does the provider forward the message to its final destination? We already mentioned that a servlet would receive the message. So, the provider will invoke another HTTP request to the destination servlet's URL.

JAXM defines two listener interfaces to standardize the way messages are received:

❑   `javax.xml.messaging.ReqRespListener`
❑   `javax.xml.messaging.OnewayListener`

They are pretty similar – both of them provide a method called `onMessage()`.

*A method with this name also exists on every message-driven bean.*

This method is called whenever a message arrives at the receiver for processing. In both cases, the parameter that is passed with this message is a `javax.xml.soap.SOAPMessage` object. The only difference is that in the case of the `javax.xml.messaging.ReqRespListener` interface, the `onMesssage()` method returns another SOAPMessage (in other words, the response), whereas the `javax.xml.messaging.OnewayListener` interface does not return anything.

Here is the `javax.xml.messaging.ReqRespListener` interface:

```
package javax.xml.messaging;

import javax.xml.soap.SOAPMessage;

public interface ReqRespListener {
   public SOAPMessage onMessage(SOAPMessage message);
}
```

and here is the `javax.xml.messaging.OnewayListener` interface:

```
package javax.xml.messaging;

import javax.xml.soap.SOAPMessage;

public interface OnewayListener {
   public void onMessage(SOAPMessage message);
}
```

Note that both of the interfaces are there for reasons of convenience; we are not required to use them. However, our code will be more portable across different JAXM implementations if we take advantage of them. Plus, if we don't use these interfaces, we have to define our own.

Another convenience class that JAXM provides for receiving JAXM messages over HTTP, is the `javax.xml.messaging.JAXMServlet` class. This class provides a default implementation for the `doPut()` method that will extract a `javax.xml.soap.SOAPMessage` from the incoming HTTP request and forward it to the `onMessage()` method. The `javax.xml.soap.SOAPMessage` object is built using a `javax.xml.soap.MessageFactory` object, just like we used before when we sent a message.

So, how do we use this servlet class for implementing our own receiver? We can create a new class that inherits from `javax.xml.messaging.JAXMServlet` and implement either the `javax.xml.messaging.ReqRespListener` or the `javax.xml.messaging.OnewayListener` interface, depending on whether a response will be provided or not. In our example, we will create a servlet that will not return any response to the caller, thus it will implement the `javax.xml.messaging.OnewayListener` interface, like so:

```
import javax.servlet.*;
import javax.servlet.http.*;

import javax.xml.messaging.*;
import javax.xml.soap.*;

import com.sun.xml.messaging.jaxm.soaprp.*;

public class MyReceiverServlet extends JAXMServlet implements OnewayListener
```

For a closer look at what goes into the servlet class, let's walk through an example.

## Try It Out – Receiving Asynchronous Messages

Here is an example of a servlet that can receive asynchronous JAXM messages:

**1.** Save the listing shown below in a file called `MyReceiverServlet.java`:

```java
import javax.servlet.*;
import javax.servlet.http.*;
import javax.xml.messaging.*;
import javax.xml.soap.*;
import com.sun.xml.messaging.jaxm.soaprp.*;

public class MyReceiverServlet extends JAXMServlet
    implements OnewayListener {

  private ProviderConnectionFactory pcf;
  private ProviderConnection pc;

  public void init(ServletConfig servletConfig) throws ServletException {
    super.init(servletConfig);

    try {
      pcf = ProviderConnectionFactory.newInstance();
      pc = pcf.createConnection();
      setMessageFactory(new SOAPRPMessageFactoryImpl());
    } catch (JAXMException e) {
      throw new ServletException(e.getMessage());
    }
  }

  public void onMessage(SOAPMessage message) {
    try {
      message.writeTo(System.out);
    } catch (Exception e) {
      System.out.println("Exception occurred! " + e.getMessage());
    }
  }
}
```

**2.** In order to compile this class we will need to add to our classpath the `javax.servlet` packages that can be found within Tomcat:

```
javac -classpath %classpath%;%CATALINA_HOME%\common\lib\servlet.jar
    MyReceiverServlet.java
```

**3.** We will also need to deploy this servlet into Tomcat in order for it to run, so we'll create a simple web application for this purpose. Create a WEB-INF directory and place the following `web.xml` file within it:

```xml
<?xml version="1.0" encoding="ISO-8859-1"?>

<!DOCTYPE web-app
    PUBLIC "-//Sun Microsystems, Inc.//DTD Web Application 2.2//EN"
    "http://java.sun.com/j2ee/dtds/web-app_2_2.dtd">

<web-app>
    <servlet>
        <servlet-name>
            MyReceiverServlet
        </servlet-name>
        <servlet-class>
            MyReceiverServlet
        </servlet-class>
    </servlet>

    <servlet-mapping>
        <servlet-name>
            MyReceiverServlet
        </servlet-name>
        <url-pattern>
            /receiver
        </url-pattern>
    </servlet-mapping>
</web-app>
```

**4.** Copy the compiled `MyReceiverServlet` class into a `\classes` subdirectory of WEB-INF so we have the following structure:

```
\WEB-INF
        \web.xml
        \classes
                \MyReceiverServlet.class
```

**5.** Now use the `jar` command to create a WAR file from the top-level directory containing the WEB-INF folder:

```
jar -cf Ch08.war WEB-INF
```

**6.** Then copy the `Ch08.war` file into Tomcat's `\webapps` directory.

**7.** Before we can restart Tomcat we also need to configure the correct destination URL for the receiver in the `provider.xml` file. This will make sure that the JAXM provider will deliver the message to the correct URL. Modify the `<Endpoint/>` element we added before as follows:

```
<Endpoint>
  <URI>
    http://localhost:8080/myservice
  </URI>
  <URL>
    http://localhost:8080/Ch08/receiver
  </URL>
</Endpoint>
```

**8.** Restart Tomcat and then rerun our `TestJAXMAsync` client from before:

```
java TestJAXMAsync
```

We'll get the same result in the client window, but now in Tomcat's window we will see:

## How It Works

For the servlet to be able to receive messages and build `javax.xml.soap.SOAPMessage` objects from it, it must create a `javax.xml.messaging.ProviderConnection` object and derive a `javax.xml.soap.MessageFactory` object from it. We only need to do this once for the lifetime of the servlet, so we will use the servlet's `init()` method to create these objects.

```
private ProviderConnectionFactory pcf;
private ProviderConnection pc;

public void init(ServletConfig servletConfig) throws ServletException {
  super.init(servletConfig);
```

```
      try {
        pcf = ProviderConnectionFactory.newInstance();
        pc = pcf.createConnection();
        setMessageFactory(new SOAPRPMessageFactoryImpl());
      } catch (JAXMException e) {
        throw new ServletException(e.getMessage());
      }
    }
```

One interesting statement to note here is:

```
    setMessageFactory(new SOAPRPMessageFactoryImpl());
```

As we mentioned earlier, the `javax.xml.messaging.JAXMServlet` convenience class creates a `javax.xml.soap.SOAPMessage` from the incoming HTTP request. It needs a `javax.xml.soap.MessageFactory` object to do that. Our servlet class uses the `setMessageFactory()` method to set this factory object.

The only other thing we need is the `onMessage()` method implementation. Here is where we process the incoming message:

```
    public void onMessage(SOAPMessage message) {
      try {
        message.writeTo(System.out);
      } catch (Exception e) {
        System.out.println("Exception occurred! " + e.getMessage());
      }
    }
```

# Web Services over JMS

So far, we have covered the asynchronous innovation of web services. More specifically, we have looked at how to asynchronously send a SOAP-formatted message and how to receive one.

This sounds exactly like the description of a scenario that uses the Java Message Service (JMS). JMS provides interfaces for sending and receiving messages, both synchronously and asynchronously. JMS is just an interface (we can think of it as an API on top of messaging middleware), and it is independent of any communication protocol that is used to implement it. J2EE application servers typically come with an embedded JMS provider, that is, code that implements the JMS interface.

Thus, for asynchronous web services, using JMS as the underlying messaging infrastructure makes perfect sense; even more so, since the J2EE Enterprise JavaBean specification describes so called Message-Driven Bean. Explaining exactly what an MDB is and how it works goes well beyond the scope of this book; however, we can think of it as a message receiver that sits there and waits for messages to arrive on a queue or a topic. As soon as a message arrives, it will be forwarded to the MDB, which can then process it in a transactional manner.

Since we need to discuss it again, the following diagram shows again how this works (recall we looked at this picture at the beginning of this chapter):

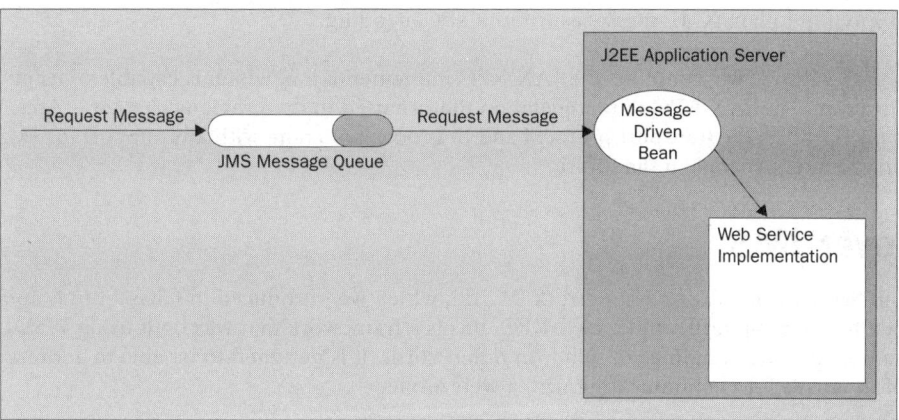

# JAXM over JMS

Now that we've developed our own sender and receiver applications using JAXM, the previous diagram should start making a lot of sense to us. Instead of creating a servlet that accepts HTTP requests with the SOAP message as its content, we deploy an MDB into the J2EE container.

While the deployment of these solutions is different, the concept is the same. We can easily imagine how we could develop a provider for JAXM that takes messages from a client and sends them to a JMS queue or topic. The destination would then be this queue's name instead of a URL. From the queue, an MDB reads the request and forwards it to the actual receiver.

Thus, the MDB would play exactly the same role that our `javax.xml.messaging.JAXMServlet` played in the previous section. Neither the client sending the request, nor the web service that receives the message would look any different, since all of this handling is hidden in the provider.

However, the reference implementation for JAXM does not come with a JMS provider. The most obvious starting point to look for a JAXM over JMS provider is for us to check with the JMS implementation and J2EE application server vendors. JAXM is relatively new, so we can expect to see more products coming out that support it in the near future.

# JAX-RPC over JMS

Another option to take advantage of the asynchronous capabilities of JMS would be to use the JAX-RPC interfaces, which we have described in Chapter 6. JAX-RPC supports one-way style operations – for example, the `javax.xml.rpc.Call` class offers a method called `invokeOneWay()`, which takes a number of input parameters and returns no response. It also takes an arbitrary string as the target endpoint address (through the `setTargetEndPointAddress()` method), so that we can pass a JMS queue name instead of a URL there.

However, note that in the case of JAX-RPC, it is assumed that we are invoking a remote function (as opposed to sending a message). This means the request message is always assumed to contain a number of (potentially encoded) parameters for the remote function invocation. JAXM, on the other hand, allows us to build plain XML messages without any encoding.

On top of the above, we would need a JAX-RPC implementation, which is capable of using JMS as a transport layer. The JAX-RPC implementation that we used in the previous chapter – Apache Axis – focuses on HTTP as the transport protocol and thus does not come with any support for JMS. However, this scenario might change in the future.

# WSIF over JMS

The Web Services Invocation Framework (WSIF), which we introduced in Chapter 6, is another candidate for JMS support. Unlike JAX-RPC, this is a framework that was built using WSDL documents with multiple protocol bindings in mind. In other words, it is designed to be able to address different kinds of protocols for communicating with a web service.

Presently, WSIF does not define protocol bindings for JMS; however, this can be expected to change soon. WSIF is in the process of being turned into an open source project by Apache, and support for JMS is already in the pipeline. As in the case of JAX-RPC, this is unlikely to result in a client API change. What will change is the runtime implementation, which will process and interpret JMS based bindings.

This can happen in two ways – through SOAP over JMS or native JMS.

## SOAP over JMS

This style of JMS-based web service invocation will use SOAP envelopes as the message format between a requester and the provider of a service. In this respect, it will be very similar to the way web services invocations are done today – a SOAP message is built, with all of the header and body elements that are needed, but instead of being sent to a destination via HTTP, it is sent to a JMS queue.

## Native JMS

In this case, there is no SOAP. Instead, all the message elements are serialized into a binary format and sent to the JMS queue, without ever being turned into an XML-based message. This style is likely be a lot faster than using SOAP, since no XML parsing is necessary. A binary object representation will almost always be faster than the readable, tagged XML format.

However, this also requires that both the requester and the provider of a service agree on how the message is serialized. If we assume that the requester is a Java application, it will create serialized Java objects. This normally means that we also need a Java program to deserialize these objects and turn them into something the web service can understand.

In other words, this style of JMS-based web service implementation, while being faster, requires Java code on both sides of the equation.

WSIF plans to support both styles in the near future, so check with the WSIF site at http://cvs.apache.org/viewcvs.cgi/xml-axis-wsif/ for more details on this.

# J2EE Web Services over JMS

Both JAX–RPC and WSIF focus on the requester of a web service. WSIF exclusively talks about the requester, without providing any support for hosting or provisioning of a service. JAX–RPC defines how a web service is mapped into a Java interface, but it does not define how a service is deployed into a run time environment. This is left to the implementation.

At the time of this writing, work is under way to define how a J2EE application container handles web services. This work is happening as part of the Java Specification Request (JSR) number 109. For the latest draft of the JSR109 specification, go to http://jcp.org/jsr/detail/109.jsp. In its first version, this JSR will not address how to host JMS-based web services, but this will change over time. However, for the time being all J2EE application server vendors will probably come up with their own way of supporting JMS for asynchronous web services.

# Summary

In this chapter, we have seen how web services can be invoked asynchronously. This is very useful in scenarios where the requester does not depend on a response being returned right away (if at all), and/or when the service execution takes a very long time. Allowing the requester to do other work in the meantime provides for better optimization of computing resources.

This leads to a programming model that is different from the one that we had discussed so far. Here, systems are more loosely coupled than in the synchronous case, namely a 'message-based' web services programming model that takes the interaction between applications as an exchange of messages rather than as an invocation of a remote function.

The Java API for XML-based Messaging (JAXM) is an effort to standardize this programming model for the Java world. It supports both a synchronous and an asynchronous messaging model. The asynchronous model requires the use of a so-called provider, which is responsible for the delivery of a message to its final destination. JAXM assumes the use of SOAP-formatted messages. The SOAP-dependent part of the API was split off into a separate specification, called the SOAP with Attachment API for Java (SAAJ). Both JAX-RPC and JAXM depend on SAAJ-JAX-RPC for synchronous, RPC-style interaction and JAXM for asynchronous, message-style interactions.

We have seen an example of a client sending a SOAP message via the JAXM API, as well as an example of receiving a JAXM message over HTTP.

Finally, we discussed how the Java Message Service (JMS) could be used as the transport layer for message-based asynchronous web service communication. This can happen on various levels and in various ways, be it as an additional provider underneath JAXM, or be it as another binding element in WSDL, which can then be interpreted by a WSIF client. JMS can be used both with and without formatting a message in SOAP. While SOAP is more flexible because of its standardized, self-describing nature, a binary (or native) format will most likely be faster and more efficient.

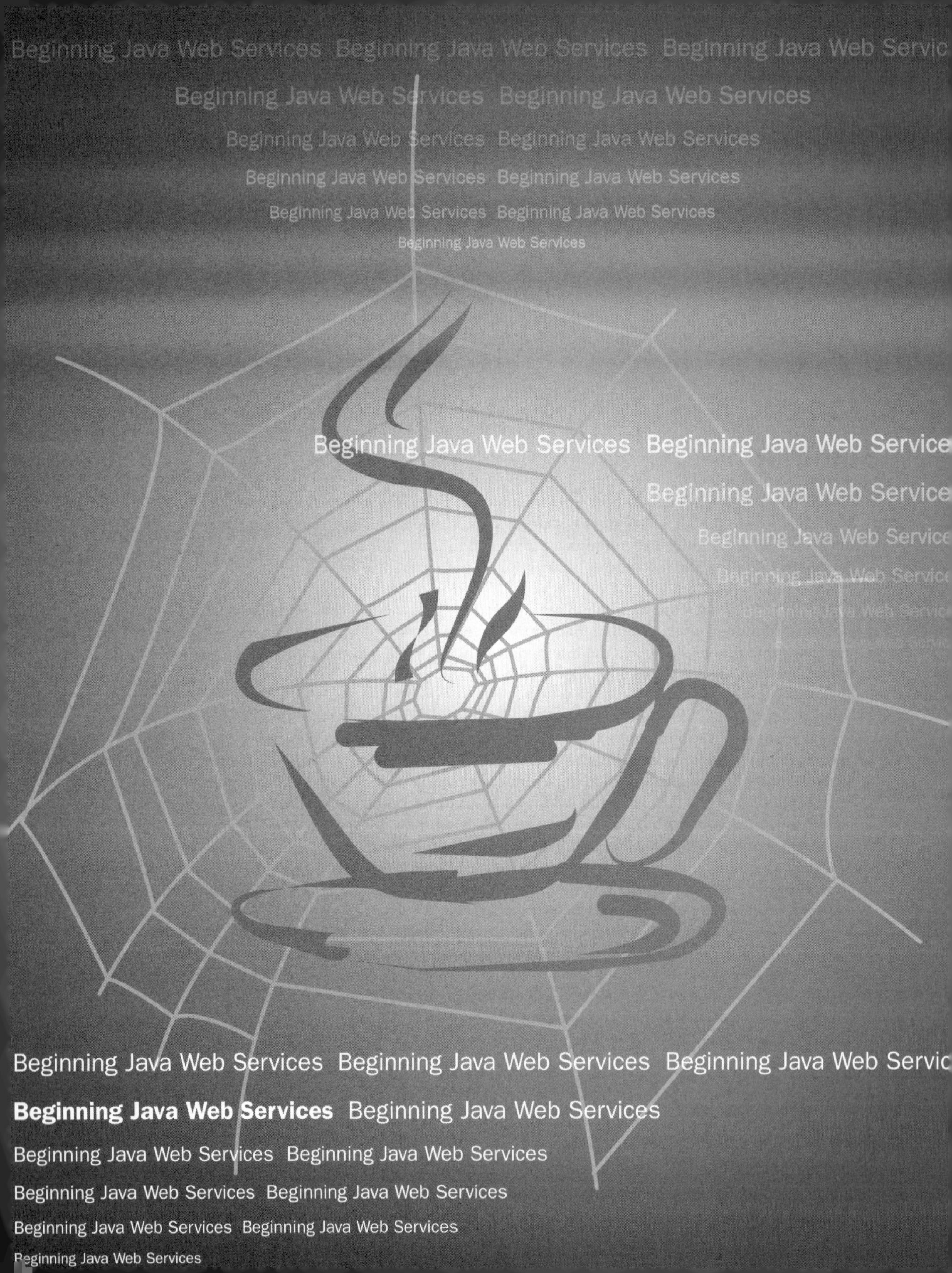
Beginning Java Web Services Beginning Java Web Services Beginning Java Web Servic
Beginning Java Web Services Beginning Java Web Services
Beginning Java Web Services Beginning Java Web Services
Beginning Java Web Services Beginning Java Web Services
Beginning Java Web Services Beginning Java Web Services
Beginning Java Web Services
Beginning Java Web Services Beginning Java Web Service
Beginning Java Web Service
Beginning Java Web Service
Beginning Java Web Servic
Beginning Java Web Services Beginning Java Web Services Beginning Java Web Servic
Beginning Java Web Services Beginning Java Web Services
Beginning Java Web Services Beginning Java Web Services
Beginning Java Web Services Beginning Java Web Services
Beginning Java Web Services Beginning Java Web Services
Beginning Java Web Services

# Securing Web Services

One of the critical aspects of enterprise applications that needs to be addressed with utmost care is security. Security covers a wide variety of enterprise application behavior including authentication, authorization, integrity, confidentiality, non-repudiation, auditing, and single sign-on.

Most of these security concerns existed long before the advent of web services. Over the years powerful security solutions have evolved to address these security issues. These solutions include message digests, digital signatures, symmetric/asymmetric key cryptography, digital certificates, SSL, and so on. Most of these technologies are relevant in the web services world for providing transport-level security.

However, the traditional security solutions deal with messages as a whole. For example, it is pretty straightforward to generate the digital signature or a message digest of an entire XML document and transmit it over wire. But the power of XML lies in the way it can represent hierarchical data. In hierarchical data we may want to encrypt only certain parts of the document and not the whole document. For example, in an XML document representing a purchase order, we may want to encrypt only sensitive information such as a credit card number. This is extremely important as web services normally work in federated environments and the propagation and routing of web services through various intermediaries depend on the information present in the header blocks of the SOAP envelopes representing those web services. In such cases we may want to encrypt only the payload data instead of encrypting the whole message.

The more recent XML and web services security specifications such as XML Signature, XML Encryption, WS-Security, and SAML are build on top of the concepts introduced by the traditional security solutions to provide secure means of transmitting XML data. XML Signature and Encryption are W3C initiatives to provide encryption and digital signature functionality to parts of XML documents.

WS-Security forms the foundation of a set of specifications initiated by IBM, Microsoft, and Verisign, to provide security solutions for web services. SAML is an OASIS specification for propagating security contexts such as authentication and authorization information.

In this chapter we will cover the various security issues relevant to writing web services and the security solutions that address these issues. Namely:

❑ Security issues

❑ Traditional security solutions

❑ HTTP authentication methods

❑ Web services security scenarios

❑ XML security specifications

❑ WS-Security and related specifications

❑ Security Assertion Markup Language

# Setting Up the StockCore Client

In this chapter we will be using the stock core example we developed in Chapter 2 to illustrate the various aspects of security. We will use this example to illustrate:

❑ How web services can be accessed over SSL

❑ How we can provide authenticated access to web services using both standard HTTP authentication methods and custom authentication methods

❑ How we can use WS-Security to sign parts of a SOAP envelope representing the web service request from the client that is verified by the server

In most of the examples we will be using Axis and Tomcat. However, for the WS-Security example we will be using WSTK and Tomcat. WSTK uses Axis as its web services framework. Please refer to earlier chapters on how to install and configure Axis and WSTK.

## Try It Out – Stock Quote Service Client

**1.** The source code for the client class `GetQuote.java` is shown below:

```
package com.wrox.jws.stockcore;
```

Import the required Axis classes:

```
import org.apache.axis.AxisFault;
import org.apache.axis.client.Call;
import org.apache.axis.client.Service;
import org.apache.axis.encoding.XMLType;
import org.apache.axis.utils.Options;
```

Import the required JAX-RPC classes:

```
import javax.xml.rpc.ParameterMode;
import javax.xml.namespace.QName;

import java.net.URL;

public class GetQuote {

  public static void main(String args[]) throws Exception {
```

The program expects the symbol and endpoint URL as mandatory command-line arguments. We can optionally pass the user name and password as well:

```
if(args == null || args.length < 2) {
   System.out.println("Usage: java GetQuote symbol url user password");
   System.exit(0);
}

String symbol = args[0] ;

URL url = new URL(args[1]);
```

Create the service and call:

```
Service  service = new Service();

Call call = (Call) service.createCall();
```

Set the endpoint URL and the operation name:

```
call.setTargetEndpointAddress( url );
call.setOperationName(new QName("StockQuoteService", "getQuote"));
```

Set the in and out parameters:

```
call.addParameter("symbol", XMLType.XSD_STRING, ParameterMode.IN );
call.setReturnType(XMLType.XSD_STRING);
```

Set the user name and password if specified:

```
if(args.length == 4) {
   call.setUsername(args[2]);
   call.setPassword(args[3]);
}
```

Invoke the stock quote service and print the results:

```
System.out.println(call.invoke( new Object[] {symbol}));

  }
}
```

**2.** Ensure that we have all the JAR files present in the \lib directory of the Axis installation in the classpath as well as a JAXP-compliant parser such as Xerces.

**3.** Compile the class using the following command (assuming you're in a \src directory):

```
javac -d ..\classes GetQuote.java
```

*You may compile the class to wherever you choose, but please bear in mind that you will need to modify later command-line arguments in order to locate it. We have stored it in* com\wrox\jws\stockcore\GetQuote.class, *so this is what our command line will reflect.*

This is the class we'll use in most of our examples without making any changes to the code. We will provide the various security services to the web service and client by altering the deployment information and command-line arguments.

### How It Works

The Axis Service class implements the JAX-RPC Service interface and provides a dynamic interface for invoking web services. This class provides a variety of constructors for passing the WSDL location and service name. However, we have used the empty constructor and set the required information manually rather than using the WSDL location. We use the service object to create the call object:

```
Service service = new Service();
Call call = service.createCall();
```

The Axis Call class implements the JAX-RPC Call interface. We use the methods defined in the Call interface for setting the web service endpoint URL, operation name, user name, and password, and register the names and types of the web service arguments and the return value. The endpoint URL is normally mapped to the Axis servlet on the web container:

```
call.setTargetEndpointAddress( url );
call.setOperationName(new QName("StockQuoteService", "getQuote"));
call.addParameter("symbol", XMLType.XSD_STRING, ParameterMode.IN );
call.setReturnType(XMLType.XSD_STRING);

if(args.length == 4) {
  call.setUsername(args[2]);
  call.setPassword(args[3]);
}
```

Finally we use the call object to invoke the web service dynamically and print the result:

```
System.out.println(call.invoke( new Object[] {symbol}));
```

## Setting Up Axis and WSTK

Before we can install our stock core service on Axis and WSTK we need to make the required classes and data available on the web container in which we run our web service. This section assumes that you have installed and configured Axis and WSTK on Tomcat as explained in the earlier chapters.

Recall from Chapter 3, that the files we need are:

```
stockcore.jar
stock_quote.xml
```

For WSTK, copy the JAR to the `%CATALINA_HOME%\webapps\wstk\WEB-INF\lib` directory the XML file to the `%CATALINA_HOME%\webapps\wstk\WEB-INF\classes\` directory.

Now that everything is set up as we need it, the subsequent sections will look at how we deploy the web service in varying configurations to provide various security services such as authorization, integrity, confidentiality, and so on.

# Security Issues

In enterprise application development, the term security is used in a wide variety of contexts. Writing secure applications involves addressing a whole host of application behavior related to security and privacy. In this section we will have a look at the various aspects of enterprise application behavior that are related to security.

## Authentication

Authentication is the process by which the claims of an entity's identity are verified, when it participates in communication with another entity. The entity that is authenticated is called the **principal** and the information used to identify the principal is the **credentials**. Credentials can be passwords, digital certificates, or security cards.

The credentials provided by the principal are normally compared against a store that contains principals and credentials. These stores include databases, LDAP directory services, and so on. If the credentials provided by the principal matches those supplied in the store, the principal is given access to the system. In very simple terms a user accessing the system will provide their user ID and password to the system. The system will compare this information to the data in a user table stored in the database. If the user ID and password pair provided by the user matches one in the database, the user is granted access to the system.

Once the principal is authenticated, the next step is to verify whether the principal has enough authority to access the system. This is verified by a process called **authorization**.

## Authorization

Authorization defines the access rights of an authenticated principal. For example, a customer logging on to an online shopping system would be able to buy things using the system. However, an administrator would have more rights than the customer, in order to perform administrative tasks. Authorization relies on the rights defined for authenticated principals.

# Data Integrity

When two parties are involved in exchanging data electronically, it is of utmost importance that the data is not modified in any way while in transit. The commonest way for data integrity to be compromised is by what, in security terms, is known as the "Man-in-the-Middle-Attack". In this case someone intercepts the data sent by the sender, alters it, and resends it to the receiver. The receiver would have no knowledge that the data from the original sender was tampered with. This concept is extremely important in the web services world where data is exchanged over the Internet. Data integrity is normally ensured using message digests and digital signatures.

# Data Confidentiality

Data confidentiality is another security aspect as important as data integrity. Where data integrity makes it extremely difficult for an attacker to tamper with the data, data confidentiality makes sure that even if the data is intercepted, it is difficult for the intercepting party to decipher the original content. This is important in exchanging confidential information such as credit card numbers and financial transactions. Data confidentiality is generally achieved using cryptography where the sender encrypts the data before sending it and the receiver decrypts it using some shared key information.

# Non-repudiation

Security solutions that provide non-repudiation services prove the occurrence of a transaction. Non-repudiation leaves digital trails identifying the originator and recipient of a transaction and the information that was exchanged. This makes originating entities accountable for transactions. Non-repudiation is normally achieved using digital signatures, signature chains, and certificate authorities. All the previous concepts are covered in detail in later sections.

# Auditing

It is impossible to write a system that is perfectly secure. We have to strike the balance between cost and security by making it more difficult for attackers to tamper with the security of the system than is worth their while. However, things can go wrong and in the event of security being compromised, there should always be enough auditing information describing when, where, and how the security was compromised so that the security hole can be detected and appropriate measures taken. Auditing provides a log of all important events within the application so that it is possible to use the audit trails to analyze when, where and how security was breached.

# Single Sign-on

Single sign-on allows us to authenticate ourselves at one server and thereafter our security credentials (authorization/authentication information and so on) are automatically carried over to other web sites we visit. Single sign-on/sign-in is a security requirement that is very relevant in a federated system of web services. However, one major disadvantage of using single sign-on is that if the security at the authenticating service is breached, the intruder gains access to all the other services as well. This means single sign-on provides a single point of failure.

# Traditional Security Solutions

We have seen the key security issues in developing enterprise-level web services. In this section we will provide an overview of the traditional security solutions that are relevant for web services. Please note that these solutions are classified as traditional because they existed before the advent of web services. In the following sections we will cover the shortcomings of traditional security solutions and look at the latest developments in providing security in the XML/web services world.

Traditional security solutions that address most of the above security issues, mainly in point-to-point scenarios include:

- Hashing
- Cryptography
- Digital Signatures
- Public Key Certificates
- Secure Socket Layer

## Hashing

Hashing is the process of transforming a set of data into a fixed length digest, so that it is practically impossible for digests generated from two different sets of data (even if they only differ by a single character, as illustrated in the example below) to be identical:

```
M1 = "Cat on a hot tin roof"
M2 = "Cat on a rot tin roof"
H1 = h(M1)
H2 = h(M2)
H1 != H2
```

H1 is the hash of M1 and H2 is the hash of M2. Even though M1 and M2 are very similar, it is practically impossible for H1 and H2 to be the same. This means that when we send our data and then the message digest to someone, it is impossible for anyone else to intercept the data in the middle and alter it, so that the message digest of the altered message generated using the same hashing function is same as that of the old one. Message digests are often used with digital signatures to provide data integrity and authentication.

There are industry-standard algorithms for performing hashing functions such as Secure Hash Algorithm (SHA), RSA-MD5-Message Digest Algorithm.

## Bulk/Symmetric Encryption

Encryption is the process of generating a cipher of a block of data, typically via the use of secret encryption keys. Decryption is the reverse process; generating the original clear text from the cipher. In cryptographic terms clear text is the original data and cipher text is the encrypted data. The secrecy of data is ensured by the secrecy of the key and not the secrecy of the algorithm used to encrypt/decrypt data. There are also industry-standard algorithms for encrypting/decrypting data using a variety of techniques.

**315**

Symmetric encryption is a very efficient mechanism of encrypting/decrypting data. In symmetric key encryption, the sender and receiver share the same secret key. The sender encrypts the data using the key to generate the cipher text and the receiver decrypts the cipher text using the same key to get the original data. This is shown below:

$$C = f(M)_K$$

$$M = f^{-1}(C)_K$$

In the above snippet $f$ is the encryption/decryption algorithm, $M$ is the clear text, $C$ is the cipher text and $K$ is the key used for encryption. This is illustrated in the following diagram:

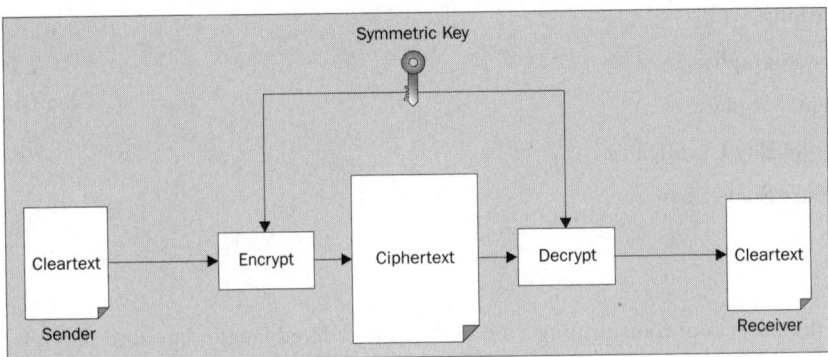

Even though, symmetric encryption is fast and efficient, there is a security concern regarding the exchange of secret keys. Generally, first the secret key has to be exchanged using more secure methods such as asymmetric encryption, since if the key is somehow discovered then transmissions are no longer secure. The key is then used for symmetric encryption to exchange data. This is the technique used in HTTPS, which is a secure version of HTTP that uses SSL. HTTPS and SSL are explained in detail in a later section.

# Asymmetric Encryption

Asymmetric Encryption also known as Public Key Cryptography is a more secure way of encrypting/decrypting data. Here instead of using a single key, a pair of keys is used. The owner of the pair keeps one of the keys and distributes the other key to the people with whom they wish to exchange data. The first key is called the private key and the second one is called the public key. When someone sends data to the owner of the key pair, they encrypt it with the public key. Now the encrypted data can be decrypted only using the owner's private key. It is of utmost importance that the owner of the key pair should ensure that the private key is stored securely as the integrity of the private key is critical. This is illustrated below:

$$C = f(M)_{PUBLIC\ KEY}$$

$$M = f^{-1}(C)_{PRIVATE\ KEY}$$

In the above snippet $f$ is the encryption/decryption algorithm, $M$ is the clear text and $C$ is the cipher text. Even though there exists a mathematical relation between the keys, it is computationally impractical to deduce one from the other. This is illustrated in the following diagram:

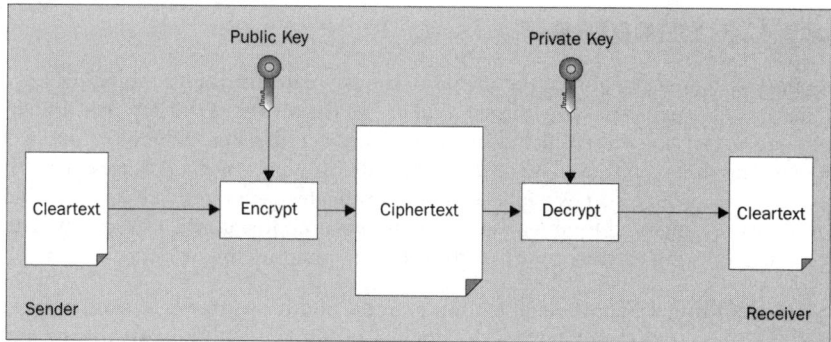

Asymmetric encryption though more secure is slow and computationally expensive. Hence it is normally used for exchanging the secret key used for bulk encryption.

The RSA (Rivest, Shamir, and Adleman) algorithm is a popularly used algorithm for public key encryption.

# Digital Signatures

Digital signatures use public key cryptography for ensuring data integrity. However, here the private key is used for encrypting the data and the public key for decrypting it. However, as encrypting the whole data using the private key is slow and computationally expensive, first a message digest is created using hashing and then the message hash is encrypted using the private key. This is illustrated in the diagram shown below:

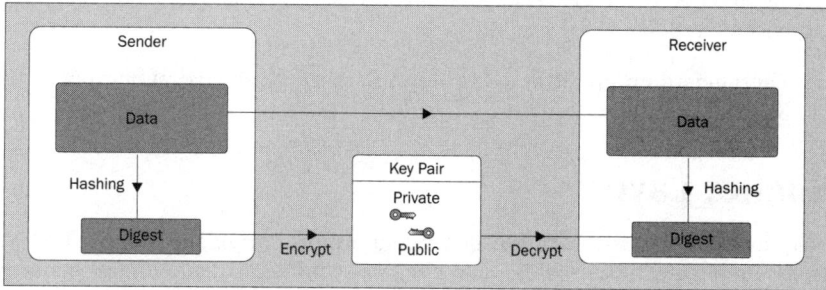

The sender creates the message digest, encrypts it with the private key, and sends the data and the encrypted digest to the receiver. The receiver decrypts the encrypted digest using the public key and compares it against the digest generated from the data that is received. Someone who sits in the middle can't tamper with encrypted digest unless they have the private key of the sender. If they tamper with the data, the receiver can easily identify it by comparing the digests.

Please note that digital signatures ensure data integrity and not confidentiality.

# Public Key Certificates

In the last section on digital signatures, the owner of the key pair distributes the public key to the individuals that would originate secure correspondence to the owner of the key pair. Public key certificates are used to ensure the authenticity of the public keys. These certificates include the public key, information about the owner, and the expiration date of the certificate. Key pairs and certificates can be generated by tools such as `keytool`, which comes with the JDK. Certificates generated like this are called self-signed certificates as they are generated by the owner and there is no information to warranty that the certificate received by a receiver is in fact the original certificate generated by the owner.

We will explain this using a hypothetical example. Suppose Meeraj needs to send a document to Sean securely. He generates a message digest of the document, signs it with his private key and sends the document, signature and public key certificate to Sean. However, Henry intercepts the data in the middle, amends the document, generates a message digest, signs it with his private key, and sends the new document, signature and *his* public key certificate to Sean claiming that it is from Meeraj. Sean will verify the amended data successfully using the new public key certificate, unaware of what happened in the middle.

This is where certificate authorities such as Verisign come into the picture. So our hypothetical situation changes. Let's say that Sean already has the public key of Andre whom he trusts. So Meeraj gets his certificate digitally signed by Andre before sending it to Sean. Now Sean can verify that the certificate originally belongs to Meeraj as it is signed by Andre. Here Andre takes the role of a Certificate Authority (CA).

Normally recipients keep a list of root CA certificates for verifying public key certificates. For example, JDK comes with a file called `cacerts`, which contains five Verisign root CA certificates. Normally, instead of having one CA, there will be a hierarchy of CAs. For example, Craig may sign the public key of Andre and Nicola may sign Craig's public key.

The international standard for public key certificates is called X.509 and public key certificates are often referred to as X.509 Certificates.

# Secure Socket Layer

Secure Socket Layer, or SSL, is a transport-dependent protocol originally proposed by Netscape for the secure transmission of data. SSL provides data integrity, confidentiality, authentication, and non-repudiation. Data confidentiality is ensured using encryption, and integrity by using hashing functions. Clients can authenticate the server and the server can optionally authenticate the client. Non-repudiation is provided using digital signatures and public key certificates.

SSL contains a record protocol and a handshake protocol. The record protocol defines the format of the messages exchanged between the client and the server. The communication between the client and the server is dictated by a set of parameters called a cipher suite. The information defined by the cipher suite includes following details:

- ❑ The key exchange algorithm
- ❑ The encryption algorithm
- ❑ The digest algorithm

When the connection is first established the cipher suite will be SSL_NULL_WITH_NULL_NULL. For example, SSL_RSA_WITH_RC4_128_MD5 means it will use RSA key exchange algorithm, MD5 message digest algorithm and an RC4 key encryption algorithm. Please note that some of the strong encryption algorithms are subject to export regulations in the United States.

During the handshake protocol depicted in the following diagram, the server and client exchange a series of messages to decide on the cipher suite and a key that will be used for bulk encryption prior to the actual data exchange. Please note that SSL uses public key encryption only to exchange a key that will be used to bulk encrypt/decrypt the original data to improve efficiency:

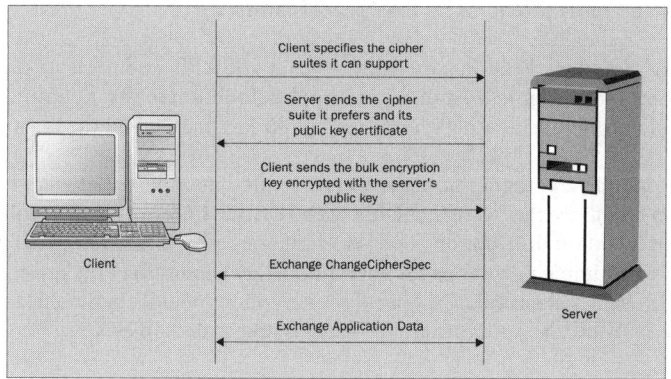

In the above diagram we can see that:

❑ The client connects to the server and sends the cipher suites it can support.

❑ The server picks the strongest cipher suite that it can support and sends it back to the client along with the server's public key certificate. This public key may be signed by a root CA. The client verifies the certificate against its root CA database.

❑ Then it generates a key that will be used for bulk encryption, signs it with the server's public key, and sends it to the server. If the key is not already in use, the client and server exchange the ChangeCipherSpec message confirming the cipher suite. If the key generated by the client is already in use, the server informs the client and the client will generate a different key.

❑ The client and server then exchange data using bulk encryption using the generated secret key.

HTTPS is secure way of using HTTP over SSL.

## SSL and Java

Normally when using HTTP between a server and client browser such as Internet Explorer, the browser software will take care of the intricacies of SSL such as verifying the public key certificate of the server against the root CA database, generating the bulk encryption key, etc. However, if we are writing Java applications that use HTTPS to connect to secure servers, we can't use the plain sockets available with the JDK. For this we should install **JSSE (Java Secure Socket Extension)** from Sun, which is an implementation of SSL. Java sockets use a factory-based approach, and their behavior can be controlled by setting system properties without making a lot of changes to the client code. JDK 1.4, however, is bundled with JSSE so it is not necessary to install JSSE separately.

In a later section we will look at using JSSE for making our stock quote service available through HTTP and enabling the `GetQuote` client to access it without making any changes.

# Java and Cryptography

Most of the web services security specification relies on XML security specifications such as XML digital signature and encryption. These in turn depend on traditional cryptographic concepts. Most of the Java implementations of these specifications therefore rely on the cryptographic tools and API provided by the Java 2 Platform, Standard Edition. Hence it would be a good idea to have an overview of the security API and tools provided by the Java 2 Platform.

The Java 2 Platform, Standard Edition, provides a variety of APIs and tools to support cryptography. The security API provides a whole host of cryptographic functionalities including hashing, encryption/decryption, digital signatures, certificate, and key management.

In pre-JDK 1.4 releases, the cryptographic classes were divided into those that were available with the standard distribution and those that were available with **JCE 1.2.1 (Java Cryptographic Extension)**. JDK 1.4 bundles JCE with the standard distribution. The Java Cryptography Extension (JCE) is a set of packages that provide a framework and implementations for encryption, key generation and key agreement, and Message Authentication Code (MAC) algorithms. Support for encryption includes symmetric, asymmetric, block, and stream ciphers. The software also supports secure streams and sealed objects.

Cryptographic classes in the core distribution provide the following functionalities:

- **Message digests**
  Used for generating hashes of specified data

- **Key pair generation**
  Used to generate private-public key pairs

- **Digital signatures**
  Used to generate and verify digital signatures

- **Key factories**
  Used for key creation from key specifications

- **Certificate factories**
  Used to create public key certificates

- **Keystore management**
  Used for managing keystores containing private keys, certificates, and so on

- **Secure random/pseudo-random number generation**
  Used to generate random and pseudo-random numbers

The JCE classes provide the following functionalities:

- **Asymmetric and symmetric ciphers**
  Used for public key and bulk encryption

- **Secret key factories**
  Factories for secret keys

❑ **MAC algorithms**
Used for message authentication codes

❑ **Key agreement protocol**
Provides functionality for key agreement protocol

Two tools that come with J2SE standard installation that are very useful in providing cryptographic functionalities are `keytool` and `jarsigner`, which are available in the `\bin` directory of the JDK installation. For example, `keytool` can be used for:

❑ Creating key pairs

❑ Creating self-signed certificates

❑ Issuing CSR (Certificate Sign Requests) to CAs

❑ Importing public key certificates for verification

❑ Importing trusted certificates from root CAs to `cacerts`

## Java Cryptography Provider Architecture

The **Java Cryptographic Architecture (JCA)** meets the following objectives:

❑ Provider independence and interoperability

❑ Algorithm independence

As we have already seen, there are several industry-standard algorithms to provide the same cryptographic functionality. For example, we can use either SHA or MD5 for generating message digests. Similarly there can be a number of implementations that support the MD5 algorithm. For example, the JCA provides an API that is independent of both algorithm and implementation.

JCA allows us to plug in new implementations without having to modify our code; all that we need to do is to edit the `java.security` file in the `\lib\security` directory of the JRE installation. In the JCA vocabulary, these implementations are called providers. The standard JDK distribution from Sun supports the following algorithms:

❑ Digital Signature Algorithm (DSA)

❑ Implementations of MD5 and SHA-1 message digest algorithms

❑ DSA key pair generator DSA algorithm parameter generator

❑ Certificate factory for X.509 certificates

The Sun provider is registered in the file `java.security` as shown below:

```
security.provider.1=sun.security.provider.Sun
```

The literal 1 after `security.provider` indicates the order in which the providers are searched for a specific algorithm implementation. For example, if we have the following providers registered:

```
security.provider.1=sun.security.provider.Sun
security.provider.2=com.ibm.crypto.provider.IBMJCE
```

and we ask for the MD5 algorithm for message digests, first the Sun provider is asked for an implementation and if it doesn't support it, the IBM JCE provider is asked. Please note that whenever we install a new provider we should make the provider classes available to the classloader. Generally having the classes as installed extensions does this.

We can also manage the providers dynamically by using the `addProvider()` and `insertProvidetAt()` methods on the class `java.security.Security`. Please note that providers added in this manner are not persistent. The method `getProviders()` can be used to get a list of all installed providers.

## Engine Classes

In the last section we have seen how JCA provides implementation independence using the provider architecture. In this section we will have a look at how algorithm independence is achieved for various cryptographic functionalities. Algorithm independence is achieved in JCA using engine classes that provide specific cryptographic functionalities. The core engine classes bundled with the JDK standard API are:

❏ `java.security.MessageDigest`
Used for providing hashing functionality

❏ `java.security.Signature`
Used for signing and verifying digital signatures

❏ `java.security.KeyPairGenerator`
Used for generating public and private keys

❏ `java.security.KeyFactory`
Used for converting opaque cryptographic keys into key specifications

❏ `java.security.cert.CertificateFactory`
Used for creating public key certificates

❏ `java.security.KeyStore`
Used for managing keystores, which are used in Java for storing certificates, key pairs, and so on

❏ `java.security.AlgorithmParameters`
Used for managing parameters to various cryptographic algorithms

❏ `java.security.AlgorithmParameterGenerator`
Used for generating parameters specific to various algorithms

❏ `java.security.SecureRandom`
Used for generating random numbers

The engine classes that come with JCE are:

❏ `javax.crypto.Cipher`
Used to provide encryption and decryption functionality

❏ `javax.crypto.KeyAgreement`
Used to provide functionality for key exchange protocol

- ❏ `javax.crypto.KeyGenerator`
  Used for symmetric key generation

- ❏ `javax.crypto.Mac`
  Used to provide MAC algorithm

- ❏ `javax:crypto.SecretKeyFactory`
  Used as a factory for secret keys

These classes provide static `getInstance()` methods to instantiate their objects, and take the algorithm name as their arguments. For example if we want to perform a hashing function using the MD5 algorithm, we will use the `MessageDigest` engine class as follows:

```
MessageDigest md = MessageDigest.getInstance("MD5");
```

This will ask each of the installed providers for a message digest engine class that supports the MD5 hashing algorithm in order of preference and return an appropriate instance. If a provider that supports the required algorithm is not found an exception is thrown.

## Java Cryptographic Tools and Files

In this section we will have a look at the various files and tools used by the Java 2 SDK for providing cryptographic functionality. The main files used by the Java 2 SDK for providing cryptographic functionalities are listed below:

- ❏ `keystore`
  As we mentioned earlier, this is a database that stores private keys and certificate chains used to authenticate their public keys. Keystores can be of different formats, depending on the providers we use. The default Sun provider uses a flat-file format called JKS (Java Keystore). Keystores are protected by passwords and each private key in the keystore is protected by its own password.

  Keystores can be manipulated using the engine class `java.security.KeyStore` that is available in JCA.

  It can also be manipulated using the `keytool` utility that comes with JDK. By default the `keystore` is stored in the user's home directory. The implementation and location of the keystores are specified in the `java.security` and `java.policy` files in the `\lib\security` directory of the JRE respectively.

- ❏ `cacerts`
  This is a `keystore` file that contains root CA certificates that can be used for authenticating certificate chains. JDK ships with five Verisign root CA certificates in the `cacerts` `keystore`. This is located in the `\lib\security` directory of the JRE.

- ❏ `security.properties`
  The security properties, such as installed providers and keystore type, are defined in the file `java.security` stored in the `\lib\security` directory of the JRE.

In this section we have seen a high-level overview of the cryptographic functionalities provided by the Java 2 Platform. In the subsequent sections we will see how these things fit into the broader world of web services security.

# Accessing a Web Service Over HTTPS

In this section we will have a look at how to make the stock quote service accessible through HTTPS. We will be using Tomcat and Axis to deploy the web service, but before we can make our web service accessible through HTTPS we need to enable HTTPS on Tomcat.

## Enabling HTTPS on Tomcat

We need to perform the following steps to enable HTTPS on Tomcat:

- ❏ Install JSSE (Please note that you don't need to do this if you are using JDK 1.4)
- ❏ Create the key pair
- ❏ Make configuration changes on Tomcat

### Try It Out – Install JSSE

JSSE can be downloaded from the Javasoft web site. The latest version is 1.0.3. Please follow the following steps to install JSSE:

1. Unpack the downloaded ZIP file to your local drive. This will create a directory called `jsse1.0.3` that will contain a `lib` directory. The `lib` directory will contain the files `jcert.jar`, `jnet.jar` and `jsse.jar`.

2. We will install these files as installed extensions. To do this, copy these files to the `lib\ext` directory of your JRE.

3. Now we will register the JSSE provider in the `java.security` file in the `lib\security` directory of the JRE by adding the following entry. Depending on the number of registered providers the numeric following the string `security.provider` will vary:

   `security.provider.3=com.sun.net.ssl.internal.ssl.Provider`

### Create Certificates and Key Stores

In the section on SSL, we saw that the servers use public key encryption for key exchange. Before we can use Tomcat with HTTPS, we need to generate the keystore and certificate for Tomcat in order to use SSL. By default Tomcat looks for the key by alias `tomcat` in the default keystore called `.keystore` in the user's home directory. The command below will generate the key pair and public key certificate after you have answered the questions it asks in order to generate your certificate (note that you will have to add a store password and a key password when prompted):

```
keytool -genkey -alias tomcat
```

This will generate a key called `tomcat` in the default keystore with a self-signed certificate. Normally we would want get our public key certificates signed by a CA and import them to our keystore. However, here we will use the self-signed certificate. This means that a client browser will pop a message saying the certificate is untrusted; we can click OK and continue as normal.

## Try It Out – Configure Tomcat

1.  To enable HTTPS on Tomcat you need to add the following entry into the `server.xml` file in the `conf` directory. This should be added under the Tomcat standalone service in the configuration file. Normally this entry is commented in the configuration file and we just need to uncomment it. However, we should specify the keystore password:

```
<Connector
  className="org.apache.catalina.connector.http.HttpConnector"
  port="8443"
  minProcessors="5"
  maxProcessors="75"
  enableLookups="true"
  acceptCount="10"
debug="0"
scheme="https"
secure="true">
<Factory
  className="org.apache.catalina.net.SSLServerSocketFactory"
  clientAuth="false"
  protocol="TLS"
  keystorePass="password"/>
</Connector>
```

2.  To test whether SSL is configured properly we can access the URL https://localhost:8443. Please note that we use https instead of http and the port number is 8443. The browser will display the Tomcat home page as shown below:

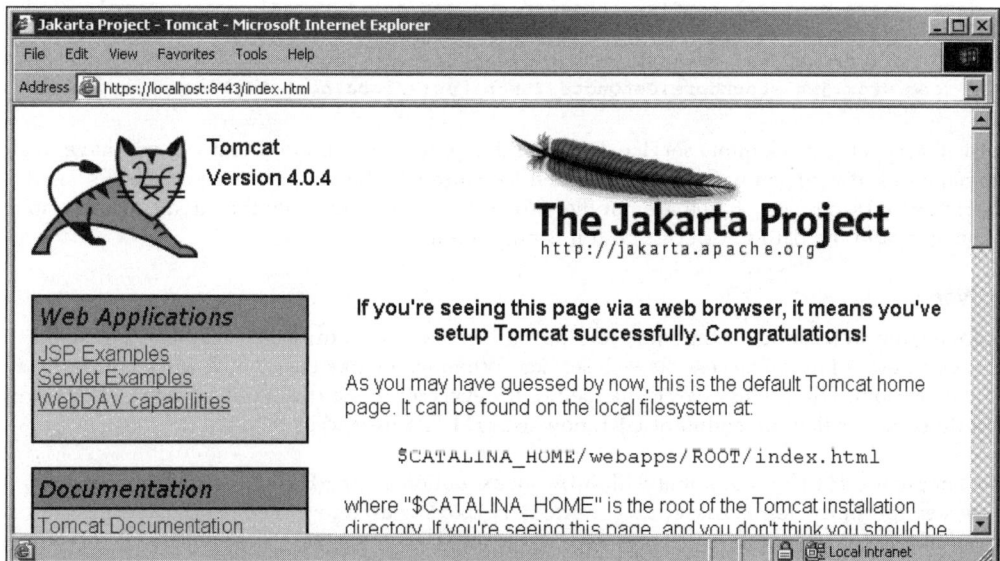

The padlock sign on the right shows that the site is accessed using HTTPS.

## Try It Out – Web Services and HTTPS

In this section we will deploy our web and access it using HTTPS.

**1.** To deploy the web service, store the contents shown below in a file called `ServerDeploy.wsdd`:

```
<deployment xmlns="http://xml.apache.org/axis/wsdd/"
  xmlns:java="http://xml.apache.org/axis/wsdd/providers/java">

  <service name="StockQuoteService" provider="java:RPC">
    <parameter name="className" value="com.wrox.jws.stockcore.StockCore"/>
    <parameter name="allowedMethods" value="getQuote"/>
  </service>

</deployment>
```

Make sure that you have all the Axis JAR files and a JAXP parser in the classpath as explained in the earlier section and run the following command to deploy the web service:

```
java org.apache.axis.client.AdminClient
    -lhttp://localhost:8080/axis/services/AdminService ServerDeploy.wsdd
```

**2.** Since we have already compiled the client class `GetQuote.java` in an earlier section of this chapter, we can access the web service by running the following command. Please make sure that you have Axis JAR file, a JAXP parser, and the current directory in the classpath:

```
java -Djava.protocol.handler.pkgs=com.sun.net.ssl.internal.www.protocol
    -Djavax.net.ssl.trustStore=c:\Beginning_JWS_Examples\Chp09\.keystore
    -Djavax.net.ssl.trustStorePassword=password
  com.wrox.jws.stockcore.GetQuote IBM https://localhost:8443/axis/services/
```

This will access the stock quote service and print the quote. Bear in mind that you will have to alter this command to suit your setup. For example, your keystore may be held in `C:\Documents and Settings\<username>` if you are not the only user on your machine; the password will also need to be changed, and the path to `GetQuote` if it is not the same.

### How It Works

Deploying the web service is the same routine stuff we have seen in earlier chapters. The main difference here is how we access the web service. When we invoke the client class, we pass the symbol and the endpoint URL. This URL is mapped to the Axis servlet in the Axis `web.xml` file. However, the main difference is that the endpoint URL now uses HTTPS instead of HTTP.

If we simply use HTTPS, our client will throw an exception stating HTTPS is an unrecognised protocol. The system property `java.protocol.handler.pkgs` is used to force the use of secure sockets instead of normal sockets.

What is the use of `javax.net.ssl.trustStore` and `javax.net.ssl.trustStorePassword` system properties you may ask? As mentioned earlier, Tomcat is using a self-signed certificate instead of one signed by a root CA. However, when the client-side JSSE framework receives the public key certificate from Tomcat it will look at the `cacerts` file for verification. It won't find anything in the `cacerts` file to verify the certificate and will throw an exception. Hence we are using the aforementioned properties to look into the default keystore for the trusted certificate.

> **In this example both the client and server use the same keystore. In a real-life scenario, you will have to export the server's public key and import it to the client's keystore. In this case the trust store should be set to the client's keystore.**

# HTTP Authentication Methods

Even though the web services specification doesn't mandate HTTP as the transport protocol, HTTP is still the most popularly used transport protocol in the web services world. In this section we will have a look at the various methods available within HTTP to provide transport level point-to-point security and how the J2EE servlet specification supports these authentication methods. HTTP provides the following authentication methods for a client to authenticate a server.

## Basic Authentication

This is the method specified in the HTTP 1.1 specification and is based on a user name and password. In this method, the HTTP server requests the client to authenticate itself. As part of this challenge, the server sends a string identifying the realm to which the client is to be authenticated. In J2EE web applications this realm name is defined in the web deployment descriptor.

In basic authentication the user name and password are transmitted from the client to the server in simple base64 encoding, which is fundamentally insecure as it doesn't use any strong encryption schemes and it doesn't provide any mechanism for the client to authenticate the server.

## Digest Authentication

This is very similar to basic authentication and the only difference is that the credential information (the user ID and password) is transmitted in an encrypted manner and hence is more secure.

## HTTPS Client Authentication

This is a highly secure authentication scheme using HTTPS. This requires the client to possess the public key certificate corresponding to the private key owned by the server.

## Servlet Support for HTTP Authentication Methods

The servlet specification supports all of the aforementioned authentication methods. It adds in a new form-based authentication method to control the look and feel of the screen used by the client browser for obtaining the users' security credentials.

The servlet specification defines role-based security where a collection of web resources is associated with specific roles. These roles are mapped to physical users using a servlet container-specific technique.

The security policies for the web applications that act as web services can be controlled using the web deployment descriptor for the web application. The example below shows the deployment descriptor excerpt that allows normal users to view the WSDL file and only special users to invoke the web service by defining different security policies for the WSDL and endpoint URLs:

```
<security-role>
  <role-name>special</role-name>
</security-role>

<security-role>
  <role-name>normal</role-name>
</security-role>

<security-constraint>

  <web-resource-collection>
    <web-resource-name>WSDL URL</web-resource-name>
    <url-pattern>/MyWebService/ws.wsdl</url-pattern>
  </web-resource-collection>

  <auth-constraint>
    <role-name>normal</role-name>
    <role-name>special</role-name>
  </auth-constraint>

</security-constraint>

<security-constraint>

  <web-resource-collection>
    <web-resource-name>Endpoint URL</web-resource-name>
    <url-pattern>/MyWebService/Service</url-pattern>
  </web-resource-collection>

  <auth-constraint>
    <role-name>special</role-name>
  </auth-constraint>

  <user-data-constraint>
    <transport-guarantee>CONFIDENTIAL</transport-guarantee>
  </user-data-constraint>

</security-constraint>

<login-config>
  <auth-method>CLIENT-CERT</auth-method>
</login-config>
```

In the above example, the WSDL URL is accessible to users defined with special and normal roles whereas only special users can invoke the web service. Further to this, the transport for web service invocation should guarantee data confidentiality. The possible values for the transport-guarantee element are NONE, INTEGRAL, and CONFIDENTIAL. The authentication method used is CLIENT-CERT.

# Component-Level Security

Even if we rely on transport-level security, it is always better to put belt and braces on our web services' security by securing the back-end components that implement the web services. In the J2EE world, if we are using EJBs to implement the web services, we can use the method permission element in the EJB deployment descriptor to provide role-based access to the EJB methods as shown below:

```
<assembly-descriptor>

  <security-role>
    <role-name>special</role-name>
  </security-role>

  <method-permission>
    <role-name>special</role-name>
    <method>
      <ejb-name>WebServiceEJB</ejb-name>
      <method-name>webServiceMethod</method-name>
    </method>
  </method-permission>

</assembly-descriptor>
```

The deployment descriptor excerpt shown above states that the `webServiceMethod()` on `WebServiceEJB` can be invoked only by authenticated principals with the role `special`.

## Try It Out – An Authenticated StockQuote Service

In this section we will have a look at how to allow access to our stock quote web service to only authenticated users.

As we saw in the earlier example, the web service is accessed through the URL https://localhost:8443/axis/services/. The non-HTTPS equivalent of this is http://localhost:8080/axis/services. If we look at the deployment descriptor for the axis web application we see that this URL is mapped to the Axis servlet. So one obvious way to restrict access to the web service is to restrict this URI. However, this will restrict access to all other web services as well as the admin service for deploying web service. Hence we will create a new URI for accessing the stock quote service and restrict that one only.

**1.** First we will modify the Axis web deployment descriptor to apply our new security policies. This file can be found in the `%axisDirectory%/webapps/axis/WEB-INF` directory and is called `web.xml`. Add the following changes to the deployment descriptor:

```
<servlet-mapping>
  <servlet-name>AxisServlet</servlet-name>
  <url-pattern>/services/secure</url-pattern>
</servlet-mapping>

<security-constraint>
```

```
   <web-resource-collection>
     <web-resource-name>Secure resources</web-resource-name>
     <url-pattern>/services/secure</url-pattern>
     <http-method>GET</http-method>
     <http-method>POST</http-method>
   </web-resource-collection>

   <auth-constraint>
     <role-name>ws_user</role-name>
   </auth-constraint>

 </security-constraint>

 <login-config>
   <auth-method>BASIC</auth-method>
 </login-config>
```

The listing above states that the BASIC authentication will be used for authenticating users and for accessing the URI /services/secure we should have the role ws_user.

**2.** Now that we have defined our security policy, we need to create users and roles that map to our security policy. By default Tomcat uses a memory realm, which is loaded from the file tomcat-users.xml available in the conf directory. Add the following entry to create a new user with the required role:

```
<user name="meeraj" password="chelsea" roles="ws_user" />
```

Now restart Tomcat for our new security policies to take effect.

**3.** To access the web service we can use the same client as in the HTTPS example. However we will pass different command-line arguments as shown below:

```
java com.wrox.jws.stockcore.GetQuote IBM
        http://localhost:8080/axis/services/secure meeraj chelsea
```

Please note that here we can use either the HTTP or HTTPS URLs. If we are using the HTTP URL we don't need to set all the system properties specific to HTTPS. However, for both cases we should specify the user name and password. Also note that now we use the secure URL instead of the earlier URL. This will access the web service and print the quote.

If you pass an incorrect password or user name, you will get a SOAP fault with an HTTP code 401 stating unauthorized access.

### How It Works

The first thing we did was to use standard J2EE web application techniques to create a secure URI that is mapped to the Axis servlet. We also specified that only users with ws_user role might access this web service as shown in the following deployment descriptor:

```
<security-constraint>

  <web-resource-collection>
    <web-resource-name>Secure resources</web-resource-name>
    <url-pattern>/services/secure</url-pattern>
    <http-method>GET</http-method>
    <http-method>POST</http-method>
  </web-resource-collection>

  <auth-constraint>
    <role-name>ws_user</role-name>
  </auth-constraint>

</security-constraint>
```

Then we created a user with the required role in the Tomcat memory realm by editing the `tomcat-users.xml` file. So, when we invoked the client we specified the restricted URL and also specified the user name and password.

The client code uses the `call` object for setting the user name and password:

```
if(args.length == 4) {
    call.setUsername(args[2]);
    call.setPassword(args[3]);
}
```

The Axis client-side framework will actually set this information in the HTTP header so that the servlet container can extract it and use it for authentication and authorization purposes.

## Custom Authentication Methods

In the last example we saw how to use standard HTTP authentication methods for providing restricted access to our web service. However, there may be scenarios where we want to implement more powerful authentication logic. For example, we may want to let a particular user access a particular web service only a fixed number of times a day. There is no way we can achieve this using standard HTTP authentication techniques.

Most of the web services platforms such as Axis, WSTK, WLS, and so on provide powerful functionality called handlers for pre and post processing SOAP messages during the web services invocation. These components use the Decorator pattern and work in a similar way to servlet filters. These components can be used for a variety of purposes such as metering, auditing, logging, encryption, signatures, and authentication.

### Axis Handler Architecture

Axis handlers can be used for processing the following:

- ❏ A SOAP request before it leaves the client
- ❏ A SOAP request before it reaches the server
- ❏ A SOAP response before it leaves the server
- ❏ A SOAP response before it reaches the client

**331**

The diagram below taken from the Axis documentation shows a view of the Axis handler architecture:

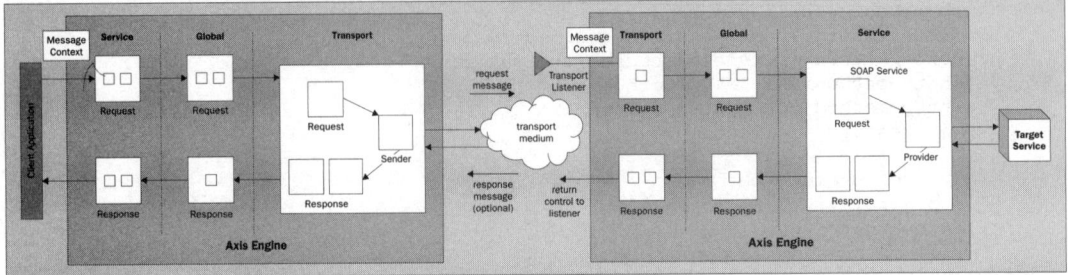

Handlers can be configured both on the client and/or the server side. They can be configured for a transport, globally for all the services, or for a specific service. The handlers implement the interface `org.apache.axis.Handler`, which defines a variety of methods. The main method is the `invoke` method that passes a reference to the message context. The message context can be used for a variety of purposes such as accessing the SOAP envelope, or the security credentials for the current thread.

> **A detailed coverage of Axis handler architecture is beyond the scope of this chapter.**
> **Please refer to the Axis architecture documentation available with the Axis**
> **installation bundle for more details.**

Axis comes with two handler implementations called `SimpleAuthenticationHandler` and `SimpleAuthorizationHandler` that illustrate the use of handlers for implementing custom authentication logic. These handlers use two files called `users.lst` and `perms.lst`, available in the `WEB-INF` directory of the Axis web application. In the following example, we will use these handlers to provide restricted access to the stock quote service.

## Try It Out – Custom Authentication

1.  To deploy the web service, store the contents shown below in a file called `ServerDeploy.wsdd`:

```
<deployment xmlns="http://xml.apache.org/axis/wsdd/"
  xmlns:java="http://xml.apache.org/axis/wsdd/providers/java">

  <service name="StockQuoteService" provider="java:RPC">
    <parameter name="className" value="com.wrox.jws.stockcore.StockCore"/>
    <parameter name="allowedMethods" value="getQuote"/>
    <parameter name="allowedRoles" value="meeraj"/>

    <requestFlow name="checks">
      <handler
        type="java:org.apache.axis.handlers.SimpleAuthenticationHandler"/>
      <handler
        type="java:org.apache.axis.handlers.SimpleAuthorizationHandler"/>
    </requestFlow>
  </service>

</deployment>
```

**2.** To deploy the web service, make sure that you have all the Axis JAR files and a JAXP parser in the classpath as explained in the earlier section and run the following command to deploy the web service:

```
java org.apache.axis.client.AdminClient
    -lhttp://localhost:8080/axis/services/AdminService ServerDeploy.wsdd
```

**3.** We need to edit the `users.lst` file in the `WEB-INF` directory of the Axis web application and add the following entry (or your own name and password depending on how you set things up in the `ServerDeploy.wsdd` file):

```
user 1 pass1
user2
user3 pass3
meeraj chelsea
```

**4.** To access the web service we can use the same client as in the HTTPS example. However we will pass different command-line arguments as shown below:

```
java com.wrox.jws.stockcore.GetQuote IBM
       http://localhost:8080/axis/services/ meeraj chelsea
```

Please note that here we can use the normal URL for accessing the service. This will access the web service and print the quote. If we pass an incorrect password or user name, we get a SOAP fault stating unauthorized access.

### How It Works

The above example is very similar to the one that uses basic authentication but has a few differences. The main difference is in the deployment descriptor where we specify only the user `meeraj` can access the stock quote web service:

```
<parameter name="allowedRoles" value="meeraj"/>
```

Then we configure a set of handlers that are invoked before the web service as shown below:

```
<requestFlow name="checks">
  <handler
    type="java:org.apache.axis.handlers.SimpleAuthenticationHandler"/>
  <handler
    type="java:org.apache.axis.handlers.SimpleAuthorizationHandler"/>
</requestFlow>
```

The snippet above states that the authentication and authorization handlers should be invoked before accessing the web service. These handlers will extract the user name and password set by the client from the message context, and compare them against the information stored in the `users.lst` and `perms.lst` files. If they don't match, a SOAP fault authentication failure is thrown. This is illustrated in the diagram shown overleaf:

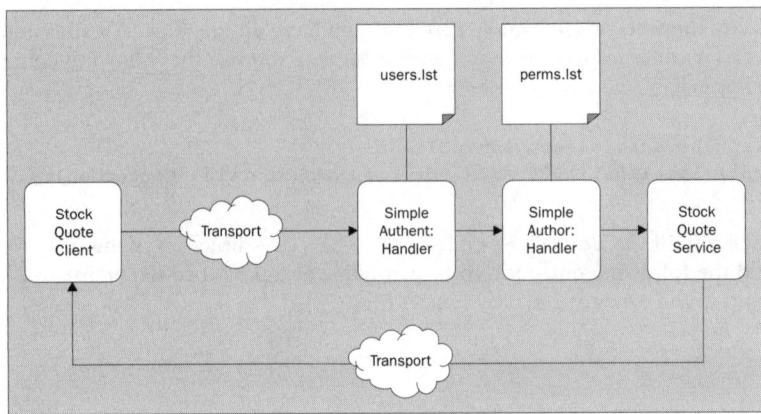

# Shortcomings of Traditional Security Methods

The traditional security solutions we have discussed so far in this chapter provide an efficient point-to-point security at transport level in exchanging information. However, in the web services world we are really talking about end-to-end security. A SOAP envelope that represents a web service request may go through a number of intermediaries before it reaches the ultimate recipient:

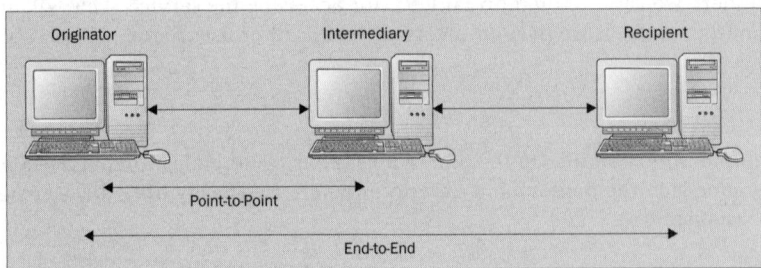

As mentioned in the beginning of this chapter, one of the most important aspects of XML is its ability to represent hierarchical data structures and to navigate to arbitrary data elements using DOM, XPath, and so on. Once the whole document is encrypted, this powerful aspect of XML is lost as the whole XML structure is now converted into a binary chunk of data.

Several organizations have been working actively on extending the traditional security solutions, to meet the various aspects of XML security requirements. Due to their efforts, a number of specifications have evolved over the last couple of years. These include:

❑   Security Assertion Markup Language from OASIS (http://www.oasis.org)

❑   XML Digital Signatures from the W3C (http://www.w3c.org)

❑   XML Encryption from W3C the (http://www.w3c.org)

❑   XML Key Management from the W3C (http://www.w3c.org)

❑   WS-Security from IBM, Microsoft, and Verisign

In the next section we will have a look at the various XML security specifications from W3C and the XML security specifications implementation from IBM – XML Security Suite. Most of these specifications build on the traditional security techniques such as digital signatures, message digests, and asymmetric and bulk encryption.

# XML Security Specifications

In this section we will mainly cover XML Signature and XML Encryption standards. Please note that the more specific web services security specifications such as WS-Security and the security assertion specifications such as SAML utilize the functionality offered by the XML security specifications.

# Canonical XML

Before we delve into the details of XML signature and encryption, we will have a quick overview of **canonical XML**. As we have seen in previous sections, signing the message digest of the data with the owner's private key generates digital signatures; mainly for checking data integrity and non-repudiation.

Similarly public key encryption involves encrypting the data with the recipient's public key and the message recipient, in turn, using the private key to decrypt the encrypted message. We have also seen that a small change in the original message will cause the message digest algorithm to generate an entirely different hash value.

In the context of XML documents, two documents can have the same content even if their textual representations are not the same. A simple example would be where the second document is formatted differently from the first. Hence if we generate message digests for the two documents, they will result in different hash values.

The canonical XML specification defines a method of generating XML documents in a form that identifies logically identical documents as having the same content despite the variations in physical formatting. Both XML signature, and encryption, work on the canonical form of the documents, so that the generated hash values are the same for two documents with identical logical structure, even if they vary in physical structure.

# XML Signature

XML signature is a W3C recommendation describing the creation and representation of digital signatures in XML. The signatures may represent any arbitrary XML and non-XML data. They can be detached from the data that is signed, or in the case of XML, data being signed can be part of the XML document. If the signature is not detached it can either envelope the data that is signed or can be enveloped by the data that is signed. Basically, XML signature defines a way of associating keys with data that is signed.

## XML Signature Syntax

XML digital signatures use references to link signature values to signed data. The data that is signed is first hashed and the hash value is placed in an element. This element is then digested and cryptographically signed.

XML digital signatures use the `Signature` element for representing signatures. The basic structure of the `Signature` element is shown below:

```
<Signature ID>
  <SignedInfo>
    <CanonicalizationMethod/>
    <SignatureMethod/>
    <Reference URI>
      <Transforms/>
      <DigestMethod/>
      <DigestValue/>
    </Reference>
  </SignedInfo>
  <KeyInfo>
  <Object ID/>
</Signature>
```

The `URI` attribute in the `Reference` element is used to link the signature to the signed data. If the signed data is available in the same document as the signature, the `URI` points to the `ID` attribute of the data that is signed.

❑ The `SignedInfo` element encapsulates all the information related to the signature.

❑ The `CanonicalizationMethod` element defines the algorithm used to canonicalize the XML data that is signed.

❑ The `SignatureMethod` identifies the algorithm used to sign the hash of the data that is signed. The algorithms supported include RSA-SHA1,and DSA-SHA1.

❑ The `Reference` element points to the data that is signed using the `URI` attribute and contains the digest algorithm that is used for hashing the data defined by the `DigestMethod` element and the digest value included in the `DigestValue` attribute. It may also contain one or more `Transform` elements identifying the processing applied to the data before it was digested.

❑ The optional `KeyInfo` element may be used to specify the key that should be used to validate the signature. The contents of this element vary depending on the signature algorithm that is used.

### An XML Signature Example

The listing below shows the XML Signature that is generated from an XML document. The programmatic signing of the document to generate the signature and then the verification of the signature is covered in a later section:

```
<emp:Signature xmlns:emp="http://www.w3.org/2000/09/xmldsig#">
  <emp:SignedInfo>
    <emp:CanonicalizationMethod
      Algorithm="http://www.w3.org/TR/2001/REC-xml-c14n-20010315">
    </emp:CanonicalizationMethod>
```

The signature method that is used is DSA-SHA1:

```
    <emp:SignatureMethod
      Algorithm="http://www.w3.org/2000/09/xmldsig#dsa-sha1">
    </emp:SignatureMethod>
```

The URI #1 points to the data that is signed:

```
<emp:Reference URI="#1">
  <emp:Transforms>
   <emp:Transform
    Algorithm="http://www.w3.org/TR/2001/REC-xml-c14n-20010315">
   </emp:Transform>
  </emp:Transforms>
```

The digest algorithm that is used is SHA1:

```
<emp:DigestMethod
  Algorithm="http://www.w3.org/2000/09/xmldsig#sha1">
</emp:DigestMethod>
```

This is the digest value:

```
<emp:DigestValue>ew6TRCmxglhpUeXvo6LgSy3cZlk=</emp:DigestValue>
 </emp:Reference>
</emp:SignedInfo>
```

This is the signature value:

```
<emp:SignatureValue>
 c4lNWEbbm/OB6YfNRi6lI7jHiNMzM0gVQWSAggN9ForXMg4aoEusqw==
</emp:SignatureValue>
<emp:KeyInfo>
```

This element defines the public key value:

```
<emp:KeyValue>
  <emp:DSAKeyValue>
    <emp:P>
      /X9TgR11EilS30qcLuzk5/YRt1I870QAwx4/gLZRJmlFXUAiUftZPY1Y+r/F9bow9s
      ubVWzXgTuAHTRv8mZgt2uZUKWkn5/oBHsQIsJPu6nX/rfGG/g7V+fGqKYVDwT7g/bT
      xR7DAjVUE1oWkTL2dfOuK2HXKu/yIgMZndFIAcc=
    </emp:P>

    <emp:Q>
      12BQjxUjC8yykrmCouuEC/BYHPU=
    </emp:Q>

    <emp:G>
      9+GghdabPd7LvKtcNrhXuXmUr7v6OuqC+VdMCz0HgmdRWVeOutRZT+ZxBxCBgLRJFn
      Ej6EwoFhO3zwkyjMim4TwWeotUfI0o4KOuHiuzpnWRbqN/C/ohNWLx+2J6ASQ7zKTx
      vqhRkImog9/hWuWfBpKLZl6Ae1UlZAFMO/7PSSo=
    </emp:G>

    <emp:Y>
      CrgJnP+zC6Zc5AjlTA26vdJ+Ui/qR5xlOiYCpV6MSXuweMhWYH5DVr9te1O9hiWDG9
      vwHSkMvoo9Ub7nQ8xqBoLn/YIesho+7Vmua7EBepew5Crq1qgMOWZiay/1Jgs/BFg5
      AaKbXBMakMmDFzHaqrjID7eFDbVARouW+6XHnAg=
    </emp:Y>

  </emp:DSAKeyValue>
</emp:KeyValue>
```

This contains the X.509 certificate information that contains the public key:

```
<emp:X509Data>
  <emp:X509IssuerSerial>
    <emp:X509IssuerName>
      CN=Kunnumpurath\, Meeraj,OU=E-Solutions,O=EDS,L=Milton
      Keynes,ST=Bucks,C=UK
    </emp:X509IssuerName>
    <emp:X509SerialNumber>
      1026516428
    </emp:X509SerialNumber>
  </emp:X509IssuerSerial>

  <emp:X509SubjectName>
    CN=Kunnumpurath\, Meeraj,OU=E-Solutions,O=EDS,L=Milton
    Keynes,ST=Bucks,C=UK
  </emp:X509SubjectName>
  <emp:X509Certificate>
MIIDJDCCAuICBD0vZcwwCwYHKoZIzjgEAwUAMHgxCzAJBgNVBAYTAlVLMQ4wDAYDVQQIEwVCdWNr
czEWMBQGA1UEBxMNTWlsdG9uIEtleW5lczEMMAoGA1UEChMDRURTMRQwEgYDVQQLEwtFLVNvbHV0

...

/YIesho+7Vmua7EBepew5Crq1qgMOWZiay/1Jgs/BFg5AaKbXBMakMmDFzHaqrjID7eFDbVARouW
+6XHnAgwCwYHKoZIzjgEAwUAAy8AMCwCFBhQ48ng00bCmtgEDUb0ga2tT/QsAhQ9SWHM+3/WIzQ7
8WXo7nnBWuSC/Q==
  </emp:X509Certificate>
  </emp:X509Data>
</emp:KeyInfo>
```

This is the data that is signed, and referenced by the `Reference` element's `URI` attribute. The signed data is enclosed in the `Object` element:

```
<dsig:Object xmlns:dsig="http://www.w3.org/2000/09/xmldsig#" Id="1">
  <employee>
    <name>Claudio Ranieri</name>
    <department>Football Club</department>
    <company>Chelsea Village</company>
    <position>Manager</position>
    <salary>100000000</salary>
  </employee>
</dsig:Object>
</emp:Signature>
```

## Reference Verification

The steps involved in reference verification are listed below:

❑ The contents of the `SignedInfo` element are canonicalized using the specified algorithm

❑ For each reference the data is obtained using the `URI` attribute

❑ This data is digested using the specified digest algorithm

❑ The digest is compared against the digest value specified in the `SignedInfo` element

The public key can be retrieved from a variety of sources:

❑ From an external source such as a `keystore`

❑ From the information present in the `KeyInfo` element

# XML Encryption

XML encryption specifies a means of encrypting data and representing it in XML format. The data that is encrypted may be XML documents, elements, element content, or any arbitrary data. The encrypted information is enclosed in the `EncryptedData` element, which will replace the element, or the element content, in the encrypted XML document. If the whole XML document is encrypted this element will become the document element.

The basic structure of the `EncryptedData` element is shown below:

```
<EncryptedData Id Type>
  <EncryptionMethod/>
  <ds:KeyInfo>
    <EncryptedKey/>
    <AgreementMethod/>
    <ds:KeyName/>
    <ds:RetrievalMethod/>
    <ds:*>
  </ds:KeyInfo>
  <CipherData>
    <CipherValue/>
    <CipherReference URI/>
  </CipherData>
  <EncryptionProperties/>
</EncryptedData>
```

❑ The `Type` attribute of `EncryptedData` element identifies whether the element, content, or any arbitrary data is encrypted.

❑ The `EncryptionMethod` element identifies the algorithm used to encrypt the data.

❑ The `KeyInfo` element can be used to hint which decrypting program to use to obtain the key to decrypt the data. This can be elements such as the plain key value (most unlikely), the encrypted key using `EncryptedKey` element, or the alias name identifying the private key of the owner in the case of asymmetric encryption.

❑ The `CipherData` element will contain the encrypted data.

## An XML Encryption Example

The listing below shows an encrypted XML document, with a particular element encrypted:

```
<?xml version="1.0" encoding="UTF-8"?>
<employee>
  <name>Claudio Ranieri</name>
  <department>Football Club</department>
  <company>Chelsea Village</company>
  <position>Manager</position>
```

The encrypted element identifies the encrypted content as an XML element:

```
<EncryptedData Id="ed2"
  Type="http://www.w3.org/2001/04/xmlenc#Element"
  xmlns="http://www.w3.org/2001/04/xmlenc#">
```

The algorithm used is RSA:

```
<EncryptionMethod
  Algorithm="http://www.w3.org/2001/04/xmlenc#rsa-1_5"/>
```

The KeyInfo element identifies the private key alias used to decrypt the data:

```
<KeyInfo xmlns="http://www.w3.org/2000/09/xmldsig#">
  <KeyName>MyKey</KeyName>
</KeyInfo>
```

The CipherData element contains the encrypted data:

```
<CipherData>
  <CipherValue>BQYjtLafz8a15ClaCZ1iFi9UY7EwZTPHUBe9VA+jT90kAo3nV
    NPUtVG0olC0Ro6mowsjlEohGnM11qUHUZRShPrl+SVOr8vOIGFcYvE447Jifd
    1TWtvRfeQTezmt6gt7fuBNu3xieB9PtcKv0pdQ7zDCitjDz9YWhRLfRMnljLI=
  </CipherValue>
</CipherData>
</EncryptedData>
</employee>
```

# WS-Security

WS-Security is the first among a set of security specifications initiated by IBM, Microsoft, and Verisign, which address specific security issues in the context of web services. These include authentication, authorization, privacy, trust, integrity, federation, secure communication channels, and auditing.

These specifications are built on top of the web services technologies such as SOAP and WSDL as well as the XML security specifications such as XML Signature and Encryption. These specifications address end-to-end security solutions in a federated web services world, rather than the point-to-point to transport-level security provided by traditional security solutions such as SSL.

The diagram below depicts the web services security specifications stack:

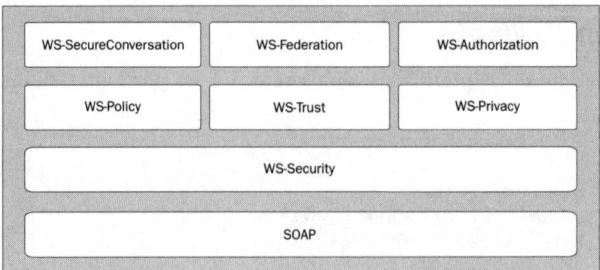

The only specification that is currently available is WS-Security; so let's look at the various blocks shown in the diagram above:

❑ **WS-Security**
Defines a secure messaging model. This extends SOAP to add security-related headers to SOAP envelopes. This security-related information includes signed and unsigned security tokens such as PK certificates, Kerberos tickets, user name/password, as well as digital signatures and encryption headers defined in accordance with the XML Signature and Encryption specifications.

❑ **WS-Policy**
Concentrates on the security policies and constraints defined by endpoint and intermediate players.

❑ **WS-Trust**
Enables web services to interoperate by defining a framework for trust models.

❑ **WS-Privacy**
Defines how web services and service consumers define privacy preferences.

❑ **WS-SecureConversation**
Defines how to manage and authenticate message exchanges.

❑ **WS-Federation**
Deals with trust relationships in a heterogeneous federated environment.

❑ **WS-Authorization**
Deals with authorization information and policies.

As we mentioned, WS-Security extends the SOAP messaging structure to provide message integrity, confidentiality, and authentication. It also provides an extensible mechanism of attaching security tokens with SOAP messages. As well as this, it provides facilities to encode binary security tokens such as X.509 certificates and Kerberos tickets. The listing below shows a simple example of sending a user name and password in a SOAP envelope as defined by the WS-Security specification:

```
<s:Envelope xmlns:s="http://www.w3c.org/2000/12/soap-envelope">
  <s:Header>
    <wsse:Security
      xmlns:wsse="http://schemas.xml.soap.org/ws/2002/04/secext">
      <wsse:UserNameToken>
        <wsse:UserName>Meeraj</wsse:UserName>
        <wsse:Password>wroxauthor528</wsse:Password>
      </wsse:UserNameToken>
    </wsse:Security>
  </s:Header>
  <s:Body>
    ...
  </s:Body>
</s:Header>
```

# Security Header Block

As we can see the `Security` element in the
`http://schemas.xml.soap.org/ws/2002/04/secext` namespace is used to pass security tokens inside the SOAP header. The contents of this header include security claims and signatures by which the sender of the message asserts the knowledge of a key. The contents of the security header block may be targeted to any receiver. The intended recipient of the header block can be specified using the standard SOAP actor attribute. A message may have more than one security header block.

However, no two security header blocks can have the same actors defined. Only one security header block may be defined without an actor attribute, and any intermediary, or the endpoint recipient, can consume this. This header block should not be removed before the message reaches the ultimate recipient.

The general structure of the security header block is shown below:

```
<s:Envelope xmlns:s="http://www.w3c.org/2000/12/soap-envelope">
  <s:Header>
    <wsse:Security
      xmlns:wsse="http://schemas.xml.soap.org/ws/2002/04/secext"
      S:actor="…"
      S:mustUnderstand="...">
      ...
    </wsse:Security>
  </s:Header>
  ...
</s:Header>
```

The contents of the `Security` element are not designed to provide extensible types of security information. Instead, it allows additional attributes to provide the extensibility mechanism. The WS-Security specification defines the following set of elements that can be used within the security header block:

- ❑ UserNameToken
  This is used for providing a user name and optional password information. The password can be sent either as clear text or a hash value.

- ❑ BinarySecurityToken
  This is used for encoding binary security tokens such as X.509 certificates, and Kerberos tickets.

- ❑ SecurityTokenReference
  This is used to provide reference to other services from which security tokens can be retrieved.

- ❑ ds:KeyInfo
  This belongs to the XML Signature namespace and is used to provide information regarding the keys for X.509 certificates among others.

- ❑ ds:Signature
  This is also from the XML Signature namespace and is used for providing digital signatures.

- ❑ xenc:ReferenceList, xenc:EncryptedKey, and xenc:EncryptedData
  These belong to the XML Encryption namespace and are used to provide encrypted information.

Let's now look at an example that demonstrates some of the topics we have covered.

# WS-Security in the StockQuote Service

In this section we will see how to sign the body part of the SOAP envelope representing the stock quote request on the client side. We will also look at how we send the signed information and the public key certificate of the signer, as a header block of the same SOAP envelope, to the stock quote service, in accordance with the WS-Security requirements for passing security tokens. The stock quote service will verify the signature using the certificate present in the SOAP envelope.

This is all achieved using the WSTK implementation of WS-Security. WSTK 3.2 provides two Axis handlers that can be used for processing binary security tokens according to the WS-Security requirements:

❑  `com.ibm.wstk.axis.handlers.SecurityReceiver`
    This can be used for verifying XML signatures and decrypting XML encrypted data

❑  `com.ibm.wstk.axis.handlers.SecuritySender`
    This can be used for generating XML signatures and creating XML encrypted data

The diagram below depicts the high-level architecture of using XML signature to create a digital signature of the stock request body part on the client side, and how it is verified on the server:

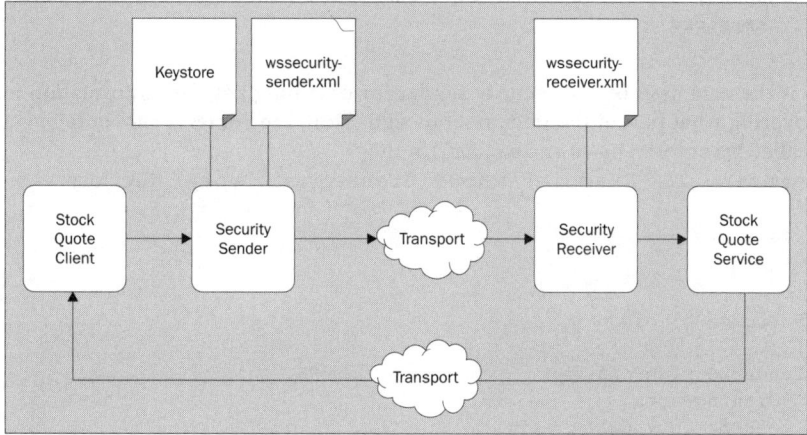

It is explained as follows:

❑  The client invokes the web service through the client-side security sender handler.

❑  The security sender first reads the `wssecurity-sender.xml` file to obtain information about which part of the document to sign and the key information required to sign the data.

❑  Then it accesses the keystore specified in the XML file and gets the private key and corresponding public key certificate for the key alias specified in the `config` file.

❑  The private key is used to sign the specified part of the SOAP request, and the signature and public key are added to that as a SOAP header block, as specified by the WS-Security specification.

❑  This envelope is then sent to the server.

❑    On the server the security receiver handler is invoked before the web service.

❑    This handler will access the `wssecurity-receiver.xml` file to find out how to verify the signature.

❑    If the signature is verified successfully, an information message is printed on the server and the service is invoked and the data is sent back to the client.

We will print the SOAP envelope before and after signing on the client side to illustrate the above process.

## Try It Out – Deploying and Accessing the Web Service

This section assumes that you have installed and configured WSTK successfully with Tomcat. Please refer to the earlier chapters for details on installing and configuring WSTK. Deploying and accessing the web service will involve the following steps:

**1.**    The command below will generate the key pair and public key certificate for you with the alias `meeraj`:

```
keytool -genkey -dname "CN=Meeraj Kunnumpurath, OU=I Solutions, O=EDS, L=Milton
Keynes, S=Bucks, C=UK" -alias meeraj -storepass password -keypass password -
keystore .keystore
```

**2.**    This is the data used by the security sender for obtaining keystore information and discovering what part of the document to sign. Store the contents shown below and store in a file called `wssecurity-sender.xml` in the `\Beginning_JWS_Examples\Chp09\SignedStockQuote\` directory:

```xml
<?xml version="1.0"?>
<clientbinding>
  <service-ref>
    <port-qname-binding>

      <SenderServiceConfig>
        <SigningParts>
          <Reference part="body"/>
        </SigningParts>
      </SenderServiceConfig>

      <SenderBindingConfig>
        <SigningKey>
          <KeyStore type="jks"
            path="c:/Beginning_JWS_Examples/Chp09/
                  SignedStockQuote/.keystore"
            storepass="password"/>
          <PrivateKey alias="meeraj" keypass="password"/>
        </SigningKey>
      </SenderBindingConfig>

    </port-qname-binding>
  </service-ref>
</clientbinding>
```

This configuration information states that the body part of the SOAP document should be signed using the private key identified by the alias `meeraj` in the keystore `\Beginning_JWS_Examples\Chp09\SignedStockQuote\.keystore`. Please note that the absolute path of this XML file should be specified in the client deployment descriptor, as we will see in a later section.

**3.** Now to create the server handler configuration data. This is the data used by the security receiver for obtaining information on how to verify the signature. Store the contents shown below in a file called `wssecurity-receiver.xml` in the `\Beginning_JWS_Examples\Chp09\SignedStockQuote\` directory:

```xml
<?xml version="1.0" encoding="UTF-8"?>
<wsbinding>
  <ws-desc-binding>
    <pc-binding>

      <ReceiverServiceConfig>
        <RequiredSignedParts>
          <Reference part="body"/>
        </RequiredSignedParts>
      </ReceiverServiceConfig>

      <ReceiverBindingConfig>
        <TrustAnchorList>
        <TrustAnyCertificate/>
        </TrustAnchorList>
      </ReceiverBindingConfig>

    </pc-binding>
  </ws-desc-binding>
</wsbinding>
```

The configuration information above states that the body part of the SOAP document should be verified using the public key certificate present in the document. Please note that the absolute path of this file should be specified in the client deployment descriptor, as we will see in a later section.

**4.** To deploy the service first store the contents shown below in a file called `ServerDeploy.wsdd`:

```xml
<deployment xmlns="http://xml.apache.org/axis/wsdd/"
xmlns:java="http://xml.apache.org/axis/wsdd/providers/java">
```

Define the security receiver handler and specify the absolute path to the configuration file:

```xml
<handler name="wssecurity-receiver"
  type="java:com.ibm.wstk.axis.handlers.SecurityReceiver">
  <parameter
    value="C:/Beginning_JWS_Examples/Chp09/
              SignedStockQuote/wssecurity-receiver.xml"
  name="configPath"/>
</handler>
```

Define the service with the handler to be invoked before the service:

```
<service name="StockQuoteService" provider="java:RPC">
  <requestFlow>
    <handler type="wssecurity-receiver"/>
  </requestFlow>
  <parameter value="com.wrox.jws.stockcore.StockCore" name="className"/>
  <parameter value="getQuote" name="allowedMethods"/>
</service>

</deployment>
```

**5.** Now run the `wstkenv` batch file present in the `bin` directory of WSTK to set up the required environment variables. Run the command shown below to deploy the service:

```
java -classpath %WSTK_CP% org.apache.axis.client.AdminClient
    -lhttp://localhost:8080/wstk/common/services/AdminService
     ServerDeploy.wsdd
```

**6.** To deploy the client chain, first store the contents shown below in a file called `ClientDeploy.wsdd`:

```
<deployment xmlns="http://xml.apache.org/axis/wsdd/"
xmlns:java="http://xml.apache.org/axis/wsdd/providers/java">
```

Define the handler to log the request and response to a file:

```
<handler name="log" type="java:org.apache.axis.handlers.LogHandler"/>
```

Define the security sender handler and specify the absolute path to the configuration file. This will also print the SOAP envelope before and after signing:

```
<handler
  name="wssecurity-sender"
  type="java:com.ibm.wstk.axis.handlers.SecuritySender">
  <parameter
    value="C:/Beginning_JWS_Examples/Chp09/
            SignedStockQuote/wssecurity-sender.xml"
    name="configPath"/>
  <parameter value="true" name="printBefore"/>
  <parameter value="true" name="printAfter"/>
</handler>
```

Define the service along with the request and response handler chain:

```
<service name="urn:StockQuoteServiceClient">
  <requestFlow>
    <handler type="log"/>
    <handler type="wssecurity-sender"/>
  </requestFlow>
  <responseFlow>
    <handler type="log"/>
  </responseFlow>
</service>

</deployment>
```

**7.** Now run the `wstkenv` batch file present in the `bin` directory of WSTK to set up the required environment variables. Run the command shown below to deploy the service:

```
java -classpath "%WSTK_CP%" org.apache.axis.utils.Admin client
    ClientUndeploy.wsdd
```

**8.** The client class in this case is slightly different, as the client now invokes the web service through the client handler instead of accessing it directly:

```
package com.wrox.jws.stockcore;

import org.apache.axis.AxisFault;
import org.apache.axis.client.Call;
import org.apache.axis.client.Service;
import org.apache.axis.encoding.XMLType;
import org.apache.axis.utils.Options;

import javax.xml.rpc.ParameterMode;
import javax.xml.namespace.QName;

import java.net.URL;

public class GetQuote {

  public static void main(String args[]) throws Exception {

    if(args == null || args.length < 2) {
      System.out.println("Usage: java GetQuote symbol url user password");
      System.exit(0);
    }

    String symbol = args[0] ;

    URL url = new URL(args[1]);

    Service  service = new Service();

    Call call = (Call) service.createCall();

    call.setTargetEndpointAddress( url );
```

Now the client accesses the handler first and the handler will access the web service depending on the endpoint URL:

```
call.setOperationName(new QName("urn:StockQuoteServiceClient",
    "getQuote"));
call.addParameter("symbol", XMLType.XSD_STRING, ParameterMode.IN );
call.setReturnType(XMLType.XSD_STRING);

if(args.length == 4) {
  call.setUsername(args[2]);
```

```
        call.setPassword(args[3]);
    }

    System.out.println(call.invoke( new Object[] {symbol}));

  }
}
```

**9.** Compile the client class as usual. To run the client class, run the `wstkenv` batch file present in the `bin` directory of WSTK to set up the required environment variables. Run the command shown below to deploy the service:

```
java -classpath %WSTK_CP% com.wrox.jws.stockcore.GetQuote IBM
    http://localhost:8080/wstk/common/services/StockQuoteService
```

This will invoke the web service, print the request SOAP envelope before and after signing, and print the result:

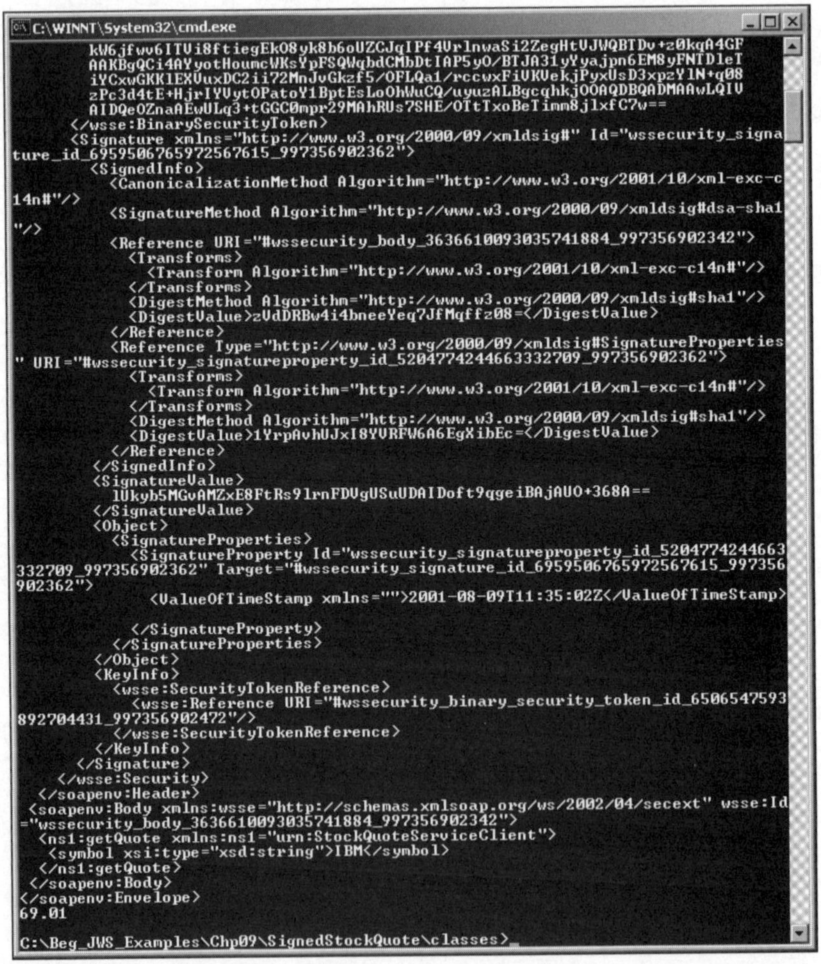

On the server side, the security receiver will verify the message and print a success message to the Tomcat console. Additionally, all the request and response messages will be stored into a file called `axis.log` in the current directory.

### How It Works

The best way to demonstrate what is happening here is by looking at the contents of the `axis.log` file, as it will show us what is happening throughout the procedure. The contents of this file are shown below:

```
=========================================================
= Elapsed: 38060 milliseconds
```

This is the request message:

```
= In message: <?xml version="1.0" encoding="UTF-8"?>
<soapenv: Envelope xmlns:SOAP-ENC="http://schemas.xmlsoap.org/soap/encoding/"
  xmlns:soapenv="http://schemas.xmlsoap.org/soap/envelope/"
  xmlns:xsd="http://www.w3.org/2001/XMLSchema"
  xmlns:xsi="http://www.w3.org/2001/XMLSchema-instance"
  soapenv:encodingStyle="http://schemas.xmlsoap.org/soap/encoding/">
<soapenv:Header>
```

The WS-Security security header is used to store the binary security token containing the public key certificate of the private key used to sign the data:

```
<wsse:Security xmlns:wsse="http://schemas.xmlsoap.org/ws/2002/04/secext"
  soapenv:mustUnderstand="1">
  <wsse:BinarySecurityToken EncodingType="wsse:Base64Binary"
Id="wssecurity_binary_security_token_id_5557806051649257235_1028127480620"
    ValueType="wsse:X509v3">
    MIIDDTCCAssCBD1H6a8wCwYHKoZIzjgEAwUAMGwxEDAOBgNVBAYTB1Vua25vd24xEDAO
    BgNVBAgTB1Vua25vd24xEDAOBgNVBAcTB1Vua25vd24xEDAOBgNVBAoTB1Vua25vd24x
    EDAOBgNVBAsTB1Vua25vd24xEDAOBgNVBAMTB1Vua25vd24wHhcNMDIwNzMxMTM0NDE1
    ...
    kUgABeC/3gFgaH5fGpdcFs9IpFc26EbRKud8joNToqSE7BRAreBOGNPv1CYqcZA2r5dG
    Fg4hIeUwZpxp9finV7cAgKfh3zHNFXnJoprQscP9x2fJOXdddw78O4L+uoK41DYKI4cX
    1WaEj47JIAoBMAsGByqGSM44BAMFAAMvADAsAhQVL09r6nmjkZHHtqDQUb+RHUcQXwIU
    Qiqe54Ckrd2pHjmYmQkbUdkS4aY=
  </wsse:BinarySecurityToken>
```

This element uses the XML Signature semantics to store the signature information:

```
<Signature xmlns="http://www.w3.org/2000/09/xmldsig#"
  Id="wssecurity_signature_id_2868516446223760635_1028127480510">
  <SignedInfo>
    <CanonicalizationMethod Algorithm="http://www.w3.org/2001/10/xml-
      exc-c14n#"/>
      <SignatureMethod Algorithm="http://www.w3.org/2000/09/xmldsig#dsa-
        sha1"/>
```

The reference URI points to the ID attribute of the SOAP body part that is actually signed:

```
<Reference
  URI="#wssecurity_body_1374006965804613176_1028127480510">
  <Transforms>
    <Transform Algorithm="http://www.w3.org/2001/10/xml-exc-
      c14n#"/>
  </Transforms>
```

This is the digest method that is used:

```
<DigestMethod
  Algorithm="http://www.w3.org/2000/09/xmldsig#sha1"/>
<DigestValue>VmwBN8J936LQP6O1/E/IK4cbN4c=</DigestValue>
</Reference>
<Reference
  Type="http://www.w3.org/2000/09/xmldsig#SignatureProperties"
URI="#wssecurity_signatureproperty_id_7160021005214925315_1028127480510">
  <Transforms>
    <Transform Algorithm="http://www.w3.org/2001/10/xml-exc-
      c14n#"/>
  </Transforms>
  <DigestMethod
    Algorithm="http://www.w3.org/2000/09/xmldsig#sha1"/>
  <DigestValue>dxKPmsgw3pjHcJqi+WwmqawzoEA=</DigestValue>
</Reference>
</SignedInfo>
```

This is the actual digital signature:

```
<SignatureValue>
  a5mYeRAsjnw3OoLp2PIjjMWU26AJTY3XtrU9MvuxmEKfJc8h7UWEpQ==
</SignatureValue>
<Object>
  <SignatureProperties>
    <SignatureProperty
Id="wssecurity_signatureproperty_id_7160021005214925315_1028127480510"
Target="#wssecurity_signature_id_2868516446223760635_1028127480510">
      <ValueOfTimeStamp xmlns="">2002-07-
        31T02:58:00Z</ValueOfTimeStamp>
    </SignatureProperty>
  </SignatureProperties>
</Object>
<KeyInfo>
  <wsse:SecurityTokenReference>
    <wsse:Reference
URI="#wssecurity_binary_security_token_id_5557806051649257235_1028127480620"
    />
  </wsse:SecurityTokenReference>
</KeyInfo>
</Signature>
</wsse:Security>
</soapenv:Header>
```

This is the information that is signed and is identified by the `Id` attribute:

```
<soapenv:Body xmlns:wsse="http://schemas.xmlsoap.org/ws/2002/04/secext"
    wsse:Id="wssecurity_body_1374006965804613176_1028127480510">
<ns1:getQuote xmlns:ns1="urn:StockQuoteServiceClient">
    <symbol xsi:type="xsd:string">IBM</symbol>
</ns1:getQuote>
</soapenv:Body>
</soapenv:Envelope>
```

This is the response from the stock quote web service:

```
= Out message: <?xml version="1.0" encoding="UTF-8"?>
<soapenv:Envelope xmlns:soapenv="http://schemas.xmlsoap.org/soap/envelope/"
    xmlns:xsd="http://www.w3.org/2001/XMLSchema"
    xmlns:xsi="http://www.w3.org/2001/XMLSchema-instance">
    <soapenv:Body>
      <ns1:getQuoteResponse
        soapenv:encodingStyle="http://schemas.xmlsoap.org/soap/encoding/"
        xmlns:ns1="urn:StockQuoteServiceClient">
        <getQuoteReturn xsi:type="xsd:string">69.01</getQuoteReturn>
      </ns1:getQuoteResponse>
    </soapenv:Body>
</soapenv:Envelope>

=========================================================
```

# SAML

**SAML**, or **Security Assertion Markup Language** is an XML-based framework for exchanging security information, mainly in a federated environment. It is an OASIS specification addressing the following issues:

❑   Single sign-on

❑   Authorization services

❑   Back office transactions

Security information is expressed in terms of assertions about subjects. Subjects can be any entity that has an identity in a security domain. Assertions state whether a subject has been authenticated, or is authorized to access a resource, or has a specified set of attributes. The main types of assertions are:

❑   **Authentication Assertion**
For example, an issuing authority asserts that subject, Fred Flintstone, was authenticated at 10:00 in the morning using a rock swipe card. An example of an SAML excerpt asserting this authentication is shown below:

```
<saml:Assertion
  MajorVersion="1"
  MinorVersion="0"
  AssertionID="123"
```

```
    Issuer="Acme.com"
    IssueInstant="2001-12-12T:10:00:00Z">
    <saml:Conditions
      NotBefore="2001-12-12T:10:00:00Z"
      NotAfter="2001-12-12T:10:15:00Z"/>
    <saml:AuthenticationStatement
      AuthenticationMethod="RockSwipe"
      AuthenticationInstant="2001-12-12T:10:04:00Z">
      <saml:Subject>
        <saml:NameIdentifier
          SecurityDomain="Acme.com"
          Name="FredFlintstone"/>
      </saml:Subject>
    </saml:AuthenticationStatement>
</saml:Assertion>
```

❑ **Attribute Assertion**

For example, an issuing authority asserts that Fred Flintstone's (the subject's), department is Heavy Lifting. Here the department is the attribute and the value is Heavy Lifting. An example of SAML attribute assertion is shown below:

```
<saml:Assertion
  MajorVersion="1"
  MinorVersion="0"
  AssertionID="123"
  Issuer="Acme.com"
  IssueInstant="2001-12-12T:10:00:00Z">
  <saml:Conditions
    NotBefore="2001-12-12T:10:00:00Z"
    NotAfter="2001-12-12T:10:15:00Z"/>
  <saml:AttributeStatement>
    <saml:Subject>
      <saml:NameIdentifier
        SecurityDomain="Acme.com"
        Name="FredFlintstone"/>
    </saml:Subject>
    <saml:Attribute
      AttributeName="Department"
      AttributeNamespace="Acme.com">
      <saml:AttributeValue>Heavy Lifting</saml:AttributeValue>
    </saml:Attribute>
  </saml:AttributeStatement >
</saml:Assertion>
```

❑ **Authorization Decision Assertion**

This asserts on the authority of a subject to perform an action on a resource. For example the subject Fred Flintstone is given access to fiddle the payroll information:

```
<saml:Assertion
  MajorVersion="1"
  MinorVersion="0"
  AssertionID="123"
```

```
Issuer="Acme.com"
IssueInstant="2001-12-12T:10:00:00Z">
<saml:Conditions
   NotBefore="2001-12-12T:10:00:00Z"
   NotAfter="2001-12-12T:10:15:00Z"/>
<saml:AuthorizationDecisionStatement
   Decision="Permit"
   Resource="Payroll">
   <saml:Actions Namespace="Acme.com/Payroll">
     <saml:Action>Fiddle</saml:Action>
   </saml:Actions>
   <saml:Subject>
     <saml:NameIdentifier
        SecurityDomain="Acme.com"
        Name="FredFlintstone"/>
   </saml:Subject>
</saml:AuthorizationDecisionStatement>
</saml:Assertion>
```

# Assertion Exchange Protocol

SAML uses a request-response protocol for acquiring assertions. Assertions queries are sent using the assertion request messages and the responses are received as assertion statements. The excerpt below shows an authentication assertion request:

```
<samlp:Request
  MajorVerion="1"
  ...>
  <samlp:AuthenticationQuery>
    <saml:Subject>
      <saml:NameIdentifier
         SecurityDomain="Acme.com"
         Name="FredFlintstone"/>
    </saml:Subject>
  <samlp:AuthenticationQuery>
</samlp:Request>
```

The response to this request will contain an authorization assertion statement as well as status messages indicating the state of the assertion. Similar types exist for attribute and authorization decision assertions.

# Protocol Bindings

The baseline binding for encoding SAML encoding requests and responses is SOAP over HTTP. Other bindings, including raw HTTP, will follow in course of time. Vendors have started supporting SAML in their products for providing security services such as single sign-on, authentication, back-office transactions, and do on. JSAML is a Java implementation of SAML that is available for free from Netigrity (http://www.netigrity.com).

# Summary

In this chapter we have covered the various security issues in the context of web services. First we started by discussing basic security concerns and had a look at the traditional security solutions that addressed these issues. Then we had a look at the Java support for traditional security solutions. We looked at the shortcomings of traditional security solutions in solving the issues in the web services world.

After that we looked at the various XML specifications that form the foundations for the latest web services security specification. We concluded the chapter by looking at WS-Security and SAML, the two most dominant security specifications currently targeting the web services world.

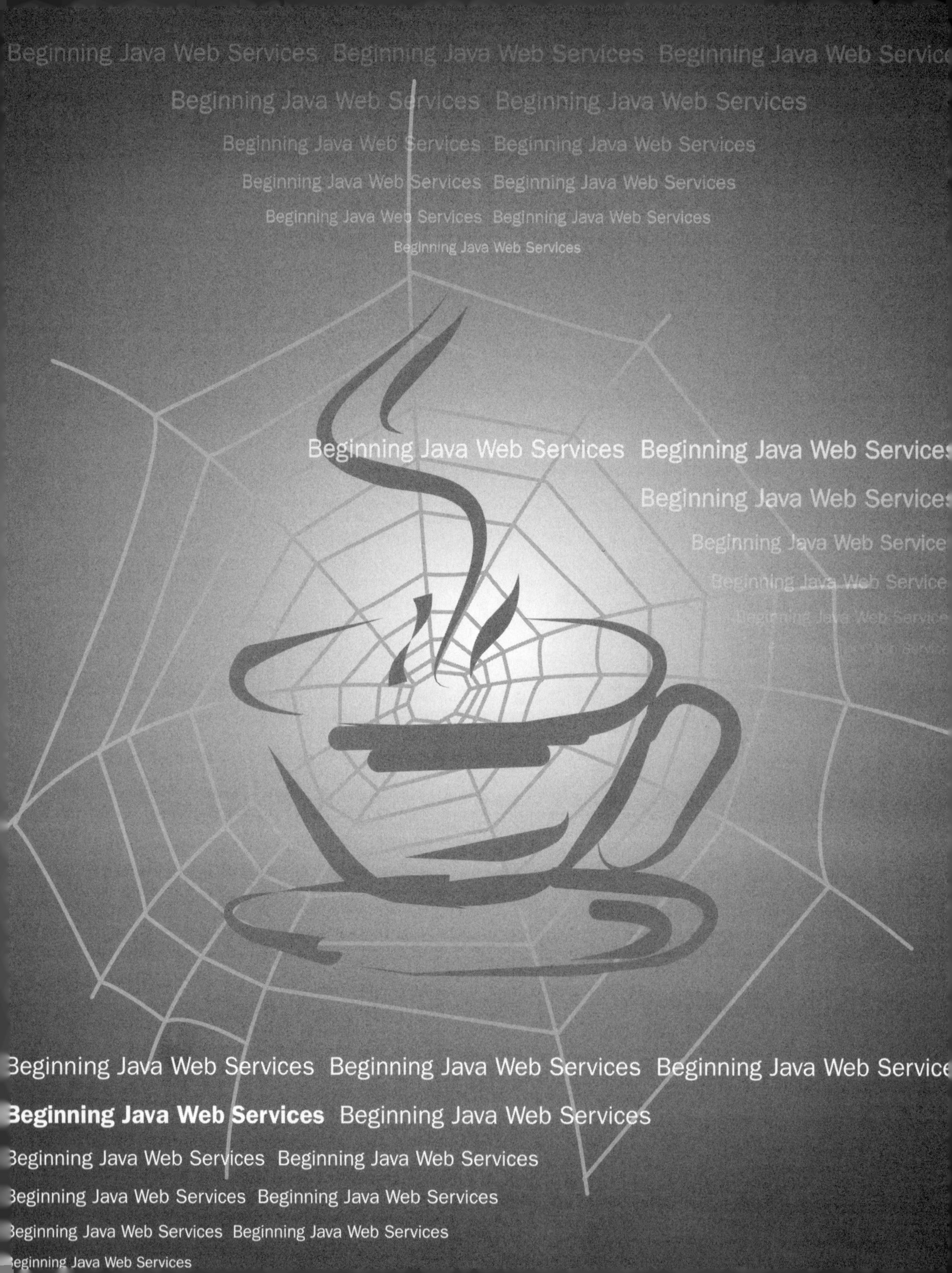
Beginning Java Web Services Beginning Java Web Services
Beginning Java Web Services Beginning Java Web Services
Beginning Java Web Services Beginning Java Web Services
Beginning Java Web Services Beginning Java Web Services
Beginning Java Web Services Beginning Java Web Services
Beginning Java Web Services
Beginning Java Web Services Beginning Java Web Services
Beginning Java Web Services
Beginning Java Web Services Beginning Java Web Services
Beginning Java Web Services Beginning Java Web Services
Beginning Java Web Services Beginning Java Web Services
Beginning Java Web Services Beginning Java Web Services
Beginning Java Web Services Beginning Java Web Services
Beginning Java Web Services

# Web Services Products and Tools

The previous chapters of this book had focused on the fundamentals of web services with illustrative examples using Java, SOAP, and XML. This chapter will focus on a number of tools available commercially that can make the design, development, and deployment of web services a simple, straightforward task.

After completing the last nine chapters, you should have a firm grasp of the complexities involved in developing web services, and are now ready to see how easy it can be. In this chapter we will be looking specifically at:

- ❑ BEA WebLogic Workshop
- ❑ IBM WebSphere Application Developer
- ❑ IBM WebSphere SDK for web services

All of the tools that we examine here can be downloaded over the web. Some are trial software, with a limited lifespan while others are freeware. It is not the intent of the author or Wrox to endorse any specific product nor will we make any comparisons between these products. Our intent is to illustrate some of the ways in which available tools make the development of web services simpler, by providing graphical interfaces, generating WSDL and SOAP messages, and other conveniences.

## An Example

The easiest way to understand the capabilities of a tool is to try it with a simple example. In this case, we'll go back to the checking account example from Chapter 1. We'll create a simple API that allows us to create an account, enter transactions, get a balance, and get a transaction listing. We'll take a look at how this plays out in the various tools.

In order to store our transaction information, we are going to need a database. The figure below shows a data model for our application. The database is very simple. It consists of an ACCOUNT table, a TRANSACTIONS table, and a TRANSACTION_TYPE table for lookup information. The ACCOUNT table has an ACCOUNT_NUMBER attribute as the key field and a simple character attribute for the OWNER. The TRANSACTION_TYPE table has two attributes – a TRANS_CODE for a key and a TRANSACTION_TYPE field to describe the transaction. The TRANSACTIONS table holds all the transactions for our system.

All of the fields are part of the key, which is a simplification, and results in the inability to put in matching transaction types on the same day (for example, two withdrawals from an ATM of $100 each) but it's not too much of a simplification, and saves us from having to come up with a mechanism for generating a transaction number. Attributes of the TRANSACTIONS table include the ACCOUNT_NUMBER, the TRANS_CODE from the TRANSACTION_TYPE table, the TRANSACTION_DATE, the TRANSACTION_AMOUNT, and the TRANSACTION_DESC, a description of the transaction.

The following is a diagram of this structure:

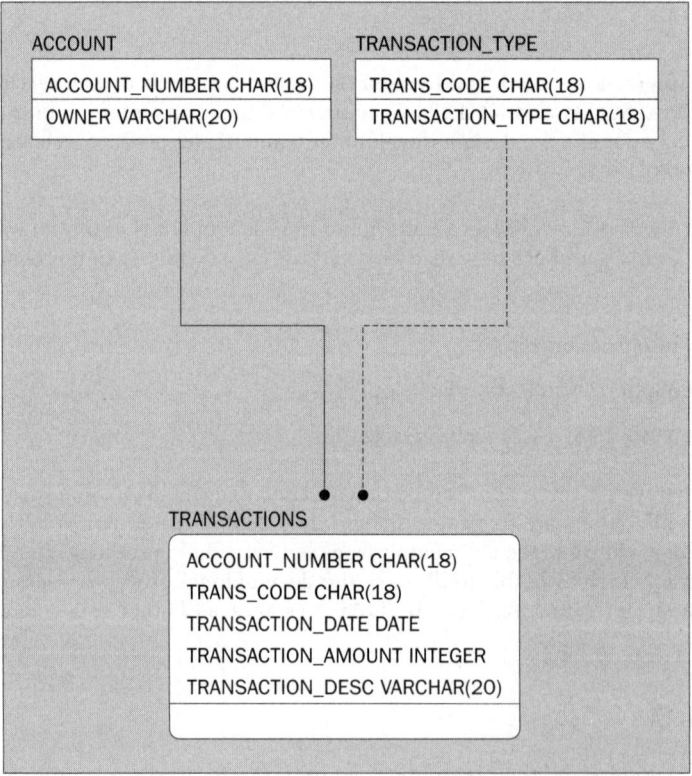

Now that we have a database design, we need a database to hold our information. We will be using MySQL; however, please feel free to use any database of your choice. The latest version of MySQL can be obtained from http://www.mysql.com. For more details on MySQL please refer to *Beginning Databases with MySQL* from *Wrox Press (ISBN 1-86100-692-6)*.

# Create the Checking Database

Now that we have selected the database server, let's create a new database, which we will be using throughout this chapter.

## Try It Out – Create the Database

**1.** To create the database, we will execute the following SQL query:

```
CREATE DATABASE CHECKING;
```

**2.** Now that the database exists, we need to build the tables. For this we will again execute a SQL script. The entire script is shown below:

```
USE CHECKING;

CREATE TABLE ACCOUNT
(
  ACCOUNT_NUMBER  CHAR(18) NOT NULL,
  OWNER  VARCHAR(20),

  PRIMARY KEY (ACCOUNT_NUMBER)
);

CREATE TABLE TRANSACTION_TYPE (
  TRANS_CODE  CHAR(18) NOT NULL,
  TRANSACTION_TYPE  CHAR(18),

  PRIMARY KEY (TRANS_CODE)
);

CREATE TABLE TRANSACTIONS (
  ACCOUNT_NUMBER  CHAR(18) NOT NULL,
  TRANS_CODE  CHAR(18) NOT NULL,
  TRANSACTION_DATE  DATE NOT NULL,
  TRANSACTION_AMOUNT  INTEGER NOT NULL,
  TRANSACTION_DESC  VARCHAR(20) NOT NULL,

  PRIMARY KEY (ACCOUNT_NUMBER, TRANS_CODE, TRANSACTION_DATE,
    TRANSACTION_AMOUNT, TRANSACTION_DESC)
);
```

**3.** Now that the database tables exist, we'll populate a few rows for testing purposes. If all goes right, we'll have three transaction types, one account, and three transactions. Here's the script:

```
INSERT INTO TRANSACTION_TYPE VALUES ('DEBIT', 'Debit transaction');
INSERT INTO TRANSACTION_TYPE VALUES ('CREDIT', 'Credit transaction');
INSERT INTO TRANSACTION_TYPE VALUES ('CHECK', 'Check');

INSERT INTO ACCOUNT VALUES ('1','Sean Rhody');
```

```
INSERT INTO TRANSACTIONS VALUES ('1', 'CREDIT', "2002-06-18", 1000,
   'Opening Balance');
INSERT INTO TRANSACTIONS VALUES ('1', 'DEBIT', "2002-06-18", -500,
   'ATM Withdrawal');
INSERT INTO TRANSACTIONS VALUES ('1', 'CHECK', "2002-06-18", -250,
   '#1001');
```

Note that our checkbook only deals in INTEGER values. Also note that we must have a negative value for the transaction amount of a DEBIT or a CHECK. This lets our code be very basic – we don't have to look at the transaction type to determine the sign of the transaction amount. If we get everything correct, a simple SQL statement will show us with a balance of $250. If we execute this statement:

```
SELECT Sum(transaction_amount) as CHECKBOOK_BALANCE
FROM transactions WHERE account_number = '1'
```

we get the result as shown below:

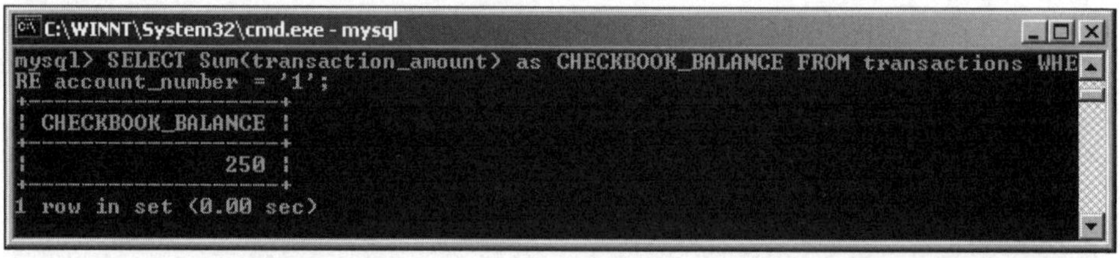

Now that we've got a database to work with, we can see how to develop web services using some tools.

# BEA WebLogic Workshop

We can download BEA WebLogic Workshop from the site http://developer.bea.com/products/product.jsp?highlight=wlw.

WebLogic Workshop is designed to be a high-level tool for corporate developers and business analysts. It features a graphical interface that allows us to build web services in a fairly intuitive fashion by wiring components and services together. It provides the underlying WSDL and SOAP definitions and automatically deploys to WebLogic Application Server 7.0, which is included with Workshop.

## Installation

The Workshop comes with a straightforward installation utility. Simply click on the executable to bring up the installation program.

Like most wizard-based installations, this is a multiple step process. We accepted most of the defaults, including the location of the BEA Home, (C:\bea). This home represents the root of the file system that BEA uses to deploy all of its files. It's where the actual deployed code will reside.

We are also asked to select an installation type. Again, we choose the default one – **Typical Installation**. In most cases this is desirable, as most of the reference materials will be based on the typical installation. There are times where more complex circumstances (such as multiple developers, or shared file systems, may warrant a custom installation.

Finally we have to choose the location of the WebLogic Platform. This is actually the location of the WebLogic Application Server. Again, it's important to remember this, because all of the scripts will refer to this directory:

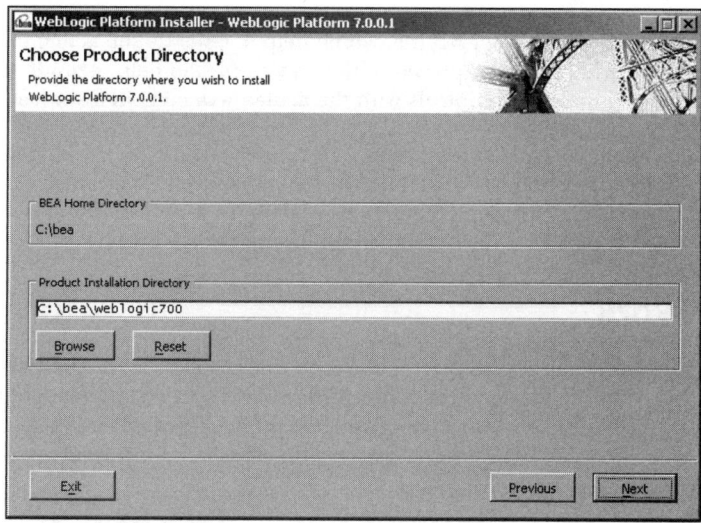

Once we've got the installation completed, we can start the Workshop by accessing the menu choice Start | Programs | BEA WebLogic Platform 7.0 | WebLogic Workshop | WebLogic Workshop. This opens the development environment, as shown below:

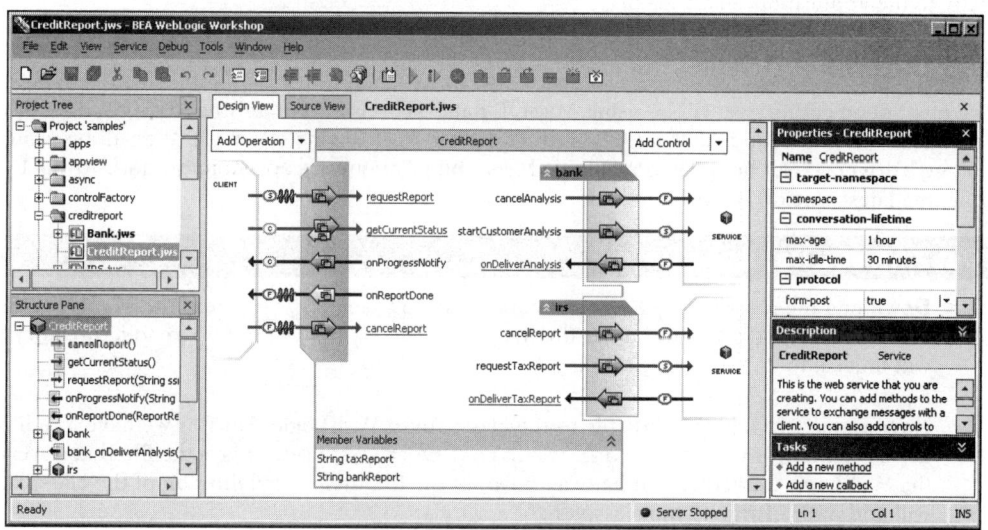

The Workshop is designed to allow us to do most of our work through menus, links, and dialog boxes, rather than spending too much time writing Java code. If we look under the covers, we'll see that it creates EJBs for us, but it's not something we would notice while creating the code.

The previous image shows one of the examples in full view. When we create a new web service, the Workshop creates a file called a .jws (Java Web Service) file. We can edit this, but again, not entirely directly. Some editing is done via properties on the right-hand side of the interface. Additionally, editing is done by writing code in the Source View panel. There are also dialog boxes or wizards that generate code.

Workshop inserts special tags into the JWS file, which help it generate the actual implementation, similar to the code that early Java IDEs placed in the .java files to help them do things, such as synchronize graphic development of controls with the actual Java code in a source file.

In brief, Workshop is about controls and services. We create web services, add methods, callback functions and member variables, and work with a variety of controls. We can string one web service into another, or access existing EJB implementations as well. In just a few pages, we will be creating the Checking web service, but first we need to do a little preparation work.

# Preparation Work

On the bottom of the Workshop screen there's a section that displays either Server Running or Server Stopped. If the server is not running, we can start it from the Tools | Start WebLogic Server menu choice. It may take a little while to start up because, behind the scenes, Workshop is running a cmd file to start the server. Knowing this is important, because the classpath for the server is set in this command file, and we'll be altering it in the next few steps.

While we will be doing most of our work in the WebLogic Workshop, we're going to have to do some work in WebLogic Application Server itself. That's because this is where we define database connections. Later versions of Workshop will probably have a database connectivity feature, but the present version lacks the ability to allow us to define our database information. So we have to go directly to the application server itself.

## Add the Database Driver

As we mentioned earlier, we will be using MySQL database server. For getting MySQL to work with WebLogic, we will have to add MySQL's JDBC driver to WebLogic's classpath. We will be using the mm.mysql driver. It can be freely downloaded from http://mmmysql.sourceforge.net/. At the time of writing, the latest version is 2.0.14.

### Try It Out – MySQL Database Driver

1.  Download the mm.mysql-2.0.14-you-must-unjar-me.jar from the MySQL site http://www.mysql.com/ and unjar the file mm.mysql-2.0.14-bin.jar to a directory (we will unjar it to C:\mysql\jdbc).

2.  Now we have to add this JAR file to the classpath of WebLogic. For this we have to edit the file C:\bea\WebLogic700\server\bin\StartWLS.cmd. This is the file that starts up the WebLogic Server. About halfway down in the file there is a definition of the classpath. We will add our JAR file to the classpath:

```
@rem Set first two positional parameters to SERVER_NAME and ADMIN_URL
if not "%1" == "" if "%SERVER_NAME%" == "" set SERVER_NAME=%1
if not "%2" == "" if "%ADMIN_URL%" == "" set ADMIN_URL=%2
```

```
set CLASSPATH= %JAVA_HOME%\lib\tools.jar;C:\mysql\jdbc\mm.mysql-2.0.14-
bin.jar;%WL_HOME%\server\lib\weblogic_sp.jar;%WL_HOME%\server\lib\weblogic.jar;%C
LASSPATH%
```

```
set PATH=.;%WL_HOME%\server\bin;%JAVA_HOME%\bin;%PATH%
@rem Import extended environment
if exist extEnv.cmd call extEnv.cmd
```

Without these changes, WebLogic will not be able to find the mm.mysql driver. We have to stop and start WebLogic Server for this change to take effect.

**3.** Once we've done so, we're ready to define the database components we'll need. To do so, open a browser and type http://localhost:7001/console. This brings up the WebLogic Server Console, using the default WebLogic port (7001), which is a JSP application:

> By default, during installation, the initial user name and password are set to
> `installadministrator`.

**4.** Logging into the server provides us with the console, which is part JSP, and part applet. In order to be able to use our database, we need to do the following:

- ❑ Configure a connection pool
- ❑ Configure either a data source or a transaction data source
- ❑ Ensure that the connection pool is targeted at the correct server
- ❑ Ensure that the data source is targeted at the correct server
- ❑ Restart the server

In earlier releases, we worked with a database connection directly, but now we can work through a data source, which is connected to a connection pool. A connection pool enables sharing of a small set of database connections by a larger group of users. Since connections are only used periodically, we can typically service a much larger set of clients with a small number of connections.

A connection pool is used to mitigate the inherent expense associated with the process of opening database connections. Where the developer writes code to open and use connections, the work of the pool goes on behind the scenes by reallocating existing connections rather than creating new ones. The pool expands automatically if more simultaneous connections are required than the pool would normally provide.

**5.** To create a connection pool, go to the Services Configurations section on the main page. Then select the Connection Pools link, which is listed under the JDBC heading:

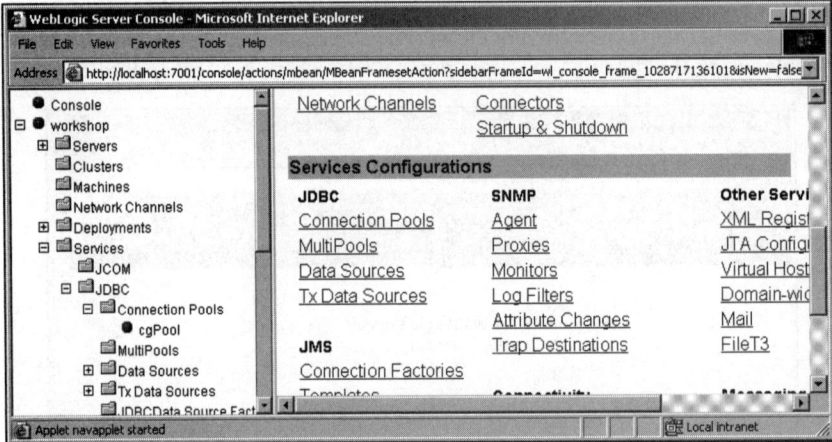

**6.** This brings up the connection pool page, where we can create a new connection. To create a new connection pool click on the Configure a new JDBC Connection Pool link:

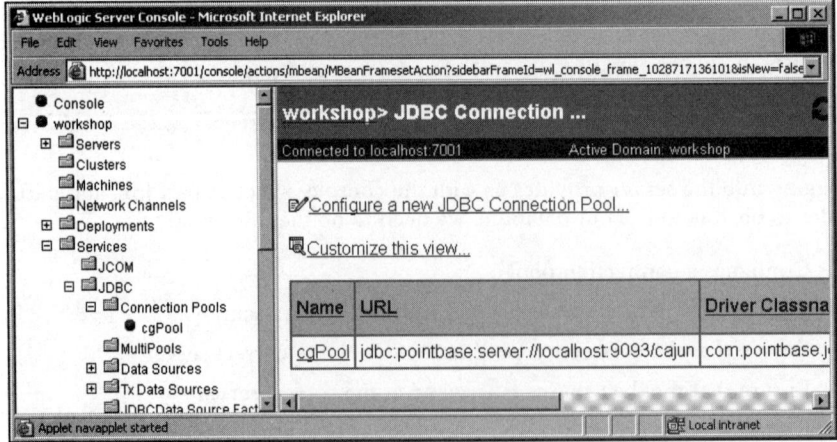

**7.** We need to define the parameters for the connection pool. We can define the name as anything we like, but for our example we will be using `CheckingPool`:

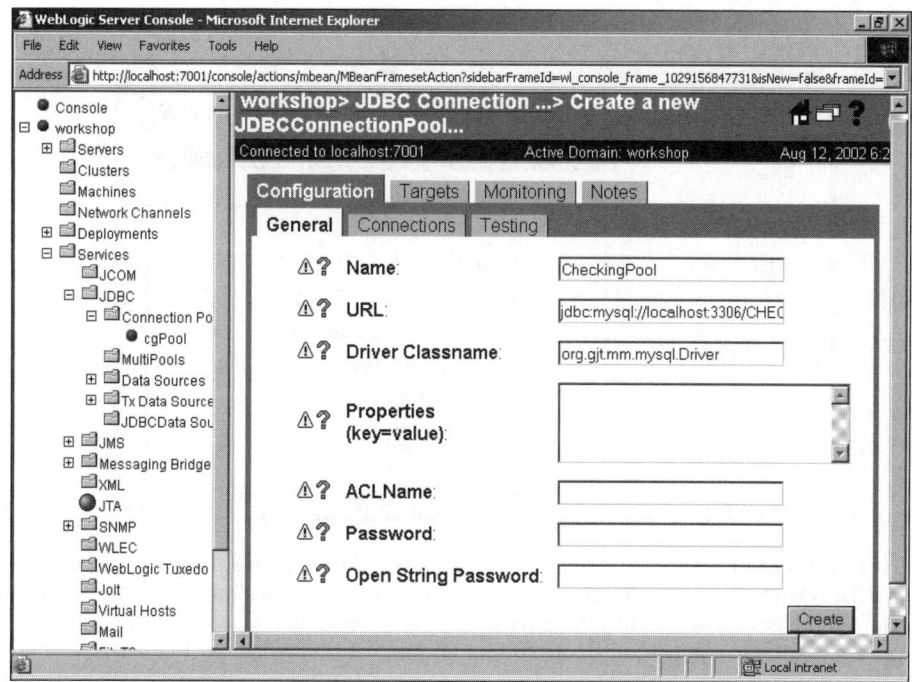

The URL tells the pool which instance to connect to – in this case we want `jdbc:mysql://localhost:3306/CHECKING?user=sa&password=wrox123`.

> Please note that in the URL, you will have to replace **'sa'** and **'wrox123'** by your database login name and password.

The Driver Classname should be `org.gjt.mm.mysql.Driver`, as we are using the MM.MySQL driver. Remember Java is case sensitive so be use to use the appropriate case.

The Properties section allows us to define other parameters but we will leave it blank. We can also leave ACL Name, Password, and Open String Password blank.

**8.** Once we've configured the connection pool, we need to attach it to a data source. There are two types of data sources – transactional, and non-transactional. The former allows participation with the transaction management mechanism of the J2EE container. It's not strictly necessary for us to use a transactional source, as we're not doing multiple SQL calls or anything, which would require an atomic transaction, but the setup of both sources is identical. If we did decide to use transactions later, we are covered if we use a transactional source right from the start.

To create the data source, we can expand the JDBC section of the tree on the left, and click on TX Data Sources, and then select Configure a new JDBC Tx Data Source, which brings up the screen shown below:

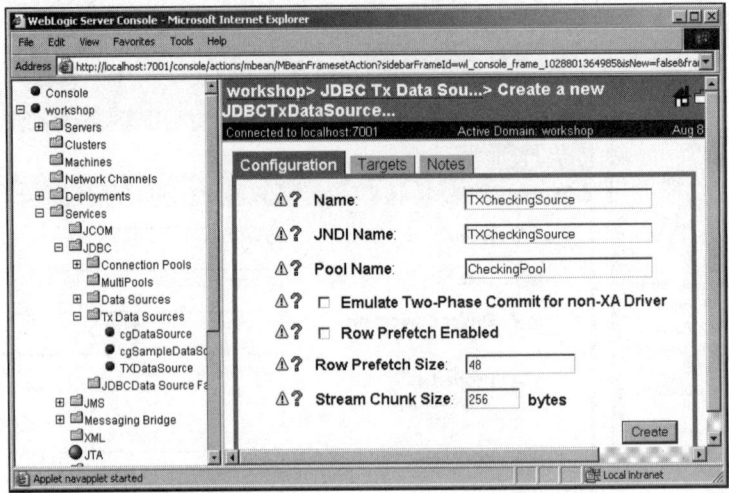

This allows us to designate an internal name; we will use `TXCheckingSource`. It also allows a JNDI Name, which is what the Workshop will use. Again, we'll use `TXCheckingSource`. The Pool Name is what links the data source to a connection pool; we'll use our `CheckingPool` connection pool. The remaining values can be left blank.

**9.** We now need to make sure that we have actually targeted the server for the connection pool and the data source correctly; otherwise we'll generate errors. This section is critical, if we fail to deploy the components to the target server, then our code will not work.

To do this, go back to the `CheckingPool` connection pool, which we had earlier made, and click on the Targets tab to bring up the screen shown below:

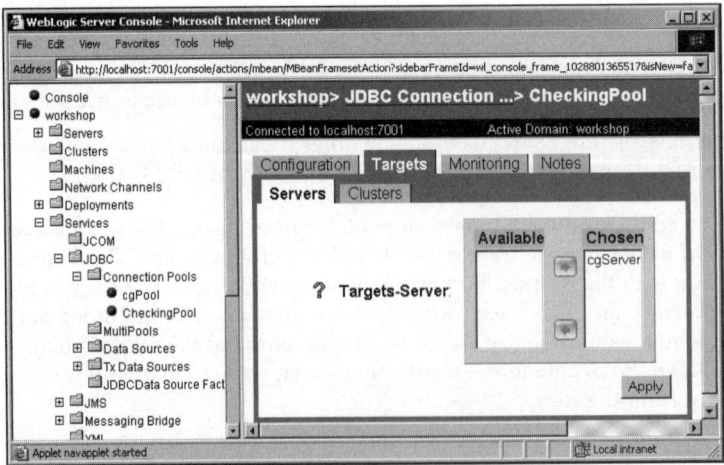

This screen allows us to designate which servers the pool will be deployed to. In our case there is only one available server, cgServer, which is the default server. So we will be selecting it. Note that it's possible to run multiple servers on a single machine, and they do not have to be symmetric (not every component needs to be deployed on every server).

**10.** Likewise, we need to target the server for the data source; we will do in a similar fashion. We can reach this screen by clicking on the JDBC folder, expanding the TX Data Source folder, then clicking on the TXCheckingSource data source and finally clicking on the Targets tab:

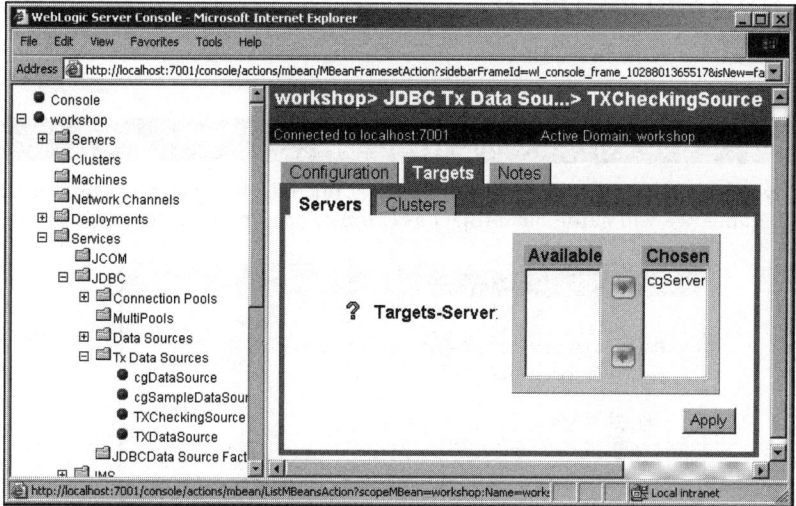

**11.** We should now stop and start the server from the Tools menu of Workshop. Once this is done, log in again and click on Servers, then the cgServer icon. Click on the Services tab and then select JDBC. If all is well we should see the CheckingPool service listed, like this:

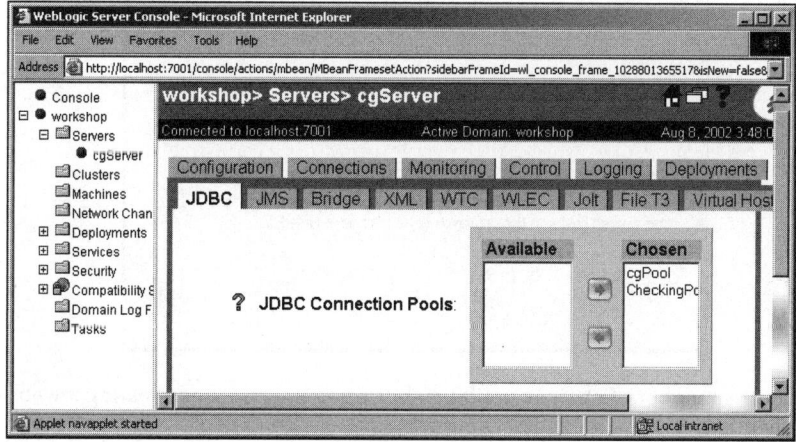

Now we're ready to develop a web service using this connection pool.

## *Troubleshooting Tips*

Most of the common causes of problems lie in getting the classpath right and in ensuring that the connection pool and data source are deployed correctly. When WebLogic starts, it displays a console window. We can see the classpath displayed in the messages generated here; though it can be a little tricky to read them. Use the Target tabs in the JDBC section to ensure that the services are properly deployed – it's easy to miss one and have our whole day ruined when our web service fails.

# Creating the Web Service

Now for the moment we've been waiting for – let's use the Workshop to create a web service.

## Try It Out – Create a Web Service Using Workshop

**1.** Start by selecting New Project from the File Menu. This brings up a dialog box asking for the project name; we will name our project as Checking. The next screen is shown below:

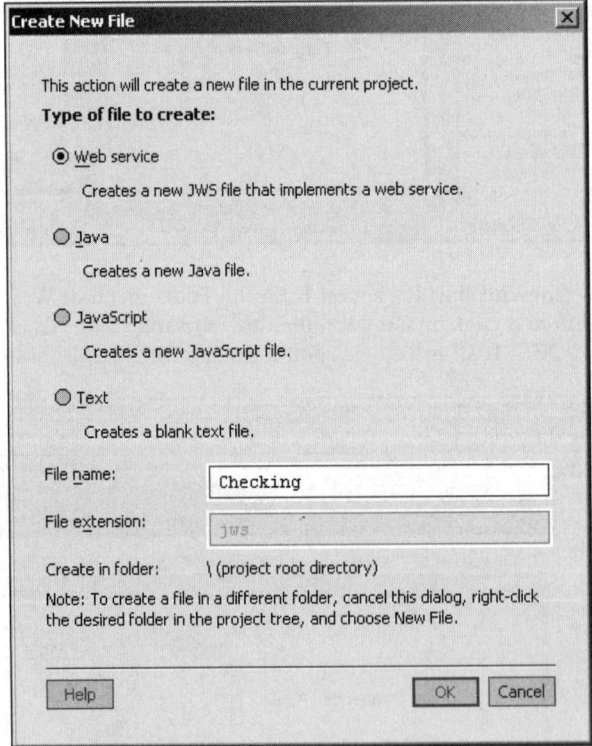

There are a number of choices available, but we're interested in creating a web service, so we'll pick that, also we will enter the File name as Checking.

**2.** We are now looking at a partially completed web service:

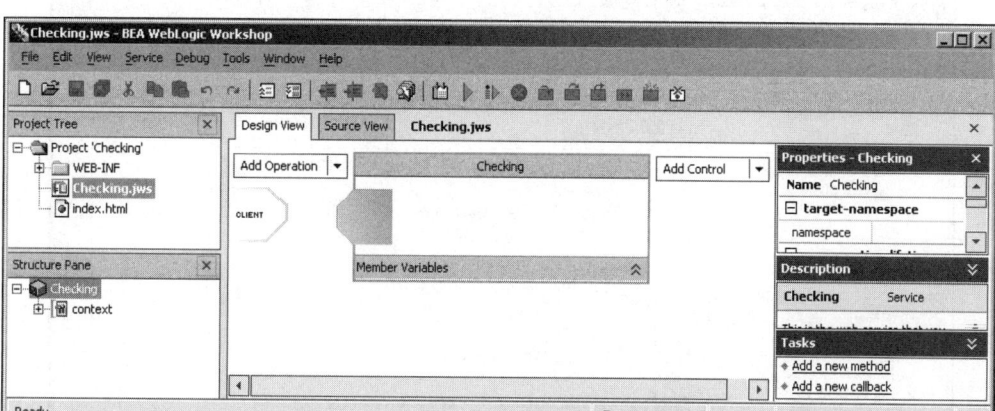

As we can see from the above screenshot, in the **Design View** there are two drop-down menus; on the left is the **Add Operation** dropdown, and on the right is the **Add Control** dropdown. The **Add Operation** dropdown allows us to add either methods or callbacks. Methods are for synchronous operations; callbacks are for asynchronous operations.

**3.** To add a new method, click on the **Add Operation** drop down and select **Add Method**. This adds a new method, which we will rename as `createAccount`. This method will be responsible for creating a new account in the `Account` table.

**4.** The figure below shows the effect of right clicking on the arrow. We can select Go to Code in .jws as the option in order to edit the function:

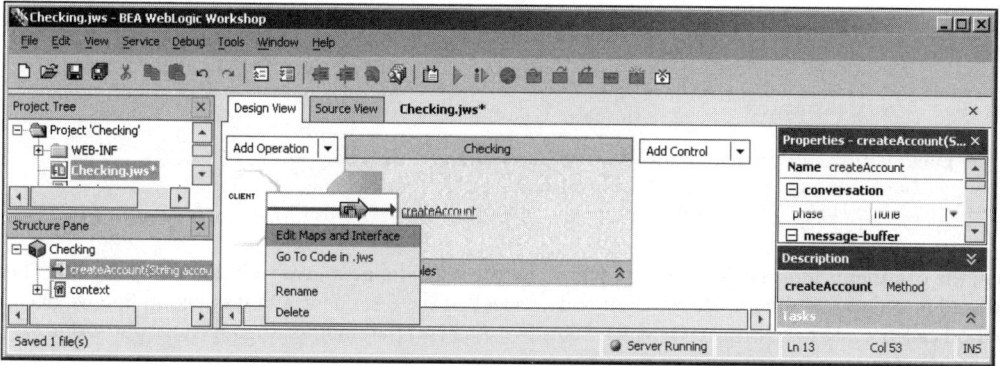

The figure below shows the `createAccount()` method in the editor. As mentioned earlier, the Workshop inserts tags (for example, `@jws:operation`) into the source file to help it generate the code it needs to deploy the web service:

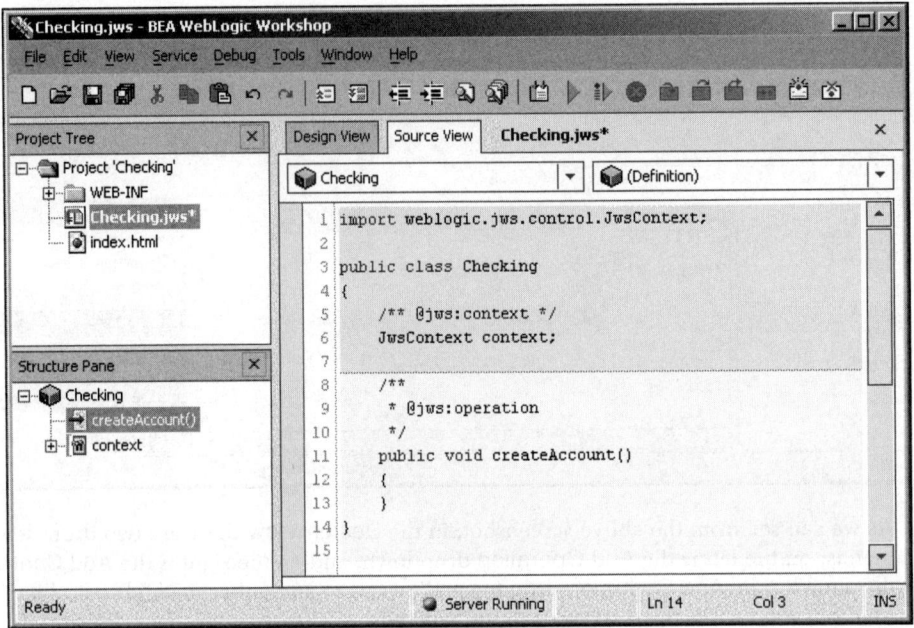

Do not remove these tags as the editor and the underlying code generation rely on them.

**5.** Now let's modify the `createAccount()` method. What we want is an account number and an owner name, both of which are strings. We want to store this in the database, creating a new account in the `Account` table. To do this, we're going to need a database control. We'll get to that in a minute, but first let's look at the code for the method:

```
/**
 * @jws:operation
 */
public void createAccount(String accountno, String owner) {
  CheckingControl.insertAccount(accountno, owner);
}
```

First, the comments (normal Javadoc comments, by the way) define a Java web service operation. These tags are used in generating the implementation code, as well as the test client. On the second line we declare a method called `createAccount()` which takes two `String` parameters, `accountno` and `owner`.

The single line of code within the method accesses the database control and calls a function on it to insert a new account. The method is shown in the screenshot opposite. We can see that Workshop highlights the method under development in a different color. It does some rudimentary syntax checking and can catch and flag simple errors. For example, if we forget to define the type of the parameter, Workshop will flag the name with a small red mark.

It's also possible to see the mapping of XML messages to the methods. The figure below shows the mapping of XML to the `createAccount()` method. Note that we don't have to do this ourselves – as the method parameters are defined, they are automatically mapped to XML:

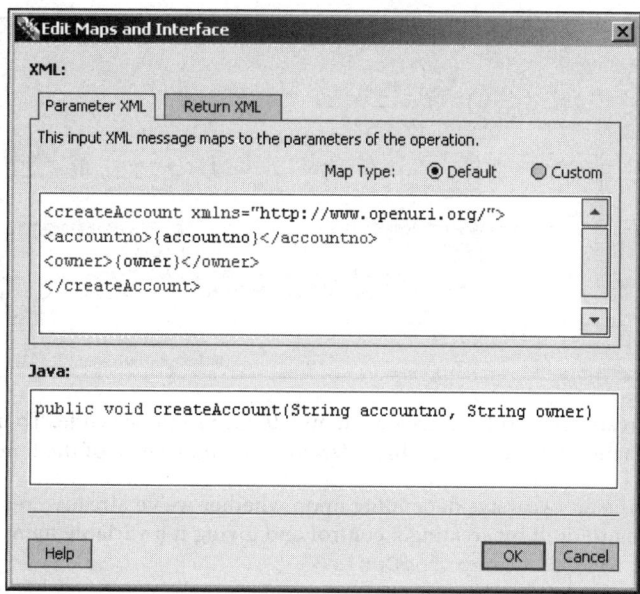

Now let's look at adding a control.

## Adding a Control

Workshop comes with five types of controls, and they are as follows:

| Control | Function |
| --- | --- |
| Service | Used to turn another web service into a control for use in the current web service under development. This allows us to treat any web service as just another component in our toolkit. |
| Timer | Allows us to provide delay or time services. It's useful mainly for testing or for setting up time-dependent responses in asynchronous services. |
| Database | Takes a JNDI data source and turns it into a control. As we will see, we can write SQL statements that become methods of the control. |
| EJB | Allows us to utilize an Enterprise JavaBean as a control within our web service. This is extremely useful for migrating existing J2EE applications to web services. |
| JMS | Allows the inclusion of JMS messaging services within a web service. The combination of EJB and JMS controls allows web services to wrapper almost every facet of J2EE Development. |

Let's create the database control that we need to support our Checking web service.

**1.** Click on the **Add Control** dropdown and select **Add Database Control** like this:

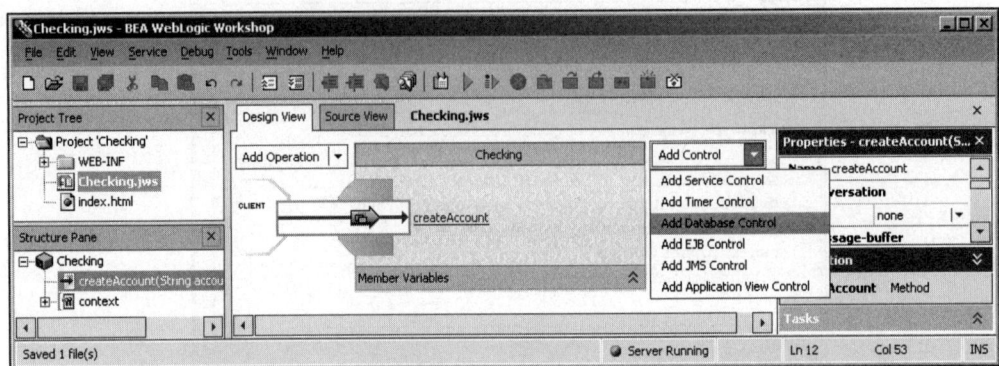

When we create a control, we create a template for use in our code. To utilize this template, we have to actually create a variable reference for an instance of the template.

**2.** We can do this in two ways depending upon whether we've already created a control or not. We are going to do it by creating a control and giving it a variable name at the same time; in this case we will call it CheckingControl.

**3.** As we are creating a new control, we click on the second radio button and give it a name – CheckingCTRLControl. If, the control already existed we would have to click on the first option. Finally, we need to tie it to our JNDI data source, TXCheckingSource:

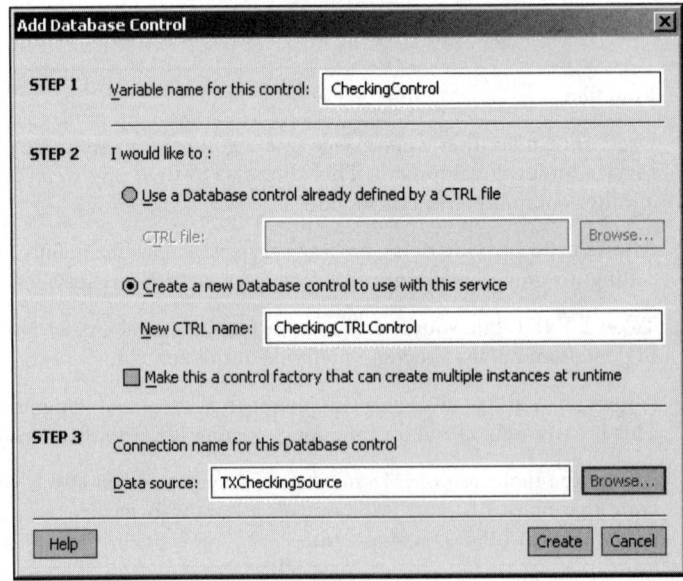

**4.** The result is a new control on the left, in the project tree, as well as a new component shown on the right in the Design view. But this component is nothing more than a connection – it does not have any methods that we can connect to the web service to help implement our requirements.

**5.** Note that the component does have base class methods that may be useful in certain cases. But it has no SQL statement-related methods yet. In order to do something useful, we need to add a method to the Control. We do so by right-clicking on it and selecting **Add Method**. In this case we're going to create a method named `insertAccount()`, which we'll use to create an account in the database:

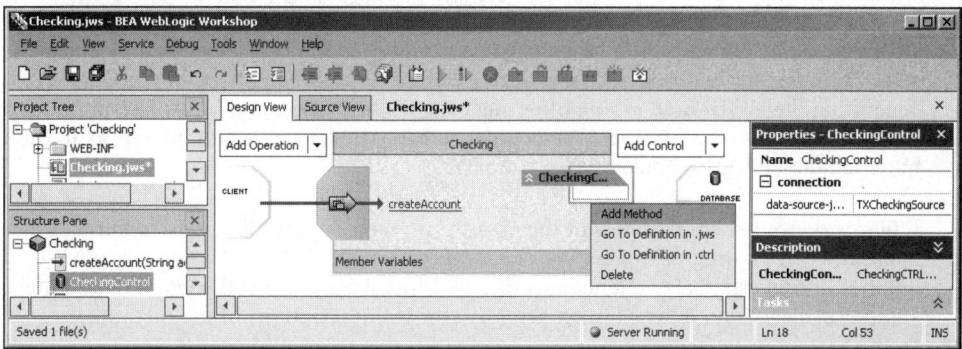

**6.** After we've added the method in the design view, we right-click on it and bring up the **Edit SQL and Interface** dialog box. This dialog allows us to write the Java method definition and tie it to the SQL to be executed. In this case, we take the two `String` parameters, `accountno` and `owner`, and use them to create a new record.

Notice below in the SQL that we write that we use the two parameters that are defined in the Java section. In the SQL section, if we want to use them we need to enclose them in braces { } to indicate the use of a parameter. Our SQL statement is as follows:

```
INSERT INTO ACCOUNT (account_number, owner)
VALUES ({accountno},{owner})
```

This is shown in the screenshot below:

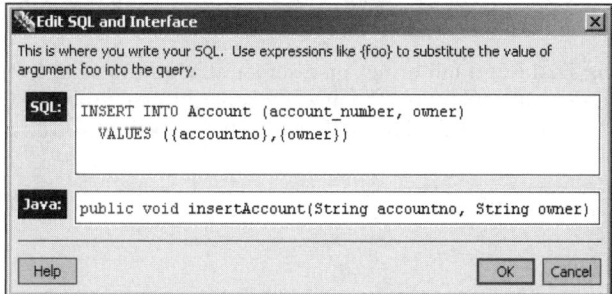

Yes, we've really created a web service that can create a new checking account within our database – and we did it with one line of Java code and two lines of SQL. Now all we have to do is test it.

# Testing the Web Service

You might be thinking that we've missed a step. After all, where is the WSDL? What about a UDDI entry? We haven't seen any SOAP messages; and don't we have to write a client to test with? These are all good thoughts. But we don't need to worry since Workshop has it covered.

## Try It Out – Test the Web Service

**1.** On the toolbar, there's a little green triangle pointing to the right; the execute button. Clicking this button creates and runs a client for our web service, which Workshop deploys for us, generating the WSDL and all the other necessary information and implementation. Clicking the button brings up a browser. We could also bring this up manually by typing in the URL http://localhost:7001/Checking/Checking.jws.

**2.** Either way, we get an overview of the Checking web service. There are a number of options open to when viewing this page. We can get access to the WSDL (shown below). We can get a number of suggestions for clients, including a Workshop Control file (so we could include it in another project), and a Java Proxy. We can also see descriptions of the methods:

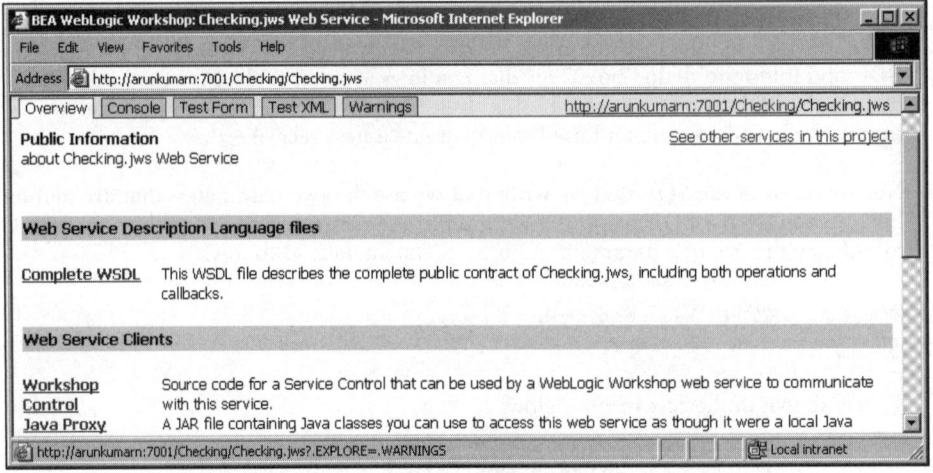

**3.** Clicking on the **Test Form** tab brings up a screen that allows us to test our web service. To do so, we entered the value 1003 for the new account number, and WROX Press Account as the owner. We then clicked the button that calls the createAccount() method:

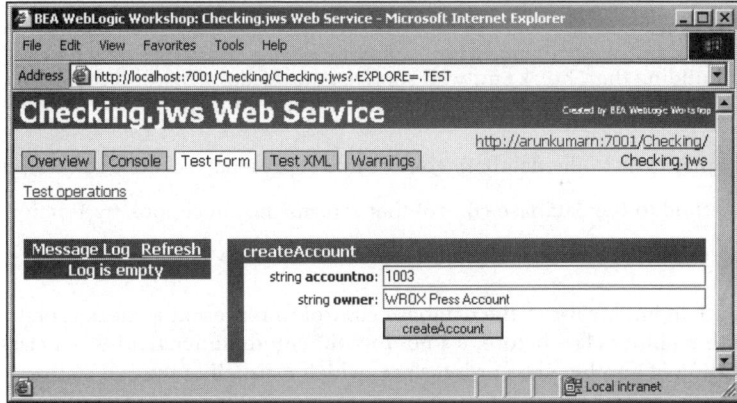

**4.** The results are shown below. Since there is no return value the result is not very interesting, but if there were an error, we'd see a lot more information:

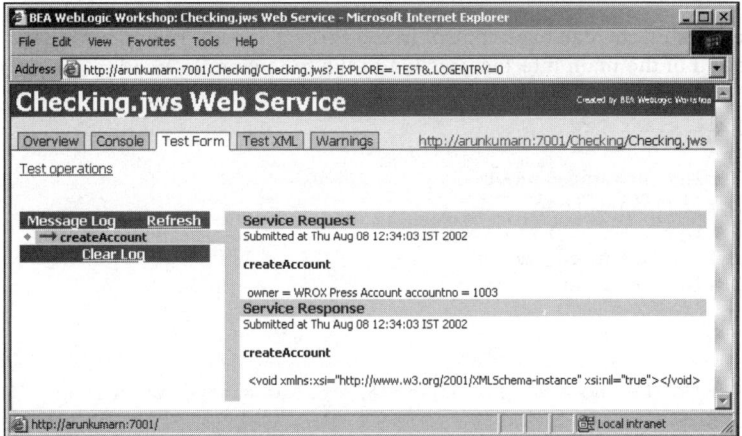

**5.** Finally, we will go to the MySQL prompt and execute the following SQL query:

```
SELECT * FROM ACCOUNT
```

**6.** This gives us the follow resultset, which shows our new account, created in the database:

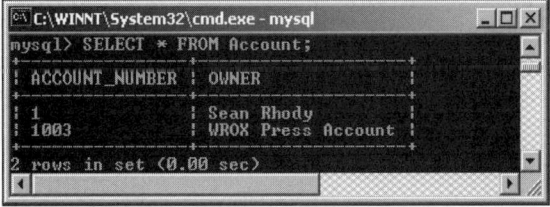

and thus we've tested our web service.

# Returning Data

Our next step in building the Checking web service is to create a method that provides a list of transactions for a particular account. To do this, we'll do the following:

❑   Add an inner class to the database control that represents a checkbook transaction

❑   Add a method to the database control that returns the checkbook transaction information

❑   Add a method to the web service that returns the data to the client

To begin, we'll add an inner class to the database control to represent a checkbook transaction. If you've never worked with an inner class before, it's not too difficult to understand. It's a class that is declared inside the declaration of another class or interface, which is usually returned as the results of a method.

For example, when we get a resultset from a JDBC call, what is returned implements the interface resultset, but is actually an inner class. Inner classes are useful for localizing the implementation and in our case, for use as structures to hold data.

**1.**   Double-click on the database control in the Project Tree to open its code file. Beneath the declaration of the main interface, we'll add the following Java code:

```
static public class Trx {

    public String account_number;
    public String trans_code;
    public String transaction_date;
    public int transaction_amount;
    public String transaction_desc;

    public Trx(){}

    public Trx(String acctno, String code, String tdate, int amount,
        String desc) {

        account_number = new String(acctno);
        trans_code = new String(code);
        transaction_date = new String(tdate);
        transaction_amount = amount;
        transaction_desc = new String(desc);
    }
}
```

The inner class is called Trx. It consists of five data members that correspond almost exactly to the definition of the Transactions table in the database. Almost, in this case, because we're going to treat the transaction date as a String rather than a java.sql.Date class, this simplifies handling.

**2.** Now that the Inner Class exists, we'll add a new method to the database control. Click on the drop-down listbox on the right of the control in the Design View to add a new method named `getTransactions()`. Then right click on the method and select **Edit SQL and Interface**. This brings up the dialog box as shown below:

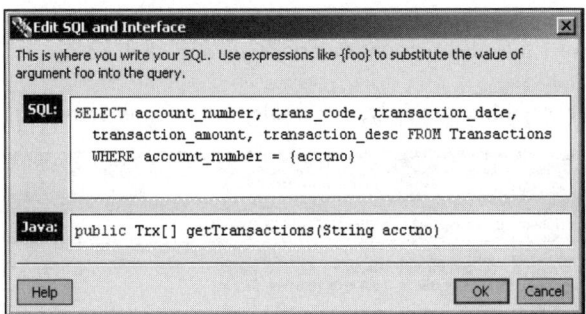

Let's look at the SQL:

```
SELECT account_number, trans_code, transaction_date,
  transaction_amount, transaction_desc FROM Transactions
WHERE account_number = {acctno}
```

It should be straightforward. We are selecting all of the fields of the `Transactions` table by name so we know the exact order. We are using the parameter `acctno`, which is defined in the method heading. This returns a resultset of the transactions for a particular account. The method heading is fairly simple as well:

```
public Trx[] getTransactions(String acctno)
```

It declares a method, `getTransactions()`, that returns an array of `Trx`, the inner class that we declared earlier. It takes one argument, a string that is the account number that we're interested in.

**3.** Now it's time to add a method to the web service to use the database control. Click on the dropdown to the left of the web service and select **Add Method** and create a new method called `listTransactions()`. Then click on the new link to edit the method:

```
/**
 * @jws:operation
 */
public CheckingCTRLControlControl.Trx[] listTransactions(String acctno)
{
    return CheckingControl.getTransactions(acctno);
}
```

This method is simply a wrapper for the database operation. Note that we have to fully qualify the return type – the inner class has no visibility outside the interface in which it's declared. We take a single string argument for the account number, and call the `getTransactions()` method of the database control.

## Test It

Now that the method is complete, let's test it.

**1.** Click on the green triangle to start the test browser.

**2.** Enter a value of 1 into the account number field and click on the listTransactions button.

**3.** If we've done everything correctly, our results should look something like this:

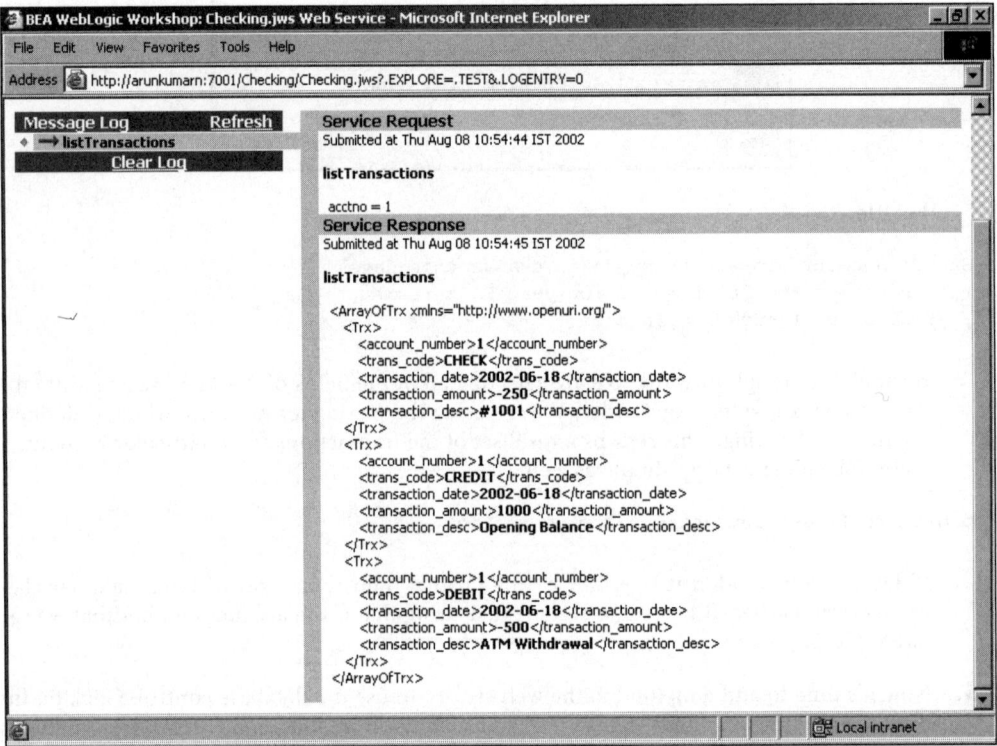

Once again, we've created a real, working method in just a few lines of code.

## The WSDL File

Before we move on, let's examine the WSDL file.

**1.** We need to start the client (click on the green triangle on the toolbar). The WebLogic Server also needs to be running.

**2.** WebLogic Workshop will bring up a browser with the generated client. Click the Overview tab, then click on the link for complete WSDL to see the generated WSDL file:

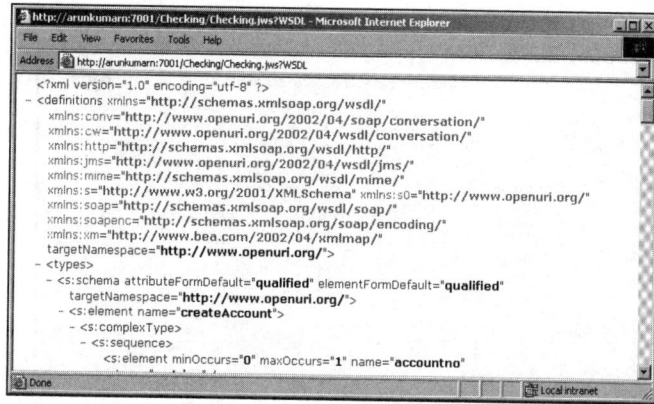

That's it. We're all done! Let's have a quick summary of what we have seen of the WebLogic Workshop.

### Finishing Up

WebLogic Workshop Beta allows us to create and deploy web services graphically in a Java environment, while writing only a minimal amount of code.

We've learned how to do the following using WebLogic Workshop:

❑   Create a new web service

❑   Create database controls to access data sources provided by the WebLogic server

❑   Add methods to the web service

❑   Tie methods in the web service to methods in the database control

❑   Generate a test client

❑   Use inner classes to represent complex data sets

❑   Test our web service

# IBM WebSphere Studio Application Developer

Similar to the BEA Workshop, IBM provides a development IDE that automates many of the tasks associated with creating a web service. This environment is called the WebSphere Studio Application Developer.

## Download and Installation

You can download the WebSphere Studio Application Developer from the IBM web site (http://www-3.ibm.com/software/ad/studioappdev/). For convenience IBM has divided the application, which is large, into five core downloads (about 65MB apiece), and three optional downloads. Each download is an executable file that will unpack files into a directory. You need to run each executable, then use Windows Explorer to go to the directory and run the Setup.exe file. This brings up a typical installation wizard, which asks you where to install, and confirms several choices. For example, you will be asked for your primary development role. In our case select Web Services Developer:

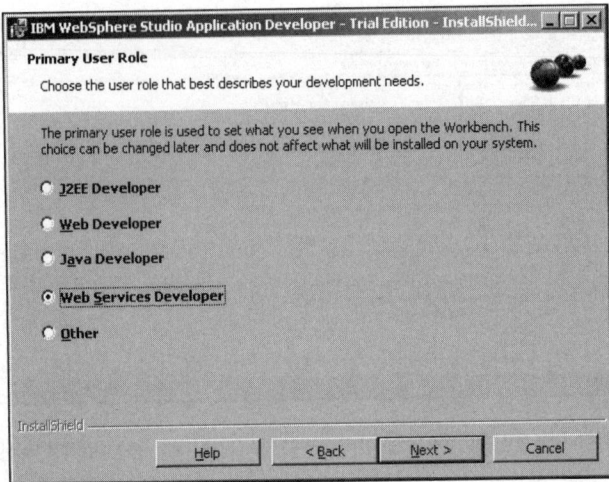

Once installed, WebSphere Studio is activated by selecting Start | Programs | IBM WebSphere Application Developer | IBM WebSphere Application Developer – Trial Edition. As you might expect, the trial edition is a time sensitive release that expires after 60 days.

# Building a Web Service

The executable brings up a multi-paned development environment:

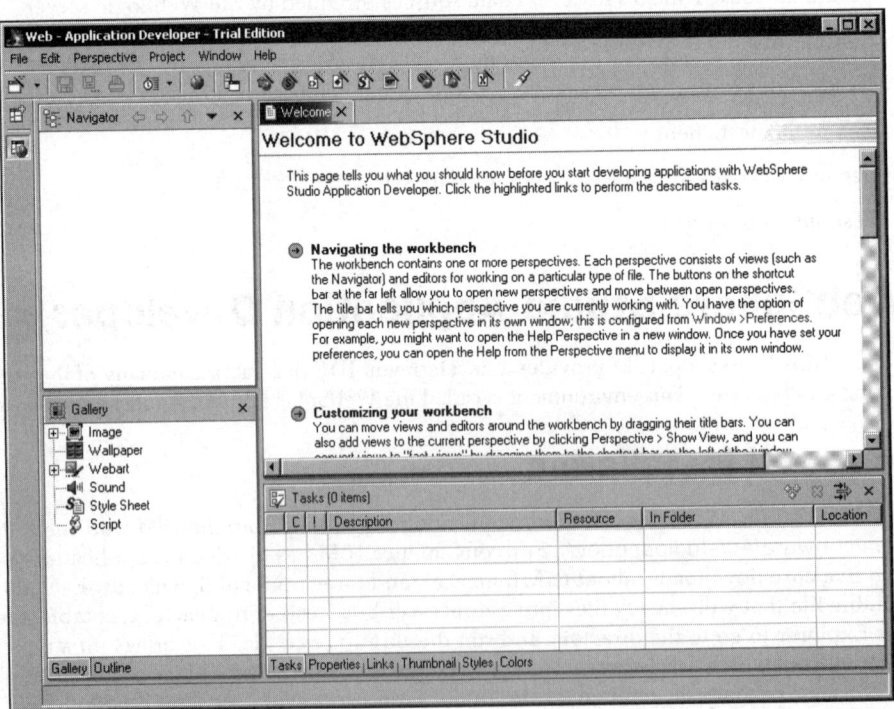

The IDE understands Java quite well, and is context sensitive. It does not have the pop-up completion facilities of other editors, so you'll have to type out all of your variable names and package declarations. Creating a web service is fairly simple in WebSphere Studio. We'll perform the following steps:

❏   Create a new Web Project.

❏   Create and compile new Java file to implement the service

❏   Generate the web service using a wizard which creates the WSDL, Java proxy, test client and runs the service in an internal server

❏   Test the service using a generated JSP client

Without further ado, let's begin with the first task.

## Create the Project

Now let look at developing our Checking web service.

**1.**   The first step in the process is to create a new Web Project. From the File menu select New, and then Project. This brings up the dialog box below:

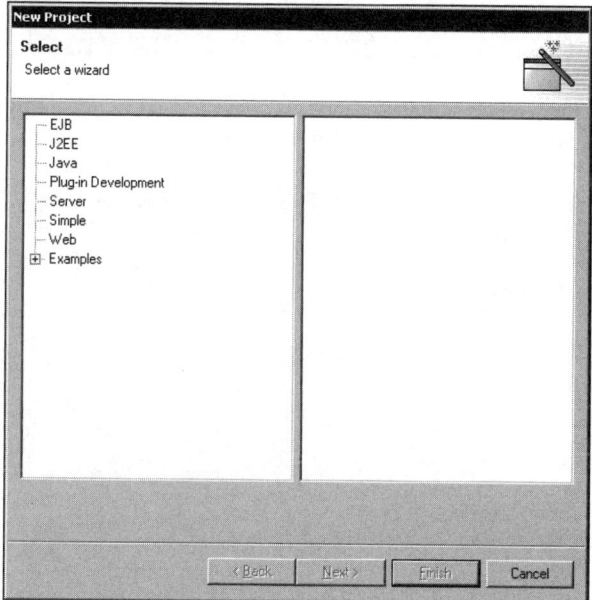

Select Wcb, and then Web Project, and click Next.

*Note that WebSphere Studio does not distinguish here between a Web Project and a Web Services project – perhaps in the next release some differentiation will occur. There are enough similarities due to the deployment environment that this choice is fairly good for web services in any event. For example, using this project generates the WEB-INF file structure necessary to deploy to the built-in Apache Tomcat server.*

**2.** Name the project `CheckingProject`:

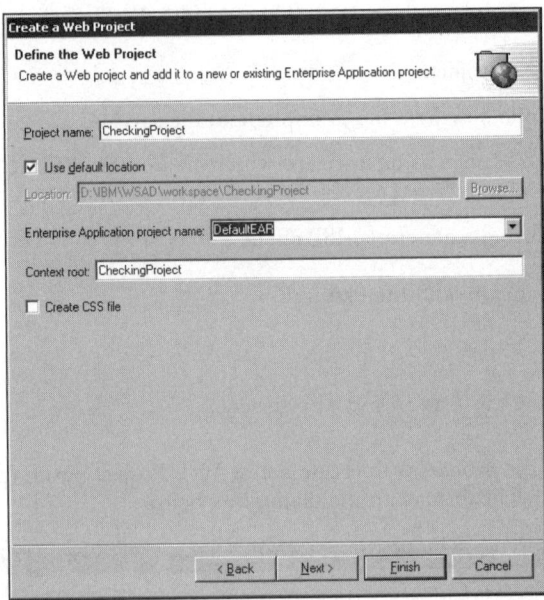

**3.** We can accept the wizard defaults for the rest of the project so just hit Finish now. This will create the project and open the environment. You can see the environment itself in the screenshot below:

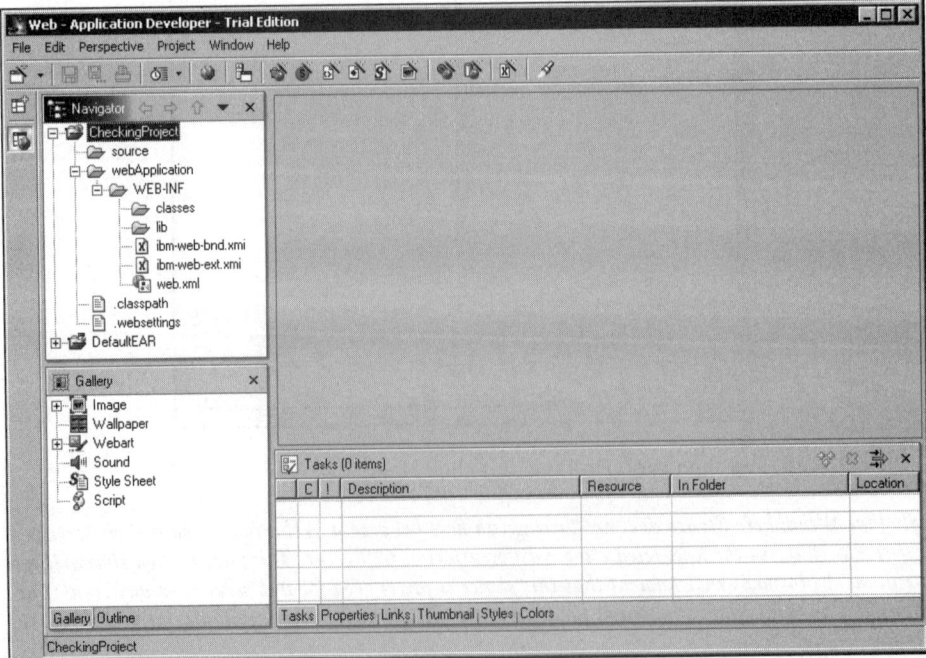

**4.** Since we're going to access the database from our service, we need to include the database driver in the list of libraries for the server.

In order to configure our server we need to start one up. Right-click on our **CheckingProject** folder in the **Navigator** pane and select **Run on Server**. This will start our web project on a new server instance. Consequently a new folder will appear in the **Navigator** pane for servers. Expand this until you can see the **defaultInstance.wsi** file:

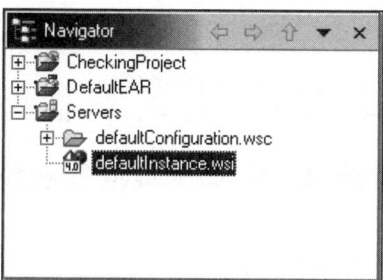

**5.** Open up the **defaultInstance.wsi** file (double-click it) and switch to the **Paths** tab. Hit the **Add External JARs** button in the lower **Class Path** window and browse to the MySQL JDBC driver JAR file and add it:

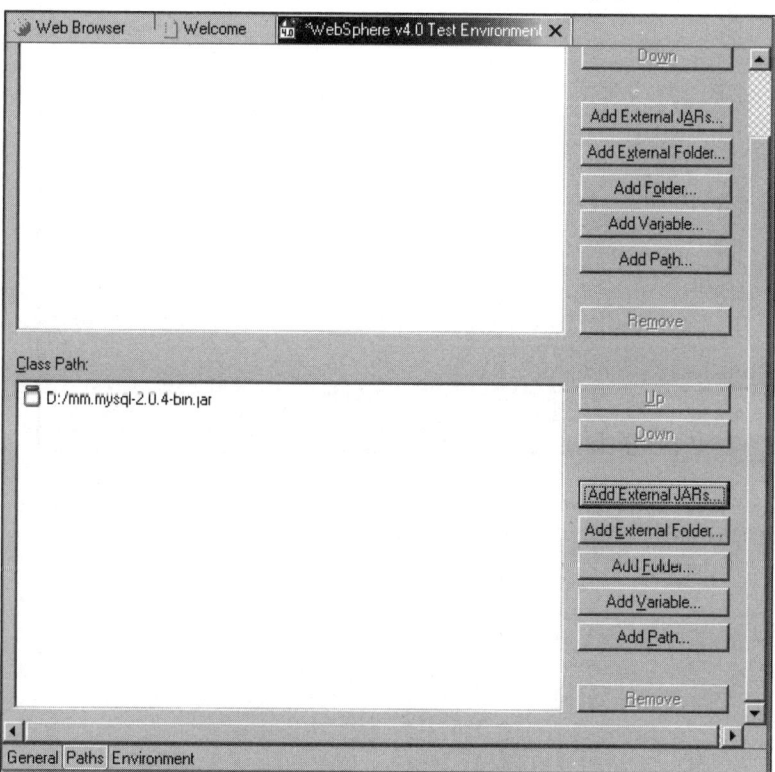

Now when we start our server again it will be able to load our JDBC driver.

> **Of course if you are using a database other than MySQL then add the relevant JAR file here for your database of choice.**

## Create the Solution Implementation File

Our next order of business is to create a Java class that implements the service.

**1.** Click on File | New | Other to open the New dialog box, then click on Java and then on the `servlets` directory and on Java Class to create a new class:

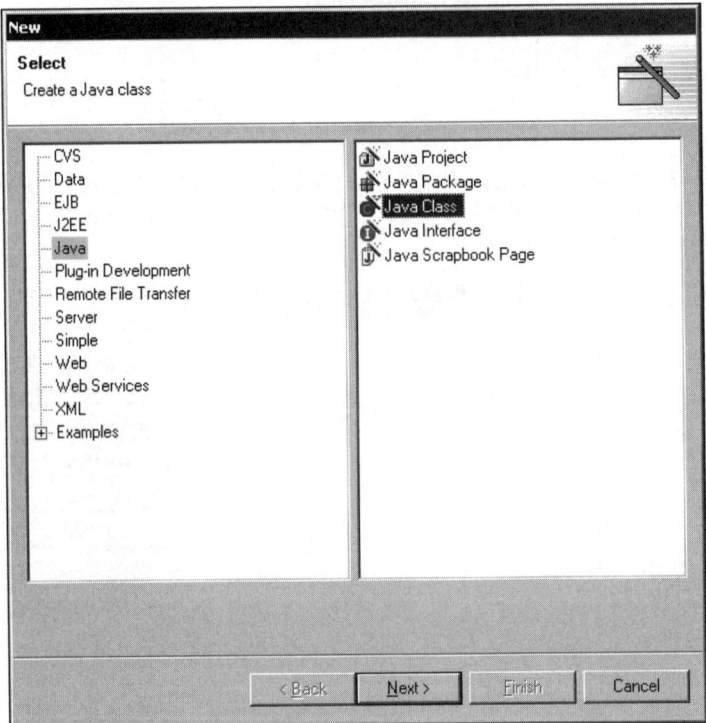

**2.** Click on Next and name the new class `CheckingImpl` and place it in the source folder for our project (use the Browse button), then click Finish:

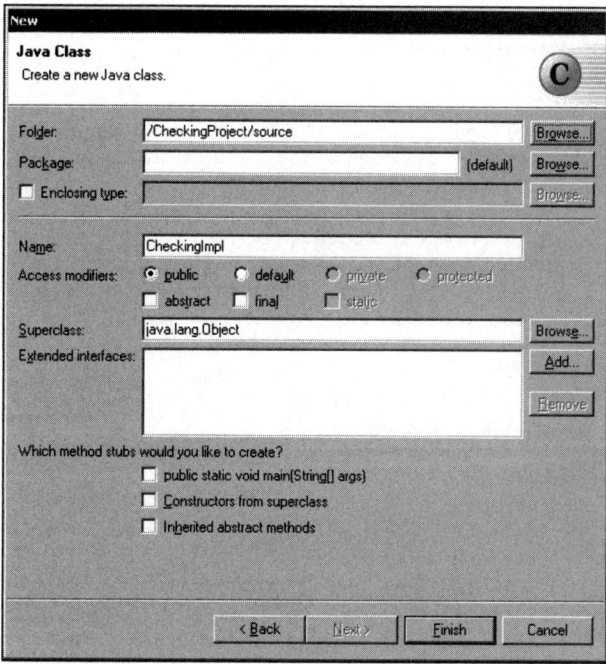

**3.** Now we need to write the code for the service implementation. We'll create two methods, createAccount() and getTransactions() to illustrate various concepts. The complete listing is shown below:

```
import java.sql.*;

public class CheckingImpl {

  public CheckingImpl(){}

  public void createAccount(String accountno, String owner) {

    try {
      Class.forName("org.gjt.mm.mysql.Driver").newInstance();
      String url = "jdbc:mysql://localhost:3306/CHECKING?" +
                   "user=sa&password=wrox123";
      Connection con = DriverManager.getConnection(url);
      Statement stmt = con.createStatement();
      String SQL = "INSERT INTO Account (account_number, owner) " +
                   "VALUES ('" + accountno + "', '" + owner + "')";
      stmt.execute(SQL);
      con.close();
    } catch (Exception e) {
      System.out.println("Exception: " + e);
    }
  }
}
```

```
public String getTransactions(String acctno) throws Exception {
  String results = "<transaction-list>";

  try {
    Class.forName("org.gjt.mm.mysql.Driver").newInstance();
    String url = "jdbc:mysql://localhost:3306/CHECKING?" +
                 "user=sa&password=wrox123";
    Connection con = DriverManager.getConnection(url);
    Statement stmt = con.createStatement();
    String SQL = "SELECT account_number, trans_code, transaction_date, " +
                 "transaction_amount, transaction_desc FROM " +
                 "Transactions WHERE account_number = '" +
                 acctno + "'";

    results += "<SQL>" + SQL + "</SQL>";
    ResultSet rs = stmt.executeQuery(SQL);

    while (rs.next()) {
      results += "<transaction>";
      results += "<account_number>" + rs.getString("account_number") +
                 "</account_number>";
      results += "<trans_code>" + rs.getString("trans_code") +
                 "</trans_code>";
      results += "<transaction_date>" + rs.getString("transaction_date") +
                 "</transaction_date>";
      results += "<transaction_amount>" + rs.getInt("transaction_amount")
                 + "</transaction_amount>";
      results += "<transaction_desc>" + rs.getString("transaction_desc") +
                 "</transaction_desc>";
      results += "</transaction>";
    }

    rs.close();
    con.close();

  } catch (Exception e) {
    results += "<exception>" + e.getMessage() + "</exception>";
  }
  results += "</transaction-list>";
  return results;
  }
}
```

**4.** Save the project. This will also compile it.

Let's examine the first method. The `createAccount()` method is used to create a new account within the database. It accepts a string representing the account number and a string with the owner information as parameters. It begins by connecting to the database using standard JDBC methods. After creating a `Connection`, a `Statement` instance is created, which is used to actually invoke a SQL statement. The SQL statement is created by including the parameters within a string variable, and then executed with a call to the `execute()` method of the `Statement`. Finally, the `Statement` and the `Connection` are closed:

```
        public void createAccount(String accountno, String owner) {

          try {
            Class.forName("org.gjt.mm.mysql.Driver").newInstance();
            String url = "jdbc:mysql://localhost:3306/CHECKING?" +
                        "user=sa&password=wrox123";
            Connection con = DriverManager.getConnection(url);
            Statement stmt = con.createStatement();
            String SQL = "INSERT INTO Account (account_number, owner) " +
                        "VALUES ('" + accountno + "', '" + owner + "')";
            stmt.execute(SQL);
            con.close();
          } catch (Exception e) {
            System.out.println("Exception: " + e);
          }
        }
```

We'd also like to implement a method that returns data. The getTransactions() method does just that. The method accepts a single parameter – a String that is the number of the account that we are interested in obtaining a list of transactions for. We start by connecting to the database, as in the createAccount() method, and creating a Connection and a Statement object. We build up a query in a string and include the account number.

As this SQL statement returns results (as opposed to the INSERT statement we used in the createAccount() method) we need to call the executeQuery() method instead of execute(), and we get back a resultset from the method.

We're storing the results of this method in a string called results. We'll format it as XML, so it can be parsed if desired. We will include the SQL statement (this is useful in debugging) as well as the data (if any). In the case of an exception, we return that information instead.

Processing the resultset is straightforward. We use a while loop to go through the records, and add each attribute from the resultset to the results string. Note that we are asking for the date as a String, rather than a Date – it's easier to process this way and we don't intend to use it as a java.sql.Date class anyway. When we're done with the data, we close the results string and return it:

```
        public String getTransactions(String acctno) throws Exception {
          String results = "<transaction-list>";

          try {
            Class.forName("org.gjt.mm.mysql.Driver").newInstance();
            String url = "jdbc:mysql://localhost:3306/CHECKING?" +
                        "user=sa&password=wrox123";
            Connection con = DriverManager.getConnection(url);
            Statement stmt = con.createStatement();
            String SQL = "SELECT account_number, trans_code, transaction_date, " +
                        "transaction_amount, transaction_desc FROM " +
                        "Transactions WHERE account_number = '" +
                        acctno + "'";

            results += "<SQL>" + SQL + "</SQL>";
```

```
      ResultSet rs = stmt.executeQuery(SQL);

      while (rs.next()) {
        results += "<transaction>";
        results += "<account_number>" + rs.getString("account_number") +
                   "</account_number>";
        results += "<trans_code>" + rs.getString("trans_code") +
                   "</trans_code>";
        results += "<transaction_date>" + rs.getString("transaction_date") +
                   "</transaction_date>";
        results += "<transaction_amount>" + rs.getInt("transaction_amount")
                   + "</transaction_amount>";
        results += "<transaction_desc>" + rs.getString("transaction_desc") +
                   "</transaction_desc>";
        results += "</transaction>";
      }

      rs.close();
      con.close();

    } catch (Exception e) {
      results += "<exception>" + e.getMessage() + "</exception>";
    }
    results += "</transaction-list>";
    return results;
  }
```

## Generating a Web Service

The next step in the process is to generate the web service.

**1.** To do this, right-click on the CheckingImpl.java file in the IDE's Navigator pane and select New | Other, then from the New dialog choose Web Services and then Web Service.

**2.** Upon pressing Next, choose a Java bean web service and our web project. You should also select Launch the Universal Test Client and Generate a Sample if you want to test the service (which we do) or see sample client code that is generated:

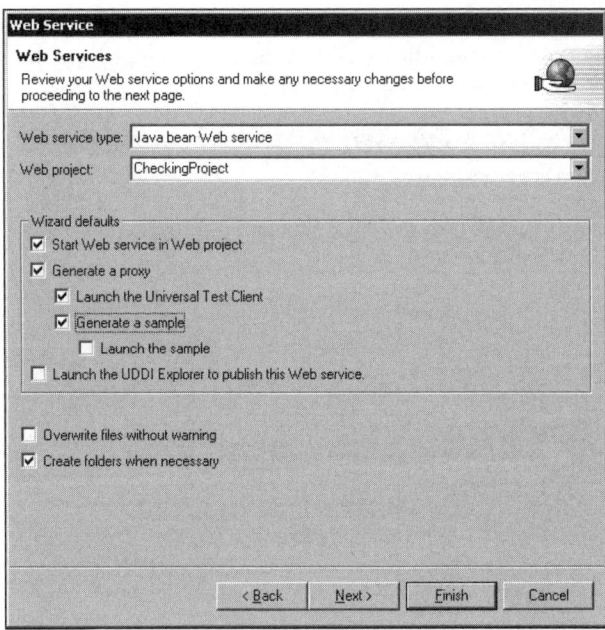

**3.** The next step is to select the bean to use as the web service. Notice that we have to select a single bean – we can't spread our web service over multiple classes. Of course, we can get around this in code, by invoking other classes, but there must be a single service file to work with. In our case our `CheckingImpl` class will be already selected (if not then browse to select it):

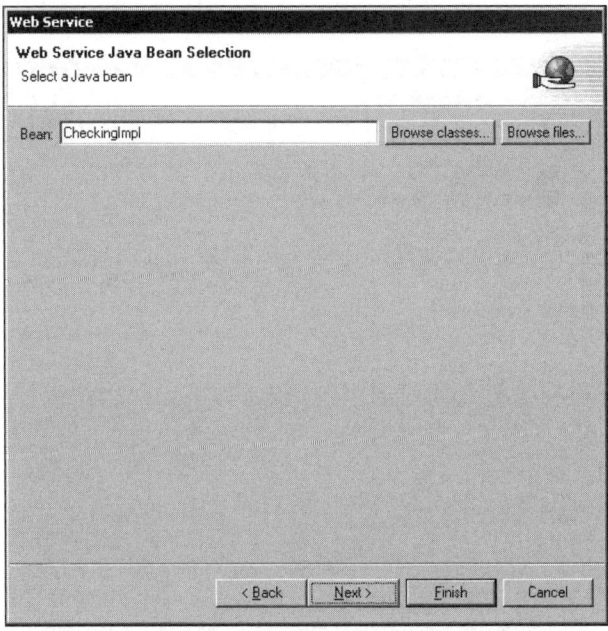

**4.** Next we set up the web services aspects of the service. WebSphere Studio generates all of the information you see, so you don't need to change anything. Note that the WSDL is broken into two files – a service file and a binding file:

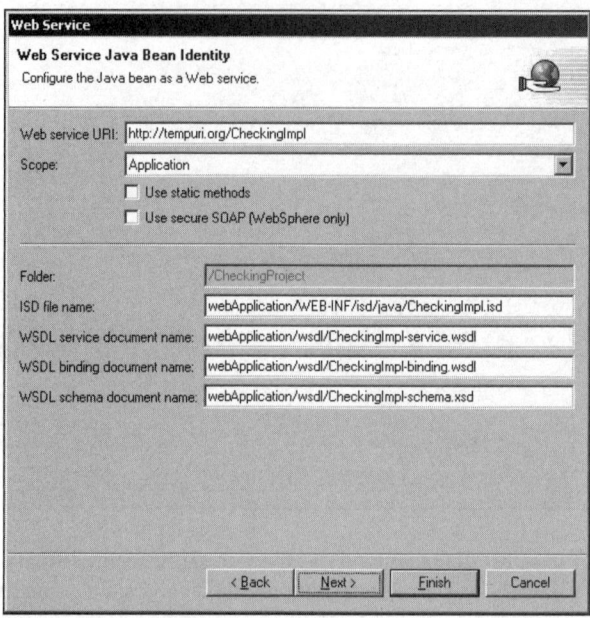

**5.** The next step is to select the methods to publish. Since our service has only service methods (in other words there are no helper methods) we select all the methods:

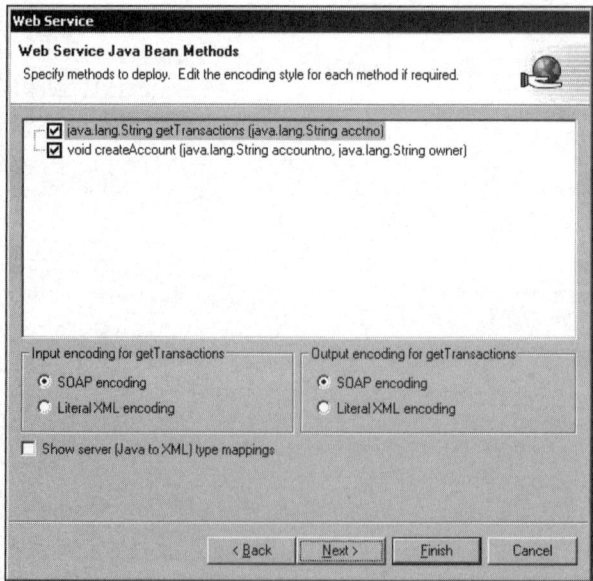

*If the dialog registers no methods on the bean then you will need to quit the wizard and go back and save the project first (thus compiling the class) before restarting the wizard.*

**6.** Now we look at the proxy generation. We need to tell the wizard what port in the binding to talk to. Since we only have a single `Port` in our generated binding, this is simple – the port is already pre-selected by the wizard. This step generates a file called `proxy.soap.CheckingImplProxy`. This class can be used if we wanted to build a Java client that uses the web service – it wrappers the methods and encapsulates the web service interface into a Java class:

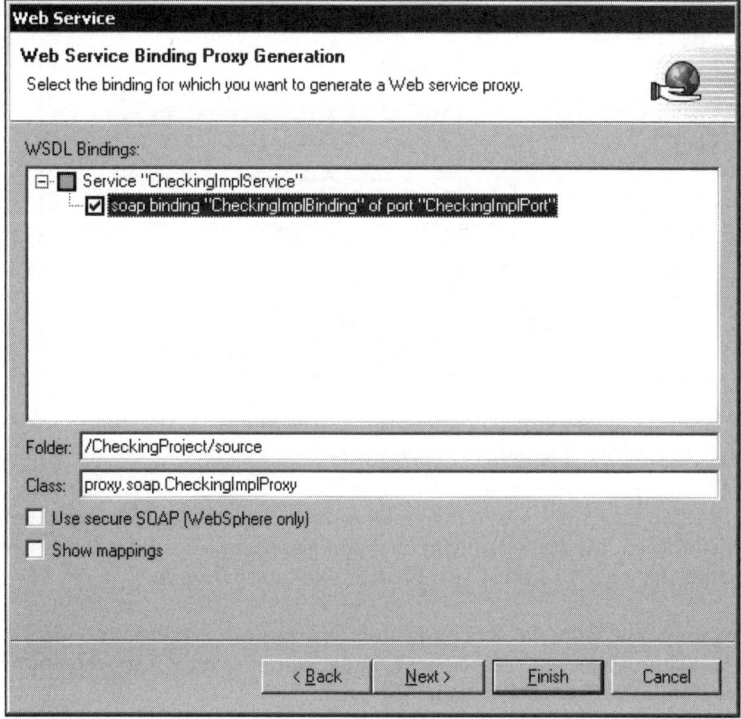

**7.** We can also generate a sample application, which consists of a set of JSP files. Note that we need the proxy we created above in order to actually create the JSP. Generating a sample creates four JSP files, a frame, and three frame sections:

- ❑   `Input.jsp` – The input parameters for each method.
- ❑   `Methods.jsp` – A list of methods.
- ❑   `Result.jsp` – The results of a method invocation.
- ❑   `TestClient.jsp` – The frame that holds the other three files. Launch this file to test the web service.

If you select the **Generate a Sample** checkbox, the sample application will be launched once the service is deployed. Make sure this box is checked.

**391**

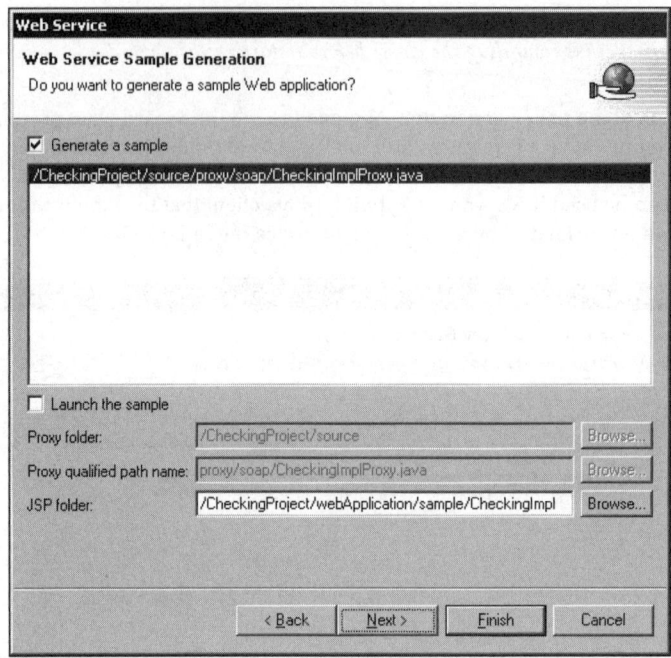

*If you forgot to check this box, or want to run the test client at a later time, simply select the* TestClient.jsp *file in the IDE, then right-click and select* Run on Server.

**8.** Finally, we can hit **Finish**. Once the generation is complete, assuming you checked the **Launch** checkbox, the JSP client is launched. WebSphere Studio provides an internal browser, which loads the TestClient.jsp file from an internal server.

If you examine the **Console** section of the IDE, you can see the WebSphere Application Server launch information. WebSphere Studio provides a built-in web application server to run your web service, as well as your JSP client:

**9.** To test the web service, select one of the methods to invoke. In the image below, we selected the getTransactions() method, and entered an account number of 1, then hit **Invoke**, which produced the **Result** section in the lower frame. You can see the string that the method returns as a result of the lookup. If you haven't added any transactions to the database, you should get three transactions back since we created three transactions when we first loaded the database:

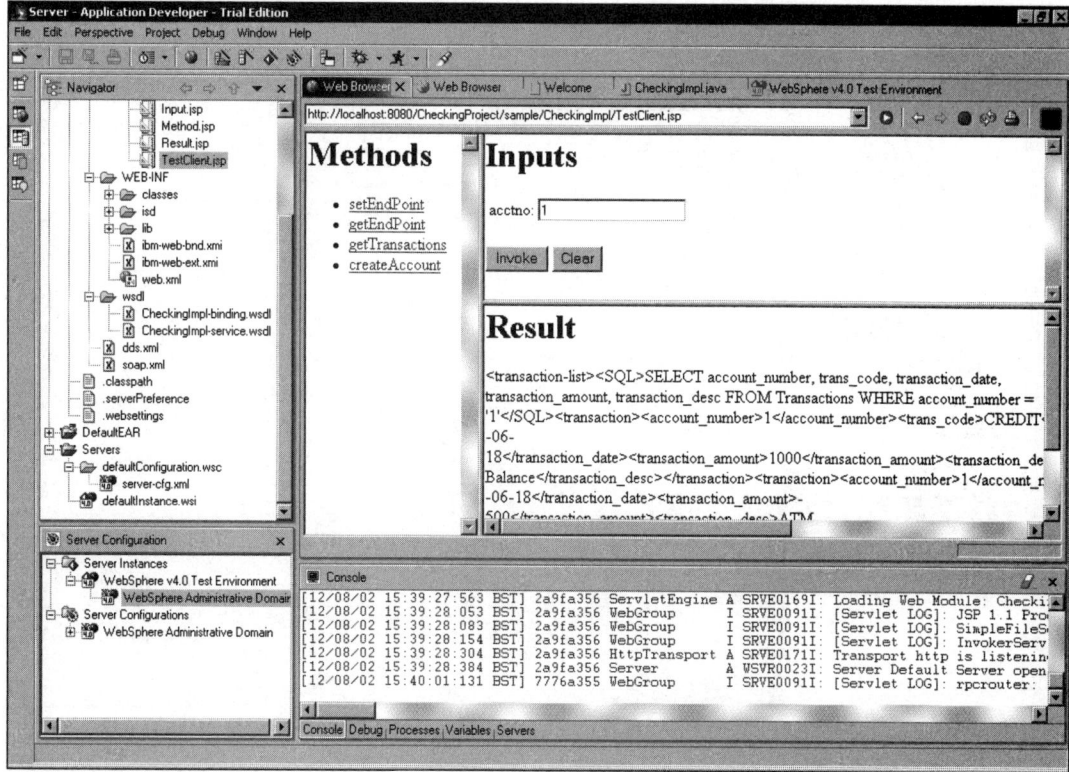

# Finishing Up

Before we move on, let's examine the WSDL file. This is a simple task in WebSphere Studio – click on the WSDL file located under the WSDL folder in the webApplication folder (in the Navigator pane), and double-click the `CheckingImpl-Binding.wsdl` file. The IDE displays the WSDL in an XML editing window (if you'd rather see a plain text version of the WSDL then right-click the file and select Open With | Default Text Editor):

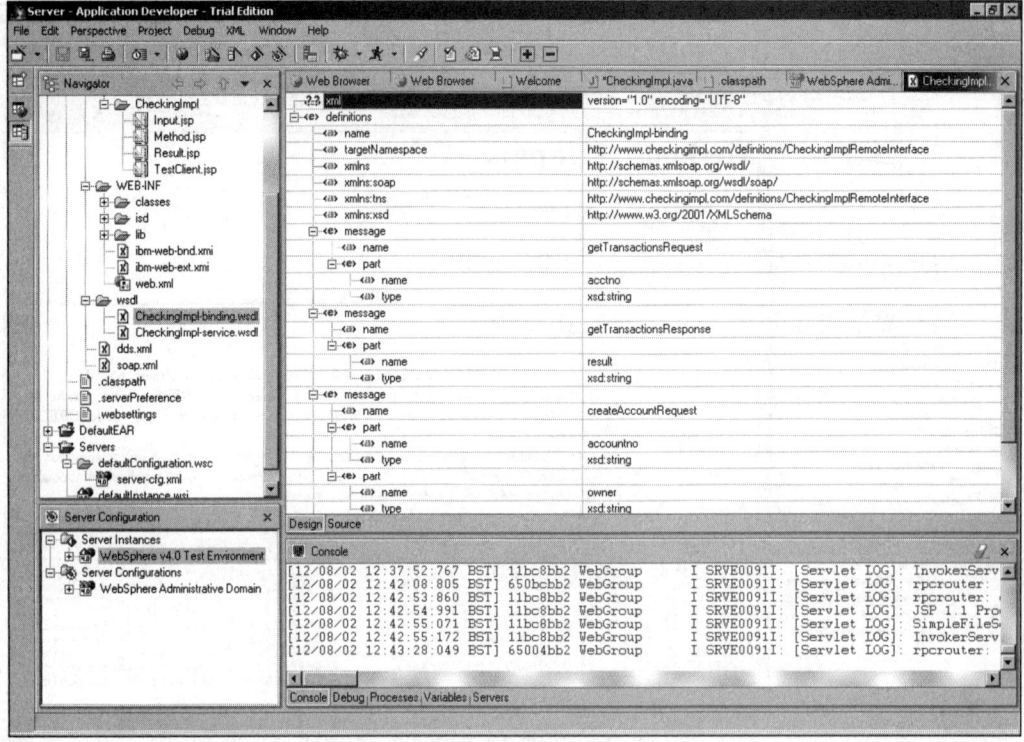

That's it. We're all done! Let's have a quick summary of what we have seen of the IBM WebSphere Studio Application Developer. This environment allows us to create and deploy web services in a Java environment.

We've learned how to do the following:

❑ Create a web project in WebSphere Studio

❑ Create a new web service by creating a Java class

❑ Generate WSDL, a Java proxy, and a sample application

❑ Test our web service

# IBM WebSphere SDK for Web Services

Another alternative available from IBM is the IBM WebSphere SDK for web services. This is a set of tools (mostly the Axis toolset discussed earlier in the book), as well as a lightweight version of WebSphere suitable for deploying web services. We'll examine this as a more programming-oriented approach to deploying web services, one that doesn't hide the details quite as much.

# Downloading and Installing

We can download the WSDK from the following URL
http://www-106.ibm.com/developerworks/webservices/wsdk/

1.  As usual with the IBM site, we'll need a name and password. The download is a file named
    `ibm-wsdk-131-w32.exe`. This is a self-extracting zip file, which will launch a brief
    installation routine. The routine will ask for the location for the SDK; we have chosen
    `C:\WSDK`:

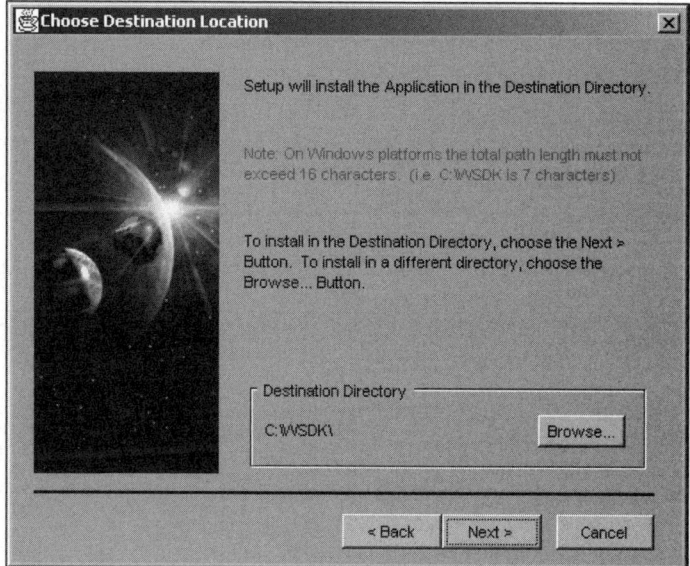

*The WSDK is limited to a total character length of 16 for installation purposes so don't choose a
long name.*

2.  Once the WSDK is installed we need to configure the server. Select Start | All Programs | IBM
    WebSphere SDK for web services | Configure WSDK to launch the configuration routine.
    This brings up the following screen:

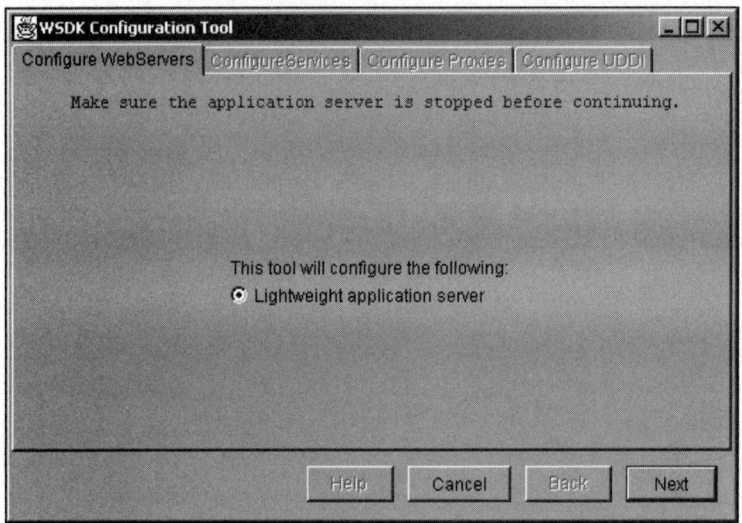

**3.** We've got no real choices on this screen; click Next to continue. That brings up the screen below:

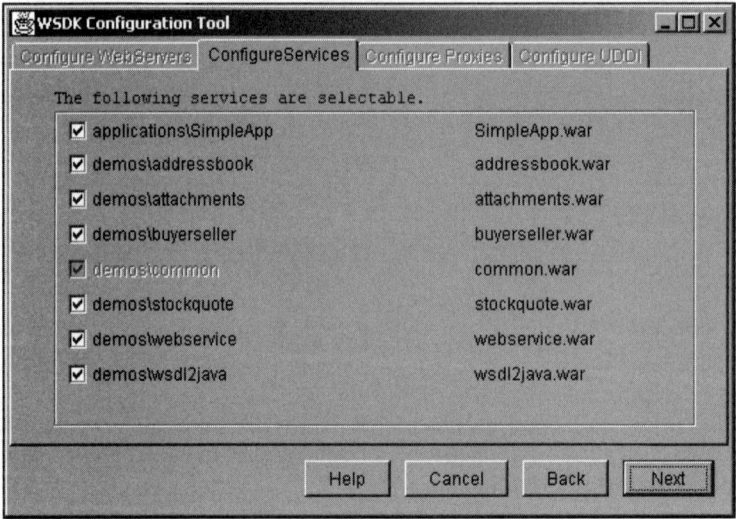

**4.** We can choose to install or uninstall any of the demonstration applications. As they all provide some useful value in understanding the toolset, we'll install them all. Clicking Next brings up the Proxies screen:

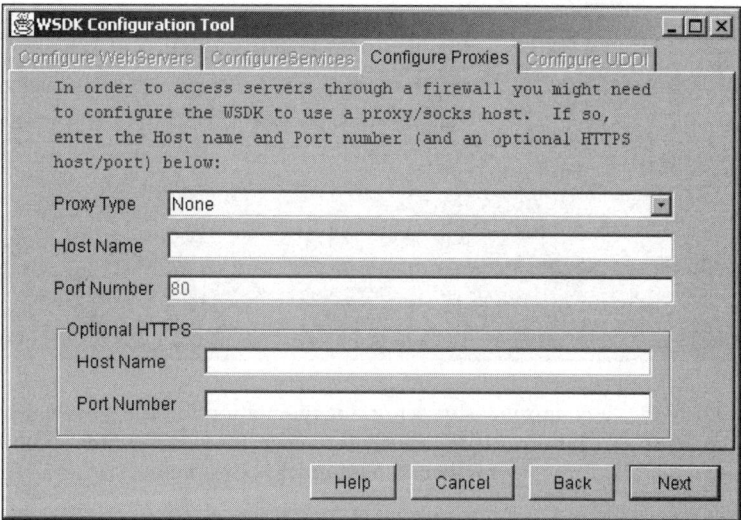

**5.** This screen allows us to set up our server in case there is a firewall, or proxy server between the WebSphere server and the Internet. In our case there isn't so we continue as is:

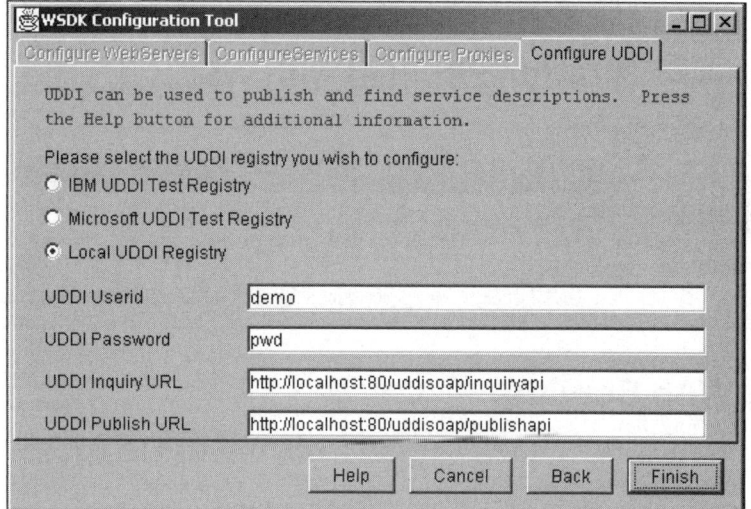

**6.** This screen allows us to set up the UDDI registry we want to work with. Since we're doing experimental work rather than actual production coding for public consumption, we'll use the Local UDDI registry. This is the default, and all of the values are provided by the IDE. Simply click Finish to conclude the configuration.

**7.** Once this is done, we can launch the server by selecting Start | Programs | IBM WebSphere SDK for web services | Start AppServer. The AppServer is a console application. When it's running, it will look something like this:

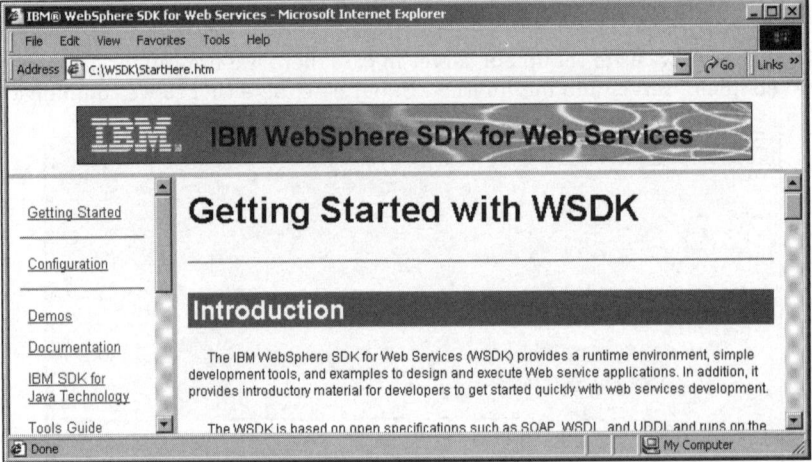

8. IBM also provides a comprehensive set of documentation for the WSDK, which we can access by clicking Start | Programs | IBM WebSphere SDK for web services | Start Here. It launches an HTML-based set of documentation, as shown below:

# Creating a Web Service

Creating a web service under the WSDK is a series of steps. We will do the following:

1. Establish the directory structure: We'll set up a set of directories under the appropriate directory in the WSDK distribution so the server can host the files

2. Create the Implementation class: As we did before, we'll create a Java class to represent the service

3. Create the WSDL descriptions: To work with UDDI, the WSDK needs the WSDL to be separated into two files – the interface and the implementation

**4.** Create the Axis Deployment Descriptor: We'll be using the underlying Axis implementation, and will need a deployment descriptor for our service

**5.** Deploying the Service WAR: We'll deploy the Service Web Archive (WAR) to the proper directory so that the service can operate

**6.** Register the Service with Axis: This will deploy our code as a web service

**7.** Publish the Service: We'll publish the service to UDDI

**8.** Create Java Client: We'll test the service using a Java client

Now let's see how these steps work.

## Establish the Directory Structure

The first step in the process is to create the appropriate directory structure. We need to create this structure under the WSDK_HOME\Services directory. If we installed WSDK in C:\WSDK, then this is C:\WSDK\Services. We'll start by creating our directory – NewTesting. Next we'll add all of the needed subdirectories. The finished structure looks like this:

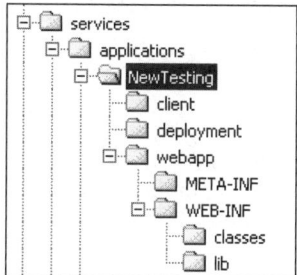

With our directory structure in place, the next step is to create a Java class that implements the logic.

## Create the Implementation Class

Once again, we'll create a simple service that creates a new account in our Checking database. To do so, we'll create file called NewTesting.java:

```
import java.sql.*;

public class NewTesting {
  public String getMessage() {
    return "Hello there!";
  }
}
```

```
public String createAccount( String owner) {
  String tracking = "starting";
  try {
    tracking="createAccount";
    Class.forName("org.gjt.mm.mysql.Driver").newInstance();
    String url =
      "jdbc:mysql://localhost:3306/CHECKING?user=sa&password=wrox123 ";
    tracking = "Connected: Owner: " + owner;
    Connection con = DriverManager.getConnection(url);
    Statement stmt = con.createStatement();
    String accountno = "1234";
    tracking = "Ready to try";

    String SQL = "INSERT INTO Account (account_number, owner)
      VALUES ('" + accountno + "', '" + owner + "')";
    tracking = "SQL is: " + SQL;
    stmt.execute(SQL);
    con.close();
    tracking = "complete";
    return "1234";

  } catch (Exception e) {
    System.out.println("Exception: " + e);
    return tracking + e;
  }
 }
}
```

In order to have the JDBC driver (in our case mm.mysql-2.0.14-bin.jar) on the server classpath, we need to modify the appserver.bat file in the C:\WSDK\bin directory. We will add the archives to the line that defines the classpath, as shown below:

```
:setcp
set WSDK_CP=%WSDK_CP%;%WAS_HOME%\lib\webcontainer.jar;C:\mysql\jdbc\
  mm.mysql-2.0.14-bin.jar;
```

As we can see, we have added the JAR file at the end of the classpath definition. If we run our application and get JDBC errors, it's likely that we've either forgotten this step, or got the path wrong.

Our next step is to create the WSDL.

## Create the WSDL Descriptions

Although we can describe this with a single WSDL file from our perspective, the WSDK needs two different files, which help the UDDI registry differentiate between interface and implementation. It uses one file to represent the business entry and the other to represent the tModel. To create the WSDL files, we can either code by hand, or use the java2wsdl tool. In order to use this tool, WSDK_HOME\bin must be in our path. The command is shown overleaf:

```
Java2wsdl -N "http://NewTesting" -n "http://NewTesting-interface" -o
c:\wsdk\services\applications\NewTesting\NewTesting_interface.wsdl -O
c:\wsdk\services\applications\NewTesting\NewTesting_impl.wsdl -L
"http://localhost:80/NewTesting/NewTesting_interface.wsdl" -1
"http://localhost:80/NewTesting" NewTesting
```

The table below lists the `Java2wsdl` options on the command line as a quick reference:

| Option | Description |
| --- | --- |
| N | Describes the target namespace for the WSDL files. |
| n | Specifies the target namespace for the interface portion of the WSDL files. |
| o | Specifies the WSDL output file for the interface portion of the WSDL description of the web service. |
| O | Specifies the WSDL output file for the implementation portion of the WSDL description of the web service. |
| L | Specifies the WSDL output file for the interface portion of the WSDL description of the web service. |
| m | Specifies the method or methods published by the WSDL. |
| 1 | Specifies the implementation class for the web service. |

The correct result of our previous command is two files in the directory `C:\WSDK\Services\applications\NewTesting\webapp`:

❑ `NewTesting_Impl.wsdl`

❑ `NewTesting_Interface.wsdl`

Our next step is to create the Axis Deployment Descriptor.

## Create the Axis Deployment Descriptor

The WSDK uses the Axis SOAP implementation as the SOAP engine for the WSDK. Axis requires a file known as a Web Services Deployment Descriptor (WSDD) to deploy a web service; we covered this in Chapter 3. For our purposes, we will create a deployment descriptor called `deploy.wsdd` and place it in the `C:\WSDK\services\applications\NewTesting\deployment` directory. Here is the listing for the `deploy.wsdd` file:

```
<m:deploy xmlns:m="AdminService">

  <service name="mcosage" pivot="RPCDispatcher">
    <option name="className" value="NewTesting"/>
    <option name="methodName" value="createAccount"/>
  </service>
```

```
    <beanMappings xmlns:sa="urn:NewTesting-types">
      <sa:NewTesting classname="NewTesting"/>
    </beanMappings>

  </m:deploy>
```

Our next step is to try to deploy our code as a service.

# Deploying the Web Service

There are a few files we'll simply copy over into our directory structure, as they don't change at all. These files are basic configuration files, so we don't need to modify them for our purposes. We'll copy them from `WSDK_HOME\services\applications\SimpleApp`.

From this root, these files are:

- ❏ `webapp\META-INF\import.xml`
- ❏ `webapp\WEB-INF\ibm-web-bnd.xmi`
- ❏ `webapp\WEB-INF\ibm-web-ext.xmi`
- ❏ `webapp\WEB-INF\server-config.wsdd`
- ❏ `webapp\WEB-INF\wsdkProperties.xml`
- ❏ `webapp\WEB-INF\lib\*` – these are a series of JAR files.

At this point we've created the implementation file, the WSDL and the WSDD. Now we will make use of these files to actually deploy and test a web service using the WSDK. In order to do that we will need to create a `web.xml` file. This file tells the web server (WebSphere) to map requests to the Axis servlet. This is really a simple description file that describes a web application. We set the display name to `NewTesting`, and then set up the servlet processing, which uses the Axis toolkit.

The listing for the `web.xml` file is shown below:

```
<?xml version="1.0" encoding="UTF-8"?>

<!DOCTYPE web-app PUBLIC "-//Sun Microsystems, Inc.//DTD Web Application
  2.3//EN" "http://java.sun.com/j2ee/dtds/web-app_2.2.dtd">
  <web-app>
  <display-name>NewTesting</display-name>

  <servlet>
    <servlet-name>Axis</servlet-name>
    <servlet-class>org.apache.axis.transport.http.AxisServlet</servlet-
      class>
  </servlet>

  <servlet-mapping>
    <servlet-name>Axis</servlet-name>
    <url-pattern>/services/*</url-pattern>
  </servlet-mapping>
```

```
    <mime-mapping>
      <extension>wsdl</extension>
      <mime-type>text/xml</mime-type>
    </mime-mapping>

    <mime-mapping>
      <extension>xsd</extension>
      <mime-type>text/xml</mime-type>
    </mime-mapping>
</web-app>
```

This file tells the Axis toolkit how to handle different types of requests, and basically hands them off to the servlet handler.

With that completed, we can now deploy the service.

## Deploying the Service WAR

To deploy the service, we need to rerun the configuration utility. If the server is running, shut it down, and then run the configuration utility again. Step through until we get to the **Configure Services** tab. This time we should see the `applications\NewTesting` service listed. Make sure this is selected and continue through the configuration process. This will deploy the Service WAR file, which is created in the `WSDK_HOME\EAR` directory. Our next step is to register the service with Axis.

> *As mentioned earlier, if any changes are made to the implementation, we will need to rerun the configuration utility, as this utility creates the WAR file for us. Changes made are not automatically included – the WAR file must be re-created in order for the updates to be used.*

## Register the Service with Axis

To register the service, we use the command `axisDeploy`. This command registers our service, using the `deploy.wsdd` file that we created in the previous section. To do so, go to the deployment subdirectory of `NewTesting` and execute the following command:

```
AxisDeploy deploy.wsdd -lhttp://localhost:80/NewTesting/services/
        AdminService
```

The next step is to publish the service.

## Publishing the Service

To publish and test the service, we'll borrow heavily from the example client in the `SimpleApp` directory. We'll create a new client, which will:

❑ Publish our service interface

❑ Publish our service provider

❑ Publish our service implementation

❑   Test the service

❑   Unpublish all our information

To do all this, we'll create a test class as a client.

# A Java Client

In the C:\WSDK\services\applications\NewTesting\client directory, we'll create a file
called NewTestingClient.java. Let's examine this in stages. There are actually nine methods in the
client; we'll look at them all briefly, but the requestService() method is what is of particular
interest to us, as it is the actual invocation of the service. The methods are:

❑   Class Definition

❑   main()

❑   publishServiceImplementation()

❑   publishServiceInterface()

❑   publishServiceProvider()

❑   unPublishServiceImplementation()

❑   unPublishServiceInterface()

❑   unPublishServiceProvider()

❑   requestService()

We'll examine each of these below:

### Class Definition

To create this class we borrowed heavily from one of the WSDK examples:

```
import com.ibm.uddi4j.wsdl.definition.ServiceInterface;
import com.ibm.uddi4j.wsdl.definition.ServiceDefinition;
import com.ibm.uddi4j.wsdl.client.UDDIWSDLProxy;
import com.ibm.uddi4j.wsdl.client.ServiceProviderNotFoundException;
import com.ibm.uddi4j.wsdl.provider.ServiceProvider;
import com.ibm.uddi4j.wsdl.util.TModelKeyTable;

import org.uddi4j.util.KeyedReference;
import org.uddi4j.util.CategoryBag;
import org.uddi4j.datatype.Name;

import org.apache.axis.client.AdminClient;
import org.apache.axis.client.Service;
import org.apache.axis.client.Call;
import org.apache.axis.AxisFault;

import javax.xml.rpc.namespace.QName;

import java.util.Vector;
```

```
import java.net.URL;
import java.net.MalformedURLException;


public class NewTestingClient {

  // URL's for the various WebServices elements
  private static String wsdlServiceInterfaceURL =
    "http://localhost:80/NewTesting/NewTesting_Interface.wsdl";
  private static String serviceInterfaceName =
    "http://localhost:80/NewTesting/NewTesting_Interface";
  private static String serviceProviderName = "Whatever name you want.";
  private static String wsdlServiceImplURL =
    "http://localhost:80/NewTesting/NewTesting_Impl.wsdl";
  private static String soapServerURL =
    "http://localhost:80/NewTesting/services/AdminService";
  private static String soapDeploymentDescriptor =
    "../deployment/deploy.wsdd";
  private static String serviceName;


  // needed for the UDDI key element
  private static String tModelKey;
  private static String keyName;
  private static String keyValue;


  // required for creating a proxy to the UDDI service registry
  private static String UDDI_INQUIRY_URL =
    "http://localhost:80/uddisoap/inquiryapi";
  private static String UDDI_PUBLISH_URL =
    "http://localhost:80/uddisoap/publishapi";
  private static String UDDI_USERID ="demo";
  private static String UDDI_CRED ="pwd";
  private static String TRANSPORT_CLASS =
    "org.uddi4j.transport.ApacheAxisTransport";


  // to store the category bag representing the UDDI entry
  private CategoryBag categoryBag;
  // store the UDDIWSDLProxy
  private UDDIWSDLProxy uddiWsdlProxy;
  // store the Call object for invocations
  private Call call = null;

  static {
    // initialize the elements needed for the UDDI key element
    tModelKey = TModelKeyTable.getTModelKey("NAICS");
    keyName  = "Whatever you want.";
    keyValue = "12345"; // any number
  }
```

We can see that the code makes use of much of the `uddi4j` libraries, as well as the `axis` libraries. We define a number of static variables, which represent things like URLs of various components. There are also strings to represent the names of UDDI elements. The section that shows the service registry information is important, as these variable values must match the definition in the server configuration.

Now let's look at what happens when this class is instantiated. As seen below, the class creates a UDDI element, and sets the name of the tModel. It also creates a proxy interface to the UDDI registry, which the other functions will make use of later:

```
/**
 *   Default constructor
 */
public NewTestingClient() {

  // create the object which are used a lot throughout this code
  // create the UDDI key element
  KeyedReference keyedReference = new KeyedReference(keyName, keyValue);
  keyedReference.setTModelKey(tModelKey);

  // now create a CategoryBag and set the keyed reference
  categoryBag = new CategoryBag();
  categoryBag.add(keyedReference);

  // create a proxy interface to the UDDI service registry

  try {
    uddiWsdlProxy = new UDDIWSDLProxy(UDDI_INQUIRY_URL,
      UDDI_PUBLISH_URL, UDDI_USERID, UDDI_CRED, TRANSPORT_CLASS);
  } catch(Exception e) {
    e.printStackTrace();
  }
}
```

The execution of the program is contained in the main() method.

### The main() Method

This method creates a new instance of the client, then publishes the services and invokes the service request, and finally it unpublishes all of the services:

```
public static void main(String[] args) {
  NewTestingClient sac = new NewTestingClient();
  sac.publishServiceInterface();
  sac.publishServiceProvider();
  sac.publishServiceImplementation();
  sac.requestService();
  sac.unpublishServiceImplementation();
  sac.unpublishServiceProvider();
  sac.unpublishServiceInterface();
}
```

### Interface Publishing

Our first step is to publish the actual interface. We use the wsdlServiceInterfaceURL to point to the location of the service, and the categoryBag containing the UDDI key element that was created in the constructor. Now that we have a service, we can publish it using the UDDI proxy that was instantiated in the constructor as well:

**406**

```
      void publishServiceInterface() {
        System.out.println("Publishing service interface ...");

        try {
          // create the service interface
          ServiceInterface serviceInterface = new
            ServiceInterface(wsdlServiceInterfaceURL, categoryBag);

          // Publish the service interface
          serviceInterface = uddiWsdlProxy.publish(serviceInterface);

          System.out.println("<<< Service interface " + wsdlServiceInterfaceURL
                            + " was published. >>>");

        } catch(com.ibm.uddi4j.wsdl.client.UDDIWSDLProxyException e) {
          System.out.println("<<< Service interface " + wsdlServiceInterfaceURL
                            + " was NOT published. >>> " + e);

        } catch(com.ibm.uddi4j.wsdl.definition.InvalidServiceDefinitionException
            ex) {
          System.out.println("<<< Service interface " + wsdlServiceInterfaceURL
                            + " was NOT published. >>> " + ex);
        }
      }
```

Our next step is to publish the provider.

### Provider Publishing

Now we attempt to publish the provider. We create a vector to hold the name of the service provider, and attempt a UDDI lookup of the provider using the method findAllServiceProviders().

If we find the provider, we use it, if not we create a new provider. Finally we publish the provider to UDDI as well:

```
      void publishServiceProvider() {
        System.out.println("Publishing service provider ...");

        // create a vector to use for the proxy find
        Vector providerNameVector = new Vector();
        providerNameVector.add(new Name(serviceProviderName));

        try {
          // Find the service provider
          ServiceProvider[] serviceProviderList =
            uddiWsdlProxy.findAllServiceProviders(null, providerNameVector, null,
            null, null, null, true);

          // if no service provider found create one

          if (serviceProviderList == null) {
            // Create service provider
```

```
            ServiceProvider serviceProvider =
              new ServiceProvider(serviceProviderName, serviceProviderName,
                categoryBag);

            // Publish the service provider
            uddiWsdlProxy.publish(serviceProvider);
            // Display publish completed message
            System.out.println("Service provider " + serviceProviderName +
                                " was published.");
          } else {
            // service provider already created
            System.out.println("Service provider " + serviceProviderName +
                                " already published.");
          }

        } catch(com.ibm.uddi4j.wsdl.client.UDDIWSDLProxyException e) {
          System.out.println("<<< Service provider " + serviceProviderName +
                              " was NOT published. >>> " + e);
        }
      }
```

### Implementation Publishing

Here we'll make use both of the `uddi4j` classes and axis to publish our service. First we'll define a new service definition, which we'll use towards the end to publish the service. We create an axis `Call`, which is the object we'll use eventually to invoke the axis services to register our code in the SOAP server, which is distinct from the UDDI registry. Finally, once the SOAP registration is completed, we register the implementation in UDDI:

```
void publishServiceImplementation() {
  System.out.println("Publishing service implementation ...");
  ServiceDefinition serviceDef=null;

  try {
    // create a service definition (note we use the category bag created in
    // publishServiceInterface()
    serviceDef = new ServiceDefinition(wsdlServiceImplURL, categoryBag);
  } catch(com.ibm.uddi4j.wsdl.definition.InvalidServiceDefinitionException
      ex) {
    System.out.println("<<< Service implementation " + wsdlServiceImplURL +
                        " was NOT found. >>> " + ex);
    return;
  }

  // create an axis admin client
  AdminClient admin = new AdminClient();
  // get the Call object so we can set the endpoint - the Call object acts
  //(under the covers) as our proxy to deploy the service.
  Call call = admin.getCall();

  // deploy the service in the SOAP server
```

```
try {
  // set the endpoint for any Axis calls on this service
  call.setTargetEndpointAddress(new URL(soapServerURL));
  // process the Axis deployment descriptor
  String str = "";
  try {
    str = admin.process(soapDeploymentDescriptor);
  } catch(Exception ex) {
    System.out.println("Error processing Axis deployment descriptor : "
                        + ex);
    return;
  }

  if ( str.indexOf("<Admin>Done processing</Admin>") == -1 ) {
    System.out.println("Axis fault detected");
    return;
  }
  System.out.println(" <<< Service " + wsdlServiceImplURL +
                      " deployed. >>>");
} catch (MalformedURLException e) {
  System.out.println(" <<< Cound not deploy service " +
                      wsdlServiceImplURL + " because of exception " + e
                      + " >>>");
  return;
}

/* now publish the service to the UDDIWSDLProxy - note again how similar
 *this is to previous code */

// create the vector
Vector providerNameVector = new Vector();
providerNameVector.add(new Name(serviceProviderName));

try {
  // Find service provider
  ServiceProvider[] serviceProviderList =
    uddiWsdlProxy.findAllServiceProviders(null, providerNameVector, null,
    null, null, null, true);

  if (serviceProviderList != null) {
    // Publish the service
    serviceDef = uddiWsdlProxy.publish(serviceProviderList[0],
      serviceDef);

    // get the service name and store it
    serviceName = serviceDef.getName();

    System.out.println("<<< Service " + wsdlServiceImplURL +
                        " published. >>>");
  } else {
    System.out.println("<<< Service Provider " + wsdlServiceImplURL +
                        " not found. >>>");
  }
```

```
    } catch(com.ibm.uddi4j.wsdl.client.UDDIWSDLProxyException e) {
      System.out.println("<<< Service provider " + wsdlServiceImplURL +
                         " was NOT published. >>> " + e);
    } catch(com.ibm.uddi4j.wsdl.definition.InvalidServiceDefinitionException
        ex) {
      System.out.println("<<< Service provider " + wsdlServiceImplURL +
                         " was NOT published. >>> " + ex);
    }
  }
```

Now let's discuss the removal of the various registrations.

### Implementation Removal

To remove the implementation, we work backwards. First we remove the UDDI registration with a call to the function unpublish(). Then we remove the implementation from the axis SOAP server with a call to undeployService(). Note that we create a number of objects along the way to do the lookups; similar to objects we created when publishing. In production code we might consider making these instance variables as well to reduce the work we do:

```
void unpublishServiceImplementation() {

  System.out.println("Unpublishing service implementation ...");
  /* first we need to unpublish the service provider */
  // create the vector
  Vector serviceNameVector = new Vector();
  serviceNameVector.add(new Name(serviceName));

  try {
    // Create service definition
    ServiceDefinition[] serviceDefinitionList =
      uddiWsdlProxy.findAllServices(null, null, null, null, null, null,
      serviceNameVector, true);

    if (serviceDefinitionList != null) {
      // Create service provider
      ServiceProvider serviceProvider =
        uddiWsdlProxy.findServiceProvider(serviceDefinitionList[0]);

      if (serviceProvider != null) {
        // unpublish the serviceProvider
        uddiWsdlProxy.unpublish(serviceProvider, serviceDefinitionList[0]);
        System.out.println("<<< Service " + serviceName +
                           " was unpublished. >>>");
      } else {
        System.out.println("<<< SERVICE PROVIDER FOR " + serviceName +
                           " NOT FOUND. >>>");
        return;
      }
    } else {
      System.out.println("<<< SERVICE " + serviceName + " NOT FOUND. >>>");
      return;
```

```
    }
  } catch(com.ibm.uddi4j.wsdl.client.UDDIWSDLProxyException e) {
    System.out.println("<<< Service interface " + serviceName +
                    " was NOT unpublished. >>> " + e);
  }

  /* now we need to undeploy the service */
  try {
    // Create the SOAP service manager proxy which will be used to undeploy
    // the service and set it's endpoint
    AdminClient admin = new AdminClient();
    admin.getCall().setTargetEndpointAddress( new URL(soapServerURL) );

    try {
      // Undeploy the service in the SOAP server using the specified service
      // name
      admin.undeployService( serviceName );
    } catch(Exception ex) {
      System.out.println("Exception encountered undeploying from Axis : "
                      + ex);
    }

    // Indicate whether or not the service was undeployed
    System.out.println("<<< Service " + serviceName +
                    " was unpublished. >>>");
  } catch(java.net.MalformedURLException e) {
    System.out.println("<<< Service " + serviceName +
                    " was NOT unpublished. >>> " + e);
  }
}
```

Once the implementation is removed, we can remove the provider.

### Provider Removal

This is also straightforward – we find the service, and we call `unpublish()` to remove it:

```
/**
 * Unpublish the service provider form the UDDI - note how similar this is
 * to publishServiceProvider()
 */
void unpublishServiceProvider() {
  System.out.println("Unpublishing service provider ...");

  try {
    // create a vector to use for the proxy find
    Vector providerNameVector = new Vector();
    providerNameVector.add(new Name(serviceProviderName));

    // Find the service provider
    ServiceProvider[] serviceProviderList =
      uddiWsdlProxy.findAllServiceProviders(null, providerNameVector, null,
      null, null, null, true);
```

```
      if (serviceProviderList != null) {
        // Unpublish the service provider
        uddiWsdlProxy.unpublish(serviceProviderList[0]);
        System.out.println("Service provider " + serviceProviderName +
                           " was unpublished.");
      } else {
        System.out.println("Service provider " + serviceProviderName +
                           " is invalid.");
      }
    } catch(ServiceProviderNotFoundException e) {
      // Display error message
      System.out.println("<<< SERVICE PROVIDER " + serviceProviderName +
                         " NOT FOUND. >>>");

    } catch(com.ibm.uddi4j.wsdl.client.UDDIWSDLProxyException e) {
      System.out.println("<<< Service provider " + serviceProviderName +
                         " was NOT published. >>> " + e);
    }
  }
```

Now we can remove the interface too.

### Interface Removal

We achieve this with a call to unpublish():

```
/**
 * Unpublish the service interface from UDDI
 */
void unpublishServiceInterface() {
  System.out.println("Unpublishing service interface ...");

  try {
    // Find the service interface we are trying to unpublish
    ServiceInterface[] serviceInterfaceList =
      uddiWsdlProxy.findAllServiceInterfaces(null, serviceInterfaceName,
      null,null,true);

    if (serviceInterfaceList != null) {
      // Unpublish the service interface
      uddiWsdlProxy.unpublish(serviceInterfaceList[0]);
      System.out.println("<<< Service interface " + serviceInterfaceName +
                         " was unpublished. >>>");
    } else {
      System.out.println("<<< Service interface " + serviceInterfaceName +
                         " not found. >>>");
    }
  } catch(com.ibm.uddi4j.wsdl.client.UDDIWSDLProxyException e) {
    System.out.println("<<< Service interface " + serviceInterfaceName +
                       " was NOT published. >>> " + e);
  }
}
```

Now we can see how we actually use a web service in Java.

### Service Invocation

We start out by creating a `Call` object, which is our proxy to the service. We set up a `PortQN`, which represents the port in our WSDL definition. We select the operation we want to attempt (there can be more than one obviously in a web service) via a call to `setOperation()`. We actually use the web service by calling the `invoke()` method. Then we print the result, using `System.out.println()`, to the console:

```
public void requestService() {
  try {
    String  namespace = "http://NewTesting" ;
    QName  serviceQN = new QName( namespace, "NewTestingService" );

    Service service = new Service(new URL(wsdlServiceImplURL), serviceQN);

    QName portQN = new QName( namespace, "message" );

    // This Call object will be reused for all invocations
    if ( call == null ) call = (Call) service.createCall();

    // Now make the call...
    System.out.println("Invoking service >> " + serviceName + " <<...");
    call.setOperation( portQN, "createAccount" );
    String retVal = (String) call.invoke( new Object[] {"SPQR"} );
    System.out.println("Result returned from call to " + serviceName +
                     " -- " + retVal);
  } catch(java.net.MalformedURLException e) {
    System.out.println("Error invoking service : " + e);

  } catch(javax.xml.rpc.ServiceException e2) {
    System.out.println("Error invoking service : " + e2);

  } catch(java.rmi.RemoteException e3) {
    System.out.println("Error invoking service : " + e3);
  }
}
```

That's it; we are all done for this example. Let's quickly discuss what we have seen in this section.

We can see that the IBM WebSphere SDK for web services provides a great deal of power and flexibility in the ability to create and deploy web services. This flexibility comes at the price of more coding and synchronization as we create Java, WSDL, WSDD, and XML messages to manage the service.

We provided some initial insight into the software packages provided by IBM, including UDDI4J and AXIS. In addition to these APIs, we've covered some of the tools (such as `java2wsdl`) in other chapters in the book.

# Finishing Up

Let's have a quick summary of what we have seen of the IBM Web Services Toolkit. This environment allows us to create and deploy web services developed in Java.

We've learned how to do the following using the WSTK:

- Create a new web service by creating a Java class
- Create a directory structure to support our web service
- Create WSDL to support our web service
- Deploy a Java class as a web service
- Register the web service with Axis
- Write a Java client to access our web service
- Test the web service with our Java client

# Summary

We've examined three different products that make it possible to create web services using Java. BEA WebLogic Workshop provided a high-level drag and drop interface that makes web service development largely about connecting components rather than coding. IBM WebSphere Studio Application Developer provides a more code-related approach to web services development, and is more focused on writing Java code, while providing convenient automation of many tasks in the development and testing of web services.

The IBM Web Services Toolkit is the most code-intensive of the tools we examined, and lacks a GUI or other productivity tools, but does provide incredible control of the web services environment. Different developers will want to use a different one of these tools depending upon their need for speed and power.

There are also a number of other tools available to the Java programmer that we didn't have space to include. These tools include:

- Iona XMLBus
  It is available from http://www.iona.com

- GLUE and GAIA by The Mind Electric
  They are available from http://www.themindelectric.com

- SUNOne Studio
  It is available from http://www.sun.com

- Borland JBuilder and Enterprise Server
  Available at http://www.borland.com

These tools all provide some capability to create, manage, or deploy web services with varying degrees of automation. What degree is best is a choice that remains up to you.

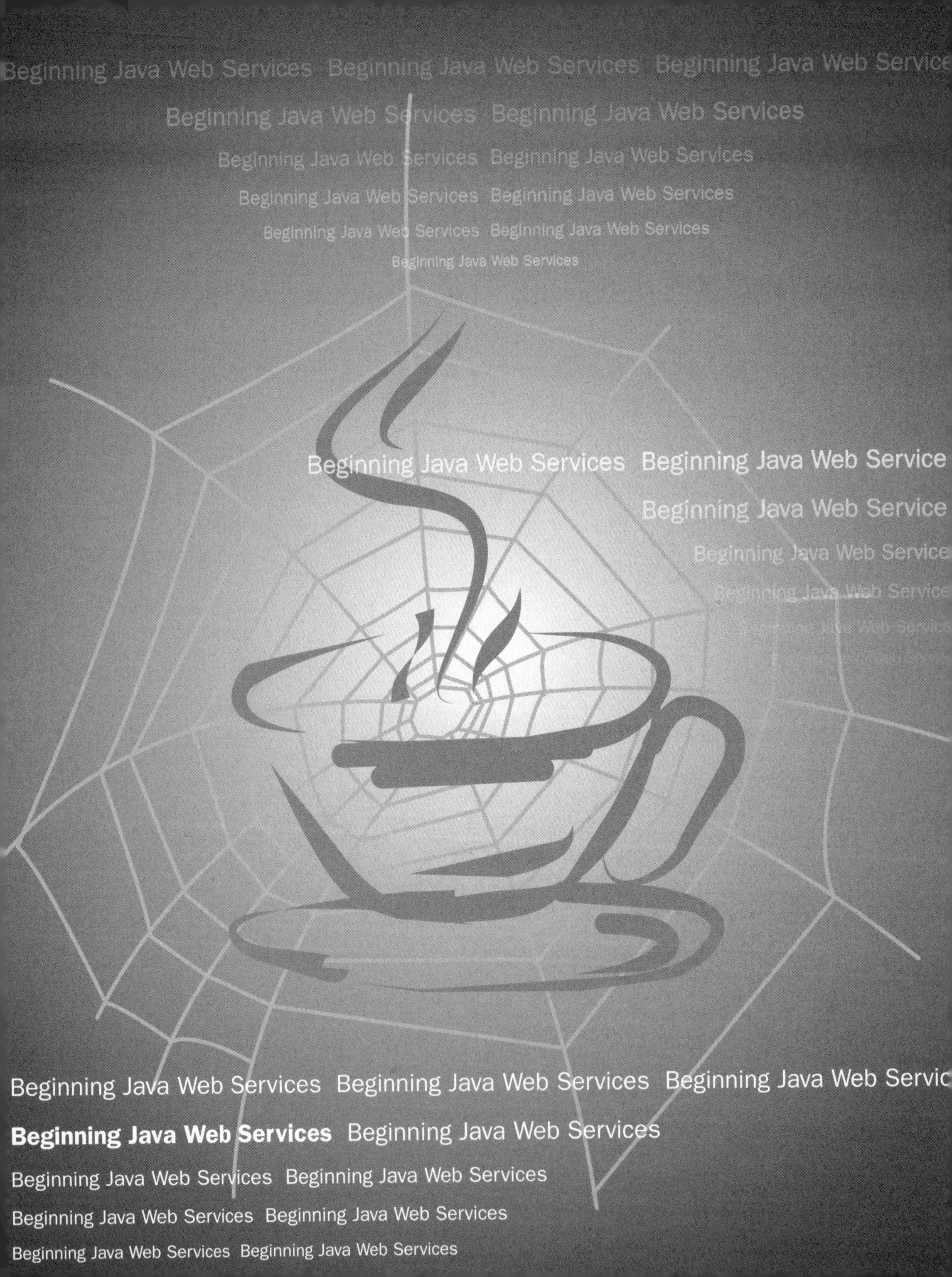
Beginning Java Web Services Beginning Java Web Services Beginning Java Web Service
Beginning Java Web Services Beginning Java Web Services
Beginning Java Web Services Beginning Java Web Services
Beginning Java Web Services Beginning Java Web Services
Beginning Java Web Services Beginning Java Web Services
Beginning Java Web Services
Beginning Java Web Services Beginning Java Web Service
Beginning Java Web Service
Beginning Java Web Service
Beginning Java Web Services Beginning Java Web Services Beginning Java Web Servic
Beginning Java Web Services Beginning Java Web Services
Beginning Java Web Services Beginning Java Web Services
Beginning Java Web Services Beginning Java Web Services
Beginning Java Web Services Beginning Java Web Services

# Case Study – Application Integration

So far in this book we have covered the various technologies and tools that are used for implementing web services. In this chapter, we will be discussing a case study to illustrate the use of web services for integrating a set of disparate applications within an enterprise. The case study will focus on leveraging the services provided by an existing set of applications, with the web services technology, to perform Enterprise Application Integration (EAI).

The case study will be deployed on BEA WebLogic 7.0 server and WebLogic Workshop. An evaluation copy of the WebLogic server and Workshop can be downloaded from http://www.bea.com/.

In this case study we will use WebLogic Workshop to package three existing applications as web services. These applications will then be accessed through their web services interface to build a brand new web-based shopping system, which will leverage the services provided by these applications. The three applications that are integrated to build the online shopping system are:

- ❑ A database application that stores catalog information
- ❑ A J2EE application that processes credit card payment
- ❑ A proprietary messaging system that is used for order processing

In the course of this chapter we will learn how to expose these applications as web services with a minimum amount of effort, and how these applications can be easily accessed from J2EE web applications through their web services interface.

## Internal and External Web Services

Before we delve into the various intricacies of our case study, we will have a quick look at the two scenarios in which web services are more popularly used.

When the web services hype started gaining momentum, everyone was excited about companies implementing, describing, publishing, discovering, and consuming web services on the Internet and forming dynamic businesses. These types of web services, where the producers and consumers are different companies, are called **external web services**.

However, in most practical scenarios, forming business partnerships involves many formal procedures and processes. This realization leads to new business collaboration standards and specifications such as ebXML and BizTalk, which address issues not dealt by the basic web services technologies like XML, SOAP, WSDL, UDDI, etc.

External web services mainly provide services that are accessed by trading partners. For example, www.xmethods.com provides a public registry of external web services that can be accessed over the public network. Examples for external web services include services that provide stock quotes, weather forecasts, and so on. External web services may be free or commercial. Commercial web services can adopt different payment models, including payment per invocation, as well as a subscription-based model.

For example, if we are developing an online system for trading security instruments, we may enter a trading agreement with Reuters or FT to access their web services for providing the latest quote for the specified security.

However, at the time of writing, lots of products are coming into the market, which use web services technologies to provide end-to-end EAI solutions. In such scenarios, the consumers and producers of web services are the applications running within an enterprise. Such web services are called **internal web services**. For example, we may have an application that manages the production unit of our company interfacing with the inventory system, using web services.

The diagram below depicts the use of external and internal web services:

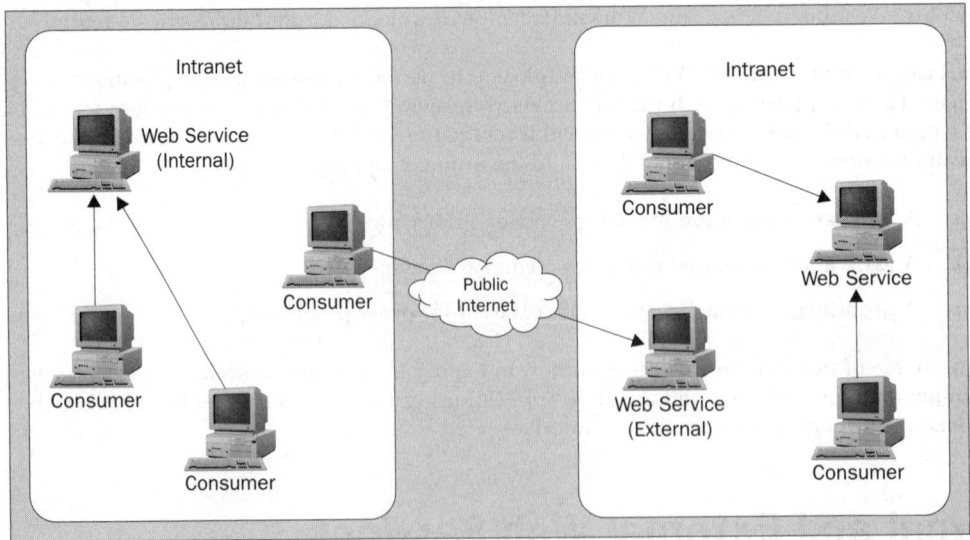

Since web services use platform-neutral, language-neutral, and vendor-neutral technologies such as XML, HTTP, SOAP, and WSDL, they are very well suited for integrating disparate, heterogeneous, and disconnected applications within an enterprise. On top of this, most of the mainstream J2EE server vendors offer support for web services and provide easy-to-use tools that can be used for exposing standard J2EE components like EJBs and JMS destinations via web services. The diagram below depicts how web services can fit into an existing J2EE infrastructure:

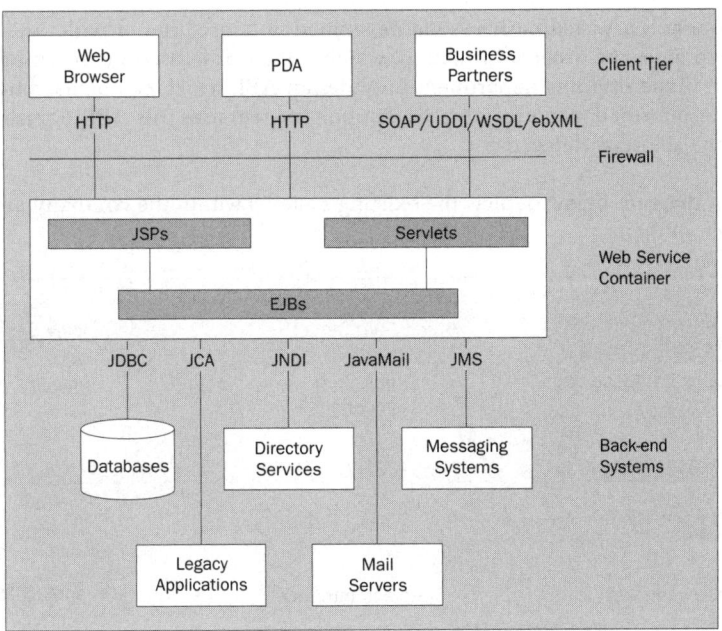

The seamless integration of web services with existing J2EE technology components, contributes highly towards leveraging the power of existing solutions and components to build a web services-based EAI solution.

Over the past years one of the most critical problems with EAI solutions has been the dependence on proprietary vendor API and plug-ins. Most of the time application developers were writing 'glue' code to get the EAI solutions from various vendors to work with their applications. Web services and associated technologies provide a vendor-neutral and open standard solution, which can leverage the existing infrastructure of enterprises to provide an elegant EAI solution.

Let's now move on to discuss our case study, which, as we mentioned earlier, will make use of web services to integrate a set of disparate internal applications and expose them as a web application.

# Case Study Overview

Acme Corporation, our fictitious case study corporation, currently provides catalog-based shopping services to its customers. It delivers printed copies of catalogs containing the products on offer to its customers, and the customers place orders over the telephone. The orders are processed by desk clerks, who validate the payment details and use an in-house system to control the shipping of the order.

**419**

The company has an in-house J2EE-based system that connects to various credit card providers to process credit card payment. The system provides a simple stateless interface implemented using a J2EE session EJB component.

The products available in the catalog are stored in a MySQL database. The company has a system written in C that connects to the database and prints the catalog information.

The shipping system is a Visual Basic system developed in-house, that provides the desk clerks an easy-to-use interface to enter the order information, which is later processed by the shipping department. The system used in the shipping department provides an API, which can be used by external systems for pushing order information. Currently, the shipping system uses this API to push the order information to the shipping department.

The deployment diagram below depicts the existing systems within the company and the interfaces provided by each of them:

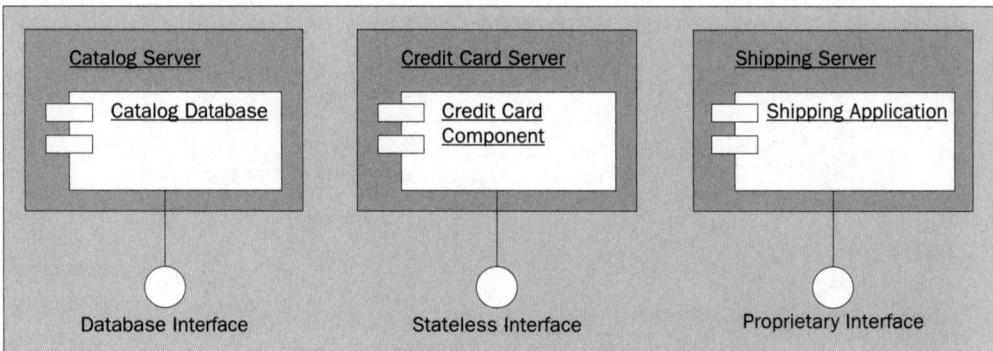

The company has now made a decision to make some of its services available to the public over the Internet. It has also decided to integrate the existing disparate set of applications to provide a new end-to-end online shopping solution to its customers. It has also been agreed upon to use the Web Services technology for integrating the existing applications in a loosely coupled manner.

The component diagram opposite depicts how the existing applications may be integrated using the web services technology: The current interface to the shipping system is currently very slow and will not be acceptable in a web-based solution. Hence, as part of the new system, it has also been decided to improve the transaction throughput of the system by providing an asynchronous interface.

This component diagram depicts the proposed architecture of the new system:

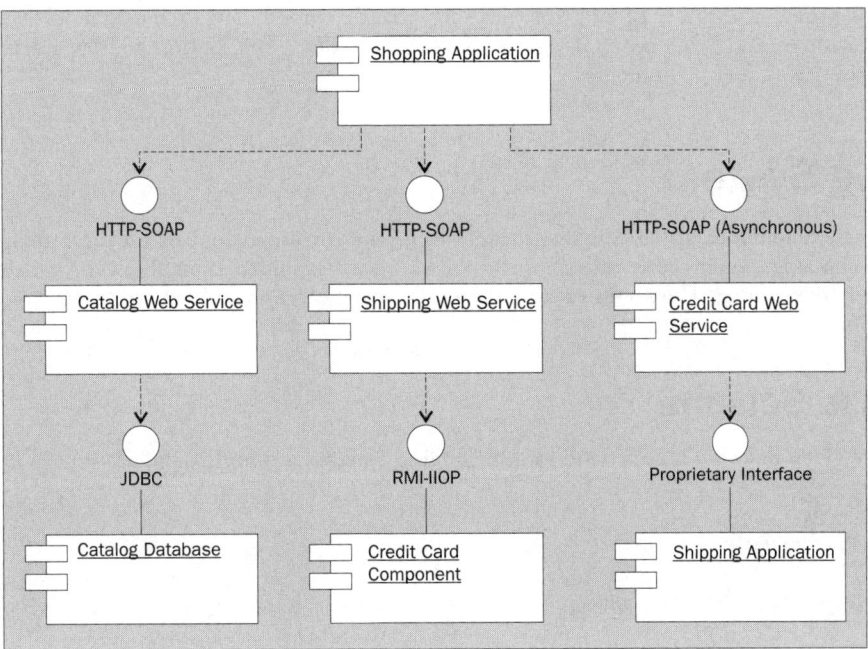

In short, we can summarize the situation as:

❏ The online shopping application will access the catalog application through a web service using SOAP over HTTP. At the moment, the catalog information is stored in a database, but the SOAP-based web service that can be accessed using standard web services invocation technologies such as JAX-RPC and JAXM, will access the database using JDBC to provide the necessary catalog information.

❏ The credit card application provides a stateless session EJB interface that will be exposed as a standard SOAP-based web service that can be accessed using JAX-RPC or JAXM. The web service will use the standard RMI-IIOP protocol for accessing the EJB component.

❏ The shipping application currently provides a proprietary interface. This will also be accessed from a SOAP-based web service. The web service will provide message buffering and an asynchronous invocation facility to improve performance and transaction throughout.

Acme Corporation has decided to use the BEA Workshop and WebLogic Server for developing and deploying its web services and shopping application, as its existing applications currently run on WebLogic. BEA WebLogic Server is a proven platform for developing scalable and robust J2EE applications and also provides a robust environment for deploying web services.

BEA Workshop is an IDE for assembling, developing, debugging, deploying, and testing enterprise class web services. Workshop also allows you to expose standard J2EE components like EJBs, JMS destinations, and JDBC data sources as web services accessible through standard protocols like JAX-RPC and JAXM with the minimum amount of effort. For more details on BEA WebLogic, please refer to Chapter 10

WebLogic provides a variety of tools for exposing existing components such as stateless session EJBs, JMS destinations, and Java classes as web services that are described, published, discovered, and invoked using standard technologies.

# Catalog System

First, we will take a look at the database that stores the information required for the catalog system. The database contains a single table called `Product`, which stores information about the various products available in the catalog. The section below shows the structure of the table used for storing the catalog information.

# Database Schema

The script given below will create the `Product` table and insert sample data into it:

```
CREATE TABLE Product (
  code varchar(30),
  name varchar(30),
  description varchar(60),
  price double);
```

The table stores a unique code identifying the product, the name of the product, a description for the product, and the price of the product:

```
INSERT INTO Product VALUES ('PR01', 'T-Shirt', 'Hooded T-Shirt', 123.45);
INSERT INTO Product VALUES ('PR02', 'Jacket', 'Leather Jacket', 234.56);
INSERT INTO Product VALUES ('PR03', 'Trousers', 'Denim Straights', 345.67);
INSERT INTO Product VALUES ('PR04', 'Trainers', 'Cross Mountain Trainers',
  456.78);
INSERT INTO Product VALUES ('PR05', 'Tights', 'Denim Tights', 567.89);
```

> *We have used MySQL for storing the table and data shown above. However, you can make use of any relational database with a valid JDBC-compliant driver. By running the scripts given above, you can create the table and populate it with the sample data.*

# Develop the Catalog Web Service

In this section we will develop the catalog web service, which will connect to the database and provide the catalog information to the web service clients. In this section we will be performing the following tasks:

❑  Configure a datasource within WebLogic server to connect to the database

❑  Create a new web services project in WebLogic Workshop

❑  Create a new web service that will provide the catalog information

❑  Deploy and test the web service

❑  Generate the proxies that can be used by clients for accessing this web service

## Configure the Datasource

Datasources are used in J2EE for getting connections to the database. They implement the `javax.sql.DataSource` interface. Normally either the JDBC provider or the J2EE server vendor provides classes that implement this interface. In most cases J2EE servers provide tools for configuring datasources and making them available for JNDI lookup. The clients that require connecting to databases can look up these datasources using JNDI calls and use them for creating connections to databases. Please refer to *Professional Java Server Programming* from Wrox Press (ISBN 1-86100-537-7) for an in-depth coverage of JDBC and JNDI.

In Chapter 10, we have seen how to configure datasources within the WebLogic server. For this web service we need to configure a datasource called `productDataSource` to connect to the database containing our `Product` table (for more details on configuring datasources within WebLogic please refer to Chapter 10).

## Create a New Web Services Project

In this section we will create a new web services project in Workshop that will contain all the three web services used in this case study. For this we need to perform the following steps:

**1.** Start the database server containing the `Product` table and data (in our case it will be MySQL)

**2.** Start the WebLogic server in the workshop domain by running the `%WLS_HOME%\WebLogic700\samples\workshop\startWebLogic.cmd` where `%WLS_HOME%` is the directory in which we have installed WebLogic server and Workshop

**3.** Start the Workshop IDE either using the shortcuts available on the start menu

Once the Workshop IDE is up and running, we will create our project. For this click on the File menu and select the New Project option. This will open a dialog box asking us to enter the name of the project. In this dialog box enter `ShoppingWS` and click OK:

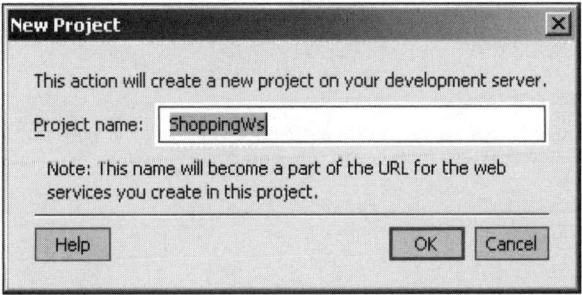

This will create the following file structure:

```
%WLS_HOME%\Weblogic7000\samples\workshop\applications\ShoppingWS
%WLS_HOME%\Weblogic7000\samples\workshop\applications\ShoppingWS\WEB-
INF\lib
%WLS_HOME%\Weblogic7000\samples\workshop\applications\ShoppingWS\WEB-
INF\classes
```

Now a dialog box will pop up, click the Cancel button of this dialog box. Then, in the tree on the left-hand side of the IDE right-click on the root item and select New Folder from the pop-up menu. Create a folder called catalog. In this folder we will be storing the required files for the catalog web service. Repeat the process to create folders shipping and creditCard for the files implementing the shipping and credit card web services respectively.

## Create the Catalog Web Service

In this section we will create the catalog web service. For this, right-click on the catalog folder in the tree on the left-hand side of the IDE, and then click on the New File item in the popup menu. This will display a dialog for entering details about the file we are going to create. The Web Service radio button will be selected by default. Enter the name of the file CatalogWS and click OK:

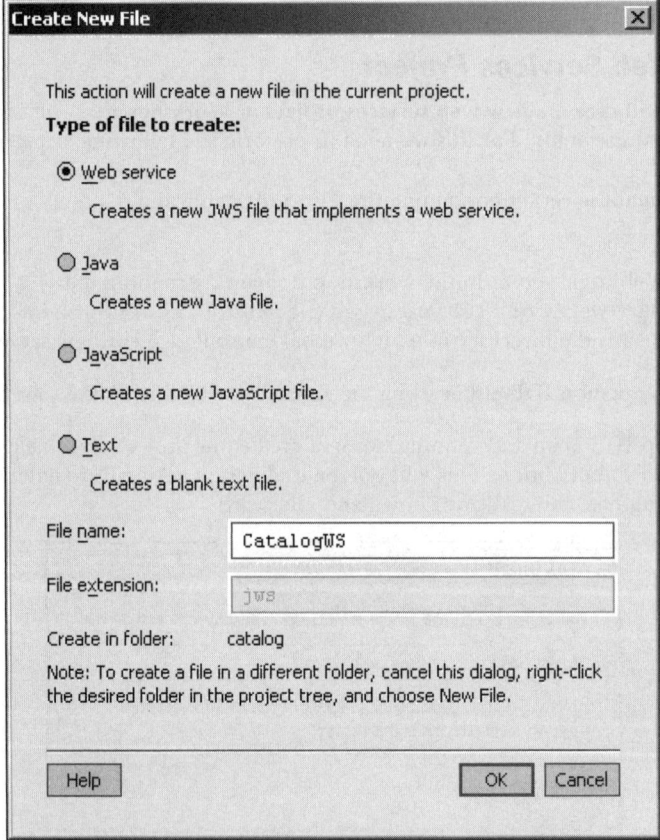

Now the IDE will display the design view of the web service in the middle pane. In the property pane on the right-hand side enter the target namespace of the web service as catalog.

### Add the getCatalog() Method and the Database Control

Now we will add the getCatalog() method, which will be exposed by the web service to its clients. For this click on the **Add Operation** drop-down box in the middle pane and select the **Add Method** item. Enter the name of the method as getCatalog.

Next we will add the database control that we need for connecting to the database from the web service. For this click on the **Add Control** drop-down box on the right-hand side of the middle pane and select the **Add Database Control** item. This will display a dialog box for entering the details of the database control.

In the dialog box enter the variable name of the control as productDataSource. This will be the name by which we will be referring to the control from within our web service. Select the radio button for creating a new control and enter the name of the control as ProductDataSource. This will create a new file called ProductDataSourceControl.ctrl under the catalog folder. This control can be reused in other web services as well. Select the productDataSource that was configured within WebLogic by clicking the **Browse** button. Now click **OK**:

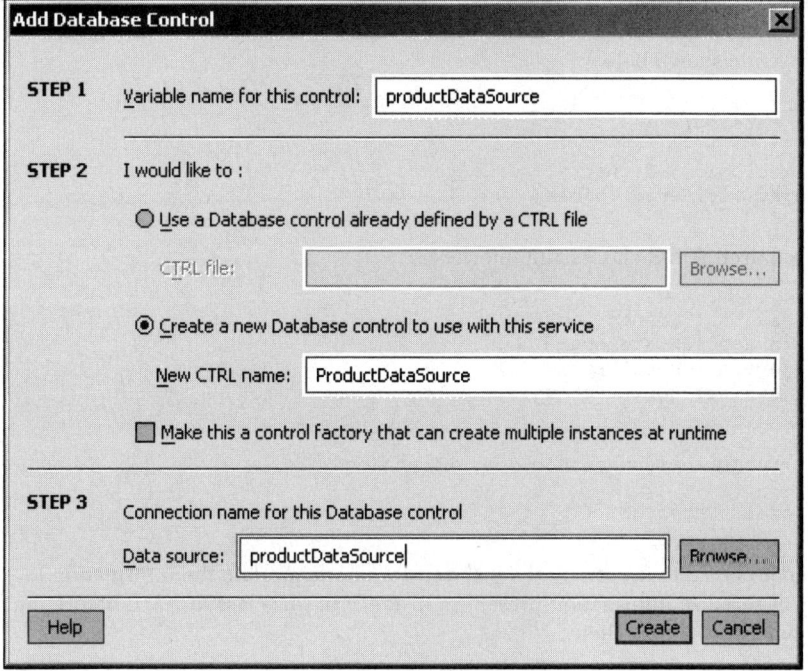

The figure below shows the design view of our web service with the operation on the left side and the control on the right side:

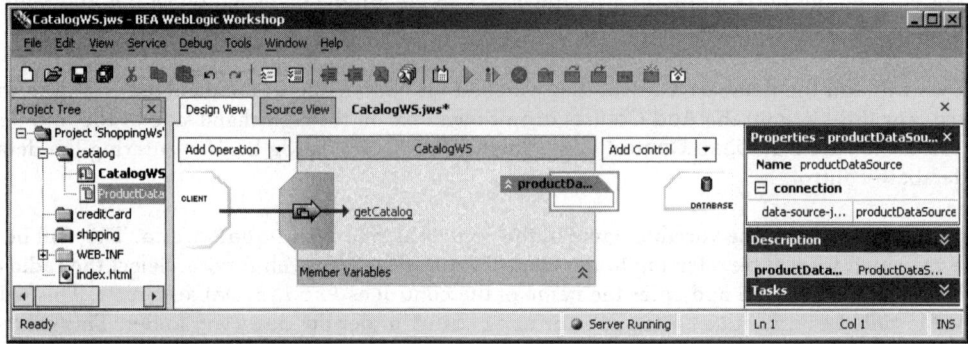

## Add Code to the Web Service

In this section, we will be adding code to our web service for connecting to the database and returning the catalog information to the clients. For this, click on the **Source View** tab of our catalog web service and enter the code shown below:

```
package catalog;

import weblogic.jws.control.JwsContext;
import java.io.Serializable;
```

Import the required JDBC classes and interfaces:

```
import java.sql.Connection;
import java.sql.Statement;
import java.sql.ResultSet;
import java.sql.SQLException;
/**
 * @jws:target-namespace namespace="catalog"
 */
public class CatalogWS {
```

This is an inner class that is used by the web service to encapsulate the information for each product. WebLogic will serialize information present in instance of this class to XML before the web service response is send back to the client:

```
    public static class Product implements Serializable {
```

This represents the unique code for each product:

```
        private String code;
        public String getCode() { return code; }
        public void setCode(String val) { code = val; }
```

This represents the name of the product:

```
private String name;
public String getName() { return name; }
public void setName(String val) { name = val; }
```

This represents the description for the product:

```
private String description;
public String getDescription() { return description; }
public void setDescription(String val) { description = val; }
```

This represents the price of the product:

```
private double price;
public double getPrice() { return price; }
public void setPrice(double val) { price = val; }
}
```

This is the datasource control we will use for connecting to the database. This line of code was automatically generated by the web service when we added the database control in design view:

```
/**
 * @jws:control
 */
private ProductDataSourceControl productDataSource;

/** @jws:context */
JwsContext context;
```

This is the operation exposed by the web service. WebLogic Workshop generated the shell of this method when we added the method in the design view:

```
/**
 * @jws:operation
 */
public Product[] getCatalog() throws SQLException {
```

Get a connection from the datasource and use the connection to create a statement:

```
Connection con = productDataSource.getConnection();
Statement stmt = con.createStatement();
```

Execute the SQL query to get the number of products in the database:

```
ResultSet res = stmt.executeQuery("SELECT COUNT(*) FROM PRODUCT");
res.next();
Product products[] = new Product[res.getInt(1)];
```

Execute the SQL query to get all the product details from the database, loop through the result set, and create the array of products:

```
res = stmt.executeQuery("SELECT * FROM PRODUCT");
for(int i = 0; i < products.length && res.next(); i++) {
  Product product = new Product();
  product.setCode(res.getString(1));
  product.setName(res.getString(2));
  product.setDescription(res.getString(3));
  product.setPrice(res.getDouble(4));

  products[i] = product;
}
```

Close the database resources:

```
res.close();
stmt.close();
con.close();
```

Return the array of products:

```
    return products;
  }
}
```

## *Test the Web Service*

In this section we will test whether our web service is working properly. Click on the **Debug** menu and select the **Start** option. This will open the web service home page in a browser window. This page has four tabs:

- ❑ Overview
  This tab provides links for viewing the WSDL for the web service, downloading client proxies, and so on

- ❑ Console
  For controlling the various logging and persistence aspects of the web service

- ❑ Test Form
  This will provide functionality for testing the web service using HTTP GET and POST

- ❑ Test XML
  This will provide functionality to test the web service by sending raw XML

We will test our web service using the **Test Form** tab. For this, click on the **getCatalog** link located on the tab. This will execute the web service and display the result in the browser as shown:

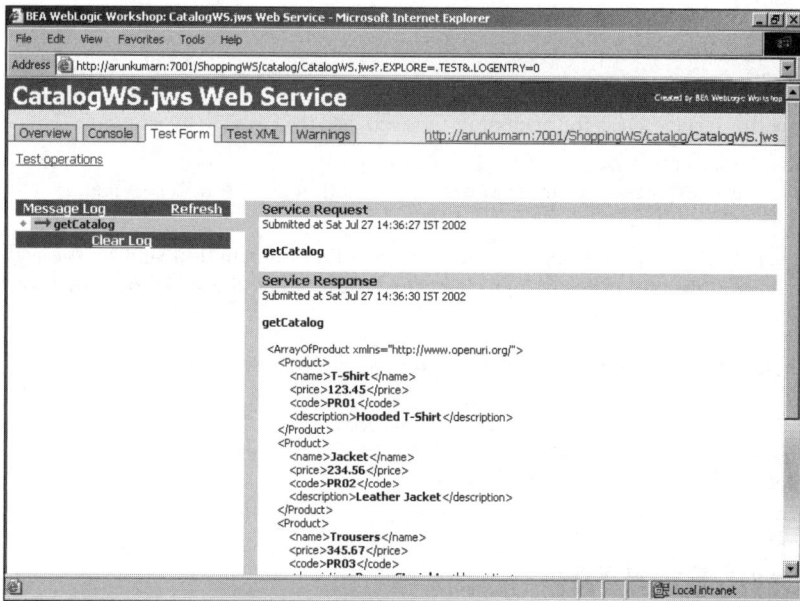

## Generate Client Proxy

Now we will generate the client proxy JAR file for accessing the web service from clients. We will use this JAR file later in the shopping application for accessing the web service. For this click on the Overview tab and then on the Java Proxy link:

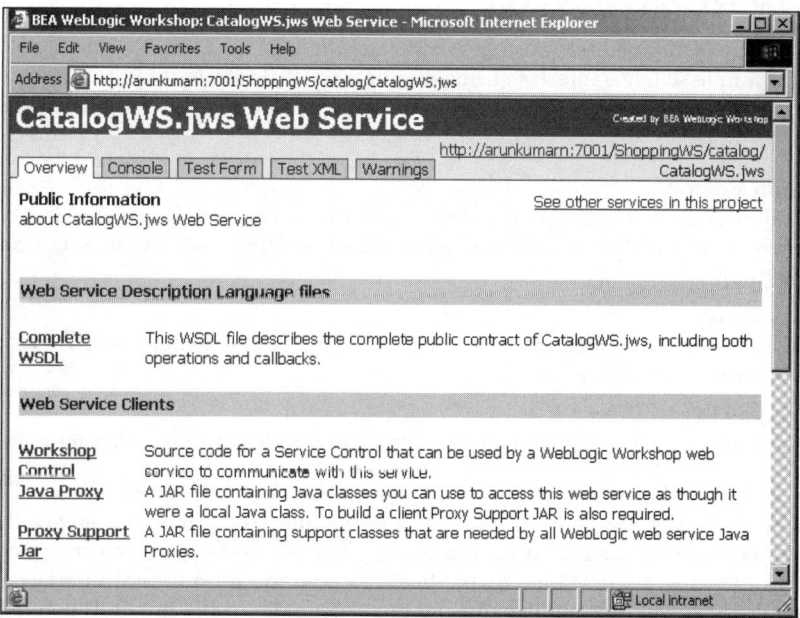

Save the generated JAR file under the name `CatalogClient.jar`. This JAR file contains three classes inside and is used for accessing the web service:

❑ `WebLogic.proxies.jws.CatalogWS`
This is the service class for accessing the web service.

❑ `WebLogic.proxies.jws.CatalogWSSoap`
This is the interface used for invoking the operation on the web service.

❑ `catalog.Product`
This is the client-side representation of the product information sent by the web service. The client-side stubs and other helper classes will deserialize the XML data received from the web service to generate instances of this class.

The snippet below shows how the catalog web service can be accessed from the client:

```
CatalogWS_Impl catalogWS = new CatalogWS_Impl();
CatalogWSSoap catalogWSSoap = catalogWS.getCatalogWSSoap();
Product[] products = catalogWSSoap.getCatalog();
```

# Credit Card System

In this section we will be implementing the credit card application as a web service. First we will have a look at the backend component that implements the web service and then we will look at exposing this component as a SOAP-based web service.

## Credit Card Session Bean

As we have already mentioned the existing credit card application is implemented as a J2EE application and provides a simple stateless interface using-session EJB. EJBs are part of the J2EE technology suite and are used for building transactional business components. The EJB specification provides three types of EJBs:

❑ **Session Bean**
Session beans act as extensions to the clients that invoke the beans. Session beans can either be stateless or stateful. Stateful session beans remember their instance state across multiple invocations.

❑ **Entity Bean**
Entity beans are components that can be shared by multiple clients and are used for modeling persistent domain objects.

❑ **Message-Driven Bean**
Message-driven beans are components activated by asynchronous JMS messages.

Both session and entity beans provide a client view that can be accessed by clients. This is achieved by using the home and component interface. The home interface provides methods that govern the life cycle of a bean like creating, finding, removing the bean, and so on. The component interface defines the business method provided by the bean. In addition to these two interfaces, an EJB needs a bean implementation class that implements the business logic for the methods defined in the component interface.

For our credit card session bean we need to write the component interface, home interface, and bean implementation class. Please note that a comprehensive coverage of EJB is beyond the scope of this chapter and the book. For a detailed coverage of EJBs refer to *Professional EJB* from *Wrox Press (ISBN 1-86100-508-3)* for more details.

### Component Interface

The listing below shows the component interface for the session bean. The interface defines a single method specifying the credit card number to debit, and the amount that needs to be debited. It returns a Boolean value indicating whether the payment was processed successfully:

```
package com.acme.creditcard;

import javax.ejb.EJBObject;
import java.rmi.RemoteException;

public interface CreditCardService extends EJBObject {
```

The component interface defines the business method used by the clients for authorizing credit card payments:

```
    public boolean debit(String cardNo, double amount) throws RemoteException;
}
```

### Home Interface

The code for the home interface is shown below:

```
package com.acme.creditcard;

import javax.ejb.EJBHome;
import javax.ejb.CreateException;
import java.rmi.RemoteException;

public interface CreditCardServiceHome extends EJBHome {
```

Define the lifecycle method to create an instance of the bean:

```
    public CreditCardService create() throws CreateException, RemoteException;
}
```

Since the catalog service is going to be implemented as a stateless component, the home interface defines a no-argument create() method.

## Bean Implementation Class

The source file for the bean implementation class is shown below:

```
package com.acme.creditcard;

import javax.ejb.SessionBean;
import javax.ejb.SessionContext;

import java.util.Random;

public class CreditCardServiceEJB implements SessionBean {
```

These are the lifecycle methods that need to be implemented from the `SessionBean` interface:

```
public void ejbActivate() {}
public void ejbPassivate() {}
public void ejbRemove() {}
public void setSessionContext(SessionContext ctx) {}

public void ejbCreate() {}
```

The business method implementation:

```
public boolean debit(String cardNo, double amount) {
  return new Random().nextBoolean();
}
}
```

## Standard Deployment Descriptor

The code below lists the standard `ejb-jar.xml` deployment descriptor:

```
<?xml version="1.0"?>

<!DOCTYPE ejb-jar PUBLIC
  "-//Sun Microsystems, Inc.//DTD Enterprise JavaBeans 1.1//EN"
  "http://java.sun.com/j2ee/dtds/ejb-jar_1_1.dtd">

<ejb-jar>

  <enterprise-beans>
    <session>
```

The name of the EJB:

```
<ejb-name>CreditCardService</ejb-name>
```

The home interface:

```
<home>com.acme.creditcard.CreditCardServiceHome</home>
```

The component interface:

```
        <remote>com.acme.creditcard.CreditCardService</remote>
```

The bean class:

```
        <ejb-class>com.acme.creditcard.CreditCardServiceEJB</ejb-class>
```

Define the bean as stateless:

```
        <session-type>Stateless</session-type>
      </session>
    </enterprise-beans>

  </ejb-jar>
```

### WebLogic Deployment Descriptor

The code below lists the WebLogic-specific deployment descriptor `WebLogic-ejb-jar.xml` for the session EJB:

```
<?xml version="1.0"?>

<!DOCTYPE WebLogic-ejb-jar PUBLIC
  "-//BEA Systems, Inc.//DTD WebLogic 7.0.0 EJB//EN"
  "http://www.bea.com/servers/wls700/dtd/WebLogic700-ejb-jar.dtd">

<WebLogic-ejb-jar>

  <WebLogic-enterprise-bean>
    <ejb-name>CreditCardService</ejb-name>
```

Define the JNDI name for looking up the home interface:

```
        <jndi-name>CreditCardServiceHome</jndi-name>
    </WebLogic-enterprise-bean>

</WebLogic-ejb-jar>
```

## Building and Deploying the EJB

In this section we will build and deploy our EJB on WebLogic server. For this, first we need to compile the component interface, home interface, and bean class. Please make sure that while compiling these classes, we have the `weblogic.jar` file in our classpath:

```
set classpath=%classpath%;%BEA_HOME%\server\lib\weblogic.jar
```

*%BEA_HOME% is where we have installed WebLogic 7.0.*

We will change to the %jwsDirectory%\Chp11\CreditCardService\src directory and compile the files:

```
javac -d ..\classes CreitCardSercice.java
javac -d ..\classes CreditCardServiceHome.java
javac -d ..\classes CreditCardServiceEJB.java
```

After compiling the classes, create the following directory structure inside the \classes directory:

```
/com/acme/creditcard/CreditCardService.class
/com/acme/creditcard/CreditCardServiceHome.class
/com/acme/creditcard/CreditCardServiceEJB.class
/META-INF/ejb-jar.xml
/META-INF/WebLogic-ejb-jar.xml
```

Then in the %jwsDirectory%\Chp11\temp run the jar command to create a JAR file with structure as shown above.

```
jar cf CreditCardService.jar *
```

Copy the JAR file to %WLS_HOME%/Weblogic700/samples/workshop/applications to deploy the EJB.

# Develop the Credit Card Web Service

In this section we will develop the credit card web service, which will use the EJB to process credit card payments issued by the web service clients. We will perform the following tasks:

❑ Create a new web service that will process credit card information

❑ Deploy and test the web service

❑ Generate the proxies that can be used by clients for accessing this web service

## Create the Credit Card Web Service

Now we will create the credit card web service. For this right-click on the creditcard folder in the tree on the left-hand side of the IDE and click on the New File item in the popup menu. This will display a dialog for entering details about the file we are going to create. The Web Service radio button will be selected by default. Enter the name of the file CreditCardWS and click OK. Now the IDE will display the design view of the web service in the middle pane. In the property pane on the right-hand side enter the target namespace of the web service as creditCard.

### Add the debit() Method and the EJB Control

Now we will add the debit() method, which will be exposed by the web service to its clients. For this, click on the Add Operation drop-down box in the middle pane and select the Add Method item. Enter the name of the method as debit.

Before we can use the EJB control for accessing the credit card EJB we need to make the client view of the EJB available to our web services project. For this we need to copy the `CreditCardService.jar` file to `%WLS_HOME%/WebLogic700/samples/workshop/applications/ShoppingWS/WEB-INF/lib` directory. After this we will have to restart both WebLogic server and Workshop.

Now we will add the EJB control that we need to access the credit card EJB. For this, click on the **Add Control** drop-down box on the right-hand side of the middle pane and select the **Add EJB Control** item. This will display a dialog box for entering the details of the EJB control. In the dialog box enter the variable name of the control as `creditCard`. This will be the name by which we will be referring to the control from within our web service.

Select the radio button for creating a new control and enter the name of the control as `CreditCard`. This will create a new file called `CreditCardControl.ctrl` under the `creditcard` folder. This control can be reused in other web services as well. Select the `CreditCardServiceHome` by clicking the **Browse** button against the JNDI name. This will automatically populate the home and remote interfaces. Then click OK:

The figure below shows the design view of our web service with the operation on the left side and the control on the right side:

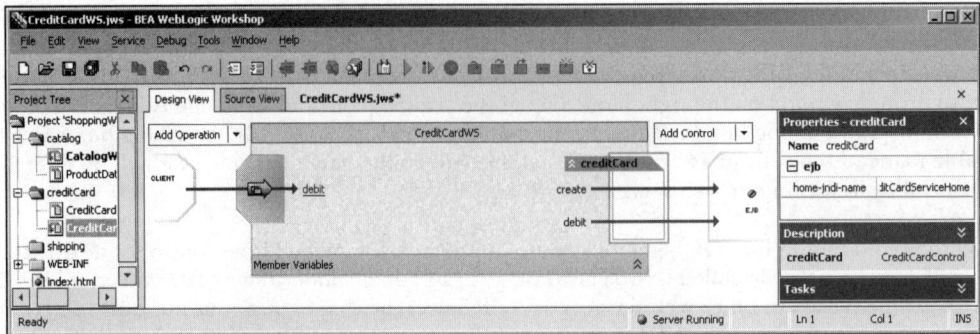

## Add Code to Web Service

In this section we will add code to our web service, for using the credit card EJB for processing the credit card payment. Click on the **Source View** tab of our credit card web service and enter the code shown below in the text editor:

```
package creditcard;

import weblogic.jws.control.JwsContext;
import java.rmi.RemoteException;

/**
 * @jws:target-namespace namespace="creditCard"
 */
public class CreditCardWS {
```

This is the EJB control we will be using for processing credit card payment. These lines of code were automatically generated by the web service, when we added the EJB control in the design view:

```
/**
 * @jws:control
 */
private CreditCardControl creditCard;

/** @jws:context */
JwsContext context;
```

This is the operation exposed by the web service. WebLogic Workshop generated the shell of this method when we added the method in the design view:

```
/**
 * @jws:operation
 */
public boolean debit(String ccNo, double amount) throws RemoteException {
```

Use the EJB control to call the method on the credit card EJB to process the payment:

```
        return creditCard.debit(ccNo, amount);
    }
}
```

## Test the Web Service

In this section we will check whether our web service is working properly. For this, click on the Debug menu and select the Start option. This will open the web service home page in a browser window. We will test our web service by using the Test Form tab that displays a form for entering the credit card number and amount as shown below:

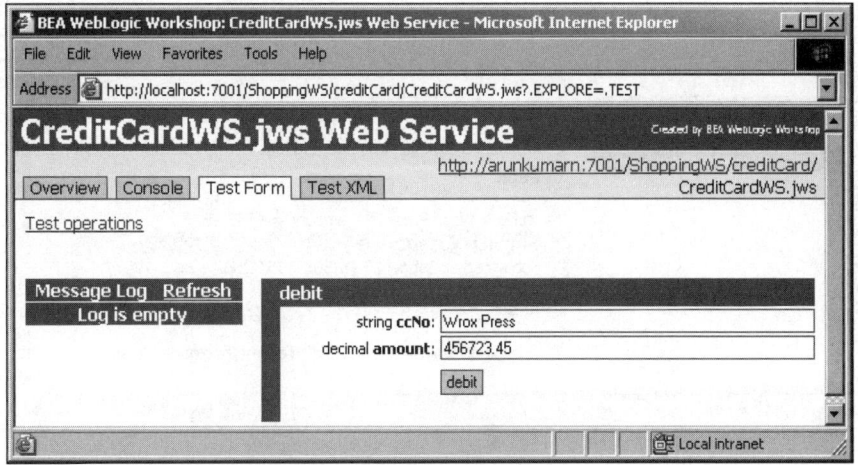

Submit the form by clicking on the debit button. This will execute the web service and display the result in the browser as shown below:

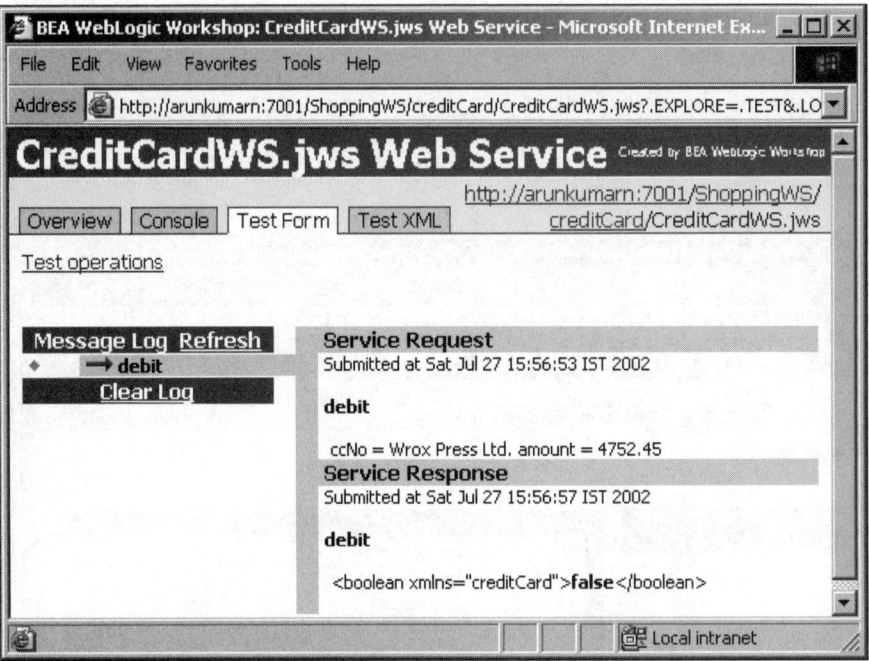

## Generate Client Proxy

Now we will generate the client proxy JAR file for accessing the web service from the clients. We will be using this JAR file later in the shopping application for accessing the web service. For this, click on the Overview tab and select the Java Proxy link. Save the generated JAR file under the name `CreditCardClient.jar`. There are two classes in this file that we will be using for accessing the web service:

- ❏ `WebLogic.proxies.jws.CreditCardWS`
  The service class for accessing the web service

- ❏ `WebLogic.proxies.jws.CreditCArdWSSoap`
  The interface used for invoking the operation on the web service

The code snippet below shows how the catalog web service can be accessed from the client:

```
CreditCardWS_Impl creditCardWS = new CreditCardWS_Impl();
CreditCardWSSoap creditCardWSSoap = creditCardWS.getCreditCardWSSoap();
creditCardWSSoap.debit("0000 0000 0000 0000", 456.76);
```

# Shipping System

As we have already mentioned the shipping system provides a proprietary API for its client systems. We have also mentioned that the performance of the shipping system is time intensive and it has an unacceptable level of performance to be used in a web application scenario. In this section we will wrap the shipping system in a web service and demonstrate how it can be invoked asynchronously from clients by using a queuing mechanism.

> **Please note that the implementation of the system is not shown in this chapter. We simulate the delay in accessing the shipping system by letting the thread sleep for thirty seconds within the web service.**

# Develop the Shipping Web Service

In this section we will develop the credit card web service, which will use the EJB to process credit card payments issued by the web service clients. For this we will perform the following tasks:

❏ Create a new web service that will process shipping order

❏ Deploy and test the web service

❏ Generate the proxies that can be used by clients for accessing this web service

## Create the Shipping Web Service

In this section we will create the shipping web service. For this, right-click on the shipping folder in the tree on the left-hand side of the IDE and click on the New File item in the pop-up menu. This will display a dialog for entering details about the file we are going to create. The Web Service radio button will be selected by default. Enter the name of the file ShippingWS and click OK. Now the IDE will display the design view of the web service in the middle pane. In the property pane on the right-hand side enter the target namespace of the web service as shipping.

### Adding the placeOrder() Method

Now we will add the placeOrder() method that will be exposed by the web service to its clients. For this, click on the Add Operation drop-down box in the middle pane and select the Add Method item. Enter the name of the method as placeOrder.

Now we will see how to add asynchronicity and message buffering facilities to the web service. In the Workshop, IDE methods can be declared as asynchronous by setting the message buffering property to true in the method's property sheet. These methods return immediately to the client before executing the body of the method.

The method arguments are stored in an internal buffer for the method to process them later. Asynchronous methods are required to have void return type. WebLogic uses internal JMS queues for storing the buffered messages. When we use message buffering, all the argument types should be serializable.

The figure below shows the design view of our web service with the operation on the left side and the control on the right side:

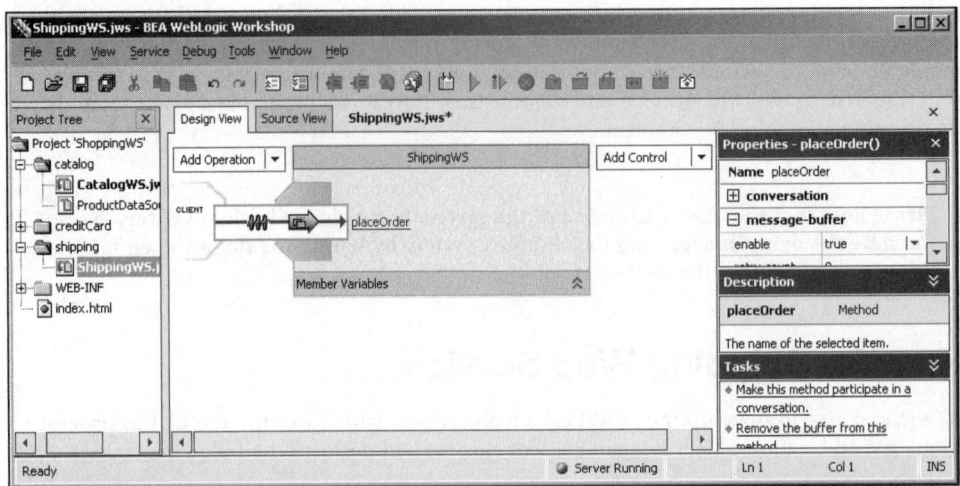

Please note that the graphic representing the method call for placeOrder() is different from that for getCatalog() and debit() in the previous web services. This indicates that the placeOrder() method implements message buffering and is invoked asynchronously.

### Adding Code to our Web Service

In this section we will add code to our web service for processing the order. For this click on the Source View tab of our credit card web service and enter the code shown below in the editor:

```
package shipping;

import weblogic.jws.control.JwsContext;

import java.io.Serializable;

/**
 * @jws:target-namespace namespace="shipping"
 */
public class ShippingWS {
```

This inner class represents the address to which the order is to be sent:

```
    public static class Address implements Serializable {
```

The name of the person:

```
        private String name;
        public String getName() { return name; }
        public void setName(String val) { name = val; }
```

The street:

```
    private String street;
    public String getStreet() { return street; }
    public void setStreet(String val) { street = val; }
```

The city:

```
    private String city;
    public String getCity() { return city; }
    public void setCity(String val) { city = val; }
```

The county:

```
    private String county;
    public String getCounty() { return county; }
    public void setCounty(String val) { county = val; }
```

The post-code:

```
    private String postcode;
    public String getPostcode() { return postcode; }
    public void setPostcode(String val) { postcode = val; }
    }
```

This inner class represent each item in the order:

```
    public static class Item implements Serializable {
```

Unique item code:

```
    private String code;
    public String getCode() { return code; }
    public void setCode(String val) { code = val; }
```

Item quantity:

```
    private int quantity;
    public int getQuantity() { return quantity; }
    public void setQuantity(int val) { quantity = val; }
    }
    /** @jws:context */
    JwsContext context;
```

This is the web service method invoked by clients for placing orders, by passing the address and array of items. WebLogic will accept the incoming SOAP request and deserialize the XML representing the data to the relevant objects. Please also note that the method supports message buffering:

**441**

```
/**
 * @jws:operation
 * @jws:message-buffer enable="true"
 */
public void placeOrder(Address address, Item[] items) {
```

This is just to simulate the delay in processing the order. Even though the thread sleeps for thirty seconds, the client gets the control back immediately after invocation due to message buffering:

```
  try {
    Thread.sleep(30 * 1000);
  } catch(InterruptedException ex) { }

  System.out.println("Order processed.");
  }
}
```

## Test the Web Service

In this section we will check whether our web service is working properly. For this, click on the **Debug** menu and select the **Start** option. This will open the web service home page in a browser window. We will test our web service using the **Test XML** tab as WebLogic is unable to display the form because the web service expects complex data types. In this page we can write the XML code that represents the data and submit the data to the web service. WebLogic provides a template XML document that represents the web service's input as shown below:

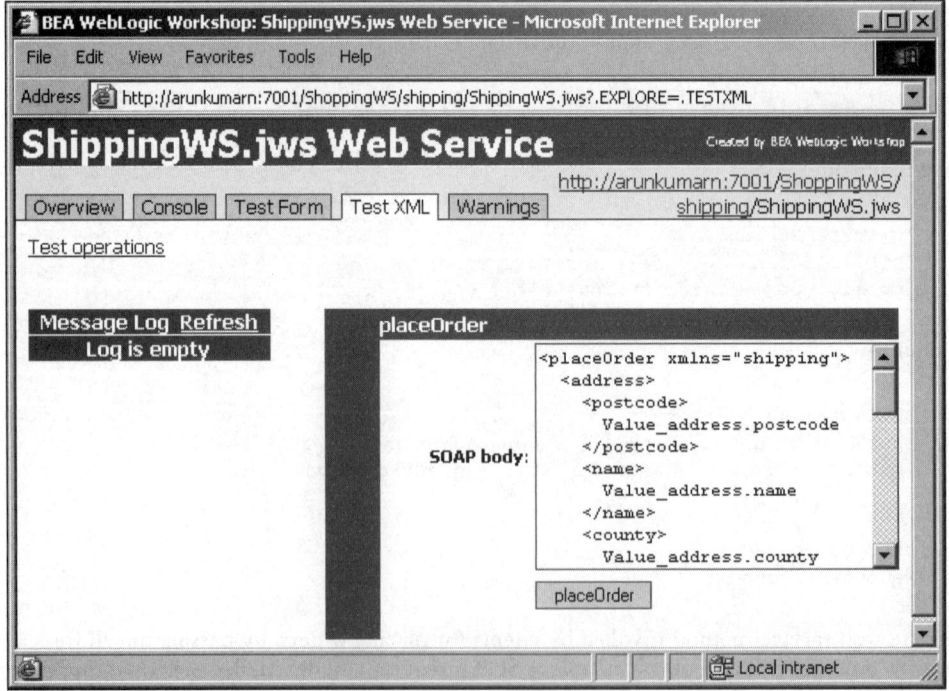

Submit the form by clicking on the placeOrder button. This will execute the web service and display the result in the browser as shown below:

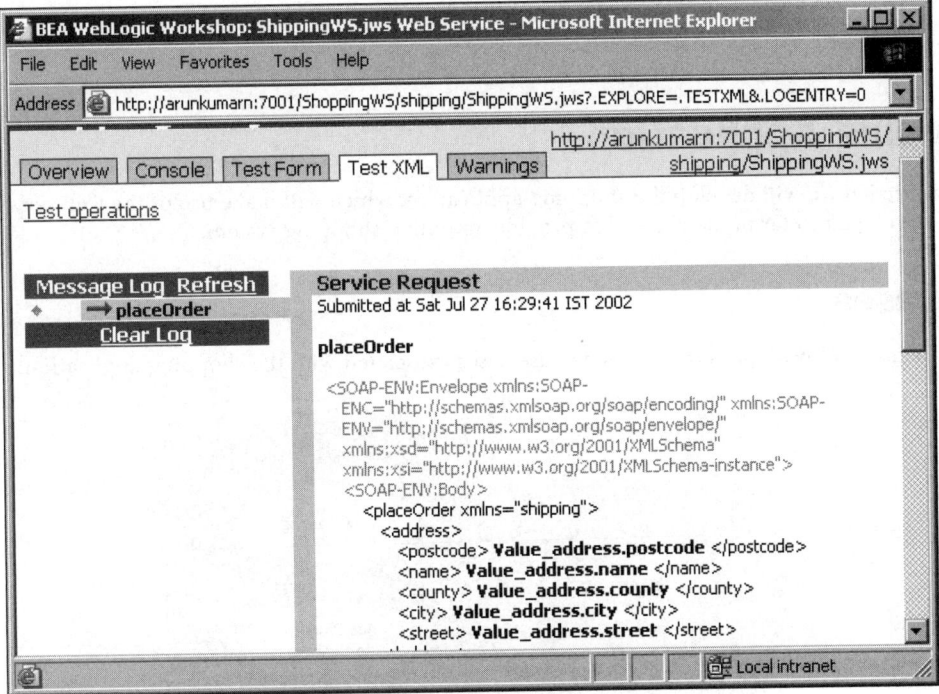

## Generate Client Proxy

Now we will generate the client proxy JAR file for accessing the web service from the clients. We will use this JAR file later in the shopping application for accessing the web service. For this, click, on the Overview tab and select the Java Proxy link. Save the generated JAR file under the name `ShippingClient.jar`. There are four classes in this file that we will be using for accessing the web service:

❏   WebLogic.proxies.jws.CreditCardWS
The service class for accessing the web service.

❏   WebLogic.proxies.jws.CreditCArdWSSoap
The interface used for invoking the operation on the web service.

❏   shipping.Address
This class is the client-side representation of the address information to the web service. The client-side stubs and other helper classes will serialize the class to XML before sending to the web service.

❏   shipping.Item
This class is the client-side representation of the item information to the web service and works in the same way as the Address class.

The code snippet below shows how the catalog web service can be accessed from the client:

```
ShippingWS_Impl shippingWS = new ShippingWS_Impl();
ShippingWSSoap shippingWSSoap = shippingWS.getShippingWSSoap();
shippingWSSoap.placeOrder(address, items);
```

# Shopping Application

In this section we will develop the shopping application, which will make use of the web services we have developed so far in the chapter to provide an online shopping system.

## Use Cases

The diagram below depicts the high-level use cases associated with the shopping application:

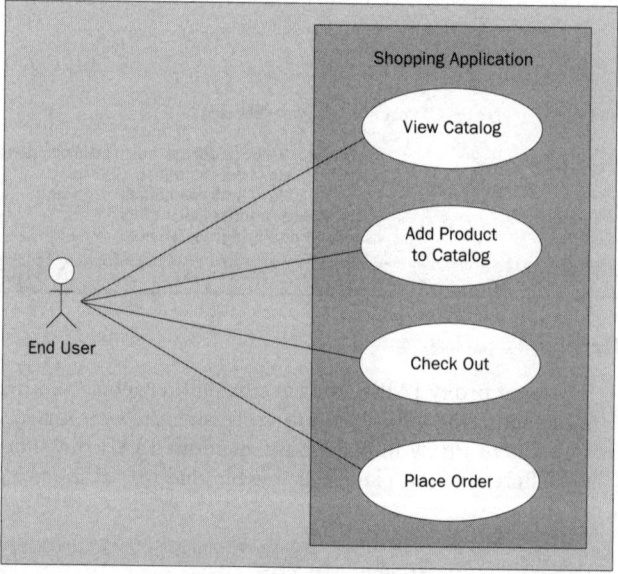

The end users can visit the web site and browse through the catalog. From the catalog they may choose to add items to the shopping cart and then check out. The system will then display the current cart, and prompt for the payment and dispatch address details. On submitting the order form, the system will authenticate the payment details and instruct the shipping system to deliver the order.

## Architecture

The user actions on the client browser are transformed to requests to specific servlets. Depending on the requests, these servlets access the underlying web services to send or retrieve data. The retrieved data is stored as request- or session-scope beans and the request is forwarded to the JSP that renders the next view. The JSP retrieves the data from the request scope bean and renders them as HTML.

A typical set of interactions is listed below:

- ❏   The end user accesses the application by requesting the catalog
- ❏   The catalog servlet accepts the request and asks the catalog web service for the latest catalog
- ❏   This data is stored as a request-scope bean and forwarded to the catalog JSP
- ❏   The user adds an item to the shopping cart
- ❏   The request is sent to the add-to-cart servlet
- ❏   This servlet adds the item to the cart and forwards it to the catalog servlet
- ❏   The end user decides to check out
- ❏   The request is sent to the checkout servlet that stores the order details as a request-scope bean and forwards the request to the checkout JSP
- ❏   The user decides to place the order
- ❏   The request is sent to the place-order servlet
- ❏   This servlet accesses the credit card web service to authenticate the payment and then accesses the shipping web service to dispatch the order

This is depicted in the collaboration diagram shown below:

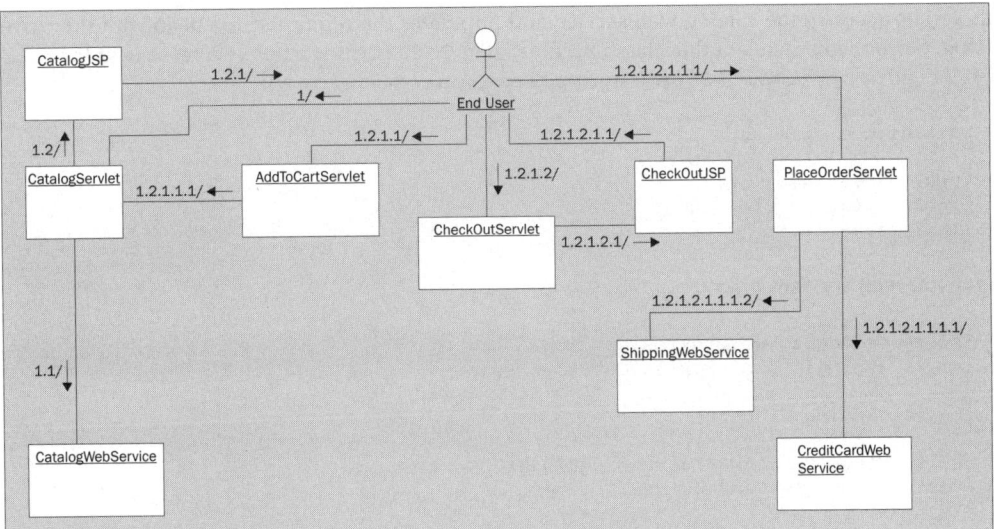

# Application Classes

Now we will have a look at the various classes and interfaces that constitute the shopping application.

## Attributes

This interface enumerates the various bean names used to store session-scope data. Store the contents of this class in a file called `Attributes.java` (it is in the `%jwsDirectory%\Chp11\ShoppingApplication\src`):

```
package com.acme.shopping;

public interface Attributes {
```

This is the name under which the catalog details are stored as a session-scope bean:

```
    public static final String CATALOG = "CATALOG";
```

This is the name under which the shopping cart details are stored as a session-scope bean:

```
    public static final String CART = "CART";
```

This is the name under which the order details are stored as a session-scope bean:

```
    public static final String ORDER = "ORDER";
}
```

## CatalogServlet

This servlet accesses the catalog web service and populates the request scope bean with the current catalog. Store the contents of this class in a file called `CatalogServlet.java` (it is in the `%jwsDirectory%\Chp11\ShoppingApplication\src` directory):

```
package com.acme.shopping;

import javax.servlet.*;
import javax.servlet.http.*;
import java.io.*;
```

Import the web services proxy:

```
import weblogic.jws.proxies.CatalogWS_Impl;
import weblogic.jws.proxies.CatalogWSSoap;

import catalog.Product;

public class CatalogServlet extends HttpServlet {
  private ServletContext ctx;

  public void init(ServletConfig config) throws ServletException {
    super.init(config);
    ctx = this.getServletContext();
  }

  protected void processRequest(HttpServletRequest req,
    HttpServletResponse res)throws ServletException, IOException {
```

Get the current session:

```
        HttpSession sess = req.getSession();
```

Use the client proxy for the catalog web service to get the list of products by invoking the web services. Store the list of products as a session scope bean:

```
        CatalogWS_Impl catalogWS = new CatalogWS_Impl();
        CatalogWSSoap catalogWSSoap = catalogWS.getCatalogWSSoap();
        sess.setAttribute(Attributes.CATALOG, catalogWSSoap.getCatalog());
```

Forward the request to the catalog JSP:

```
        ctx.getRequestDispatcher("/Catalog.jsp").forward(req, res);
    }

    protected void doGet(HttpServletRequest req, HttpServletResponse res)
        throws ServletException, IOException {
      processRequest(req, res);
    }

    protected void doPost(HttpServletRequest req, HttpServletResponse res)
        throws ServletException, IOException {
      processRequest(req, res);
    }
}
```

## Catalog.jsp

This JSP code displays the current catalog. Store the contents of this class in a file called `Catalog.jsp` (it is in the `%jwsDirectory%\Chp11\ShoppingApplication\src`):

```
<%@page import="com.acme.shopping.Attributes"%>
<%@page import="catalog.Product"%>

<html>
  <head><title>Product Catalog</title></head>
  <body>
    <table border="1">
```

Retrieve the catalog:

```
      <%
        Product[] products =
          (Product[])session.getAttribute(Attributes.CATALOG);
        for(int i = 0;products != null && i < products.length;i++)
        {
      %>
```

Loop through the catalog and render the details of products:

```
        <tr>
          <td><%= products[i].getName() %></td>
          <td><%= products[i].getDescription() %></td>
          <td><%= products[i].getPrice() %></td>
          <td>
```

Render the link to add the item to the shopping cart:

```
          <a href="addToCart?code=<%= products[i].getCode() %>">
          Add
          </a>
        </td>
    </tr>

    <% } %>
  </table>
```

Render the link to check out:

```
    <a href="checkOut">Check Out</a>

  </body>
</html>
```

## AddToCartServlet

This servlet adds the selected item to the shopping cart. Store the contents of this class in a file called AddToCartServlet.java (it is in %jwsDirectory%\Chp11\ShoppingApplication\src):

```java
package com.acme.shopping;

import javax.servlet.*;
import javax.servlet.http.*;
import java.io.*;
import java.util.*;

public class AddToCartServlet extends HttpServlet {

  private ServletContext ctx;

  public void init(ServletConfig config) throws ServletException {
    super.init(config);
    ctx = this.getServletContext();
  }

  protected void processRequest(HttpServletRequest req,
      HttpServletResponse res) throws ServletException, IOException {
    HttpSession sess = req.getSession();
```

Get the selected item code:

```
String code = req.getParameter("code");
```

Get the cart from the user's session:

```
HashSet cart = (HashSet)req.getSession().getAttribute(Attributes.CART);
```

If the cart is not present, create a new cart:

```
if(cart == null) cart = new HashSet();
```

Add the selected item to the cart:

```
cart.add(code);
```

Add the cart back to the session:

```
sess.setAttribute(Attributes.CART, cart);
```

Forward the request to the catalog JSP:

```
    ctx.getRequestDispatcher("/Catalog.jsp").forward(req, res);
  }

  protected void doGet(HttpServletRequest req, HttpServletResponse res)
      throws ServletException, IOException {
    processRequest(req, res);
  }

  protected void doPost(HttpServletRequest req, HttpServletResponse res)
      throws ServletException, IOException {
    processRequest(req, res);
  }
}
```

## CheckOutServlet

This servlet processes the request when the user decides to proceed to checkout. Store the contents of this class in a file called `CheckOutServlet.java`:

```
package com.acme.shopping;

import javax.servlet.*;
import javax.servlet.http.*;
import java.io.*;
import java.util.*;
import catalog.Product;

public class CheckOutServlet extends HttpServlet {
```

```
    private ServletContext ctx;

    public void init(ServletConfig config) throws ServletException {
      super.init(config);
      ctx = this.getServletContext();
    }

    protected void processRequest(HttpServletRequest req,
        HttpServletResponse res) throws ServletException, IOException {
      HttpSession sess = req.getSession();
```

Get the shopping cart from the user's session:

```
    HashSet cart = (HashSet)sess.getAttribute(Attributes.CART);
    if(cart == null || cart.isEmpty()) {
      PrintWriter writer = res.getWriter();
      writer.println("Shopping cart is empty");
      writer.close();
      return;
    }
```

Get the current catalog:

```
    Product[] products = (Product[])sess.getAttribute(Attributes.CATALOG);
    HashSet order = new HashSet();
    for(int i = 0; products != null && i < products.length; i++) {
      Iterator it = cart.iterator();
      while(it.hasNext()) {
        String code = (String)it.next();
        if(code.equals(products[i].getCode()))
          order.add(products[i]);
      }
    }
```

Populate the session with the details of the currently selected items:

```
    sess.setAttribute(Attributes.ORDER, order);
```

Forward the request to the checkout JSP:

```
    ctx.getRequestDispatcher("/CheckOut.jsp").forward(req, res);
  }

  protected void doGet(HttpServletRequest req, HttpServletResponse res)
      throws ServletException, IOException {
    processRequest(req, res);
  }

  protected void doPost(HttpServletRequest req,
      HttpServletResponse res) throws ServletException, IOException {
    processRequest(req, res);
  }
}
```

## CheckOut.jsp

This JSP accepts the payment details, shipping address, and the number of items that are ordered. Store the contents of this class in a file called CheckOut.jsp:

```
<%@page import="com.acme.shopping.Attributes"%>
<%@page import="catalog.Product"%>
<%@page import="java.util.*"%>

<html>
  <head><title>Product Catalog</title></head>
  <body>
    <form action="placeOrder">
      <table border="1">
        <tr>
          <td colspan="3" align="right">Quantity</td>
        </tr>
```

Loop through the list of currently selected items and render a form showing the details and entering the quantities of selected items required:

```
<%
  HashSet order =
     (HashSet)session.getAttribute(Attributes.ORDER);
  Iterator it = order.iterator();
  while(it.hasNext())
  {
     Product product = (Product)it.next();
%>

<tr>
  <td><%= product.getName() %></td>
  <td><%= product.getDescription() %></td>
  <td>
    <input type="text" name="<%= product.getCode() %>"/>
  </td>
</tr>
<% } %>
```

Render the form elements for capturing the billing and shipping details:

```
<tr>
  <td colspan="2" align="right">
    <b>Name</b>
  </td>
  <td>
    <input type="text" name="name"/>
  </td>
</tr>
<tr>
```

```
            <td colspan="2" align="right">
              <b>Street</b>
            </td>
            <td>
              <input type="text" name="street"/>
            </td>
          </tr>
          <tr>
            <td colspan="2" align="right">
              <b>City</b>
            </td>
            <td>
              <input type="text" name="city"/>
            </td>
          </tr>
          <tr>
            <td colspan="2" align="right">
              <b>County</b>
            </td>
            <td>
              <input type="text" name="county"/>
            </td>
          </tr>
          <tr>
            <td colspan="2" align="right">
              <b>Postcode</b>
            </td>
            <td>
              <input type="text" name="postcode"/>
            </td>
          </tr>
          <tr>
            <td colspan="2" align="right">
              <b>Credit Card No:</b>
            </td>
            <td>
              <input type="text" name="creditCard"/>
            </td>
          </tr>
          <tr>
            <td colspan="2" align="right">
            </td>
            <td>
              <input type="submit" value="Place Order"/>
            </td>
          </tr>

      </table>

  </body>
</html>
```

## *PlaceOrderServlet*

This servlet processes the request when the user decides to place an order. The servlet accesses the underlying web services for authenticating credit card payment and dispatching the shipment. Store the contents of this class in a file called `PlaceOrderServlet.java`:

```
package com.acme.shopping;

import javax.servlet.*;
import javax.servlet.http.*;
import java.io.*;
import java.util.*;

import java.net.URL;
```

Import the web services proxies:

```
import weblogic.jws.proxies.CreditCardWS_Impl;
import weblogic.jws.proxies.CreditCardWSSoap;
import weblogic.jws.proxies.ShippingWS_Impl;
import weblogic.jws.proxies.ShippingWSSoap;

import shipping.Address;
import shipping.Item;
import catalog.Product;

public class PlaceOrderServlet extends HttpServlet {

  private ServletContext ctx;

  public void init(ServletConfig config) throws ServletException {
    super.init(config);
    ctx = this.getServletContext();
  }

  protected void processRequest(HttpServletRequest req,
      HttpServletResponse res) throws ServletException, IOException {
    HttpSession sess = req.getSession();
```

Get the shopping cart from the session:

```
HashSet cart = (HashSet)sess.getAttribute(Attributes.CART);
if(cart == null || cart.isEmpty()) {
  PrintWriter writer = res.getWriter();
  writer.println("Shopping cart is empty");
  writer.close();
  return;
}
```

Get the order details from the session:

```
HashSet order = (HashSet)sess.getAttribute(Attributes.ORDER);
if(order == null || order.isEmpty()) {
  throw new ServletException("Unable to find order");
}
```

Create the `Address` object from the request parameter:

```
Address address = new Address();
address.setName(req.getParameter("name"));
address.setStreet(req.getParameter("street"));
address.setCity(req.getParameter("city"));
address.setCounty(req.getParameter("county"));
address.setPostcode(req.getParameter("postcode"));

ArrayList itemList = new ArrayList();
```

Iterate through the order and calculate the total amount:

```
double total = 0;
Iterator it = order.iterator();
while(it.hasNext()) {
  Product product = (Product)it.next();
  int quantity =
  Integer.parseInt(req.getParameter(product.getCode()));

  Item item = new Item();
  item.setCode(product.getCode());
  item.setQuantity(quantity);
  itemList.add(item);

  total += quantity*product.getPrice();
}
```

Create the list of items to be ordered:

```
Item[] items = new Item[itemList.size()];
for(int i = 0;i < items.length;i++) items[i] = (Item)itemList.get(i);
```

Process the credit card payment and if successful, place the order:

```
try {
  if(!debitAccount(req.getParameter("ccNo"), total)) {
    PrintWriter writer = res.getWriter();
    writer.println("Credit card authorisation failed");
    writer.close();
    return;
  } placeOrder(address, items);
} catch(Exception ex) {
  throw new ServletException(ex);
}

PrintWriter writer = res.getWriter();
writer.println("Your order has been successfully processed");
writer.close();
return;
```

```
    }

    protected void doGet(HttpServletRequest req,
        HttpServletResponse res) throws ServletException, IOException {
      processRequest(req, res);
    }

    protected void doPost(HttpServletRequest req,
        HttpServletResponse res) throws ServletException, IOException {
      processRequest(req, res);
    }
```

This method uses the credit card web service proxy to invoke the web service for processing payment:

```
    private boolean debitAccount(String ccNo, double amt) throws Exception {
      CreditCardWS_Impl creditCardWS = new CreditCardWS_Impl();
      CreditCardWSSoap creditCardWSSoap = creditCardWS.getCreditCardWSSoap();

      return creditCardWSSoap.debit(ccNo, amt);
    }
```

This method uses the shipping web service proxy to invoke the web service for placing the order:

```
    private void placeOrder(Address address, Item[] items) throws Exception {
      ShippingWS_Impl shippingWS = new ShippingWS_Impl();
      ShippingWSSoap shippingWSSoap = shippingWS.getShippingWSSoap();
      shippingWSSoap.placeOrder(address, items);
    }
  }
```

# Deployment Descriptor

The deployment descriptor, web.xml, contains the following details:

- ❏ The servlet definitions
- ❏ The servlet mappings
- ❏ Servlet context listener declaration
- ❏ Context parameters specifying the endpoint URL and WSDL locations for the various web services

Servlet definitions:

```
<!DOCTYPE web-app PUBLIC
  "-//Sun Microsystems, Inc.//DTD Web Application 2.3//EN"
  "http://java.sun.com/dtd/web-app_2.3.dtd">
<web-app>
```

Add-to-cart servlet:

```
<servlet>
  <servlet-name>addToCart</servlet-name>
  <servlet-class>com.acme.shopping.AddToCartServlet</servlet-class>
</servlet>
```

Catalog servlet:

```
<servlet>
  <servlet-name>catalog</servlet-name>
  <servlet-class>com.acme.shopping.CatalogServlet</servlet-class>
</servlet>
```

Checkout servlet:

```
<servlet>
  <servlet-name>checkOut</servlet-name>
  <servlet-class>com.acme.shopping.CheckOutServlet</servlet-class>
</servlet>
```

Place-order servlet:

```
<servlet>
  <servlet-name>placeOrder</servlet-name>
  <servlet-class>com.acme.shopping.PlaceOrderServlet</servlet-class>
</servlet>
```

URL mappings:

```
<servlet-mapping>
  <servlet-name>addToCart</servlet-name>
  <url-pattern>/addToCart</url-pattern>
</servlet-mapping>

<servlet-mapping>
  <servlet-name>catalog</servlet-name>
  <url-pattern>/catalog</url-pattern>
</servlet-mapping>

<servlet-mapping>
  <servlet-name>checkOut</servlet-name>
  <url-pattern>/checkOut</url-pattern>
</servlet-mapping>

<servlet-mapping>
  <servlet-name>placeOrder</servlet-name>
  <url-pattern>/placeOrder</url-pattern>
</servlet-mapping>

</web-app>
```

# Building and Deploying the Application

In this section we will build and deploy our web application on WebLogic server. For this first we need to compile the classes. Please make sure that you have the `weblogic.jar` file in your classpath, while compiling these classes as well as the web service proxy JAR files:

```
set classpath=%BEA_HOME%\server\lib\weblogic.jar;.\CatalogClient.jar;
\CreditCardClient.jar;.\ShippingClient.jar
```

After setting the classpath, we will change to the directory `%jwsDirectory%\Chp11\ShoppingApplication\src` and compile the files:

```
javac -d ..\classes Attributes.java
javac -d ..\classes CatalogServlet.java
javac -d ..\classes AddToCartServlet.java
javac -d ..\classes CheckOutServlet.java
javac -d ..\classes PlaceOrderServlet.java
```

Once we have compiled the classes, create the following directory structure:

```
/Catalog.jsp
/CheckOut.jsp
/WEB-INF/web.xml
/WEB-INF/lib/CatalogClient.jar
/WEB-INF/lib/CreditCardClient.jar
/WEB-INF/lib/ShippingClient.jar
/WEB-INF/classes/com/acme/shopping/Attributes.class
/WEB-INF/classes/com/acme/shopping/StarupListener.class
/WEB-INF/classes/com/acme/shopping/CatalogServlet.class
/WEB-INF/classes/com/acme/shopping/PlaceOrderServlet.class
/WEB-INF/classes/com/acme/shopping/AddToCartServlet.class
/WEB-INF/classes/com/acme/shopping/CheckOutServlet.class
```

Then run the `jar` command to create a WAR file with structure shown above:

```
jar cf Shopping.war *
```

Copy the WAR file to `%WLS_HOME%/Weblogic700/samples/workshop/applications` to deploy the EJB.

# Running the Application

The application can be accessed by the URL http://localhost:7001/Shopping/catalog:

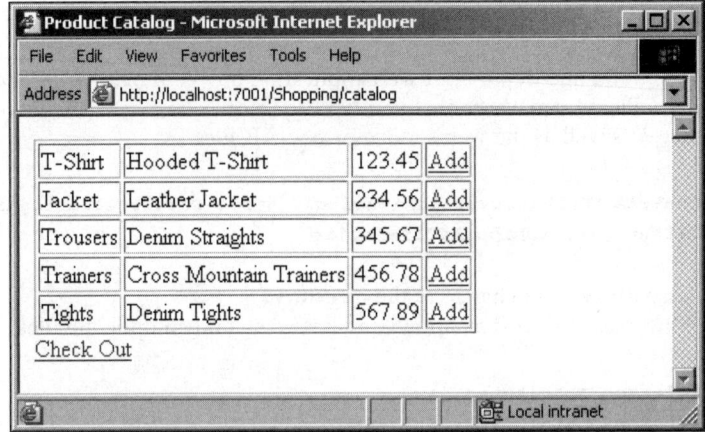

After adding the items to the cart click on the Check Out link:

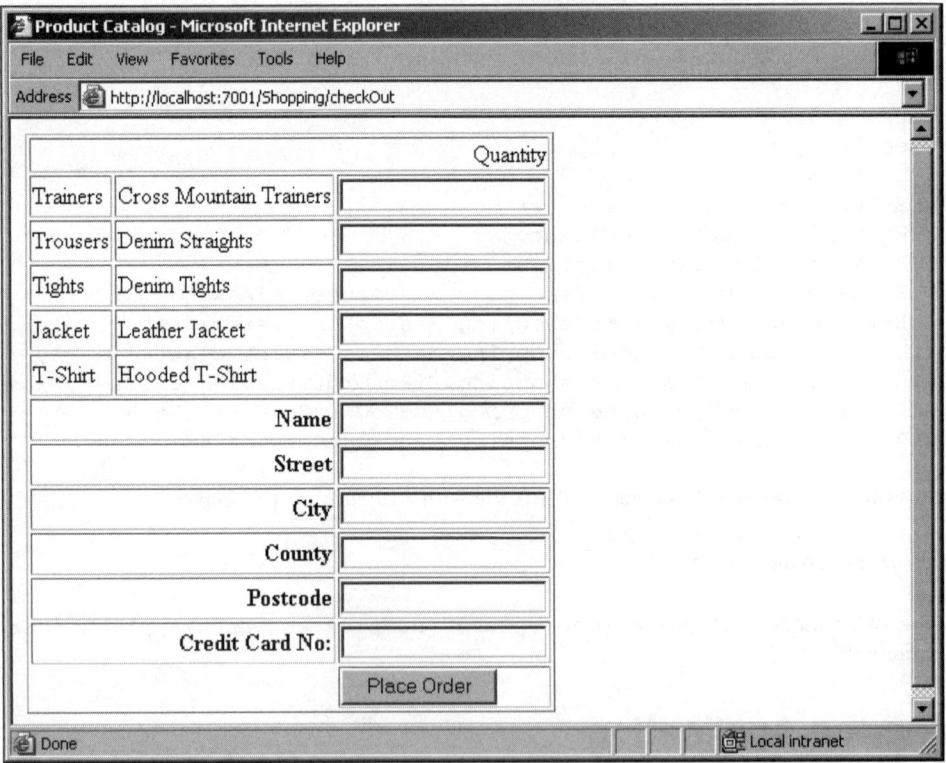

Enter the required information and submit the form. If the payment is processed successfully we can see the order details in the WebLogic console window.

# Summary

In this chapter we have developed a full-fledged case study using web services for integrating a set of disparate applications within an enterprise. We looked at exposing standard J2EE components such as datasources and EJBs as SOAP-based web services. In the case study we developed a web application that leveraged the services provided by a set of existing applications, and covered the use of web services for integrating the new application with a set of existing applications.

We have seen how to use WebLogic Workshop for developing, deploying, and testing web services. We also looked at developing asynchronous web services to improve the transaction throughput and performance in web-based applications.

Beginning Java Web Services Beginning Java Web Services Beginning Java Web Services
Beginning Java Web Services Beginning Java Web Services
Beginning Java Web Services Beginning Java Web Services
Beginning Java Web Services Beginning Java Web Services
Beginning Java Web Services Beginning Java Web Services
Beginning Java Web Services
Beginning Java Web Services Beginning Java Web Services
Beginning Java Web Services
Beginning Java Web Services
Beginning Java Web Services
Beginning Java Web Services Beginning Java Web Services Beginning Java Web Services
Beginning Java Web Services Beginning Java Web Services
Beginning Java Web Services Beginning Java Web Services
Beginning Java Web Services Beginning Java Web Services
Beginning Java Web Services Beginning Java Web Services

# Index

# H

# I

# J

# Notes

Notes

# ASP Today

## The daily knowledge site for professional ASP programmers

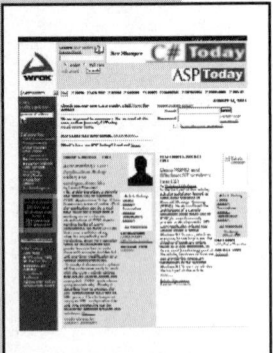

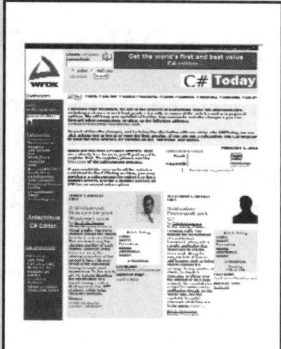
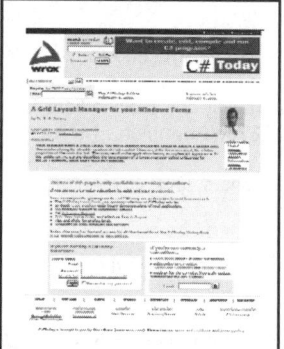

# p2p.wrox.com
## The programmer's resource centre

# A unique free service from Wrox Press
## With the aim of helping programmers to help each other

Wrox Press aims to provide timely and practical information to today's programmer. P2P is a list server offering a host of targeted mailing lists where you can share knowledge with four fellow programmers and find solutions to your problems. Whatever the level of your programming knowledge, and whatever technology you use P2P can provide you with the information you need.

**ASP**
Support for beginners and professionals, including a resource page with hundreds of links, and a popular ASP.NET mailing list.

**DATABASES**
For database programmers, offering support on SQL Server, mySQL, and Oracle.

**MOBILE**
Software development for the mobile market is growing rapidly. We provide lists for the several current standards, including WAP, Windows CE, and Symbian.

**JAVA**
A complete set of Java lists, covering beginners, professionals, and server-side programmers (including JSP, servlets and EJBs)

**.NET**
Microsoft's new OS platform, covering topics such as ASP.NET, C#, and general .NET discussion.

**VISUAL BASIC**
Covers all aspects of VB programming, from programming Office macros to creating components for the .NET platform.

**WEB DESIGN**
As web page requirements become more complex, programmer's are taking a more important role in creating web sites. For these programmers, we offer lists covering technologies such as Flash, Coldfusion, and JavaScript.

**XML**
Covering all aspects of XML, including XSLT and schemas.

**OPEN SOURCE**
Many Open Source topics covered including PHP, Apache, Perl, Linux, Python and more.

**FOREIGN LANGUAGE**
Several lists dedicated to Spanish and German speaking programmers, categories include. NET, Java, XML, PHP and XML

## How to subscribe:
### Simply visit the P2P site, at http://p2p.wrox.com/

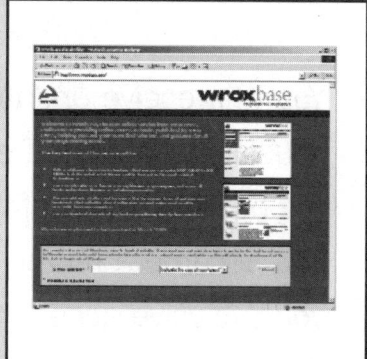
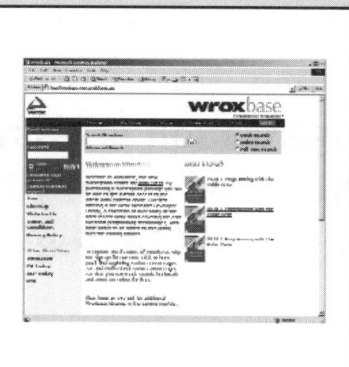

**wrox**

Programmer to Programmer™

Registration Code: 75314N0N19H89701

Wrox writes books for you. Any suggestions, or ideas about how you want
information given in your ideal book will be studied by our team.
Your comments are always valued at Wrox.

Free phone in USA 800-USE-WROX
Fax (312) 893 8001

UK Tel.: (0121) 687 4100        Fax: (0121) 687 4101

## Beginning Java Web Services – Registration Card

Name _____

Address _____

_____

_____

City _____ State/Region _____

Country _____ Postcode/Zip _____

E-Mail _____

Occupation _____

How did you hear about this book?

☐ Book review (name) _____

☐ Advertisement (name) _____

☐ Recommendation _____

☐ Catalog _____

☐ Other _____

Where did you buy this book?

☐ Bookstore (name) _____ City _____

☐ Computer store (name) _____

☐ Mail order_____

☐ Other _____

What influenced you in the purchase of this book?

☐ Cover Design ☐ Contents ☐ Other (please specify):

_____

How did you rate the overall content of this book?

☐ Excellent ☐ Good ☐ Average ☐ Poor

What did you find most useful about this book? _____

_____

What did you find least useful about this book? _____

_____

Please add any additional comments. _____

_____

What other subjects will you buy a computer book on soon?

_____

What is the best computer book you have used this year?

_____

**Note:** This information will only be used to keep you updated
about new Wrox Press titles and will not be used for
any other purpose or passed to any other third party.

Check here if you DO NOT want to receive support for this book ▐

**wrox**

Programmer to Programmer™

Note: If you post the bounce back card below in the UK, please send it to:

Wrox Press Limited, Arden House, 1102 Warwick Road,
Acocks Green, Birmingham B27 6HB. UK.

*Computer Book Publishers*